SMALL BUSINESS MANAGEMENT

A GUIDE TO ENTREPRENEURSHIP

THIRD EDITION

Nicholas C. Siropolis
Cuyahoga Community College

HOUGHTON MIFFLIN COMPANY Boston
Dallas • Geneva, Illinois
Lawrenceville, New Jersey • Palo Alto

Cover photo by Peter Simon/PHOTOTAKE

All photos inside text, unless otherwise noted, are by Karabinus & Associates, Inc.

Printed in the U.S.A.

Library of Congress Catalog Card Number: 85-80697

ISBN: 0-395-35717-9

EFGHIJ-D-898

DEDICATED TO:
Shirley, my mother, and my sister, Helen

CONTENTS

PREFACE

This book is for those men and women who someday may go into business for themselves and for those who are already in business for themselves but who wish to strengthen their entrepreneurial and managerial skills. It is designed expressly for courses and programs called Small Business Management, Starting a New Venture, and the like, offered by two-year community and technical colleges and four-year colleges and universities.

Although many colleges require an Introduction to Business course as a prerequisite, others do not. This means that for some students a course in entrepreneurship—or small business management—will be their first and perhaps only exposure to the business world. For this reason, the text is written in such a way that the material can be grasped by students having little or no background in business.

The text covers the entire spectrum of entrepreneurship, ranging from the business plan to computers, from marketing research to social responsibilities. Coverage of these subjects and others is deep enough to challenge students and ensure a working knowledge. To excite the student's interest, the text makes wide use of graphics and true-to-life examples. Equally important, the text is written in a style that invites enthusiastic reading and study.

Thanks to the suggestions of reviewers as well as of professors who used the second edition, we made many changes in this third edition. We also rewrote most topics to update them and to make them more comprehensive. As in the first and second editions, we have strived to supply a textbook that reflects the letter and spirit of the entrepreneurial tradition, a textbook that is teachable and readable, content-rich and stimulating. We have also strived to convey to students the conviction that entrepreneurship is a vitally important endeavor.

The book is divided into three parts. The first three chapters give an overview of entrepreneurship. The next seven chapters discuss the problems of launching a new venture, and the remaining ten chapters deal with the problems connected with managing an ongoing venture. Each of the twenty chapters contains two short cases, and one comprehensive case. (See the chapter guide on the next page.)

The sixty cases are based on actual experiences of entrepreneurs and

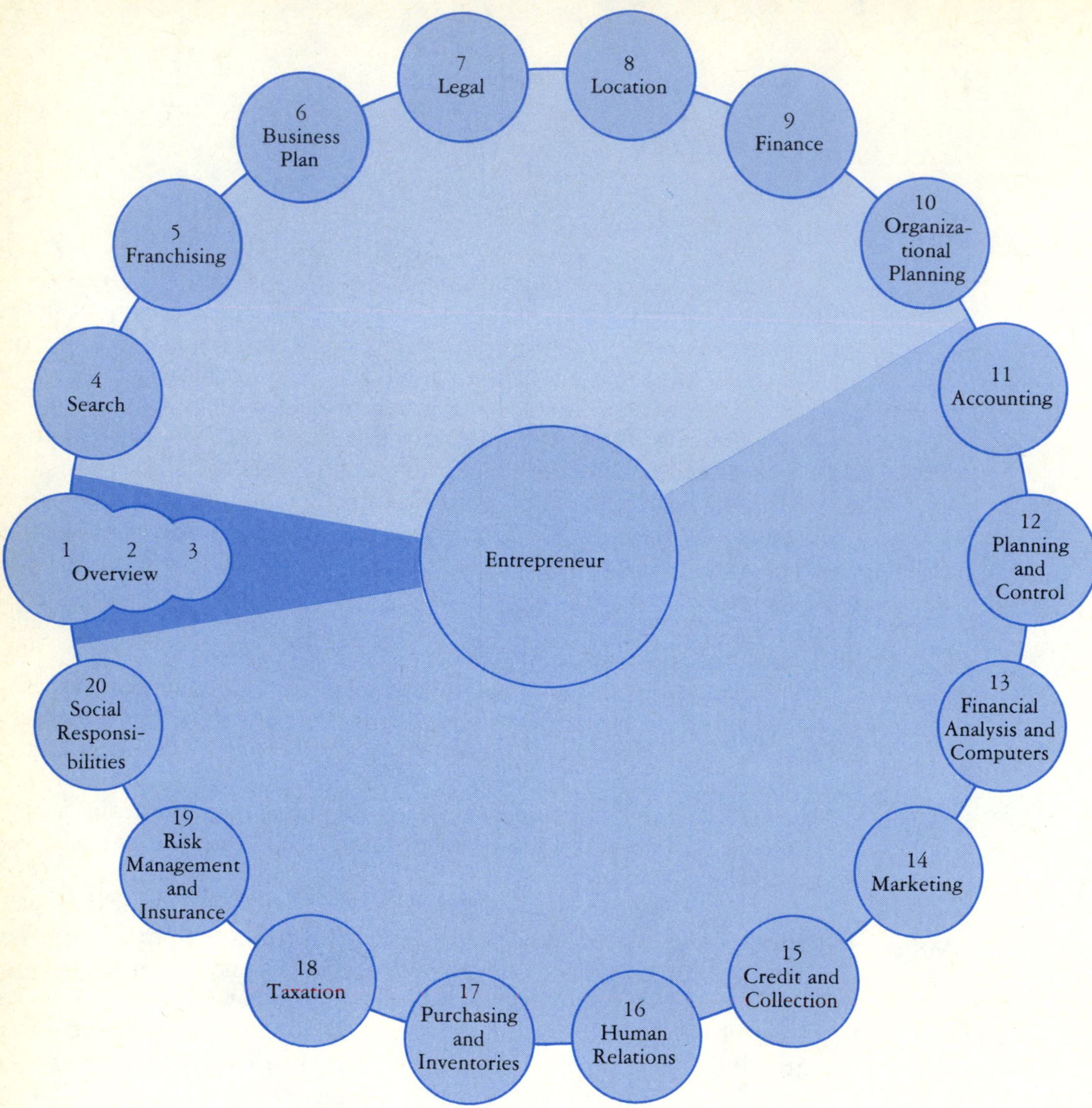

people in small business. The comprehensive cases describe how the entrepreneurs began their ventures, how they progressed with them, and the directions in which they are moving with their ventures. These cases have financial statements, including ones that show how the entrepreneurs financed their ventures at the start. Many of the cases also show examples from business plans used by the entrepreneurs. Students generally like the case method of instruction because it focuses, not on memorization, but on thinking through true-to-life business problems and opportunities.

Finally, we invite your comments and criticisms. That way, we can better provide you with materials that lend themselves to the teaching and learning of entrepreneurship. We sincerely appreciate your suggestions.

Acknowledgments

This book is by no means the work of one person. Many have contributed to its development. Let me mention just a few:

- ☐ The entrepreneurs who gave so freely of their time and energies to supply me with case material.
- ☐ The faculty and staff at Cuyahoga Community College, who enabled me to create an accredited curriculum devoted to entrepreneurship. I am especially indebted to Darl Ault, Elizabeth Boyer, Mildred Brown, John Coleman, Walter Johnson, Kenneth Killen, Kermit Lidstrom, Joseph Malone, Robert Parilla, George Plavac, Robert Sexton, Richard Shapiro, Booker Tall, and Lowell Watkins.
- ☐ The Greater Cleveland Growth Association, where I first got the idea to create an entrepreneurship curriculum. In particular, I am indebted to Melvin Roebuck, with whom I have had a long professional relationship. Others that I am indebted to are Michael Benz, John Robinson, and Ramesh Shah.
- ☐ The U.S. Small Business Administration, which never failed me in my numerous requests for help. In particular, I am grateful to Eleanor Bozik, S. P. Fisher, Hudson Hyatt, and Norman McLeod.
- ☐ Vincent Panichi of John Carroll University and Ciuni and Panichi, Inc., who so generously helped me with updating the chapter on taxation.
- ☐ Reviewers whose numerous criticisms were so creatively helpful to me. I am especially indebted to A. Keith Strasser, Moorpark College; Richard E. LaBarre, Ferris State University; James Christensen, Delta College; David V. Aiken, Hocking Technical College; John J. Buckley, Orange County Community College; and Bernard W. Weinrich, St. Louis Community College at Forest Park; Ernest H. Brass, III, Lake Erie College.

To all of these men and women and their organizations, my heartfelt thanks.

NICHOLAS C. SIROPOLIS

PART 1 AN OVERVIEW OF SMALL BUSINESS

1 SMALL BUSINESS IN A FREE ENTERPRISE SOCIETY

QUESTIONS FOR MASTERY

Why is the study of small business important?

How is small business defined?

What is the role of small business in our economy?

What is the relationship between small business and big business?

Why do small businesses succeed or fail?

If America is to be civilized, it must be done by the business class.

Alfred North Whitehead

Small business enjoys a tradition of infinite variety and solid achievement. It thrives everywhere. So vital is small business that few, if any, parts of our economy could go on without its products and services. Small business is also a civilizing influence, rising above dollars and cents to enrich the lives of men and women the world over.

PLACE OF SMALL BUSINESS IN HISTORY

In the vast sweep of human history, small business has received scant attention. Few historians have bothered to record its contributions to society, even though the first known piece of writing on it appeared more than 4,000 years ago. It described how bankers loaned money at interest.[1] Since then, small businesspersons have spent countless hours pouring out products and services to benefit the consumer.

Small business flourished in almost all ancient cultures. The Arabs, Babylonians, Egyptians, Jews, Greeks, Phoenicians, and Romans excelled at it. Their products and services, however, were often shoddy and slipshod. Consumers often were cheated and defrauded. The result was that small businesses became objects of scorn.

Into this controversy stepped Hammurabi, King of Babylon. In 2100 B.C., he drafted a code of three hundred laws to protect consumers and small businesspersons, especially against fraud. Carved on marble columns eight feet high, the original code now resides at the Louvre Museum in Paris, though much of it has been erased by time. A sampling of Hammurabi's laws follows:

> If outlaws hatch a conspiracy in the house of a wineseller and she does not arrest them and bring them to the palace, that wineseller shall be put to death.
>
> If a builder has built a house for a man and does not make his work perfect; and the house which he has built has fallen down and so caused the death of the householders, that builder shall be put to death.[2]

These two laws underscore the truth of the saying that "the more times change, the more they stay the same." Indeed, the need to protect consumers from business and business from consumers is as vital today as in Hammurabi's time. Note also that the first law deals with businesswomen and their social responsibilities toward government.

Small Business Ignored

Although crowded with achievement, small-business history has never fired the public mind. Greek and Roman historians virtually ignored small business. In their view, ideas and military deeds were the stuff of history. Yet it was largely through small business that civilization was spread to all four corners of the then-known world. Small businesses brought to the have-nots such things as Babylonian astronomy, Greek philosophy, the Jewish calendar, and Roman law.

In the centuries that followed, even the Roman Catholic church held small businesspersons in low esteem. The church branded retailers as sinners because they did nothing to improve a product; but still they charged higher prices than did the maker of the product. And, until the nineteenth century, the church often spoke against the practice of charging interest on loans.

Although now held in higher esteem than ever before, small business remains overshadowed by professions such as medicine and law. In her classic history of businesses—big and small—Miriam Beard points out:

> Physicians are now wrapped in such dignity that the public forgets how recently they occupied the status of barbers. Lawyers have climbed from the solicitor-family relation to a solemn eminence. . . . Not so the businessman; he still struggles on, unfathered and unhallowed. He is his own ancestor, and, usually, his memory does not reach back even to the last business crisis.[3]

A Change in Image

Today, however, small business enjoys more esteem and prestige than ever before. Educators, journalists, and politicians alike have begun to underscore its achievements and opportunities, its promise and problems. Perhaps the best measure of its new-found prestige was the White House Conference on Small Business held in 1980. Called at the urging of President Jimmy Carter, this conference brought together 1,683 delegates from all 50 states, most of them small businesspersons. At the conference, they made 60 recommendations covering such diverse subjects as:

- Taxation and education
- Innovation and federal procurement

This conference likely never would have taken place but for the "rising tide in the spirit of individual enterprise in America . . ."[4] So influential was the conference that the U.S. Congress has passed into law 40 of the 60 recommendations.[5] For example, the U.S. Congress enacted such landmark pieces of legislation as:

- The Small Business Innovation Research Act, which sharply boosts small business's share of federal research work
- The Regulatory Flexibility Act, which requires federal agencies to take small business into account when writing or reviewing rules and regulations

Another measure of small business's new-found prestige is the recent birth of dozens of publications devoted to small business. Until the late 1970s, there were hardly any, and certainly none had any popularity. Today, one of the most successful is *Inc.* magazine. For instance:

> *Inc.*'s total paid circulation was 300,000 three years after its birth in 1979. Each of the nation's leading business magazines such as *Fortune* and *Business Week* took roughly 25 years to reach that level of paid circulation. The fact that *Inc.* has done it in three years is in my view a reflection of how hungry American small business has been to have a magazine of its own.[6]

DEFINITIONS OF SMALL BUSINESS

Small business defies easy definition. Typically, we apply the term *small business* to so-called mom-and-pop stores such as neighborhood groceries and restaurants, and we apply the term *big business* to such giants as IBM and General Motors. But between these two extremes fall businesses that may be looked upon as big or small, depending on the yardstick and cutoff point used.

Common Yardsticks

There are a number of common yardsticks:

Total assets: The total cash, inventory, land, machinery, and other resources held by a business.
Owners' equity: The total investment made by investors. For example, in a corporation, investors would generally be the shareholders who buy stock and creditors would generally be those who either lend money or supply credit.
Yearly sales revenues
Number of employees

Each yardstick has its points. But *number of employees* has more in its favor than any of the others. Among other things, this yardstick is:

Inflation proof: It is unaffected by changes in the purchasing power of the dollar.
Transparent: It is easy to see and understand.
Comparable: It allows good comparisons of size between businesses in the same industry.
Available: It is easy to get from businesses.

If we accept number of employees as the yardstick of size, what should the cutoff point be? Five hundred is the number recommended by the U.S. Department of Commerce and widely used by Chambers of Commerce; so in this textbook, we will call a business small if it employs fewer than 500 persons, unless noted otherwise.

Almost all definitions require some qualification. Ours is no exception. To qualify as small, a business not only should employ fewer than 500 persons but should also be:

Independently owned: It should not be part of another business.

Independently managed: Small businesspersons should be free to run their businesses as they please.

This second qualification rules out many franchises. One of the hardy myths about franchising is that owners work for themselves. That is not always so. An investor who buys a franchise must often live up to numerous contractual obligations, such as keeping certain store hours, paying monthly fees to the franchisor, and preparing monthly performance reports. In these cases, the true boss is the franchisor, not the franchisee.

The SBA's Definitions

Let us now look at some other definitions of small business, namely those laid down by the U.S. Small Business Administration (SBA). This federal agency was created by the U.S. Congress in 1953 to help small business thrive. To meet this goal, the SBA offers programs designed to help small businesses upgrade their managerial skills and borrow money.

For businesses seeking loans, the SBA has drawn up definitions of smallness to fit virtually every industry. A partial list appears in Exhibit 1.1. Note the SBA's use of different yardsticks and cutoff points. Exhibit 1.2 condenses these definitions into broad industry groups.

These definitions are by no means hard and fast, and they can be relaxed in exceptional cases. In 1966, for example, the SBA classified American Motors as small to enable the company to bid on certain government contracts. At the time, American Motors ranked as the

EXHIBIT 1.1

SBA Standards of Smallness for Selected Industries

Manufacturers	**Employing Fewer Than**
Petroleum refining	1,500 persons
Electronic computers	1,000
Macaroni and spaghetti	500
Wholesalers	**Employing Fewer Than**
Sporting goods	500 persons
Furniture	500
Paints and varnishes	500
Retailers	**Earning Sales of Less Than**
Grocery stores	$13.5 million a year
Automobile agencies	11.5
Restaurants	10.0
Services	**Earning Sales of Less Than**
Computer-related services	$12.5 million a year
Accounting services	4.0
Television repair	3.5

Source: "U.S. Small Business Administration: Small Business Size Standards," *Federal Register*, Vol. 49, No. 28 (Washington, D.C.: U.S. Government Printing Office, February 9, 1984), pp. 5024–5048.

EXHIBIT 1.2

SBA Standards of Smallness

Industry Group	Number of Employees	Yearly Sales Revenues (millions of dollars)
Manufacturing	50 to 1,500	—
Wholesaling	500	—
Retailing	—	3.5 to 13.5
Services	—	3.5 to 14.5

nation's sixty-third largest manufacturer, with 32,000 employees and sales revenues of $991 million. The SBA justified its judgment by applying a seldom-used test of smallness—namely, that a business qualifies as small if it does not dominate its industry. American Motors easily met that test.

Note in Exhibit 1.2 that many of the SBA's definitions really cover medium-sized businesses. For example, a manufacturer employing 1,000 persons probably has sales revenues in excess of $50 million a year. Few laypersons would view such a business as small.

THE BRIGHT SIDE OF SMALL BUSINESS

Returning to our earlier, simpler definition of a small business as one that employs fewer than 500 persons, let us now place this number in focus. How many businesses are that small? How many people does small business employ?

As shown in Exhibit 1.3, more than 99 percent of the nation's 16 million businesses are small—even if we define a small business as one that employs fewer than 100 rather than 500. The total of 16 million businesses includes farms, franchises, and professional firms. Turning to Exhibit 1.4, note that there are as many part-time nonfarm businesses as there are full-time nonfarm businesses.

Clearly, small business is a vital force in the economy. Further evidence of its vitality is the fact that small business employs roughly half of the nation's workforce.[7]

EXHIBIT 1.3

Percentages of Small Businesses

Percentage of Businesses	Number of Employees Fewer Than
88.9%	10 persons
94.7	20
99.2	100
99.9	500

Source: U.S. Department of Commerce, *Enterprise Statistics* (Washington, D.C.: U.S. Government Printing Office, 1977), Series ES77-1, Table 5, p. 142.

EXHIBIT 1.4 *Make-up of Small Business Population*

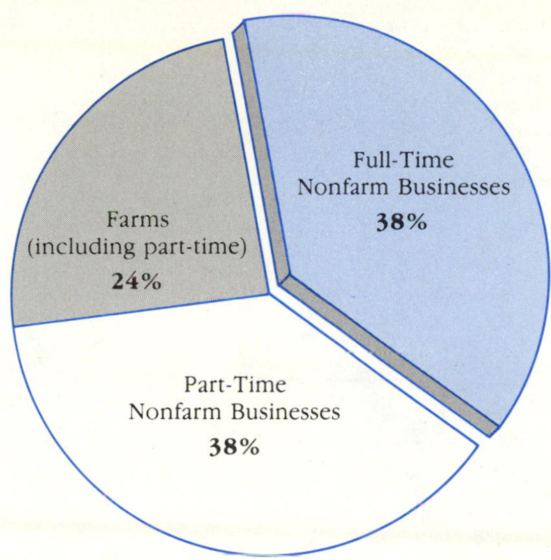

Source: Adapted from National Federation of Independent Business Research and Education Foundation, "Small Business in America," (Washington, D.C., 1981).

Financial Performance

In terms of sheer numbers, then, small business far outstrips big business. But how well are small businesses doing? Are they falling behind, keeping pace with, or moving ahead of big business? These questions are hard to answer with precision.

Even so, the evidence suggests that small business outearns big business. Some proof appears in Exhibit 1.5. On the average, small manufacturers earn a higher return on owners' equity than large manufacturers do. In other words, for each dollar they put in, small-business investors earn more than do big-business investors. Although we lack hard data showing why small manufacturers do better, we can offer these two major reasons:

- In many industries, small business can respond more quickly and at less cost than big business to the quickening rate of change in products and services, processes and markets.
- Small business has become more attractive to talented, individualistic men and women.

We lack similar data comparing the performance of small and big business in nonmanufacturing industries such as retailing, services, and wholesaling. But we believe, for these same two reasons, that small businesses in these industries are also doing well.

EXHIBIT 1.5 *Comparison of Financial Performance*

Since 1964 small manufacturers have consistently outperformed big manufacturers.

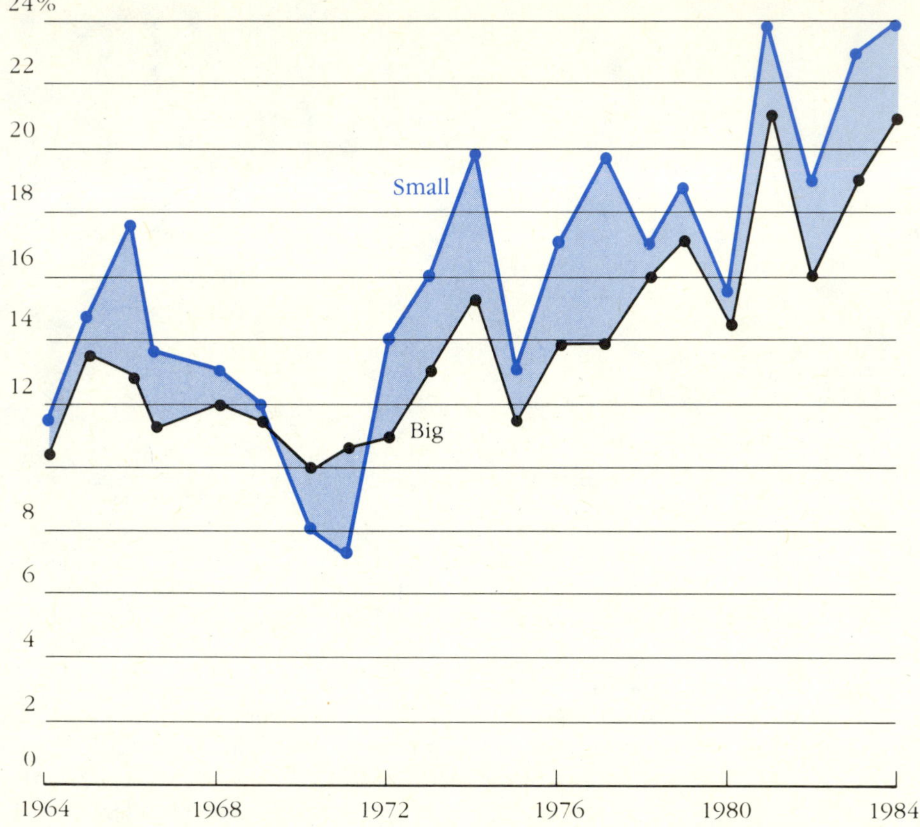

Source: Federal Trade Commission, *Quarterly Financial Reports for Manufacturing Corporations* (Washington, D.C.: U.S. Government Printing Office, 1964–1984), Table 5.

Innovation

Small business sparks our economy. Often creative and resourceful, small businesspersons tend to be mavericks. They are likely to:

- Cut prices when others follow the price leader
- Innovate when others are content to sit on their hands
- Reject suggestions from competitors to set just one price

Often, it is the mavericks who push back the frontiers of knowledge. Ideas are their stock in trade. In fact, study after study shows that major inventions are as likely to come from either small businesses or individuals as from big businesses. "Most studies show that . . . size adds little to research intensity and may actually detract from it in some industries."[8] For example, General Electric, the world's largest electrical manufacturer, credits small businesses with many of its product ideas, including the invention of electric toasters, ranges, refrigerators, dishwashers, vacuum cleaners, and deep freezers.[9] Small businesses or individuals also invented the personal computer, the stainless steel razor blade, the transistor radio, the photocopying machine, the jet engine, and the quick photograph. Their ingenuity gave us the helicopter, power steering, the automatic transmission, air conditioning, cellophane, and even the 19-cent ballpoint pen.

Since 1953, small businesses have accounted for half of all major inventions, according to studies made by both the U.S. Department of Commerce and the U.S. Office of Management and Budget.[10] Moreover, a study by the National Science Foundation found that small businesses produce 24 times as many inventions for each research dollar as many of the biggest businesses.[11]

Inventiveness of Big Business

Clearly, we are all better off for the presence of millions of small businesses in our economy. Their ingenuity enriches our lives. Of course, big business enriches our lives as well. For evidence, we need look no further than DuPont and IBM, whose ingenious new products and processes are legion.

The very size of many big businesses, however, may discourage innovation. For example, "An auto industry with millions of dollars invested in great stamping dies to turn out steel bodies has no incentive to embrace the technology of plastics."[12]

Big businesses seldom suppress invention (ideas) and innovation (application of ideas). But they cannot put every new invention straight into production just because it outdoes a current product. They must wait until new ways and new products are so superior that the changeover can be made without a steep rise in price. If we could start from scratch, we doubtless could have a much better automobile than we have. But the scrapping of entire automobile plants is too far-fetched even to think about.

Dependence of Big Business on Small Business

Our economy depends on small business for much more than invention and innovation. For one thing, small business employs tens of millions of men and women. For another, it sells most of the products made by big manufacturers to consumers. In addition, it provides big business with many of the services, supplies, and raw materials it needs. General Motors, for example, buys from more than 30,000 suppliers, most of whom are small. Why? Because big business cannot supply them as cheaply as small business. Some of the products and services that small business can supply more cheaply are:

- Those whose sales volume is small
- Those that demand close personal contact with customers
- Those that must meet each customer's unique specifications

Small Business Creates Jobs

In the popular view, it is not small business but big business that creates most new jobs. This view is false. Professor David L. Birch of the Massachusetts Institute of Technology found that between 1969 and 1976:

- Small businesses with 20 or fewer employees created 66 percent of all new jobs in the nation. In New England alone, such businesses created 99 percent of all new jobs. But—
- Middle-sized and big businesses created few new jobs.[13]

These results are striking, based as they are on data files of 5.6 million businesses. In Professor Birch's words, "It appears that the smaller corporations . . . are aggressively seeking out most new opportunities, while the larger ones are primarily redistributing their operations."[14]

Another study found that small, young, high-technology businesses create new jobs at a much faster rate than do older, larger businesses.[15]

EXHIBIT 1.6 *Job Creation*

Young, high-technology businesses create jobs at a much higher rate than do mature businesses.

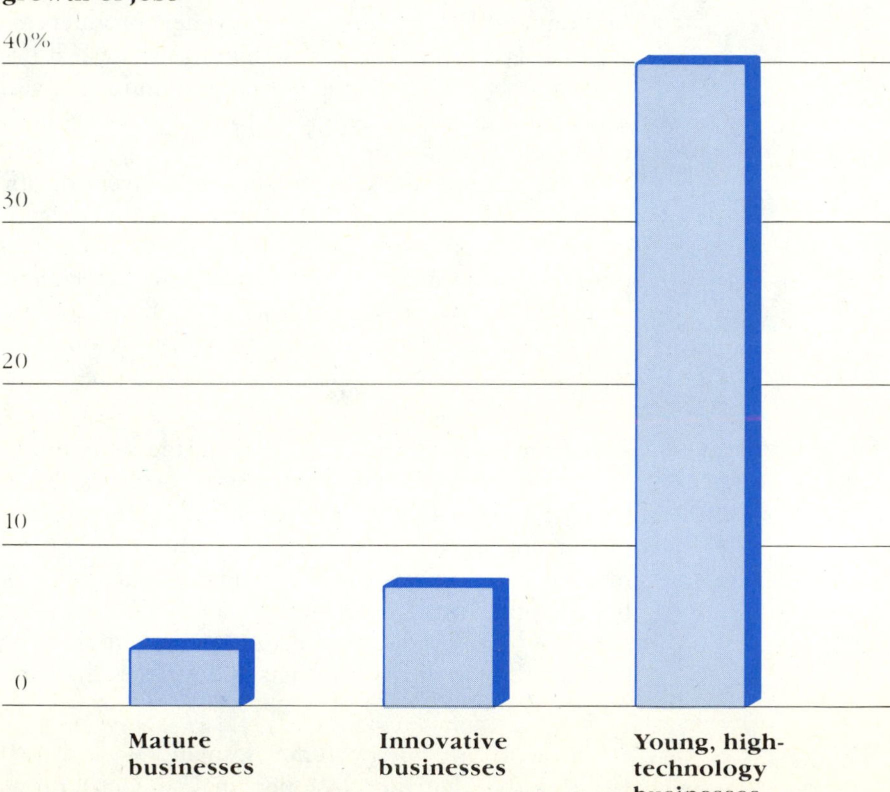

Source: U.S. Department of Commerce, *Recommendations for Creating Jobs Through the Success of Small, Innovative Businesses* (Washington, D.C.: U.S. Government Printing Office, March 1980), p. 88.

High-technology businesses, such as chemistry and electronics, require a high degree of scientific or engineering knowledge in order to succeed. Their ability to create jobs quickly is dramatized in Exhibit 1.6.

Still another measure of small-business vitality is the increasing number of businesses formed each year since 1960. New business incorporations crossed the 600,000 mark for the first time in 1983.[16] This number is roughly triple the number in the early 1960s. However, this total covers mature as well as newly founded businesses:

- Mature businesses born as either sole proprietorships or partnerships that incorporated later
- New businesses that incorporated at birth

THE DARK SIDE OF SMALL BUSINESS

Financial performance, innovation, responsiveness and job creation form the bright side of the picture. In contrast, the dark side reflects the problems unique to small business. Many small businesses die in their infancy. In fact, of the 600,000 new businesses born each year in the United States, only half live as long as 18 months and only one in five lives as long as ten years.[17]

Why so high a death rate? Perhaps the chief reason is ease of entry. In fact, it is often easier for people to go into business for themselves than to find an employer. No law stops them from choosing themselves as boss. And they may choose almost any line of business they like best. They may have 20 years of experience in that line or none at all. They may do a textbook job of researching their markets or plunge in with no information at all. They may be millionaires or penniless. Yet, regardless of their qualifications, freedom of opportunity guarantees them the right to launch their own venture.

But, as economists often point out, freedom of opportunity means not only the freedom to succeed, but also the freedom to fail. Failure to see this reality often causes untold stress, trauma, and tragedy.

Surface Causes of Failure

Should we somehow screen would-be small businesspersons before the marketplace does its own screening? No. The right to make wrong choices lies at the heart of our economic system. Without this right, initiative and incentive would soon dry up and our free enterprise system would then cease to be free.

What are some of the reasons so many fledgling businesses die? What do experts like Dun & Bradstreet identify as the cause of business failure? *Bad management.* Dun & Bradstreet has more than a century of experience in reporting on the financial health of businesses. In fact, they keep up-to-date credit ratings on 5.3 million businesses, and so they are uniquely qualified to judge why small businesses fail. They have found that businesses fail for the very same reasons year after year. These reasons are

EXHIBIT 1.7

Causes of Business Failures

Percentage of Business Failures	Cause of Failure	Explanation
44%	Incompetence	Inability to run the business—physically, morally, or intellectually
17	Lack of managerial experience	Little, if any, experience managing employees and other resources before going into business
16	Unbalanced experience	Not well-rounded in marketing, finance, purchasing, and production
15	Inexperience in line	Little, if any, experience in the product or service before going into business
1	Neglect	Too little attention to the business, due to bad habits, poor health, or marital difficulties
1	Fraud or disaster	Fraud: misleading name, false financial statements, premeditated overbuy, or irregular disposal of assets. Disaster: fire, flood, burglary, employees' fraud, or strike (some disasters could have been provided against through insurance)
6	Unknown	
100%		

Source: The first two columns are from *The Business Failure Record* (New York: Dun & Bradstreet, 1981), p. 12. Reprinted by permission of Dun & Bradstreet Corp.

listed in Exhibit 1.7. Note that the first four reasons add up to bad management. All told, this is the reason for 92 percent of failures.

According to Dun & Bradstreet, bad management often is evidenced by such problems as heavy operating expenses or slow-paying customers, a poor location or competitive weaknesses, inventory difficulties or excessive fixed assets.

Impressive as these statistics may be, pointing an accusing finger at bad management, they merely camouflage the real reason so many businesses die young. Ease of entry is the chief cause, and bad management is merely an effect.

Are Small Business Failures Really Failures?

Though widely accepted, Dun & Bradstreet's statistics on failure may be open to question. In the words of Professor Albert Shapero of Ohio State University:

> The fact is that no one knows the start-up rate or the failure rate. In fact, we don't even know what "failure" means. Do we mean bankruptcy?

But many people go out of business without declaring bankruptcy, working like hell to settle every debt even though they have to close the doors of their business.

Others close because their owners reach retirement age and have no one to turn the company over to. Still others shut down because they're bored. Are these business failures?

And is failure really failure? Many heroes of business failed at least once. Henry Ford failed twice. Maybe trying and failing is a better business education than going to a business school that has little concern with small business and entrepreneurship.[18]

Big-Business Growth

Still another worrisome statistic is big business's share of the nation's economic pie. According to the Federal Trade Commission (FTC), the nation's top 200 manufacturers boosted their share of manufacturing assets to 61 percent in 1982 from 48 percent in 1950.[19] That comes to a stunning 27 percent increase in concentration of assets in 32 years. We can only conclude that small businesses, at least in manufacturing, are finding it harder and harder to compete against big businesses. Although the FTC's analysis focuses on manufacturing, similar trends toward concentration are apparent in both wholesaling and retailing. For example, the fifty largest retail businesses owned 32 percent of all retail assets in 1977.[20]

Perhaps small businesses fail to keep pace with the growth of big businesses primarily because they are not prepared to handle increased managerial demands. It is one thing to manage a shop of 10 employees and quite another to manage a shop of 100. With only 10 employees, small businesspersons generally have visual control over everyone and everything under them.

But once their business grows to, say, 100 employees, small businesspersons must rely on more sophisticated ways to plan and control their business. Unfortunately, they often lack the managerial skills to recognize, hire, and tap the talents they need to survive and grow.

In contrast, presidents of billion-dollar corporations are more likely to be professional managers. Skillful in the best and latest managerial tools, they orchestrate the talents of dozens of knowledgeable workers to solve problems and pursue opportunities.

Minorities and Women in Small Business

Historically, minorities and women have always played a disproportionately small role in small business. Although they have made some progress, they have a long way to go before they participate in small business to the full extent of their dreams and goals. For example:

- Blacks own only 2.3 percent of the nation's 16 million businesses. Yet they make up 11 percent of the total population. What is more, their businesses account for 0.4 of one percent of the total yearly sales volume in the nation.[21]

- Women own only 7.1 percent of the nation's businesses. Yet they make up 51 percent of the total population. They account for 6.6 percent of the total yearly sales volume.[22]

Similarly, statistics for Hispanics and Native Americans show a disproportionately low share of the business world.

THE FUTURE OF SMALL BUSINESS

The future looks bright for small business. It will probably hold its strong position in the economy because of:

- Its ability to generate new ideas, new products, and new services that benefit consumers
- Its ability to create new jobs
- Big business's increasing dependence on small business for supplies, services, and raw materials
- Rising individualism among the young. More and more, business school graduates prefer to work for themselves than for somebody else.

These observations lack statistical support. We cannot peer into the future, but we can predict that small business will probably continue to spark progress in our economy.

It is unlikely, however, that small-business failures will slow down. The example of successful small businesses will continue to attract the unqualified as well as the qualified in increasing numbers. As our population expands, we can expect a steady rise in the total number of small businesses.

The Importance of Education

Our economy is likely to continue to become more scientific and therefore more complex. The rising flood of new knowledge, new managerial tools, and new managerial lifestyles will make obsolete many managerial practices as well as many products and services. So small businesspersons will have to be better prepared to master change. Colleges and universities have already begun to meet this need. In fact, according to a survey by Professor Karl H. Vesper of the University of Washington, in 1978, 137 universities offered courses on how to launch new businesses. Only eight universities had offered these courses ten years earlier.[23] Today, the total number of such universities probably runs into the hundreds.

In contrast to the universities, most of the nation's 1,231 community colleges offer at least one accredited course in small business management. A few even offer associate degrees in that discipline. And one school, Cuyahoga Community College, requires most business majors to take a course in small business management as part of its core curriculum.

The SBA will also continue to help small business with its many programs to upgrade skills and lend money. In addition, state and local governments will play an increasingly creative role, especially in stimulating inventions and their development into strong, healthy businesses that provide jobs.

Help will also come from an unexpected quarter: big business. In fact, some big businesses already are helping finance small businesses. Others are likely to follow suit. But their interest will be limited largely to small businesses with big brains—that is, high-technology companies that promise to grow at a fast rate. Such high-risk companies usually have a new product or service that promises to make a major breakthrough in the marketplace. Some spectacular examples in the past were Xerox, Sony, and Polaroid.

The future will also see the rise of small business as a new and unified political force at the local, state, and federal levels. One likely result is the passage of laws and policies that encourage risk taking and innovation by small business. At the federal level, small business has already won recognition as a political force.

SUMMARY

Small business had its crude beginnings more than 40 centuries ago in the civilization of the eastern Mediterranean. Although crowded with achievement, small-business history has never captured the public mind, at least not to the extent that law and medicine have. But this gap is narrowing as small business begins to win recognition as a creative force in our economy.

Small business is at the center of modern society, touching all our lives. Few if any parts of our economy could run without its endless flow of products and services. More important, its ingenuity sparks invention and innovation; studies show that major ideas and inventions are as likely to come from small business as from big business. Riding a wide wave of creativity, small business will continue to spawn new products and new services to benefit consumers.

Of the nation's 16 million businesses, 99 percent qualify as small; that is, they employ fewer than 500 persons. About 600,000 new businesses are born each year, but half die within 18 months. The main reason for this high death rate is the ease with which unqualified people may start new businesses.

Contrary to popular opinion, small business is flourishing in the shadow of big business. One study shows that, on the average, small manufacturers are more profitable than big manufacturers.

The future of small business looks bright. In ever-increasing numbers, men and women will make their careers in small business. And they will be better prepared to make the most of their opportunities, thanks largely to better education and better help from the many groups devoted to giving small business a helping hand.

DISCUSSION AND REVIEW QUESTIONS

1. Write a short paragraph indicating what you believe you are likely to get out of a course in small business management.
2. Should small business be as highly regarded as medicine and law? Why?
3. Does small business dominate the business world? Why?
4. Define these terms: *small business, return on owners' equity, invention, innovation, total assets, freedom of opportunity, ease of entry.*
5. On the basis of your own observations, is small business thriving or declining? Justify your answer.
6. What guarantees the existence of small business?
7. Why, on the average, are small manufacturers more profitable than big manufacturers?
8. Why do so many small businesses fail in the first few years of their existence? Explain fully.

9. Why was the U.S. Small Business Administration created by Congress?
10. Why is small business becoming an increasingly strong voice in political circles?
11. Should all men and women be screened before they go into business for themselves? Why?
12. How does the definition of small business used in this textbook differ from the SBA's definitions? How did you define a small business before you read this chapter?
13. Should small businesspersons be concerned with political forces and their effects? Why?
14. How does small business serve as a barrier against monopoly?
15. Why is the study of small business especially vital for those who plan to launch their own venture?

NOTES

1. Edward C. Bursk, *The World of Business* (New York: Macmillan, 1963), I, 2.
2. G. R. Driver and John C. Miles, *The Babylonian Laws* (Oxford: The Clarendon Press, 1955), II, 83.
3. Miriam Beard, *A History of the Business Man* (New York: Macmillan, 1938), I, 1.
4. White House Commission on Small Business, *Report to the President: American Small Business Economy: Agenda for Action* (Washington, D.C.: U.S. Government Printing Office, April 1980), p. 9.
5. Charles R. McDonald, "It's Time for Conference II," *Inc.* (July 1984), p. 16.
6. Letter written to each delegate of the 1980 White House Conference on Small Business by Milton D. Stewart, who cofounded the conference in his capacity as chief counsel of the U.S. Small Business Administration (January 14, 1982).
7. U.S. Small Business Administration, *The State of Small Business: A Report of the President* (Washington D.C.: U.S. Government Printing Office, 1984), p. 12.
8. Leonard Weiss, quoted in Mark J. Green, *The Closed Enterprise System* (New York: Bantam Books, 1972), pp. 22–23.
9. Theodore K. Quinn, *Giant Business: Threat to Democracy* (New York: Exposition Press, 1953), p. 116.
10. U.S. House of Representatives Committee on Small Business, *Future of Small Business in America* (Washington, D.C.: U.S. Government Printing Office, August 1979), p. 7.
11. U.S. Senate Committee on Small Business, *Small Business and Innovation* (Washington, D.C.: U.S. Government Printing Office, June 1979), p. 42.
12. Jerry S. Cohen and Morton Mintz, *America, Inc.* (New York: Dial Press, 1971), p. 49.
13. David L. Birch, *The Job Generation Process* (Cambridge, Massachusetts: M.I.T. Program on Neighborhood and Regional Change, 1979), p. 8.
14. Ibid.
15. U.S. Department of Commerce, *Recommendations for Creating Jobs Through the Success of Small Innovative Businesses* (Washington, D.C.: U.S. Government Printing Office, March 1980), p. 88.
16. "New Incorporations," *The Wall Street Journal* (November 19, 1984), p. 1.
17. These statistics are "rough estimates" made by Dun & Bradstreet in 1969 and reported in *The Wall Street Journal* on April 10, 1969.
18. Albert Shapero, "Numbers That Lie," *Inc.*, May 1981, p. 16.
19. U.S. Department of Commerce, *Statistical Abstract of the United States* (Washington, D.C.: U.S. Government Printing Office, 1984), p. 538.

20. U.S. House of Representatives Committee on Small Business, *Future of Small Business in America* (Washington, D.C.: U.S. Government Printing Office, August 1979), p. 15.

21. U.S. Department of Commerce, *Statistical Abstract of the United States* (Washington, D.C.: U.S. Government Printing Office, 1984), p. 534.

22. Ibid.

23. Quoted by David E. Gumpert, "Future of Small Business May Be Brighter than Portrayed," *Harvard Business Review*, July–August 1979, p. 176.

CASE 1A *Academy Specialties, Inc.*

Each year since its birth in 1978, Academy Specialties, a furniture reupholstery company, has increased both its sales revenues and its after-tax profits. In 1983, its after-tax profits were $18,100 on sales revenues of $128,500. Founders Shirley Bosko and Dorothy Werblow are now wondering whether it would be wise to expand sales by diversifying into related fields. In 1984, Ms. Werblow was chosen by the U.S. Small Business Administration (SBA) as its Small Businessperson of the Year.

Background

In 1978 Ms. Bosko and Ms. Werblow first thought about running their own small business. At the time, both women worked for a franchising company that sewed vinyl restaurant tablecovers and sold them to franchisees. Ms. Bosko was the company's office manager and Ms. Werblow its plant manager.

Despite what Ms. Werblow describes as a "fabulous product," the franchising company fell victim to its own success—it expanded so rapidly that it overextended itself financially. The result was bankruptcy, and both women were left without jobs.

Their joblessness was short-lived. Upon discovering that their former employer had left dozens of orders for tablecovers unfilled, they decided to invest $900 each for shop space, a sewing machine, a vendor's license, and other assets to start their own business. They named their company, Academy Specialties, Inc. Why? "Because it got at the top of the Yellow Pages and off to a good start," says Ms. Werblow. The business's beginning balance sheet appears in Exhibit 1A.1.

As they expected, when they filled the backlog of orders, they found themselves with few repeat orders. It was clear that most of the franchisees had found local producers of tablecovers. "Some franchisees were awful to us," says Ms. Werblow. "They thought we were naive, although we produced a high-quality tablecover, on time."

EXHIBIT 1A.1

Academy Specialties, Inc.: Beginning Balance Sheet (August 15, 1978)

Assets		Equities	
Cash	$ 700	Liabilities	$ 0
Inventory	200	Owners' equity	1,800
Sewing machine	500		
Cutting table	200		
Other	200		
Total	$1,800	Total	$1,800

A Crucial Product Decision

With orders for tablecovers dwindling, the two women had to make a major operating decision. They both wanted to continue running their own business. As Ms. Bosko says, "the thought of looking for a job depressed us deeply. We dreaded inflexible work schedules, ornery bosses, and office politics . . . It was a real gutsy thing. We were scared to death. Neither of us had any other means of support, so we were determined to make a go of it."

They needed to develop another product—something else to do with their cutting table and sewing machine. They both wanted to continue working with fabric, but not to make tablecovers, since, as Ms. Werblow says, "making tablecovers is both boring and repetitious."

It was Ms. Bosko who first suggested that their company specialize in furniture reupholstery. "We started by brainstorming a little to figure out just where our skills might best be used," says Ms. Bosko. "We soon realized that a lot of offices out there would have bruised or damaged chairs that needed refurbishing and fixing."

First, however, the two women had to overcome a major obstacle—neither one knew much about reupholstery. They both enrolled in night classes at a local high school to learn all they could about reupholstery and then practiced what they learned on an antique chair at their shop.

Their Niche in the Marketplace

They were aware that no upholsterer in town was aggressive in filling the need that most offices had for furniture repair. "They were order takers, waiting for decorators to call them," says Ms. Werblow. "If that was so, then we were sure we could take that business away from them by simply going after it aggressively. Office reupholstery was a completely untapped market."

The two women decided to test their convictions by canvassing every business in the city's bustling downtown district. "To our delight," says Ms. Werblow, "we discovered that businesses were indeed happy to find someone willing to replace just the damaged part of their chairs, thereby restoring their value." Ms. Bosko visited such major corporations as Eastman Kodak, General Electric, IBM, McDonald's, and U.S. Steel with few turning her away.

Her visits had several purposes. First, she wanted to make office managers aware they had the need for furniture reupholstery. Second, she informed them that Academy Specialties was prepared to fill that need. "Our sales pitch was that replacing furniture is a capital expenditure like a typewriter," says Ms. Werblow. "We pointed out that redoing their chairs comes out of the maintenance budget. Our service is as consumable as the typewriter ribbon." Finally, she added that Academy Specialties would gladly do the smallest of jobs. "We told them that we are *the* shop to which they should give all their business," says Ms. Werblow.

A Difficult Beginning

All the while, the two women were barely scraping by financially. "We starved the first year," says Ms. Werblow. "So much so that I even began doubting myself. I even asked myself, 'Did this nonsense make sense?' I almost gave it all up. Without Shirley to pick me up when I was down, I'm not sure I would have persevered."

For some time, the two women worried that they would not be able to pay the rent; so in the hope that it would lead to a larger, continuous use of their services, they accepted repair jobs as small as armrests. Cash flow was so slow that they did not have $50 to buy a stapler; so, they used only tacks in their repairs. They also had to overcome the anger and frustration at being robbed four times, twice losing all of their hand tools and office equipment. "Even with all these headaches," says Ms. Bosko, "I was not about to trade my lot for a plush sales manager's job with an established company marketing a glamorous product. I'd rather be in my own business, not under somebody else's thumb. I like knowing that all the benefits and pats on the back are for Dorothy and me."

Indeed, had either Ms. Bosko or Ms. Werblow been of a different frame of mind and instead re-entered the job market, it is likely that they would have found new jobs quickly, since employers would have found their academic credentials to be impressive. Ms. Bosko attended Kent State University, and Ms. Werblow graduated from Baruch College, College of the City of New York, with a major in business administration.

A Momentous Decision

With sales limping along the first year, the two women made what they believe to be their most important operating decision. Until then, they had worked in tandem, both sharing the production and the marketing aspects of their business. From then on, their duties would be separate:

- Ms. Bosko would be in charge of marketing the company's services. Her duties would range from making sales calls to making pick-ups and deliveries in her Chevette hatchback. She would also help the customers select fabrics. Her only advertising piece would be a bright pink card, since "hot pink doesn't get lost in the shuffle."
- Ms. Werblow, on the other hand, would be in charge of "getting out the work." She would run the shop, doing all of the furniture reupholstering. "I'm not suited to selling," she says. "My personality is such that I seek solitary environments. I'm a perfectionist at heart, so I'm better suited to production and doing high-quality work than I am at knocking on office doors to get orders."

This organizational decision worked. By the end of the first year, sales revenues had increased sharply and each woman was able to draw a salary of $100 a week, roughly the federal minimum wage at the time. Their organizational chart, unchanged since 1978, appears in Exhibit 1A.2.

Marketing Style

Although both women had studied business administration in college, they did not use a traditional, textbook marketing approach. In their eagerness

EXHIBIT 1A.2 *Academy Specialties, Inc.: Organizational Chart*

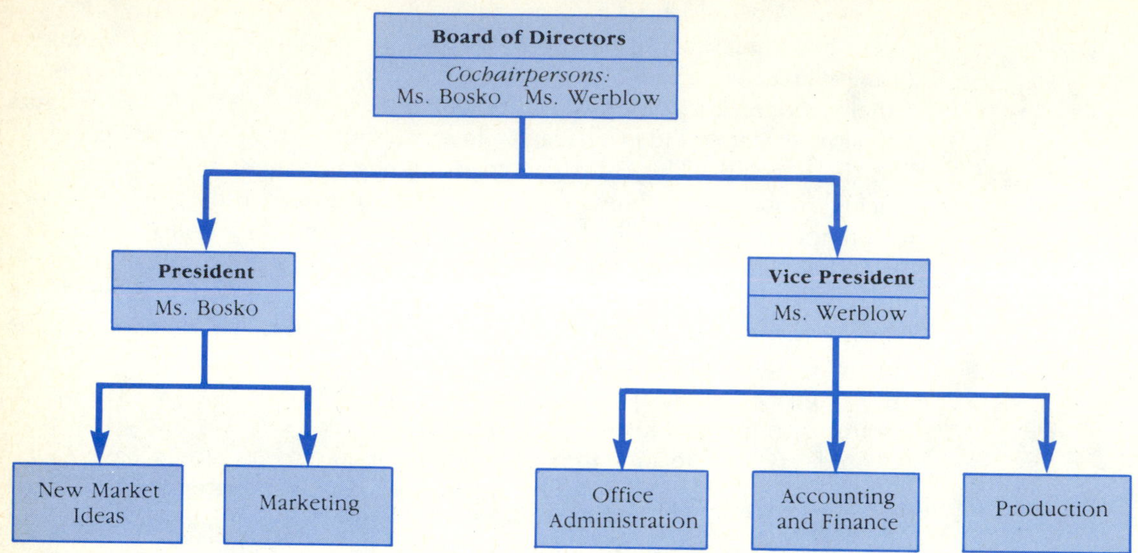

to land clients, they shunned both advertising and sales promotion. Instead, they focused their energies almost entirely on personal selling and, later, on public relations. A recent newspaper article described them as follows:

> Ms. Bosko and Ms. Werblow are known to lawyers, doctors, corporate executives, and restaurant owners throughout the area as the "dynamic duo." Need a new look for that shabby office furniture? Tired of those tattered bar stools? Call the owners of Academy Specialties, the wonder women of reupholstery.
>
> Their miracles with fabric have earned them near-celebrity status. As they walk down the street, people say, "Hey, there go the nutty girls who redid the chairs in our office." One executive chased Ms. Bosko through the city's public square, yelling, "Shirley, you have to help me! We're having inspection in a week. Please do something."

Indeed, they have never let a customer down. They answer telephones in the middle of the night, and even work round the clock to meet clients' deadlines. An especially tough job came from a restaurateur who wanted twelve new banquette seats and backs upholstered for the grand opening of his new restaurant—the next day. Ms. Bosko and Ms. Werblow quickly determined a strategy for the job, instructed the carpenter to order the materials, and came to the restaurant to complete the upholstering overnight. "The carpenter was building the seats at the very same time as we were working," says Ms. Bosko. "He took one look at us and couldn't believe that we were upholstering faster than he could do the carpentry work."

A Typical Assignment

The two women purposely developed a reputation for uniqueness. In addition to invading the "male-dominated world of business," they are willing to do any task, however menial, that is necessary to complete a job, as this quotation from a recent magazine article demonstrates:

> Shirley Bosko makes pick-ups and deliveries in her Chevette hatchback. "We've stopped traffic enough times," says Ms. Bosko. "People wave and say, 'There they go again.'"
>
> On Mondays, Ms. Bosko often will walk into an office, decked out in her three-piece suit and briefcase, ready to make the sale. She helps the customer select fabric and makes all the arrangements. "Fine, my crew will be by tomorrow," she tells him.
>
> The client is in for a shock the next day when "the crew"—Ms. Bosko—shows up in jeans and sneakers, carrying her equipment. When she is dressed in these clothes, secretaries sometimes stare. One woman remarked in a condescending voice, "I can't believe the things your company makes you do."*

Occasionally, sexism complicates their efforts to land new clients. Once an attorney agreed to meet with Ms. Bosko, just so he could ask her for a tennis date. "All it takes is one off-color comment that I don't laugh at and they know we mean business," says Ms. Bosko. Some men also try what Ms. Bosko calls the "cutesy-pie approach." "We don't go for that either," says Ms. Bosko. "Some of them are thinking, 'Boy, the audacity of those women.' They really wonder, 'Can two middle-class suburban women really pull this off?' Yes, we sure can."

Financial Performance

The two partners are proud of their business's performance. Sales revenues and after-tax profits have both gone up every year since they founded it in 1978. Their yearly financial performance is summarized here and graphed in Exhibit 1A.3.

Year	Sales Revenues	After-Tax Profits
1978	$ 23,100	$(2,700)
1979	37,300	700
1980	58,700	3,300
1981	88,300	9,700
1982	107,600	14,400
1983	128,500	18,100

They are especially pleased that profits have increased yearly, along with sales. "We make every effort to be financially productive," says Ms.

* Maria Riccardi, "Nothing's Shabby about Their Work," *The Plain Dealer* (October 10, 1982), p. 1-C.

EXHIBIT 1A.3 *Academy Specialties, Inc.: Financial Performance*

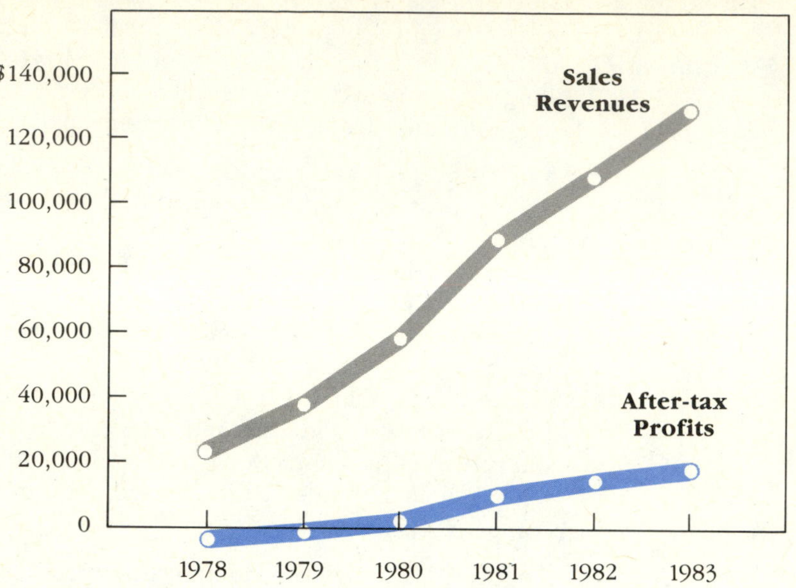

Werblow. "I keep exact records of materials, labor, and time so that I can see whether we make a profit on each job."

Indeed, as the partner who runs the office, Ms. Werblow has tried "at all times to bring big-business methods to our little shop." She keeps detailed cost records, cash flow charts, and inventory controls; and she reads magazines for small businesses such as *Inc.*, to find the latest ideas, methods, and management tips that she can apply in the business.

So cost-conscious is Ms. Werblow that she does all her own bookkeeping to save on accountant's fees. She now employs three women in production, two of whom she hired because they were receiving benefits from the federal program, Aid for Dependent Children (AFDC). "By hiring AFDC mothers," says Ms. Werblow, "I also earn tax credits."

She knows at all times how much is owed the business by customers as well as how old each bill is. Similarly, she knows to the penny how much the business owes to suppliers. "If my accounts payable are less than my accounts receivable, then I'm making a profit," says Ms. Werblow.

Although she does the bookkeeping herself, she pays a certified public accountant to prepare the business's tax returns. Recently, from the detailed books kept by Ms. Werblow, the accountant prepared these financial statements covering operations for the past three years:

- Income statements, as shown in Exhibit 1A.4
- Balance sheets, as shown in Exhibit 1A.5

EXHIBIT 1A.4

Academy Specialties, Inc.: Three-year Income Statements

	1981	1982	1983
Sales revenues	$88,300	$107,600	$128,500
Cost of sales	22,900	25,800	31,500
Gross profit	$65,400	$ 81,800	$ 97,000
Operating expenses:			
Wages	$19,400	$ 26,000	$ 30,500
Insurance	4,600	5,400	6,000
Automobile	3,900	4,600	6,000
Utilities	5,000	5,200	5,400
Payroll taxes	2,800	3,800	4,400
Depreciation	2,300	2,300	4,300
Office	3,000	2,900	3,800
Rent	3,600	3,600	3,600
Supplies	2,100	2,200	2,500
Repairs and maintenance	1,600	1,800	1,900
Sales promotion	1,300	1,700	1,900
Bank fees	1,000	1,300	1,800
Advertising	1,100	1,300	1,700
Employee welfare	1,000	1,200	1,600
Legal and accounting	900	1,000	1,100
Licenses	200	200	200
Total operating expenses	$53,800	$ 64,500	$ 76,700
Profit before taxes	$11,600	$ 17,300	$ 20,300
Federal income taxes	2,000	2,900	2,200
Profit after taxes	$ 9,600	$ 14,400	$ 18,100

Ms. Werblow does not believe she needs a microcomputer to help with the bookkeeping. "It takes me just minutes each day to update our books," says Ms. Werblow. "Besides, all I have to do is look around the shop to see what my assets and liabilities are."

Volunteer Activities

Although she regularly logs a 60-hour workweek and rarely takes a vacation, Ms. Werblow nevertheless finds time to volunteer her services and talents for causes that she "strongly believes in." She has embraced the promotion of entrepreneurship among women almost single-mindedly, never turning down an opportunity to speak about the need for women to become independent through entrepreneurship.

It was Ms. Werblow's belief in this cause that led her and several other women entrepreneurs to form the Women's Business Ownership Association (WBOA) in her city. Now boasting more than 150 members, the WBOA has become the most active women's business group in the city. Ms. Werblow goes one step further and calls the WBOA "the *only* entrepreneurial group in town. Sure, there are other entrepreneurial groups, mostly male-dominated, but they are not truly entrepreneurial. By

EXHIBIT 1A.5

Academy Specialties, Inc.: Three-year Balance Sheets

	Year-end		
Assets	1981	1982	1983
Current assets			
Cash in bank	$ 2,200	$ 4,000	$ 7,300
Accounts receivable	1,100	3,400	9,700
Inventory	2,300	3,500	8,800
Total current assets	$ 5,600	$10,900	$25,800
Fixed assets			
Furniture and fixtures	$12,600	$12,600	$22,600
Automobiles	15,500	15,500	15,500
Less: Accum. depreciation	(6,800)	(9,000)	(13,300)
Total fixed assets	$21,300	$19,100	$24,800
Total assets	$26,900	$30,000	$50,600
Equities			
Current liabilities			
Accounts payable	$ 700	$ 200	$ 1,000
Taxes payable	1,400	700	1,800
Notes payable, shareholders	10,300	200	800
Total current liabilities	$12,400	$ 1,100	$ 3,600
Owners' equity			
Common stock	$ 1,000	$ 1,000	$ 1,000
Retained earnings	13,500	27,900	46,000
Total owners' equity	$14,500	$28,900	$47,000
Total equities	$26,900	$30,000	$50,600

that I mean their membership includes big law firms, big CPA firms, and big family-owned businesses. Are they entrepreneurial? I don't believe so."

Currently its vice president, she also sees the WBOA as a vehicle for "renewing" herself. Monthly meetings are devoted almost exclusively to networking and to education. Seminars and workshops focus on such topics as:

- How to approach your banker for a loan
- How to motivate your employees
- How to succeed

Of her many activities, Ms. Werblow is proudest of the Women's Business Ownership Educational Conference. Held yearly, this conference attracts as many as 500 women, most of them "eager to find out what it takes to become a successful entrepreneur." At the 1985 conference, two of the workshops were conducted by Ms. Bosko and Ms. Werblow:

- Ms. Bosko spoke about: *Selling Your Product or Service: Sell Hard, Keep It Light, and Close the Sale.*
- Ms. Werblow spoke about: *Do-It-Yourself Marketing Research: What Is It and How Can It Help You? It's for Everyone.*

The entire conference is organized, staffed, and carried out by women. "We believe that successful women entrepreneurs offer the best role models for aspiring women entrepreneurs," says Ms. Werblow. Indeed, of the 72 speakers at the 1985 conference, only one was male.

Small Businessperson of the Year

Each year, the regional office of the SBA selects a Small Businessperson of the Year. In 1984, Ms. Werblow was chosen. "I can't begin to tell you how thrilled I was," says Ms. Werblow. "It was one of the most exciting things that ever happened to me, to be recognized like that."

In screening candidates for the Small Businessperson of the Year Award, the SBA applies a set of strict standards, including:

- *Staying power*—Several years as an established and profitable business.
- *Increase in sales revenues*—An indication of continued growth.
- *Innovativeness of product or service offered*—Illustrations of creativity and imagination.
- *Response to adversity*—Examples of problems faced by the business and the solutions used by the entrepreneur.
- *Contributions to community-oriented projects*—Evidence that the small businessperson has volunteered personal resources to help improve a community's quality of life.
- *Growth in number of employees*—The impact of the business on the community's job market.

Ms. Werblow won the award, despite competition with many other small businesspersons with businesses much larger than hers. Submitted by the WBOA, hers was the only presentation packet that the SBA judges rated "exceptional."

Looking to the Future

Academy Specialties, Inc., is in no hurry to grow. As shown earlier, in Exhibit 1A.3, both its sales revenues and after-tax profits have grown steadily since 1978. "Sure I would like to have a pet rock," says Ms. Werblow, "but I prefer to grow slowly. Making a lot of money is not a big thing with me or Shirley. I would rather visit the Grand Canyon. Nor are we building the business to leave it to somebody."

Their idea of slow and controlled growth is to double sales revenues and after-tax profits every five years. "That means it would take us 15 years to reach that magical sales level of a million dollars," says Ms. Werblow. "We don't know exactly how we're going to accomplish that little feat, but we'll find a way, Shirley and I."

Recently, Academy Specialties received a special order from a steel manufacturer to make covers for microcomputers. The unexpected order ignited Ms. Werblow's imagination. "Hundreds of thousands of microcomputers are sold every year," says Ms. Werblow. "What an enormous market that is, and with no competition." She charged the steel manufacturer $28 a cover, although material costs were only $3 a cover. "Like light bulbs, I charge what the traffic will bear," says Ms. Werblow.

The company has just begun providing such services as drapery cleaning, window treatments, and carpet cleaning. "These services are logical extensions of what we do now," says Ms. Werblow. "But we must be careful not to overextend ourselves. We must never lose sight of the fact that reupholstery is the core of our business."

Nor do the partners plan to move out of their high-crime location, even if growth justifies their moving to a safer part of town. "We're going to be part of this area's renaissance," says Ms. Werblow. A view of Ms. Bosko and Ms. Werblow in their shop appears in Exhibit 1A.6.

Questions

1. What are the company's prospects?
2. What are the key elements in the success of this kind of business?
3. Comment on the entrepreneurial qualities of Ms. Bosko and Ms. Werblow.
4. Analyze the company's financial performance.
5. Comment on Ms. Bosko's and Ms. Werblow's plans for the future.

EXHIBIT 1A.6 *Academy Specialties, Inc.: Dorothy Werblow and Shirley Bosko in their shop*

CASE 1B *Adam Smith*

Following are selected excerpts from a cover story about free enterprise that appeared in *Time* magazine:

> In [Adam] Smith's* view, the great motivator of economic activity is "the uniform, constant, and uninterrupted effort of every man to better his condition"—or, bluntly, self-interest. Only this drive moves men to produce the goods that society needs.
>
> As [Adam Smith] put it: "It is not from the benevolence of the butcher, the brewer, or the baker, that we expect our dinner, but from their regard to their own interest. . . ."
>
> Self-interest expresses itself as the drive for profit and produces that great marvel, the self-regulating market. If consumers are free to spend their money any way they wish—and businessmen can compete uninhibitedly for their favor—then capital and labor will flow "naturally" . . . into the uses where they are most needed.
>
> If consumers want, say, more bread than is being produced, they will pay high prices and bakers will earn high profits. Those profits will lure investors to build more bakeries. If they wind up turning out more bread than consumers want to buy, prices and profits will fall and capital will shift into making something that consumers need and desire more—shoes, perhaps.
>
> Thus the businessman seeking only his profit is "led by an invisible hand to promote an end which was no part of his intention"—the common good. . . .
>
> [Adam Smith's] system was designed to enthrone not the businessman but the consumer. . . . he advocated complete laissez-faire.† Government, he said, should stop trying to regulate trade, cease all intervention in the market, and let free competition work its wonders.

Questions

1. Is the above an accurate description of the operation of today's economy? Does today's economy differ? If so, how?
2. Identify at least one flaw in Adam Smith's system.

Source: "Can Capitalism Survive?" *Time*, July 14, 1975, p. 53.

CASE 1C *Gibraltar Industries—How Big Is Small?*

Staying small is essential for Gibraltar Industries, Inc., a major supplier of fire-, chemical-, and heat-resistant clothing for the military. It is vital to be

* Adam Smith was a Scottish philosopher who wrote the classic, *The Wealth of Nations*, in 1776. In it, he describes how a free economy works.

† *Laissez faire* is a French phrase meaning "letting people do as they please without intervention."

classified as small because the U.S. Department of Defense reserves 95 percent of apparel contracts for small businesses exclusively. So, if Gibraltar loses its status as a small business, it also loses the major source of its sales revenues.

Its competitors insist that Gibraltar is a big business posing as a small one to get contracts under the federal small-business set-aside program. The program is supposed to help small firms by reserving a "reasonable portion" of federal purchases for small businesses to bid on.

The U.S. Small Business Administration (SBA) has had trouble deciding just how large or small Gibraltar is. At one point, the SBA ruled that Gibraltar no longer qualified as a small business. It exceeded the 500-employee limit for apparel makers when its three affiliated companies' labor forces were included.

But three weeks after its ruling, the SBA re-certified Gibraltar as a small business, noting that it had "substantially" changed its relationships with its affiliates.

Lawyer Dennis Riley, who represents one of Gibraltar's competitors, has called these changes "a sham." He says that Gibraltar's maneuvers make a mockery of the set-aside program and the size standards. Gibraltar's board chairman, Wallace Forman, says that he *must* maneuver like this or the company will lose a huge amount of sales.

The set-aside "has become a sort of welfare program," Mr. Forman claims. The recipients are trapped in it. If I tried to escape, I would starve to death."

Questions

1. Should Gibraltar be allowed to bid on contracts that are set aside for small business? Why?
2. Has the set-aside program become a "sort of welfare program" as Mr. Forman says?

Source: Adapted from Sanford Jacobs, "Concern Fights to Stay 'Small' so It Can Keep U.S. Contracts." *The Wall Street Journal*, Dec. 13, 1982, p. 1 of Section 2. Reprinted by permission of The Wall Street Journal,

2 THE ENTREPRENEUR

QUESTIONS FOR MASTERY

What is an entrepreneur?

What are the main traits of successful entrepreneurs?

What is the difference between entrepreneurship and management?

What problems do minorities and women have as entrepreneurs?

What are the rewards and hazards of being an entrepreneur?

Every man has business and desire, such as it is.

William Shakespeare

Successful men and women come from backgrounds so broad and complex that analysis of what it takes to create a successful business has been imprecise. Experts often try to pinpoint those traits that favor success and those that do not. But most have only been able to conclude that good managers run successful small businesses and poor managers run unsuccessful ones.

Some scholars, however, have researched the matter meaningfully, to help answer such elusive questions as these: What kinds of men and women are likely to found successful businesses? Can business success be taught? If so, how?

DEFINITION OF ENTREPRENEURS

Today, we take for granted the meaning of the word *entrepreneur*. It suggests spirit, zeal, ideas. But we tend to apply the word loosely to describe anyone who runs a business—for example, the person who presides over General Motors, owns a corner fruit stand, owns a McDonald's franchise, or hawks magazine subscriptions from a home telephone.

In the past, the word *entrepreneur* enjoyed a purer, more precise meaning. It described only those who created their own business. In fact, the *American Heritage Dictionary* defines an entrepreneur as "a person who organizes, operates, and assumes the risk for business ventures," as Henry Ford and Steven Jobs did.

Henry Ford, Entrepreneur

Mr. Ford created his first two businesses in 1899 and 1901 to make racing cars. In one car, he raced 90 miles an hour, a feat unheard of at that time. He became a celebrity overnight, and his success led him to believe there was a barrel of money in the business. Unfortunately, there was not; both companies later folded.

Clearly, Mr. Ford mistook his market. The racing car market was too small. Next, he turned his energies to putting the world on wheels. In 1903, at age 40, Mr. Ford raised $28,000 and began the Ford Motor Company, this time to make a car for the masses. The philosophy underlying his venture has been described as follows:

> A car for the multitude . . . large enough for the family . . . a car to lift farm drudgery off flesh and blood and lay it on steel and motor.[1]

Mr. Ford met his goal by 1908, when he built the cheap and sturdy Model T automobile. It revolutionized our way of life. Priced as low as $260, the Model T soon crowded out the horse and buggy. It also tore down the walls between city and farm. In short, it changed the face of the land. Today, superhighways thread the continent, and one hundred million cars help people pursue almost any way of life.

What kind of man was Henry Ford? Above all, he had a burning desire to succeed. Success itself meant more to him than the field in which he achieved it. That may also account for his many other interests, ranging from airplanes and car racing to American furniture and rubber plantations.

A resilient man, Mr. Ford was a two-time loser before he became a winner. He reveled in risk-taking, in trying something new and making it work. Although he was never more than a tinkerer and mechanic, he was brilliantly intuitive. He had an uncanny ability to search out the mass market, and he saw that the best way to reach such a market was by selling cars at less than $500, at prices low enough to fit the consumer's pocketbook. It was this vision that brought about the mass production of cars.

Steven Jobs, Entrepreneur

What Henry Ford did for the automobile industry, Steven Jobs did for the personal computer industry. In the 1980s, the personal computer industry erupted as decisively as did automobiles in the 1920s and television in the 1950s. The entrepreneur who triggered the eruption was Steven Jobs.

Mr. Jobs's entrepreneurial vision enabled him to exploit a market that such giants as IBM and Hewlett-Packard had previously ignored entirely. These entrenched businesses wanted to market their computers only to large organizations that made large purchases. They did not want to sell to the masses, dismissing the idea of personal computers as being too sophisticated for most consumers and therefore too risky for their business.

Mr. Jobs changed all that. Like Henry Ford, he was convinced that he could sell to the masses. The idea so intrigued Mr. Jobs that, in 1976, he joined forces with an electronics engineer, Stephen Wozniak, to design a desktop computer that would have mass appeal. It would be priced low enough to reach markets that had never considered buying computers before. One such market was the nation's 16 million small businesses.

Mr. Jobs and Mr. Wozniak named their new venture Apple Computer Corporation. Working out of a garage in Cupertino, California, on the tiny budget of less than a thousand dollars, both men worked like dynamos to make their venture successful. In a short time, they defined the computer product, raised the money, organized the manufacture, and developed a marketing strategy.

They succeeded phenomenally. There was indeed a mass market that hungered for the personal computer. So much so that it took the Apple Computer Corporation just seven years to rack up sales revenues of a billion dollars a year. The Apple computer soon became a household word. And, Mr. Jobs made the cover of *Time* magazine in 1982. In his recent book on the entrepreneurial spirit, author George Gilder had this to say about Mr. Jobs:

> An adopted son of California parents, Mr. Jobs had reached his eminence after a long period of searching in the wilderness for gurus and genetic forebears, sampling vegetarianism and primal scream therapy, and slouching through the 1970s in jeans and sandals. All the emotional turmoil and restless energy of his youth—the rebellion, the failures,

the guilt, the betrayals—suddenly fused into an irrepressible force of creation.[2]

Pure Entrepreneurs

Like Henry Ford and Steven Jobs, pure entrepreneurs also launch their own ventures from scratch. They nurse them into successful businesses by their instinct for opportunity, sense of timing, hard work, and idea-producing ability. They quicken the development of our economy. And they seem motivated not merely by profit but also by the "desire to found a private dynasty, the will to conquer in a competitive battle, and the joy of creating."[3]

As a nation, we often put pure entrepreneurs like Mr. Ford and Mr. Jobs on a pedestal. Novelists and economists alike glorify them. The Horatio Alger tales, for example, dramatize the entrepreneurial habit of

EXHIBIT 2.1 *Well-Known Examples of Pure Entrepreneurs*

These entrepreneurs had life-improving ideas and made them work. They all began small.

Entrepreneur	Product	Comment
Thomas Alva Edison		The hardest won of Mr. Edison's 1093 patents was invention of the bulb that would light up the world. He also fathered the motion picture and recording industries.
Miles Lowell Edwards		Mr. Edwards, a retired engineer, and Albert Starr, a heart surgeon, worked together to integrate pumping technology and the human heart. Their artificial valve now helps tens of thousands of hearts to keep pumping.
Benjamin Franklin		Almost 200 years after Mr. Franklin glued together two sets of spectacles, no one has been able to improve the basic design of bifocal lenses.
Whitcomb L. Judson		Mr. Judson nearly went bankrupt selling his new zippers because they tended to pop open unexpectedly. An electrical engineer refined the idea, and the business eventually was named Talon, Inc.

Source: Adapted from an SBA exhibit at the National Geographic Society in Washington, D.C. (May 1980).

winning through hard work and education. In addition, economists credit the pure entrepreneur with pushing our economy ahead in giant steps. Some well-known examples of other pure entrepreneurs appear in Exhibit 2.1.

In this textbook, we define pure entrepreneurs as men and women who create a venture from the raw materials of their own ideas and hard work. Others, of course, may also qualify as entrepreneurs, but not as pure ones. These others would include:

- Those who take over a business after the founder retires, dies, or sells out—but who continue to build and innovate
- Those who run a franchise independently of the franchisor

Entrepreneurship and the Entrepreneur

Let us pause here to distinguish between the terms *entrepreneur* and *entrepreneurship*. Although in this textbook we regard entrepreneurs mostly as those who launch new ventures, entrepreneurship is far more widely practiced—among old businesses as well as new ones, and among big businesses as well as small ones. In the words of Professor Nathaniel H. Leff, "Entrepreneurship is the capacity for innovation, investment, and expansion in new markets, products, and techniques."[4]

This definition means that an entrepreneur is at work whenever someone takes risks and invests resources to make something new, design a new way of making something that already exists, or create new markets.

Management and Entrepreneurship

Nor is entrepreneurship the same thing as management. The first job of the manager is to make a business perform well. The manager takes given resources—such as manpower and money, machines and materials—and orchestrates them into production. In contrast, the first job of the entrepreneur is to bring about change on purpose. As Economist Irving Kristol has suggested:

> More and more, chief executives refer to themselves as "managers," sometimes even "professional managers." Well, if that indeed is what they are . . . then they are wildly overpaid. A good executive . . . is above all an energetic and shrewd entrepreneur, seeking out—no, creating—new opportunities for profitable economic transactions. It is only the possession of this talent . . . that justifies the high salaries they receive.[5]

ENTREPRENEURIAL TRAITS

Neither Henry Ford nor Steven Jobs is a typical entrepreneur. In fact, no two entrepreneurs are precisely alike. In the words of Professor Peter F. Drucker, noted author-lecturer-consultant:

> Some are eccentrics, others painfully correct conformists; some are fat and some are lean; some are worriers, some relaxed; some drink quite

> heavily, others are total abstainers; some are men of great charm and warmth, some have no more personality than a frozen mackerel.[6]

Though taken out of context, Professor Drucker's words underline the futility of painting a word picture of the typical entrepreneur. Precious little is known about entrepreneurs, about the kinds of men and women who go into business for themselves. How do they get started? Why do they do it? Is it because, in Henry David Thoreau's phrase, they "lead lives of quiet desperation" and desire something new and different? Are they society's rejects who "instead of becoming hobos, criminals, or professors make their adjustment by starting their own business"?[7]

To be sure, many seek escape from boring, dead-end jobs. This is especially true of those who in their middle years face up to the fact that they will never climb to the executive suite, write a Broadway play, or make a million dollars. They feel frustrated and ponder the possibility of a new career—perhaps entrepreneurship.

Example: Caroline Jones, cofounder of Mingo-Jones Advertising Inc. in New York, began in 1968 as a secretary at J. Walter Thompson Company, one of the nation's largest advertising agencies. The only route out of the secretarial pool then, she says, was copywriting. After completing a training course at J. Walter Thompson, she became the agency's first black female copywriter.

By the time she cofounded Mingo-Jones Advertising Inc. in 1977, she had accumulated a breadth of experience. She had held jobs at several other large advertising agencies, advancing to account executive. "I knew I'd hit my plateau then," she says.

Today, her agency has a dozen clients, including Kentucky Fried Chicken and the Miller Brewing Company. Sales revenues are about $22 million a year. "I didn't have any role models," says Ms. Jones. "But I also didn't have anyone telling me that what I wanted to do was impossible."[8]

Or are entrepreneurs overachievers, drawn to the challenge of creating their own venture rather than escaping from previous failure? Studies at Harvard University and Massachusetts Institute of Technology found that entrepreneurs are not likely to come from the pool of society's rejects. In fact, entrepreneurs enjoy a "generally higher than average level of success in their previous employment."[9]

This finding suggests that it is not outside pressures that force successful people to become entrepreneurs. If they decide to go into business for themselves, they usually do so for good reasons. They may prefer not to be ciphers in somebody else's business, or they may want to exploit an invention themselves. Society's rejects, however, often go into business for the wrong reasons, with outside pressures playing a strong role. They may decide to go on their own only after being demoted, passed up, or fired. Not all fail. Many succeed, sometimes spectacularly.

Example: An unemployed paperhanger in Hammond, Indiana, one day in 1939 invented a large, boxlike machine that could simultaneously freeze and dispense ice cream. He sold the rights to a manufacturer in Illinois. This merger produced the first Dairy Queen, and by 1984 there were more than 5,000 outlets all across America.[10]

Clearly, men and women become entrepreneurs for a variety of reasons. However, their desire for self-expression appears to be a common thread. This desire helps explain why more than half of all the nation's wage earners prefer to work for themselves rather than somebody else.[11] Yet few become entrepreneurs. In fact, most overachievers choose to work for somebody else. Why?

Perhaps most are dreamers, sitting on a cloud with their feet dangling in air. A more likely reason is that their horizons are defined by monthly mortgage payments and broken washing machines. Many cannot give up their jobs without risking their home life. Besides, how can they sacrifice pensions and company-paid insurance? So, early on, they become emotionally incapable of taking that fateful first step—unless forced to do so by some crucial event, such as the loss of a job.

Key Entrepreneurial Traits

Of the men and women who do become entrepreneurs, why are so few successful? As mentioned in Chapter One, many new businesses die in infancy. In fact, half die within 18 months of birth. What is it, then, that makes for success instead of failure? Can we pinpoint the key traits of successful entrepreneurs? If we could, then we might predict what kinds of men and women are most likely to succeed as entrepreneurs.

To begin with, successful entrepreneurs are likely to be overachievers. Like Henry Ford and Steven Jobs, they burn with the desire to excel. In his landmark study of entrepreneurs, Professor David C. McClelland of Harvard University found that they are likely to do well if they are also:[12]

- Reasonable risk-takers
- Self-confident
- Hard workers
- Goal setters
- Accountable
- Innovative

These traits defy sharp separation. Each trait shades off into the others like the colors of a spectrum. Just as it is impossible to tell where red shades into orange, so it is with these traits.

Successful Entrepreneurs are Reasonable Risk Takers

Any new business poses risks for entrepreneurs. They may succeed or they may fail, and they cannot foresee which it will be.

For protection, entrepreneurs are likely to take the middle ground. How? For one thing, they shun ventures in which the odds against them are high. One such situation is the automobile industry. Few entrepreneurs would try to come up with a pollution-free automobile to vie with Detroit's billion-dollar automobile industry, because their chance of success would be practically nonexistent.

At the same time, most entrepreneurs shun a sure thing, because the satisfaction from such a task would be too small to justify the effort. Entrepreneurs are not likely to be found performing routine chores like sorting buttons or grinding coffee.

Even though entrepreneurs generally choose ventures that fall between these two extremes, they tend to go in the direction of high risk. They are likely to prefer ventures in which risk of failure is high, but not too high. Why? Because they recognize that they are more likely to gain both satisfaction and success from tasks that fit their own skills. That is what makes them reasonable risk takers. Like mountain climbers who test their abilities against a terrain that matches yet stretches their knowledge and experience, entrepreneurs are reasonable adventurers.

Example: In 1967, while an accountant with a large firm, Thomas Fatjo founded the company that would eventually become the largest solid-waste disposal enterprise in the country. Called Browning-Ferris Industries (BFI), this company grew, by 1984, to 15,500 employees and sales revenues of $953 million.

To accomplish such dynamic growth, Mr. Fatjo, in effect, created a brand-new national industry. He had observed that most waste-removal companies were very small, local operations, typically owned by men in their fifties, without money to modernize or expand.

Mr. Fatjo reasoned that these companies and their cash-poor owners stood to gain immensely from the money and expert knowledge provided by a buy-out. And BFI stood to grow by buying as many companies as it possibly could. Averaging five acquisitions a month, each a *moderate* risk in his eyes, Mr. Fatjo was able to create the first national waste-disposal company.[13]

Contrary to popular belief, entrepreneurs generally avoid ventures that are pure gambles. They would rather depend on themselves than on Lady Luck. There is no way, for example, to influence the roll of a pair of dice—unless, of course, they are loaded. Entrepreneurs prefer to shape events by their own actions. They want to make things happen rather than let them happen.

Successful Entrepreneurs are Self-Confident

Entrepreneurs believe in themselves. They have confidence that they can outdo anyone in their field. They tend not to accept the status quo, believing instead that they can change the facts. Often, they believe the odds are better than the facts would justify. The old New York Yankees used this strategy, and their winning habits once dazzled the world of sport. But they often won with mediocre ballplayers, prompting sportswriters to say: "Those pinstripe uniforms convince a ballplayer that he's better than he ought to be." This description captures the essence of the entrepreneur.

Example: Few industries are as fiercely competitive as the entertainment industry. Even the SBA shies away from helping to finance entertainment businesses since the industry is so volatile. One entrepreneur who has succeeded spectacularly, despite the odds, is Berry Gordy.

Supremely confident in his abilities, Mr. Gordy founded Motown Industries in Detroit in 1964. Today, his company is the nation's largest black-owned business. With talent from Detroit's inner city, Mr. Gordy established the "Motown sound." And within the past two decades, his music has become universally accepted as the "sound of young America."

One measure of Mr. Gordy's success is that during Motown's first decade, roughly 75 percent of some 600 records released by the company landed on the national sales charts—a staggering figure compared to an industry-wide average of 2 to 5 percent. Among the artists he discovered and developed are The Supremes, Diana Ross, The Temptations, Stevie Wonder, The Jackson Five, and Rick James.[14]

Successful Entrepreneurs are Hard Workers

Few people in our society work harder than entrepreneurs. Many big-business executives put in long hours, too, but entrepreneurs seem to put in even longer hours, driven by their desire to excel.

According to one study, top executives work an average of 60 hours a week. Although we lack similar data on entrepreneurs, it is likely that they work even longer, especially during the first few years. Only when their venture is firmly rooted in the marketplace do they taper off. Even then, however, entrepreneurs tend to be compulsive workers, especially when a crisis flares up. Mentally, they rarely are away from their office. In her study of hard workers, Dr. Marilyn Machlowitz of Yale University found that:

> During the New York City power blackout in 1977, many entrepreneurs still worked compulsively. Despite radio warnings to stay home, they had gone to work, often to find that they had to walk up 20 to 30 flights of stairs because the elevators were down.[15]

Dr. Machlowitz also found that it is a mistake to assume that hard workers never have any leisure. "They have reversed the relationship that America has with work. It is far better to live for the 50 weeks a year that you work than for the 2 weeks you are off."[16] To Winston Churchill, hard workers were "fortune's favorite children whose work and pleasures are one."

Not that entrepreneurs always work harder. They do so only when their own skills can shape events. If a situation lacks challenge, they leave it alone.

Successful Entrepreneurs are Goal Setters

Psychologists often define happiness as striving toward meaningful goals, not necessarily the achievement of those goals. This definition of happiness fits many entrepreneurs. Happiest with goals in front and not behind them,

EXHIBIT 2.2 *Entrepreneurial Goal Setting*

they rarely feel that they have arrived. As shown in Exhibit 2.2, the process of setting and achieving goals repeats itself among entrepreneurs.

To entrepreneurs, merely choosing a new, meaningful goal is self-renewing. Planning and carrying out the steps needed to reach the goal are stimulating. The result is often the opening of a door that leads to still another goal—as in the following example:

Example: Joseph Hrudka's story is a classic, all-American rags-to-riches saga. It is also something he has lived twice. In 1964, at age 25, he turned an interest in drag racing and a five-dollar investment into a multimillion-dollar automotive gasket business. In six years, he was worth $17 million and his company went public.

Just as the popularity of home auto-repair began to decline, Mr. Hrudka sold out to W.R. Grace Company, the New York conglomerate. He received $12 million from the deal, and the other $5 million went to the other stockholders.

Did he retire? No. A goal setter, Mr. Hrudka became active in the stock market and launched two new businesses. Meanwhile, W.R. Grace was not having much luck with the gasket company and, in 1981, sold it back to Mr. Hrudka for $4 million.

Once again, timing was everything. Automotive do-it-yourselfing was on the upswing again and within four years Mr. Hrudka's little company was publicly traded once again. As far as he knows, no one has ever taken the same company public twice. Today, Mr. Hrudka has a net worth in excess of $125 million. In 1984, CBS Television's "60 Minutes" featured his entrepreneurial successes.[17]

Entrepreneurs like Mr. Hrudka are compulsive achievers. Once they have met a goal, they lose interest in further effort in that area because it gives them little sense of achievement. They work hard if they feel challenged.

Successful Entrepreneurs are Accountable

Entrepreneurs generally want full credit, or full discredit, for their success or failure. Steady feedback on their performance enables entrepreneurs to remain accountable. To measure their performance, entrepreneurs may use any one of several yardsticks, among them return on investment and rate of profit growth. These yardsticks, of course, may cut two ways, giving proof not only of success but also of failure.

What they measure is profitability, for it is profits that best tell entrepreneurs how well they are doing in the marketplace. As suggested by Exhibit 2.3, profits really serve only as a yardstick of performance, not as a

EXHIBIT 2.3 *Accountability*

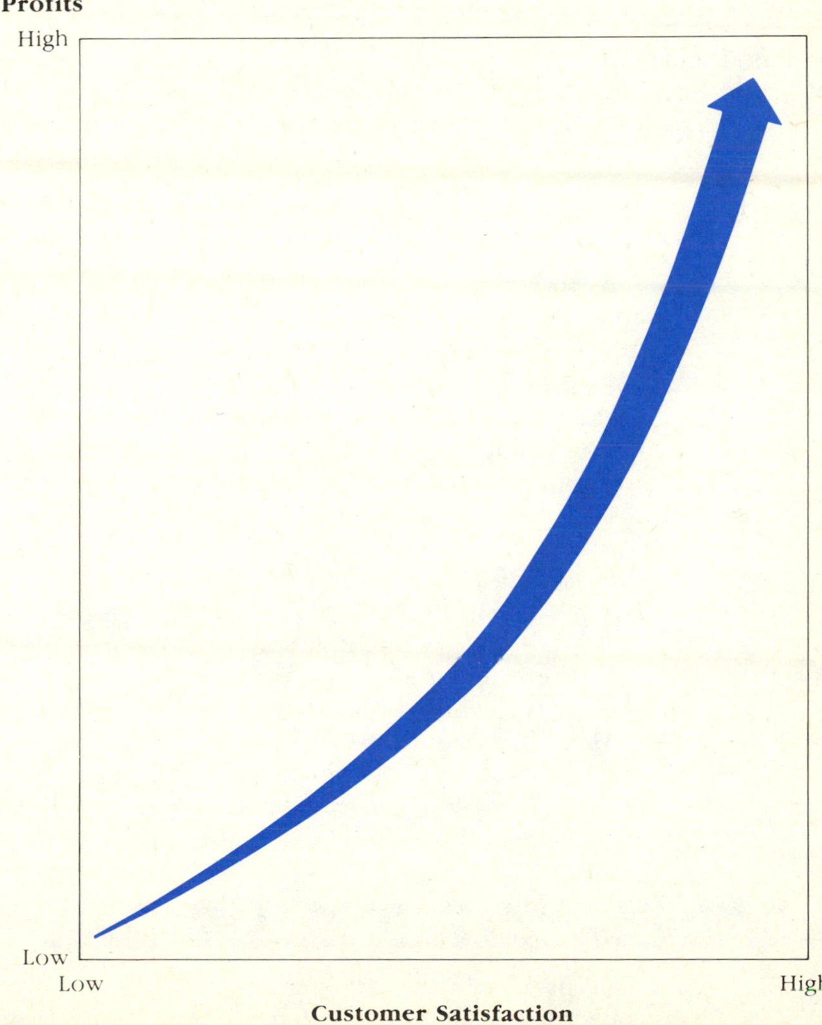

goal. In the words of Marvin Bower, a management consultant:

> Profits are really a measure of the competitive value of a company's contribution to users, distributors, and the public. And, it is only by maximizing that contribution that a company can maximize its profits. In other words, concentrate on things that produce a profit rather than on profit itself. Perhaps using profit as a measure instead of a goal is a distinction without a difference. Maybe so. But it is a useful distinction to guide the thinking of entrepreneurs.[18]

Profits play another role, as a reward for successful risk taking. Entrepreneurs deserve some return (profits) on their investment, just as individual savers deserve some return (interest) on their savings accounts. Entrepreneurs, moreover, deserve a higher return because they risk failure, whereas individual savers usually do not.

Successful Entrepreneurs are Innovative

To the lay mind, innovation is generally the most distinctive entrepreneurial trait. As exemplified by Henry Ford, entrepreneurs tend to tackle the unknown; they do things in new and different ways; they weave old ideas into new patterns; they offer more solutions than alibis.

In practice, however, the role of the entrepreneur often differs from the role of the innovator. Although innovation may be vital to being entrepreneurial, it becomes entrepreneurial only when carried into production to benefit consumers. For example, although Americans invented the transistor, it was the Japanese who benefited most from making, selling, and adapting the transistor to new products.

> **Example:** It is Steven Jobs, more than anyone else, who kicked open the door and let the personal computer move in. But, Mr. Jobs did not make the revolution alone. He did not even make the machine that made the revolution, the Apple II, the personal computer that along with its other skills seemed to mint money.
>
> Stephen Wozniak, age 32, Mr. Jobs's friend and cofounder who looks like a Steiff Teddy bear on a maintenance dose of marshmallows, created the Apple II. He worked from some pre-existing technology, scaling it down radically and making it affordable to consumers as well as corporations.
>
> "Steve didn't do one circuit, design, or piece of code," says Mr. Wozniak, who was widely regarded as the true technological wizard in Mr. Jobs's corporate Oz. "He's not really been into computers, and to this day he has never gone through a computer manual. But it never crossed my mind to sell computers. It was Steve who said, 'Let's hold them up in the air and sell a few.'"[19]

DEVELOPING ENTREPRENEURS

This profile of the successful entrepreneur gives only a partial answer to the question, What makes the entrepreneur tick? A more rounded answer requires a look at the social origins of entrepreneurs.

Psychologists say that entrepreneurs are likely to come from families in which parents set high standards for their children's performance, encourage habits of self-reliance, and avoid being strict disciplinarians.

But what determines how parents set standards? Why do some parents stress achievement and others not? Probably because their social or ethnic group believes in it. For example, persons of Jewish background have been known to make every sacrifice to give their children an education. In fact, Judaism stresses education and achievement.

The need to achieve crops up in all ethnic groups, but more so in some than in others. For example, Armenians and Chinese, Greeks and Jews tend to become entrepreneurs. Other minority groups have lagged as entrepreneurs. The main reasons are easy to pin down. For one, minority groups have long held business in low esteem.

Minority groups have also lacked business skills and attitudes, mainly because they have had little exposure to the ways of business. Historically, the plight of minorities has prevented the development of such skills and attitudes. The plantation system in the South, for example, offered blacks no experience with money, no incentive to save, and no idea of progress—none of the experiences that would prepare them for urban living.

Small wonder, then, that their share of the business world has been so small. Just how small is apparent from the statistics cited in Chapter One: Blacks own just 2.3 percent of the 16 million businesses in the nation, even though they account for 11 percent of the total population.

Some Progress

There are signs, however, that blacks may soon be entering the entrepreneurial world in record numbers. Their attitudes toward business and entrepreneurship are beginning to change dramatically. Take this headline that appeared in a monthly magazine devoted to blacks in business:

Black Students Are Bullish on Business[20]

As recently as 1965, black college students overwhelmingly preferred to major in either the liberal arts or education. No more. As borne out by Exhibit 2.4, they now prefer business administration and the sciences in increasing numbers. Although these statistics cover 41 black colleges, students at other colleges and universities show similar trends toward business and the sciences. To cite one dramatic example, in 1950 the Harvard Business School had just 2 black students; in 1980, there were 66.

Barriers for groups long denied equal access to entrepreneurial opportunities are dissolving. Women, for example, are heading for business careers in record numbers. A survey by the University of California and the American Council on Education found that women students majoring in business mushroomed from 3 percent in 1966 to 17 percent in 1980.[21]

Similar data on other minority groups—Hispanics and Native Americans in particular—are unavailable. Even so, some progress seems to be taking place, although not as dramatically as in the cases of blacks and women. Community colleges in particular have pioneered educational

EXHIBIT 2.4

The Rise of Black Students in Business and the Science

Course of Study	1976	1979
Business Administration	16.7%	21.5%
Engineering and Computer Sciences	6.9	11.0
Sociology	10.2	9.5
Education	14.4	9.0

Source: United Negro College Fund, "Black Students Are Bullish on Business," *Black Enterprise*, February 1980, p. 52.

programs to help bring Hispanics and Native Americans into the nation's economic mainstream—as they have done with blacks and women.

Helped along not only by educational institutions but by the federal government as well, a surge in entrepreneurship among minorities is likely:

Example: Black managers climbing the corporate ladder are finding that it often doesn't reach as high as they want to go. Many are jumping off to start their own businesses, betting that they can rise higher and faster as entrepreneurs. Charles T. Grant, the immediate past president of the National Black MBA Association, tells blacks in corporate America: "You've got to take the riskier assignments and prove yourself over and over again. If you show results, you'll get promoted at first, but sooner or later you'll hit a bottleneck and know that's as far as any black is going to go in the company. Then you've got to decide whether to keep banging on the door to go higher, or to go it alone."

Just a decade ago, corporate America was where ambitious blacks wanted to be. Business schools were enrolling black students, and corporations were integrating their management ranks. Between 1972 and 1982, federal statistics show, the number of blacks classified as managers and officials surged 83 percent, to 445,000.[22]

Individual Versus Group Achievement

So far, our discussion of entrepreneurs has centered on the individual achiever at the expense of group achievers. This emphasis is natural, mainly because most psychological research stresses the individual achiever. Another reason is that team spirit seems to be out of fashion, even in athletics. Yet there is impressive evidence that some men and women achieve more as members of groups than they do as individuals. In the words of one psychologist:

> In spite of the theories of psychologists, administrators, and educators, our society does not run on individual achievement alone. I fear that our beliefs that it does have led us to assume that people who can't cut the mustard on their own initiative can't cut it at all.[23]

In some circumstances, entrepreneurs may achieve more when they work as a group rather than as individuals. Such group effort often helps individuals to overcome their fear of failure or kindle their desire to achieve.

Rewards and Hazards of Entrepreneurship

In general, entrepreneurs like nothing better than the psychological satisfaction of being their own boss. Esteemed by friends and relatives alike, their self-image mirrors that esteem.

Financially, successful entrepreneurs often outdo big-business executives. Rather than save money or dabble in stocks, entrepreneurs are likely to plow profits back into their ventures to keep them growing. They are often more interested in seeing their equity in the business increase than in drawing big monthly paychecks.

These are the chief rewards of entrepreneurship. But what of the hazards? Launching a new venture always carries some risk of failure. There is no such thing as a perfectly safe investment. As a rule, the riskier the venture, the greater the potential profit. If the entrepreneur succeeds, profits may be high; if not, their life savings may be lost. For some, failure is tragic; to others, it is an opportunity to begin anew. Henry Ford, for example, failed twice before he successfully launched Ford Motor Company. Ralph Waldo Emerson wrote, "Valor consists in the art of self-recovery." Even so, many men and women cannot take failure in their stride; it shatters their ego, dulls their drive, weakens their will. With each personal tragedy, society loses also.

ON SELF-ANALYSIS

Libraries overflow with books that tell bosses how best to pick their workers. But, for some reason, writers fail to offer any advice on how best to pick oneself as boss. Yet this decision is of first importance. In the words of Louis L. Allen:

> The man who begins a small business has *selected himself* to run the show. . . . In almost every case I have seen, the man who has done this selecting is neither qualified by training and inclination nor by objective reasoning to make such a judgment. This, more than any single ingredient in a small business, accounts for the high rate of failure. . . .
>
> When a man picks himself as "the boss" he has made a fateful choice—one on which the fortunes of his enterprise will rise or fall.[24]

In Arthur Miller's Pulitzer Prize-winning play *Death of a Salesman*, the widow of Willy Loman asks her son, Biff, "Why did he do it? Why did he kill himself?" Biff replies, "Poor guy, he never knew who he was."

Like Willy Loman, few would-be entrepreneurs look long and hard at themselves, mainly because there is so little to measure themselves by, except for some checklists. But these are so trivial that few aspiring entrepreneurs would take them seriously. One checklist, for example, asks about neatness, cleanliness, clothing, mannerisms, breath, posture, height, and weight.

Clearly, such questions fail to help the would-be entrepreneur evaluate himself or herself as a potential entrepreneur. But there is a test, brief and to the point, that we recommend highly. Appearing in Exhibit 2.5, this test has ten pairs of statements. For each pair, circle the one you agree with. This description of the test is purposely sketchy. You will see why when your instructor analyzes your responses.

EXHIBIT 2.5

Self-Analysis

In each pair of statements, circle the one you agree with.

1. a. Promotions are earned through hard work and persistence.
   b. Making a lot of money is largely a matter of getting the right breaks.
2. a. Many times the reaction of teachers seems haphazard to me.
   b. In my experience, I have noticed that there is usually a connection between how hard I study and the grades I get.
3. a. The number of divorces indicates that more and more men and women are not trying to make their marriages work.
   b. Marriage is largely a gamble.
4. a. When I am right I can convince others.
   b. It is silly to think that one can really change another person's basic attitudes.
5. a. In our society, a man's future earning power depends on his ability.
   b. Getting promoted is really a matter of being luckier than the next guy.
6. a. I have little influence over the way other people behave.
   b. If one knows how to deal with people, they are really quite easily led.
7. a. Sometimes, I feel that I have little to do with the grades I get.
   b. The grades I make are the results of my own efforts; luck has little or nothing to do with it.
8. a. People like me can change the course of world affairs if we make ourselves heard.
   b. It is only wishful thinking to believe that one can influence what happens in society at large.
9. a. A great deal that happens to me is probably a matter of chance.
   b. I am the master of my fate.
10. a. Getting along with people is a skill that must be practiced.
    b. It is almost impossible to figure out how to please some people.

Source: Julian B. Rotter, "External Control and Internal Control," *Psychology Today*, June 1971, p. 42.

SUMMARY

Most men and women would like to go into business for themselves, but few do. Of those who do, few succeed. Even so, becoming a successful entrepreneur is not impossible. The odds favor the person who is an overachiever. Such people are also likely to be:

- Reasonable risk takers
- Self-confident
- Hard workers
- Goal setters
- Accountable
- Innovative

Entrepreneurs inspired the energy that spans the American continent. It was entrepreneurs like Henry Ford and Steven Jobs who pushed our economy ahead in giant steps.

Entrepreneurs spring from every walk of life, and each ethnic group boasts its own successful entrepreneurs. But some ethnic groups tend to have more entrepreneurs than others. For example, Armenians and Chinese, Greeks and Jews tend to go into business for themselves. But other minority groups and women tend not to, mainly because until recently most entrepreneurial opportunities were closed to them.

Other social factors also appear to influence entrepreneurial success. Psychologists say that entrepreneurs are likely to have parents who set high standards for their children's performance, encourage habits of self-reliance, and avoid being strict disciplinarians.

The chief reward of entrepreneurial success is the satisfaction of a job well done, reflected especially in a profitable performance. The chief hazard is entrepreneurial failure, which may shatter the ego and destroy life savings.

Evaluating oneself as an entrepreneur is an important task, aided in this chapter by a special test.

DISCUSSION AND REVIEW QUESTIONS

1. In what ways are entrepreneurs necessary to the health and growth of our economy?
2. Do you agree that franchisees are not pure entrepreneurs? Why?
3. Write a paragraph on the traits of an entrepreneur you know well.
4. Define the terms *entrepreneur, reasonable risk taker, gamble, accountability, profit, entrepreneurship, management.*
5. What is it in men and women that responds so deeply to the call of entrepreneurship?
6. Which entrepreneurial trait do you believe is most necessary for success? Why?
7. What are the rewards and hazards of entrepreneurship?

8. How do entrepreneurs and managers differ?
9. Why do so few men and women actually become entrepreneurs, even though most of them say they would prefer to work for themselves rather than for someone else?
10. Do you agree that profits are *not* a goal of doing business? Explain, using an example.
11. Are innovators necessarily also entrepreneurs? Explain, using an example.
12. In what ways do the six entrepreneurial traits overlap?
13. How can parents influence entrepreneurial behavior in their children?
14. Why are there so few entrepreneurs among minority groups and women?
15. Why is education so vital to entrepreneurial success?

NOTES

1. *Ford at Fifty* (New York: Simon & Schuster, 1953), p. 104.
2. George Gilder, *The Spirit of Enterprise* (New York: Simon & Schuster, 1984), p. 161.
3. Joseph A. Schumpeter, *The Theory of Economic Development,* trans. Redvers Opie (Cambridge, Mass.: Harvard University Press, 1934).
4. Quoted by Office of Economic Research, The New York Stock Exchange, *Economic Choices for the 1980s* (January 1980), p. 9.
5. Irving Kristol, "Business vs. the Economy," *The Wall Street Journal,* June 26, 1979, p. 18.
6. Peter F. Drucker, *The Effective Executive* (New York: Harper & Row, 1966), p. 22.
7. Orvie F. Collins and David G. Moore, quoted by Patrick R. Liles, *New Business Ventures and the Entrepreneur* (Homewood, III.: Richard D. Irwin, 1974), p. 2.
8. Adapted from Carol Hymowitz, "Many Blacks Jump Off the Corporate Ladder to be Entrepreneurs," *The Wall Street Journal,* August 2, 1984, p. 14.
9. Herbert A. Wainer and Paul V. Tiplitz, master's theses at Massachusetts Institute of Technology, 1965, quoted by Patrick R. Liles, *New Business Ventures and the Entrepreneur*, p. 3.
10. Daniel J. Boorstin, *The Americans: The Democratic Experience* (New York: Random House, 1973), pp. 431–432 (updated).
11. The Gallup Report (Princeton, N.J.: The Gallup Organization, July 1979), p. 1.
12. David C. McClelland, *The Achieving Society* (Princeton, N.J.: Van Nostrand, 1961).
13. Adapted from Craig R. Waters, "Fleshing Out an Empire," *Inc.,* October 1984, pp. 53–54.
14. Adapted from Samuel C. Certo and others, *Business,* (Dubuque, Iowa: Wm. C. Brown Publishers, 1984), p. 78.
15. Janet Gardner, "A Workaholic—and Happy That Way," Cleveland *Plain Dealer,* March 14, 1980, p. 1-D.
16. Ibid.
17. Donald Sabath, "Mr. Gasket Back in the Driver's Seat," Cleveland *Plain Dealer,* December 4, 1984, p. 1-E.
18. Marvin Bower, *The Will to Manage* (New York: McGraw-Hill, 1966), pp. 62–63.
19. "The Updated Book of Jobs," *Time,* January 3, 1983, p. 25.
20. United Negro College Fund, "Black Students Are Bullish on Business," *Black Enterprise,* February 1980, p. 52.
21. "Record Number of Freshmen Heading for Business Careers," Cleveland *Plain Dealer,* January 20, 1980, p. 8-A.
22. Carol Hymowitz, "Many Blacks Jump Off the Corporate Ladder to be Entrepreneurs," *The Wall Street Journal* (August 2, 1984), p. 1.
23. Alvin F. Zander, "Team Spirit vs. the Individual Achiever," *Psychology Today,* November 1974, p. 68.
24. Louis L. Allen, *Starting and Succeeding in Your Own Business* (New York: Grossett & Dunlap, 1968), pp. 8–9.

CASE 2A *Weaver Screen-print*

Mark and Helen Weaver began their silk-printing venture in 1982. Their venture lost money in 1984, although sales revenues approached $100,000. "I'm not a smashing success yet," says Mr. Weaver, "but then again, I'm satisfied. In fact, I think I can double or triple sales in two years by expanding out of my plant into retailing."

To do that, though, Mr. Weaver may have to quit his job at Lubrizol Corporation. He has two years to go before he can "legally" retire and still get his pension benefits. Says Mr. Weaver, "I'm not sure what to do, how best to balance my desire for inner peace against my retirement benefits."

Background

There was little in the Weavers' background to indicate they would someday become entrepreneurs. Both began their business careers at the same rayon manufacturing company, where Mr. Weaver worked as a chemist and Mrs. Weaver as a laboratory technician.

Shortly after they met there in 1950, they married and soon expanded their family to include two sons. One job change later found Mr. Weaver working as a project engineer for Lubrizol Corporation, a large chemical manufacturer. Mrs. Weaver also changed jobs to work for a large department store selling children's apparel.

At Lubrizol, Mr. Weaver rose from project engineer to warehousing manager. In 1981, after 22 years with the company, Mr. Weaver suddenly realized that he would rise no higher. He was now 49 years old.

"I saw for the first time that I would never become a vice president," says Mr. Weaver. "Lubrizol is a great company to work for, but you've got to be a chemical engineer or a chemical researcher to get anywhere in the company. The top executives are mostly from one engineering school. So I began to look around."

In his search for a better job, Mr. Weaver soon found that his age worked against him. "Who wants to hire a 49-year-old?" says Mr. Weaver. Blocked off in one direction, he began to overflow with ideas in another. "Overnight, I made up my mind to go into business for myself. Just like that! Of course, I first talked it over with my wife and, without a moment's hesitation, she said yes. In fact, she even offered to quit her job at the department store where she enjoyed nine years of seniority. Working as a team, we just knew we couldn't fail."

Choice of Industry

For weeks, Mr. Weaver pondered what kind of industry to go into. When he was in his twenties, he had often thought about someday opening his own restaurant. He had moonlighted for five years at a drive-in restaurant, working at every job, including cook and dishwasher. But after watching so many restaurants fail, he had concluded long ago that a restaurant would be "too big a gamble. They're too faddist. They're popular for five years, then they go under."

Then, opportunity beckoned. As president of the Little League Baseball League in his hometown, Mr. Weaver observed that the printing on the players' uniforms kept peeling off. So he approached the sporting goods retailer who had sold them the uniforms to find out why.

The retailer told Mr. Weaver that he was having a terrible time getting high-quality silk printing on T-shirts. "It came to me right there and then," says Mr. Weaver, "that if he was having trouble, then other sporting goods retailers had the same problem also. Wow, that very moment my thoughts jelled!"

In the next breath, Mr. Weaver asked the retailer a question: "Would you buy silk printing from me if I guarantee its quality?" "You better believe I would," replied the retailer. "I'll not only buy from you—if you guarantee the quality—but I'll also give you a guaranteed sales contract each year. If I buy less than the guarantee, I'll pay you the difference. And, if I buy more than the guarantee, I'll still pay you the difference. You can't lose. Now, what do you think of a deal like that?"

"You just put me in business," laughed Mr. Weaver. "Would you put your offer in writing?" The retailer did, although he left out any mention of a guaranteed sales contract.

A Learning Experience

Of course, the Weavers now had themselves a problem: How and where to launch their new silk-printing venture? They knew nothing about silk printing. In fact, they had never seen it done before.

Undaunted, the Weavers spent "every spare second" for a month reading and studying every article and book they could find about the art of silk printing. Here, the public library proved to be especially helpful.

After absorbing all they could, they then leafed through the Thomas Register to get the names of local suppliers of silk-printing equipment. "We had to start somewhere," says Mr. Weaver. "I was sure that suppliers would help us get started if it meant we'd be customers."

And that is precisely what happened. Armed with the letter of intent from the sporting goods retailer, the Weavers landed a supplier who:

- Suggested how best to design a silk-printing plant
- Specified precisely what pieces of equipment the Weavers would need
- Suggested that they hire a "22-year-old who knows silk printing inside out"

"The supplier gave us quite an education," says Mr. Weaver. "So, just two weeks after talking to him, we took out a second mortgage on our house, borrowed $40,000 from the bank, and ordered the equipment from the supplier. We never even looked at another supplier." To justify the $40,000 loan, the Weavers gave the bank the statement that appears in Exhibit 2A.1.

EXHIBIT 2A.1

Weaver Screen-Print:
Justification for $40,000 Loan as Presented to the Bank

- We request a loan of $40,000.
- Our minimum operating expenses per year will be:

$ 8,000	Operating expenses
7,200	Loan payments
6,000	Lease payments
3,000	Utilities
3,000	Miscellaneous expenses
500	Insurance premiums
$27,700	Total operating expenses

- Necessary business volume to break even:

$$\text{Breakeven volume} = \frac{\$27{,}700 \text{ total expenses per year}}{\$1.50 \text{ sales price per unit}}$$

= 18,470 units per year
= 1,540 units per month
= 70 units per day (assuming 22 business days per month)

The breakeven volume above can be achieved by the Weaver family, so no salary is necessary.

- There is no apparent competition in Lake County.
- The purchased equipment can produce 475,200 units per year, requiring 10 employees at $4.00 an hour.
- Expected volume the first year is 90,000 units, or sales of $135,000. This sales figure is attainable because of a handshake agreement with Koenig Sporting Goods to sell them at least 60,000 units per year at $1.50 per unit.

In Business at Last

It was now March 1982. One month later, the Weavers leased 1,000 square feet of space in an industrial park zoned for light manufacturing. "We first looked for an abandoned gas station, but we couldn't find one that was suitable, so we settled on an industrial park," says Mr. Weaver.

At the same time, they hired the "silk-printing expert" the supplier had recommended. By July 4, "everything was in place," and the Weavers opened for business. Their beginning balance sheet appears in Exhibit 2A.2.

EXHIBIT 2A.2

Weaver Screen-Print: Beginning Balance Sheet (July 4, 1982)

Assets		Equities	
Cash	$13,800	Accounts payable	$ 1,000
Printing supplies	2,000	Mortgage loan	40,000
Office supplies	500	Owners' equity	1,500
Plant equipment	24,000		
Prepaid rent	1,200		
Other	1,000		
Total assets	$42,500	Total equities	$42,500

When they began, the Weavers had just the retailer's letter of intent and *no* customers. Mr. Weaver continued to work days at his old job. Mrs. Weaver, on the other hand, quit her job with the department store to become the new venture's manager. They named their venture Weaver Screen-Print.

With overhead costs to cover, the Weavers' chief worry was how best to go about marketing their services. "We had to get customers in a hurry," says Mr. Weaver, "or else we'd run out of cash. So I thumbed through the Yellow Pages and worked up a list of every sporting goods store in the county—44 in all. Then I began paying a few of them a visit, cold."

The Weavers' first customer was a yacht club that wanted this message emblazoned across each of 48 T-shirts:

Cruizin
Boozin
Snoozin

EXHIBIT 2A.3 *Weaver Screen-Print: View of Screen-Print Process*

EXHIBIT 2A.4

Weaver Screen-Print: 1984 Income Statement

Sales revenues		$91,600
Operating expenses		
Salaries and wages	$39,400	
Materials and supplies	18,900	
Utilities	7,900	
Rent	7,800	
Professional fees	5,300	
Depreciation	5,300	
Payroll taxes	3,500	
Interest	2,200	
Office supplies	800	
Property tax	700	
Freight	500	
Insurance	400	
Miscellaneous	200	92,900
Operating loss		$ 1,300

With that order, and Mr. Weaver's after-hour visits to prospective customers, business began to pick up. By the end of 1982, the Weavers "managed to break even." Word had spread that they guaranteed their performance, a rarity in the industry.

This strategy did, indeed, give the Weavers a competitive edge. So much so that the large sporting goods retailer followed through on his original promise to sign a guaranteed sales contract. By the fall of 1984, Mr. Weaver was landing one half of all prospective customers he visited on his monthly round of sales calls. "If only I had more time," says Mr. Weaver, "I just know I could get many more customers." Financial statements for 1984 appear in Exhibits 2A.4 and 2A.5. The seasonality of their sales is shown in Exhibit 2A.6.

Taking Stock

Now that their revenues are approaching $100,000 a year, the Weavers are "taking stock of our business. We've grown so fast that we have to pause and see where we want to be, two or three years down the road," says Mr. Weaver. Looking back, the Weavers believe their three years in business have been "highly rewarding."

They do regret one thing, however. A competitor sued the Weavers for printing on T-shirts the logo, "Cleveland, You've Got to Be Tough!" The competitor claimed it had the copyright for the message, suing the Weavers for $500,000. In its suit, the competitor asked the U.S. District Court to "seize all plates, molds, and matrices used for marking the shirts and any T-shirts stored" by the Weavers.

As it turned out, the suit was settled quietly out of court for just $29.75. "Would you believe," says Mr. Weaver, "that they sued us for $500,000 over an order on which we made just $29.75?" But they ended up paying legal fees of $2,000.

EXHIBIT 2A.5 *Weaver Screen-Print: Balance Sheet (December 31, 1984)*

Assets			**Equities**		
Current assets			Liabilities		
Cash	$ 2,900		Note payable	$50,000	
Accounts receivable	8,080		Payroll taxes	830	$50,830
Supplies inventory	2,300	$13,280			
Fixed assets			Owners' equity		(1,650)
Printing equipment	$35,820				
Automobile	2,590				
Improvements	380				
Office equipment	130				
	38,920				
Less: accumulated depreciation	3,100	35,820			
Deposit		80			
Total assets		$49,180	Total equities		$49,180

To achieve revenues of nearly $100,000 a year, the Weavers had to expand their original idea of doing only direct printing on T-shirts. They also began to do transfers, promotional printing, and sewing of decals and numbers—all on T-shirts, uniforms, and jackets.

"We now offer a complete service," says Mr. Weaver. To meet the demand for expanded services, the Weavers had to expand their shop space

EXHIBIT 2A.6 *Weaver Screen-Print: Seasonality*

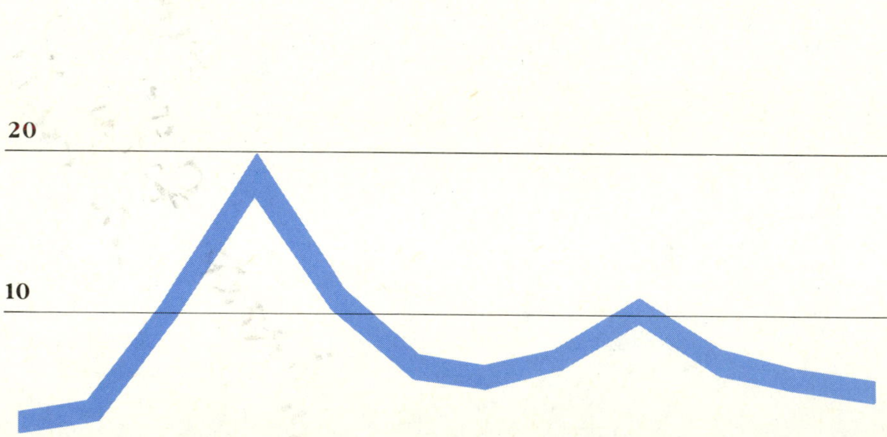

from 1,000 to 3,500 square feet. It cost them $34,000 to buy the latest silk-printing equipment. "I'm always looking for ways to invest in equipment of the latest technology," says Mr. Weaver. "Our competitors don't. Their equipment is so old it's held together by baling wire. Our equipment is one of the major reasons our quality is so good."

A Critical Time

The Weavers believe this is a critical time in the life of their venture. It is now the spring of 1985. They are convinced they can double or triple revenues, if only they had the time to market their services. "I'm really in a puzzle," says Mr. Weaver. "With more time, I'm sure I could do a better job of selling. The only time I've got is after hours, when I'm done working at my other job at Lubrizol. I'm not sure whether to quit or not. I have just two years to go before I can retire legally and receive the pension benefits I'm entitled to."

The Weavers lack a marketing plan. "We don't need one," says Mr. Weaver. "Ours is a seat-of-the-pants operation. We just go from day to day; and so far, things have worked out well. I'm a do-it-yourselfer. I even put in all the equipment myself. My wife and I never needed legal help to get started. We just went ahead and did it. We're equal partners, she and I. Nothing's on paper, and we like it that way.

"Our business philosophy may be summed up in one word: trust. We trust our employees, and they trust us. We also trust our customers, and they trust us. That's the Japanese way." Mr. Weaver once spent two years in Tokyo with the U.S. Army.

Optimistic Outlook

To double or triple revenues, the Weavers are giving "serious thought" about expanding into retailing. "We might set up a dummy store in the city," says Mr. Weaver. "We could sell T-shirts with standard prints like the Superman logo and cartoon characters like Peanuts and Popeye. The exposure would be great."

To carry off such an expansion, the Weavers are counting heavily on their reputation as high-quality silk printers. Their quality has been so high that they have rarely lost a customer. "Even the few customers we lost have referred others to us," says Mrs. Weaver. She says the keys to their success are:

- Fast service—just one-week delivery for custom work
- The best equipment available
- Guaranteed performance
- Good, loyal employees

Questions

1. What are the strengths of Weaver Screen-Print? Its weaknesses?
2. Comment on the Weavers' justification for a $40,000 loan (see Exhibit 2A.1).

3. Should Mr. Weaver quit his job with the Lubrizol Corporation and devote full time to his venture? Why or why not?
4. How well has Weaver Screen-Print performed financially? What questions does your financial analysis raise?
5. Outline a step-by-step plan for the Weavers to follow before launching the expansion they are now considering, focusing on the questions they should answer before making the decision.

CASE 2B *John Vitt*

For the past six years, John Vitt has pursued his desire to own a Zero's fast-food franchise. Zero's, Inc. has 450 franchised outlets, mostly in the East and Midwest. These outlets sell mostly hamburgers, french fried potatoes, and milk shakes. Mr. Vitt is 49 years old. In January 1985, he received this letter from a Zero's executive:

> Dear John:
>
> We have received and reviewed your work history with Zero's that you pursued in your desire to become a licensee. After consulting with our people, we have decided that we cannot now consider you favorably for a Zero's license.
>
> We sincerely appreciate your interest in Zero's and sincerely hope you will understand that our decision was a difficult one to make.
>
> John, good luck in your career-seeking efforts.
>
> Sincerely,
> Richard R. Rhine
> Licensing Manager
> Zero's, Inc.

The news left Mr. Vitt speechless. For six years, he had pursued, single-mindedly, his goal to own a Zero's franchise. To prepare himself for the franchise, he had taken the following steps:

- He moonlighted for five years at a Zero's franchise in Syracuse, learning all he could about fast-food service.
- He studied small business management at a local community college for six years, eventually earning a two-year associate degree. He made the dean's list every quarter.
- He made three trips to Zero's headquarters in Philadelphia for interviews.
- He had amassed personal assets worth $135,000 and owed no one.

"I'm really at a loss why they turned me down," says Mr. Vitt. "I'm a good family man, active in civic affairs, a churchgoer, and a union steward. Everybody looks up to me, even my five children. And I also have a little business on the side, as a plasterer. I know it wasn't the money, because I could've scraped together the $60,000 cash required for a franchise."

A Zero's brochure contains the following profile of a typical franchisee:

> The entrepreneur awarded a Zero license gains the prestige of operating under a nationally known reputation and of receiving strong corporate support.
>
> Our selection process focuses on matching the right place with the right person. We know what kind of person will get along well in which community—and we place him where his chances for success will be best.
>
> Our licensees enthusiastically accept the responsibility of a 10-year license and a 10-year lease on a Zero's restaurant. They eagerly become active in community affairs. All are on-the-job owners. Some have a restaurant background; but most come from backgrounds as diverse as chemistry and the army, law and professional football. In fact, about 85 percent have never been connected with the food industry before.
>
> Our licensees are good decision makers with the ability to recruit, train, and motivate the 20 to 40 full- and part-time employees that work for them.

Questions

1. What should Mr. Vitt do now?
2. Why did Zero's turn down Mr. Vitt's application for a franchise?
3. Could Mr. Vitt made a go of a Zero's franchise? Why?

CASE 2C *Jeffrey Brooks*

Jeffrey Brooks has a dilemma. At the age of 26, he had resigned from a lucrative managerial position and opened a small men's-clothing store. After a couple of difficult years, the business flourished. He eventually opened three more clothing stores and then sold the company for a handsome profit.

But three months of boredom convinced Mr. Brooks that he was not ready to retire. He took a managerial position with a big company but again realized that he wanted to be his own boss. Using the remaining profits from the sale of his clothing stores, he struck out on his own once again. This time he decided to open a construction firm.

The business got off to a decent start but soon floundered. Mr. Brooks quickly came to the conclusion that although he was a good manager, he knew little about the technical side of things.

So, Mr. Brooks entered into an agreement with Paul Hansen, his general foreman, whereby Mr. Hansen became a partner in the company. Mr. Brooks was to provide managerial know-how while Mr. Hansen attended to operations.

After five years of this arrangement, the two men began to quarrel over how the company should be managed. Mr. Brooks sold out to Mr. Hansen and, at the age of 45, retired again.

Shortly after his forty-seventh birthday, Mr. Brooks decided that his retirement had been premature. He was again restless and wanted to get back into business. This time he decided to open a restaurant.

The town in which Mr. Brooks lives is a medium-sized community dominated by a large state university. The success of his first business was partially attributable to the fact that he attracted the student business. His construction firm also did much of its work for the university.

For the restaurant venture, however, Mr. Brooks saw an opportunity to move away from the university. He recognized that all the restaurants around town were planned to appeal to the university community, so he reasoned that there existed a sizable demand for a quality restaurant designed to attract non-university patrons.

Mr. Brooks purchased a building across town from the university and, six months later, opened an adult-oriented restaurant featuring steaks and fresh seafood. The restaurant was a tremendous success from the very first. Mr. Brooks attracted a large and loyal following.

By the time he reached the age of 56, Mr. Brooks had put away enough money to assure his comfort and security for the rest of his life. Further, he has just received a very attractive offer from another party to buy the restaurant. Mr. Brooks has two weeks to make a decision about whether to accept the offer.

Questions

1. Should Mr. Brooks sell the restaurant? Why?
2. Why has Mr. Brooks been so successful with his various enterprises?

Source: Ricky W. Griffin, *Management* (Boston: Houghton Mifflin, 1984), pp. 694–695.

3 SMALL BUSINESS AND INDUSTRY

QUESTIONS FOR MASTERY

How do products and services flow between manufacturers, wholesalers, retailers, services, and consumers

How are products and services classified?

Where are the most promising entrepreneurial opportunities?

How vital is it to keep up with the knowledge explosion?

What may the world be like in the year 2000?

No profit grows where there is no pleasure taken; in brief, Sir, study what you most affect.

William Shakespeare

Entrepreneurs energize our economy, thriving in almost every industry. Entrepreneurial opportunities, however, are greater in some industries than in others. To illustrate these opportunities, in this chapter, we will examine four major industry groups and their relationships to one another and to the consumer.

MAJOR INDUSTRY GROUPS

Before we look at each industry group in detail, let us first define them briefly.

Manufacturing: Manufacturers convert raw materials into products. These products may then be sold to another manufacturer, to be used as raw materials for still another product. Or they may be sold unchanged to wholesalers, retailers, or even directly to consumers. An example is the manufacture of nylon stockings, parachutes, and toothbrushes out of coal, air, and water.

Wholesaling: Wholesalers are middlemen between manufacturers and retailers. The popular view of the wholesaler as someone who sells at big discounts at off-list prices is incorrect. Rather, wholesalers buy products from manufacturers, store them, and then sell them either to retailers or to consumers. As it passes from the manufacturer to the wholesaler and then to the consumer, the product stays unchanged but the wholesaler provides services to the retailer, such as fast delivery or credit financing, that enhance the value of the product. An example is the wholesaler who stores a farmer's fruit and vegetables for resale to a wider market of grocers than the farmer could economically reach.

Retailing: Retailers buy product from either wholesalers or manufacturers and sell it to consumers. Retailers in turn add value to the product by offering services to the consumer, such as personal attention, wide selection, or credit terms. An example is the department store that sells consumers a host of products ranging from toothpaste to shirts to home computers.

Services: Service firms do not deal in a product. Instead, they sell personal skills to manufacturers, wholesalers, and retailers as well as to consumers. An example is the tax preparer who guides taxpayers through Form 1040.

Note in Exhibit 3.1 how these four industry groups differ in terms of personnel and money, materials and machines. As a rule, manufacturing businesses are the hardest to establish and services are the easiest. To make toothpaste, the entrepreneur must invest not only in personnel but also in raw materials and machines. To prepare tax forms, however, entrepreneurs need only invest in their own training and perhaps some reference material; they can run their businesses out of storefronts or even from their homes.

EXHIBIT 3.1 *How Major Industry Groups Differ*

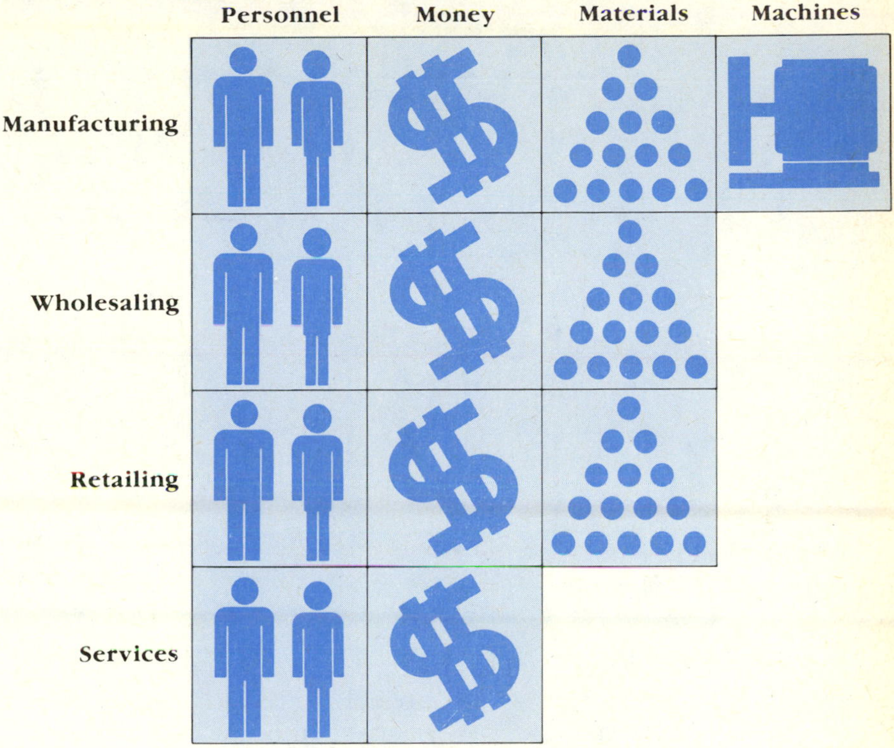

The differences are by no means as sharp as shown here. In fact, industry groups often overlap and blur together. One example is the laundry industry, which uses equipment like washing machines and presses; yet it is a *service* and not a manufacturing industry.

In Exhibit 3.2, note how manufacturers, wholesalers, and retailers link together to serve consumers. Tubes of toothpaste may move from manufacturers to drug wholesalers and finally to drug stores where consumers may buy them. Men's suits may move directly from garment makers to men's shops. Note, also, that services reach out to all industry groups as well as to consumers.

MANUFACTURING

Manufacturing, more than any other industry group, lends itself to bigness, and for a good reason. Because of the investment required in equipment, energy, and raw materials, it takes much more money to start a manufacturing venture. Automobile manufacture, for example, calls for millions of

EXHIBIT 3.2 *Flow of Products and Services Between Industry Groups*

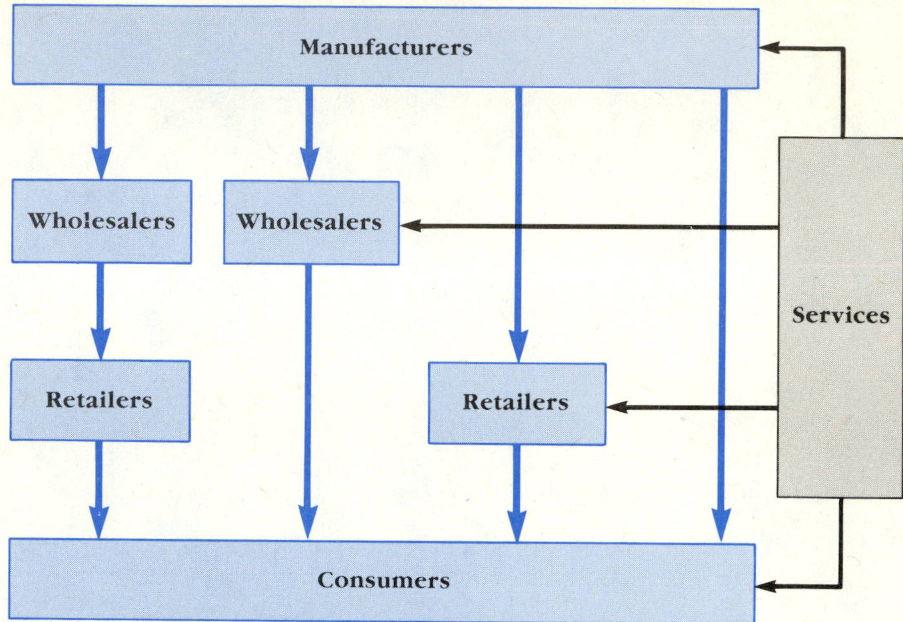

dollars of investment and hundreds of workers before the first automobile can roll off the assembly line. Such requirements shut out most entrepreneurs. True, Henry Ford began on a shoestring of just $28,000. But today, it is all but impossible to begin from scratch in competition with giants like Ford Motor Company.

Just how strongly does big business dominate the world of manufacturing? The nation's top 500 manufacturers account for:

- Two-thirds of the total sales revenues generated by manufacturers
- Three-fourths of the total number of employees in manufacturing

Even so, many entrepreneurs do well in manufacturing. It is not uncommon for entrepreneurs to outdo big business in such innovative industries as chemicals, electronics, and toys.

Example: In personal computers, entrepreneurs are doing well against such giants as IBM and Texas Instruments. In fact, it was entrepreneur Steven Jobs who brought out the first personal computer in 1976. It was only after computers became a runaway success that big business began making its own models.

With so much money at stake, the risks are generally much greater in manufacturing than in wholesaling, retailing, or services. But, often, so are the rewards. It is not uncommon for small manufacturers to earn more than a 20 percent return on their investment. Such high returns tend to favor those industries that turn out a steady flow of new ideas and new products. They expect change, and they help it happen.

Tradition, not change, dominates such old industries as sawmills and bakeries, clothing and machine tools. These industries tend to be marginal, with many businesses just breaking even. Few entrepreneurs are drawn to such industries, although they seem to offer opportunities because they are ripe for change.

Example: In the early 1950s, one entrepreneur saw opportunity in an old industry's problems. He began his own business to make machinery for the sawmill industry. He chose the sawmill industry because it had changed little since the Civil War and there was ample room for innovation. He modernized the design of sawmill machinery, offering sawmill operators equipment tailored to their specific needs. His strategy was to sell machinery unavailable from any other manufacturer.

The success of his strategy is evident in the growth of his business—from just 3 employees originally to 104 by the time that he sold out.

Such entrepreneurial success often attracts the attention of big business. Most big businesses are aware of the innovations that flow from small manufacturers. In fact, Ford Motor Company, Exxon, and many others have set up special departments to find innovative manufacturers, either to buy into or to buy out. On both sides, a buy-out may be favorable:

- For a big business, it may be a way to invest profits or to diversify into something new.
- For the entrepreneur, it may be a way to realize capital gains or to retire.

The purchase of small businesses by big business does not always benefit the consumer, however.

Example: Until the 1950s, hundreds of textile entrepreneurs made cotton and woolen fabric of almost every conceivable color, style, and weave. If garment makers failed to find what they wanted at one textile mill, they could go to another mill in search of style and elegance. Today, such variety and competition no longer exist. A handful of big businesses has bought out almost all small mills and converted them to focus on the manufacture of fabrics made from manmade fibers like nylon and polyester. Because such fibers lend themselves to mass production of the same style, color, and weave, consumers now find similar clothes in virtually every store.

In general, manufacturing offers more opportunities for innovation than any other industry. Retailing and wholesaling rank last, while services lie in between.

WHOLESALING

Small business dominates wholesaling. Businesses with fewer than 100 employees account for nearly 80 percent of the number of employees in wholesaling. This high percentage stems from the fact that wholesalers are mostly caretakers; they need fewer employees for a given volume of business than do manufacturers or retailers.

As caretakers, wholesalers buy product in bulk from manufacturers, store it in a place convenient to retailers, and then sell it as retailers call for it. Besides having few employees, a wholesaler usually has few customers, although most tend to be large-volume, repeating customers.

Entrepreneurs who try their hand at wholesaling normally do so only after a long apprenticeship. It takes time to master the subtleties of negotiating low purchase prices, winning the confidence of retailers, and anticipating their needs. There are few instant wholesalers.

Often, wholesaling is a balancing act in which the entrepreneur is either calming the feathers of a retailer whose promised goods have failed to arrive or chasing after suppliers who have failed to deliver. Despite the frenzy, many entrepreneurs prosper, especially those few who innovate.

EXHIBIT 3.3 *Small Business Employment by Industry Group*

Businesses with fewer than 100 employees account for most of the employment in wholesaling, services, and retailing.

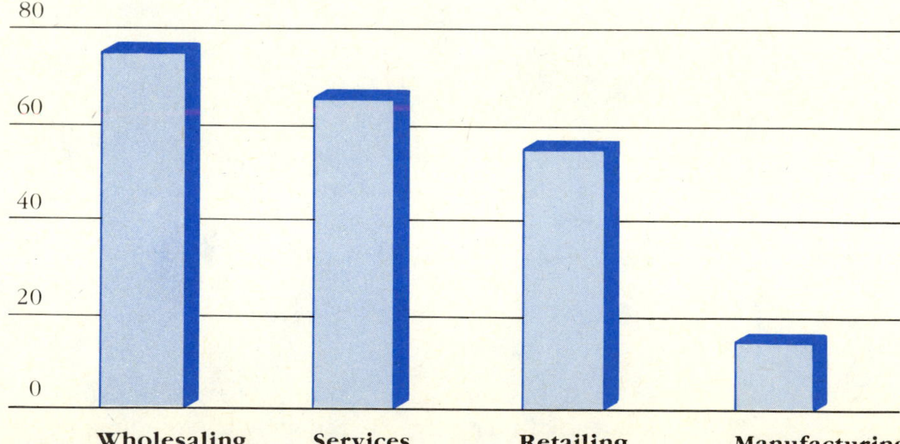

Source: U.S. Department of Commerce, *Enterprise Statistics* (Washington, D.C.: U.S. Government Printing Office, 1977), E372-1, Table 5, p. 142.

Example: Entrepreneurs have opened specialty pharmaceutical houses that deliver prescription items to druggists four times a day. Such fast service enables druggists to eliminate inventories of slow-moving drugs.

Exhibit 3.3 shows how small business dominates not only wholesaling but also retailing and services. Note, however, that small business accounts for less than 20 percent of the total employment in manufacturing.

RETAILING

As shown in Exhibit 3.3, businesses with fewer than 100 employees account for more than 50 percent of all employees in retailing. Most of them have fewer than five employees. Moreover, there are hundreds of different kinds of retailers, ranging from wig shops to automobile agencies, from custard stands to department stores.

Although sometimes called "the nation's biggest small business," retailing nonetheless has spawned some giant businesses. Two examples are department-store chains like Sears and J.C. Penney. Big chains also stand out among groceries, restaurants, and variety stores.

Even so, small retailers are holding their own. Almost as many men and women, for example, work in small grocery stores as in large chains like A&P.

Some entrepreneurs do quite well in retailing, such as the innovative entrepreneurs who start discount drug stores and convenience food stores that open at 8 A.M. and close at midnight. As a rule, however, few retailers pursue innovation with regularity, unlike manufacturers in growth industries like chemicals and electronics.

Specialty shops are especially attractive to retailing entrepreneurs because such shops enable them to focus their resources in depth on a narrow segment of the market rather than spread those resources too thinly over a wider spectrum. For example, a retailer may sell suits styled only for men taller than 6 feet 2 inches, but in so doing, may offer a broader selection and better fit than the department store with which it competes.

Many entrepreneurs go into retailing with an eye to multiplying one store into many as quickly as possible. They do so chiefly by selling franchises to investors. That way, entrepreneurs can expand without putting up too much of their own money. Franchising is often a shortcut to growth.

Example: Specializing in nothing but microwave ovens and accessories, Friedman's Microwave Ovens of Oakland, California has expanded dramatically. Begun in 1976, Friedman's mushroomed to more than 80 franchises in just four years.

The key to Friedman's success is its microwave cooking classes that come free-for-life to everyone who buys an oven at Friedman's. "There's no doubt," says founder Arthur Friedman, "that a lot of people have ruined a lot of food in a microwave oven, and that has given microwaves a bad name. So here in our schools we try to convince people that there are no mysteries about microwaves—it's only common sense." Clearly, the Friedman strategy has paid off.[1]

SERVICES

Of all the industry groups, services generally are the easiest to go into. Many can be run from a home or a storefront office. Examples are telephone-answering services and management consulting firms. Such businesses require little, if any, investment.

Other services, such as motels and professional athletic teams, require much more investment. For example, new professional football franchises go for as much as $40 million.

Like retailing, the different kinds of services number into the hundreds, ranging from shoeshine parlors to car rental agencies, from marriage counselors to brain surgeons. Services are the fastest growing part of our economy. If we count all the men and women who work for nonprofit organizations, services today account for more than 50 percent of the nation's total workforce. Ours is the first economy in history in which services dominate.

Services hold a magnetic attraction for the entrepreneur. Unlike retailing, services are open to innovation. And no other industry group offers entrepreneurs a higher return on their investment in time. Often, they can do it independently, without having to work with others. That is why they are drawn to such fields as computer services and the law, accounting and management consulting.

Example: A pioneer in personal computing, Portia Isaacson of Richardson, Texas, foresaw the trend toward widespread business use of microcomputers. She felt confident enough in 1976 to gamble on opening one of the nation's first computer stores.

In 1980, Ms. Isaacson left retailing and founded her own technology forecasting and consulting firm—Future Computing. Her firm specializes in product and strategic planning for clients—including leading computer and electronics equipment manufacturers and retailers.[2]

Like retailing, services lend themselves to franchising; for many kinds of services, it is the least costly way to expand, as the following franchisor has found.

Example: The American obsession with being thin continues to fatten the wallets of weight-loss franchisors. Currently, there are 21.1 million adults who are overweight or obese in the United States. Andrew Kostecka, a commodity industry specialist at U.S. Department of Commerce, explains that the market for weight-loss centers is growing, since people have more leisure time and "are more health conscious and better educated."

One franchisor who has succeeded spectacularly in this market is Diet Center of Rexburg, Idaho. Begun in 1972, Diet Center has grown to 1,910 franchises in the United States and Canada. It is selling new centers at the rate of four a week.[3]

Big business offers little threat to the survival of small service businesses. The greater threat is posed by the consumer who turns do-it-yourselfer. In some cases, entrepreneurs fight back by creating new, hard-to-copy services. Beauty shops, for example, have created hair styles that defy imitation by do-it-yourselfers.

So far, we have talked about retailing and services as if they were separate industry groups that do not overlap. This is not always so, as borne out by these examples:

- Professional football teams sell not only entertainment but also foot-long hot dogs and 98-page programs featuring player rosters and photographs.
- Motels sell not only a night's lodging but also razor blades and steak-and-potato dinners.
- Service stations sell not only gasoline and motor oil but also services, such as fixing flat tires and balancing wheels.

Since the lines separating services from other industry groups often overlap and blur, it is sometimes hard to classify businesses into the neat categories of manufacturing, wholesaling, retailing, or services.

CLASSIFICATION OF SERVICES NOT NORMALLY CLASSIFIED AS SUCH

So far, we have discussed only those industries that are normally classified as services. Other industries may also fall into this category.

For our purposes in examining the nature of various industries and their accessibility to entrepreneurs, we will group these industries under services. They logically belong there, although it could be argued that construction and utilities also qualify under manufacturing. For example, a carpenter may translate an architect's drawings (services) into a two-story house (manufacturing). Building the house also requires other craftspeople to put in plumbing and electrical wiring (services).

Communication

Communications media such as magazines, newspapers, television, and radio are dominated by big business. Their very nature limits opportunities for new ventures. But their lure is so great that some entrepreneurs try their hand at starting, say, a new magazine featuring hot-rod cars or a new suburban newspaper featuring local happenings.

Example: In 1953, Hugh Hefner hocked his furniture for $600, scraped together $10,000 more, and started his own magazine. Its name? *Playboy*. The first issue in 1953 sold 54,000 copies. By 1983, *Playboy* had a circulation of 5,200,000 and sales revenues of $349 million.

Construction

Most construction contractors are small. And contrary to popular opinion, small business is the nation's biggest builder. This is especially true among electrical, painting, and plumbing contractors. Big business is not absent from the construction industry, however. For example, giant general contractors build skyscrapers like the Sears Tower in Chicago or blast through mountain ranges to build superhighways like the Pennsylvania Turnpike.

General contracting holds the greatest attraction for pure entrepreneurs in construction, mostly because of the challenges it offers. For example, a general contractor may take an architect's plans for a domed football stadium, translate them into hundreds of materials, and then contract out the construction work to dozens of subcontractors.

Subcontracting also attracts the entrepreneur, often because it requires little investment beyond tools and skill. A painting subcontractor, for example, need only invest in a pickup truck, a ladder, a brush, and some cans of paint.

Construction also attracts entrepreneurs because it appeals to their desire for creative satisfaction. A carpenter building a hencoop, for example, gets a deeper satisfaction from the work than someone tightening bolts on an assembly line. When the hencoop is finished, it often belongs more to the carpenter than to the person who hired him or her, continuing to bring pleasure long after the job is completed.

Finance

Finance, too, is dominated by small business. Most of the nation's 15,000 commercial banks are small. Almost every town has one. But banking also has its giants. In 1984, San Francisco's Bank of America had assets of $121 billion, more than the combined holdings of all the small banks in the country. Note how humbly the Bank of America began:

Example: In 1904, Amadeo Peter Giannini opened his first branch in a remodeled saloon. His bank catered to the needs of the little person and to small business. As they grew rich, so did his bank. Today, the Bank of America is the nation's second largest bank.

Commercial banking no longer has much attraction for entrepreneurs. It is too hard to get into, since federal and state laws often require commercial banks to raise as much as $2.5 million before opening their doors for business. Even so, many entrepreneurs do make their mark in finance, but in other areas, such as venture capital, stock brokerage, mortgage lending, finance companies, and investment banking.

Of these, venture capital has perhaps the strongest appeal for entrepreneurs. In their view, what could be more creative fun than to risk money on a new idea or a new product? Note the difference between banks and venture-capital firms:

- Banks rent money.
- Venture-capital firms risk money.

Venture-capital firms seek out new enterprises, especially those backed by new ideas and keen talent. Banks, on the other hand, avoid them because by law they cannot take chances with their depositors' money.

Insurance

This industry's statistics boggle the mind. Insurance is the nation's greatest reservoir of money, with more than $580 billion in assets. The industry's 2,100 companies have sold policies totaling an astronomical $4.6 trillion. Few of the companies are small.

Tens of thousands of insurance agents, however, represent insurance companies and sell policies. All are independent small businesspersons.

Insurance holds some attraction for the entrepreneur, but not much. The entrepreneurs who do well usually sell group life insurance or group medical insurance. Group policies enable organizations to insure each of their workers for far less than the cost of insurance for an individual.

Real Estate

A popular form of investment, real estate has grown into a $105 billion-a-year industry. Servicing it are more than 120,000 real estate firms. Most of them are small, with just a handful of employees. Such firms normally work as finders. For example, if a family wants to sell their house, the real estate agent's job is to find them a buyer.

Entrepreneurs, however, generally prefer commercial rather than residential sales. And they are likely to go in as developers, not brokers. The explosive growth of shopping centers after World War II was mostly the work of entrepreneurs. More than 24,000 shopping centers now dot the country.

Transportation

Like the insurance industry, transportation is made up almost entirely of big businesses. The reason is obvious: it takes millions of dollars just to establish a railroad or an airline. A few small businesses have been successful in transportation, such as taxi companies and helicopter short-hop services.

The opportunity that entrepreneurs are exploring in transportation has been opened up by the combination of suburban sprawl, the energy crunch, and inadequate mass transit. Entrepreneurs are filling the gap with door-to-door autobus service that involves picking up passengers, taking them to work or to shopping centers, and then returning them home.

Utilities This is the only industry that almost entirely shuts out the entrepreneur. With the exception of telephone companies, utilities are monopolies in virtually every community. Gas and electric companies are closely controlled and regulated by state laws that also give such utilities the exclusive right to serve a community.

A LOOK AT THE FUTURE

What will tomorrow be like? What products and services will consumers want 10 or 20 years from now? Which industries will lend themselves to entrepreneurial adventure?

Looking into the future is high art. Knowledge is now exploding so quickly that industry leaders must look 5, 10, or 20 years ahead just to keep up. In fact, our store of knowledge is doubling every five years, or several hundred times faster than in the 1920s. By contrast, in the Stone Age, the knowledge of primitive human beings doubled every 100,000 years.[4]

Futurism itself has become a growth industry for entrepreneurs. The Library of Congress, which has its own futures research group, has estimated that there are nearly 100 small firms devoted to some aspect of futures research. One such firm has already helped more than 500 government and corporate clients to peer into the future.[5]

Futurists foresee a world far different from today's. Some of their predictions about the year 2000 follow.

On People The nation's population will stop growing, peaking at 270 million. Cities and suburbs will cluster together to form so-called megalopolises. For example, the coastal strip between Boston and Washington will seem to become one city, with little farmland in between. Such megalopolises will be home for eight out of ten people. Many men and women will work at home as computer networks spread.

Our society will continue to mature. By the year 2000, 17 percent of the total population will be 60 years old and over. Only 28 percent will be under 20 years old.

On Demographics The South and the West will continue to grow, at the expense of the other regions. Two out of three new jobs between 1975 and 1985 sprang up in those regions. The frost-belt states will counter these trends with a host of incentives to attract industry.

On Transportation Two dramatic changes will slowly begin to take place in transportation: the production of automobiles powered by electricity, and the design of hovercraft that ride on cushions of air.

On Food Beef consumption will lessen as frogmen raise fish in a network of underwater pens. These underwater farmers will then grind their nutrition-rich crop into a host of many-tasting foods. The magic of chemistry will impart flavors to please any palate—from garlic to champagne, from mustard to beefsteak.

On Shopping Today's supermarkets will diminish in number as homemakers begin shopping by videophone. These phones will enable homemakers to scan, price, and order groceries without leaving their kitchens. This practice will spread to other retailing industries, especially to department stores and drugstores.

On Information The microprocessor, a computer smaller than a thumbnail, will change the life of every man, woman, and child on earth. A marvel of technology, this computer can process mountains of information with lightning speed. By the year 2000, it will cause changes such as these:

- Computers will help scientists solve major problems in biology, chemistry, and physics.
- Electronic books will begin to replace printed books.
- Electronic mail will replace much of the postal service.
- Robots will run much of the machinery now run by humans.
- Taxpayers will file paperless returns by computer.
- Telephones built into watches will become a reality.

Libraries and filing cabinets will begin to give way to computers with amazing memories. These storehouses of information will be available to every person who wants them—by dialing a coded number from their homes.

Computers that listen and respond to human speech will also become widespread by the year 2000. Such computers will give entrepreneurs access to large data bases through the telephone network, while providing for the control of complex machines by vocal command. These systems will be helpful in the day-to-day control of business operations. They will also make sophisticated devices for the handicapped possible.

> **Example:** Consider a conversation between a computer and its users concerning the inventory of a warehouse. The computer "knows" how many of each item are on hand and where each article is stored. Its data base also lists costs and suppliers.
>
> The users have questions that the computer can answer, such as, "Do we have any blue pencils in stock?" The computer's response might be: "There are 14 cases of blue pencils in bay 13."[6]

On Work The number of working men and women will drop from 40 percent today to 30 percent. The drudgery of manual labor, the monotony of clerical work, and the dullness of assembly lines will be borne by versatile computers. The computer will also invade the executive suite, replacing many middle managers.

With the arrival of the computer age, lifestyles will also change sharply. For example, the average person will spend a lifespan of 75 years as follows: one third becoming educated, one third working at a job, and one third enjoying retirement.

Many families will be independently wealthy. Thanks to government benefits, even nonworking families will be well off. Median family income will approach $20,000 a year (in 1985 dollars).

On Medicine Science and medicine will combine their talents to all but free the world of bacterial and viral disease. Artificial hearts and lungs will be available to everyone who needs them. Pocket radar will enable the blind to see and the deaf to hear. Chemical therapy will cure the mentally retarded.

On the Environment A garbage-disposal revolution is also in the offing. Consider that we make more garbage than steel in a year. By law, every municipality will have to recycle all of its garbage. One benefit will be the burning of combustible materials to produce electrical energy.

Almost everyone likes to play the game of future. We are no exception. Although forecasts such as this one must be taken with a grain of salt, they do hint at answers to this key question: In what industries lie the best opportunities for entrepreneurial adventure in the future?

There is no way to answer this question with military precision. We can only guess. But it seems that entrepreneurs will be drawn to those industries prepared for strong upward trends in:

- Affluence and leisure
- Individualism
- Urbanization
- Technology

We will take up each of these trends in the next chapter, when we deal with the search for a venture.

SUMMARY

Although small business thrives in almost every industry, it is stronger in some than in others. The requirements of each industry group—the initial financial investments in personnel, materials and equipment—determine just how strong the presence of small business is. In terms of number of employees, small business dominates three of the four major industry groups: wholesaling, retailing, and services. It is less strong in manufacturing, mostly because of the large sums of money needed to get started.

Entrepreneurial opportunities abound in virtually every industry. In any industry, small businesses are most successful when they are innovators. In manufacturing, for example, small businesses compete well in high-technology industries such as chemicals and electronics. Services, because of their ease of entry, attract many entrepreneurs and are the fastest growing part of our economy.

Life in the year 2000 will differ sharply from life today. The knowledge explosion will continue to spark change at an accelerating rate, thanks largely to the remarkable versatility of the computer.

DISCUSSION AND REVIEW QUESTIONS

1. Which industry group appeals most to you? Why?
2. Do you agree that entrepreneurial opportunities will broaden in the future? Why?
3. Why have service industries grown so rapidly?
4. Define the terms: *manufacturing, wholesaling, retailing, services, venture capitalist, futurist, megalopolis.*
5. What is the difference between venture capital and bank loans? Which is better for the entrepreneur? Why?
6. Why do manufacturing industries generally lend themselves to big business?
7. Why may some old industries like textiles be attractive to entrepreneurs?
8. Which of the four major industry groups—manufacturing, retailing, services, or wholesaling—is likely to attract the innovative entrepreneur? Explain.
9. Is there always a sharp distinction between retailing and services? Explain.
10. Comment on the reasonableness of our forecast for the year 2000.
11. What do manufacturers, wholesalers, retailers, and services have in common? In what ways do they differ? Give your own examples.
12. Many consumers believe that restaurants are a service business. Is this true? Explain.
13. Identify and briefly describe some of the dramatic changes that have taken place in your community in the past five years. How have these changes influenced entrepreneurial opportunities?
14. Should every entrepreneur be a futurist? Why? How do you plan to keep up with the knowledge explosion?
15. Is it reasonable to call the age we live in the computer age? Explain.

NOTES

1. Adapted from John Bachman, "Friedman's Microwave Ovens," *Franchising Today,* April 1981, p. 19.
2. Adapted from "Spotlight: Portia Isaacson," *Output,* April 1981, p. 54.
3. Adapted from Carol Steinberg, "Weight Loss Centers Earn Fat Profits," *Venture,* December 1984, p. 152.
4. Martin Levin, "Phoenix Nest," *Saturday Review,* June 22, 1968, p. 4.
5. Paul Dickson, "The Future Revised," *Northwest Orient Magazine,* January 1979, p. 10.
6. Stephen E. Levinson and Mark Y. Liberman, "Speech Recognition by Computer," *Scientific American,* April 1981, p. 64.

CASE 3A *ColeJon Mechanical Corporation*

ColeJon was founded in 1976 as a remodeling firm. Just seven years later, as a maintenance service firm, ColeJon's sales revenues reached $4,753,000. This record of fast growth earned for its two founders, Lonzo Coleman and James Jones, national recognition in 1984 as Minority Contractors of the Year. President Ronald Reagan honored them at the White House, calling them "outstanding business owners."

Mr. Coleman and Mr. Jones believe that ColeJon is now poised to become one of the nation's largest contractors. By 1988, they expect sales revenues to increase six-fold, to $28 million a year. About 75 percent of their sales, however, stem from government contracts and just 25 percent from the private sector. "I wish we could reverse that ratio," says Mr. Coleman. "The question is, How?"

Background

In 1976, Mr. Coleman first thought about becoming an entrepreneur. Although he had a steady job as a pipefitter, he saw that his opportunities as a tradesman were limited. An apprentice for five years and later a master pipefitter, Mr. Coleman could aspire only to be foreman for contractors specializing in maintenance service.

"I realized there was no way I could become an executive if I remained a pipefitter," says Mr. Coleman. "No way I could reach the boardroom. I knew, too, that the main reason employers hired me was to satisfy EEO* requirements on a particular project. The total lack of opportunity kept preying on my mind. More than ever, I was convinced that I could succeed at what I wanted to be, but only if I started my own business."

That same year, Mr. Coleman met Mr. Jones while they were working together, installing a heating system at a local college. Mr. Jones had apprenticed for four years as a sheet-metal worker and was now a master tradesman. He soon shared with Mr. Coleman the frustration with his lot as a tradesman.

Mr. Jones fully agreed with Mr. Coleman that "there were many talented people working in subservient roles who would never be able to use their talents and receive the proper recognition." The chemistry between the two men was such that, on the very day they first met, they made up their minds to become partners and start their own business.

At the time, both men had secure jobs with reliable incomes. Mr. Coleman, for example, earned $25,000 a year as a pipefitter. Now his wages, as well as Mr. Jones's, would drop to zero.

The Early Years

So it was that, in 1976, Mr. Coleman and Mr. Jones scraped together $5,000 each to start their own remodeling firm. They named their firm *ColeJon*, which is a contraction of their surnames: *Cole*man and *Jon*es. "It

* Equal Employment Opportunity

EXHIBIT 3A.1 *ColeJon Mechanical Corporation: 1977 Income Statement*

Sales revenues from contracts	$56,100
Cost of contracts	43,500
Gross profit	$12,600
Operating expenses	5,100
Profit before taxes	$ 7,500
Federal income taxes	0
Profit after taxes	$ 7,500

truly gave us and our families a sense of pride to form a company named after us," says Mr. Coleman.

The two men harbored no illusions about the sacrifices they would be called upon to make. Mr. Coleman mortgaged his house and Mr. Jones borrowed money from relatives. "We couldn't go to the movies anymore," says Mr. Coleman. "My wife learned how to cook hamburgers in a hundred different ways. Without our wives, I doubt that we would have survived the first year. They truly were supportive and never complained about the change in our lifestyles, severe as it was."

Two months passed before the two men landed their first job, the installation of air conditioning systems in 13 stores in a shopping center. "We made just $500 profit from that job," says Mr. Jones. Their firm's first-year income statement and end-of-year balance sheet appear in Exhibits 3A.1 and 3A.2.

"Even though things often looked bleak our first year in business," says Mr. Coleman, "not once did Jim and I consider giving up and folding our firm. To us, that would have been a fate worse than death. We would persevere." Mr. Jones adds, "Perseverance is what made ColeJon survive and succeed, and it has paid off handsomely."

EXHIBIT 3A.2 *ColeJon Mechanical Corporation: Balance Sheet (December 31, 1977)*

Assets			Equities		
Current assets:			Current liabilities:		
Cash	$17,700		Accounts payable	$12,700	
Accounts receivable	16,100		Payroll taxes payable	1,600	
Other	200	$34,000	Accrued expenses	1,600	
			Other	4,000	$19,900
			Shareholders' loans		$ 8,000
Fixed assets:					
Equipment	$ 2,700		Owners' equity		
Less: Accumulated depreciation	300	$ 2,400	Common stock	$ 2,000	
			Retained earnings	7,300	$ 9,300
Other assets:					
Deposits, organization		$ 800			
Total assets		$37,200	Total equities		$37,200

Education

Both Mr. Coleman and Mr. Jones believe that "lack of preparation" was the main reason for their failure during the first year. They were not prepared to run a business of their own. Neither man had ever supervised anyone before, and had certainly never managed a business.

"I did learn about the ways of business by observing the contractors I had worked for," says Mr. Jones. "But it was a negative learning experience. The contractors were such poor managers that I learned what *not* to do, especially in the treatment of tradesmen like myself. They rarely trusted me and other tradesmen to put in a full day's work."

Ironically, it was the contractors that Mr. Jones had worked for that helped him decide to launch his own venture. "I just knew I could do better," says Mr. Jones. "I just knew that I was a motivator, that I could help others to excel. What better way to use that talent than in a business of your own?"

Mr. Coleman and Mr. Jones have similar educational backgrounds. Both are graduates of large urban high schools who did well in their studies. Although encouraged by their teachers to go on to college, both men ignored the advice and instead decided to learn trades and earn money in order to marry and raise families soon after graduation.

They have not ignored education since. Mr. Coleman now believes that education should be a "continuous thing" and he takes courses as he needs them at a local college. He has studied small business management, marketing, construction management, and engineering design. Mr. Jones also has taken courses to improve his technical skills.

Both men also attend seminars regularly all over the country. "What I like most about these seminars is the networking," says Mr. Coleman. "Jim and I get to meet with other contractors to share information and solutions to problems. We often come away feeling excited about what we learned. In essence, Jim and I have learned to learn and learned to think for the rest of our lives."

Bonding Problem

Bonding companies, which protect customers and suppliers by selling bonds for certain percentages of the contract prices, have traditionally influenced business for contractors. The three main kinds of bonds are:

- Bid bonds, which assure customers that contractors are prepared to work according to the terms of their contracts if their bids are successful.
- Payment bonds, which assure suppliers that they will be paid by the bonded contractors.
- Performance bonds, which assure customers that jobs will be completed by the bonded contractors according to plans and specifications.

These same bonds, however, create difficulties for new contractors who seek business. The U.S. Small Business Administration (SBA) describes these problems in this way:

> The effect that bonding companies have had on contractors is evident in the area of competition. The customer, by requiring that the contractor

be bonded, is more or less assured of adequate completion of the job. Therefore, contractors are compared on the basis of price. Also, commercial banks are often more lenient to bonded contractors.

Bonding companies usually require the contractor to have proven experience and the organizational financial capacity to complete the project. This can be a real stumbling block to the new contractor.

With the widespread use of bonding requirements, the competition that is generated often leads the inexperienced contractor to submit bids that are unrealistically low. One or two such mistakes often can spell bankruptcy.

The SBA, by the way, has a surety bond program designed to help small and emerging contractors who might have previously been unable to get bonding. The SBA is authorized to guarantee up to 90 percent of losses incurred under bid, payment, or performance bonds on contracts up to $500,000.*

In the early days, ColeJon was faced with the problem of bonding in securing contracts. "As much as anything else, the bonding restraints imposed upon us kept us from growing," says Mr. Jones. "The odd thing was, we could do the work, but we couldn't get the bonding that would let us do the work." Mr. Coleman adds, "The bonding restraint was like a millstone round our necks. The most we could get was a $25,000 bond, based on our personal assets, mine and Jim's. That meant we could only bid on $10,000 jobs."

Catch-22

Mr. Coleman and Mr. Jones tried to take advantage of the standard bond market, but they were turned down because of their inexperience as contractors. "It was a classic Catch-22 situation," says Mr. Jones. "We couldn't get work because we couldn't get bonding; and we couldn't get bonding because we couldn't get work. Amazing!" Later, the SBA granted aid to Mr. Coleman and Mr. Jones through its surety bond program and enabled the two men to succeed.

"Credibility is something you can't put dollars and cents on," says Mr. Coleman. "Jim and I spent, and still spend, most of our waking hours building up our credibility. We got our first job bidding low, just so we could gain some credentials, some credibility. It was a $3,000 job and we made no money. That first year was so rough, I did not draw a single penny of salary. Nor did Jim."

In 1978, their third year of business, the two men created an informal advisory council to give them the managerial help they needed for success. "We had too many managerial shortcomings, Lonnie and I," says Mr. Jones, "so we vowed to do something about it. For instance, our financial statements were such a mess that bankers laughed at them." In particular, they had little knowledge of project management or cost estimation for

* U.S. Small Business Administration, *Business Plan for Small Construction Firms* (Washington, D.C.: U.S. Government Printing Office, 1974), p. 7.

projects. These skills are crucial for contractors, as the SBA confirms:

> Whether an entrepreneur succeeds as a contractor—makes a profit or not—depends to a great extent on his or her bidding practices. Therefore, the contractor must make careful and complete estimates.
>
> Many of the more successful contractors attribute their success to their estimating procedures. They build the job on paper before they submit a bid. In doing this, they break the job down into work units and pieces of material. Then, they assign a cost to each item. The total of these costs will be the direct project cost.
>
> Contractors must also figure on the indirect costs of a job. For instance, they will have overhead expenses such as the cost of maintaining an office, trucks, license fees, and so on. The estimate should also consider any interest charges that contractors will pay on money they borrow to get the job underway.
>
> There are also insurance fees to pay, surety bond premiums, travel expenses, advertising costs, office salaries, lawyer's fees, and so on. These must also be paid out of the contractor's sales revenues.
>
> The decision whether to bid on a particular job should be determined by several factors. First, does the contractor have the capacity to complete the job on schedule and according to specifications? The contractor should beware of overextending himself or herself out of business. He must operate within his known capabilities. On any job, he must follow all the details of the work himself, or find competent supervision.*

Professional Help

The first and only professional that Mr. Coleman and Mr. Jones added to their advisory board was their attorney, Bernard Mandel, who is also an expert in cost accounting. In the first two years with ColeJon, Mr. Mandel did not charge for his services.

"What a super guy Bernie is," says Mr. Coleman. "He never even realized we could afford to pay him. He just went on doing such legal work as writing subcontractors' agreements, filing legal papers, and resolving disputes—as if we still could not afford his services. Of course, all this has changed and Bernie now charges us his normal fee."

"We've always had pressing legal problems," says Mr. Coleman. "It's the nature of the industry. It's comforting to know that all I have to do is pick up the phone and ask Bernie for help. He can handle anything, even negligence suits against disreputable suppliers.

Federal Markets

After three years of lackluster performance, in 1979 ColeJon's fortunes took a decided turn for the better. With Mr. Mandel's help, Mr. Coleman and Mr. Jones decided to devote almost all their marketing efforts to federal contracts, since the federal government is the world's largest buyer of

* U.S. Small Business Administration, *Business Plan for Small Construction Firms* (Washington, D.C.: U.S. Government Printing Office, 1974), pp. 6–7.

products and services. And, one of the SBA's major responsibilities is to see that small businesses like ColeJon obtain a fair share of this vast federal market. To obtain their fair share, Mr. Coleman and Mr. Jones drafted a marketing strategy consisting of these steps:

- To learn about federal markets. They wrote to Washington and ordered such helpful documents as the *Small Business Subcontracting Directory*, the *Small and Disadvantaged Business Utilization*, and the *Commerce Business Daily*.
- To talk with specialists at the SBA and attend every workshop and seminar on federal markets that they could.
- Watch awards of major contracts to large companies in their area. Such companies contract directly with numerous subcontractors like ColeJon.
- Prepare descriptive literature or brochures about ColeJon's capabilities in the federal market. In order to do so, they learned about the process of landing federal contracts and assessed ColeJon's ability to provide services.
- Make frequent visits to small business specialists at the various federal agencies in their trading area.
- Carefully study the terms of contracts, to make sure ColeJon can satisfy them to the letter.

The SBA's 8(a) Program

The federal program that appealed most to Mr. Coleman and Mr. Jones was the SBA's 8(a) program, which directs federal procurement dollars to minority-owned businesses. This program has been highly controversial, as these excerpts from *The Wall Street Journal* suggest:

> Mention 8(a) and people who have heard of it are likely to think of a program that made millionaires of a handful of minority entrepreneurs who balked at leaving the program after their companies had gotten several hundred million dollars apiece in government business.
>
> It's the program remembered for advancing millions of dollars to put the inexperienced and ill-suited into businesses that didn't work, with the result that they defaulted on contracts—souring procurement officers on the program and squandering taxpayers' money.
>
> That, of course, is one side of 8(a), so called for the section of federal law that created it. But it isn't the whole story of 8(a) or the 2,600 companies whose owners have been certified as economically and socially disadvantaged and eligible to be awarded government contracts without competitive bidding.*

The other side of the SBA's 8(a) program is that it enables minority entrepreneurs to succeed. "Without such help," says Mr. Jones, "we never would have made it."

* Sanford L. Jacobs, "Company Sees Beneficial Side of Much-Maligned SBA Plan," *The Wall Street Journal*, June 18, 1984, p. 21.

Mr. Mandel again volunteered his services to guide Mr. Coleman and Mr. Jones through the maze of paperwork required by the SBA. Applying for certification as an 8(a) contractor involved giving detailed information about their firm and about themselves. The SBA's regional office then determined that ColeJon was eligible—a decision that later was reviewed and approved in Washington.

Mr. Coleman and Mr. Jones soon began landing government jobs, both local and federal. They overdid every job to build their credibility in the marketplace. At the same time, they expanded their business to include service maintenance, as described in their brochure:

> ColeJon designs and installs state-of-the-art plumbing, heating, air conditioning and fire protection systems, as well as power and process piping. ColeJon provides contract maintenance to industry and governmental units, protecting their mechanical "lifelines" against failure through constant vigilance.

Financial Performance

Sales began to soar as word spread in government circles that ColeJon performed well. Bonding was no longer a problem, since ColeJon had won certification by the SBA as an 8(a) contractor. ColeJon's yearly financial performance is summarized here and graphed in Exhibit 3A.3:

EXHIBIT 3A.3 *ColeJon Mechanical Corporation: Financial Performance*

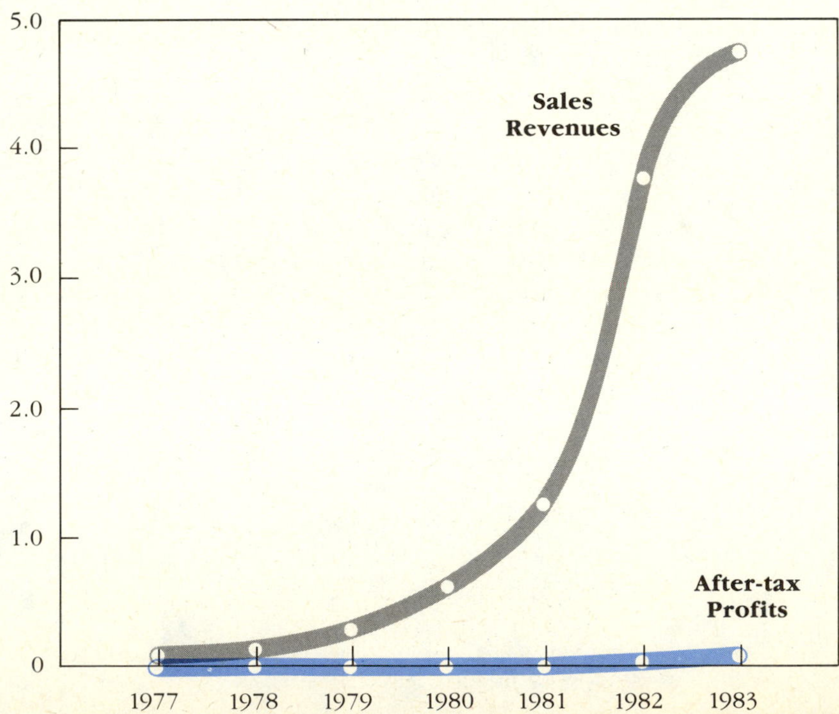

Year	Sales Revenues	After-Tax Profits
1977	$ 56,100	$ 7,500
1978	82,300	(3,300)
1979	252,700	(8,600)
1980	601,500	(9,100)
1981	1,248,400	(10,800)
1982	3,756,800	71,500
1983	4,753,000	71,600

"We're proud of this record, Jim and I," says Mr. Coleman. "Never in our wildest dreams did we expect to be the founders of a multimillion-dollar corporation in so short a time. Our perseverance really paid off. When we started, all we could get was a bonding line of $25,000; would you believe that we now have a bonding line of $1,500,000? When we started, we could bid on nothing larger than a $10,000 job; now it's up to $1 million."

Today, ColeJon's largest service maintenance contract is with NASA's Lewis Research Center, which requires 80 employees. In addition, the company provides maintenance at the Environmental Protection Agency in Narragansett, Rhode Island. Its other clients include such giant corporations as Republic Steel and Union Carbide.

Mr. Coleman and Mr. Jones are especially proud of the fact that they have never lost a client. "Once we land a job," says Mr. Jones, "the client sticks with us and keeps renewing our contract. What better proof of our acceptance in the marketplace?"

Motivating Employees

Both Mr. Coleman and Mr. Jones credit much of their success to their methods of organization. "I'm a fiend for organization," says Mr. Coleman, "and I'm a good motivator." His philosophy on employee motivation is as follows:

- To avoid either deception or rationalization among employees by relying on solid reasons and arguments.
- To give employees options, not orders, while at the same time retaining authority.
- To respect confidences, always making the effort to create trust by keeping the flow of information open.
- To build mutually satisfying relationships with employees and respect their individual purposes and needs.

The two men recognize that each employee has unique gifts and that their firm must allow employees to use these gifts. As a result, one often hears such words as "trust" and "mutual respect" throughout ColeJon.

"The moral of such a working philosophy is clear," says Mr. Jones. "If we treat our employees the way they themselves would like to be treated, our employees will then return the compliment in the form of productive and high-quality work. A work atmosphere not based on such

EXHIBIT 3A.4 *ColeJon Mechanical Corporation: Organizational Chart*

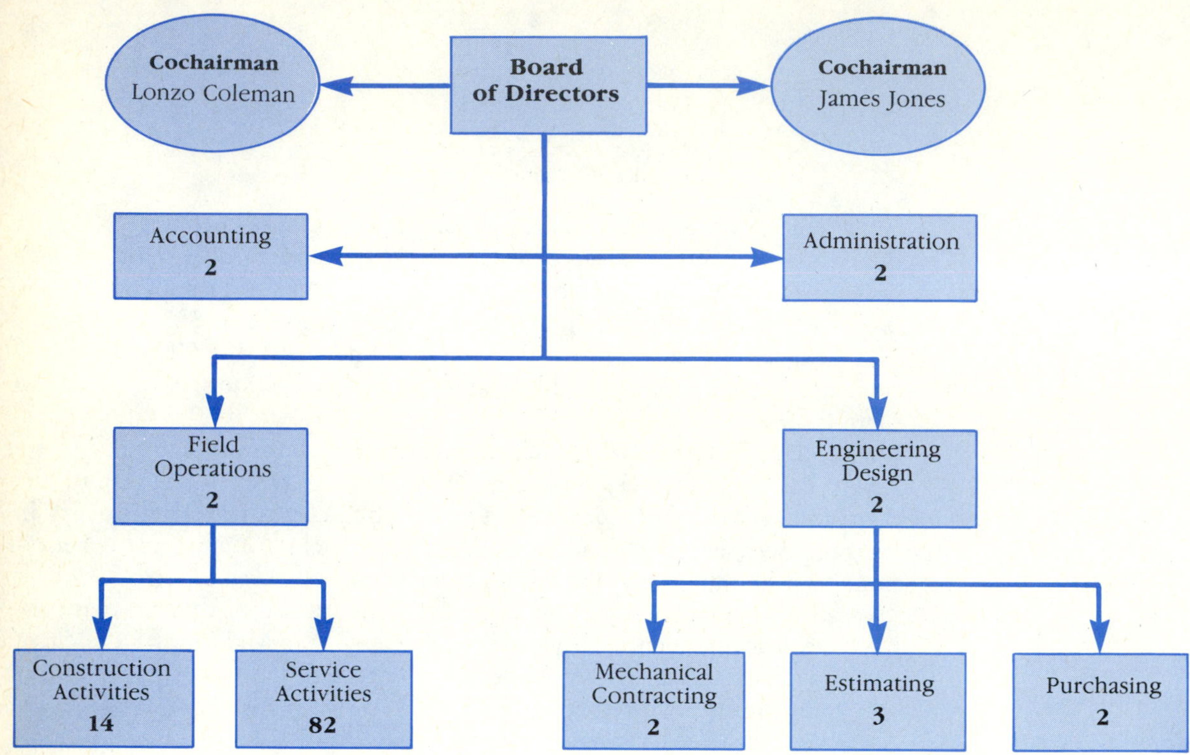

sensitivity is like a marriage without mutual respect. It's bound to collapse like a house of cards."

And, they hire only foremen, foreladies, and managers whose working philosophy coincides with theirs. "We go to great lengths, Lonnie and I, to hire the right person for the right job," says Mr. Jones. "We tell every job candidate that we look for managers who will fondle a job the same way we would if we were doing the job ourselves, away from the office."

It was this idea that led them to hire a seasoned mechanical engineer as a consultant in every facet of project management. "His formal knowledge of bidding and of project management was just what we needed to perform efficiently," says Mr. Coleman.

The engineer had once owned a small business himself and been a chief engineer with a major contractor. Mr. Coleman and Mr. Jones filled the slots shown in the organizational chart in Exhibit 3A.4 with men and women of this caliber.

Control

To control ColeJon's performance, both men recognize the need for feedback at various stages of project management. As sole owners of ColeJon, they must plan, direct, and control each project efficiently.

Throughout this managerial process, ColeJon also needs constant financing, so their controls must supply them with the information they need to keep ColeJon's operations "on the money."

To manage each job efficiently, they analyze job costs to make sure it will turn a profit. "That is why good records are so important," says Mr. Coleman. "How can we possibly bid intelligently on a job unless we know what the costs are?"

As ColeJon grew, their information and recordkeeping needs became ever larger and more complex. So, although all of ColeJon's accounting is done in-house, most of it is done by a minicomputer programmed to generate:

- Quarterly income statements and balance sheets for the entire company
- Profit and cost comparisons of all projects
- Quarterly operating budgets
- Daily cash position
- Cash forecasts
- Payroll

"The computer is our firm's memory," says Mr. Jones. "Most of our historical data is locked into the computer's memory. All we have to do is press a few keys to recall the data we need, especially for bid estimation."

The Future

"We want to be one of the country's major contractors," says Mr. Coleman. "We started out as remodelers, changed to service maintenance, and now may move into development programs for the federal government." By 1988, Mr. Coleman and Mr. Jones expect sales revenues to reach $28 million a year, up from $4,753,000 in 1983. ColeJon's income statements for 1981, 1982, and 1983 appear in Exhibit 3A.5.

EXHIBIT 3A.5

ColeJon Mechanical Corporation: Three-year Income Statements

	1981	1982	1983
Sales revenues from contracts	$1,248,400	$3,756,800	$4,753,000
Cost of contracts	1,077,700	3,157,700	3,585,500
Gross profit	$ 170,700	$ 599,100	$1,167,500
Operating expenses	183,700	483,200	979,100
Operating profit	$ (13,000)	$ 115,900	$ 188,400
Interest expense	7,400	17,700	18,700
Profit before taxes	$ (20,400)	$ 98,200	$ 169,700
Federal income taxes	(9,600)	26,700	98,100
Profit after taxes	$ (10,800)	$ 71,500	$ 71,600

EXHIBIT 3A.6 *ColeJon Mechanical Corporation: Dependence on Government Markets*

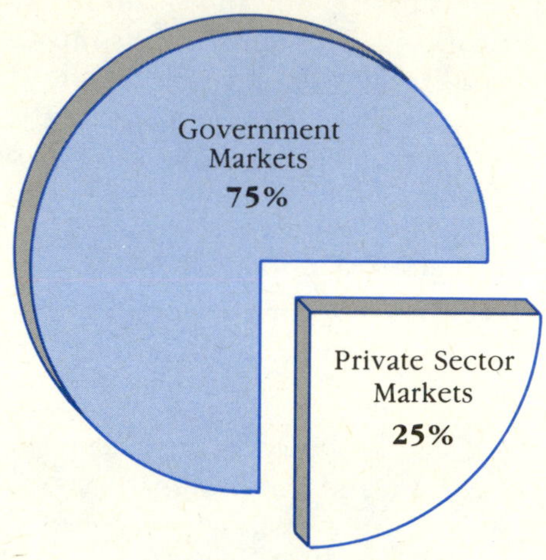

Although work for local and federal government clients has been largely responsible for ColeJon's success, Mr. Jones worries about that relationship. As shown in Exhibit 3A.6, roughly 75 percent of ColeJon's sales revenues come from government contracts and only 25 percent from the private sector. "I would like to see that ratio reversed," says Mr. Jones. "Right now, ColeJon is highly vulnerable. The SBA's 8(a) program, for example, runs for just five years. When this program dries up, we've got to make up for the loss of business by landing more private sector clients. That means we'll have to become even more competitive than we are now. Set-aside programs like 8(a) can't last forever."

Mr. Jones worries, too, that ColeJon is not as fully accepted in contract maintenance as it should be. "Just the other day, we had four auditors looking at our books, at our operations," says Mr. Jones. "We're always being investigated to see if we're capable." Views of Mr. Coleman and Mr. Jones as well as a client's building appear in Exhibit 3A.7.

Questions

1. Comment on the need for federal programs like the 8(a) program.
2. What are ColeJon's prospects?
3. Analyze ColeJon's financial performance.
4. What accounts for ColeJon's success?
5. What advice would you give Mr. Coleman and Mr. Jones regarding their plans for growth?

EXHIBIT 3A.7 *ColeJon Mechanical Corporation: Views of Lonzo Coleman and James Jones and a Client's Building*

CASE 3B *Ellen Wagner*

At age 33, Ellen Wagner wants to shift careers. She now works as a certified public accountant (CPA) for a large auditing firm. "The pay is good," says Ms. Wagner. "And I get to meet a lot of top executives, but I'm tired of looking at numbers all day long. It's getting to me. I want to do something new and different."

Ms. Wagner soon called up her accounting professor at the University of Michigan for advice. "I'm not sure where to start," began Ms. Wagner. "But I've made up my mind to give up the accounting profession. I'm just not cut out for it. It's too confining. Does that shock you?"

"No," replied the professor. "Tell me, do you have any idea what you'd like to do?"

"That's why I'm calling," said Ms. Wagner. "I thought you might give me some guidance. As a CPA, I've audited the books of a lot of entrepreneurs. I really admire them. One of my clients, for example, started with just one employee to make electronic gadgetry. And would you believe, in just 13 years, he has expanded to 270 employees. He built his business with his own two hands, literally. It must give him a lot of satisfaction."

"Is that what you'd like to do, go into business for yourself?" asked the professor.

"Yes, I would," replied Ms. Wagner. "But all I know is accounting. How do you suggest I start?"

"Well," said the professor, "why don't you look at some of the fragmented industries. You know, industries like real estate where no single firm has more than, say, 1 percent of the total market. Fragmented industries are generally inefficient and could use someone of your talents. Another point about fragmented industries is that they're usually easy to go into. They often require little beginning capital."

"Thanks for the advice," said Ms. Wagner. "Real estate sounds like a good place to start. I have only $22,000 in stocks and savings, so I can't think too much about going into other industries, especially manufacturing. Besides, I'm not mechanically inclined. I can't even fix a leaky faucet. You know, it's a good thing I'm still single."

The idea of going into some aspect of the real estate industry intrigued Ms. Wagner. She vaguely recalled reading in *The Wall Street Journal* that industry leaders see the development of franchises as a revolution in real estate. "You know, someday there'll be a McDonald's of the real estate world," said Miss Wagner, "and it could be me."

Questions

1. What should Ms. Wagner do now?
2. Do you think the professor's advice was sound? Why or why not?

CASE 3C *Joan and Laura*

Joan and Laura enjoyed fine art, felt they had good taste in decorating, and knew many artists whose work they wanted to promote. To capitalize on what they called their "passion for art," Joan and Laura decided to go into business for themselves. It was their thought to:

- Decorate the offices of businesspersons who lacked the time or taste to do it themselves.
- Offer to decorate the offices free of charge if the businesspersons bought the art through Joan and Laura. Otherwise, they would charge a flat hourly fee for their decorating services.

For the art, they would charge a 40 percent commission, which is what art dealers charge.

Question What questions will Joan and Laura need to answer to turn their idea into a business?

Source: This case was prepared by Carol Rivchun, Director of the Small Business Management Center of the Greater Cleveland Growth Association.

PART 2 STARTING A NEW VENTURE

SEARCH FOR A NEW VENTURE

QUESTIONS FOR MASTERY

Why is it important to answer the question "what business am I in?" thoughtfully and precisely?

What specific industries are likely to prosper in the future?

What are the two major ways of going into business for oneself?

How does one evaluate the financial worth of a business?

How does one patent an invention?

Let us watch well our beginnings,
and results will manage themselves.
Alexander Clark

As the saying goes, "a thousand-mile journey begins with but a single step." So must a new venture. The first step may be the decision to become an entrepreneur. The next step may be to choose a product or service. Then the would-be entrepreneur must decide whether to:

- Buy an existing business, or—
- Start from scratch

This chapter focuses on these two ways of going into business—after first dealing with choice of product or service. This chapter also explains how to evaluate a venture and how to deal with the problems of patenting an idea.

CHOICE OF PRODUCT OR SERVICE

Early on, the entrepreneur must answer this question: What business should I be in? This may seem like an absurd suggestion. "If there's one thing I know," said one entrepreneur, "it's what business I'm going into." However, entrepreneurs often *think* they know what business they have chosen without closely analyzing their choice. To show why entrepreneurs must make conscious decisions, let us look at this example:

Example: Anthony DiBiasio started a business selling and renting boats. He thought he was going into the marina business. But when he got into trouble and asked for outside help, he learned that he was not really in the marina business. Instead, Mr. DiBiasio was in several businesses. He was in the restaurant business with a dockside cafe—serving meals to boating parties. He was also in the real estate business—buying and selling lots up and down the coast. And he was in the boat-repair business—buying parts and calling in a mechanic to help him. The fact was that Mr. DiBiasio was trying to be all things to all people. With this approach, he was spreading himself thin.

Before he could make a profit, Mr. DiBiasio had to decide *what* business he really was in and concentrate on it. After much study, he saw that his business was really a recreation shopping center. From that point on, profits began to flow.[1]

A vital first step for would-be entrepreneurs is to define their business with precision and brevity. In this regard, Robert Townsend, a former board chairman of Avis Rent-A-Car Corporation, had this to say:

> We defined our business as "renting and leasing vehicles without drivers." This let us put the blinders on ourselves and stop considering the acquisition of related businesses like motels and travel agencies. It also showed us that we had to get rid of some limousine and sightseeing companies that we already owned.[2]

Choosing a product or service requires entrepreneurs to look closely at their own skills and at industry trends to see how well they mesh. Questions that they might ask themselves include:

- Do I really want to run that kind of business?
- Do I really want to sell that kind of product or service?
- Do I really want to do that kind of work?

As mentioned in Chapter Three, it is most likely that entrepreneurs will be attracted to those industries that will capitalize on the upward trends in affluence and leisure, individualism, urbanization, and technology. Let us now look at these trends, one by one.

Affluence and Leisure

Ours is truly an affluent society and it is likely to be even more affluent by the year 2000. The gap between the haves and the have-nots will narrow, not only in the United States but also abroad. As affluence grows, so will leisure time. Which industries are likely to seize on this upward trend? Let us name just a few:

- Recreation and travel
- Banking and stock brokerages
- Real estate
- Luxury and specialty goods
- Education
- Health spas and beauty salons
- Restaurants
- Sporting goods and hobbies
- Performing arts and entertainment
- Publishing

Individualism

More and more, men and women will choose to work for themselves rather than for someone else. With more leisure time, they may choose to moonlight by setting up their own businesses. Many will work out of their homes. Industries most likely to benefit from this trend include:

- Law
- Management consulting
- Accounting and tax preparation
- Mail order
- Telephone answering services
- Computer programming
- Financial services

Urbanization

Many more persons will be living in urban areas by the year 2000; and, as a result, consumers will be more sophisticated in their buying habits. They will seek the highest quality products and services. The following industries will probably benefit from increased consumer sophistication:

- Equipment rental
- Pet shops
- Day care centers
- Housing construction
- Fashion clothing, gourmet foods, and boutiques
- Home computers, electronic gadgetry, and stereo systems

Technology

The nation's laboratories will continue to invent new gadgets, new machines, new products. Many of these will be so complex as to defy servicing by do-it-yourselfers. So strong growth is foreseen in many service industries, including:

- Plumbing
- Television and appliance repair
- Electronics servicing
- Automobile repair
- Lawn care

The fast growth of technology will attract many entrepreneurs to manufacturing also. As inventors come up with new products, the need for entrepreneurs to make and market them will intensify. Most new products will spring from such industries as:

- Chemicals
- Environmental control and energy-saving equipment
- Computers, automated machines, and electronics
- Medical equipment
- Office equipment
- Robotics, biotechnology, and communications

High Technology in Perspective One area that will continue to grow dramatically is high technology entrepreneurship. The U.S. Department of Labor defines a high technology venture as any company that:

- Spends twice as much for research and development as the average for all manufacturing companies; or—
- Counts among its employees at least five percent who have four-year college degrees in either the engineering sciences, such as chemical and electrical engineering, or in the basic sciences, such as chemistry and physics.

In the public mind, high technology generally conjures up images of such emerging industries as robotics, biotechnology, and telecommunications. It is such industries, marked by rapid and sometimes dizzying change, that have dominated the news and captured the public's attention. Yet, of the 600,000 new ventures being founded yearly, no more than

EXHIBIT 4.1 *The Hierarchy of Technology*

High technology industries require a base of medium, low, and no technology industries.

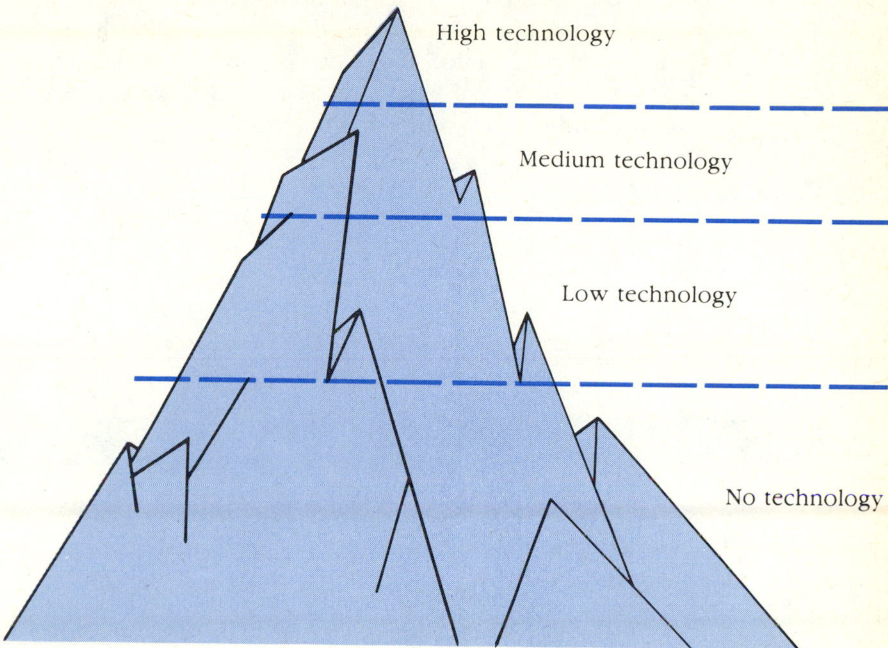

1.5 percent—about 10,000 a year—are high technology companies. The remaining 590,000 new ventures include:

- Medium technology companies, such as makers of surgical instruments or small robotized foundries for special-purpose castings
- Low technology companies, such as financial-service firms or toy makers
- No technology companies, such as new ethnic restaurants or garbage pick-up and disposal services.[3]

In short, high technology may be the mountaintop in our economy as the creator of tomorrow's jobs. To succeed, however, it must rest on a massive mountain, like the one shown in Exhibit 4.1, supported by the growing workforce in the medium, low, and no technology companies. These lower levels of technology are as vital to our economy as high technology, and they abound with entrepreneurial opportunities.

General Outlook

From now until the year 2000, more entrepreneurial opportunities than ever before can be expected. Competition surely will be keener, but it will be so healthy as to stimulate the birth of new ventures.

This optimism must be tempered, however, by the knowledge that some industries are rapidly passing out of the hands of small business into those of big business—as seems to be happening with personal computers.

Trends toward bigness are bound to affect many areas of manufacturing, some areas of retailing and wholesaling, and a few areas of services. However, new entrepreneurial opportunities will more than offset such trends. In fact, even the older industries, usually thought of as backward, offer entrepreneurial opportunities. Two such industries are textiles and insurance. Both are changing so rapidly that they are now part of the high technology revolution. For example:

- In textiles, cloth is being cut by laser beams and looms are driven by computers programmed to duplicate the irregularities of hand weaving.
- In insurance, firms now offer a wide variety of policies that would have been impossible before the arrival of computers.[4]

BUYING OUT AN EXISTING BUSINESS

After choosing a product or service and making sure that the choice fits their skills and desires, entrepreneurs must decide whether to buy an existing business or to start a business from scratch.

Lawyers and bankers often advise entrepreneurs to buy out a business rather than start from scratch. The reason is that existing businesses are much less risky. The odds are better because a successful, existing business has already:

- Proven its ability to draw customers at a profit
- Established healthy relationships with bankers, suppliers, and the community

The track record of an existing business surpasses the guesswork required to evaluate the prospects of a fledgling business. Past records, however, do not eliminate risk. "Any fool can buy a business," said Royal Little, the former president of Textron. "The question is whether the business you buy will be successful."[5]

Mr. Little points up the sticky problem of evaluating a business before buying it. To help resolve this problem, entrepreneurs should follow a procedure like the one in Exhibit 4.2. Note that our discussion has already covered the first step in the procedure: the choice of product or service. We will now discuss the remaining steps.

Understanding a Seller's Motives

Sellers commonly hide their true motives for selling. They often give good rather than true reasons for selling. Some owners, seeing that technology may soon outdate their product or service, will say they want to retire to California or they want to teach small business management at a local

EXHIBIT 4.2 *Deciding Whether to Buy an Existing Business*

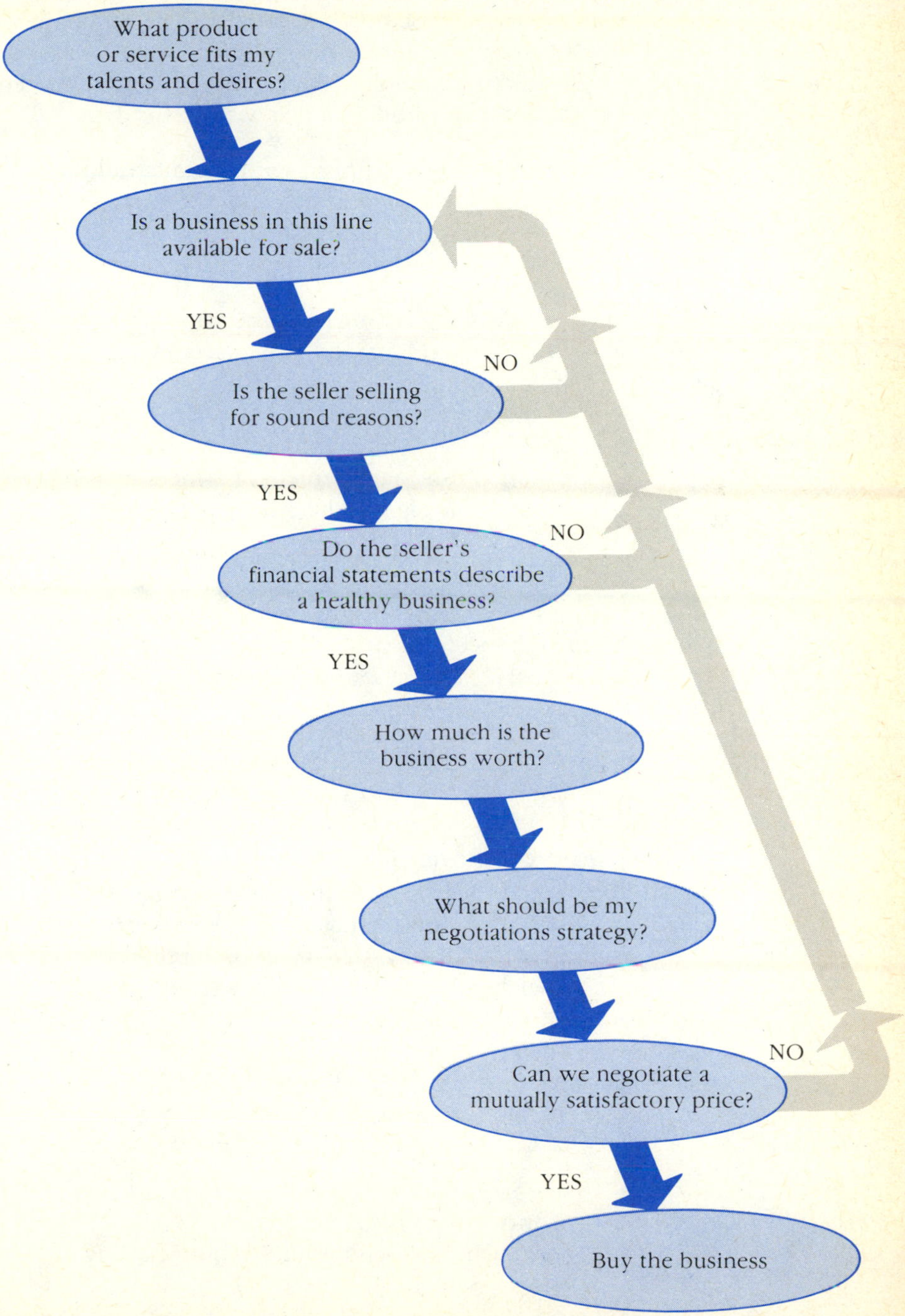

What product or service fits my talents and desires?

Is a business in this line available for sale?

YES

Is the seller selling for sound reasons?

NO

YES

Do the seller's financial statements describe a healthy business?

NO

YES

How much is the business worth?

What should be my negotiations strategy?

Can we negotiate a mutually satisfactory price?

NO

YES

Buy the business

college. In most cases, though, fear underlies their desire to sell:

- Fear about the financial future of their business and family
- Fear that because they are company-rich though cash-poor, wealth built up over a lifetime would be lost
- Fear that technology, once simple, is now too complex to cope with
- Fear that the product or service is outdated[6]

Owners rarely express their fears; instead they hide them and stress the good reasons for selling. So buyers must search out the real reasons. Otherwise, they may lack any basis for deciding whether they can solve the problems of the business to be acquired. Among the valid business reasons why owners want to sell are:

> **Personal and career reasons:** Owners may wish to convert their holdings in a family-held business to cash.
> **Management succession:** Owners may doubt the ability of younger men and women in the business to carry on profitably in the future.
> **One-person management:** Owners may realize that their business is getting too big for them and, because of their own managerial shortcomings, they cannot continue to strengthen the business themselves.[7]

Evaluating Financial Aspects of a Business

Let us now turn to the equally important problem of evaluating the financial aspects of a business. Financial evaluation raises the following questions:

- How healthy is the seller's business?
- How profitable has it been?
- How much is it worth?

Role of Financial Statements To help answer such questions, buyers should begin with the seller's financial statements. Many buyers blindly accept any financial statements bearing an accountant's signature. Remember, however, that an accountant works chiefly as an advisor. They may make suggestions but they cannot stop sellers from using any accounting methods that best serve their own purposes.

The idea that businesspersons may more or less select the profit level of their business may seem a bit odd. But owners have this right. Few owners habitually juggle their books, but there are many ways by which profits can be overstated or understated legally. For example:

- Inventories may be accounted for in a half-dozen ways, each affecting profits differently.
- Assets such as machines and buildings may be written up or down in value.
- Depreciation may be speeded up or slowed down.

One buyer, speaking from bitter experience, said:

> We have studied companies for months before making an acquisition. We have made audits, sent in our controller, paid attention to every financial detail—or so we thought. In each case we found out something after we took over that we did not know before the deal was closed. Some of the differences between what we thought we were buying and what we did buy were major. We have learned. But this we believe sincerely. Financial statements *don't* really answer any questions, they just allow you to ask them.[8]

These problems are especially severe in small family-owned businesses. Here, accounting practices tend to vary widely. Owners may take every possible deduction to cut taxes, or they may use the fastest depreciation allowances permitted by the U.S. Internal Revenue Service, or they may expense rather than capitalize their costs.

Auditing The buyer's first step in evaluating the financial aspects of a business should be to find out what adjustments need to be made to the seller's financial statements. To do that, the buyer should get the seller's income statements and balance sheets for, say, the past five years. These statements show, at least on paper, the seller's financial health, as well as profitability. Armed with these statements, the buyer should now examine, and question, such information as:

- Bills owed by customers—to make sure they are collectible
- Inventories—to make sure of their existence and their quality
- Equipment—to make sure every piece of equipment works and is not held together by baling wire
- Bank loans, bills owed to suppliers, and other debts—to make sure payment can be made
- Leases, licenses, franchises, and contracts—to make sure they can be transferred
- Public records—to make sure the seller is the titleholder of record, has no tax liens against the property, has no outstanding product warranties, has no payments due under purchase contracts, and so on

A Team Effort To carry out this audit, the buyer normally needs the help of two professionals: an accountant and a lawyer. Their services are indispensable. Although the fees of such professionals are high, their knowledge may spare the buyer the pain of buying the wrong business. Their judgment is by no means flawless, but they can reduce the odds of making the wrong choice.

As shown in Exhibit 4.3, investigation of the seller's business should be a team effort. It is the buyer's responsibility to make sure that his efforts mesh with those of the accountant and the lawyer. The buyer often forgets the accounting and legal aspects of the buy-out; the lawyer tends to be

EXHIBIT 4.3 *Suggested Procedure for Investigating a Potential Acquisition*

Investigation of a potential acquisition should be a team effort, involving the buyer, a lawyer, and an accountant.

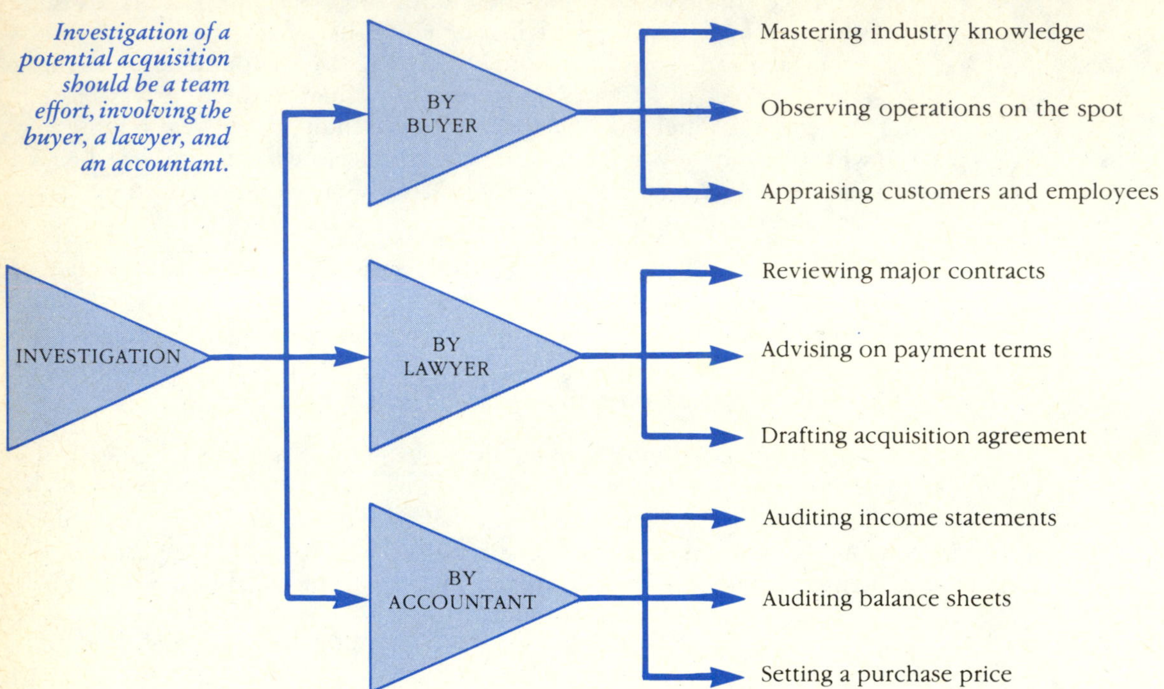

absorbed in the legal aspects; and the accountant tends to focus on the audit. The buyer must never lose sight of the need to exchange and correlate all information collected on the seller's business.

Example: The accountant, as she reviews the financial information, may uncover possible federal income tax deficiencies for past years by the seller. The buyer and the lawyer should be given immediate knowledge of that fact. The lawyer then proceeds to protect the buyer—by contract—against the assumption of any legal obligations to pay back taxes. In turn, the buyer then evaluates the effect of the tax deficiencies on the seller's business. Is the business still viable and desirable?[9]

Setting a Price

Having thoroughly examined and questioned the financial records of the seller's business, the buyer must tackle the problem of pricing it. Again, evaluating a seller's business is much more art than science. The questions

- What is the seller's business worth?
- What can the business be bought for?

. . . cannot be answered with precision since many factors, often incapable of measurement, influence the price placed on a business by both buyer and

EXHIBIT 4.4 *Traditional Approaches for Pricing a Potential Acquisition*

The entrepreneur should price a potential acquisition from both the buyer's and the seller's viewpoints.

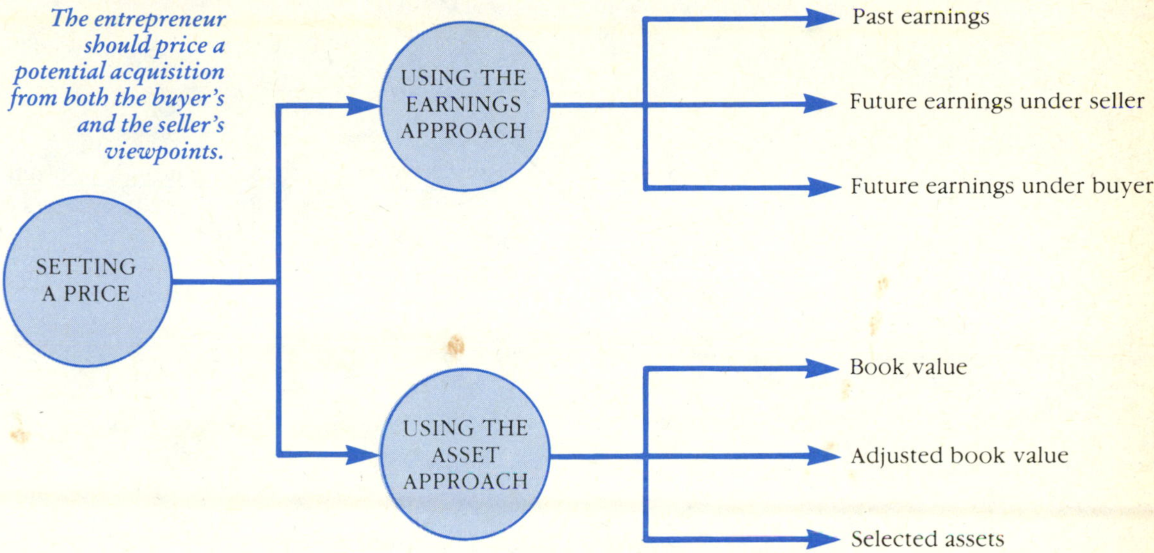

seller. Thus, there is no best way to price a business. Buyers must look at businesses from both their own viewpoints and those of the sellers.

In pricing a seller's business, the buyer may use either of two traditional approaches: earnings[10] or assets. As shown in Exhibit 4.4, the earnings approach requires the buyer to focus only on earnings, either past or future. The asset approach, on the other hand, requires the buyer to focus on assets only, without regard to their earning power.

Earnings Approach

Capitalizing Profits This earnings method assumes that the entrepreneur or buyer is really buying a series of yearly profits when purchasing a business. It requires entrepreneurs to ask themselves: What am I willing to pay for the chance to earn a certain profit each year for, say, the next 10 years? To clarify the meaning of this question, let us look at this example:

Example: Suppose a buyer estimates that a bookstore will earn $10,000 a year after taxes for the next 10 years. What should the buyer pay the seller for this opportunity? To answer this question, the buyer should first estimate what return to expect on the investment. Let us assume that she expects a 15 percent return on investment, after income taxes. Why does she expect 15 percent? Perhaps because the buyer has other opportunities that will return at least that much. Or perhaps because the buyer simply wants that much return even though the next best opportunity may be a bank that returns 10 percent on savings. Or perhaps because 15 percent is the seller's current return on owners' equity.

We can now arrive at the purchase price by capitalizing the buyer's estimate of average yearly future profits:

$$
\begin{aligned}
\$10{,}000 &= 15\% \times \text{Purchase price} \\
\text{Purchase price} &= \$10{,}000 \div 15\% \\
&= \underline{\underline{\$67{,}000}} \text{ (rounded)}
\end{aligned}
$$

Capitalizing profits is a popular earnings method, although it often gives misleading results. For one thing, buyers may estimate after-tax profits in any one of several ways, among them:

- Last year's profits only
- The average yearly profits for the past five years
- The average yearly projected profits for the next five years, estimated on the basis of past profits
- The average yearly projected profits for the next five years, based on the buyer's belief that his or her superior managerial skills will boost profits

The first two ways have little to recommend them in logic because they fail to take into account any changes that will occur as a result of the transfer of ownership. Although the third way does suggest that the future will be different, only the fourth way recognizes the key role of the entrepreneur. Generally, entrepreneurs buy a business only if convinced their managerial skills will improve the performance of the business.

Personal Return With the capitalizing profits method, we looked at return on investment only from the business's viewpoint. Another earnings method would be to look at return only from the perspective of the buyer's personal gain. This method stresses the cash flow—or its equivalent—that the buyer would earn by buying a business. The *personal return* method assumes that the entrepreneur stands separate and apart from the business and its profits.

The capitalizing profits method relates after-tax profit to total investment. But it is a flawed estimate of return in that entrepreneurs often invest little of their own money. It is often useful to think of return more as a personal return on the entrepreneur's investment only. Following are some ways that entrepreneurs may earn a return on their investment:

- Perquisites, meaning such fringe benefits as an automobile, season tickets to football games, and the like
- Dividends and interest
- Salary

Example: A seller offers her toy-making business to an entrepreneur for $100,000. After some study, the entrepreneur estimates that his yearly personal return would be:

$24,000	salary
4,000	perquisites
2,000	interest on long-term loan
$30,000	total personal return (cash flow or its equivalent)

Now let us assume that $100,000 is the seller's firm price for the business and that the entrepreneur plans to finance the purchase price in this way:

- $20,000 cash sale of stock to himself, keeping 60 percent of the business for himself
- $60,000 cash sale of stock to others, giving them just 40 percent of the business
- $20,000 long-term loan from the entrepreneur to the business

Now what would the entrepreneur's personal return on his investment be? His return may be estimated as follows:

$$\text{Personal return} = \$30,000$$
$$\text{Personal investment} = \$40,000 \text{ (including loan)}$$

$$\text{Personal return on investment} = 75\% \text{ a year } \left(\frac{\$30,000}{\$40,000} \times 100\right)$$

So far, we have focused on two earnings methods. *Capitalizing profits* stresses after-tax profits expressed as a percentage of total business investment. *Personal return* stresses the entrepreneur's personal return expressed as a percentage of personal investment. Let us now describe the asset approach to pricing a business.

Asset Approach

This approach ignores earnings and instead focuses on the seller's assets, such as buildings, equipment, inventories, and accounts receivable. It gives little thought to a business's future earnings. Although often not recommended, the asset approach is popular because it is easier to use than the earnings approach, which requires the buyer to perform the complex task of forecasting earnings in order to price a business. The three traditional asset methods—book value, adjusted book value, and selected assets—will now be described.

Book Value *Book value* is the difference between what a business possesses (assets) and what it owes (liabilities). It is the fastest way to price a business, since the buyer needs only to look at the seller's latest balance sheet. This method is full of pitfalls, however, because it tells the buyer nothing about the true worth of a business. For example, a business may have a book value of $100,000 and still be worthless—because its assets are incapable of creating customers at a profit. Even so, book value does offer a good beginning for estimating a purchase price. Remember, however, that the entrepreneur is more interested in buying profitability than assets such as land, buildings, and machines.

Adjusted Book Value This asset method adjusts for any significant differences between book and market value of assets such as land, buildings, and equipment. Market value measures what the assets could now be sold for, regardless of book value. For example, a buyer may adjust the price of land recorded in the seller's books at its original cost, since its value has appreciated greatly.

Selected Assets With this asset method, the buyer selects only the seller's assets that he believes he needs. Unwanted equipment and inventories remain with the seller. In this way, the buyer evaluates only parts of the seller's business, not the whole thing.

Negotiating a Price

When entrepreneurs have estimated what to pay for a business, they have only just begun. They must now get down to the nitty-gritty of negotiating a price with the seller. Unless buyer and seller are of like mind, there may well be a wide gap between what the buyer believes the business is worth and what the seller believes it is worth.

Negotiations are rather like a game of chess. It is an intellectual exercise. The buyer must think out a strategy, anticipate the seller's reactions, and develop effective countermoves in advance. In thinking out their strategy, buyers should begin by looking at numbers such as these:

- Ceiling price—What is the business worth today with new and superior management?
- Best price—What is the business worth today with current management?
- Book value—What is the business worth today on paper?

Sellers, of course, will come up with their own numbers. For reasons of sentiment if not greed, sellers are likely to inflate the asking price. For the buyer, no matter how well prepared, it is hard to see through such a practice.

Although negotiations may depend on numbers, the buyer must also look closely at the seller's human side. The seller may, for example, seek ironclad assurances that:

- The business name (which often is also the seller's name) will continue after the sale
- Certain employees, especially relatives, will enjoy continued job security
- Product or service quality will continue to be improved

It is the buyer's job to tell which human factors matter most to the sellers. They may balk unless convinced the buyer will meet these nonfinancial demands. Remember, sellers usually are also entrepreneurs. They mold businesses in their own image, and probably spend much of their lives doing so. Often, they see businesses as personal monuments. As shown earlier in Exhibit 4.2, the wise buyer balances the human aspects of the business with the financial aspects in price negotiation.

Human aspects do have their price. For example, if the buyer agrees to keep nonworking relatives on the payroll, two salaries must be paid for one position. The buyer should negotiate a lower purchase price to offset the added cost.

Even after all this give-and-take, buyer and seller may still be miles apart on price. Their ability to agree hinges on their skills at the negotiating table and on how they see each other's strengths and weaknesses.

STARTING FROM SCRATCH

This is the road traveled by the pure entrepreneur, for whom founding and molding a business poses a much greater challenge than taking over an existing business. Pure entrepreneurs seek a business that is truly their own creation. They crave the creative satisfaction that comes from planting an idea and then making it grow into a strong and sturdy business.

To be sure, the risks are also greater. As mentioned earlier, newborn ventures are less likely to succeed than takeovers. With a takeover, records may give the buyer some idea of how healthy and profitable the business is. But, with a new venture, the best an entrepreneur can do is guess at what the profits will be. It may be intelligent guesswork, but it is guesswork nonetheless. There are some practical reasons why entrepreneurs may prefer to begin from scratch, among them:

- To avoid the ill effects of a prior owner's errors
- To choose their own banker, equipment, inventories, location, suppliers, and workers—without being bound by commitments and policies made by the previous owner
- To create their own loyal customers

How does the entrepreneur evaluate the prospects of a new venture? According to the SBA, the first condition for business success is:

> . . . the existence of a real, and not merely an apparent, business opportunity. This means that his venture must sell a product or a service needed and desired by consumers. It also means that his venture must draw enough customers who will buy at a price high enough and at a volume high enough to make a profit.[11]

To do that, entrepreneurs must study their market to estimate such things as total market, share of market, and sales revenues. This is difficult, even for businesses the size of General Motors and Du Pont, let alone the small entrepreneur. Still, it must be done.

With a takeover, entrepreneurs have past records that may tell them what the sales revenues were during the past five years, and, more important, whether revenues are going up, standing still, or going down. From such information, entrepreneurs may then predict their yearly revenues by assuming that revenues will either:

- Follow past trends; or—
- Outdo past trends

But when starting from scratch, entrepreneurs must put in a lot of effort to get information about their markets. Before estimating their revenues, for example, entrepreneurs should answer such questions as these:

- Who are my customers?
- Where are they?
- How many of them are there?
- What percentage will buy from me?
- At what price will they buy my product or service?
- In what quantities will they buy?

Getting answers to these and related questions is called marketing research. As discussed in Chapter Six, marketing research probably is the most important step in the preparation of a business plan. More will be said about this tool in that chapter as well as in Chapter Eight on location and Chapter Fourteen on marketing.

INVENTION AND THE ENTREPRENEUR

Many entrepreneurs are also inventors. Often, such entrepreneurs must decide whether to apply for patents, giving them the exclusive rights to their inventions. Patenting a product, however, takes time and money. Before launching a new venture, entrepreneurs should weigh both the benefits and the costs of patenting an invention by answering the questions listed here and shown in Exhibit 4.5:

- Is my product patentable?
- Do I need or desire patent protection?
- How do I go about getting such protection?
- If I do get a patent, can I keep competitors from circumventing it?

For legal protection, entrepreneurs should hire a patent attorney. Although entrepreneurs can get a patent themselves, the process is so

EXHIBIT 4.5 *Some Practical Questions*

Entrepreneurs should weigh both the benefits and the costs of patenting an invention.

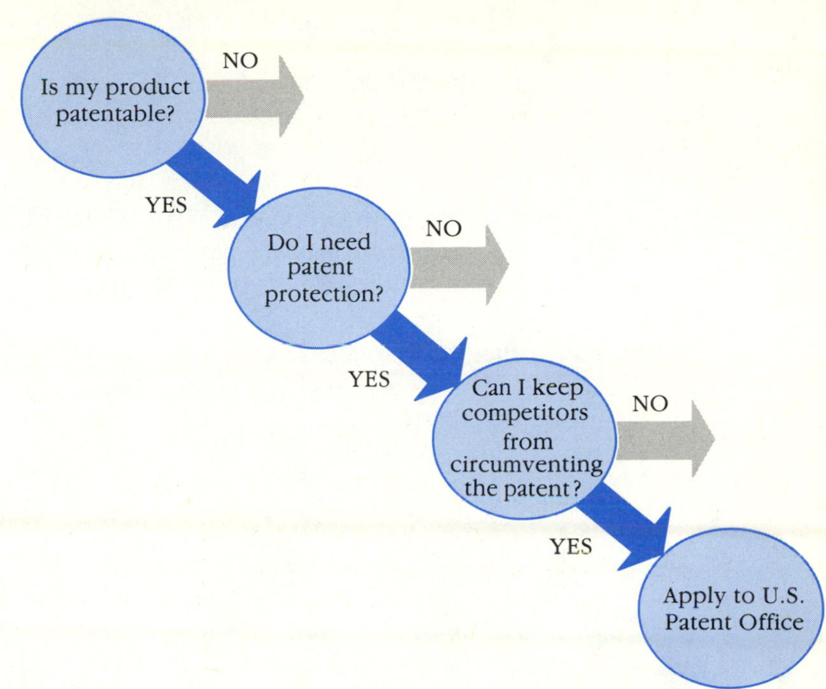

complex that they would be wise to leave it to an attorney. Summarized below are some guidelines that every inventor-entrepreneur should follow, as prepared by the Patent, Trademark and Copyright Research Institute of George Washington University.

The Patenting Process

Assume that an entrepreneur has invented a new hydraulic bumper device that absorbs automobile collisions up to 30 miles an hour. The law says that, to be patentable, the device must be new, useful, and not obvious. If the new device appears to meet these standards, the entrepreneur should take the following steps:

Make a Record The entrepreneur should fix the time the device was invented, since they may need to prove this later. The entrepreneur should also write out a description of the hydraulic bumper device and illustrate it with sketches. Finally, the description and illustrations should be signed and dated in the presence of knowledgeable witnesses.

Be Sure the Invention Is Practical The entrepreneur should learn enough about the automobile market to be sure there is some chance that the device will be used. Can it be made more cheaply than others on the market? Does it involve engineering problems for the manufacturer? Entrepreneurs should avoid patenting products that will not create customers at a profit.

Get a Patent Attorney The entrepreneur should seek out an attorney from the *Directory of Registered Patent Attorneys and Agents*[12] which lists patent attorneys by state and city.

Have a Search Made The entrepreneur should ask the patent attorney to get copies of existing patents on hydraulic bumper devices that might stop the entrepreneur from getting a patent.

Prepare an Application If the search suggests that this hydraulic bumper device is the first of its kind, the entrepreneur should ask the patent attorney to prepare the formal application for a patent. The application must include:

- A petition, which is a request for a patent, addressed to the Commissioner of Patents of the U.S. Department of Commerce.
- The specification, which describes the entrepreneur's hydraulic bumper device, explains how it works, and describes how it is constructed.
- The claims of patentability, which define the entrepreneur's invention. Such claims are intended to tell how the hydraulic bumper device differs from all other such devices not only on the market but disclosed in patents, magazines, and other publications.
- An oath, which the entrepreneur signs before a notary public. The oath requires the entrepreneur to swear that he believes himself to be the first and sole inventor of this hydraulic bumper device.

The patenting process is complex, costly, and time-consuming. In fact, it takes an average of two years from the time the entrepreneur files the application with the Commissioner of Patents until the patent is received. Should the entrepreneur's patent application conflict with another patent, it may take much longer than two years.

Once the patent is granted, the entrepreneur has the "right to exclude others from making, using, or selling the invention throughout the United States."[13] Such patent rights last 17 years. After the patent expires, anyone may make, use, or sell the hydraulic bumper device without the entrepreneur's permission. The 17-year term may not be extended except by special act of Congress.

Meanwhile, competitors may try to "design around" the invention. To succeed, and thus avoid infringing on the entrepreneur's patent, a competitor need only eliminate a single element of the entrepreneur's patent claims.

Problems in the Patent System

When the Congress created the patent system in 1790, the system was designed "to encourage citizens to invent and to disseminate information on their inventions throughout the new nation for its overall good."[14]

The patent system has often come under dispute. Some federal judges, for example, believe that patents work against the public good. The Antitrust Division of the U.S. Department of Justice seems to share that view. They seem to be saying that monopolies are bad; and since patents are monopolies, patents are bad.

We believe otherwise. Without the incentive to invent, talented entrepreneurs are less likely to channel their creative energies into new products. In the words of Intellectual Property Owners, Inc.:

> The purpose of the patent system is to encourage inventions and their marketing by granting patent holders exclusive rights to their patentable products or processes. These rights are being subverted by a growing clash between the nation's patent and antitrust laws.
>
> There is a growing acceptance that patent use should be tested by antitrust law criteria—a viewpoint which severely and unnecessarily limits the manner in which a patent holder can control his property.
>
> Certain members of the judiciary and the U.S. Department of Justice . . . have succumbed to this interpretation, thus seriously eroding the patent incentive.[15]

How serious is this erosion of the patent incentive? One study for the U.S. Department of Commerce suggests that the incentive to invent and innovate has slowed down dramatically. The following statistic shows that many men and women have, indeed, lost their desire to invent:

- The number of patents granted yearly to Americans has dropped 22 percent since 1976.[16]

Whatever the reasons for this 22 percent drop, there is a strong need to keep the inventive spirit alive. Much of the nation's economic magic depends on men and women who are free to invent and who are given the prospect of generous rewards, protected by a strong patent system.

SUMMARY

Would-be entrepreneurs may go into business for themselves in one of two ways: either by buying an existing business or by starting a business from scratch. But before choosing one or the other, entrepreneurs must first select a product or service. They must ask themselves the critical question: What business should I be in?

An intelligent answer requires entrepreneurs to look closely at their strengths and desires, as well as at industry trends. Aspiring entrepreneurs must be aware of these trends to better prepare themselves for the opportunities in high, medium, low, and no technology fields.

Buying an existing business poses fewer risks than launching a new venture, since an existing business has records of past successes and failures. For example, a buyer may look at the seller's balance sheets, count inventories, inspect equipment, and observe customer buying habits.

To price an existing business, prospective buyers may use either the earnings or asset approach. The earnings approach is superior because it focuses on future earnings; the asset approach looks only at assets, ignoring their earning power.

Once entrepreneurs have set a price, they must then engage in the delicate art of negotiation, taking into account both the financial and human needs of the seller.

To pure entrepreneurs, starting from scratch has the greater appeal. They prefer to pick their own product or service, their own location, workers, suppliers, and so on.

Many entrepreneurs double as inventors of products. Before launching their ventures, such entrepreneurs should decide carefully whether to patent their inventions. The patenting process is complex, costly, and time-consuming and usually requires the help of a patent attorney.

DISCUSSION AND REVIEW QUESTIONS

1. Why might you, as a would-be entrepreneur, prefer to buy an existing business rather than start from scratch?
2. Why does the seller of a business often give good rather than real reasons for wanting to sell?
3. Would you consult with an attorney and an accountant before buying a business? Why or why not?
4. Define these terms: *audit, capitalizing profits, perquisites, personal return on investment, high technology, book value, marketing research.*
5. Which is a better approach to pricing a business: earnings or assets? Why?
6. Why should every entrepreneur answer the question, "What business should I be in?"
7. Briefly describe the various ways of arriving at a purchase price for an existing business.
8. How important are nonfinancial considerations in negotiating the purchase price of an existing business? Explain.
9. Why do bankers and lawyers generally advise entrepreneurs to buy an existing business rather than to start from scratch?
10. Briefly describe how you would go about evaluating the prospects of a new venture.
11. Before buying a business, why is it vital to audit the seller's books? Which items in the seller's business deserve a close look? Why?
12. In your community, which products and services seem to be growing

faster than others? How do they compare with those noted in the beginning of the chapter?

13. Describe the patenting process.
14. Is it necessarily a good idea to patent an invention? Why?
15. What is the first condition for business success?

NOTES

1. Adapted from U.S. Small Business Administration, "Business Plan for Retailers," *Management Aid No. 2.020* (Washington, D.C.: U.S. Government Printing Office, 1982) p. 2.
2. Adapted from Robert Townsend, *Up the Organization* (New York: Alfred A. Knopf, 1970), p. 129.
3. Peter F. Drucker, "Europe's High-Tech Delusion," *The Wall Street Journal*, September 14, 1984, p. 24.
4. John S. DeMott, "The High-Tech Challenge," *Time*, December 24, 1984, p. 38.
5. James H. Perry, *Acquisition-Merger Study* (Wilmington, Del.: Atlas Chemical Industries, December 13, 1963), p. 25.
6. Adapted from Myles L. Mace and George G. Montgomery, *Management Problems of Corporate Acquisitions* (Boston: Division of Research, Harvard Business School, 1962), pp. 37–56.
7. Adapted from Mace and Montgomery, pp. 37–56.
8. Mace and Montgomery, p. 184.
9. Charles A. Scharf, *Acquisitions, Mergers, Sales, and Takeovers* (Englewood Cliffs, N.J.: Prentice-Hall, 1981), p. 75.
10. Earnings are synonymous with after-tax profits.
11. Adapted from U.S. Small Business Administration, *Success and Failure Factors in Small Business* (Washington, D.C.: U.S. Government Printing Office, 1979), pp. 2–3.
12. This directory is available from the Superintendent of Documents of the U.S. Government Printing Office in Washington, D.C. 20402.
13. U.S. Department of Commerce, *Patents* (Washington, D.C.: U.S. Government Printing Office, 1972), p. 24.
14. Theodore L. Bowes, "Help for the Patent System," *NAM Reports*, March 18, 1974, p. 6.
15. Ibid.
16. U.S. Department of Commerce, *Statistical Abstract of the United States* (Washington, D.C.: U.S. Government Printing Office, 1984), p. 552.

CASE 4A *Karabinus & Associates, Inc.*

In 1984, Karabinus & Associates, a photographic studio, earned sales revenues of $58,730 and before-tax profits of $8,960. Its founder and president, Joseph Karabinus, is dissatisfied with this performance. "I've been in business for myself now for six years, and I should be doing a lot better. What should bother me—and it doesn't—is that I could be earning much more with less work and risk by working for somebody else—in fact, at least twice as much. I'm really good at what I do."

Background

Although now 40 years old, Joseph Karabinus first became an entrepreneur when he was just 13. Entirely on his own initiative, he had established a photographic studio in the basement of his parents' home. "I had a habit I couldn't afford," says Mr. Karabinus, "so I began selling my services to students. I charged them a nickel for each wallet-sized photograph. My dad, though, didn't like the idea of my becoming a photographer; he wanted me to be an electrical engineer.

"So I worked around him by appealing to my mom. She was so soft-hearted that she let me buy a $200 press camera. Believe me, 27 years ago, that was a lot of money to spend on a 13-year-old upstart like me. Somehow, my dad never found out how much it cost. Good thing, too, because he was a strict disciplinarian, a patriarch from the old school, and he would have hit the ceiling."

Earning top grades in high school, Mr. Karabinus decided to further his education. He chose a university that had an undergraduate program in photography. "My mind was made up to become a professional photographer, in every sense of the word *professional*," says Mr. Karabinus.

"Funny thing, though, I had to take courses in such mind-bending subjects as chemistry and physics—to get my college degree. And, to this day, I don't know why such courses were required." He was graduated in the top third of his class, earning a bachelor of fine arts degree with a major in photography.

Momentarily Sidetracked

Soon after graduation, Mr. Karabinus married his high school sweetheart and began raising a family. Although he yearned to establish his own professional studio, Mr. Karabinus was convinced "it would be sheer madness to starve charmingly while I was struggling to make it as a professional photographer."

So he went to work for an aerospace company, Thompson-Ramo-Wooldridge, Inc. (TRW). "I never thought I'd ever work for a corporation that big," says Mr. Karabinus. Indeed, TRW is one of the top 100 corporations in the country, with sales of more than $5 billion a year. TRW had hired him to work in the industrial photography department.

Mr. Karabinus stayed there for 12 years. "It seemed like an eternity," says Mr. Karabinus. "From day one, it was a frustrating experience. The work was mundane, to say the least. True, I was doing what I like best, taking photographs, but the psychic satisfaction just wasn't there.

"Nobody seemed to care about quality. It was annoying to work for bosses whose standards were so much lower than mine. There I was, a college graduate, reduced to taking photographs of stuff like broken hardware, test rigs, and new electronic instrumentation for TRW's advertising brochures. The pay was good, but I just couldn't stand it."

Finally Breaking Away

Against the advice of his family, Mr. Karabinus quit his job with TRW. "When I told my boss that I was quitting," says Mr. Karabinus, "he told me how sorry he was to see me leave. I reminded him that I had done the same kind of photographic work for 12 years. Just think, I had one year's experience 12 times over. That's not growth. Then, my boss reminded me that TRW had once laid off everybody else in my department but me. That's how much they thought of me and my work.

"To go it alone, I knew my family had to support my decision completely, without compromise. They did, eventually, although at first they tried hard to discourage me from striking off on my own. But, after 12 years of leading a compromised life, there was no alternative for me. They saw that it was now or never for me."

In Business for Himself

When he opened his doors for business in 1978, Mr. Karabinus was so cash-poor that he had to borrow all his start-up costs—$6,000 at 9 percent interest. "It was a five-year signature loan," says Mr. Karabinus. "I didn't even have to mortgage my house. I'm sure the bank was impressed by my ability to earn money—if I really had to—to pay off the loan. They trusted me." His beginning balance sheet appears in Exhibit 4A.1.

Two problems, besides financing, were (1) where best to locate and (2) how best to organize legally. After talking with a friend of his who was also an entrepreneur, Mr. Karabinus decided to locate in the basement of his home, until "my sales volume justified my moving away to larger quarters." He also decided to form a sole proprietorship, because "it's a lot simpler than forming a corporation."

EXHIBIT 4A.1

Karabinus & Associates, Inc.: Beginning Balance Sheet (April 15, 1978)

Assets		Equities	
Cash	$1,400	Accounts payable	$ 500
Photographic supplies	1,100	Long-term loan	6,000
Camera equipment	3,600	Owner's equity	0
Office equipment	300		
Other	100		
Total assets	$6,500	Total equities	$6,500

With $3,600 worth of camera equipment in his basement, Mr. Karabinus was fully equipped to satisfy customers in need of photographic services. "Of course, I never told the prospective clients I approached that my studio was next to the washer in my basement," says Mr. Karabinus. "If I had, they would have labeled me an amateur and not a professional. Believe me, image is important."

Defining His Business

Indeed, for the first few months he spent almost all his time "beating the bushes," explaining his photographic services. He soon found that his experience at TRW worked against him. "There, all I did was industrial photography," says Mr. Karabinus. "When prospective clients asked me what experience I had, they questioned my ability to do photographic art rather than straight industrial stuff." He had defined his business in this way:

> To create photographic art for clients who do creative work, such clients as advertising agencies, public relations firms, and architectural design firms

Mr. Karabinus was bent on "creating photographic art rather than simply taking photographs. I wanted to do unusually creative things for clients, translating their words into visual images that evoke feelings. In a real sense, I saw myself as an interpreter, an artistic interpreter at that."

After six months of being on his own, Mr. Karabinus landed only one client. The client was an architect friend of his who needed photographs taken of several ice rinks that he had designed. His income from that one job was $753.10. "It's a good thing my wife was working," says Mr. Karabinus, "or I would have been on the bread line or out driving a taxicab at night. A big part of my problem was that I knew nothing about business. I never took a single course in small-business management when I was in college."

Turnaround

A professor friend of his recommended that he enroll in a small-business program at a local college. He did so, taking all six courses devoted to small-business management. "That helped a lot," says Mr. Karabinus. "The case studies really opened my eyes, gave me direction."

One of the things he learned was the value of having a "thought-through marketing strategy. I had my priorities all wrong. I never sat down and figured out how best to attract clients." When he finally did, he came up with this strategy:

- To spend one-third of my time seeking new clients, mostly by visiting them sight unseen and armed with a sample portfolio of my best photographic art
- To update my list of existing and prospective clients each quarter, focusing on architectural firms and advertising agencies, public relations firms and downtown retail stores

- To offer clients a broader range of services by forming an informal partnership with someone knowledgeable in advertising
- To project an image of professionalism by incorporating my business and by moving into more spacious quarters downtown
- To guarantee my performance, offering to do a job over if I fail to satisfy a client's needs

This strategy seemed to work. Two years later, in 1980, revenues increased from almost zero to $19,000; and, in 1981, revenues tripled to $57,000. "I thought I was on my way," says Mr. Karabinus. "But, since 1981, my sales have been on a roller coaster ride."

- Revenues and profits since 1980 are graphed in Exhibit 4A.2.
- Condensed income statements appear in Exhibit 4A.3.
- A detailed income statement for 1984 appears in Exhibit 4A.4.

Problem Analysis

Mr. Karabinus is unsure why his "sales curve hasn't kept moving onward and upward. I'm doing all the things my professors told me to do. One thing I remember came from my small-business professor. He kept

EXHIBIT 4 A.2 *Karabinus & Associates, Inc.: Sales Revenues and Profits by Year*

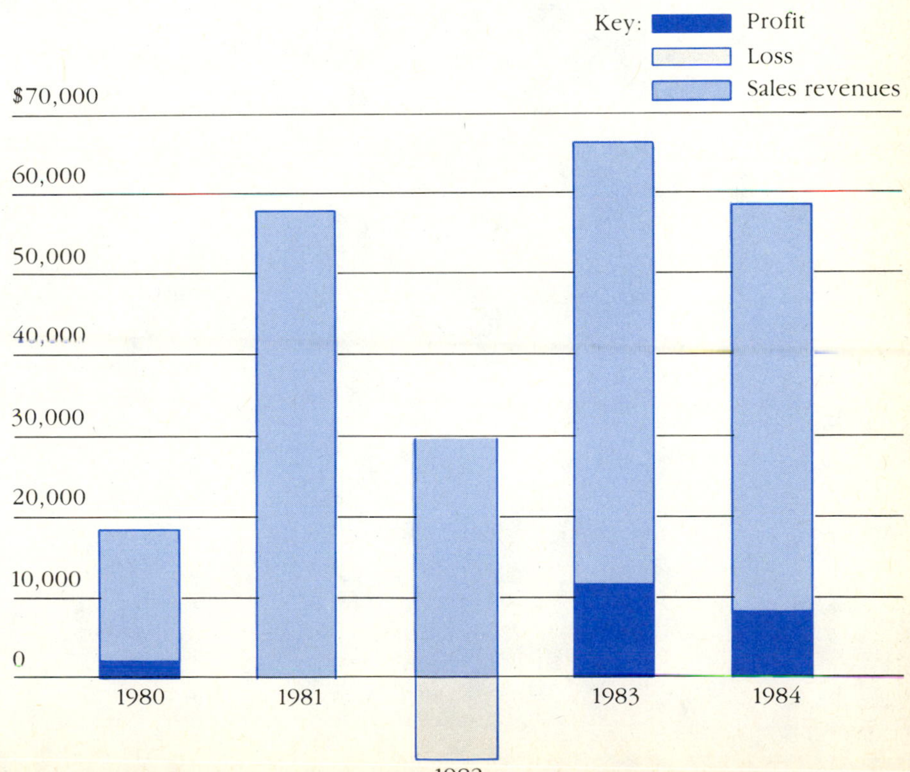

EXHIBIT 4A.3

Karabinus & Associates, Inc.: Condensed Income Statements (1980 through 1984)

	1980	1981	1982	1983	1984
Sales revenues	$19,170	$57,970	$30,240	$66,720	$58,730
Cost of sales	11,430	27,470	12,620	27,470	21,750
Gross profit	$ 7,740	$30,500	$17,620	$39,250	$36,980
Operating expenses	6,290	30,270	27,770	26,990	28,020
Operating profit	$ 1,450	$ 230	($10,150)	$12,260	$ 8,960

stressing the importance of finding a niche in the marketplace, offering clients what your competitors aren't. That's why I guarantee performance on a no-questions-asked basis.

"In an industry like mine, competition is fierce. Everybody thinks he's an expert. Anybody with a $199.50 camera can set up shop and call himself a professional photographer. It's these amateurs who muddy the waters. Most people don't realize the years it takes to be a true professional." See Exhibit 4A.5 for the quality of Mr. Karabinus's work.

EXHIBIT 4A.4

Karabinus & Associates, Inc.: Detailed Income Statement (1984)

Sales revenues		
Laboratory services	$20,160	
Advertising	19,210	
Commercial	10,090	
Industrial	3,670	
Materials	1,530	
Architectural	1,220	
Miscellaneous	2,850	$58,730
Cost of sales		21,750
Gross profit		$36,980
Operating expenses		
Salaries and benefits	$ 7,830	
Supplies	4,790	
Rent	4,410	
Maintenance	2,500	
Travel and entertainment	2,220	
Interest	2,130	
Professional services	1,510	
Utilities	1,190	
Insurance	750	
Dues and seminars	560	
Licenses	100	
Advertising	30	
Depreciation	0	28,020
Operating profit		$ 8,960

EXHIBIT 4A.5 *Karabinus & Associates, Inc.: Examples of Karabinus Quality*

One avenue that Mr. Karabinus has recently pursued is an "informal partnership" with an advertising agency run by Jeffrey Wershing. The agency is now located in a corner of the same suite of rooms that Mr. Karabinus occupies.

"Working with Jeff is an ideal arrangement," says Mr. Karabinus. "I've expanded my market. I can now say to a prospective client that if you want an advertising brochure done, I can do the *whole* thing for you—the photographic art, the layout, the written word, everything. Believe me, the

EXHIBIT 4A.6

Karabinus & Associates, Inc.: Description of a Typical Photographic Assignment

A typical job begins with the client seeking out a photographer, either with a layout in hand specifying the photographs to be taken, or with an idea in mind. In essence, the client seeks a photographer who can contribute creatively to the client's concept. One such job is described below, in Mr. Karabinus's own words:

> The job called for a fashion spread to be shot on location. My client's art director already had a location chosen but wanted to confer with me before going ahead.
>
> The location was a small, private museum-to-be, not yet ready to be opened to the public. It had fire engines, old cars, farm buildings, a general store, and a workshop stocked with antiques.
>
> The next step was to select the live models, and set the date. Because of conflicts in scheduling, my client and I chose to shoot the job on a weekend.
>
> The amount of preparation is awesome on a shoot like this. Everything that might be needed must be packed and brought with you. Everything from coffee pots and lunch meat to clothes pins and masking tape. For this particular job, we even brought an auxiliary power unit to run the strobes so we could shoot at night in the woods.
>
> We started at 8 A.M. and got back about 11 P.M. About six hours were spent actually taking pictures. I then processed the film and made contact proof sheets.
>
> Next came the long process of selecting the best photographs. I then sized the photographs to fit the proportions of the layout that my client and I had worked out jointly. The advertising copy was then set in the selected type face.
>
> Last, upon the client's approval, I sent the layout to the engraver for separations. Color keys were pulled for client approval, and the final run was made. All told, 100,000 copies of the layout were printed.

advertising industry can be lucrative; its potential is limitless. For example:

> A competing photographer working for an advertising agency recently shot two rolls of 35-mm film. He charged the agency $9,000 for just a half hour of shooting. After deducting the cost of the model and the set, his income was $4,000. Set-up time, however, took a week.

"Other photographers I know in town get as much, if not more. But it takes time to get yourself established. Now that I'm in partnership with an advertising agency, I'm sure that I'll land more clients, especially those willing and able to pay $9,000 for just a half hour of shooting." See Exhibit 4A.6 for a description of a typical job for a client.

The Need for Improvement

Another recent change is the hiring of Chrissie Spuhler. Her duties include running the receptionist desk, keeping the books, and keeping after slow-paying customers. "I hired her because she's a self-starter," says Mr. Karabinus. "She doesn't have to be told what to do. I'm away so much I needed somebody just to watch the shop."

Although his books are now up-to-date, Mr. Karabinus rarely looks at them. "I'm just too busy getting jobs and then getting them done," says Mr. Karabinus. He vows to "change my attitude and do some hard planning. I should have a budget but I keep putting it off. If my old professor ever saw how I run my little business, he would have cardiac arrest."

Questions

1. Comment on Mr. Karabinus's entrepreneurial and managerial qualities.
2. What questions would you raise after analyzing Mr. Karabinus's financial statements?
3. Comment on the quality of Mr. Karabinus's marketing research and his marketing plan.
4. Would you invest in Mr. Karabinus's venture? Why?
5. If Mr. Karabinus came to you for advice on how best to boost sales, what would you suggest he do now? Why?

CASE 4B *Gus DuPrea Shoe Store*

In January 1985, Gus DuPrea, a shoe salesman for a big department store in Chicago, was discussing his future with the sales manager of a shoe manufacturer. Mr. DuPrea confided:

> I'm unhappy. I'm making a living, but I spend $400 a week to live and this doesn't leave anything to put away. My wife and I aren't getting any younger. I've been in this store 17 years now. I'd like to have my own store, be my own boss. Do you know of any shoe stores for sale?

The sales manager told Mr. DuPrea of a store in Elko, Indiana, whose owner wanted to sell out:

> The man is retiring to Florida as soon as he can find a customer. He has already sold his other properties in town. His name is Tom Watkins, and he's been in Elko all his life. He has the only shoe store there; about all the town can handle. Tom serves the townspeople and the majority of farmers for about 10 miles around.
>
> The nearest towns are Fisher and Attumwa, both about 17 miles away, and about the same size as Elko. It's a growing area—about a 10 percent rise in population every decade. There are a few small new industries in Elko.
>
> Tom told me about the store a couple of months ago. You could buy it for $40,000 in cash. Tom says there is no point in saying how much he earns from the store. He'll give anyone all the facts and let him see for himself that, with the lower cost of living in Elko, there's enough in it to make a good living and still put a little aside.
>
> A week later, Mr. DuPrea drove to Elko and visited the store. It was not fancy, but he told his wife later, "It's a nice store. It sure looked good compared to the other stores in Elko."

Elko is the Umbagawa county seat. There are 1,776 townspeople, who make up one third of the population of the trading area. Most business activities there center on servicing the food industry. The town has shippers, farm machinery dealers, food stores, two canneries, and a flour mill.

All stores in Elko are open from 8:00 A.M. to 5:00 P.M. on Monday, Tuesday, and Thursday. Stores are open till 1 P.M. on Wednesdays, except during the fishing season, when they are closed on Wednesdays. Fridays and Saturdays are late nights, with stores staying open until 9:00 P.M.

The store is located on a busy corner of town. It has two display windows. The larger one, on Main Street, faces most of the everyday shopping traffic. Mr. Watkins usually had about 25 pairs of shoes in this window.

Soon after they met, Mr. Watkins gave Mr. DuPrea these figures:

Inventory at original retail	$50,400
Average fixed expenses	$ 9,600 per year
Store fixtures	$ 8,000
Average gross margin	35%
Expenses variable with sales	12%
Average turnover per year	2.5

Mr. Watkins took Mr. DuPrea around town and found a house for sale in a suitable neighborhood. On the level that Mr. DuPrea planned to live, he thought he could get by on $1,200 a month in Elko.

Mr. Watkins said he was so well-known that he did not have to advertise. A credit check later disclosed that Mr. Watkins did indeed have an unusually good reputation.

When he returned to Chicago, Mr. DuPrea figured that his total assets could be converted into $48,000 in cash if necessary.

Questions

1. What should Mr. DuPrea do?
2. What range of income and personal savings is Mr. DuPrea likely to receive from the store?
3. Imagine that you are an experienced retailer and an old friend of Mr. DuPrea. Assuming that you know as much as Mr. DuPrea about the offer, what questions would you raise?

Source: Case prepared by Alan S. Marcus of Taylor Business Institute in New York City.

CASE 4C *Viking, Inc.*

Ollie Ness has organized a new venture to make antipollution equipment for the chemical, oil, and steel industries. To finance his venture, Mr. Ness has raised $300,000 by selling stock to friends, $200,000 by borrowing from a bank (long-term), and has invested $50,000 himself. In exchange for that sum of money, he has received 60 percent ownership of the new venture. The other shareholders have received 40 percent ownership.

Mr. Ness expects to draw a salary of $30,000 the first year and to pay dividends of $5,000 that year. He values the use of a company car and other perquisites at $4,000 a year. He expects a net profit of $50,000 the first year.

Questions

1. What is Mr. Ness's personal return on investment the first year?
2. What is the business return on investment?
3. Which of these two estimates of return is the better measure of Mr. Ness's performance? Explain.

5 FRANCHISING

QUESTIONS FOR MASTERY

How important is franchising to the economy?

What are the different kinds of franchising systems?

What are the advantages and pitfalls of franchising?

How valuable is a lawyer's help in evaluating a franchise opportunity?

How does one best evaluate a franchise opportunity?

Help me with knowledge . . .

Robert Browning

In Chapter Four we discussed two major ways of going into business for oneself: either to start from scratch or to buy out an existing venture. A third major way is to buy a franchise.

Today, few business topics spark more controversy than franchising. Opinions about its place in the economy differ sharply: some see franchising as the last frontier of the would-be entrepreneur, and others see it as a fraud. Neither extreme is correct—the truth lies somewhere in between. This chapter will try to put franchising in proper perspective.

HISTORY OF FRANCHISING

Contrary to popular opinion, franchising did not begin with the boom of fast-food franchises like McDonald's in the 1950s. Rather, its beginnings date back to the early 1800s. However, it was in 1898, when General Motors began franchising dealerships, that modern franchising got its first real push. Still alive and well today, their franchise system boasts 10,500 dealers scattered throughout the country. Here is how franchising works:

Example: The franchised new-car dealer signs a contract with one of the car manufacturers to serve as its representative in an area. The franchised dealer then sells only that line of new cars—Buicks, for example. In some areas, the franchisee may have a double franchise and sell, say, Gremlins made by American Motors as well as Buicks made by General Motors.

Similar franchise systems were created by Rexall in 1902 and Howard Johnson in 1926—as were many oil, grocery, motel, and fast-food franchises during those years. So great has been its growth that most industries have already been touched by franchising. According to the National Federation of Independent Business, about 10 percent of the nation's 16 million businesses now run under some kind of franchise agreement; and, as shown in Exhibit 5.1, franchising accounts for 32 percent of all retail sales.

Definition of Franchising

There is no one best definition of franchising. Borrowed from the French, *franchising* originally meant being free from slavery. Today, it has several other meanings, depending on the industry. Some people even call franchising an industry, as if it were a product or service. But a typical franchise is simply an agreement between seller and buyer—an agreement that permits the buyer (franchis*ee*) to sell the product or service of the seller (franchis*or*). The International Franchise Association defines it this way:

> A franchise is a continuing relationship between the franchisor and the franchisee in which the sum total of the franchisor's knowledge, image, success, manufacturing, and marketing techniques are supplied to the franchisee for a consideration.

EXHIBIT 5.1 *Importance of Franchising in Retailing*

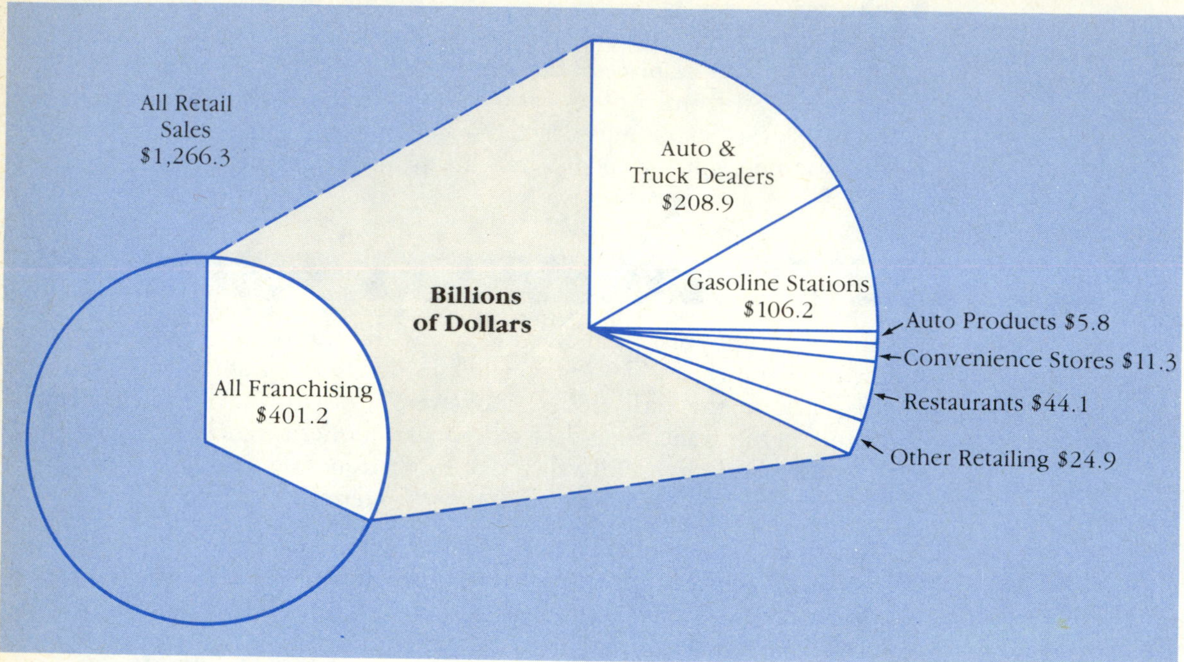

In 1984, franchising accounted for 32 percent of all retail sales.

Source: U.S. Department of Commerce, *Franchising in the Economy: 1982–84* (Washington, D.C.: U.S. Government Printing Office, 1984), p. 12.

The franchisee thus gets a ready-made business. And therein lies the appeal of franchising. The franchisee does not have to build up a business step by step as must the entrepreneur who starts from scratch. Rather, the franchisee's business is established overnight. And, it probably will be a carbon copy of all the others in the franchise chain.

For a fee, the typical franchisee gets expert help that would otherwise be too costly for his business individually, such as:

- Marketing strategy, with special emphasis on advertising
- Initial employee and management training
- Store design and equipment purchasing
- Standardized policies and procedures
- Centralized purchasing with savings
- Continued management counseling
- Location selection and advice
- Negotiation of leases
- Financing

In essence, franchising thrives because it merges the incentive of owning a business with the management skills of big business. And, personal ownership is one of the best incentives yet created to spur hard work. Shown in Exhibit 5.2 are some advantages and disadvantages of franchising.

Franchising may benefit not only the franchisee but also the franchisor. For example, it may enable the franchisor to grow rapidly by using other people's (the franchisee's) money. That is largely how giant franchisors like McDonald's and Baskin-Robbins have mushroomed into billion-dollar businesses in so short a time.

The Strength of Franchising

The International Franchising Association predicts that franchising will soon dominate retailing. Franchising also is strong in services, and to a lesser degree, in manufacturing. The following statistic from the U.S. Department of Commerce underscores its role in the economy: in 1984, there were 462,000 franchises with sales revenues estimated at $457 billion.[1]

Until recently, the word *franchising* was synonymous with fast-food outlets like McDonald's and Wendy's. But today franchising has invaded most industries. Name a product or service, and chances are there is someone who franchises it, even in old-line companies like Sears or

EXHIBIT 5.2 *Selected Advantages and Disadvantages of Franchising*

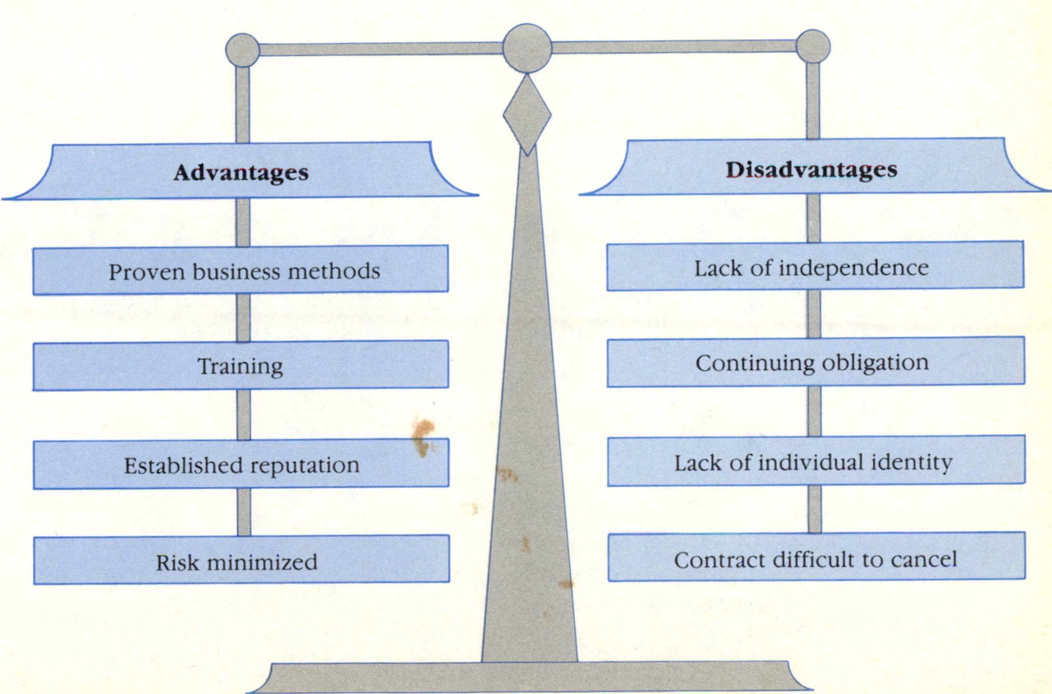

Montgomery Ward. These two companies have franchised 1,800 small-town catalogue order outlets since the mid-1960s.

Franchises are offered in industries as different as art galleries and shoe-repair shops, dating bars and personal computers. It has even spread to services for weight watching and bed-wetting control. The diversity of franchised businesses is shown in this partial list:

- Hertz car rental agencies and General Motors dealerships
- Exxon service stations, Goodyear Tire distributorships, and AAMCO transmission shops
- Holiday Inn motels and Ralston Purina restaurants
- Coca-Cola bottling plants

This discussion suggests that, for the would-be entrepreneur, franchising is often the best route to success. The failure rate is low, since the larger organization protects the franchisee by providing guidance and setting standards. According to the U.S. Department of Commerce, only 4 percent of all franchises in the country were discontinued in 1984. Yet, as this entrepreneur's experience shows, a franchise is not a sure way to success:

> Bernard Leyva seemed to have an ideal background for striking out on his own with a franchised business. Before buying two Der Wienerschnitzel restaurants in Los Angeles in 1978, he had been a Der Wienerschnitzel district manager for five years.
>
> But Mr. Leyva's restaurants did poorly—location was one factor—and his costs escalated. In 1984, Mr. Leyva quit the restaurant business. He vows never to buy a franchise again. He says that troubles with his restaurants worsened in 1980 after his building leases, which were tied to the consumer price index, ballooned to $4,100 a month from $2,900.[2]

KINDS OF FRANCHISING SYSTEMS

Franchise systems take many forms. These systems are by no means limited to chains like McDonald's and Holiday Inn. For example, franchise systems may connect:

- Manufacturer and manufacturer
  Manufacturer and wholesaler
  Manufacturer and retailer
- Wholesaler and wholesaler
  Wholesaler and retailer
- Retailer and retailer
- Services and services

Let us look first at franchise systems between manufacturer and manufacturer. Suppose a chemical manufacturer patents a new way to make ammonia. Because this process cuts the cost of ammonia manufacture by, say, 20 percent, other chemical manufacturers may want to use it. So the chemical manufacturer who invented the process may license the others to use it. The license would give them the right to use the new process in return for a fee, called a *royalty*. In this case, the licensor is really the franchisor; the licensee is the franchisee.

Another franchise system might be between manufacturer and retailer. The best example of such a system is that between automobile manufacturers and retail automobile dealerships. Still another example is service stations, which lease space and sell gasoline and oil bought under contract from oil refiners like Exxon. Franchise systems between manufacturer and wholesaler, wholesaler and wholesaler, and wholesaler and retailer operate in similar ways.

However, retail and service franchise systems like McDonald's or Holiday Inn differ markedly from manufacturer or wholesaler systems because the franchisee is really an extension of the franchisor. In such chains, each franchise resembles a company outlet, the main difference being that the franchisor invested the franchisee's money to create the outlet instead of its own money.

In contrast, with a manufacturer-to-manufacturer franchising system, franchisees are relatively autonomous. Such franchisees are all but free to do as they please. Policies and procedures may be of their own making; even the shop and equipment may be of their own design. That would not be the case with such service-to-service franchise systems as McDonald's.

MYTHS OF FRANCHISING

The Myth of Instant Wealth

The fast growth of franchising has spawned a number of myths. Perhaps the most popular one is the promise of instant riches. Get-rich-quick schemes abound. Many prey on lower-income men and women looking for a way to become rich without having to work for someone else. Take this example:

> I could tell this was no ordinary Corvette. The body was covered with blue and yellow velvet. The interior was finished floor-to-roof with blue and yellow fur. Two men in flashy double-knit suits leaned against the car's long hood and snagged lunchtime passersby as they crossed an intersection in downtown Washington.
>
> "How would you like to be able to afford a car like this?" one of the men asked me. "Sure," I answered. "Great. Give me a call," he said, and produced a card that read: "Above-average earnings for the average person. Put yourself in the successful 2%. Opportunities unlimited."[3]

These two men were franchisees of Koscot Interplanetary, Inc., selling mink-oil-based cosmetics. For $5,000, Koscot would sell an investor a distributorship. The investor could then earn money in one of two ways:

- Hire a sales force to sell Koscot cosmetics door-to-door
- Sign up other investors at $5,000 each, keeping a $2,650 commission

The two men had chosen the second way as the easier path to riches. The trouble with such a scheme is that somebody inevitably gets hurt. It benefits the few franchisees who get in early, but hurts those who get in later.

The foregoing example is extreme. But it does dramatize how unethical operators may take in the innocent with overblown promises of instant riches. It also shows why franchising sometimes causes controversy. As the Bank of America points out:

> To its protagonists, franchising is the last frontier of independent businesspeople and the most dynamic distribution method for bringing goods and services to market ever devised.
>
> To its severest critics, it is a fraudulent gimmick to separate the small investor from his funds—and worse.[4]

The Myth of Independence

Another myth is that franchisees are independent businesspersons. In many cases, this simply is not so. Franchisees generally are not free to run their business as they see fit, as mentioned earlier. They often are hamstrung by the franchisor's policies, standards, and procedures. Nor do franchisors encourage their franchisees to improve the way they do business. The Bank of America says:

> The best franchisee, as far as many franchisors are concerned, is someone who is smart enough to understand and operate the system, but not smart enough to try to improve on it.
>
> One franchisor describes the ideal franchisee as the sergeant type—midway between the general who gives the orders, and the private who merely follows them. People who want their own business to escape taking orders from others frequently see franchising as the answer. They are subsequently frustrated by their lack of autonomy. For example:
>
> - The paper work involved in preparing sales records and reports may be as extensive as that required of a paid manager of a chain outlet.
> - Inventory mix may be spelled out without regard to customer preferences.
> - The franchisee may dislike the franchisor's advertising campaign but have no say in the matter.[5]

EVALUATING A FRANCHISE OPPORTUNITY

In a real sense, franchisees do not start from scratch. When they buy a franchise, entrepreneurs generally receive a ready-made business. And, all they need do is follow the franchisor's instructions on how best to do business. Instructions cover a host of details including:

- What product or service to sell
- How to sell it
- How to control costs
- What reports to prepare
- How long to stay open each day

Nevertheless, before buying a franchise, entrepreneurs should first make sure that their decision to become a franchisee is sound. Outlined in Exhibit 5.3 is a step-by-step procedure that entrepreneurs should follow. Searching out likely franchises is the first step. The next step, self-analysis, calls for entrepreneurs to match their skills and desires to the franchise opportunity, by answering these questions:

- Do I really believe in the franchisor's product or service?
- Do I really want to be that kind of person, do that kind of work, run that kind of franchise?

Checklist These questions are just a beginning. To do a thorough job of analyzing a franchise opportunity, entrepreneurs should next go through a checklist

EXHIBIT 5.3 *Procedure for Evaluating Franchise Opportunities*

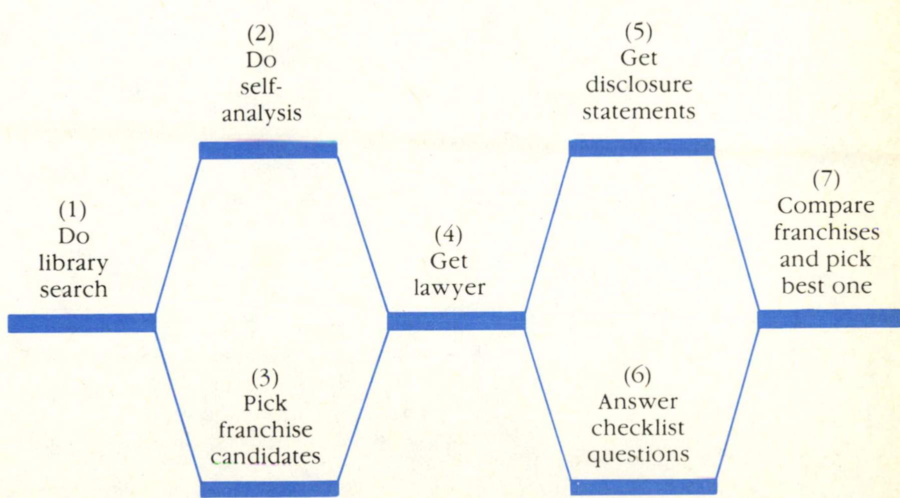

like the one in Exhibit 5.4. This checklist of 25 questions may spare the entrepreneur the pain of making the wrong decision, or of being victimized by unkept promises—as was this franchisee:

> Until 1970, Caleb Moberly was the colonel in charge of all military payrolls for the Air Force. Still, he wondered "whether I could run a business of my own." It cost him $30,000 and more work than he had ever done before to find out.
>
> Mr. Moberly and his wife opened a United Rent-All equipment center in a fast-growing suburb of Denver in October 1971. For the first year and a half, they worked seven days a week from 8 A.M. until 6 P.M. They now take occasional days off, but, he says, "you never get the work done."
>
> Yet it's not the hard work that bothers him—even if their income this year of nearly $30,000 strikes him as inadequate—because he expects to sell out for a profit of over $100,000 within a year and go back to playing

EXHIBIT 5.4

Checklist for Evaluating a Franchise

On the Franchise Opportunity Itself

1. Did your lawyer approve the franchise contract after he studied it paragraph by paragraph?
2. Does the franchise call upon you to take any steps which are, according to your lawyer, unwise or illegal in your state, county, or city?
3. Does the franchise give you an exclusive territory for the length of the franchise or can the franchisor sell a second or third franchise in your territory?
4. Is the franchisor connected in any way with any other franchise companies handling similar merchandise or services?
5. If the answer to the last question is yes, what is your protection against this second franchisor organization?
6. Under what circumstances and at what cost can you pull out of the franchise contract?
7. If you sell your franchise, will you be paid for your goodwill, or will the goodwill you have built into the business be lost by you?

On the Franchisor

1. For how many years has the franchisor been in business?
2. Does the franchisor have a reputation for honesty and fair dealing among the local entrepreneurs holding its franchise?
3. Has the franchisor shown you any certified figures indicating exact net profits of one or more going franchises, which you *yourself* checked with the franchisee?
4. Will the franchisor help you with:
   (a) A management training program?
   (b) An employee training program?
   (c) A public relations program?
   (d) Merchandising ideas?
   (e) Financing?
5. Will the franchisor help you find a good location for your franchise?
6. Is the franchisor adequately financed so that it can carry out its stated plan of financial help and expansion?

golf. He frowns at the memory of promises he says were broken by the franchisor.

"At first I didn't get the help I was told I'd get," he says. "The coordinator they sent to help me get started was completely inept." The company failed to deliver all the items for their inventory by the time the store opened, Mrs. Moberly complains.

They find United Rent-All better to work with now. "They have an excellent system for keeping track of what is in stock and how much is earned on each item, and their public image is good," they say.[6]

These entrepreneurs might have avoided the problem of unkept promises had they used a checklist like the one in Exhibit 5.4. Fortunately, their problems were not insurmountable and their franchise later prospered. Franchisees often make costly mistakes in judgment. The entrepreneur's best defense against such mistakes is the checklist.

EXHIBIT 5.4

Checklist for Evaluating a Franchise (cont.)

7. Is the franchisor a one-man company or a larger company with a trained and experienced management team—so that there would always be an experienced person as its head?
8. Exactly what can the franchisor do for you which you cannot do for yourself?
9. Has the franchisor investigated you carefully enough to assure itself that you can successfully operate one of their franchises at a profit both to them and to you?

On You—the Franchisee

1. How much equity capital will you need to buy the franchise and operate it until your sales revenues equal your expenses?
2. Where are you going to get the equity capital you need?
3. Are you prepared to give up some independence of action to get the advantages offered by the franchise?
4. Do *you* really believe you have the ability, training, and experience to work smoothly and profitably with the franchisor, your employees, and your customers?
5. Are you ready to spend much or all of the rest of your business life with this franchisor, offering its product or service to your public?

On Your Market

1. Have you made any study to find out whether the product or service which you propose to sell under franchise has a market in your territory at the prices you will have to charge?
2. Will the population in your territory increase, remain static, or decrease over the next five years?
3. Will the demand for the product or service you are considering be greater, about the same, or less in five years?
4. What competition exists in your territory for the product or service from nonfranchise firms and franchise firms?

Source: U.S. Department of Commerce, *Franchise Opportunities Handbook* (Washington, D.C.: U.S Government Printing Office, October 1984) p. xxxi.

Getting Disclosure Statements

To evaluate a franchise opportunity, entrepreneurs should ask the franchisor for its *disclosure statement*. A priceless tool, this statement should enable the entrepreneur to answer many of the questions posed in the checklist. It should also enable the entrepreneur to:

- Compare one franchise with another
- Understand what to expect from the franchisor
- Estimate the risks and costs involved

All franchisors are now required by federal law to provide disclosure statements to entrepreneurs in each state. The law requires that such statements give detailed information on 20 subjects, a sampling of which follows:

- The financial statements of the franchisor
- A description of the lawsuits in which the franchisor and its officers, directors, and management personnel have been involved
- Information about the initial franchise fee and other initial payments that are required to obtain the franchise
- A description of the involvement of any celebrities or public figures in the franchise
- A list of the names and addresses of other franchisees
- A complete statement of the basis for any profit claims made to the franchisee, including the percentage of existing franchises that have actually achieved the profits that are claimed

Need for a Lawyer

Entrepreneurs should rely on a lawyer to get through the fine print of the franchisor's disclosure statement. It would be a mistake for entrepreneurs to assume that the statement tells everything there is to know about the franchisor. Nor will it necessarily tell all about the consequences of signing a franchise contract.

So it is vital for entrepreneurs to get the help of a lawyer familiar with the legal workings of franchising. Such lawyers can also inform entrepreneurs fully about their legal rights before signing the franchise contract. Equally important, lawyers can advise entrepreneurs about their legal obligations to the franchisor. But perhaps the lawyer's most creative role is to suggest changes in the contract that would better serve and protect the entrepreneur's interest. According to the U.S. Department of Commerce:

> At the very least, you should be certain that every promise you consider important made by the franchisor and its representative is stated clearly in writing in the franchise contract. If such promises do not clearly appear in the contracts you sign, you may have no legal remedy if they are not kept; and you may be legally obligated to comply with your own continuing obligations under the franchise contract.[7]

The Franchise Contract

The contract is the backbone of any franchisor-franchisee relationship. Failure to understand its fine print may cause the entrepreneur trouble later on. It is especially crucial to ask the question: Under what conditions may the entrepreneur pull out of the franchise contract and what would it cost to pull out?

Entrepreneurs should make sure they understand what they stand to lose or gain if they should decide to pull out or if the franchisor should decide to cancel the franchise contract. Typically, franchisors reserve the right to cancel a franchise contract if the franchisee:

- Fails to reach revenue goals
- Tarnishes the image of other outlets by giving poor service to customers
- Fails to provide required weekly or monthly progress reports to the franchisor

Other, though less precise, reasons for canceling a contract include:

- The franchisee's failure to work hard and for long hours
- The franchisee's failure to work smoothly with the franchisor
- The franchisee's misuse of the franchisor's name and equipment

Typically, franchise rights run one to five years, with options to renew. An exception is McDonald's, which sells for $320,000 the right to operate a franchise at a specific site for 20 years. When the contract expires, the franchisee must put up another $320,000 or so to continue operating at the same site. Unlike McDonald's, some franchise rights run indefinitely—but generally the contract has a clause that gives either the franchisor or the franchisee the right to cancel on 30 to 60 days' notice.

Selling an Existing Program

A problem could arise, however, if the franchisee should decide to sell out before the contract runs out. Such a sale generally cannot be carried out without the franchisor's approval. This seems like a distinct drawback of franchising, as explained here:

> The right to sell or transfer the franchise determines whether or not a franchisee is truly an independent owner of a business, or merely an affiliate within a chain. Contract provisions should reflect your rights to build a profitable business and then sell it on the open market. The reputable company will do everything to protect its trademarks, patents, and uniquely developed services, but it should not—and must not—deprive you of the right to sell or transfer *your* business.[8]

Another sore point is the price at which a franchisee may be forced to sell the franchise, either to another entrepreneur or back to the franchisor. The franchisor often forces the franchisee to sell at a price lower than its value to a prospective buyer. For example, a franchise may be worth $50,000 more than its book value to a prospective buyer. If the franchise is sold who deserves the gain of $50,000, the franchisor or the franchisee?

Franchisors may claim it was their image that generated the $50,000 gain. Franchisees may counter that it was their hard work that created all that gain. To avoid such a problem, entrepreneurs should make sure they have the right to sell the franchise at the highest possible price and that they can pocket the entire selling price. McDonald's has an enlightened attitude in this regard:

Example: In 1984, a franchisee sold his McDonald's restaurant for $600,000. Its value on the books was about $200,000. The franchisee got to keep the entire capital gain of $400,000. McDonald's had an interesting though imprecise way of estimating the purchase price of the franchise. They took the most recent year's revenues and multiplied by half.

Franchisor's Training Program

Perhaps the most crucial question to consider in evaluating a franchisor relates to the franchisor's training program. Reputable franchisors like McDonald's and Baskin-Robbins provide intensive training programs, including on-the-job training at an existing outlet. Some franchisors even provide refresher training after the franchisee has been operating for some time. Exhibit 5.5 traces the sequence of steps that, ideally, franchisors should follow in training their franchisees.

The main goal of these training programs is to supply entrepreneurs with management skills they need to run a franchise profitably. Without such training, the typical, inexperienced franchisee is likely to founder and fail. Entrepreneurs should make sure their franchise contract tells precisely how and where training will take place. McDonald's, for example, provides a three-step training program:

Instruction at a training school: McDonald's has a $2 million school called Hamburger University near Chicago. After a three-week cram course in how to run a franchise profitably, franchisees receive a degree in *Hamburgerology*. Courses cover everything from how to mop the floor to how to post a ledger.

Instruction at an existing franchisee's site: McDonald's has every new franchisee spend at least one week with an established franchisee. While there, the new franchisee works at every job, from sweeping the parking lot to waiting on customers.

Instruction at own site: McDonald's provides franchisees with an experienced instructor to tide them over the rough edges of start-up. The instructor works side by side with the franchisee for at least one week—or until such time as the instructor is sure the franchisee can go it alone.

Franchisees often credit the franchisor's training for their success. Take this example:

Ginny Wehunt of Rock Hill, South Carolina has expanded a $2,500 investment in a Uniforce Temporary Personnel franchise into a business

EXHIBIT 5.5 *Franchisee Training*

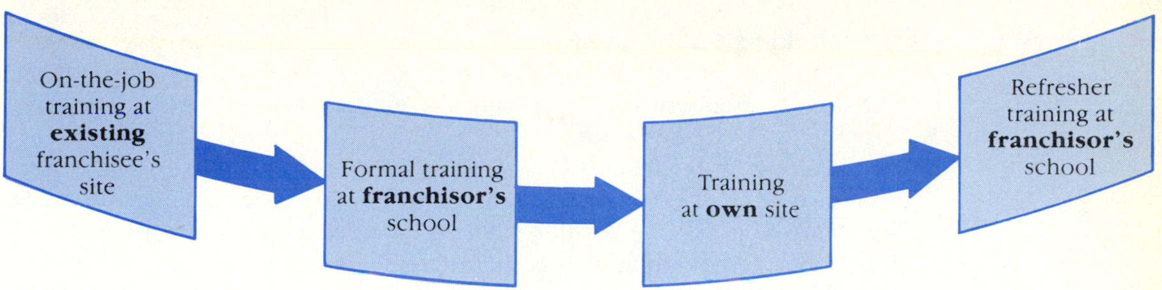

that will earn her over $150,000 this year. The four offices she now owns place as many as seven hundred temporary workers a week in clerical, industrial, technical, or medical assignments.

What sold Ms. Wehunt on Uniforce were rosy prospects for the temporary personnel business and impressive Uniforce benefits: a *good training program* for herself and any employees, an elaborate testing system for temporary workers, and a centralized system for billing clients and handling the payroll—all in return for a royalty of 10 percent.

Ms. Wehunt now has 25 employees and six-figure profits. She spends most of her time selling employers in the area on the advantages of hiring temporary workers for long-term projects; that's where her major profits lie. She visits her four offices regularly and takes special pleasure in training and promoting her employees.[9]

Costs to the Franchisee

Entrepreneurs should be sure to take pains to estimate what a franchise would cost, since franchisors often fail to tell entrepreneurs the full story. A franchisor may say, for example, that "all you need is $10,000 to buy a wall-cleaning franchise." But, the $10,000 may cover just the right to use the franchisor's trade name and way of doing business. Hidden may be such costs as equipment, lease deposits, and even the signs needed to open the franchise—not to mention the money to finance inventory or to finance customers who buy on credit.

Entrepreneurs may avoid such problems by preparing a business plan, as discussed in Chapter Six. The cash budget, a key part of the business plan, will identify all cash costs, including the franchise fee, working capital, building and equipment costs, and royalties:

The franchise fee: This gives the franchisee the right to do business at a specific address or in a specific territory. Depending on the franchise, this fee may range from zero to millions of dollars. As mentioned earlier, McDonald's charges a fee of $320,000 for a 20-year contract.

Working capital: This covers the money needed to buy inventory, pay salespersons, make lease payments, and so on until customers buy and pay up.

Building and equipment costs: The entrepreneur may pay for these in full or in part. Some franchisors lease both building and equipment to the franchisee, thus sparing the entrepreneur the need to make a large initial cash outlay. McDonald's charges a leasing fee of 8.5 percent of revenues.

Royalties: These generally range from 0 to 15 percent of revenues. In return for the royalty payment, the franchisee may get such services as advertising, financial statements, and management advice. McDonald's, for example, charges a royalty of 3 percent on revenues. Thus a franchisee with yearly revenues of $800,000 pays McDonald's $24,000 a year in royalties.

As with any other venture, financing a franchise may pose problems if an entrepreneur has little savings. Typically, the reputable franchisor wants the entrepreneur to put up at least half the money needed to get started, as equity capital. Often, the entrepreneur will try to raise the money needed by selling stock to relatives and friends or borrowing from them to buy stock in his or her own name. The remaining half may be borrowed from a commercial bank, often with the franchisor as cosigner of the note.

FRANCHISE OPPORTUNITIES FOR MINORITY PERSONS

Until the mid-1960s, there were few minority franchisees. For example, of the 30,000 retail automobile dealerships existing in 1967, only one was owned by a black. This picture has changed dramatically. By 1980, there were more than 200 minority dealerships, most of them black-owned and prospering.

Similar gains have been made in other industries, thanks to a more enlightened attitude toward minorities. In fact, more than 900 franchisors have declared that their franchises are open to all would-be entrepreneurs, regardless of race.[10] McDonald's had 220 black franchisees in 1980. There were none in 1968.

It is vital, however, not to mistake progress for arrival. Minorities have a long way to go before they own their proportionate share of franchises. To help speed things along, the federal government has been pushing franchising as a good way to improve the economic lot of minorities. Franchising offers special promise to minority men and women with little money and little experience, enabling them to have their own businesses with the backing of big-business practices.

SUMMARY

Franchising plays a vital role in our economy and may soon become the dominant form of retailing. It also is prominent in services and, to a lesser degree, in manufacturing. Currently, franchising is growing at a rate of 10 percent a year and shows few signs of slowing down significantly.

Franchising thrives because it combines the incentive of personal ownership with the management and technical skills of big business. To entrepreneurs, franchising offers a short-cut to growth. They receive ready-made businesses without having to build up slowly. To the franchisor, franchising offers quick expansion. The franchisor grows by letting entrepreneurs finance its growth through the sale of franchises.

The rapid growth of franchising has attracted dishonest as well as honest franchisors. Abusers of the system generally promise instant riches with little work, the freedom of being one's own boss, and little initial investment.

Before buying a franchise, entrepreneurs should do a thorough job of evaluating a franchise opportunity, following a procedure like this one:

- Do a self-analysis, matching personal skills and desires to the franchise opportunity
- Get legal advice to review contracts and protect one's interests
- Answer the checklist questions with the help of disclosure statements from prospective franchisors
- Select the most promising franchisor
- Negotiate a franchise contract

DISCUSSION AND REVIEW QUESTIONS

1. Explain the myths of franchising.
2. How would you evaluate a franchise opportunity?
3. Identify some franchising abuses and suggest ways to correct them.
4. Define these terms: *franchise, franchisor, franchisee, disclosure statement, franchise fee, working capital, royalties.*
5. What accounts for the rapid growth of franchising?
6. Is the franchisee an entrepreneur? Explain fully.
7. Why might you prefer to be a franchisee rather than start from scratch or buy out an existing business?
8. Why should would-be franchisees work closely with a lawyer before committing themselves to a franchise?
9. Is franchising limited to fast-food services like McDonald's? Explain.
10. Why is the franchise contract the backbone of any franchisor-franchisee relationship?
11. Why does franchising offer a good way for minorities to go into business for themselves?

12. What should a franchisor's management training program consist of to be of most benefit to the franchisee?
13. Assume you are the franchisee of a pet shop. Somebody offers to buy the shop at twice its book value. In your opinion, should you or the franchisor reap the benefit of the difference between what the franchise is worth to the buyer and its worth on the books? Explain.
14. What are some of the reasons for a franchisor to cancel a franchise contract?
15. Name the different kinds of franchising systems and describe how they differ.

NOTES

1. U.S. Department of Commerce, *Franchising in the Economy: 1982–84* (Washington, D.C.: U.S. Government Printing Office, 1984), p. 1.
2. Teri Agins, "Owning Franchises Has Pluses, but Wealth Isn't Guaranteed," *The Wall Street Journal,* October 11, 1984, p. 29.
3. Rudy Maxa, "Products Prove Second to Selling Right to Sell," Cleveland *Plain Dealer,* January 1, 1973, p. 6-B.
4. Reprinted with permission from Bank of America, NT&SA, "Franchising," *Small Business Reporter,* Vol. 9, No. 9, Copyright 1975, 1978. This report is currently out of print.
5. Ibid., p. 3.
6. Michael Creedman, "A Franchise Is a Hard Way to Get Rich," *Money,* September 1973, p. 36. Reprinted from the September 1973 issue of *Money Magazine* by special permission; © 1973, Time, Inc.
7. U.S. Department of Commerce, *Franchise Opportunities Handbook* (Washington, D.C.: U.S. Government Printing Office, October 1984), p. xxx.
8. Robert M. Dias & Stanley I. Gurnick, *Franchising: The Investor's Complete Handbook* (New York: Hastings House, 1969), p. 89.
9. Judith Jobin, "Start Your Own Business?" *Woman's Day,* April 24, 1984, p. 38.
10. U.S. Department of Commerce, *Franchise Opportunities Handbook* (Washington, D.C.: U.S. Government Printing Office, October 1984), p. xxvi.

CASE 5A *Taco Luke Franchise & Puerto Rican Development Corp.*

After only six months in business, this fast-food franchise made a before-tax profit of $18,900 on sales revenues of $79,300. This record is a source of pride to

- Adelanio Matos, the franchisee
- Luke Owens, the franchisor
- Hector Suarez, who heads the Puerto Rican Economic Development Corporation

It took them three years to launch the franchise—three years measured in miles of red tape, acres of paper, and dozens of meetings. "If I had it all to do over again, I'm not sure I would," says Mr. Owens.

But bolstered by this success after a previous failure, Mr. Owens looks forward to selling similar franchises in New York City, where 900,000 Puerto Ricans live.

Background

Mr. Owens is an unlikely entrepreneur. Until 1966, football was his passion. He played for 10 years as a professional, mostly with the St. Louis Cardinals. His performance earned him a spot as defensive tackle on the Associated Press All-Pro Team four times.

But in his ninth season, as he turned 30, Mr. Owens suddenly realized that he would soon be washed up as a player. The thought struck a chill in his heart. "I was an old man at 30," says Mr. Owens. "I knew my days with the Cardinals were numbered. So I had to do some hard thinking about what to do with the rest of my life. I owed it to my wife and kids."

At the time, many professional football players were buying fast-food franchises. "It seemed the thing to do," says Mr. Owens. "So I thought I'd look into a McDonald's franchise." At the end of the 1965 season, he visited their headquarters in Elk Grove, Illinois to see about buying a franchise.

McDonald's turned him down. "They wanted $46,000 for a franchise in St. Louis," says Mr. Owens. "I had $27,500 to put down and I could've borrowed the rest. But I never got to first base. They seemed surprised I was black."

Undaunted, Mr. Owens visited other franchisors, including Arby's, Burger Chef, Chicken Delight, and Red Barn. All turned him down. "I couldn't find anybody to take my money," says Mr. Owens.

One lesson he had learned from football was how to come back from defeat. "I was down but not out," says Mr. Owens. "I saw that I'd have to make it on my own. But I lacked experience. I had never sold milk shakes and hamburgers, much less run a business."

Opportunity Knocks

His luck turned when he met two Chicago entrepreneurs, Bruce Kirk and David Roosevelt. Mr. Roosevelt was the great-grandson of Theodore Roosevelt, the nation's president from 1901 to 1909. They had started a fast-food business in Oklahoma City called Senor Taco, serving Mexican food only. Although not yet successful there, they were already planning to sell franchises to investors like Mr. Owens.

"I told Dave Roosevelt I'd like to learn about the business first," says Mr. Owens. "He said OK. So I went down to Oklahoma City for two and a half weeks, at my own expense, to learn all I could about selling tacos. I thought it was a real opportunity for me."

Impressed with Mr. Owens's desire and talents, the two entrepreneurs agreed to sell him a franchise. The agreement called for them to finance both the building and the equipment and for Mr. Owens to pay a franchise fee of $10,000. So, in 1967, one year after he quit professional football, Mr. Owens was busy selling tacos as a franchisee.

Disaster Strikes

Then Mr. Owens found himself in trouble: Mr. Kirk was killed in a plane crash and Mr. Roosevelt was drafted into the infantry and packed off to Vietnam. With no one to look after the Senor Taco parent company, it went under.

After the shock wore off, Mr. Owens moved fast to pick up the pieces. He talked to Mr. Kirk's wife, offering to buy the assets of the defunct parent company. It took three years and $3,200 of legal fees before he finally worked out a deal suitable to all parties—not only to bill collectors and bankers but also to Mrs. Kirk and Mr. Roosevelt. The final price was $14,500. And part of the deal was a change in name, to Taco Luke. "That was a great feeling," says Mr. Owens. "I was finally my own man." The year was 1971.

But during those three years of negotiating his freedom, Mr. Owens was knocked to his knees by events beyond his control. In the summer of 1968, race riots broke out that left in their wake 11 persons dead and parts of the city ravaged by fire. "Before the riots, half my customers were black and half were white," says Mr. Owens. "But after the riots, I lost all my white customers. I knew right then that I'd be swallowed up."

Revenues dropped steadily as even blacks began to stay away:

> I watched the area change to a low-level street life. I saw things I never imagined I'd see: shootings, muggings, murders, rapes, killings, dope pushers, pimps, contract people, after-hour gamblers. You name it, I saw it. But it's a funny thing: I met some fair-minded blacks who looked up to me and liked my image as a clean guy. I was someone different to these low-life persons. And I tried to help those who let me. I found that many of them had good minds but were misdirected. In fact, I think some of them might have become managers if their energies had been channeled elsewhere.

Now on the edge of failure, Mr. Owens began to make plans to pull up stakes and go elsewhere. Neighboring fast-food franchises were having similar problems. On Mr. Owens's block were Burger Chef, Mahalia Jackson, and McDonald's. "They were all hurting," says Mr. Owens. "The rumor was that McDonald's was doing a million dollars of business *before* the riots and less than half that *after* the riots. So I just had to get out—but how?"

A Second Chance

The answer came one steamy Sunday afternoon. Business was especially slow that day, causing Mr. Owens to feel depressed and weary. But not for long. One of his customers happened to be Hector Suarez, who headed the Puerto Rican Economic Development Corporation (PREDC), described in Exhibit 5A.1. They struck up a conversation, and Mr. Owens casually said that he "had lots of problems and wished he had a way out." "I've got a way out," offered Mr. Suarez. "You'll hear from me in a week or so." When Mr. Suarez called Mr. Owens, his first words were, "Let's make a deal."

That call marked the beginning of a new lease on life for Mr. Owens. "I just knew in my bones it would work out," says Mr. Owens. "Hector was as sincere a guy as I've ever met. Would you believe we picked a site the day he phoned me? That's how fast we moved," The site was a busy intersection in the middle of the city's Puerto Rican district.

Mr. Owens had now come full circle. All along, he had wanted to put a franchise in the city's near-west side, which is almost all white—even before he opened his first outlet on the east side, which is almost all black. "I couldn't sell my good points to bankers," says Mr. Owens. "They were worried because I was black. They thought I'd bring blacks in from the ghetto. So they wanted me to locate in the black ghetto. And I went along

EXHIBIT 5A.1

The Puerto Rican Economic Development Corporation

The Puerto Rican Economic Development Corporation (PREDC) was formed in November 1969 and incorporated under state law as a nonprofit organization in February 1970. Its tax-exempt status was granted under Section 501c of the U.S. Internal Revenue Code.

PREDC is governed by a board of 26 trustees, representing 80 percent of the city's Puerto Rican leadership. This board meets every two weeks, with an average attendance of 16 trustees a meeting.

PREDC was born out of a concern for the economic future of the city's 22,000 Puerto Ricans. Survey after survey had shown that this community lagged far behind other ethnic groups, especially in new-business starts and employment.

Moreover, urban blight has stripped the community of much-needed shopping services. Empty store fronts are eyesores everywhere.

It is PREDC's goal to reverse urban blight by creating jobs and entrepreneurial opportunities throughout the Puerto Rican community.

with them, even though I knew blacks didn't know too much about Mexican food. That's one of the reasons I didn't do well in the ghetto."

So Mr. Owens and Mr. Suarez joined hands to put up a Taco Luke franchise. There was little doubt in their minds that it would succeed. After all, there were 22,000 Puerto Ricans within a half mile of the corner site they had chosen—and most of them enjoyed eating tacos.

Needs a Business Plan

Equally important, Burger King wanted the site. "When I heard that, I just knew it had to be a good site," says Mr. Owens. "They're tops at marketing research. So, in a way, their research helped me, because now I wouldn't have to make a fancy market survey."

Not so. Mr. Owens and Mr. Suarez soon found they could not move their venture to first base without a business plan. Banks, the Chamber of Commerce, and the SBA all asked for such a plan. And, of course, a key part of it is a market survey. "That really upset me," says Mr. Owens. "They just wouldn't accept the fact that Burger King had already done such a survey. My Lord, I didn't know the first thing about doing such a survey, much less about putting a plan together."

His frustration was short-lived, thanks to a college student, Angelo Lupo. A marketing major, Mr. Lupo had volunteered his services through VISTA (Volunteers In Service To America). When Mr. Lupo offered to work up a business plan for the proposed Taco Luke franchise, Mr. Owens was skeptical. "I thought he was one of those college guys with a crew-cut, white socks, wing-tipped black shoes—and a white sheet over his arm. But to my surprise he was a hip guy and very brilliant."

Mr. Lupo began working on the business plan "with jet-like energy." His life soon became a busy round of meetings and interviews to get answers to such questions as these:

- What sales revenues is the franchise likely to generate in its first year of operation?
- How soon is the franchise likely to break even?
- How much would it cost to buy the corner lot, raze the abandoned building on it, construct a building, put in a parking lot, and buy fixtures and equipment?
- What is the best way to finance these costs?
- Who is the person likely to do the best job of running the franchise?

Researching the Market

High on the list of Mr. Lupo's priorities was to get a marketing research study done. He asked the Chamber of Commerce for help. They responded by assigning their marketing consultant, Dr. William Trombetta, to do the study. "This study had to come first," says Mr. Lupo, "because it's the revenue forecast that tells you how big a building to put up, how much working capital you'll need, how many people to hire, and a host of other things."

To forecast revenues, the marketing consultant borrowed procedures worked out by the Chicago Development Corporation. These procedures are designed to help establish small businesses in low-income areas, and they focus on such things as these:

- The number of families in each census tract located in the proposed franchise's trading area (see Exhibit 5A.2)
- The median family income in each census tract
- The median percentage each family spends eating out
- The percentage of total expenditures for food that families are *likely* to spend buying tacos and other Mexican food at the proposed franchise

EXHIBIT 5A.2 *Trading Area Around Proposed Franchise Site*

The assumed trading area of the facility is outlined by a dark line, based on a five-minute driving-time radius from the proposed retail site.

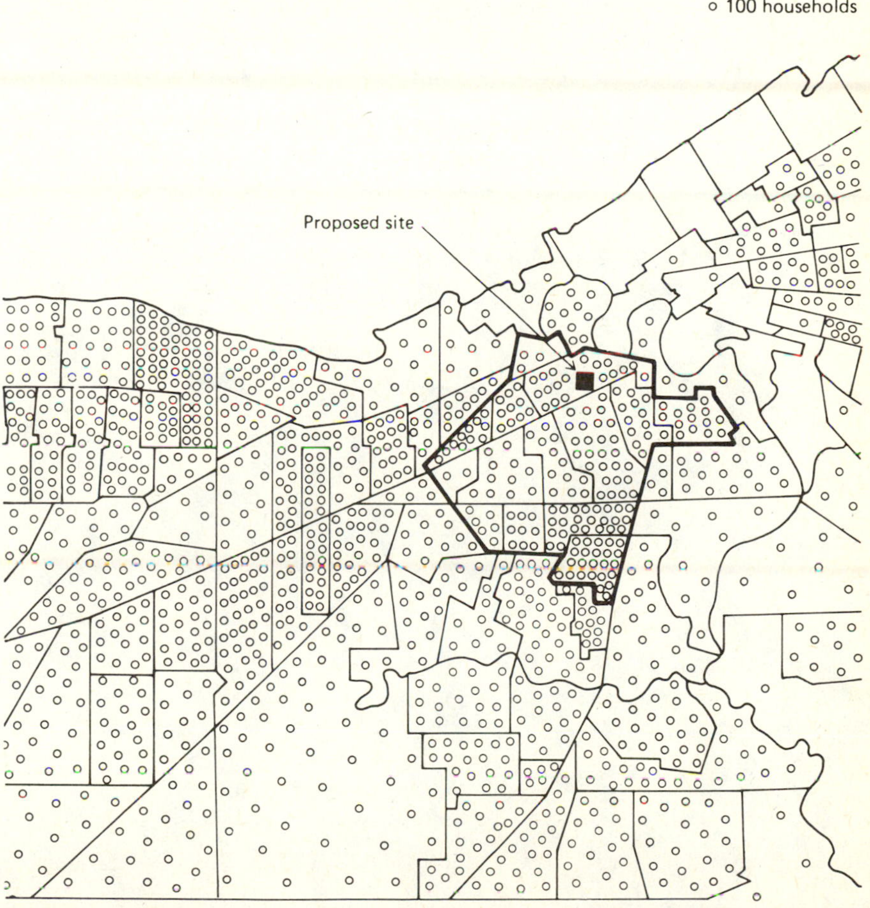

Source: Taco Luke Franchise.

EXHIBIT 5A.3 *Model for Estimating Sales Revenues*

Number of families in census tracts	×	Median income of families in census tracts	×	Percentage of family's income spent on eating out	×	Percentage of family's food expense likely to be spent at franchise	=	Sales revenue forecast for franchise

The idea was to multiply the four factors to produce a sales revenue forecast (see the model in Exhibit 5A.3).

It was no problem for the consultant to get this information. Information on the number of families in each census tract came from a local newspaper's marketing and research department. Information on median family income came from the *United States Census of Population and Housing* at the public library. And information on what percentage of a family's income is spent on food came from a report published by the U.S. Department of Labor, also available at the library.

Armed with all this information, the consultant put his desk calculator to use and came up with $4,250,000 as the total amount that families in the trading area spend on eating out. His calculations appear in Exhibit 5A.4.

EXHIBIT 5A.4 *Estimate of Market Potential*

(A) Census Tracts in Trading Area	(B) Number of Families in Each Census Tract	(C) Median Family Income	(D) Total Gross Income (B × C)	(E) Percentage of Yearly Income Spent on Eating Out	(F) Total Market Potential (D × E)
C-9	1,788	$7,630	$ 13,650,000	3.9%	$ 530,000
C-5	1,484	7,800	11,580,000	3.9	450,000
B-7	1,395	8,490	11,840,000	3.9	460,000
C-8	1,376	8,550	11,760,000	3.9	460,000
C-6	1,163	6,180	7,190,000	3.3	240,000
B-6	1,115	8,040	8,970,000	3.9	350,000
B-8	1,088	8,230	8,960,000	3.9	350,000
D-1	1,004	7,360	7,380,000	3.3	240,000
C-7	992	6,660	6,610,000	3.3	220,000
C-4	936	7,960	7,500,000	3.9	290,000
D-9	820	8,800	7,220,000	3.9	280,000
C-2	410	7,580	3,110,000	3.9	120,000
D-6	305	8,250	2,520,000	3.9	100,000
B-5	304	8,280	2,520,000	3.9	100,000
C-3	202	4,160	840,000	6.7	60,000
Total	14,382		$111,650,000		$4,250,000

Now came the hard part. The consultant had to estimate what share of the total food dollar the franchise was *likely* to get. More or less picking a figure out of the air, he settled on 5 percent. So he forecast revenues of $210,000 for the proposed franchise for its first year of operation.

Verifies Forecast

Not entirely satisfied with this textbook approach, the consultant went on to verify the forecast by making an on-the-spot traffic study with Mr. Lupo's help. In fact, Mr. Lupo stood on the corner for seven straight days in December to count:

- The number of pedestrians by the hour
- The number of passing cars by the hour

Based on this study, the consultant came up with a revenue forecast lower than his earlier one: $155,000 versus $210,000. How he got the $155,000 is explained in Exhibit 5A.5.

The consultant also looked at the quality of competing fast-food franchises in the area. He found that the only serious competition would come from a six-stool coffee shop and a stand-up sub shop. In contrast,

EXHIBIT 5A.5

Forecast of Sales Revenues from On-the-Spot Survey

A. Key assumptions*	
Average purchase by customers	$1.00
Drive-in ratio	0.5%
Walk-in ratio	1.2%
B. Pedestrian flow at proposed site	
Number of pedestrians per day	2,120
Walk-in ratio	1.2%
Walk-in trade per day	250 (2,120 × 0.12)
C. Vehicular flow at proposed site	
Number of vehicles per day	19,500
Drive-in ratio	0.5%
Drive-in trade per day	100 (19,500 × 0.005)
D. Student flow at proposed site	
Number of students at high schools	3,040
Assumed drop-in ratio	2.5%
Student trade per day	75 (3,040 × 0.025)
E. Forecast of sales revenues	
Walk-in trade	250
Drive-in trade	100
Student trade	75
Average purchase	$1.00
Number of days per year	365
Forecast of revenues	$155,000†

* These assumptions come from Mr. Owens's experience at his original outlet on the east side.
† $1.00 × 365 (250 + 100 +75) = $155,000

EXHIBIT 5A.6

Estimated Return on Investment

A.	Forecast of yearly revenues	$155,000
B.	Operating profit ratio	5.0%*
C.	Operating profit (A × B)	$7,750
D.	Total investment	$138,000
E.	Return on investment (C ÷ D)	6% a year

* Industry average

Mr. Owens's original outlet on the east side competed with such giants as Burger King, Mahalia Jackson, and McDonald's—"all this in a black area. But on the near west side, the area's Puerto Rican flavor would surely enhance the chances that an ethnically related outlet would succeed." Return-on-investment calculations appear in Exhibit 5A.6.

Financing

While this marketing study was underway, Mr. Lupo was spending most of his time on a nagging question every banker had asked him: What would it cost to start up the business?

The answer: $138,000. It took him nine months to make that estimate with the help of architects, realtors, and lawyers. The $138,000 would be invested as follows:

$ 82,500	for purchasing the corner lot, razing two old buildings, and putting in a paved parking lot
50,000	for constructing a building and buying equipment, fixtures, and furniture
5,500	for working capital
$138,000	

With the marketing and investment aspects in hand, Mr. Lupo was able to piece together the rest of the business plan. When he completed the plan, it weighed more than a pound. "I never knew there was so much red tape around," says Mr. Lupo. "I filled out enough forms to last a lifetime."

Mr. Lupo carried five copies of his business plan to the SBA, with whom he had been in touch from the day he began work on the plan. Within five months, the SBA agreed to make the $124,200 loan called for by the plan, at $5\frac{1}{2}$ percent interest. The rest, or $13,800, would be invested by members of the Puerto Rican community. The SBA requires that at least 10 percent of a new venture's total capitalization come from private investors—hence the need for seed money.

"Anthony Delfine deserves a lot of credit for getting us the loan," says Mr. Owens. "He was a loan specialist for the SBA, helping minority entrepreneurs get on their feet. Without Tony's help—and Angelo Lupo's—I wouldn't have made it."

But a year later, in 1973, the venture ran into a snag. Dealings with unskilled construction contractors led to spiraling costs in materials and labor. Mr. Lupo now estimated it would take another $29,500 to complete the project. At first, the SBA refused to approve the cost overrun. But after some discussion, the SBA approved it.

A Grand Opening

When the project was finally completed in May 1974, the Taco Luke franchise opened with the balance sheet shown in Exhibit 5A.7. A photograph of the franchise appears in Exhibit 5A.8.

The franchise opened in a splash of ceremony. The mayor praised the Puerto Rican community for its efforts at self-improvement. But few of the hundreds who attended the ceremony were aware of the sweat and heartache that had preceded it. Few knew that three long years had passed since the first meeting between Mr. Owens and Mr. Suarez until the opening of the franchise. "If I had it all to do over again, I'm not sure I would," says Mr. Owens. "It wasn't easy."

The man Mr. Suarez chose to run the franchise is Adelanio Matos. Once a grocer, Mr. Matos owns the franchise and the equipment, leasing from PREDC the building and grounds. Mr. Matos's income statement after six months in business appears in Exhibit 5A.9.

As the franchisor, Mr. Owens gets 4 percent of revenues from Mr. Matos. In turn, Mr. Owens donates one-fourth of his franchise fee to PREDC for use in other community projects. "It's the least I can do," says Mr. Owens. "They're such great people, and they helped me when nobody else would."

Bolstered by his success here, Mr. Owens plans to sell the franchise to investors in other cities with large Puerto Rican populations. Especially appealing is New York City, with 900,000 Puerto Ricans.

EXHIBIT 5A.7

Taco Luke Franchise: Balance Sheet (May 6, 1974)

Assets			**Equities**	
Current assets			Bank note	$150,750
Cash	$ 4,000			
Inventory	1,000	$ 5,000	Owners' equity	16,750
Fixed assets				
Land	$82,500			
Building	69,500			
Equipment	10,000	$162,000		
Organizational costs		500		
Total assets		$167,500	Total equities	$167,500

EXHIBIT 5A.8 *Taco Luke Franchise: Exterior View of Restaurant*

EXHIBIT 5A.9

Taco Luke Franchise: Income Statement
(May 6, 1974 to November 1, 1974)

Sales revenues		$79,300
Cost of goods sold		
Food purchases	$36,400	
Ending inventory	100	36,300
Gross profit		$43,000
Operating expenses		
Wages	$11,300	
Rent	2,800	
Franchise fee	2,000	
Insurance	1,700	
Salaries	1,500	
Supplies	1,000	
Utilities	900	
Taxes	700	
Interest	500	
Depreciation	500	
Repairs	400	
Telephone	200	
Commissions	200	
Advertising	200	
Licenses and permits	100	
Lease improvements	100	24,100
Operating profit		$18,900

Questions

1. Identify the obstacles that Mr. Owens had to overcome when he first sought to become an entrepreneur in 1966. In your opinion which obstacles still remain today?
2. Why did Mr. Owens succeed?
3. Comment on the paperwork that is needed in order to qualify for a loan from the SBA.
4. What are Mr. Owens's prospects for expanding his franchise into other Puerto Rican communities? If you were Mr. Owens, how would you go about it?
5. Comment on the franchise's performance to date.

CASE 5B *Ron Schultz*

Ron Schultz was a life-insurance salesman, modestly providing for his wife and two sons. They lived in a quiet urban neighborhood on the tight budget that many families with a limited income find necessary.

At 42 years of age, Mr. Schultz was seeking to enter a new field—one that would enable him to increase his income. One opportunity he looked at was a franchise with one of the nation's biggest automatic-transmission repair services. Investigation revealed a fast-growing market with little competition:

- New-car dealers were equipped to repair only the one make of transmission they sold. Because of their high overhead, their transmission-repair prices ran high.
- Neighborhood garages farmed out their transmission-repair work to small shops that varied sharply in quality and cost.

The potential was clear. But Mr. Schultz was bothered by his lack of a mechanical background. The franchisor's intensive training program was designed to overcome just such doubts. Spanning four weeks, the program ran 48 hours a week and covered such subjects as pricing, employee recruiting, advertising, customer service, supervision, and cost controls.

The program's objective was to familiarize the franchisee with all aspects of the transmission-repair business—with emphasis on *managing* transmission specialists rather than doing the actual mechanical work.

At the franchisor's suggestion, Mr. Schultz picked several names at random from a list of their franchisees. He visited each one at his convenience. Each franchisee seemed pleased with his own business. And each one urged Mr. Schultz to seek his own franchise with the parent company.

Further investigation indicated that the site for the new franchise could be right in Mr. Schultz's area. The tentative site boasted 40,000 registered automobiles within a 30-minute drive.

The initial cash investment for this franchise was $70,000. And the franchisor was ready to help Mr. Schultz raise the money. The $70,000 investment would cover such items as:

- Initial rental and parts inventory
- Special tools and outdoor signs
- Workbenches and office supplies

Continuing help offered by the franchisor included monthly conferences for all area franchisees to review sales progress and business proficiency.

The requirements Mr. Schultz had to meet—besides his initial $70,000 investment—were a strong desire to earn money and a knack for communicating with people.

Questions

1. What should Mr. Schultz do?
2. What advantages do you see in the franchisor's offer?
3. What disadvantages do you see in the offer?
4. What added information would you advise Mr. Schultz to get?

Source: Case prepared by the U.S. Small Business Administration.

CASE 5C *Anthony Williams*

Anthony Williams wants to own a franchise. "I don't care what kind of franchise I go into," says Mr. Williams, "just so I'm the owner. Believe me, I've been around a lot and learned a lot. I've poured steel, washed dishes, clerked at supermarkets, peddled papers, tended bar. You name it, I've done it. Of course, now I've got a steady job driving a truck for the Post Office. Been at it for eight years."

Mr. Williams is 39 years old, married, with four children. Like others in his neighborhood, he is heavily mortgaged and buys often on the installment plan—all the time betting that paychecks will keep coming in week after week.

A graduate of a local community college, Mr. Williams recalls what a professor once told him. "Franchising," said the professor, "is ideal for entrepreneurs who lack experience. Franchisors teach you all you have to know." And Mr. Williams remembers to this day the professor's statement that 99 percent of all McDonald's franchisees had *no* prior experience in the restaurant industry.

Question

Assume that Mr. Williams has come to you for advice. What would you tell him to do?

6 DEVELOPING A BUSINESS PLAN

QUESTIONS FOR MASTERY

Why write a business plan?
How do you prepare a business plan?
Can a business plan be versatile?
Why is it important to get the facts and make sound assumptions?
What is the difference between operating plans and financial plans?

If we are true to plan, our statures touch the skies.

Emily Dickinson

A business plan is an essential step for would-be entrepreneurs in turning their ideas for products or services into flourishing ventures. Planning requires entrepreneurs to *anticipate*:

- The potential market for their venture
- The potential costs of meeting the demands of that market
- The potential pitfalls in organizing the operations of the venture
- The early signals that alert them of progress or setbacks

The business plan is a rigorous exercise, based on facts, that provides the underpinnings for a successful venture.

NEED FOR PLANNING

Planning is decision-making; that is, deciding what to do, how to do it, and when to do it. It is vital for business success. As one businessman put it:

> Planning is so important today that it occupies a major part of the time of some of the most respected men in business . . . Planning allows us to master change. It forces us to organize our expectations and develop programs to bring them about.
>
> Planning is a most effective way to draw out the best in all of us—our best thinking, our best interests and aims—and to enable us to develop the most efficient way of achieving our maximum growth.[1]

The very act of preparing a business plan forces entrepreneurs to think through the steps they must take—from the moment they decide to go into business for themselves to the moment they open for business to the moments they are actively engaged in business.

A Road Map for Entrepreneurs

In many ways, the business plan resembles a road map, telling entrepreneurs how best to get from A to Z. Entrepreneurs may think: Why should I spend my time drawing up a business plan? The answer is that they cannot afford not to. A complex economy such as ours demands such a plan:

> Time was when an individual could start a venture and prosper provided he was strong enough to work long hours and had the knack for selling at prices above what materials or product had cost him. Small stores, grist mills, livery stables, and blacksmith shops sprang up in many crossroad communities as Americans applied their energy and native intelligence to settling the continent. Today, this native intelligence is still important. But, by itself, the common sense for which Americans are famous will not ensure success in a small business. Technology, the marketplace, and even people themselves have become more complicated than they were 100, or even 25, years ago.
>
> Today, common sense must be combined with new techniques in

order to succeed in the space age. Just as one would not think of launching a manned space capsule without a flight plan, so one should not think of launching a new business without a business plan.[2]

Outside Pressure

The idea of a business plan is hardly new. Big business has long been turning them out yearly by the thousands, especially for marketing new products, buying out an existing business, or expanding into foreign markets. But what is new is the growing use of such plans by entrepreneurs. Outside pressures now force them to develop their businesses on paper before investing time and money in a venture that may have little chance of success.

Outside pressures flow mainly from creditors and investors whom the entrepreneur may approach for money. Most of them ask for a business plan before entertaining a request for money. These outside pressures are healthy:

- Entrepreneurs benefit because a business plan makes them better appreciate what it may take to succeed.
- Investors and creditors also benefit because a business plan gives them better information on which to decide whether to help finance the entrepreneur.

EXHIBIT 6.1 *Who Needs a Business Plan?*

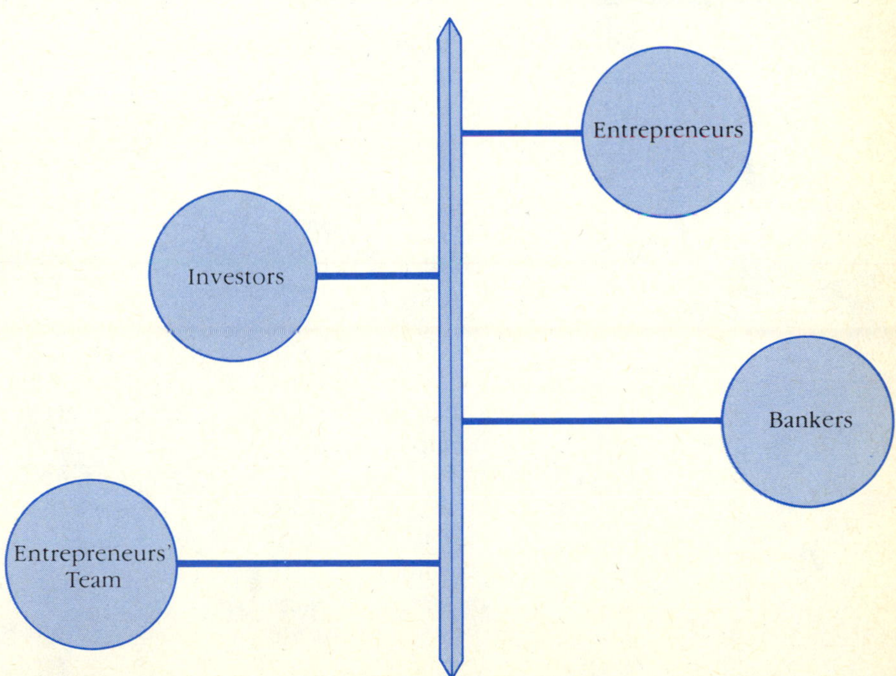

How many entrepreneurs actually prepare a formal business plan? Probably fewer than 5 percent. The remaining 95 percent plan in less structured ways. Some may do it entirely in their heads and others may simply write notes on the backs of old envelopes. But, as Dr. William R. Osgood of Northeastern University points out:

> If you are not in business but are trying to determine whether or not your business idea makes sense, or if you are getting started, the business plan is your most important task. It will help you avoid mistakes and will save you effort, time, and money.
>
> Going into business is rough—half of all new businesses fail within the first two years of operation. The best way to enhance your chances of success is to plan and follow through on your planning.
>
> Your business plan can help you avoid going into a business venture that is doomed to failure. If your proposed venture is marginal at best, the business plan will show you why and may help you avoid paying the high tuition of business failure. It is far cheaper not to begin an ill-fated business than to learn by experience what your business plan could have taught you at a cost of several hours of concentrated work. Plan what's going to happen—then do it.[3]

PARTS OF A BUSINESS PLAN

What should a business plan cover? It should be a thought-through and objective analysis of both personal abilities and business requirements for a particular product or service. It should define strategies for such functions as marketing, production, organization, legal aspects, accounting, and finance. A business plan should answer such questions as:

- What do I want and what am I capable of doing?
- What are the most workable ways of achieving my goals?
- What can I expect in the future?

There is no single best way to begin. We suggest a guide that should be changed to suit individual needs. Exhibit 6.2 recommends the steps that entrepreneurs may take to prepare a business plan, as well as the time it may take to complete each step.

Exhibit 6.3 shows how all 14 steps in Exhibit 6.2 tie together. It is apparent from the exhibit that certain key steps cannot be taken until earlier steps are completed. For example, entrepreneurs cannot research their market (Step 4), unless they first choose a product or service (Step 3), and they cannot prepare a marketing plan (Step 8), unless they first research their market (Step 4), forecast their revenues (Step 5), and choose a site (Step 6).

EXHIBIT 6.2 *Suggested Steps to Take in Developing Your Business Plan*

Step No.	Description of Steps	Completion Date	Comments
1	Decide to go into business for yourself.		
2	Analyze your strengths and weaknesses, paying special attention to your business experience, business education, and desires. Then answer this question: Why should I be in business for myself?	Third week	
3	Choose the product or service that best fits your strengths and desires. Then answer these questions: What is unique about my product or service? How do I know it is unique? What will my product or service do for customers? What will it not do? What should it do later but does not now do?	Fourth week	
4	Research the market for your product or service, to find answers to such questions as these: Who are my customers? Where are they? What is their average income? How do they buy? At what price? In what quantities? When do they buy? When will they use my product or service? Where will they use it? Why will they buy it? Who are my competitors? Where are they? How strong are they? What is the total market potential? Is it growing?	Seventh week	
5	Forecast your share of market if possible. Then forecast your sales revenues over a three-year period, broken down as follows: First year—monthly Second year—quarterly Third year—yearly Next, answer this question: Why do I believe my sales-revenue forecast is realistic?	Eighth week	
6	Choose a site for your business, then answer this question: Why do I prefer this site to other possible sites?	Eighth week	
7*	Develop your production plan, answering these questions: How big should my plant be? How should my production process be laid out? What equipment will I need? In what size? How will I control the waste, quality, and inventory of my product?	Tenth week	

(*continued*)

EXHIBIT 6.2 *Suggested Steps to Take in Developing Your Business Plan (cont.)*

Step No.	Description of Steps	Completion Date	Comments
8	Develop your marketing plan, answering such questions as these: How am I going to create customers? At what price? By what kinds of advertising and sales promotion? Through personal selling? How?	Tenth week	
9	Develop your organizational plan, answering this question: What kinds of talent will I need to make my business go? Draw up an organizational chart that spells out who does what, who has what authority, and who reports to whom.	Twelfth week	
10	Develop your legal plan, focusing on whether to form a sole proprietorship, a partnership, or a corporation; and then explain your choice.	Twelfth week	
11	Develop your accounting plan, explaining the kinds of records and reports you need and how you will use them.	Twelfth week	
12	Develop your insurance plan, answering this question: What kinds of insurance will I need to protect my venture against possible loss from unforeseen events?	Twelfth week	
13	Develop your financial plan by preparing these statements: A three-year cash budget. Show how much cash you will need before opening for business and show how much cash you expect will flow in and out of your business, broken down as follows: First year—monthly Second year—quarterly Third year—yearly An income statement for the first year only Balance sheets for the beginning and ending of the first year A profitgraph (breakeven chart), showing when you will begin to make a profit Then determine how you will finance your business and where you expect to raise money.	Fifteenth week	
14	Write a cover letter summarizing your business plan, stressing its purpose and its promise.	Sixteenth week	

* This step applies only to those entrepreneurs who plan to go into manufacturing. Otherwise, it should be omitted.

EXHIBIT 6.3 *Flow Diagram Showing How Steps in Business Plan Relate*

Shown here at 16 weeks for illustrative purposes. Clearly, the time it takes to prepare a business plan may take less or much more than 16 weeks, depending on the complexity of the venture.

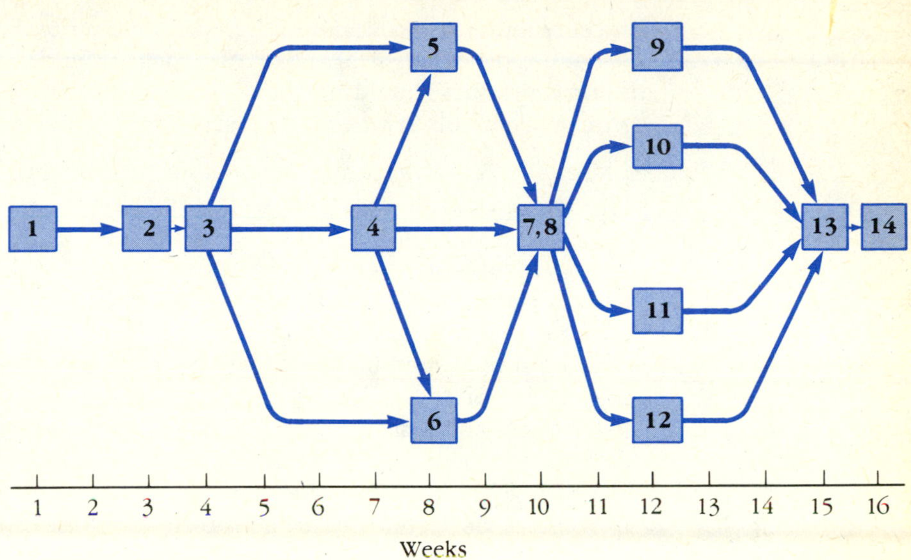

KEY:
1 Decide to go into business
2 Analyze yourself
3 Choose product or service
4 Research markets
5 Forecast sales revenues
6 Choose site
7 Develop production plan
8 Develop marketing plan
9 Develop organizational plan
10 Develop legal plan
11 Develop accounting plan
12 Develop insurance plan
13 Develop financial plan
14 Write cover letter

The guidelines in Exhibits 6.2 and 6.3 are tailored to new ventures. They are also applicable to the following situations:

- Buying an existing business—perhaps omitting Steps 3, 8, 9
- Expanding an existing business—perhaps omitting Steps 1, 2, 3, 10
- Floating additional shares of common stock—perhaps omitting Steps 1, 6, 10
- Borrowing money from a commercial bank—perhaps omitting Steps 1, 6, 10

As they follow the guidelines in Exhibits 6.2 and 6.3, entrepreneurs should keep complete notes that document all facts, back all assumptions, and give the authority for all opinions. Otherwise, entrepreneurs may lack credibility with investors and creditors.

AUTHORSHIP OF BUSINESS PLAN

Entrepreneurs themselves should prepare and write the business plan, with the help of professionals if needed. Its focus should be on its substance and the final product should not be so slick as to make investors wary of its content. These observations underscore this idea:

> **Example:** As Jerry Casilli of Genesis Capital puts it, "The value of a business plan is in the process. The important part is the thinking that goes on to come up with it."
>
> Investors and bankers usually expect a business plan to be neatly typed and purged of poor grammar, but a business plan that is too polished can raise the eyebrows of investors and bankers. "If a guy thinks form is more important than substance, then he's missing the point of a business plan," says Steven Merrill of Merrill Pickard Anderson & Eyre of San Francisco.
>
> Investors and bankers strongly advise against using outside consultants to help develop a business plan. "A professionally prepared business plan is a turn-off if the entrepreneur is not the guiding force behind it," says Dan Case, vice president at Hambrecht & Quist of San Francisco.[4]

GETTING THE FACTS

By answering the guideline questions in Exhibit 6.2, entrepreneurs can prepare a thoughtful and effective business plan. To use the guidelines well, however, they will need to get facts, opinions, and judgments. The following suggestions may be helpful.

Step 1: Deciding to Go into Business

The decision to go into business requires little fact-finding. It is recommended, however, that entrepreneurs take the self-analysis test offered in Chapter Two.

Step 2: Analyzing Oneself

Analysis of personal strengths and weaknesses also requires little fact-finding. Entrepreneurs may simply sit down and list their strengths, paying special attention to their business experience and education. On another sheet of paper, they may list their weaknesses. Next, they should analyze their readiness to start their own business.

When analyzing their strengths and weaknesses, entrepreneurs should be honest with themselves. It is often hard for them, as for others, to see their own shortcomings.

Step 3: Choosing a Product or Service

This is a critical step. As a rule, it is foolish for entrepreneurs to choose a product or service they know little about. A bad choice will severely weaken their chance of success, and learning from their mistakes can be costly. Still, some entrepreneurs do go into an entirely unfamiliar field and succeed. As a general rule, entrepreneurs should pick a product or service they:

- Know intimately because they have worked with it for years
- Are convinced will grow at a rate faster than that of the economy as a whole
- Can get excited about

It is also vital that entrepreneurs develop precise answers to these two questions:

- What is unique about my product?
- What does it offer customers that competing products do not offer?

Step 4: Researching the Market

Research is perhaps the most crucial step of all. Entrepreneurs should spare no expense in their quest for facts. The more they know about their markets, the greater their chance of creating customers at a profit.

Too often, entrepreneurs do a poor job in this vital area, tending to rely on hearsay instead of facts and thus lacking even the foggiest idea of how best to reach the customer. Many new ventures fizzle into oblivion because entrepreneurs failed to get the basic information they needed to move products out of their hands and into those of customers. Shown in Exhibit 6.4 is the typical marketing research process.

In quest of facts, it is logical to begin with the question: Who are my customers? Entrepreneurs who sweep their market with a glance and decide, "Every one of the city's million people will want my product," are

EXHIBIT 6.4 *Marketing Research Process*

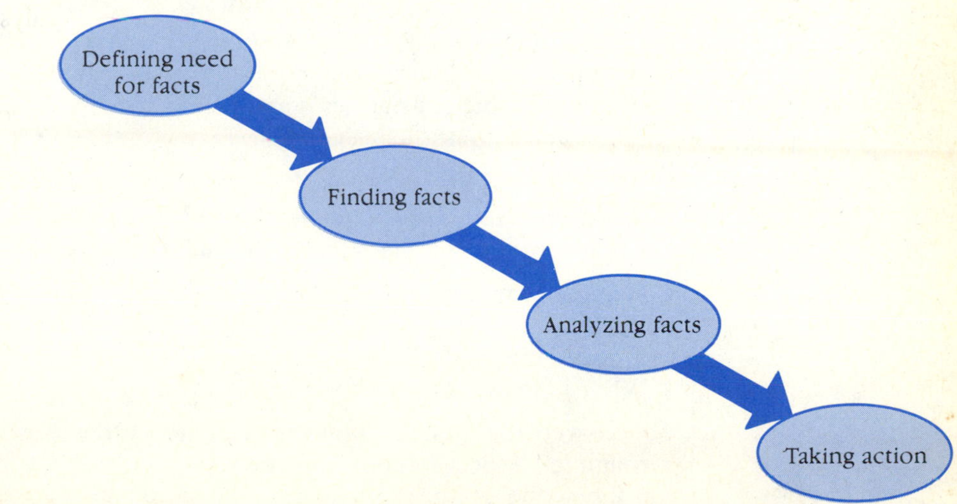

taking a casual approach that can only hamper their later efforts to define a marketing strategy. Instead, they should get facts on where customers live and shop, their average income, how they buy, at what price, why they buy, and so on. This is a tall order; but the information is not only important, it is also obtainable.

To get such information, entrepreneurs should begin with their local Chamber of Commerce. The Chamber can tell them what facts are available, either at hand or buried in government statistics. Trade associations are equally fruitful sources; they offer mountains of information, often at no cost. Virtually every industry has such an association. After collecting facts already unearthed by others, entrepreneurs should then leave their desks and do some fact-finding of their own.

Example: Let us assume an entrepreneur, who is a certified public accountant, plans to open an accounting service for small businesses only. As part of her business plan, the entrepreneur needs to estimate the total *market potential* for such a service. *Market potential* is the total dollar value of accounting services now purchased by small businesses in the marketing area. To estimate market potential, the entrepreneur should begin by talking to prospects. She may choose about 25 small businesspersons at random and visit each one to get answers to such questions as:

- Will you buy my accounting service at competitive hourly rates, if I promise my service will be quicker and better suited to your needs? If not, why?
- How much does your present accounting service charge you?

Armed with such information, the entrepreneur may now estimate her total market potential in this way:

a. Average hourly charge	= $50.00
b. Average number of hours per month of service time used by small businesses	= 4
c. Number of small businesses in sample	= 25
d. Number of small businesses in marketing area	= 5,000
e. Number of months in year	= 12
f. Yearly market potential (a × b × d × e)	= $12,000,000

Besides estimating market potential, the entrepreneur should also look at her competition, getting answers to such questions as these:

- Who are my competitors?
- Where are they?
- How strong are they?
- What kinds of accounting services do they offer?

To answer the first two questions, the entrepreneur should thumb through the Yellow Pages and visit each accounting service to get a feeling for the scope of their operations. Then, on an area map, she should pinpoint their locations.

Answers to the questions about competitors' strengths and services should come from the entrepreneur's banker, who has access to a copy of each competitor's Dun & Bradstreet report, if available. These reports offer insights into a competitor's financial strength, credit rating, and line of accounting services.

The process of fact-finding described in the example is usually called marketing research. We will discuss this vital tool more fully in Chapters Eight and Fourteen.

Step 5: Forecasting Sales Revenues

After estimating the market potential for their selected businesses, entrepreneurs should estimate what share of that market they can reasonably expect to gain. They must do so by making realistic assumptions, taking into account the number and size of competitors and the amount of time it will take them to achieve their goals. Entrepreneurs then need to express their expected market share in terms of sales revenues. A good rule of thumb is to estimate sales revenues over a three-year period, broken down as follows:

- First year—monthly
- Second year—quarterly
- Third year—yearly

These revenue figures are key estimates because they are the basis for almost all other figure estimates that the entrepreneur must make. It is vital, therefore, that revenues be estimated in a realistic way and not picked out of the air.

Example: For her accounting service, the entrepreneur might now estimate her share of market (or revenues) as follows:

a. Total market potential = $12,000,000
b. Number of competitors = 59
c. Number of competitors *plus* entrepreneur = 60
d. Share of market (a ÷ c) = $200,000

Next, the entrepreneur should estimate how long it will take her to reach that revenue level. A realistic estimate might be three years.

It bears repeating that revenue forecasts must qualify as intelligent guesswork. Unless armed with such forecasts, the entrepreneur lacks a realistic target to aim for and cannot plan such expenditures as the following:

- Buying or leasing long-lived assets such as buildings, equipment, or land
- Buying inventories and supplies
- Hiring employees
- Financing customers who may take one, two, or more months to pay their bills

Revenue forecasts must be based on assumptions as well as facts; the accuracy of a revenue forecast hinges largely on the accuracy of the assumptions that support it.

Step 6: Choosing a Site

Entrepreneurs usually have some idea, from the very start, of where best to locate their business. California, for example, may be preferred because of its climate. Or a hometown location may be preferred because life-long friendships may enable the entrepreneur to raise money and draw customers more readily than in a town of strangers. Wise entrepreneurs, however, balance personal preference with business logic. Because the two rarely match perfectly, entrepreneurs must often compromise:

> **Example:** If he is going into chemical manufacture, the entrepreneur may have to locate his plant hundreds of miles from where he prefers to live. The chemistry of his process may require ten pounds of raw materials to make one pound of chemical product, suggesting to the entrepreneur that he should locate close to suppliers in order to cut transportation costs.

Suppliers, customers, or financial support may determine regional locations. Equally important is location within a city or neighborhood. Too often, entrepreneurs jump at the first vacancy that comes along, rather than base their choice on the results of their marketing research. Location is a critical decision that can mean the difference between success or failure. We will discuss location in greater detail in Chapter Eight.

Step 7: Developing a Production Plan

The need for a production plan applies only to entrepreneurs who intend to manufacture a product. In preparing such a plan, perhaps the most critical question an entrepreneur should answer is: How big should my plant be? The estimate should be in volume of product per year and should flow logically from the revenue forecast. General practice is to use the third-year forecast, or even the fifth-year forecast, to size a plant. However, entrepreneurs may find that a five-year forecast often stretches too far into the future to be realistic.

After estimating size, entrepreneurs should lay out their production process. Efficient layout requires that equipment be arranged in ways that:

- Minimize manual handling of materials
- Make best use of workers' time
- Offer flexibility for expansion

An especially helpful tool in the planning process is a flow diagram that shows how raw materials would enter the plant, how these materials would change into product, and how product would leave the plant.

Entrepreneurs must also determine the type and size of the equipment needed for the production process. Each piece of equipment should be sized in a way that keeps the process free of bottlenecks. Equipment suppliers can generally offer expert advice on how to go about selecting and sizing equipment.

Last, entrepreneurs should lay out their plans to control the waste, quality, and inventory of their product.

Step 8: Developing a Marketing Plan

This step forces entrepreneurs to detail how they plan to create customers at a profit. If, in Step 4, entrepreneurs have painstakingly researched their markets, then their marketing plans are likely to be creative and effective. To develop a marketing plan, entrepreneurs must make use of these marketing tools:

- Distribution channels and servicing activities
- Advertising and sales promotion
- Personal selling
- Pricing

Properly combined and coordinated, these marketing tools generate sales revenues, as depicted in Exhibit 6.5. To clarify marketing plans further, let us refer to our earlier example dealing with accounting services.

Example: Let us assume that the entrepreneur estimates first-year revenues at $100,000. She then asks herself: How should I go about getting customers for my accounting service? In other words, what marketing mix should I use?

The entrepreneur knows that, on the average, her industry spends 10 percent of revenues on getting orders. This statistic tells her she should budget $10,000 for that purpose. So the next question she asks is: On what marketing tools, and in what combination, should I spend the $10,000?

EXHIBIT 6.5 *Marketing Tools*

Proper coordination of marketing tools creates sales.

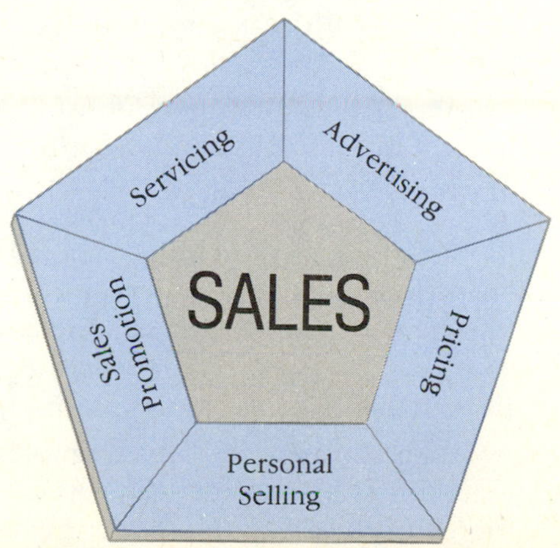

Because of the importance of personal contact in providing accounting services to small businesses, the entrepreneur might decide that three fourths of her marketing effort should be personal selling and just one fourth should be advertising. In dollar terms, she would spend $7,500 for personal selling and $2,500 for advertising.

This example is oversimplified, but at least it gives some idea of the proper approach. We will examine the marketing plan in some detail in Chapter Fourteen.

Step 9: Developing an Organizational Plan

Entrepreneurs should now assemble, at least on paper, the team they need for their new venture. First, they should spell out:

- What needs to be done to carry out their marketing and production plans
- Who reports to whom
- What qualifications are required for above-average performance in each job

Having analyzed and described their needs, entrepreneurs may now prepare an organizational chart defining who does what and who reports to whom.

The subjects of organizational planning and human relations are covered in some detail in Chapters Ten and Sixteen, respectively.

Step 10: Developing a Legal Plan

This step takes us into the legal arena. Here, entrepreneurs must decide whether to go it alone as a sole proprietor, share their venture with one or more partners, or incorporate. Each choice has its advantages and disadvantages. Which one is best hinges on a host of issues, such as personal preference, taxes, and personal wealth.

At the first opportunity, the entrepreneur should see a lawyer for advice. The lawyer should be an expert in new ventures, preferably with experience in the entrepreneur's industry. These and other legal questions are dealt with in some detail in Chapter Seven.

Step 11: Developing an Accounting Plan

Entrepreneurs often overlook the accounting side of their venture. They reason that records can be put off until tomorrow, except that tomorrow never seems to come. Entrepreneurs mistakenly prefer to work on more pressing matters such as marketing and production plans.

From the start, entrepreneurs must keep records in order to know how well their venture is doing and in what direction it is moving. Therefore, the entrepreneur should have an accountant design a record-keeping system before, and not after, the venture starts.

The system need not be complex or consist of journals and ledgers and worksheets. It can be quite simple. If the system only requires that notes and figures be kept on the backs of old envelopes, so be it—as long as these notes and figures enable the entrepreneur to keep track of the business. As a rule, the best record-keeping system is one that will:

- Ensure a high degree of accuracy
- Handle information at low cost
- Turn out reports quickly
- Minimize theft and fraud

The subject of accounting, as well as the related subject of control, are discussed in some detail in Chapters Eleven and Twelve, respectively.

Step 12: Developing an Insurance Plan

Like record keeping, insurance is a step that entrepreneurs often ignore, sometimes until well after their venture has been launched. This shortsightedness is hazardous. Entrepreneurs must protect themselves and their ventures from any unforeseen events that may threaten them, such as fire and theft.

To provide for their protection, entrepreneurs should develop a program of risk management before they launch their venture. Such a program would specify:

- Where dollar losses may occur
- How severe such losses might be
- How to treat these risks

To make sure the risk-management program is tailored to the needs of their venture, entrepreneurs should seek the help of an insurance agent and perhaps the help of a lawyer as well.

The subject of insurance is explored in much greater detail in Chapter Nineteen.

Step 13: Developing a Financial Plan

A financial plan ties together all the preceding steps by translating production, marketing, and organizational plans into dollars. In other words, the financial plan is a dollar expression of the entrepreneur's operating plans, as shown in Exhibit 6.6.

Dollars provide the common denominator by means of which dissimilar parts of a venture may be added or subtracted, multiplied or divided. For example, how could an entrepreneur possibly add together trucks and hammers, land and light bulbs unless such assets were expressed in dollars? That is one reason for preparation of a financial plan.

Dollars also enable entrepreneurs to communicate more effectively. Investors and creditors understand needs expressed in dollars far better than needs expressed in physical terms. Only when reduced to dollars does an entrepreneur's need for, say, 15,000 square feet of floor space or a 55-foot distillation column make sense.

However, dollars cannot paint a complete picture of a new venture, since some vital parts simply cannot be expressed that way. How can entrepreneurs put a dollar value on their managerial skills, for example? Yet it is these skills that often spell the difference between success or failure.

EXHIBIT 6.6 *Translating Operating Plans into Financial Plans*

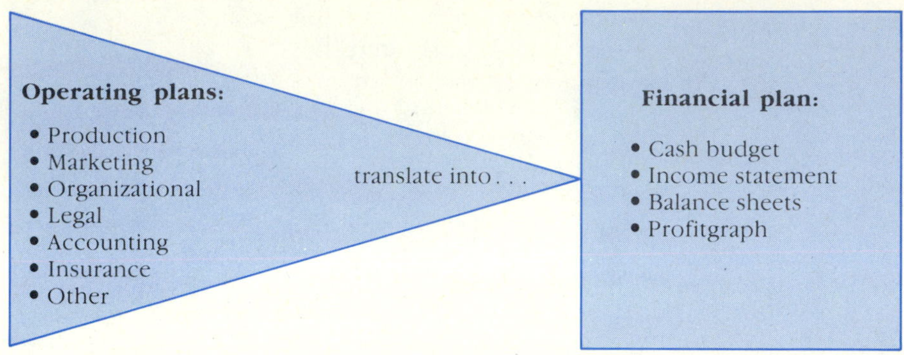

Nor can entrepreneurs put a dollar value on such intangible things as teamwork and morale, knowledge and idea-generating ability.

Entrepreneurs should know the mechanics of preparing a financial plan. It should be made up of these statements:

- A cash budget
- An income statement
- Balance sheets
- A profitgraph (breakeven chart)

The Cash Budget Of these statements, the most important one is the cash budget, because it tells entrepreneurs:

- How much money they need before they open for business
- How much money they need after they open for business

The cash budget helps entrepreneurs make sure the money will be there when bills fall due. It also acts as a signaling device, enabling entrepreneurs to pinpoint future cash shortages and surpluses. A shortage, for example, signals a need to raise more money. Otherwise, marketing and production may have to be cut back to make ends meet.

As a financial tool, the cash budget is indispensable. It not only helps entrepreneurs to spot possible cash-flow problems but also gives investors and creditors precise answers to such questions as these:

- How much money does the entrepreneur need to carry out the business plan?
- When is it needed?
- How will it be spent?
- How soon can it be repaid?

The Balance Sheet and Income Statement Besides the cash budget, entrepreneurs should also prepare two balance sheets and one income statement. Though less important than the cash budget, these statements are vital parts of every business plan. Commercial banks, in particular, appreciate balance sheets because they show:

- The dollar amounts the entrepreneur expects to spend on such assets as inventories, machines, and land
- How the entrepreneur expects to finance these assets

Entrepreneurs should prepare not one but two balance sheets—one projecting the beginning of their first year of business and the other projecting the end of their first year.

They should also prepare an income statement. This statement summarizes both expected sales revenues and expected operating expenses. The difference between revenues and expenses equals profit or loss.

The Profitgraph The last statement to be prepared is the *profitgraph*, commonly called the *breakeven chart*. We prefer the term *profitgraph* because *breakeven* suggests that entrepreneurs expect only to break even. Entrepreneurs naturally expect to do better than that.

The profitgraph shows how sales volume, selling price, and operating expenses affect profits. It also tells entrepreneurs how much product they must sell before they begin to make a profit.

Preparation of a financial plan is anything but easy, and often frustrating to the entrepreneur who lacks financial knowledge. For help, entrepreneurs should turn to their accountant or banker.

These and other financial aspects are covered in greater detail in Chapters Nine and Thirteen; the profitgraph is covered in Chapter Twelve.

Step 14: Writing a Cover Letter

Though not really part of the business plan, the cover letter nonetheless plays a vital role. It is a selling tool, addressed mostly to investors and creditors. In the letter, the entrepreneur summarizes the plan, giving special attention to its purpose and promise.

SUMMARY

As an essential step in getting their venture off the ground, would-be entrepreneurs must prepare a business plan. The business plan enables them to anticipate the opportunities, costs, difficulties, and requirements of deciding to go into business, establishing the business, and operating the business.

In essence, the business plan forces entrepreneurs to build their venture on paper first. It is a vital tool—to entrepreneurs because its preparation forces them to think about what they must do and how to do it; and to creditors and investors because it helps them decide whether to finance the entrepreneur.

To prepare the plan, the entrepreneur must pursue facts unstintingly. The plan will stand or fall on the completeness of the entrepreneur's fact-finding. In particular, the entrepreneur must dig out the facts that bear on production, marketing, organization, and legal aspects.

Help in preparing the business plan may come from accountants, lawyers, bankers, local Chambers of Commerce, and trade associations.

DISCUSSION AND REVIEW QUESTIONS

1. Why should you, a would-be entrepreneur, prepare a business plan?
2. In the business plan, which step is the most critical one? Explain.
3. Why is the cash budget more meaningful than either the income statement or the balance sheet?
4. Define these terms: *planning, business plan, market potential, marketing mix, organizational chart, cash budget, profitgraph.*
5. Why do so few entrepreneurs prepare a business plan?
6. How would you, as an entrepreneur, go about gathering facts to prepare your own business plan?
7. To what situations, other than new ventures, is the business plan applicable? Explain.
8. Why is the entrepreneur's forecast of sales revenues the single most important figure estimate?
9. Why is the business plan as important to creditors and investors as it is to the entrepreneur?
10. Why, in preparing the business plan, must entrepreneurs document all facts, back all assumptions, and give the authority for all opinions?
11. What questions does marketing research help to answer?
12. To prepare your business plan, whose professional help would you seek out? Why?
13. Do you agree that *profitgraph* is a better term than *breakeven chart*? Why?
14. In a business plan, how does the financial plan relate to operating plans?
15. What pitfall must entrepreneurs avoid when choosing a site for their venture? Explain.

NOTES

1. Harold Blancke, quoted in Marvin Bower, *The Will to Manage* (New York: McGraw-Hill, 1966), p. 46.
2. U.S. Small Business Administration, "Business Plan for Small Manufacturers," *Management Aid No. 2007* (Washington, D.C.: U.S. Government Printing Office, 1985), p. 2.
3. Adapted from William R. Osgood, *How to Plan and Finance Your Business* (Boston, Mass.: CBI Publishing Company, 1980), p. 4.
4. Adapted from Sabin Russell, "What Investors Hate Most About Business Plans," *Venture,* June 1984, p. 53.

CASE 6A *Acorn Graphics*

In June 1985, Kenneth Helms completed his studies in entrepreneurship at a local college. His goal was to launch a printing business soon after graduation. Now only 24 years old, Mr. Helms is "sure the bank will approve my loan request for $13,700."

To better prepare himself for such an opportunity, Mr. Helms wrote the following business plan, which began with a cover letter to the loan officer of a commercial bank. A view of Mr. Helms in a printing plant appears in Exhibit 6A.1.

Cover Letter to Bank

Mr. Robert Zawicki, Loan Officer
Commercial Savings & Loan Bank
One Basic Street
Strongsville, OH 44136

Dear Mr. Zawicki:

Attached is my business plan for Acorn Graphics. After reviewing my plan, you will, I am sure, agree that the potential for such a business is good.

To start my venture, I will need a bank loan of $13,700. I am sure you will also agree that my business background and technical knowledge will ensure the success of this venture.

If you have any questions, please do not hesitate to call me. Thank you for your consideration. I look forward to hearing from you shortly.

Sincerely,

Kenneth Helms

Business Plan for Acorn Graphics

Why Should I Be in Business for Myself? My past experience in working for others, plus my education and motivation, convince me that I will be able to own and manage a printing company successfully.

I now work at a medium-sized printing company, and I am involved in nearly all phases of management. I have also been employed at several other small manufacturing firms, where I participated in and studied the various operations, noting which ones are most effective and efficient.

By attending Kent State University's Business College and by majoring in entrepreneurship at Cuyahoga Community College, I have had ample classroom education in the many theories and case studies of being in business for oneself.

I am highly motivated to own and manage a business because it will enable me to make decisions based on my own ideas, experience, and research. Entrepreneurship offers unlimited income and self-esteem. For these reasons, I feel strongly that being in business for myself is my forte.

EXHIBIT 6A.1 *Kenneth Helms in a Printing Shop*

What Is Unique about My Product? From interviews with local printing companies, I have found that none visit customers regularly or pick up and deliver orders. Although one firm will deliver if the job is "large" enough, my potential customers indicate that there is a great need for this service.

If customers can place orders simply by making a telephone call, they can save themselves the annoyance of leaving the office and wasting valuable time. Most customers want quality printing at a fair price with the covenience of being able to see a salesperson at their firm. My business will do just that. I will also offer personalized design, artwork, and typesetting services. No local competitor offers such extensive in-house services. Only one has a typesetting machine on the premises.

Who Are My Customers and Where Are They Located? The majority of my customers will be other businesses and non-profit social clubs. Three major industrial parks in my marketing area will provide 70 percent of my sales. The rest of my sales will come from the many retail and service organizations in the area. I also expect 20 percent of my sales to be walk-in business, such as business cards, wedding invitations, and stationery.

As shown in Exhibit 6A.2, one industrial park is centrally located in my marketing area, while the other two are at opposite corners of the city.

Most of the retail and service businesses are centrally located in the downtown business district.

How Will My Customers Buy? I will be dealing mostly with large businesses, who stress convenience of ordering, quality of printing, and speed of delivery rather than price. My customers will usually order forms, such as invoices, purchase orders, and requisitions in large quantities. Prices will decrease with the size of the order. Generally, customers will

EXHIBIT 6A.2 *Marketing Area for Acorn Graphics*

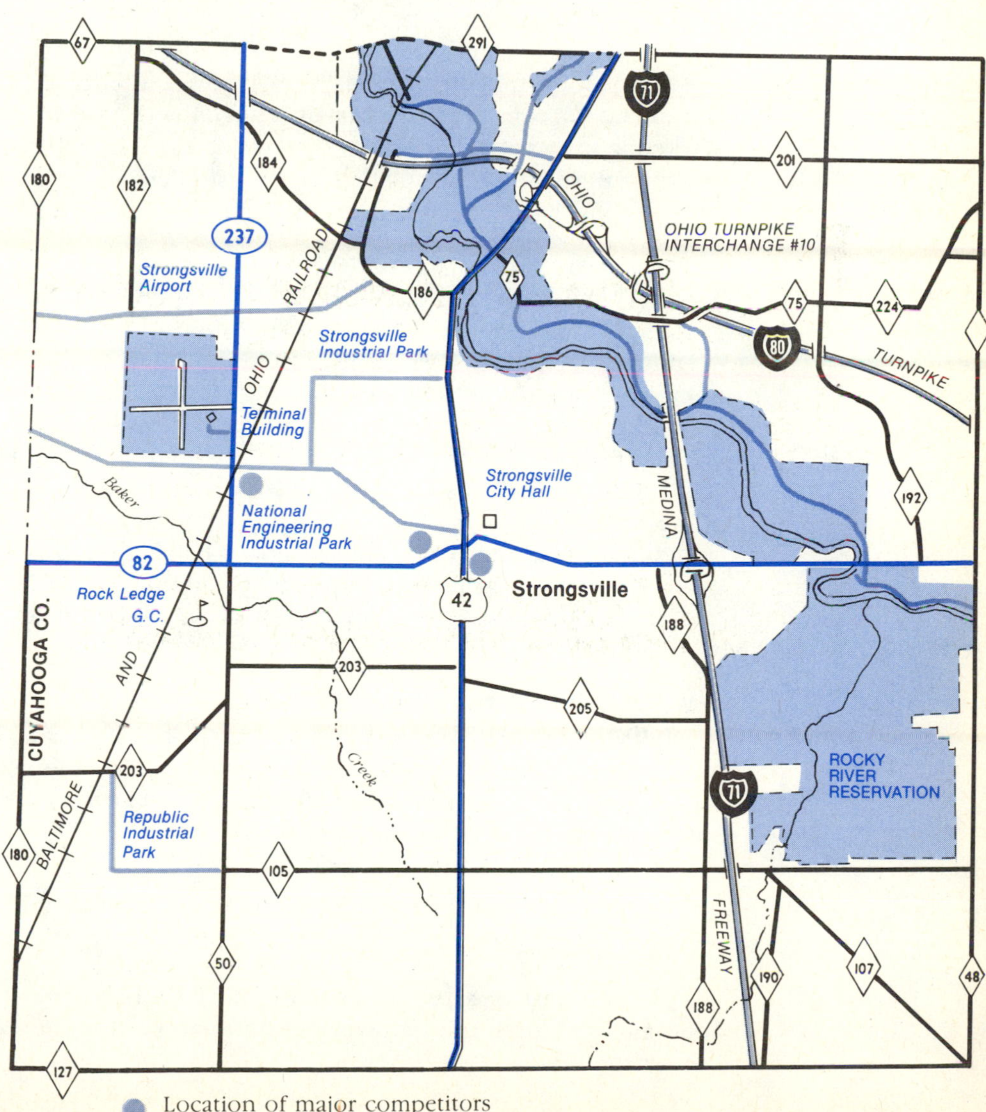

Location of major competitors

order with ample amount of lead time because they know their average usage and can easily predict when best to reorder.

For smaller-quantity items such as business cards, stationery, and fliers, my customers' main objective will be fast delivery. I have talked with potential customers who indicate that they normally purchase forms just once or twice a year, but, because of new employees, they purchase business cards 10 to 20 times a year.

Who Are My Competitors? At present, I have three major competitors located within my marketing area, as shown in Exhibit 6A.2. Two of my major competitors are franchises. After getting many quotes on a variety of printing jobs from them, I have found that I can match or beat their prices easily, even with added costs of pick-up and delivery.

The third competitor has very low prices, but offers few services. I do not intend to compete with his prices, but will instead concentrate on marketing my variety of services—artwork, typesetting, and personalized design—all with pick-up and delivery. Customers who want only inexpensive printing will probably patronize this competitor anyway.

What Is the Market Potential? From information obtained from the Strongsville Chamber of Commerce, I have found that Strongsville is the fastest-growing residential community in the county and the third-fastest in industrial growth. There is an abundance of fully-developed property immediately available in all of the industrial parks. At least two more industrial parks are planned for the area, along with a huge shopping mall and several strip shopping areas. As the community continues to grow, so will the number of my potential customers.

Small-job printing is in its infancy and is still considered to be a booming growth industry. Carl Zellers of PIANO* informed me that the demand for quick printing is expected to double by 1990. Keeping these facts in mind, my firm's growth will be limited only by my personal motivation.

What Is My Share of Market? Based on a survey of competitors by PIANO, the estimated total market potential for 1985 is $325,000 for my marketing area. When I divide this total by the number of printers, including myself, I find that, even if I were just an average performer as an entrepreneur, my share of market would be:

$325,000	=	Total market potential
÷ 4	=	Number of printers including myself
$ 81,250	=	My share of market

My forecast of sales revenues for the first three years of operations appears in Exhibit 6A.3. Note that I plan to outperform my competitors by the second year.

* Printing Industries Association of Northern Ohio

EXHIBIT 6A.3

Acorn Graphics: Three-year Forecast of Sales Revenues

- **1st Year Forecast of Sales Revenues:**

January	$ 2,200
February	3,100
March	3,500
April	4,000
May	4,400
June	4,100
July	3,800
August	3,800
September	5,400
October	5,200
November	5,600
December	4,900
Total	$50,000

- **2nd Year Forecast of Sales Revenues:**

First Quarter	$25,000
Second Quarter	22,000
Third Quarter	18,000
Fourth Quarter	26,000
Total	$91,000

- **3rd Year Forecast of Sales Revenues:**

$110,000

Where Will the Business Be Located? Since the vast majority of my customers will be other businesses, I plan to locate in an industrial park that is central to my marketing area. Such a location will help in pick-up and delivery and afford convenience to my customers.

Rent in a multitenant building in this industrial park is much less expensive than in the retail space available in the area. The savings in rent will more than justify the decrease in low-dollar, walk-in business caused by this choice of location.

The space that I rent must have air conditioning and humidity control. Such controls are essential to produce high-quality printing. Lighting must also be considered carefully in shop selection.

How Big Should My Plant Be? I will need a plant with about 2,000 square feet of area to accommodate my equipment and storage needs, as well as a reception room with a sales counter, and some room for expansion. This amount of floor space should be sufficient until my sixth year of business.

I will design the plant to minimize the handling of materials. As shown in Exhibit 6A.4, my products will flow from process to process with the smallest number of steps possible.

EXHIBIT 6A.4 *Plant Layout of Acorn Graphics*

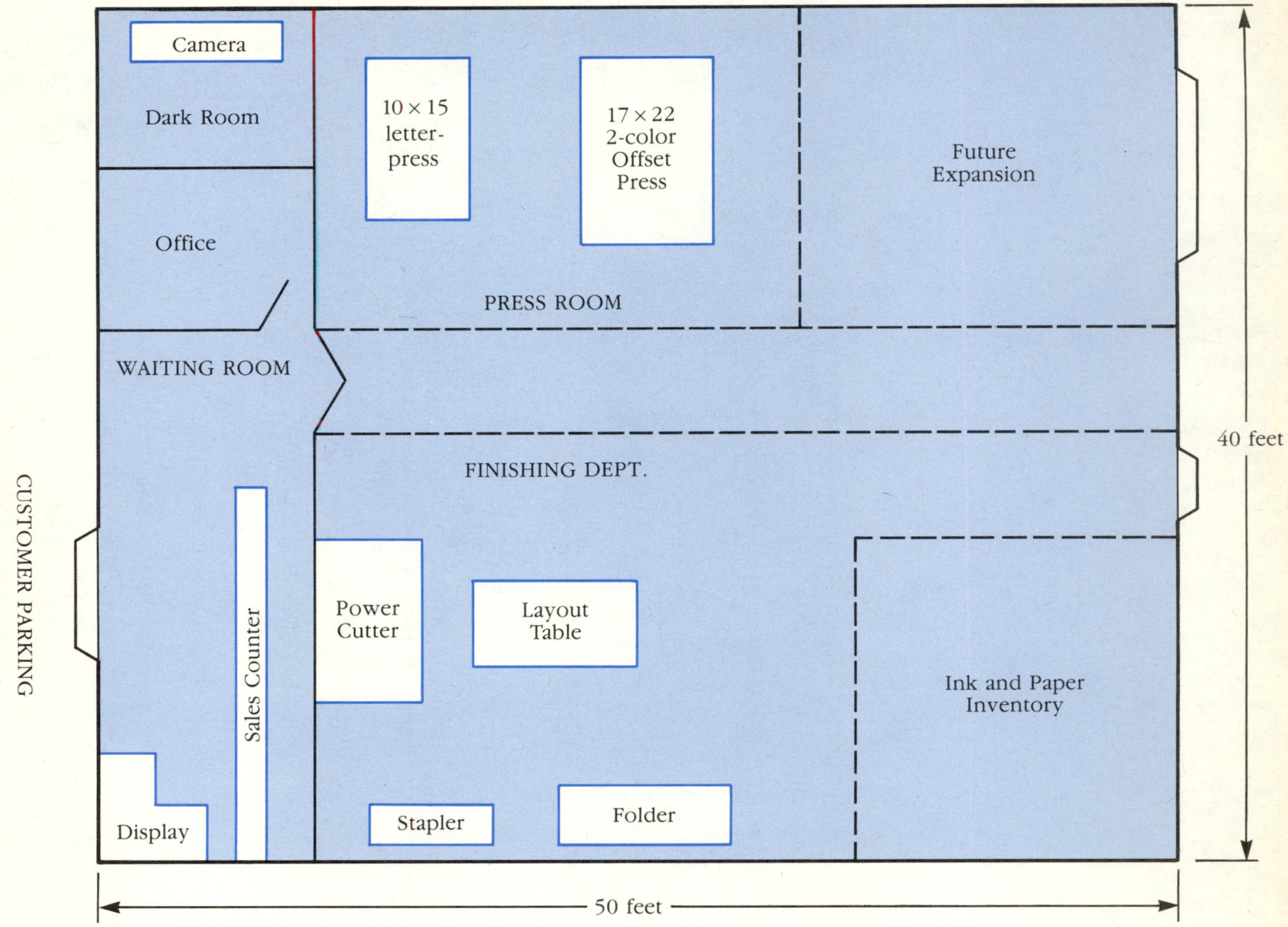

What Equipment Will I Need and What Size? My most important piece of equipment will be a two-color 17-inch by 22-inch offset printing press. Since many jobs call for two colors, I can complete most jobs in one pass with this press, saving valuable time. It is large enough to handle nearly all types of printing. I can buy this press secondhand for $4,500.

I will also need a 10-inch by 15-inch letterpress. This press will be used almost exclusively for numbering, die-cutting, embossing, and perforating. A used letterpress will cost $2,500.

The equipment needed for the bindery and finishing department is as follows:

$1,100	Eighteen-inch power cutter
550	Folder
300	Three-spindle paper drill
200	Power stapler
75	Padding vise
$2,225	Total

During the start-up phase of operation, I will contract out any typesetting that is required, until my volume dictates the purchase of a phototypesetting machine. I have found two reasonably-priced local typesetters. Typesetting can usually be marked up 50 percent on cost.

I will also need a camera and a New-Arc plate maker. The cost of these items would be $2,200. A suitable photomechanical copier, capable of reducing originals, will be rented for $110 a month.

How Will I Create Customers? During the start-up phase of my business, I will visit all manufacturers located in the three industrial parks and other parts of my marketing area. After introducing myself to the person responsible for the printing purchases, I will explain how I will be able to meet their needs, including:

- Pick-up and delivery for all jobs
- Answers to questions about printing, especially questions about business cards and letterheads
- Price quotes over the phone
- Typesetting services
- Top-quality printing
- Rush services if needed

A generous discount of 15 percent would be given on initial orders.

After visiting the manufacturers, I would enlarge my customer base by visiting all retailers in my marketing area, apprising them of my printing services and offering them the same discount. Weekly advertisements, five inches by five inches, listing my services, and occasional specials, will be run in the local newspaper.

EXHIBIT 6A.5 *Monthly Cash Flow Projection*

NAME OF BUSINESS			ADDRESS					OWNER				
Acorn Graphics			Strongsville					KENNETH HEIMS				
	Pre-Start-up Position		1		2		3		4		5	
YEAR SALES MONTH			2000		3100		3500		4000		4400	
	Estimate	Actual	Estimate	Actual	Estimate	Actual	Estimate	Actual	Estimate	Actual	Estimate	Actual
1. CASH ON HAND (Beginning of month)	10,000		10,000		1455		20		155		450	
2. CASH RECEIPTS (a) Cash Sales			400		620		700		800		880	
(b) Collections from Credit Accounts					1600		2480		2800		3200	
(c) Loan or Other Cash injection (Specify)												
3. TOTAL CASH RECEIPTS (2a+2b+2c=3)			400		2220		3480		3600		4080	
4. TOTAL CASH AVAILABLE (Before cash out) (1+3)	19000		14400		3675		3500		3655		4530	
5. CASH PAID OUT (a) Purchases (Merchandise)			2,000		350		400		420		440	
(b) Gross Wages (Excludes withdrawals)			200		250		275		275		275	
(c) Payroll Expenses (Taxes, etc.)			80		85		85		85		85	
(d) Outside Services			150		20		0		50		100	
(e) Supplies (Office and operating)			375		40		25		10		15	
(f) Repairs ard Maintenance			80		20		50		50		50	
(g) Advertising			1000		700		400		100		100	
(h) Car, Delivery, and Travel			300		200		200		200		200	
(i) Accounting and Legal			450									
(j) Rent			600		600		600		600		600	
(k) Telephone			40		40		40		40		40	
(l) Utilities			380		300		300		300		300	
(m) Insurance			240									
(n) Taxes (Real estate, etc.)			80									
(o) Interest			100		100		120		125		125	
(p) Other Expenses (Specify each)												
(q) Miscellaneous (Unspecified)			50		50		50		50		50	
(r) Subtotal			6015		2755		2545		2305		2380	
(s) Loan Principal Payment			650		650		650		650		650	
(t) Capital Purchases (Specify)			1500									
(u) Other Start-up Costs			500									
(v) Reserve and/or Excrow (Specify)												
(w) Owner's Withdrawal			250		250		250		250		250	
6. TOTAL CASH PAID OUT (Total 5a thru 5w)			8945		3655		3445		3205		3280	
7. CASH POSITION (End of month) (4 minus 6)			1455		20		55		450		1250	
ESSENTIAL OPERATING DATA (Non-cash flow information) A. Sales Volume (Dollars)			2000		3100		3500		4000		4400	
B. Accounts Receivable (End of month)			1600		2480		2800		3200		3520	
C. Bad Debt (End of month)			40		62		70		80		88	
D. Inventory on Hand (End of month)			1000		800		800		800		700	
E. Accounts Payable (End of month)			1000		500		400		500		400	
F. Depreciation			100		100		100		100		100	

SBA FORM 1100 (8-75) REF: SOP 60 10 1

TYPE OF BUSINESS	PREPARED BY	DATE
PRINTING	KENNETH HELMS	JUNE 1983

6		7		8		9		10		11		12		TOTAL		
4100		3800		3800		5400		5200		5800		4900		Columns 1–12		
Estimate	Actual	Estimate	Actual	Estimate	Actual	Estimate	Actual	Estimate	Actual	Estimate	Actual	Estimate	Actual	Estimate	Actual	
1250		2280		1155		1415		1570		2040		2425				1.
820		760		760		1080		1040		1160		980		10,000		2. (a)
3520		3280		3040		3040		4320		4160		4640		36,080		(b)
														300		(c)
4340		4040		3800		4120		5360		5320		5620		46,380		3.
5590		6320		4955		5535		6930		7360		8045				4.
460		1500		500		800		1000		1200		1100		10,170		5. (a)
275		250		250		325		320		375		350		3,420		(b)
85		80		80		100		100		120		110		1,095		(c)
100		80		120		150		180		250		200		1,400		(d)
25		220		25		25		25		25		25		835		(e)
50		50		50		50		200		100		100		850		(f)
100		200		200		200		200		400		200		3,800		(g)
200		200		200		200		200		200		600		2700		(h)
		150												600		(i)
600		600		600		600		600		600		600		7200		(j)
40		40		40		40		40		40		40		480		(k)
300		300		300		300		300		300		300		3600		(l)
		240												480		(m)
		80												160		(n)
125		125		125		125		125		125		125		1445		(o)
																(p)
50		50		50		50		100		100		100		750		(q)
2410		4165		2540		2965		3390		3885		3850		38,995		(r)
650		650		650		650		650		650		650		7,800		(s)
								500						2,000		(t)
																(u)
																(v)
250		350		350		350		350		400		400		3,700		(w)
3310		5165		3540		3965		4890		4935		4900		53,135		6.
2280		1155		1415		1570		2040		2425		3145				7.
4100		3800		3800		5400		5200		5800		4900		50,000		A.
3280		3040		3040		4320		4160		4640		3920				B.
82		76		76		108		104		116		98		1000		C.
500		900		700		700		700		600		500				D.
450		500		900		600		700		1100		1300				E.
100		100		100		100		100		100		100		1200		F.

What Personnel Will I Need? I will operate the shop alone until growth dictates the need for additional help. Then I plan to hire a college student majoring in graphic arts, perhaps through a cooperative program, whose wages would be $6.00 an hour.

How Will I Organize My Venture? I will organize my venture as a sole proprietorship, since sole proprietorships are easy to initiate. I also believe that the benefits of a sole proprietorship will outweigh those of the other legal forms of organization. Since the business will be run solely by me, I can save money initially by not incorporating. I will also be able to deduct any start-up losses from my personal income tax. Being organized as a sole proprietor will free me from such problems as taxes and government forms, and my energies can instead be channeled into improving the venture.

As my business progresses, I will eventually incorporate so I can:

- Sell the business if I desire
- Raise additional funds for expansion
- Limit my personal liability

What Kinds of Records Will I Need? After consulting a certified public accountant, I will do all the bookkeeping myself. However, I will hire the accountant to look at my books quarterly and give me advice. The financial records I will keep include:

- Sales records
- Cash receipts
- Cash disbursements (payables)
- Accounts receivable

My records will provide the information I will need to make sound decisions on the firm's financial position. The records will be simple to use and easy to understand, and I will enter information into them each night in order to keep them accurate, reliable, and consistent. I will need certain forms to operate the business, such as:

- Job tickets, explaining what each job includes. These tickets will also serve as invoices.
- Purchase orders
- Price quotation forms

How Much Cash Will I Need to Operate the Business? See Exhibit 6A.5 (pp. 178–179) for a monthly cash flow projection for the first year of operations.

EXHIBIT 6A.6

Projected Income Statement for First-year Operations

Sales revenues	$50,000
Cost of goods sold	38,000
Gross profit	$12,000
Operating expenses	11,500
Operating profit	$ 500

How Profitable Will I Be? See Exhibit 6A.6 for my projected income statement the first year. Note that I expect to earn an operating profit of $500 on sales revenues of $50,000.

How Financially Healthy Will I Be? See Exhibit 6A.7 for my projected balance sheet for the date that I first open my business. Note that the bank and I will be near-equal partners.

What is My Breakeven Point? See Exhibit 6A.8 for a profitgraph that traces the profitability of my business at different sales volumes. Note that I will begin to make a profit the moment I land more than 60 customers a month. This breakeven volume assumes the average customer order is $80.

Questions

1. Would you advise Mr. Helms to get additional information before launching his venture? What information?
2. Is Mr. Helms likely to succeed as an entrepreneur? Why?
3. Evaluate Mr. Helms's business plan as a tool to raise money? Is it thorough and complete? What suggestions would you make to improve it?
4. What are the key factors for success in this kind of business?
5. If you were the bank's loan officer, would you recommend lending Mr. Helms the $13,700 he seeks to launch his venture? Why?

EXHIBIT 6A.7

Projected Beginning Balance Sheet

Assets			**Equities**	
Current Assets			Liabilities	
Cash	$ 8,000		Bank loan	$13,700
Inventory	2,000	$10,000		
			Owner's equity	
Fixed assets			Kenneth Helms	10,000
Equipment	$11,500			
Other	2,200	13,700		
Total assets		$23,700	Total equities	$23,700

[EXH]IBIT 6A.8 *Profitgraph for Acorn Graphics*

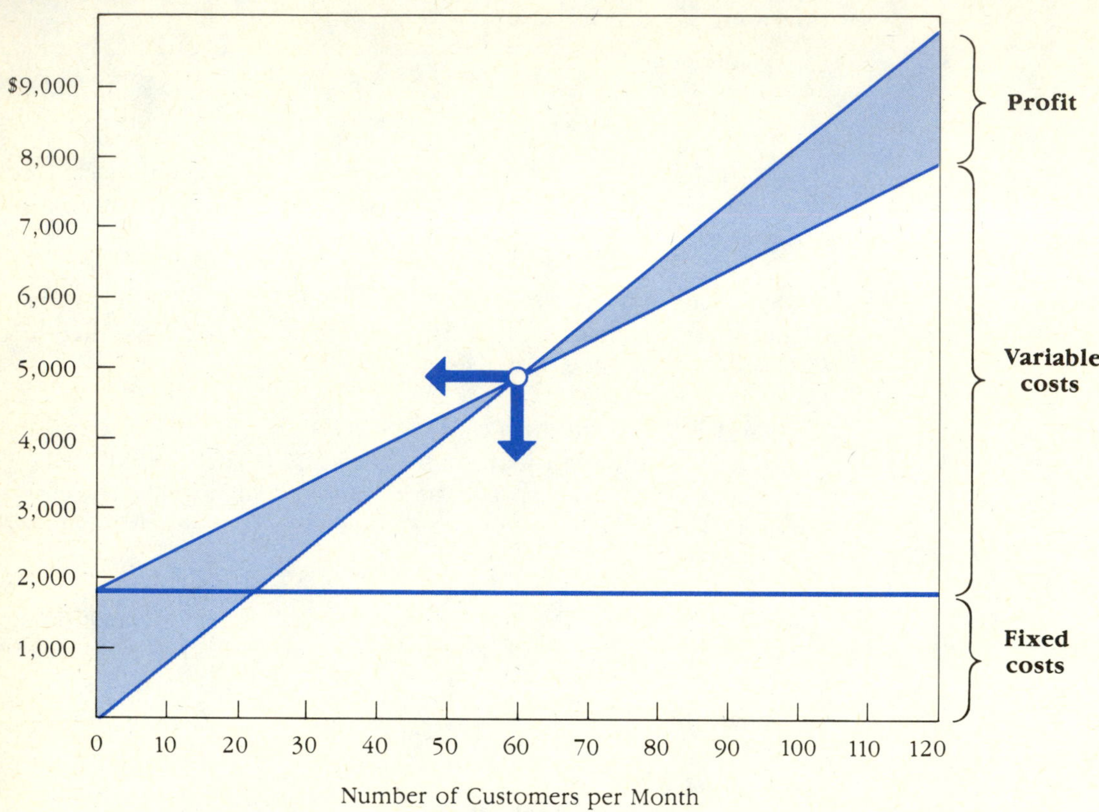

Assumptions:

- Average customer order—$80
- Monthly fixed costs—$1,800
- Variable costs per dollar of sales—$0.60

CASE 6B *Urban League Client*

The Urban League of a large southern city has a small business development center. Its purpose is to "boost the formation of new ventures among minorities." One of its business counselors, Marcia Simms, has prepared a business plan for a client who wants to expand his used-car dealership. He is seeking a $15,000 loan from the SBA, which referred him to the Urban League for help in preparing a business plan. Following are excerpts covering most of the plan as prepared for him by Ms. Simms and then submitted to the SBA.

Description of industry: Over the years, prices in the auto industry have skyrocketed to such heights that the big auto manufacturers have almost priced themselves out of the market. Despite the high prices, the public is still in the market for cars, but not so much for new cars as for reliable used cars.

In 1980, used-car dealers sold 18 million cars, which amounts to two thirds of all cars sold that year. Moreover, the increase in used-car prices was only half of the 11 percent increase in new-car prices.

The market for used cars has been a strong and growing one for the past decade, and will continue to grow.

Description of existing venture: Curtis Holmes has been in the used-car business for 20 years. He started his own business operating as Holmes's Used Car Sales in 1960. He was the first black man in the city to receive a license to sell used cars. He also maintains an auto body shop on the lot.

Competitive advantage: Used-car sales are up considerably compared to new-car sales. Prices are also up, but not so much as to hamper any possible sales. Besides selling used cars, Mr. Holmes offers such services as customizing of cars, spray painting, and revitalization of stripped-out cars for resale.

Marketing plan: Within Mr. Holmes's trading area, very little marketing will be necessary to expand used-car sales. Advertising spots on both radio and television will be his main marketing tools.

Method of distribution: Mr. Holmes sells used cars from his lot, which he owns outright. He obtains his supply of cars mainly from auto auctions held in the county once a month.

Financial information: See Exhibit 6B.1.

EXHIBIT 6B.1

Holmes's Used Car Sales: Yearly Estimates (Condensed)

Sales revenues	$150,000
Cost of sales	115,650
Gross profit	$ 34,350
Operating expenses*	20,200
Operating profit	$ 14,150

* Excludes salary for Mr. Holmes

Question On the strength of this business plan, should the SBA lend Mr. Holmes the $15,000 he seeks? Why?

CASE 6C *Decor, Incorporated*

Theodora Minelli has created a product she calls the *Old Mill*. To make and market the mill, Mrs. Minelli has formed Decor, Incorporated.

What is the Old Mill? It is a decorative centerpiece—a lighted log cabin cradled in a shallow bowl against a floral background, with water splashing softly over a motor-driven water wheel.

Mrs. Minelli believes "its rustic charm will appeal strongly to homemakers who wish to enhance the look of their living rooms." She plans to sell the mill to large discount chains at a price of $30.00 each.

Materials will cost $14.00 per mill. Overhead will run about $4,000 a month. Mrs. Minelli believes her overhead will not change over the short run, regardless of volume of production.

Question How many mills must Mrs. Minelli sell each month before she begins to make a profit?

7 LEGAL ASPECTS

QUESTIONS FOR MASTERY

How complex are the legal issues facing all small businesses?

How do you find the right lawyer?

What are the differences among sole proprietorships, partnerships, and corporations?

How do government regulations affect small businesses?

How important is it to keep up with the law?

The law is a jealous mistress.

George Sharswood

We often pride ourselves on being a nation governed by laws. So much so, that today it is all but impossible to move in many walks of life without first consulting a lawyer. Undertaking a new business venture is no exception. This chapter deals with the would-be entrepreneur's need for legal help, focusing on choosing a lawyer, deciding upon a legal form of organization, and coping with government regulations.

THE NEED FOR LEGAL ADVICE

To avoid breaking the law and to spot opportunities permitted by law, entrepreneurs need expert legal help. One of the entrepreneur's earliest acts should be to get a lawyer. Only a lawyer can help resolve the maze of legal issues raised in Exhibit 7.1, which range from questions on incorporation to questions on the rights of consumers. Entrepreneurs need not necessarily consider all of the questions listed in Exhibit 7.1. The complexity of the entrepreneur's venture determines which questions must be dealt with.

Example: An entrepreneur launching a 20-employee, million-dollar plant to make hazardous chemicals would most likely be concerned with all of the questions listed. An entrepreneur launching a part-time consulting practice working out of her own home, with herself as the sole employee, would likely be concerned with few of the questions.

Often, entrepreneurs feel they need a lawyer only when they are sued or when they sue others. This attitude is indefensible. Lawyers are by no means merely actors in tense courtroom dramas; in fact, many lawyers never set foot in a courtroom. Their more creative role is to advise entrepreneurs in such a way that it need never be necessary to go to court.

The best remedy for legal mistakes is to keep from making them. Perhaps the most apt way to describe the lawyer's role is as a kind of preventive medicine.

Choosing the Right Lawyer

Entrepreneurs should get the right lawyer months before they plan to launch their venture, and they should choose one with the same care as they would a brain surgeon. A common mistake is to select someone recommended by friends, neighbors, or relatives whose needs for legal help may differ sharply from those of the entrepreneur. These personal lawyers may not know much about new ventures, although they may be quite knowledgeable about other aspects of the law. To find the right lawyer, entrepreneurs should instead follow these guidelines:

- Seek out lawyers who are held in high esteem by the business community. The best sources of names are usually other entrepreneurs who are both seasoned and successful. As such, they are most likely to offer honest opinions about the skills of the lawyers who helped them get started.

EXHIBIT 7.1 *Selected Legal Questions*

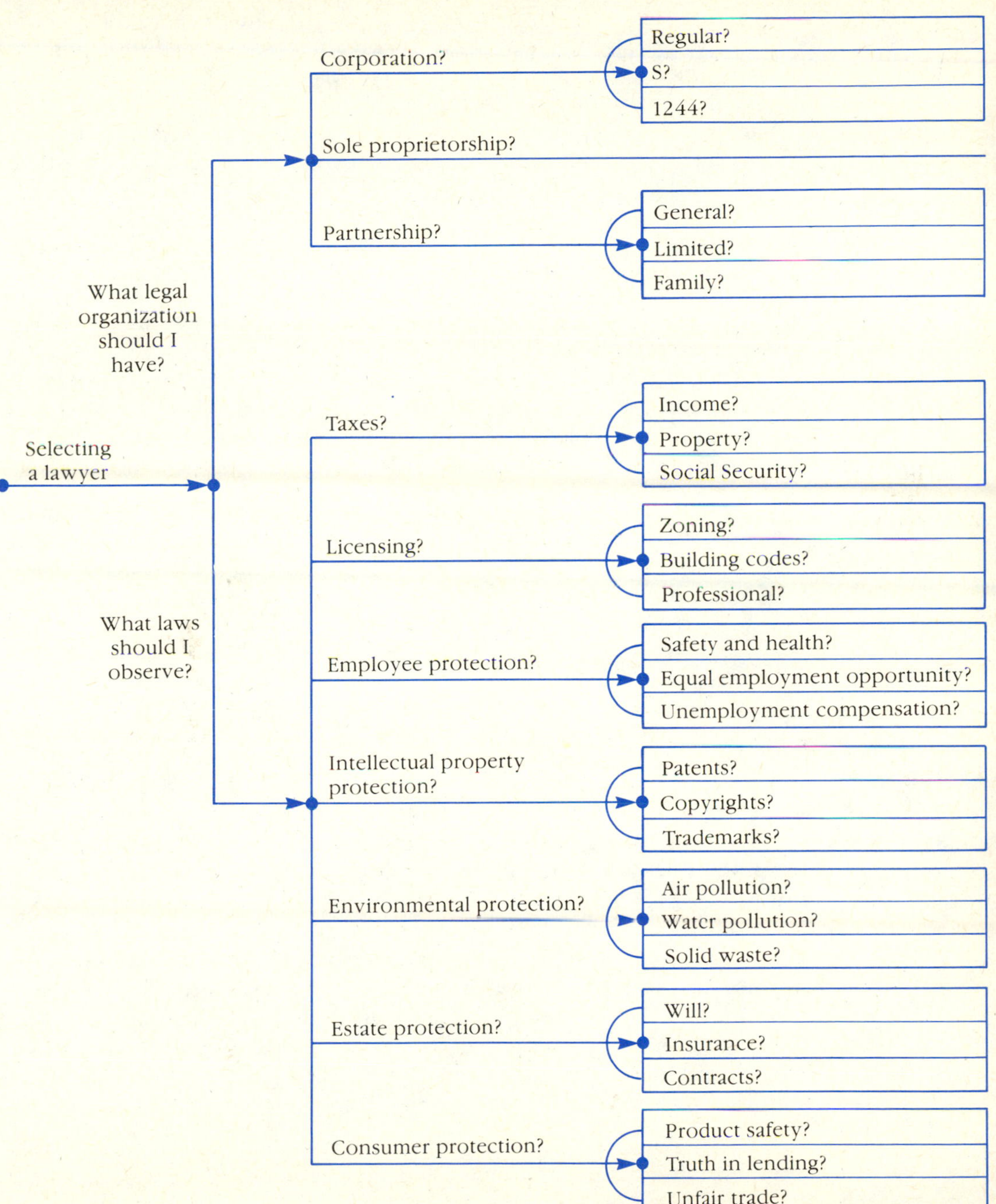

Other good sources are the loan officers of commercial banks. They generally know firsthand which lawyers are good at helping entrepreneurs get started. Professors of law are another good source.

- Check the backgrounds of lawyers who are recommended to you in the *Martindale and Hubbell Directory*. This directory is updated yearly by the American Bar Association.
- Narrow the list of names to those whose law firms are small. Such firms are likely to be more accessible, more personal, and less expensive than large firms.
- Choose the right lawyer. In making a choice, the entrepreneur should be sure that the lawyer's expert knowledge is accompanied by a reasonable match in personal chemistry. Do the parties get along?[1]

Once they choose the right lawyer, entrepreneurs are mistaken if they leave all the decisions to their lawyer. The main job of the lawyer should be to advise and to inform the entrepreneur. Only the entrepreneur should make the legal decisions, based on information provided by the lawyer. To do that wisely, the entrepreneur should become familiar with the law. As Dr. Patrick R. Liles, formerly of the Harvard Business School, suggests:

> A major difficulty for the inexperienced entrepreneur is the host of strange terms and phrases which are scattered throughout most legal documents. The novice in this kind of reading should have some understanding not only of *what* is contained in such documents, but also *why* these provisions have been included.
>
> If an entrepreneur cannot find the time or take the interest to read and understand the major contracts into which his company will enter, he should be very cautious about being an entrepreneur at all.[2]

Understanding the Legalities of Franchising and Buy-outs

The need for finding the right lawyer is just as pressing for entrepreneurs who prefer to buy a franchise or buy out an existing venture as for those who start from scratch. In fact, the need often is more pressing in franchises or buy-outs because many of the legal aspects have already been reduced to writing.

Franchise agreements often run into dozens of pages. Franchisees have little choice but to observe the franchisor's fine print. First, however, they need the help of a lawyer to translate the "strange terms and phrases" mentioned by Dr. Liles and discussed more fully in Chapter Five.

Buying out an existing venture calls for an exhaustive audit of the seller's legal documents, including deeds, sales contracts, employment contracts, purchase contracts, and the like. For example:

> Before buying a business, entrepreneurs should determine who is responsible for existing claims. They can be inherited by innocent new owners. *Case*: A company was sold while a discrimination claim was pending. *Court*: The new owners were liable for the old claim. *Reason*:

The new owners continued similar business operations, and they knew about the claim before they bought the business.[3]

Legal services are expensive, although some relief is on the way. Innovations of all kinds are now sweeping the practice of law—from prepaid legal services aimed at cutting costs to computerization of legal procedures—but it will be some time before they are practiced widely.

LEGAL FORMS OF ORGANIZATION

Choosing a legal form of organization—be it a sole proprietorship, partnership, or corporation—ranks among the entrepreneur's most vital decisions. This choice affects a number of managerial and financial issues, including the amount of taxes the entrepreneur may pay, whether the entrepreneur personally may be sued for unpaid business bills, and whether the venture dies automatically when the entrepreneur dies.

Entrepreneurs often ask, "Is there one best form of organization?" The answer is no. The best form of organization depends on the entrepreneur's likes and dislikes, the venture's needs, and the entrepreneur's tax bracket. In the words of the SBA:

> No one legal form of organization, or for that matter no combination of two or more of them, is suited to each and every small business. To try to say what is the best form for all enterprises would be like trying to select an all-purpose suit for a man.
>
> In choosing a legal form of organization, consideration to the parties concerned must be made—their likes, dislikes and dispositions, their immediate and long-range needs and their tax situations. Seldom, if ever, does any one factor completely determine which is best.[4]

Let us now look at each of the major legal forms of organization from the viewpoint of the entrepreneur. For each one, we shall focus on the advantages as well as the disadvantages.

Sole Proprietorships

Sole proprietorships are the most popular legal form of organization, accounting for 76 percent of all businesses. Because most of them are small, often employing only the entrepreneur, lay persons tend to equate small business with sole proprietorships only. However, a sole proprietorship may be as large as a million-dollar foundry or as small as a corner newsstand. Discussed below and summarized in Exhibit 7.2 are the advantages and disadvantages of sole proprietorships.

Advantages Freedom is the most striking feature of a sole proprietorship. Because they own all of a venture, sole proprietors answer to no one but themselves. They alone may reap the rewards of a successful venture or, conversely, the bitter fruit of failure.

EXHIBIT 7.2 *Sole Proprietorships: Selected Advantages and Disadvantages*

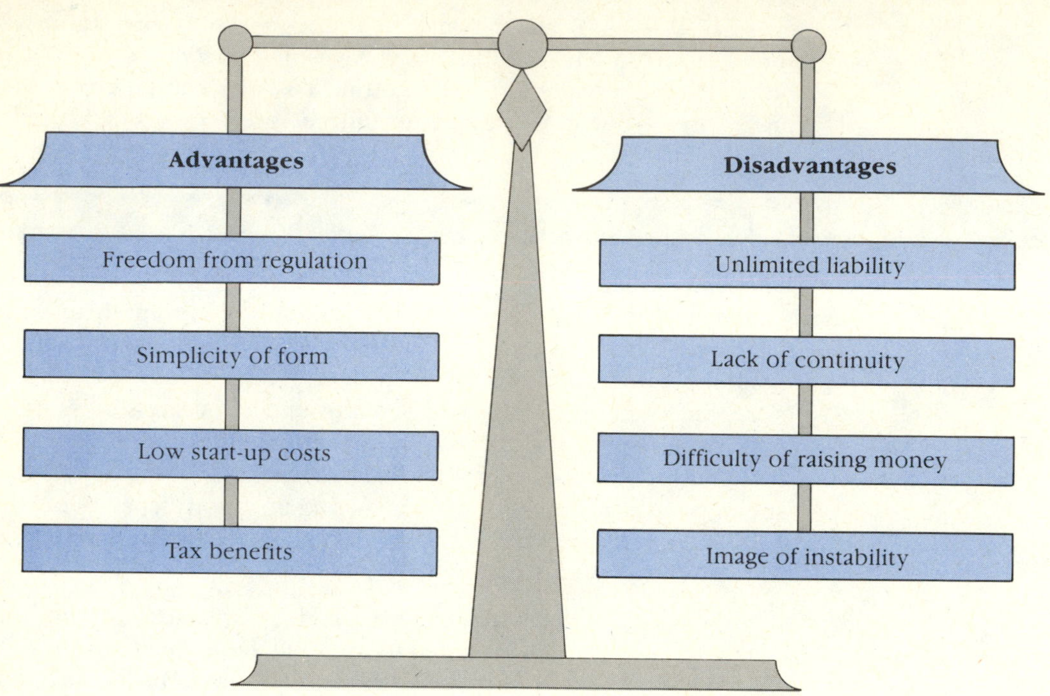

Another feature of the sole proprietorship is its simplicity. A sole proprietorship is easy to form. Often, entrepreneurs need only nail a shingle on the door telling the world they are in business for themselves. No law forces them to register with a governmental body. The lack of complex procedures is why this legal form of organization appeals so strongly to the do-it-yourself, independent-minded entrepreneur.

The sole proprietorship also offers tax benefits for new ventures likely to suffer losses before profits begin to flow. Tax laws permit sole proprietors to treat the revenues and expenses of their venture as part of their personal finances. They can cut taxes by deducting any operating losses from personal income acquired from other sources.

Still another attractive feature of the sole proprietorship is its low start-up cost. Legal fees are likely to be low, mostly because the entrepreneur is spared the high expense of incorporating. But if a venture is to be called a name other than his or her own, the entrepreneur must seek legal help to make sure the name is not already being used by another business in the same state.

Disadvantages The main drawbacks of the sole proprietorship are unlimited liability, lack of continuity, and the difficulty of raising money.

Unlimited liability: Entrepreneurs are personally liable for all debts incurred by their venture. Thus, they must pay bills out of their own pocket if their venture fails to generate enough cash flow. Creditors may step in and claim the entrepreneur's savings, house, or personal possessions. Unlimited liability is perhaps the most distasteful feature of a sole proprietorship.

Lack of continuity: Legally, a venture dies when the sole proprietor dies. It can, of course, be reorganized soon after the proprietor's death, if a successor has been trained to take over. But often, executors or heirs must liquidate because there is no one who can run the venture.

Difficulty of raising money: Sole proprietors generally find it hard to raise money not only to start up but also to expand. Commercial bankers, for example, tend to reject proprietors who are the sole strength of their venture. Bankers fear they may not be able to recover their loan if the proprietor becomes disabled.

General Partnerships

As defined by the Uniform Partnership Act, a partnership is a "voluntary association of two or more persons to carry on as co-owners a business for profit." A general partnership is really a sole proprietorship multiplied by the number of partners. It is the least popular form of organization, accounting for only 8 percent of all businesses. The most striking feature of the general partnership is its ability to grow by adding talent and money. That way, the partnership avoids one of the most serious drawbacks of a sole proprietorship—the dependence of the success of the venture on the resources of only one person. Discussed below and summarized in Exhibit 7.3 are the advantages and disadvantages of general partnerships.

Advantages

There is no legal limit to the number of partners in a venture—there may be as many as 100 or more, or as few as 2. Partners may invest equal or unequal sums of money, and they may earn profits that bear no relation to their investment. For example, in a two-person partnership, a partner with no investment may get 50 percent or more of the profits.

Like a sole proprietorship, a partnership is generally easy to organize, with few legal requirements. Even so, all partnerships begin with an agreement of some kind. It may be written, spoken, or even unspoken, but the wise entrepreneur insists on a written agreement to avoid trouble later. This agreement should spell out such things as these:

- Who invested what sums of money in the partnership
- Who gets what share of the partnership profits
- Who does what and who reports to whom
- How the partnership may be dissolved, and in that event, how assets left over would be distributed among partners
- How surviving partners would be protected from the decedent's estate

EXHIBIT 7.3 *General Partnerships: Selected Advantages and Disadvantages*

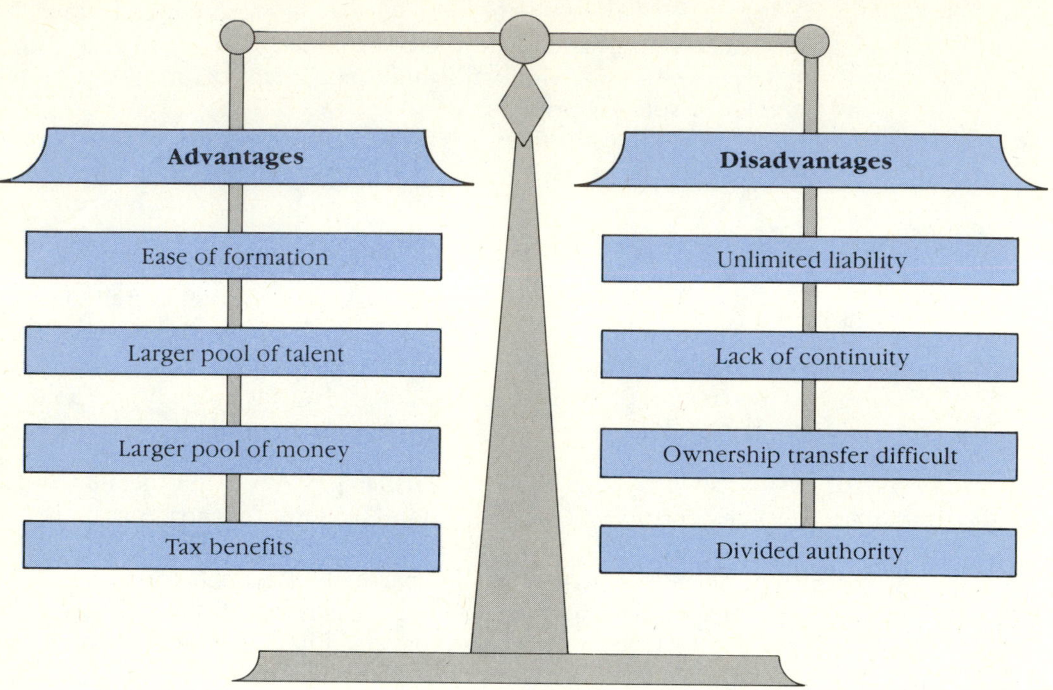

A partnership agreement is a private document. The law does not require the entrepreneur to file the agreement with a government agency, nor does it regard a partnership as a legal entity. In the eyes of the law, a partnership is simply two or more persons working together. The partnership's lack of legal standing means that the U.S. Internal Revenue Service taxes partners as individuals. This feature often attracts wealthy investors seeking a tax shelter. We will say more about tax shelters in Chapter Eighteen.

The advantages of a partnership, then, are ease of formation, a broad pool of talent, multiple sources of money, and possible tax advantages. However, there are some drawbacks to the partnership form of organization.

Disadvantages Unlimited liability is the worst drawback of a partnership. By law, each partner may be held liable for debts incurred in the name of the partnership. And if any partner incurs a debt unbeknownst to the other partners, they are all liable if the offending partner cannot pay the debt. This legal wrinkle holds even if the partnership agreement calls for all notes and bills to be endorsed by the other partners.

Example: Sidney Jordan and Robert Barron established a house-painting partnership called Bright Spot. Unwisely, they used a sprayer on a windy day and spattered dark red paint on ten automobiles parked in a lot next to the building they were painting. Mr. Jordan and Mr. Barron had to pay for the ten automobiles to be repainted. Several were expensive automobiles needing fancy paint jobs, so the bill totaled nearly $5,000.

After this disaster, Mr. Barron left town and Bright Spot went broke. Mr. Jordan was liable to pay the whole $5,000 from his own personal funds.[5]

Another drawback is lack of continuity. When one partner dies or pulls out, a partnership legally dies also even if the other partners agree to stay on. A related drawback is the difficulty of transferring ownership. Because the law regards a partnership as a sibling relationship, no partners may sell out without the consent of the other partners. A partner wishing to retire or to transfer his or her interest to a son or daughter must get the consent of the others.

The life of a partnership often depends on the ability of retiring partners to find someone compatible with the other partners to buy them out. Or the other partners may buy out a retiring partner. Failure to do so may lead to forced liquidation of the partnership. Surviving partners may also be faced with liquidation when a partner dies.

The liquidation of a partnership, however, need not cause a loss of revenues. If they wish, the surviving partners may quickly form a new partnership to retain the business of the old partnership.

Other Forms of Partnership

The entrepreneur may avoid the problem of unlimited liability by forming a limited partnership. In such an arrangement, limited partners may not take an active role in the operations of the venture, but they may invest their money without being held liable for debts made by active partners. If the business goes under, limited partners are liable only to the extent of their investment.

More complex than general partnerships, limited partnerships require legal help to organize. All partners, for example, must register in each state in which the partnership plans to do business. Limited partners must make sure they are never active in the day-to-day routine of the business. Otherwise, they risk losing their preferred status as limited partners.

Two other forms of organization have evolved to offset the defects of the general partnership. One is the *family partnership*, which enables partners to split income among members of their families to avoid high taxes. Another is the *real estate investment trust* (REIT). Managed by a trustee, REITs enjoy both continuity of life and ease of ownership transfer.

Regular Corporations

As shown in Exhibit 7.4, corporations dominate the business world. They account for 88 percent of all revenues generated by the nation's businesses, yet they make up only 16 percent of the total number of businesses.

EXHIBIT 7.4 *Relative Importance of Legal Forms of Organization*

Most businesses form sole proprietorships, but corporations account for most of the revenues.

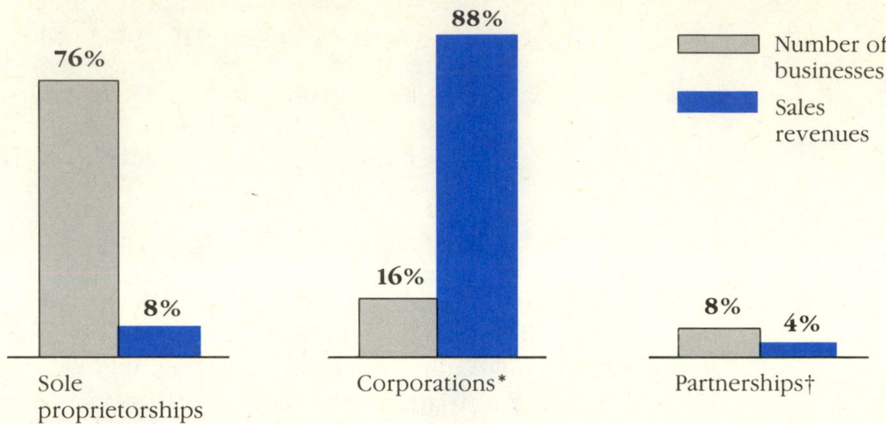

* Includes regular, S, and other corporate forms.
† Includes general, limited, and other partnership forms.
Source: U.S. Department of Commerce. *Data Book, U.S.A.* (Washington, D.C.: U.S. Government Printing Office, 1984), p. 532.

To the lay person, the corporation is the legal form of organization used only by big business. The very word *corporation* inspires awe and respect, bespeaks bigness and power. But the tiny corner newsstand has as much right to incorporate as a giant steel mill. And, it matters not whether a venture has thousands of shareholders or just one. In short, the corporation is a versatile legal tool capable of serving the entire spectrum of business.

In the words of Chief Justice of the U.S. Supreme Court, John Marshall, a corporation is "an artificial being, invisible, intangible, and existing only in contemplation of the law."[6] By these words, the Supreme Court defined the corporation as a legal person. A corporation can therefore:

- Sue and be sued
- Buy, hold, and sell property
- Make and sell products to consumers
- Commit crimes and be tried and punished for them

Discussed below and summarized in Exhibit 7.5 are the advantages and disadvantages of the regular corporation. The S-corporation and the 1244 corporation will also be discussed.

Advantages Limited liability is the most striking feature of a corporation. It limits investors' liability to their personal investments in the corporation. In the event of failure, the bankruptcy courts may seize a corporation's assets and sell them to pay debts, but the courts cannot touch the personal possessions of shareholders.

EXHIBIT 7.5 *Regular Corporations: Selected Advantages and Disadvantages*

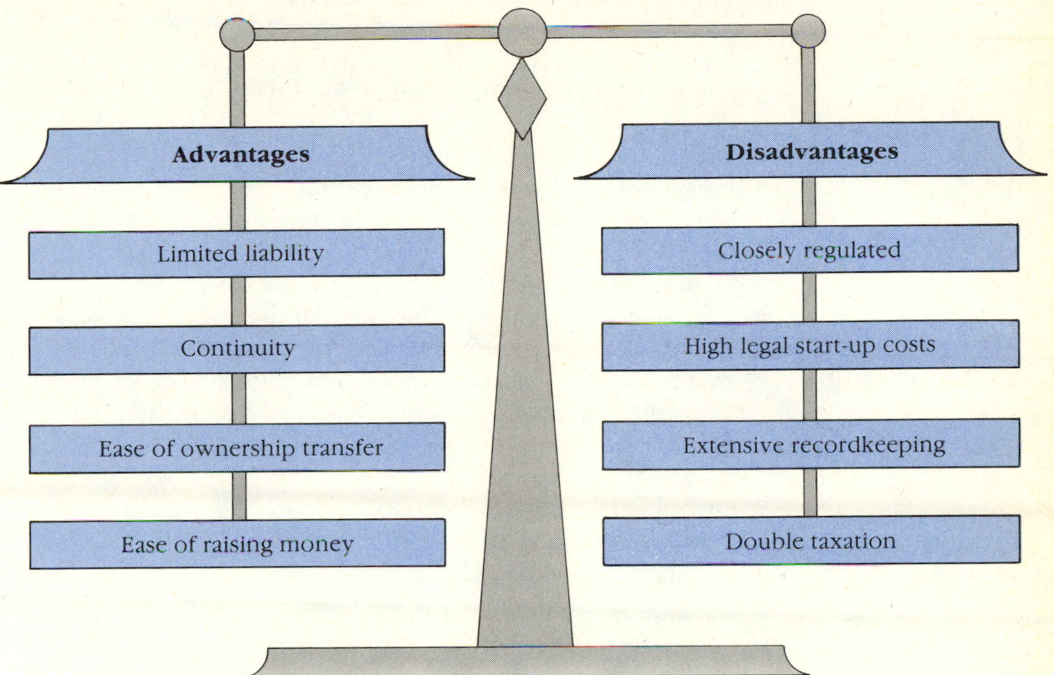

Limited liability is perhaps the major reason why lawyers often recommend the corporate form of organization. However, entrepreneurs should remember that limited liability may be meaningless in some cases. For example, if all of one's personal assets are tied up in a venture, then limited liability would offer little protection. Entrepreneurs should also remember that, no matter what legal form of organization they use, some of their personal possessions will be protected by law.

Another striking feature of the corporation is its continuity. Its life is independent of the lives of those who founded it. In other words, if the corporation prospers, it may outlive its founders. This feature stems from the fact that a corporation is a legal person. As the state's creation, it is independent of the lives of its founders and can go on forever, at least in theory.

Major Kinds of Stock A related feature is ease of ownership transfer, which takes place through the sale of stock. Corporations raise money by selling shares of stock to investors. This stock may be either *preferred* or *common*. The two kinds differ as follows:

- Preferred stock pays a fixed dividend, much like the interest payment on a loan. Preferred stockholders also enjoy priority (preference) over common stockholders as to dividends and assets if a venture liquidates. Few small corporations issue preferred stock.

- Common stock, on the other hand, is issued by every corporation. Common shareholders enjoy an ownership interest in profits and assets, though below that of all creditors and preferred stockholders. Common stock may be issued in two forms, either par value or no-par value:
- Par value stock appears in the corporation's books at a fixed amount per share—for example, $1, $10, or $100—as specified in the entrepreneur's corporate charter from the state. Except by chance, the par value of the stock bears no relation to either its market value or its book value once a corporation gets underway.
- Stated value is the amount fixed by the board of directors for no-par value stock. The stated value, like par value stock, governs the amounts to be entered in the corporation's books. The difference between par value and no-par value stock is of little practical significance.

Shareholders' Rights Each common shareholder owns part of the corporation, as evidenced by stock certificates. These certificates give common shareholders the right:

- To elect the directors of the corporation
- To cast one vote per share at shareholders' meetings
- To receive dividends in proportion to the number of common shares they hold
- To sell their shares to anyone who wants to buy them—unless the certificates say that shareholders must offer to sell them to the corporation first. Moreover, before new common stock is offered for sale, shareholders usually have the right to buy the new shares in proportion to the amount of stock they already own.

However, ownership interest does not give common shareholders the right to act for the corporation or to share in its management. General Motors, to cite an extreme example, has more than one million shareholders; only a handful of them have any voice about the way the company is run. The only way that shareholders may influence the running of the corporation is by casting their votes for directors once a year, though, in most cases, voting is meaningless—corporate managers tend to offer just one slate of directors for election.

Disadvantages Although ease of ownership transfer is one of the corporation's chief attractions, it may nevertheless complicate the life of the entrepreneur. For example, if one or more disgruntled shareholders sell their stock to someone undesirable, the entrepreneur may then be at the mercy of a person bent on overthrowing him or her. One way of sidestepping this problem is for entrepreneurs to keep the right of first refusal on all sales of stock by shareholders.

The death of a major shareholder may pose similar problems. For example, an heir or executor might insist upon direct control, possibly resulting in a takeover. To avoid such problems, entrepreneurs should buy insurance to make sure they have the money to buy out the decedent's shares.

Forming a corporation costs more than forming either a sole proprietorship or a partnership. The main reason is that legal help is needed to make sure that all state requirements are met. To begin with, a new corporation needs a charter, which is granted by the state. Legal requirements differ from state to state in many vital matters, including:

- Taxes
- Business fees
- Minimum number of directors
- Liabilities for debts
- Minimum capitalization
- Rules for issuing stock

We now see clearly why lawyers tend to favor the corporation. No other legal form offers these advantages:

- Limited liability
- Ease of raising money
- Ease of ownership transfer
- Continuity of business life

Exhibit 7.6 compares the regular corporation with the sole proprietorship and general partnership forms of organization. Note that the regular corporation is the most attractive in all ways except freedom from government regulations. Corporations are heavily regulated by law; partnerships and sole proprietorships much less so.

EXHIBIT 7.6

Relative Advantages and Disadvantages of Main Legal Forms of Organization

	Sole Proprietorship	General Partnership	Regular Corporation
Ease of transfer of ownership	Medium	Low	High
Ease of raising money	Low	Medium	High
Continuity of business life	Low	Low	High
Protection against liability for business debts	Low	Low	High
Freedom from government regulations	High	High	Low
Ease of formation	High	High	Medium

Exhibit 7.6 omits, however, the greatest potential drawback of the corporate form: double taxation. A corporation must pay income taxes on its profits, and then shareholders must pay income taxes on dividends. Dividends are not a tax-deductible expense for a corporation; they come out of after-tax profits, so dividends are taxed twice.

S-Corporations

However, entrepreneurs may avoid double taxation by forming an S-corporation. This corporate form first appeared in 1958 with the enactment of Subchapter S of the U.S. Internal Revenue Code. It soon became a popular form of organization because it not only avoids double taxation but also keeps such corporate advantages as limited liability.

An S-corporation enjoys the advantages of a corporation without its drawbacks. Because shareholders are taxed as if they were partners, an S-corporation may also serve as a tax shelter for wealthy investors during the early years of a venture.

There are, however, some strings attached to these advantages. To qualify as an S-corporation, a venture must meet some stiff legal requirements:

- It must be a domestic corporation that is not part of another corporation. In other words, it must be independently owned and managed.
- It may have no more than 35 shareholders.
- Only individuals or estates are permitted as shareholders. This requirement keeps other corporations from buying shares of its stock.
- Nonresident aliens are excluded as shareholders.

Once the venture gets underway, the entrepreneur must make sure that:

- No more than 25 percent of sales revenues come from dividends, rents, interest, royalties, annuities, or stock sales
- No more than 80 percent of revenues come from foreign nations

Many lawyers question whether the S-corporation really differs from the regular corporation. They argue that it simply is a corporation with limited size and capital structure. Even so, we believe its ability to avoid double taxation qualifies it as a separate legal form of organization, blending the regular corporation and partnership forms. Exhibit 7.7 summarizes the advantages and disadvantages of S-corporations.

1244 Corporations

To encourage investors to risk their money in small businesses, in 1958 the U.S. Congress also enacted Section 1244 of the U.S. Internal Revenue Code. Under this section, persons whose investments in a small business become worthless may treat that loss as an ordinary rather than a capital loss. This tax break now permits investment losses of up to $50,000 a year to be deducted from ordinary income. In contrast, investment losses in regular corporations can be no more than $1,000 a year. To qualify as a

EXHIBIT 7.7 *S-Corporations: Selected Advantages and Disadvantages*

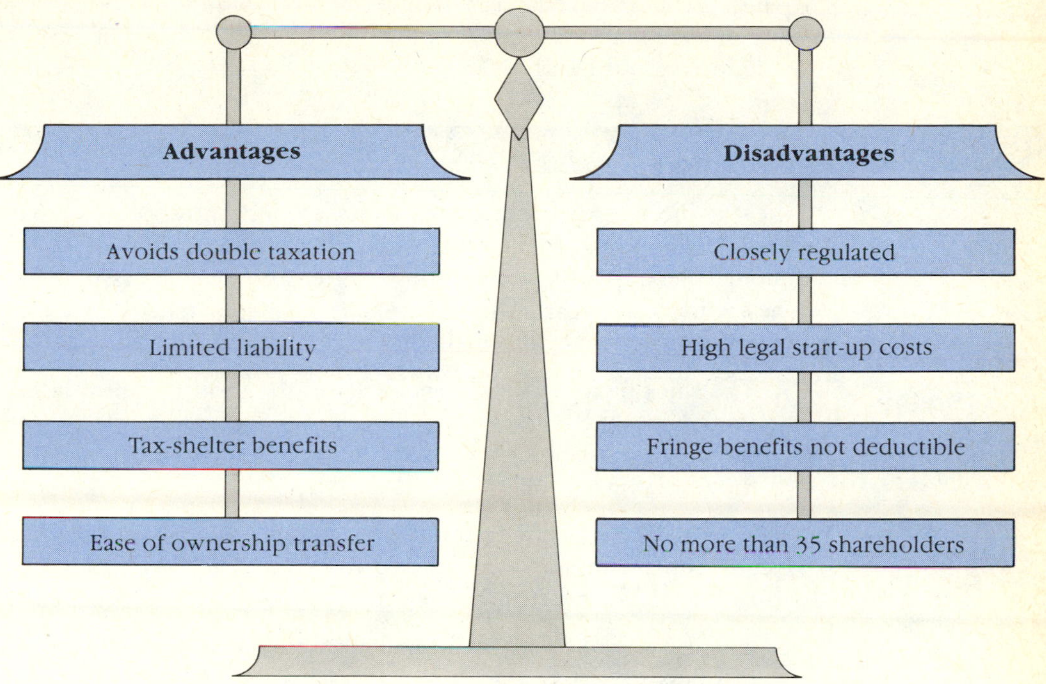

Section 1244 corporation, a small business must meet these tests, among others:

- For a new venture, no more than $1 million may be raised from sale of common stock.
- For an existing venture with common stock already outstanding, the combined value of that stock and any additional stock issued under Section 1244 must not top $1 million.
- The stock must be issued for cash or property, not in exchange for services.
- The tax break applies only to men or women—not to corporations, estates, or trusts.

As with S-corporations, 1244 corporations appeal strongly to the entrepreneur seeking money to launch a risky venture. Investors in high tax brackets are more likely to invest in the entrepreneur's venture if they know that losses, if any, will be tax-deductible as ordinary losses.

Example: An entrepreneur has just won a franchise to install a cable-television system in a small suburb of Atlanta. She needs to raise $600,000, half from commercial banks and half from private investors. She plans to attract 30 wealthy investors, all of them in the 50 percent income-tax bracket, and sell them each a $10,000 block of stock. If the entrepreneur fails, the most that each investor could lose would be $5,000, because $5,000 of the loss ($10,000 × 50%) would be tax-deductible from their personal incomes. Without Section 1244, the most that they could deduct would be $1,000.

GOVERNMENT REGULATIONS AND PAPERWORK

Few subjects spark more complaints among entrepreneurs than government regulations and the resulting paperwork. In the federal government alone, there are now more than 90 regulatory agencies issuing hundreds of new rules each year. The force of these rules is felt by every person and every business, big or small. For example:

> The rules of regulatory agencies affect the food that people eat, the cars they drive, the fuel they use, the clothes they wear, the houses they live in, the investments they make, the water they drink, and even the air they breathe.[7]

In fact, one of the fastest growing enterprises in America is the federal regulation business. According to the Center for the Study of American Business at Washington University:

> The growth of the federal regulation business would be the envy of any business executive tracking a company's sales, rising sixfold from $1.2 billion in 1971 to $7.2 billion in 1980.[8]

Regulations at Three Government Levels

Regulatory agencies exist not only at the federal level but also at the local and state levels. The complex details with which the entrepreneur must comply are exemplified here.

Example: In Houston, a small real-estate developer wants to build a number of housing units in a local subdivision. To do that, the developer must first get clearance from a local zoning board and must also file for a local construction permit. At the state level, the developer must comply with environmental protection laws and housing codes. At the federal level, the developer must comply with various U.S. Housing and Urban Development regulations and U.S. Environmental Protection Agency requirements. Federal regulations differ, depending on the size and location of the subdivision and whether the homes are planned for low, middle, or upper income buyers.[9]

Small wonder, then, that so many entrepreneurs complain about federal regulations. According to the White House Conference on Small Business in 1980:

> Many Americans see their government as too big, too remote, and too overbearing. Nowhere is this view more widely shared than in the

small-business community. Small business suffers the effects of government regulations and paperwork on:

- Competition and productivity
- Innovation and technology
- Growth and capital formation

> The cost of regulation is . . . staggering to small business because it is so vulnerable to economic fluctuations and has the fewest resources. Total cost to all business of federal regulations alone is estimated at $100 billion, with small business paying 60 percent of that sum.[10]

In the words of Vernon L. Weaver, who headed the SBA in 1980:

> Regulatory agencies make rules when they have General Motors in mind; and they forget that the tiny corner grocery store has to fill out the very same forms.[11]

Filling out forms and handling paper have become a way of life for all businesses. The SBA's Office of Advocacy surveyed 1,000 small businesses and found that those businesses had to fill out a total of 305 million federal, state, and local government forms asking 7.3 billion questions.[12]

Some relief may be on the way, at least on the federal level. For example, two of the major recommendations to come out of the White House Conference on Small Business in 1980 were:

- To require all federal agencies to analyze the cost and relevance of regulations to small business.
- To permit so-called two-tiering for all regulations. This means that, besides exempting small business, regulatory agencies would draft one set of rules for small business and another set for big business.[13]

Benefits of Regulations

To balance our discussion of regulations, we should underscore the fact that many regulations benefit both society and the entrepreneur. Few entrepreneurs would disagree, for example, with the need to:

- Ban monopolies that undercut competition
- Regulate banking practices and protect savings
- Protect the environment from pollutants
- Give women and minorities equal employment opportunities
- Help the old, the poor, and the physically handicapped lead meaningful lives
- Protect irreplaceable natural resources from exhaustion

Without government regulations, these needs and others most likely would never be met. We tend to forget that 8-year-old newsboys worked 16-hour days at the turn of the century for just $1 a day. At the time, the courts only grudgingly accepted laws designed to make working conditions more humane.

Because regulations and the paperwork they create will continue to be a fact of business life, entrepreneurs should make use of the information documented by the government forms. Data compiled by the U.S. Bureau of Census can help entrepreneurs research their markets, as did this entrepreneur:

Example: In Boston, a manufacturer of paneling who wanted to widen his market used census data to discover which areas would be best for franchising local contractors, who would use the paneling materials to convert basements into finished rooms.

First, the manufacturer used census data to learn what types of homes predominated in different areas, and whether they were built on concrete slabs or full basements. Ruling out the areas where the houses had no basements, he looked at data on family income, number of children, and number of cars.

He concentrated on families that owned more than one car—an indication that they had discretionary income to spend for home improvements. As a result of his study of census data, he then was able to grant franchises in areas that had good market potential.[14]

SUMMARY

All new ventures require a lawyer's services, and would-be entrepreneurs should not make the mistake of neglecting the legal aspects of their ventures. They should see lawyers months before they plan to launch their ventures and they should seek knowledgeable recommendations before they select lawyers. The lawyers they choose should have experience in new ventures.

Entrepreneurs should look upon such legal help as a kind of preventive medicine. The real value of lawyers is their ability to solve problems by not letting them arise in the first place.

One of the entrepreneur's first decisions should be to choose a legal form of organization. The choice of a corporation, partnership, or sole proprietorship will strongly affect how much taxes are paid, whether the entrepreneur may personally be sued, whether the venture dissolves automatically upon the founder's death, and a host of other financial and managerial issues. Lawyers generally favor the corporate form for these reasons:

- It offers limited liability.
- It lends itself to raising money.
- It outlives the venture's founders.
- It lends itself to ownership transfer.

The main drawback of the corporate form is that it suffers from double taxation. This drawback may be overcome in some cases by forming an S-corporation.

All businesses, big or small, are regulated at three government levels: local, state, and federal. Although the paperwork such regulations generate may be burdensome, entrepreneurs should turn the paperwork to their own advantage—to research their markets, for example.

DISCUSSION AND REVIEW QUESTIONS

1. Which legal form of organization do you prefer? Why?
2. Why does the public often equate big business with the corporate form of organization?
3. Interest on loans is a tax-deductible expense. Should dividends on corporate profits be treated the same way? Why or why not?
4. Define these terms: *sole proprietorship, partnership, corporation, limited liability, corporate charter, double taxation, two-tier regulations.*
5. Why do commercial bankers prefer not to lend money to sole proprietors?
6. Why might you, as a would-be entrepreneur, need legal help early in planning your venture?
7. Is there one best legal form of organization, applicable to all entrepreneurs? Explain.
8. How do regular corporations differ from S-corporations? From 1244 corporations?
9. How do general partnerships differ from limited partnerships?
10. Why should partners draw up a written partnership agreement?
11. What is the basic difference between a corporation and other legal forms of organization?
12. How would you go about getting the right lawyer for your venture?
13. Who should make the legal decisions, the lawyer or the entrepreneur? Why?
14. Why are government regulations and paperwork often a burden to entrepreneurs?
15. How do government regulations benefit the entrepreneur?

NOTES

1. Adapted from Mark N. Kaplan, "How to Get the Best Law Firm," *Boardroom Reports,* January 15, 1984, p. 9.
2. Patrick R. Liles, *New Business Ventures and the Entrepreneur* (Homewood, Ill.: Richard D. Irwin, Inc., 1984), p. 78.
3. "Trujillo v. Longhorn Manufacturing Company, Inc.," *Boardroom Reports,* January 15, 1985, p. 9.
4. Adapted from U.S. Small Business Administration, "Selecting the Legal Structure for Your Firm," *Management Aid No. 6.004* (Washington, D.C.: U.S. Government Printing Office, 1985), p. 2.

5. Adapted from Denis Clifford and Ralph Warner, *The Partnership Book* (Reading, Mass.: Addison-Wesley Publishing Company, 1982), p. 46.
6. Quoted in Lowell B. Howard, *Business Law* (Woodbury, N.Y.: Barron's Woodbury Press, 1965), p. 332.
7. "Federal Regulators: Impact on Every American," *U.S. News & World Report,* May 9, 1977, p. 61.
8. Adapted from John Cunniff, "Small Firms Devastated by Federal Regulations," Cleveland *Plain Dealer* (March 16, 1980), p. 1-E.
9. Adapted from U.S. Small Business Administration, *The Regulatory and Paperwork Maze: A Guide for Small Business* (Washington, D.C.: U.S. Government Printing Office, 1980), p. 8.
10. White House Conference on Small Business, "Issue Paper on Regulations and Paperwork" (Unpublished, January 1980), p. 140.
11. Excerpted from Mr. Weaver's talk at the White House Conference on Small Business in Washington, D.C. (January 13, 1980).
12. U.S. Small Business Administration, "Government Paperwork and Small Business" (Unpublished, December 1979), p. 3.
13. White House Conference on Small Business, *Report to the President: America's Small Business Economy* (Washington, D.C.: U.S. Government Printing Office, April 1980), p. 31.
14. Adapted from U.S. Small Business Administration, *The Regulatory and Paperwork Maze: A Guide for Small Business* (Washington, D.C.: U.S. Government Printing Office, 1980), p. 29.

CASE 7A *Manfredi Enterprises, Inc.*

In March 1980, Penelope Wadsworth received a business plan from Frank Manfredi. Ms. Wadsworth presides over Creative Ventures, a venture-capital firm; Mr. Manfredi presides over Manfredi Enterprises, a manufacturing company. Its sole product is a patented automotive device that boosts gas mileage and cuts air pollution. The purpose of Mr. Manfredi's business plan is to raise $100,000.

You have just joined Ms. Wadsworth's firm, and she has asked you to go over Mr. Manfredi's business plan. By tomorrow morning, Ms. Wadsworth wants you to recommend whether the plan merits a closer look—and why.

Background

Mr. Manfredi was born into a family of entrepreneurs. His father and uncles all ran their own businesses in Italy. Mr. Manfredi spent the first 12 years of his life in Italy and then emigrated to this country.

At the age of 18, Mr. Manfredi began his first business in Los Angeles. With mixed success, he ran a dry cleaning and shoe repair shop for three years.

Then Mr. Manfredi headed east, where he married, started a family, and worked on General Motors' assembly line. Like millions of others, he soon fell into the rhythmic lifestyle of daily work from 8:00 to 4:00, weekly paychecks, and monthly mortgage payments.

The entrepreneurial spirit that once burned bright inside him was all but dead. Then something happened to rekindle that spirit. In 1970, on a late night drive through Pennsylvania, he observed that his Chevrolet sedan ran better in the moisture-rich mountain air. When he returned home, he made up his mind to recreate "these ideal weather conditions" under the hood of his own car.

Mr. Manfredi worked on his idea in the basement of his home for seven years. The product of his labors was a booster that not only increased gas mileage but also cut air pollution. A drawing of the booster appears in Exhibit 7A.1.

Creates Own Venture

In February 1977, at the age of 51, Mr. Manfredi gave up the security of his job with General Motors for the insecurity of entrepreneurship. His immediate goal was to "raise $250,000 to make and market the booster."

A full year went by before the first booster rolled off the production line. It took that long to raise money, lease factory space, hire talent, and build production equipment. Mr. Manfredi did indeed create a company capitalized at $250,000, though only a fraction of that sum reflected paid-in

EXHIBIT 7A.1 *Manfredi Enterprises, Inc.: Drawing of Manfredi Fuel Booster*

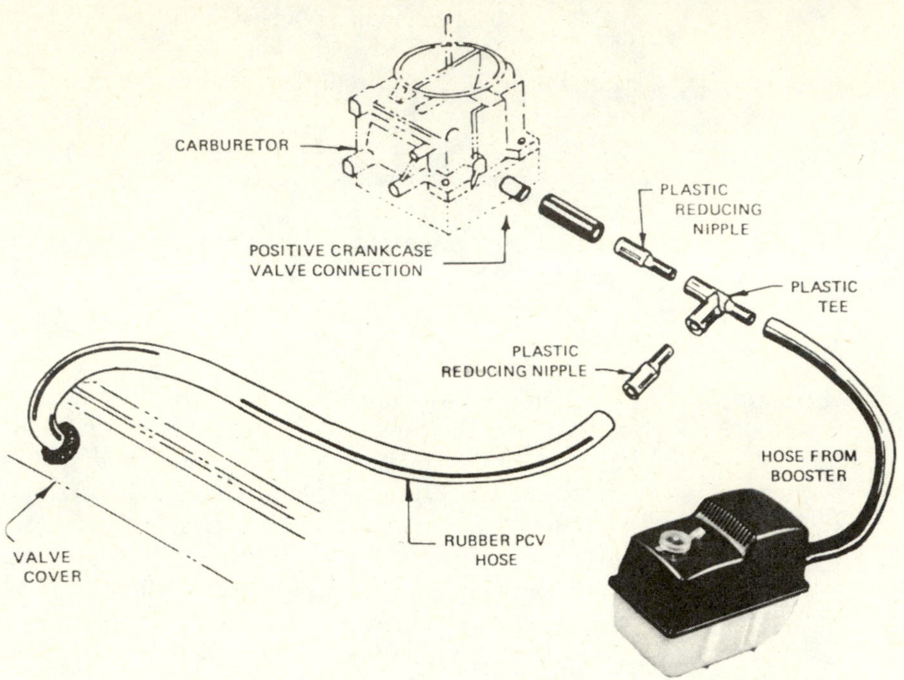

cash, as explained below. Authorized to issue 100,000 shares of common stock at a par value of $2.50 each, the company:

- Gave Mr. Manfredi 51 percent of the shares in exchange for the rights to his patent
- Gave officers and suppliers 29 percent of the shares in exchange for their services and supplies
- Sold 20 percent of these shares for cash

So, cash sales of stock represented just $50,000. Such sales were mainly to members of Local 1005 of the United Automobile Workers Union, of which Mr. Manfredi had been a member. His beginning balance sheet appears in Exhibit 7A.2.

Financial Problems

By early 1978, the company was ready to make and market the booster. Despite reams of free publicity in magazines and newspapers, sales failed to meet expectations by a wide margin. The company soon found itself in financial trouble.

EXHIBIT 7A.2

Manfredi Enterprises, Inc.: Balance Sheet (February 1, 1978)

Assets		Equities	
Patent	$127,500	Accounts payable	$ 3,100
Organizational costs	36,000	Owners' equity	250,000
Dies and forms	30,400		
Inventories	18,700		
Experimental costs	18,200		
Equipment	17,200		
Prepaid expenses	2,700		
Cash	2,400		
Total assets	$253,100	Total equities	$253,100

With its cash dwindling to zero, the company turned to a local bank for help in early 1979. The bank responded by lending the company $22,000. Of that sum, $7,000 was a personal note guaranteed by the company's board of directors.

At the same time, the company tried to float a second issue of 100,000 shares of stock, this time at a par value of four dollars a share. But because the company had suffered heavy losses, investors bought few shares of stock. The income statement in Exhibit 7A.3 shows how the company had performed.

By October 1979, the company once again found itself on the edge of failure. The bank threatened to call its loan and shareholders doubted the company's ability to exploit the booster's potential.

In spite of these difficulties, Mr. Manfredi refused to give up. Moving quickly, he persuaded his city to test the booster—with a promise that if the test succeeded, the city would have the booster installed on each of its 2,200 vehicles. Next, he convinced the bank to stretch repayment of its loan to April 1980.

The company's fortunes soon took a turn for the better. The test with the city gave these favorable results:

- On the 10 vehicles tested, the booster increased the mileage per gallon by an average of 22 percent.

EXHIBIT 7A.3

Manfredi Enterprises, Inc.: Income Statement (for year ending June 30, 1979)

Sales revenues	$18,100
Operating expenses	76,800
Operating loss	($58,700)

- On a vehicle assigned to the city's Air Pollution Control Division, the booster cut the carbon monoxide emission by 93 percent.

The Future

This success spurred Mr. Manfredi to go after venture capital. But before he could do so, he needed a business plan. "All venture-capital firms ask for one," says Mr. Manfredi. "Without one they won't give you the time of day." Within three months he had completed a plan. He sought $100,000 of venture capital—enough to carry his company through April 1981—and a venture-capital firm capable of investing its *managerial* know-how as well. "That's our most pressing need," says Mr. Manfredi.

Confident of raising the $100,000, Mr. Manfredi mailed his business plan to 15 venture-capital firms in March 1980. Excerpts appear in the following exhibits:

Exhibit 7A.4—Product Technology
Exhibit 7A.5—Marketing Strategy
Exhibit 7A.6—Rating of Booster
Exhibit 7A.7—Organizational Chart
Exhibit 7A.8—Balance Sheet
Exhibit 7A.9—Cash Budget
Exhibit 7A.10—Latest Income Statement
Exhibit 7A.11—Reorganization

Upon completing the test with the city, Mr. Manfredi offered to equip its 2,200 vehicles with the booster. Unfortunately, he was turned down because the city itself was now cash poor.

Currently, Mr. Manfredi is running another large-scale test, this one with Avis Rent-A-Car. This test covers 20 vehicles. Mr. Manfredi believes that the results of this test, coupled with those of the city test, should "remove any doubts about the booster's performance."

Questions

1. What are Mr. Manfredi's prospects?
2. Does Mr. Manfredi's business plan merit a closer look by the venture-capital firm? Why?
3. If Mr. Manfredi were to seek $100,000 from you, and you had the money, would you invest in his venture? If not, why? If yes, on what basis?
4. Comment on Mr. Manfredi's business plan. Is it thorough and precise? Has he backed up his assumptions? What additional information might you desire—and why?
5. What should Mr. Manfredi do if he fails to raise the $100,000 he seeks from venture-capital firms? Explain.

EXHIBIT 7A.4

Product Technology

Since 1887, when Willam Maxwell of England invented a rotary exhaust pump, people have tried to use water to get better performance from engines. In Maxwell's case, it was a gadget for condensing water vapor for use in steam engines. Some 36 inventions and 93 years later, Mr. Manfredi has created a device that puts moisture to good use in an automobile engine. What is so unique about it? The booster is similar to many of these other devices in its use of manifold suction to draw water into the engine, but there the similarity stops. It injects moisture-rich air rather than a liquid spray. That is the key to its performance. The explanation has to do with molecular availability.

If water is injected as a spray of droplets, only those molecules at the surface of each droplet become available for the gas-air reaction. In a droplet containing perhaps a million molecules, as few as a thousand molecules—or 0.1 percent—would be exposed to reaction.

If water is injected as moisture-rich air, the percentage of water molecules exposed to reaction would jump to as high as 10 percent. The result is more complete combustion, which brings such benefits as these:

- Greater mileage per gallon of gas
- Reduced carbon monoxide and hydrocarbon emission
- Reduced buildup of carbon in the engine

At work here is a centuries-old chemical principle, namely, the use of a catalyst (water) to quicken the rate of a reaction (gas and air). In its role as catalyst, the water molecule does not loss its individuality. Rather, it acts a little like the justice of the peace who joins couples in marriage; it helps create the union of gas and air molecules but it never becomes part of the union. Each water molecule attracts gas and air molecules and holds them together for combustion. And the more molecules of water available, the faster and more complete the combustion.

EXHIBIT 7A.5

Marketing Strategy

We have already begun to redirect our marketing strategy. Until mid-1979, our marketing efforts were directed mainly at the individual car owner. That was a mistake. The individual on the street may endorse the goals of gas economy and clean air—but not if it means dipping into a pocket and paying dollars.

On the other hand, big fleet owners *are* cost-conscious. They are interested in economy. They are interested in saving dollars. Avis Rent-A-Car, for example, estimates savings of $5 million a year on just a 20 percent increase in gas mileage. What better incentive to buy the booster?

The shift to big fleet owners as our main sales target is the most important change in marketing strategy. Other changes include:

- Building a strong regional marketing base by focusing our selling efforts on fleet owners in this state only
- Applying a marketing mix that has pricing and personal selling as its main ingredients

This strategy is working, as evidenced by two major breakthroughs—with the city and with Avis Rent-A-Car. Thanks to marketing research done by the trade magazine, *Commercial Car Journal*, we now have the names and addresses of all 182 fleet owners in this state with 10 or more vehicles.

However, our strategy lacks the one ingredient capable of bringing it to full flood—namely, a competent marketing manager.

EXHIBIT 7A.6 *Rating of Manfredi Fuel Booster*

Criterion	Rating Good	Fair	Poor
1 Marketability			
Merchandisibility	Has performance characteristics that lend themselves to promotion.		
Price	Priced low enough to enable most buyers to recover their investment through gas-cost savings in less than one year.		
Marketing strategy			Will have to set up distribution channels and marketing organization.
Number of sizes and grades	One size and grade can be used on all vehicles except diesel trucks.		
2 Durability			
Profit opportunity	Booster will have uses long enough to recover initial investment and return profits.		
Breadth of market	A national market and a potential foreign market.		
Exclusiveness of design		Protected by a patent, but it might be circumvented.	
3 Productive ability			
Equipment necessary		Company owns dies to produce booster parts but will have to buy equipment to assemble them on mass-production basis.	
Production know-how and personnel necessary	Good production know-how; more personnel needed to make booster.		
Availability of raw materials	Company can buy raw materials from wide variety of suppliers.		

EXHIBIT 7A.6 *Rating of Manfredi Fuel Booster (cont.)*

Criterion	Rating Good	Fair	Poor
4 Growth potential			
Place in market	New kind of product that will fill a pressing need not now being filled.		
Expected competitive situation			Low value added—thus enabling large, medium, and smaller companies to compete.
Expected availability of end-users	Number of end-users runs into the millions and will increase moderately.		

EXHIBIT 7A.7 *Organizational Chart*

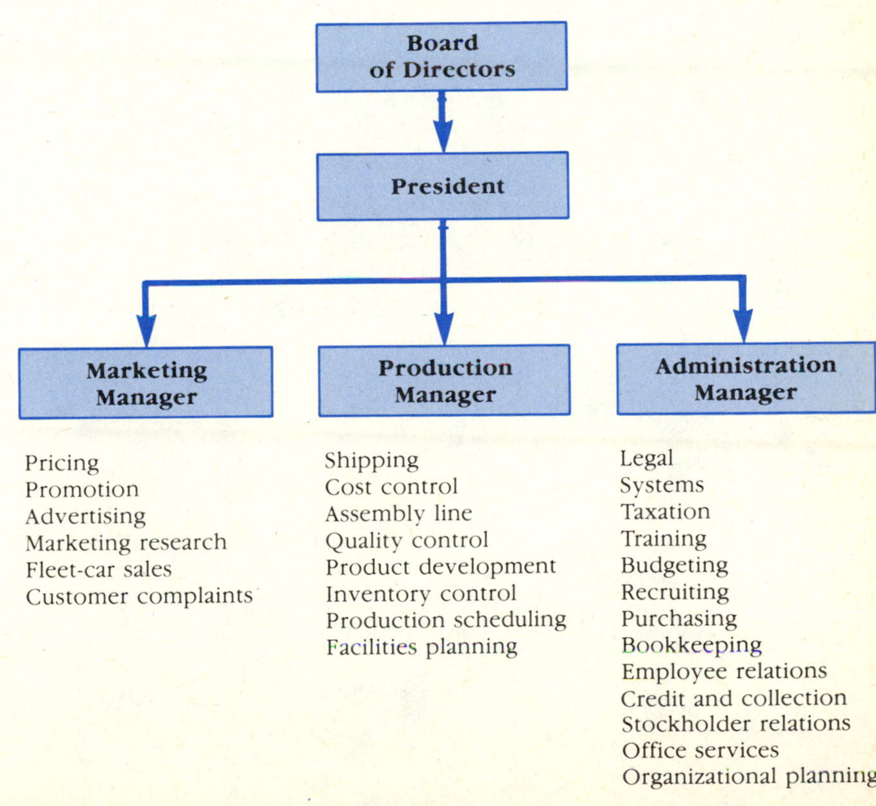

EXHIBIT 7A.8 *Balance Sheet (December 31, 1979)*

Assets			Equities		
Current assets			Current liabilities		
Inventory	$ 31,200		Note payable, bank	$ 14,500	
Cash	1,000		Note payable, officer	4,600	
Accounts receivable	900	$ 33,100	Other notes payable	1,700	
Fixed assets			Accrued taxes payable	100	$ 20,900
Dies and forms	$24,300				
Equipment and fixtures	12,100	36,400	Owners' equity		
Other assets			Common stock	$282,000	
Patent	$127,500		Deficit	(82,300)	199,700
Experimental costs	18,200				
Organizational costs	3,400				
Prepaid expenses	2,000	151,100			
Total assets		$221,000*	Total equities		$221,000*

* Rounded to nearest thousand.

EXHIBIT 7A.9 *Cash Budget (April 1980 through March 1981)*

	April	May	June	July	August
Budgeted volume, units	0	100	200	400	600
Budgeted revenue, at $40/unit	0	$ 4,000	$ 8,000	$16,000	$24,000
Cash balance at start of month	0	$18,400	$ 7,120	$17,060	$23,520
Plus collections from credit sales	0	0	4,000	8,000	16,000
Total collections plus cash balance	0	$18,400	$11,120	$25,060	$39,520
Less payments for operations					
Purchases of materials	$ 1,200	$ 2,400	$ 4,800	$ 7,200	$ 9,600
Salaries of officers	1,000	1,000	1,000	5,250	5,250
Other salaries and wages	1,500	1,900	2,300	2,700	3,100
Welfare	500	580	660	1,590	1,670
Advertising and promotion	—	2,000	1,000	1,000	1,000
Legal and accounting	1,000	1,000	1,000	500	500
Rent	700	700	700	700	700
Utilities	300	200	200	200	200
Office supplies	200	200	200	200	200
Insurance and local taxes	200	200	200	200	200
Subtotal payments for operations	$ 6,600	$10,180	$12,060	$19,540	$22,420
Less other payments					
Loan repayments		$19,100			
Equipment and experimental costs		5,000	$ 5,000	$5,000	$ 5,000
Outside consultants		2,000	2,000	2,000	2,000
Subtotal other payments		$26,100	$ 7,000	$ 7,000	$ 7,000
Total payments	$ 6,600	$36,280	$19,060	$26,540	$29,420
Cash-flow summary					
Total collections plus cash balance	$ 0	$18,400	$11,120	$25,060	$39,520
Less total payments	6,600	36,280	19,060	26,540	29,420
Surplus or deficit at month's end	($ 6,600)	($17,880)	($ 7,940)	($ 1,480)	$10,100
Investment by venture capital firm	25,000	25,000	25,000	25,000	—
Cash balance at month's end after investment	$18,400	$ 7,120	$17,060	$23,520	$10,100

EXHIBIT 7A.10

Income Statement (for six months ending December 31, 1979)

Sales revenues		$ 3,600
Cost of goods sold		3,200
Gross profit		$ 400
Expenses		
Rent	$3,000	
Salaries and wages	2,800	
Insurance and local taxes	1,600	
Supplies	1,500	
Utilities	1,400	
Advertising and promotion	700	
Legal and accounting	600	
Interest	600	
Other	200	12,400
Loss		($12,000)

September	October	November	December	January	February	March
800	1,000	1,200	1,400	1,600	1,800	2,000
$32,000	$40,000	$48,000	$56,000	$64,000	$ 72,000	$ 80,000
$10,100	$ 6,800	$ 9,140	$16,500	$28,980	$ 46,580	$ 69,500
24,000	32,000	40,000	48,000	56,000	64,000	72,000
$34,100	$38,800	$49,140	$64,500	$84,980	$110,580	$141,500
$12,000	$14,400	$16,800	$19,200	$21,600	$ 24,000	$ 26,400
5,250	5,250	5,250	5,250	5,250	5,250	5,250
3,500	4,300	4,700	5,100	5,500	5,900	6,300
1,750	1,910	1,990	2,070	2,150	2,230	2,310
1,000	1,000	1,000	1,000	1,000	1,000	1,000
500	500	500	500	500	500	500
700	700	700	700	700	700	700
200	200	300	300	300	300	300
200	200	200	200	200	200	200
200	200	200	200	200	200	200
$25,300	$28,660	$31,640	$34,520	$37,400	$ 40,080	$ 43,060
$ 2,000	$ 1,000	$ 1,000	$ 1,000	$ 1,000	$ 1,000	$ 1,000
$ 2,000	$ 1,000	$ 1,000	$ 1,000	$ 1,000	$ 1,000	$ 1,000
$27,300	$29,660	$32,640	$35,520	$38,400	$ 41,080	$ 44,060
$34,100	$38,800	$49,140	$64,500	$84,980	$110,580	$141,500
27,300	29,660	32,640	35,520	38,400	41,080	44,060
$ 6,800	$ 9,140	$16,500	$28,980	$46,580	$ 69,500	$ 97,440
—	—	—	—	—	—	—
$ 6,800	$ 9,140	$16,500	$28,980	$46,580	$ 69,500	$ 97,440

EXHIBIT 7A.11

Reorganization

Too busy keeping the company's head above water, Mr. Manfredi has had little time to reorganize his management team. But he has recently added two persons who are production and product-development experts. Working part-time, they brought the booster to its present level of quality. Until their arrival, the booster's performance had been far from flawless. Now, it is trouble-free.

Ideally, the company's organization should look like the one charted in Exhibit 7A.7. Note that the key managerial jobs, besides the presidency, would be those of:

- Marketing
- Production
- Administration

At present, Mr. Manfredi is both president and administrative manager. But because his skills lie mainly in research and development, he would rather delegate the day-to-day administration of the company to a person better talented in this area.

As to the other two managerial jobs, some progress has been made toward filling them. Either of the two persons mentioned earlier would be capable of filling the production manager's job. But the marketing manager's job is far from being filled. This job is critical, since a major reason for the company's failure to reach its potential was its failure to plan its marketing. So no effort will be spared to hire a talented individual as marketing manager.

CASE 7B Partners or Shareholders

Margaret Varadi and Helen Ludwig formed their partnership five years ago. At that time, both were working in the women's department of a major department store. Recognizing that a large market for women's wear existed in the city, they opened a small boutique in a fashionable neighborhood. Ms. Ludwig, twelve years older, did the buying and kept the books while Ms. Varadi, who was friendlier, worked mostly with the customers.

Even though each woman took only a small salary, the business did not produce much profit at first. The store gradually developed a loyal clientele, however, and became increasingly profitable as the years passed. Although both were pleased with its success, they also felt that it had to maintain a competitive edge on rival boutiques, which were springing up in other places.

The partners agreed that the shop needed remodeling and that a more diverse inventory should be carried. Of course, these changes required financing. Ms. Ludwig, who had considerable income from investments and an inheritance, suggested they dissolve their partnership and form a corporation. Ms. Ludwig reasoned that:

- Banks would lend them money more readily if they operated as a corporation.
- They could sell shares of common stock, if they wished, to raise money for growth.
- They could save on income taxes since they would pay the higher income taxes only on the part they took out as salary. The rest of the profit could remain in the business and be taxed at a lower rate until they took it out sometime in the future.
- She would be able to work less and continue to earn a good income as she neared retirement age. She would also be able to put some of the business's income into a pension plan.
- They would be better protected from potential personal liability in the event of an accident.

Questions

1. Might a bank really be more inclined to lend money to a corporation than to a partnership? Why?
2. Explain the tax responsibilities for a partnership and a corporation. Is Ms. Ludwig correct in assuming they would pay less tax as a corporation?
3. What does Ms. Ludwig mean by claiming that the corporate form would limit her personal liability?

Source: U.S. Small Business Administration, *Choosing a Form of Organization for Small Business* (Washington, D.C.: U.S. Government Printing Office, 1979), pp. 18–19.

CASE 7C *Paula Cooke*

When Richard Dosk died, his young widow became the major stockholder in his building-maintenance supplies firm—and his executive vice president, Paula Cooke, stepped up to the top job.

For 10 years, Mrs. Cooke had piloted the marketing end of the business—mainly soliciting customers by direct mail. By the time Mr. Dosk passed on, Mrs. Cooke's department—at a substantial cost—had accumulated 20,000 names of customers. Those names were in a locked file in Mrs. Cooke's office.

The widow remarried, and her husband moved into the Dosk Company. It was apparent that *he* wanted to be kingpin. Soon, Mrs. Cooke was out.

Mrs. Cooke immediately set up a rival company in which she solicited the same market—limiting it to commercial buildings. *Some* of the customers were those of the Dosk Company—which sought to protect its expensively-compiled list by running to court for an injunction.

"We want Cooke stopped from soliciting any customers of the Dosk Company," the former Mrs. Dosk cried. "Those names are highly confidential, as Cooke knows. They cost us over a half million dollars to collect."

"I'm not using that list," Mrs. Cooke insisted. "I don't have a copy. Naturally, I know some of them. I dealt with them."

"We don't believe it," replied the former Mrs. Dosk. "Here is a list of 47 of our customers that you solicited."

"Only 47 out of 1,100 commercial customers?" retorted Mrs. Cooke. "That's pure coincidence. Or maybe casual memory. Besides, anybody could pick out prospective customers. They're all listed in real estate directories."

"Not *our* list," protested the former Mrs. Dosk. "It cost Dosk Company plenty to compile it."

Question If you were the judge, how would you decide this issue? Explain.

Source: Adapted from case that appeared in *The Businessman and the Law* (now *Your Business and the Law*), published by Business Research Publications, Inc., 817 Broadway, New York, NY 10003.

8 LOCATION

QUESTIONS FOR MASTERY

Is site selection important?
How should you select a site?
What is the role of marketing research in site selection?
How does site selection differ in importance among industries?
What are the trends in shopping centers and industrial parks?

Locality seems but an accident.
Elizabeth Coatsworth

A saying common in retailing circles is that "the three most important factors in retailing success are location, location, and location." Though an exaggeration, this saying underscores the need for entrepreneurs to research their market thoroughly. Although location is indeed critical in retailing, it also plays a varied but vital role in manufacturing, services, and wholesaling as well. Only with marketing research can the entrepreneur in any industry have the information needed to choose the right location.

VARYING IMPORTANCE OF LOCATION

Characteristics Affecting Location Choice

Location is more vital in some industries than others. Certain characteristics of businesses determine the importance of location, including whether customers must travel to the business or the entrepreneur travels to the customer, whether a business offers a special product or service with little accessible competition, and whether convenience is a key selling point in what the business offers to customers.

In services like accounting and management consulting, the question of location is often trivial. A management consultant's office may be within walking distance of prospective clients or an hour's drive away. Neither distance nor accessibility affects the consultant's ability to develop new clients, because generally it is the consultant who must visit the clients to solve their problems.

Location is also trivial for ventures that offer a unique service, such as antique-furniture repair. Customers are usually willing to travel many miles to have a precious piece of antique furniture repaired or restored. The only consideration the entrepreneur must make is whether the location is accessible by automobile.

At the other extreme are industries where location may make or break a venture. It matters a great deal, for example, where a grocer locates a supermarket—it should be within walking distance for neighborhood residents, and no more than perhaps a five-minute drive for most residents in the trading area, with ample parking space available. Finally, the supermarket should not be near another supermarket.

The Role of Shopping Centers and Industrial Parks

Even in those industries where choice of location matters, entrepreneurs are becoming less able to make their own decisions. The main reason is the market trend toward shopping centers and industrial parks. This trend began just after World War II and, although it is slowing down, it shows few signs of stopping. In 1985, more than 24,000 shopping centers and more than 4,500 industrial parks dotted the country.

As a result of this trend the developer, rather than the entrepreneur, selects the location. The developer of a shopping center studies the market and decides on the mix of shops based on the needs and potential discovered in the market research. This concept is so effective that, within a generation or two, most consumers will probably be shopping at shopping centers. Just as developers of shopping centers often determine location for businesses in retailing or services, the developers of industrial parks often decide where the manufacturing entrepreneur may locate. Often, the location of the industrial park is dictated by ecological concerns, as well as access to transportation or to markets. In fact, many communities have passed laws forcing developers to meet the following requirements:

- No discharge of smoke into the air
- No despoiling of land around a plant
- No discharge of refuse, acid waste, or other pollutants into a stream
- Sufficient off-street parking concealed by landscaped and grassy areas
- Recessed loading docks so that trucks are not visible from the street

Developers of shopping centers or industrial parks must now go to great lengths to justify their proposals. Gone are the days when developers had only to make a marketing study, buy up some vacant land, and build a complex of air-conditioned shops. Many communities are now trying to slow the growth of shopping centers by claiming their right to remain residential, in contrast with developers and entrepreneurs who claim their right to free enterprise. The outcome of these conflicts will no doubt affect the pace of change in the American landscape.

MARKETING RESEARCH IN SITE SELECTION

As mentioned earlier, developers of shopping centers and industrial parks—not entrepreneurs—often decide where businesses may locate. Still, entrepreneurs can exercise their freedom of choice in areas uncontrolled by developers. As depicted in Exhibit 8.1, entrepreneurs are still free to choose:

- A geographical region
- A city within that region
- An area within that city
- A specific site within that area (except for shopping centers)

Few entrepreneurs go through a logical process of site selection. Instead, they often permit personal preference to influence their decision on where to locate. Entrepreneurs who enjoy warm weather the year round, for example, may choose to locate in the Deep South or the Southwest. Entrepreneurs who enjoy the four seasons may prefer New England or the Midwest. Others may prefer not to move at all but to locate in the very same neighborhood they were born in. Personal preference is a vital factor to be weighed in choosing a location, but entrepreneurs should not permit their biases to take the place of sound, objective research.

EXHIBIT 8.1 *Selecting a Location*

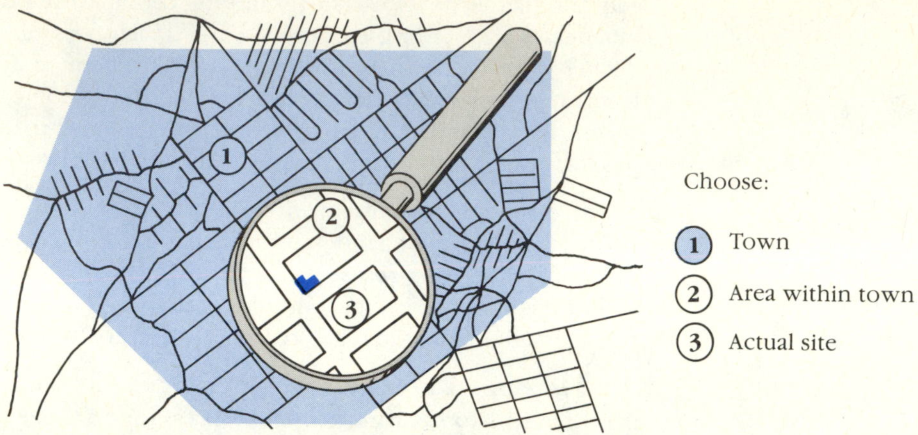

Source: Wendell O. Metcalf, Small Business Administration, *Starting and Managing a Small Business of Your Own* (Washington, D.C.: U.S. Government Printing Office, 1962), p. 16.

Selecting a Retail or Service Location

In addition to personal preference, entrepreneurs need to get and analyze the facts about their potential market before they choose a location. For example, an entrepreneur who wants to open a drugstore should seek answers to such questions as these:

On the City

- Is the city growing? If so, how fast? What parts of the city are growing most?
- What is the city's population breakdown by age, income, and occupation?
- How many drugstores are there now in the city? Where are they located? How well are they doing?
- What is the civic spirit like? Is the city progressive? Do residents work well together on civic projects?
- What is the quality of the city's schools, churches, parks, and culture?

On an Area Within the City

- What do area consumers buy when they go to a drugstore?
- What is the area's population? Is it growing? Are the people chiefly native-born or foreign?
- How do people make their living? Are they mostly white-collar workers, laborers, or retired persons?

- Are there people of all ages or are they mainly old, middle-aged, or young?
- What is the average family income? What is their total buying power?
- How many other drugstores are located in the area? How successful are they?

On a Specific Site Within the Area

- Are neighboring businesses healthy?
- How close is the nearest competing drugstore?
- Is the site surrounded by well-kept homes?
- Is there plenty of parking space available next to or near the site?
- Is the site accessible by bus?
- What zoning requirements must be met?
- How far will customers have to travel to shop in the drugstore?
- Is there a steady flow of foot traffic by the site?
- What is the floor area? Is there any room to expand?
- Can deliveries be made from the rear?
- Will the stores nearby draw customers to the site?
- Is the appearance of the site pleasing, making customers want to shop there?
- Is there a divider on the road that may discourage some potential customers?

Choosing the best location calls for painstaking attention to detail. No fact should be ignored. As depicted in Exhibit 8.1, entrepreneurs should narrow their choices to the most likely sites and then dig out the facts about each one. The following example shows how entrepreneurs may narrow their choices:

Example: An entrepreneur, Paula Lynne Berke, is thinking about opening a children's apparel store in the Dallas, Texas, area. Ms. Berke prefers to locate in the Dallas area because it offers "just the continuity of life I'm looking for." She went to college there, worked as a manager in a local department store, and is an enthusiastic supporter of the Dallas Cowboys. As part of her business plan, Ms. Berke must decide which suburb offers her the best chance of success.

Ms. Berke's marketing professor suggested that she look at the "Survey of Buying Power" prepared yearly by *Sales and Marketing Management* magazine. This survey gives data on population, income, and certain categories of retail sales for major metropolitan areas like Dallas. Since this survey is updated yearly, it furnishes needed statistics between the 10-year censuses made by the U.S Bureau of Census.

Grateful for the professor's advice, Ms. Berke visited the local library and examined their copy of the "Survey of Buying Power" for the various suburbs that are part of the Dallas area. She then narrowed her choices to three suburbs, using the data shown in Exhibit 8.2.

EXHIBIT 8.2

Data Relevant to Children's Apparel Store: (Dallas, Texas, Area)

Dallas Suburb	Age Groups 18 to 24	25 to 34	Population	Median Household Effective Buying Income
Denton	24.8	15.8	99,900	$15,021
Arlington	18.5	21.1	119,100	19,468
Collin	11.7	19.6	105,300	16,532

Of these three suburbs, Arlington looked the most favorable to Ms. Berke. It has a younger population than Collin and, although it is not quite as young as Denton, the median income is much higher. Having chosen Arlington, Ms. Berke next collected data on specific sites within the area that look the most promising.[1]

The example describes the process of marketing research, which will be discussed in greater detail in Chapter Fourteen. Marketing research is perhaps the entrepreneur's most important marketing activity, since it informs them of their markets both before and after the venture begins.

Getting and Using Information

How do entrepreneurs get the information they need to do marketing research? How do they get answers to questions like those posed in the drugstore example? We have already mentioned one source, the "Survey of Buying Power" by *Sales and Marketing Management* magazine. There are many other sources. Among the most fertile are the federal government, trade associations, and Chambers of Commerce.

The U.S. Bureau of Census, for example, provides population characteristics by census tract for all cities of 50,000 or more inhabitants. Each census tract has an average population of four to five thousand. Let us cite an example to see how entrepreneurs may use census tract data to select sites for their ventures.

Example: In Tacoma, Washington, an entrepreneur plans to launch a venture that replaces and repairs warm-air furnaces. He narrowed his search for a site to two census tracts, shown in Exhibit 8.3. Data for each tract appear in Exhibit 8.4. Which tract offers the better site for such a venture?

Tract 719.02 would be better because it has many more warm-air furnaces than Tract 718.02. Replacement and repair opportunities would be much greater in Tract 719.02.[2]

Locating a Manufacturing Plant

So far, discussion has centered on locating a retail store or a service firm. The process of deciding where to locate a manufacturing plant is more complex, and requires painstakingly thorough marketing research.

EXHIBIT 8.3 *Census Tracts in Tacoma, Washington*

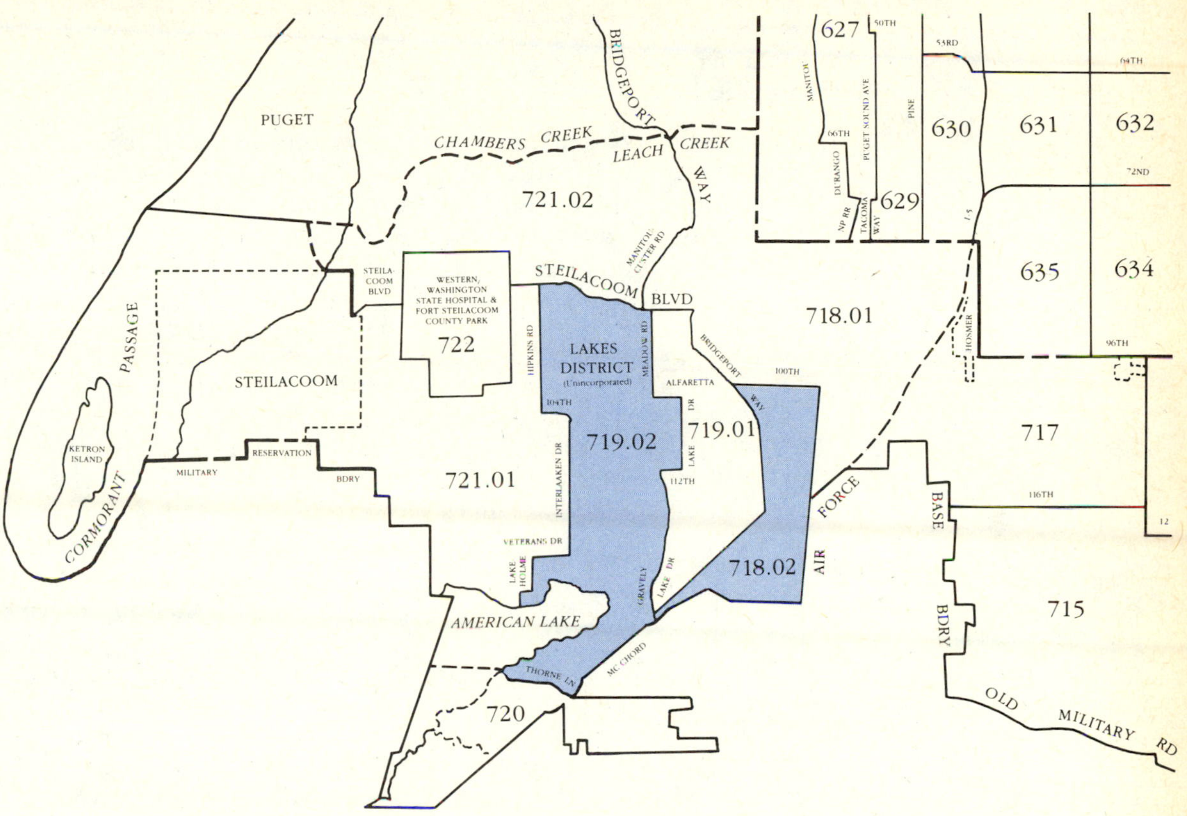

Source: U.S. Bureau of the Census.

EXHIBIT 8.4 *Selected Census Tract Data for Tacoma, Washington*

	Tract 718.02	Tract 719.02
Heating equipment		
Steam or hot water	23	206
Warm-air furnace	394	1,132
Built-in electric units	1,209	296
Floor, wall, or pipeless furnace	105	101
Other means or not heated	532	194
Total housing units	2,263	1,929

Source: Louis H. Vorzimer, U.S. Small Business Administration, "Using Census Data to Select a Store Site," *Small Marketers Aid No. 154* (Washington, D.C.: U.S. Government Printing Office, 1976), p. 9.

To find the right location for their plants, entrepreneurs generally should seek to balance three site factors:

- Sales revenues
- Manufacturing costs
- Transportation costs

These site factors vary in importance, depending on the entrepreneur's marketing area. For example, if planning to sell their product to customers within a narrow geographic area, entrepreneurs should seek the least-cost location in relation to customers and ignore the location of rivals.

Questions of markets and costs are by no means the only ones that entrepreneurs should answer. The following factors should also be considered:

Labor force: Does labor supply possess the skills I need to run my plant productively?
Community size: Should I locate in a nonmetropolitan area? What is the standard of living in the area? What is the quality of life?
Transportation: Will I have quick access to an interstate highway that enables me to make overnight delivery to markets that are far from the site?
Water pollution: What minimum levels of water-pollution control must I adhere to?
Air pollution: What kind of equipment must I install to treat emissions of air pollutants?
Land: How much land will I need not only for making my product but also for parking and for air-pollution control equipment? Should I buy more land than I need at present to provide for future expansion and as a hedge against the upward trend in land prices?
Fuel and power: Will there be ample sources of energy available now and in the future?
Taxes: What effect will state and local tax structures have on my cost of manufacture?
Financing opportunities: Will the community or the state help me finance my plant?[3]

This list of questions is by no means complete. But it does underline the complexity of picking the right location for a manufacturing plant. An example will show how the process of site selection might work:

Example: Glenn Myers, an entrepreneur, wants to build a small plant to make ammonia. A chemical engineer and a former plant manager, Mr. Myers has already done some homework on basic problems:

- Because ammonia is made by reacting natural gas with air, Mr. Myers wanted to make sure there would be an ample supply of natural gas in the future. The gas company assured him there would be.

- Because the manufacture of ammonia requires high pressures and temperatures, Mr. Myers wanted to make sure he could build such a plant. The State Development Department informed him that he could, as long as the plant was located at least one mile from the nearest family residence. That way, if an explosion did occur—a remote possibility—the lives of residents would not be endangered.
- Since hot water and other pollutants would foul the environment if discharged by the plant, Mr. Myers had to be sure that all pollutants would be neutralized. The designer of the plant assured him that pollution-control equipment placed throughout the plant would, indeed, neutralize all pollutants.

Mr. Myers has already received promises from five fertilizer manufacturers that they will buy ammonia from him if his price is lower than that of competitors. There are no competing manufacturers in the state, and Mr. Myers is sure he can underbid out-of-state competitors. Manufacturing costs will be the same regardless of location. Mr. Myers's main concern is to locate the plant in a place where the cost of transporting ammonia to the five fertilizer manufacturers is minimized.

To help him decide, Mr. Myers studied the map in Exhibit 8.5, which reveals that the five fertilizer manufacturers are located almost symmetrically about the state. The solution to Mr. Myers's location problem now becomes apparent. He should locate the ammonia plant in an area roughly equidistant from the five customers, as shown in the exhibit. Because the

EXHIBIT 8.5 *Location of Ammonia Plant in Relation to Customers*

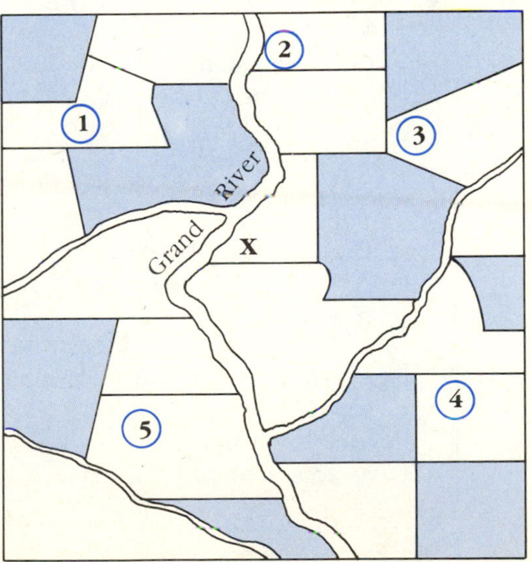

manufacture of ammonia requires a lot of water, Mr. Myers should also place the plant near the river shown.

In this example, Mr. Myers chose his plant site by inspection. In the real world, symmetrical markets and purchase areas are the exception, so choosing a site by inspection is sometimes difficult. Entrepreneurs should do an exhaustive analysis to measure the attractiveness of several likely sites, using two yardsticks:

Return on investment: What is the effect on both the revenues and the costs of each plant location? How do any changes affect potential profits?

Cost: If revenues stay the same, how does each location affect manufacturing costs?

Note the differences between locating a plant and selecting a store or office location. One major difference is that the choice of a region or community is far more important to manufacturers than the choice of a site within the community. Another difference is the lasting effect of plant location. Once a plant is built, the entrepreneur is committed to the manufacture of a certain line of products for some time. If the entrepreneur has made a poor location decision, relocation would probably mean financial collapse. Thorough research is imperative before building a plant.

Location Criteria Used by High-Technology Companies

There is little question that high-technology companies will continue to fuel the nation's economy. What do these companies look for in selecting a plant site?

Example: In 1982, the Joint Economic Committee of the U.S. Congress surveyed 691 high-technology companies to find out what criteria they use in choosing plant sites and how they evaluate the various regions of the country. As shown in Exhibit 8.6, the most important criterion is affordable labor. Other factors, in order of importance, are:

- Labor productivity
- Favorable tax climate
- Prestigious academic institutions that can provide research support
- Affordable cost of living
- Accessible transportation system
- Easy access to markets
- Limited regional regulatory controls
- Ready supply of affordable energy
- Cultural amenities
- Favorable climate
- Easy access to raw materials.

According to the report of the Joint Economic Committee, the Midwest—the epitome of smokestack America—is expected to have the

EXHIBIT 8.6 *Criteria for Selecting Plant Sites*

A sampling of 691 high-technology companies ranked 12 criteria for importance in selecting plant sites. The companies ranked each criterion either very significant, somewhat significant, or not significant. The percentages in the chart are the sum of very significant and somewhat significant percentages.

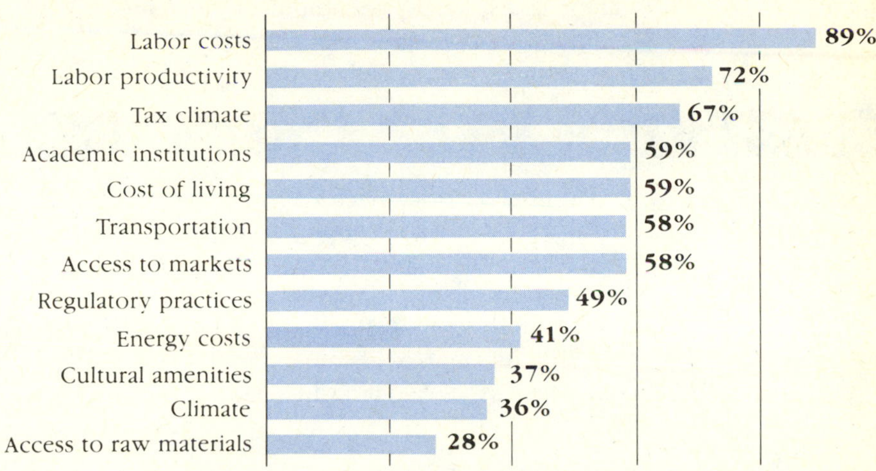

Source: Joint Economic Committee of U.S. Congress, as reported in Louis E. Boone and David L. Kurtz, *Contemporary Business* (New York, N.Y.: The Dryden Press, 1985), p. 43. Copyright © 1985 by CBS College Publishing. Reprinted by permission of CBS College Publishing.

most high-technology development in the immediate future. Although it was graded no better than fourth in any category, as shown in Exhibit 8.7, the Midwest gained the top overall ranking because other regions received such low marks for some important criteria. For instance, New England

EXHIBIT 8.7

A sampling of 691 high-technology companies ranked seven U.S. regions based on their strength in each of 12 criteria. A ranking of "1" for a region means the companies chose it to be the best in that category; "2," second best; and so on.

Rating of U.S. Regions by High-Technology Companies

	Regional Rankings						
Criterion	**New England**	**Far West**	**Mid-east**	**South-east**	**South-west**	**Mountain and plain**	**Mid-west**
Labor costs	5	7	6	1	2	3	4
Labor productivity	6	4	7	3	2	1	4
Tax climate	7	5	6	1	2	3	4
Academic institutions	1	2	3	6	5	7	4
Cost of living	6	7	5	1	2	3	4
Transportation	2	3	1	6	5	7	4
Access to markets	2	1	3	6	5	7	4
Regulatory practices	7	5	6	1	2	3	4
Energy costs	7	4	6	1	2	3	5
Cultural amenities	1	2	3	7	5	6	4
Climate	5	1	6	3	2	4	7
Access to raw materials	3	1	2	6	5	7	4

Source: Joint Economic Committee of U.S. Congress, as reported in Louis E. Boone and David L. Kurtz, *Contemporary Business* (New York, N.Y.: The Dryden Press, 1985), p. 43. Copyright © 1985 by CBS College Publishing. Reprinted by permission of CBS College Publishing.

and the Far West, which now have the highest intensity of high-technology firms, may not be able to maintain their positions because of labor costs, taxes, and the cost of living.[4]

SUMMARY

Location is a critical factor in many industries. However, because of the strong trend toward shopping centers and industrial parks, the decision where to locate is often made by the developer, not by the entrepreneur. Today, more than 24,000 shopping centers and more than 4,500 industrial parks dot the country.

Still, entrepreneurs do have some freedom of choice in areas not controlled by developers. In selecting a site, they should examine, in this order:

- A geographical region
- A city within that region
- An area within that city
- A specific site within that area

Entrepreneurs often permit their personal likes and dislikes to influence their selection. But they should never permit such personal biases to blind them to the realities of a poor location.

Entrepreneurs should research their markets before deciding where best to locate. They need to research and analyze the facts about the potential market.

Locating a manufacturing plant differs in two important ways from locating a retail store or a service. First, the choice of a region or city outweighs the choice of a site within the city. Second, the effects of a poor plant location are harder to undo than those of a poor retail or service location.

DISCUSSION AND REVIEW QUESTIONS

1. Why is location more vital in some industries than in others? Give two examples.
2. Since World War II, how has the rapid growth of shopping centers and industrial parks influenced the question of where to locate a venture?
3. Do you believe that within a generation or two, most manufacturing will take place in industrial parks? Explain.
4. Define these terms: *industrial park, developer, ecological concerns, marketing research, buying power, census tract.*
5. How would you go about selecting a site for your own venture?
6. What role does marketing research play in locating a venture?

7. If you were thinking about opening a retail store, why might you prefer to locate it near other retail stores that are healthy and prosperous?
8. Describe some of the ways you might get outside help in locating your venture.
9. In what ways is locating a manufacturing plant perhaps more critical than locating a retail store or service?
10. What role should personal preference play in locating a venture? Explain.
11. Do you believe there should be local laws inhibiting the growth of shopping centers or industrial parks? Why?
12. In locating a manufacturing plant, what site factors should the entrepreneur try to balance?
13. In site selection, what are some of the questions that a retailing entrepreneur should ask in selecting a city? An area within the city?
14. Under what conditions might locating a venture in a declining city be attractive to entrepreneurs?
15. What is meant by a "least-cost" location for a manufacturing venture?

NOTES

1. Adapted from Robert F. Hartley, *Retailing* (Boston: Houghton Mifflin, 1980), pp. 136–137.
2. Louis H. Vorzimer, U.S. Small Business Administration, "Using Census Data to Select a Store Site," *Small Marketers Aid No. 154* (Washington, D.C.: U.S. Government Printing Office, 1976).
3. Adapted from Maurice Fulton, "New Factors in Plant Location," *Harvard Business Review*, May–June 1971, p. 4.
4. Adapted from Louis E. Boone and David L. Kurtz, *Contemporary Business* (New York, N.Y.: The Dryden Press, 1985), pp. 42–44. Copyright © 1985 by CBS College Publishing. Reprinted by permission of CBS College Publishing.

CASE 8A *Chimo Enterprises, Inc.*

Chimo Enterprises is seeking a $250,000 bank loan through the U.S. Small Business Administration (SBA). Its president, Stuart Ramsay, claims he needs that sum to expand sales revenues dramatically, from $530,700 to $820,400. The company markets lawn-care, landscaping, and tree services.

To justify his loan request, Mr. Ramsay has prepared a 112-page business plan. He prepared the plan when he was participating in a strategic planning course sponsored by the small business section of the local Chamber of Commerce. Taught by Dr. Jeffrey Susbauer and Dr. Robert Baker, this course is aimed solely at entrepreneurs whose ventures are poised for growth. Both men head their own consulting firms and are well-known nationally for their knowledge of strategic planning.

Mr. Ramsay has just submitted his business plan to the SBA. The loan officer there promised to call him within ten days, to inform him of the status of his loan request. Excerpts from the plan follow.

Company History

As suggested in our beginning balance sheet, shown in Exhibit 8A.1, we began humbly as a landscape maintenance and construction company in 1976. We also plowed snow during the winter. We directed our marketing efforts mostly at large accounts such as condominiums and apartment complexes, until we won several major construction contracts for new landscaping. Then we decided to focus on that market.

In our second year of operations, we purchased a Lawn Doctor franchise. We grew rapidly in the next two years and set sales records for Lawn Doctor franchises.

In our third year of operations, we added a tree services division and developed new business by taking our existing customer base and selling additional but related services. This strategy has worked well, reducing both our marketing and transportation costs.

Since we are undercapitalized, fast growth has caused us to suffer financially. Thus, the $250,000 loan will enable us to:

- Relieve the financial strain.
- Upgrade existing equipment.

EXHIBIT 8A.1

Chimo Enterprises: Beginning Balance Sheet (June 30, 1976)

Assets		Equities	
Cash	$ 1,400	Liabilities	$ 0
Truck	5,000	Owner's equity	15,000
Landscape equipment	8,000		
Other	600		
Total assets	$15,000	Total equities	$15,000

- Reduce maintenance costs sharply.
- Market new products that match the needs of our existing customer base.

Company Mission

We aim to market a total landscaping service to commercial and residential customers, offering them lawn fertilization, landscape maintenance, and tree services. We will earn a return of 15 percent on investment from this expansion. At first we will focus on selling additional services to existing, satisfied customers within a five-mile radius of our home office. Later, as penetration warrants, we will open branches in outlying areas, thus creating job opportunities for existing employees. We will do business in an ethical way, creating a work atmosphere that enables our employees to mature professionally.

Our five-year plan calls for the opening of three branches. We expect sales revenues to reach $600,000 a year at the home office and $200,000 at each branch. This expansion will be financed mostly through funneling profits back into the business and training current employees as potential managerial candidates.

Although winter operations have centered on commercial and industrial snowplowing, we will eliminate these services in favor of more profitable lines of work, such as hydraulic deep-root tree and shrub feeding and winter antidesiccant spraying.

Description of Business

We have three operating divisions:

- Chimo landscape services division, which does home designs, new constructions, and lawn renovation work. This division specializes in high-quality, fully-guaranteed work, successfully marketed through a base of customers established by the other divisions.
- Chimo tree services division, which prunes and takes down trees. This division also specializes in such preventive work as tree spraying, hydraulic deep-root feeding, and tree surgery.
- Lawn Doctor services division, which fertilizes lawns. Using the only patented ground-metered equipment in the lawn-care industry, Lawn Doctor provides the finest custom-applied lawn programs available.

Our market focuses on homeowner accounts in a small geographic area. A feature of such accounts is that we can sell them other services once they are satisfied with the work of one division. Computer records on all prospects and customers give us a data base for marketing additional services unmatched in the industry. We expect to penetrate 10 percent of the homeowner market within a five-mile radius of our home office, expanding later to branches in outlying areas.

Our competitive position is strong, mostly because our equipment can tailor an application to a customer's specific lawn needs—a service not supplied by competitors at this time. Our salespeople evaluate lawn needs in person and make their sales presentations on the spot, resulting in a sales-to-closing ratio higher than that of our competitors.

One marketing goal is to employ salespeople throughout the year, so as to penetrate the industrial, commercial, and institutional markets more effectively. Such a salesforce would help reduce the seasonal swings in our business as well as help create a stable workforce.

Our pricing strategy is to price to customer value, by guaranteeing high-quality work. This strategy helps to retain our customer base at a level higher than that of competitors.

Major Changes in Marketing Direction

In 1983, we took a critical look at the markets we served and the services we offered. It quickly became apparent that some areas needed immediate changes. One such area was lawn mowing, which was highly unprofitable. Prices were so depressed that large buyers of lawn-mowing services were looking at price not value, so we eliminated 95 percent of all lawn-mowing operations. Similarly, we found that snowplowing prices had dropped as much as 40 percent in the past three years, so we dropped those services, too.

In 1983, the upsurge in new-home construction suggested that the market for new landscape construction would rise sharply. We decided to go into that market heavily. To date, new landscape construction sales have leaped almost 400 percent.

We also identified hydraulic deep-root feeding as a highly profitable and much-needed service for both homeowner and industrial accounts. Although still in its infancy, this market will grow quickly if we provide high-quality service. In December 1982, this new service outsold our snowplowing.

Industry Structure and Our Position

As mentioned earlier, we operate three divisions: Chimo landscape services, Chimo tree services, and Lawn Doctor services. This line of services has positioned us as a complete landscape and exterior services company. No competitor offers as much. For example, we offer such services as:

- Dethatching
- Fertilizing
- Fungus control
- Lawn renovation
- New seed and sod work
- Plug core aerating
- Soil amendments

We also offer complete design and new landscape construction. Moreover, we have a service that provides a diagnosis of shrub and tree problems and our tree services division does such work as tree removal, pruning, stump removal, tree spraying, and hydraulic deep-root feeding. Offering such a full line of services enables us to capture new business at

EXHIBIT 8A.2 *Chimo Enterprises, Inc.: Statistics on Lawn and Garden Care*

Seventy-one million U.S. households work on lawns or gardens, a $15 billion-a-year market. The most common activities:

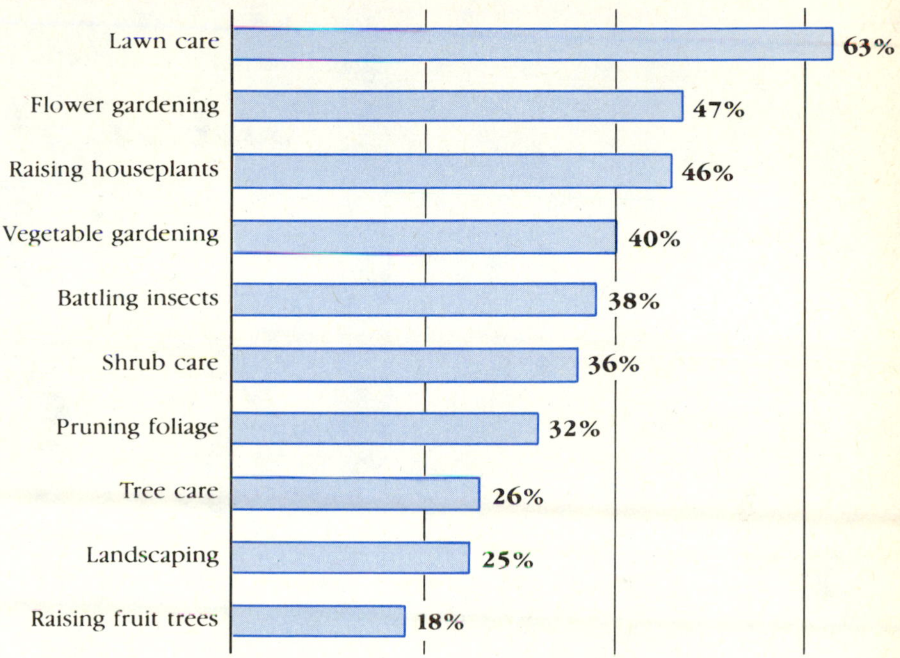

Source: National Gardening Association

reduced costs, since customers who are satisfied with one division's work will more readily buy services available from another division—as mentioned earlier. The statistics in Exhibit 8A.2 show that the markets we serve are the right ones.

In our industry, the most crucial aspect of cost control is geographic routing. Measured against an industry average of three miles per stop, our Lawn Doctor services division does well indeed. It averages less than two tenths of a mile per stop.

We control our landscape services division similarly. When we market such extra services as plug-core aerating, dethatching, and lime applications, we route our service trucks in a geographic pattern that achieves the highest number of services for the miles driven.

The tree services division markets its services similarly. Our hydraulic deep-root feeding, tree spraying, and antidesiccant spraying services are all marketed intensively at different times of the year, and the trucks are routed to achieve the highest production for the fewest miles.

Competitive Position

The market for our Lawn Doctor services division is highly competitive—at least 17 major companies vie for the same customer base. Although our prices are among the highest in the industry, we offer the best

EXHIBIT 8A.3 *Chimo Enterprises, Inc.: Lawn Doctor Services Guarantee*

services available. We have unique advantages over competitors in the following areas:

- Patented machines that "custom apply" both dry granular and liquid materials. As mentioned earlier, only our company is capable of customizing applications to individual lawn needs.
- Total landscape services. Some of our competitors offer additional services, but no one else offers a total service on a competitive basis.
- The industry's best written guarantee, as shown in Exhibit 8A.3. Note that we offer to redo any application free of charge if the customer is dissatisfied. Moreover, if the customer continues to be dissatisfied, we guarantee to refund the full cost of the last application.
- Both our name and green thumb logo, which project an image of professionalism that is seldom forgotten by customers.

Computerization

The computer boom has not escaped our eye. Because of the large number of customers, we found that it was simply too inefficient to process paper by hand. We were the first Lawn Doctor franchise in the country to install a computer.

We paid a programmer $25,000 to design programs tailored to our lawn-care business. Our computer system already carries four pages worth of data on each customer and it has the potential to carry out many more functions. The computer also produces all of our truck routing, inventory control, financial statements, financial projections, account statuses, sales invoicing, and marketing letters. Our list of computer capabilities has grown to include updating and scheduling of customer services. Each customer's file includes what was done to the lawn and when and suggests additional services that may be needed. This system enables us to serve our customers more efficiently—on time with fewer errors—and to keep better track of the lawn's progress. If a problem develops, we can resolve it quickly.

Like many operations being introduced to a computer, we expected miracles when we first installed it. We expected our staff to be able to put out reports overnight. When we realized that it just was not that simple, we sent the whole staff for a ten-week orientation program, to learn more about operating a computer system successfully. This decision for additional schooling paid off. We saved at least $10,000 in labor in the first year alone and recovered our investment in the computer system in two years. We foresee an unlimited potential for further computerization, as we install additional computer terminals, hire more employees to run them, and upgrade our operations in this way.

Like many other smaller businesses, we have discovered that computers are becoming more than just an economic advantage—they are almost mandatory. A view of our computer system appears in Exhibit 8A.4.

EXHIBIT 8A.4 *Chimo Enterprises, Inc.: A View of Kathleen and Stuart Ramsay with their Computer System*

Innovation We will continue to introduce innovative ideas that save homeowners' money while optimizing their satisfaction with the services we perform. Some examples of innovative ideas are:

- Offering improved strains of shade grass seed that correct the problem of bare ground under trees.
- Providing materials that ease the penetration of lawn roots, thus reducing the amount of water needed in summer.
- Checking acidity, alkalinity, and thatch levels routinely.
- Offering a range of corrective services to boost a lawn's endurance.

These ideas will surely beautify our customers' lawns, causing our sales to rise significantly.

Lawn care is a $5 billion-a-year industry with a growth rate of 20 percent a year, as shown in Exhibit 8A.5. It is our innovations that will always keep us ahead of our competitors.

Another new service that we plan to market is the Leaky Pipe, which is a low-cost alternative to sprinkler systems. This capillary-action, underground system may save customers up to 70 percent on water bills. Our conversations with distributors in other states have shown us that its market potential is huge. We can secure the exclusive distributorship

EXHIBIT 8A.5 *Chimo Enterprises, Inc.: Growth of Lawn-Care Industry**

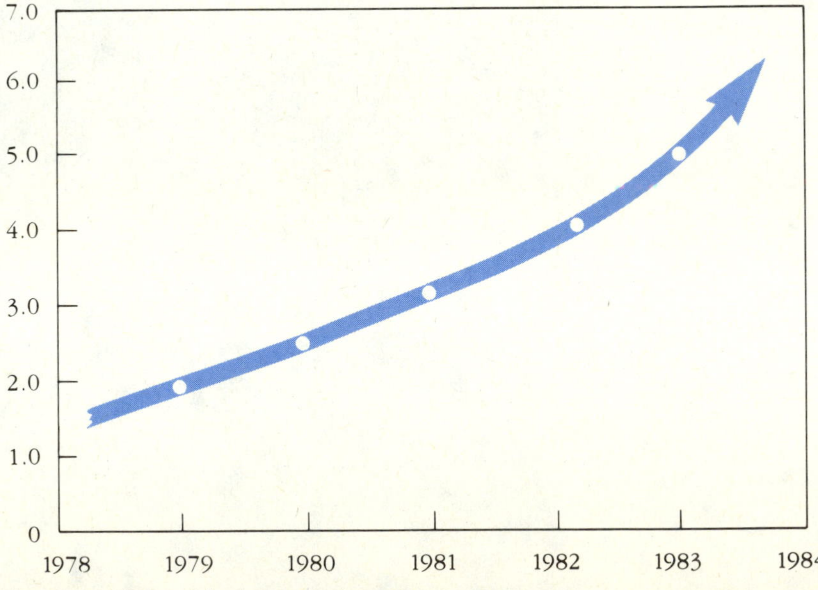

* Excludes tree services and landscape services.

covering our state. Our Green Thumb Newsletter describes the Leaky Pipe as follows:

> Totally reliable, very inexpensive, and the most effective watering system on the market today, Leaky Pipe is installed three to eight inches beneath the surface of your lawn or garden. Leaking slowly and evenly through thousands of minute pores in a flexible rubber pipe, water gently seeps into the soil from the pipe and moves by means of capillary action to the plant roots. Leaky Pipe is ideally suited for use in any lawn or garden, regardless of size. Counted among its advantages over conventional sprinkler systems are that:
>
> - Leaky Pipe saves time. It takes just a few hours to install and does its work without further effort.
> - Leaky Pipe saves water. Because neither evaporation nor runoff takes place, water savings may run as high as 70 percent.
> - Leaky Pipe saves on maintenance. Indestructibly strong and durable, it is installed wholly underground.
> - Leaky Pipe saves money. It costs much less to install than conventional sprinkler systems. Its useful life exceeds 20 years. And, it lowers water bills.

Management

Stuart Ramsay, who is the president and founder of Chimo Enterprises, was born in Montreal. While still in his teens, he left for the Canadian Arctic, where he worked as an apprentice carpenter. He received nine promotions in only three years while building the Canadian radar line.

Upon returning to Montreal, Mr. Ramsay became a district manager for the morning daily newspaper, where he worked for three years. Then, in rapid succession, he held a series of managerial jobs, each one more responsible than the preceding one:

- Manager, Branch Office, Sun Life Insurance Company in a northern Canadian mining town
- Industrial food sales representative, Procter & Gamble. With this company, he moved through the ranks to earn top honors in Canada as president of its National Sales Production Club.
- Sales manager, Commerce Label and Litho, a label and specialty printing manufacturer. He expanded the salesforce from one to nine salesmen and more than quadrupled sales.
- Commissioned salesman with Premier Industrial Corporation. Within three months he was promoted to sales manager, a position that required him to move from Canada to a midwestern U.S. city.

In 1976, Mr. Ramsay left Premier Industrial to create Chimo Enterprises, initially as a landscaping and lawn maintenance business. His interest in lawn care was sparked by a horticultural project he headed while at Sun Life Insurance.

Shortly after forming Chimo Enterprises, Mr. Ramsay purchased a Lawn Doctor franchise. Mostly because of his energetic and competitive nature, it quickly became the fastest-growing new franchise in Lawn Doctor's history.

Other Key Members of Management Team Our company's success stems largely from our management team's dedication to excellence. An organizational chart appears in Exhibit 8A.6. Our managers often work as many as 60 or 70 hours a week, especially during spring and summer. Equally important, they are overachievers who perform to the best of their abilities. The team includes:

- Kathleen Ramsay, a founder of Chimo Enterprises and its vice president. A graduate of the University of Dayton, she held a number of managerial positions before marrying Mr. Ramsay and cofounding Chimo. As a buyer for a major department store chain, she was in charge of buying and planning for eight stores in the chain. At present, Ms. Ramsay oversees such vital functions as finance, credit and collection, purchasing, systems analysis, and organizational planning.
- David Sproul, manager of all tree and landscaping services. He is a graduate of Ohio State University with a degree in landscape design and construction. His responsibilities include all field operations, new design work and landscape sales.
- Gail Lingenfelter manager of our accounting activities and computer operations. She is a graduate of Cuyahoga Community College with a degree in accounting.
- Jane Szostakowski, home office manager. She is responsible for all secretarial duties, including order entry, printing, and general office management.
- David Switzer, customer service manager. His major responsibility is to resolve all customer complaints successfully. Before joining us, he was service manager for Orkin Pest Control, where he headed a team of 12 technicians and a fleet of 10 trucks.

EXHIBIT 8A.6 *Chimo Enterprises, Inc.: Organizational Chart*

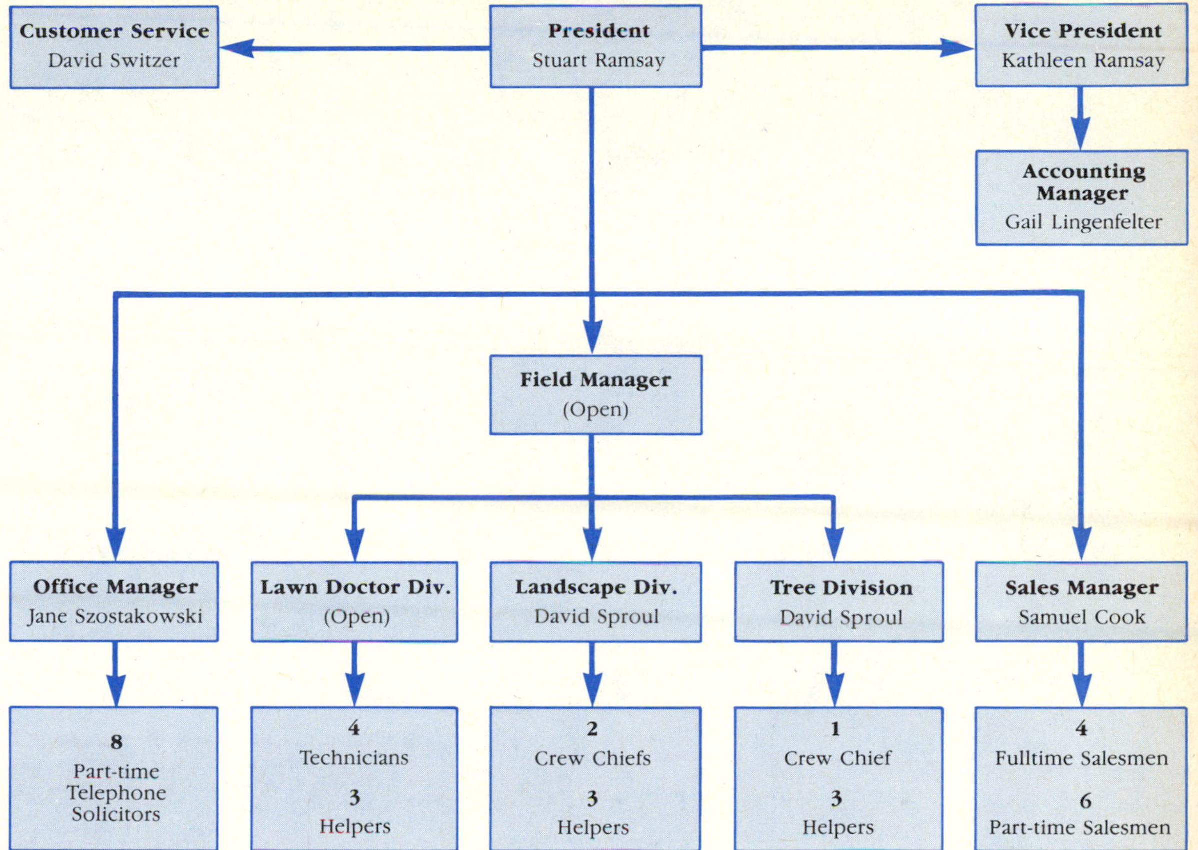

Financial Proposal

We seek a $250,000 loan, with a repayment schedule of monthly payments for seven years, through the guaranteed loan program of the SBA. We will use this money to:

- Purchase equipment and inventory
- Renovate our new office and storage building
- Update our truck fleet
- Liquidate a portion of our existing debt
- Maintain sufficient cash reserves for emergencies
- Provide adequate working capital

These uses of the loan will enable us to expand dramatically, to sales revenues of $820,400 in 1984, from $530,700 in 1983. Supporting financial

EXHIBIT 8A.7

Chimo Enterprises, Inc.: Uses of $250,000 Loan

Repayment of loan to bank	$ 76,300
Operating equipment	
3 pick-up trucks	
2 turf tamers	
1 rear-tine rototiller	
1 sod cutter	
1 motorized tree chipper	
1 stump grinder	
1 tree sprayer	
1 dump truck	
1 utility vehicle	
1 one-ton van	75,700
Working capital	53,000
Three months' cash reserve	45,000
Total	$250,000

statements appear in:

- Exhibit 8A.7 describes precisely how we will disburse the $250,000.
- Exhibit 8A.8 compares our 1984 and 1985 projected income statements with the 1983 statement.
- Exhibit 8A.9 contains our latest balance sheet, as of June 30, 1983.

Questions

1. Comment on Chimo's financial performance.
2. What accounts for Chimo's recent success?
3. Do you believe Mr. Ramsay's business plan justifies his need for a $250,000 loan? Explain fully.
4. Comment on Mr. Ramsay's entrepreneurial qualities.
5. What are the company's prospects?

EXHIBIT 8A.8

Chimo Enterprises, Inc.: Actual and Projected Income Statements

		Projected	
	1983*	1984	1985
Sales Revenues			
Lawn Doctor Division	$304,900	$501,000	$ 680,600
Landscape and Tree Division	222,800	298,400	370,000
Special projects	3,000	21,000	36,000
Total sales revenues	$530,700	$820,400	$1,086,600
Cost of sales			
Cost of services sold	$190,100	$297,500	$ 357,400
Selling expenses	33,200	42,500	59,400
Advertising expenses	29,400	38,500	54,100
Total cost of sales	$252,700	$378,500	$ 470,900
Gross profit	$278,000	$441,900	$ 615,700
Operating expenses			
Royalties	$ 30,300	$ 49,900	$ 70,400
Officers' salaries	6,300	26,400	36,000
Clerical salaries	26,100	27,200	34,000
Depreciation	21,900	28,700	26,600
Office supplies	12,200	11,500	15,300
Payroll taxes	10,700	14,600	13,900
Rent	10,400	12,000	12,600
Insurance	6,200	7,600	10,000
Telephone	9,200	8,000	8,900
Professional services	3,700	7,200	6,000
Printing	4,300	3,600	5,500
Utilities	3,600	3,200	3,300
Hospitalization	2,000	2,800	3,100
Postage	2,000	2,200	3,100
Local taxes	1,800	2,100	2,800
Travel and entertainment	4,000	1,800	2,100
Dues and licenses	2,000	1,200	2,100
Total operating expenses	$156,700	$209,800	$ 255,700
Operating profit	$121,300	$232,100	$ 360,000
Non-operating adjustments			
Interest expense	$ 30,000	$ 38,300	$ 30,400
Gain on disposal	3,500	0	0
Total adjustments	$ 26,500	$ 38,300	$ 30,400
Profit before taxes	$ 94,800	$193,800	$ 329,600

* Actual

EXHIBIT 8A.9

Chimo Enterprises, Inc.: Latest Balance Sheet (As of June 30, 1983)

Assets		
Current Assets		
Cash	$ 1,800	
Accounts receivable	135,500	
Inventories	18,400	
Prepaid expenses	16,900	$172,600
Fixed assets		
Assets under capital leases	$ 67,900	
Transportation equipment	40,000	
Machinery and equipment	26,200	
Furniture and fixtures	9,700	
Leasehold improvements	8,500	
	$152,300	
Less: Accumulated depreciation	96,500	55,800
Other assets		5,900
Total assets		$234,300
Equities		
Current liabilities		
Accounts payable	$ 62,700	
Accrued expenses	32,400	
Bank note payable	80,600	
Other notes payable	12,900	
Advertising fee payable	1,800	
Unearned revenues	118,600	
Royalty fee payable	2,800	$311,800
Long-term liabilities		
Capital lease obligations	$ 9,600	
Shareholder loans payable	70,200	79,800
Owners' Equity		
Common stock	$ 16,000	
Retained earnings	(173,300)	(157,300)
Total equities		$234,300

CASE 8B *Parrie Chemical Company*

After 13 years as an executive with two major chemical corporations, James Parrie decided to go into business for himself. His business plan completed, Mr. Parrie tentatively made two decisions::

- To manufacture nitrogen chemicals
- To locate his plant on the shores of Lake Erie, near Buffalo, New York

Mr. Parrie chose nitrogen fertilizers because he knew the product line thoroughly. He had managed a plant that made nitrogen chemicals such as urea and ammonia, which were sold mostly to fertilizer manufacturers. Before that, he had worked as a marketing researcher in agricultural chemicals. "I really have a gut feeling for the fertilizer industry," says Mr. Parrie.

Mr. Parrie chose upstate New York "not because I'm a lifelong New Yorker but because I'm sure I can adequately serve the midwestern farm belt from the region." He plans to ship fertilizer throughout the Midwest, mainly through distributors who supply farmers.

He chose Buffalo "because I grew up there. But that's not the only reason," adds Mr. Parrie. "Rail and water facilities are good, and there's also a large supply of semiskilled workers. Too, my contacts in Buffalo are good. The banks have offered to help finance my plant, and the city fathers have agreed to give me some tax advantages if I locate there."

Mr. Parrie's prospects looked good except for one major problem. "The city fathers suddenly became concerned about the wastes my plant would be discharging into Lake Erie," says Mr. Parrie. "Several chemical companies were already facing criminal prosecution from the state of New York for dumping pollutants into the lake."

Mr. Parrie ignored this problem until recently, but now he must design special equipment to neutralize the wastes from his proposed plant. He found that the additional pollution-control equipment would cost \$120,000, which would bring the total plant cost to \$720,000. He also estimated that additional energy, labor, and maintenance would cost \$10,000 a year.

Because before-tax profits would average about \$70,000 a year, Mr. Parrie is beginning to have doubts about locating in his home town of Buffalo. He spoke with a plant-location consultant, who suggested he look at plant sites in certain other midwestern states where "they're eager to attract new industry and aren't as worried about pollution." He also spoke to one of the city fathers, who suggested that he pass the added cost on to customers.

Questions

1. What should Mr. Parrie do now?
2. What alternatives does Mr. Parrie have?
3. What additional information would help Mr. Parrie decide what to do?

CASE 8C *Woolley Appliance Store*

The Woolley Appliance Store is a locally-owned home appliance outlet that has been in business for 18 years. It is located in Pelham, a town of 20,000 people. For the last five years, the store's yearly sales revenues have topped \$500,000.

Its owner, Sarah Woolley, has controlled the business since she founded it. Recently, she has considered expanding her business by opening a new outlet in Emmett, a town not far from Pelham. Emmett has a population roughly equivalent to that of Pelham, but does not have an appliance store.

Ms. Woolley is eager to enter this new market before someone else does. During the past several months she has been compiling buying power information for the Emmett market. Using the data in Exhibits 8C.1, 8C.2, and 8C.3, she has compared the buying power of the two markets for last year and this year.

EXHIBIT 8C.1

Disposable Income, Savings, and Discretionary Purchasing Power

	Pelham		Emmett	
Items	Last Year	This Year	Last Year	This Year
Per capita	$5,450	$5,200	$3,025	$3,500
Personal savings (as percent of disposable income)	0.06	0.07	0.03	0.04
Discretionary purchasing power (as percent of aggregate consumer purchasing power)	0.40	0.45	0.20	0.25

EXHIBIT 8C.2

Percent of Families in Selected Income Classes: (Last Year)

Income	Pelham	Emmett
Under $10,000	10	25
$10,000–$15,000	25	35
$15,000–$25,000	30	20
$25,000–$35,000	20	15
Over $35,000	15	5

EXHIBIT 8C.3

Patterns of Consumer Spending for Selected Products: (as percentage of total consumer expenditures)

Expenditure	Pelham	Emmett
Housing	14.5	13.7
Food for home consumption	16.1	18.2
Household appliances	1.4	0.9
Recreation	6.3	5.5
Clothing	10.3	8.6

Questions

1. Indicate the relevance of each of the exhibits to Ms. Woolley's decision.
2. What recommendation would you make to Ms. Woolley concerning the opening of an appliance store in Emmett? Give specific reasons for your recommendation.
3. What factors other than buying power should Ms. Woolley evaluate before making her decision?

Source: Adapted from William M. Pride and O. C. Ferrell, *Marketing: Basic Concepts and Decisions*, 2nd ed. (Boston: Houghton Mifflin, 1980), pp. 611–612. Used by permission.

9 FINANCING

QUESTIONS FOR MASTERY

Why does one need a financial plan?

How does one estimate the amount of money needed to launch a new venture?

What is the difference between equity capital and debt capital?

What are the various ways of raising money?

How do federal agencies like the SBA help entrepreneurs finance their ventures?

Money is the seed of money.

Jean Jacques Rousseau

Like many works of art, a business begins on a piece of paper. The would-be entrepreneur may sit down and design a small electronics plant to meet customer needs and make a fine product, but without money, the entrepreneur's plant may never become a reality. That is why entrepreneurs should understand how to estimate the amount of money they need and then how to go about raising that money.

This twin problem fascinates entrepreneurs, perhaps more so than any other part of launching a new venture. This fascination may stem from a romantic view of how some multimillion-dollar businesses have begun on shoestrings of just a few thousand dollars. Apple Computer Corporation, for example, began with only $600 in 1976.

Despite its romantic aspects, financing a new venture frustrates many entrepreneurs. Often, they do not know where to begin, or if they do know, they go at it haphazardly. It is one purpose of this chapter to help relieve that frustration.

ESTIMATING MONEY NEEDS

Before they can estimate how much money they need, entrepreneurs must know what they plan to do. Unfortunately, many entrepreneurs do not, often because they have failed to work out a business plan. Yet the very act of preparing such a plan enables entrepreneurs to crystallize their thinking on how best to launch their ventures. It forces them to move logically and systematically from the stage of dreams and ideas to that of concrete action. It is the concreteness of the business plan that assists entrepreneurs in determining their financial needs.

The centerpiece of the business plan is the *cash budget*, which translates operating plans into dollars. Without a cash budget, entrepreneurs have no way of estimating their financial needs. So vital are cash budgets that few investors or creditors will entertain a request for money without one. More than any other way, the cash budget enables them to decide intelligently whether to finance the entrepreneur. The cash budget, for example, helps the banker get answers to these questions:

- How much money do you need?
- How will you spend the money?
- How soon will you pay us back?

Entrepreneur's Reluctance to Budget

The process of budgeting has many guises. Some individuals divide the money from their weekly income into piles that they then place in envelopes earmarked for groceries, clothes, entertainment, and so on. The federal government engages in a lengthy procedure of debate and compromise between the Congress and the president. Many giant corporations proceed in an orderly system that reflects both long- and short-range goals.

What they are all doing is budgeting, or financial planning. Yet, although such planning is widely practiced among individuals, government, and big business, it is little used by entrepreneurs. One reason for their reluctance to budget may be their discomfort with numbers. To many entrepreneurs, financial skill is something best left to Wall Street. In commenting on this attitude, the Bank of America says:

> Running any business today demands certain technical skills. Purchasing demands technical skill. Production demands another technical skill; selling . . . still another technical skill. You feel at home with these skills—they are tangible evidence that you are in business.
>
> But there is another skill that plays a big part in how you do—and sometimes, whether you do—business. And that is financial skill. It is not a tangible, see-in-action skill, like the others. But rather, it is a "think" skill . . . The biggest problem with this particular "think" skill is that it intimidates most people. The mere language of finance . . . sounds so official, important, and difficult that many businesspersons automatically assume it is beyond their understanding. They feel that anything so obviously "textbookish" is better left to the professionals.[1]

With this attitude, it is hardly surprising that so many entrepreneurs find themselves in trouble from the start. Yet they often blame investors and creditors for their plight, not themselves. An entrepreneur might say, "If only I had $10,000, I could really make my idea work." Generally unprepared, such entrepreneurs can make little effort to convince potential investors and creditors of their need for money. But the odds favor the prepared entrepreneur. As Branch Rickey, former owner of the old Brooklyn Dodgers, once said, "Luck is the residue of design."

Budget Preparation

We introduced budget preparation in Chapter Six. Let us now discuss the details of how to work up a cash budget. Before they can begin to develop cash budgets, entrepreneurs must first spell out their operating plans, defining their production, marketing, staffing, accounting, and legal goals. Note that these are all key parts of the business plan.

Before we describe the process of translating these plans into dollars, let us first point out two limitations of budgeting:

- All budgets depend on estimates of what entrepreneurs think will happen in the future. However, they cannot always predict what will happen. Their budgets can be no better than their estimates of what the future holds, so entrepreneurs should be as thorough as possible in their efforts to prepare workable operating plans.
- Budgets cannot account for the effects of intangible qualities or unpredictable events. They cannot reflect how skilled and able the entrepreneur may be, nor can they reflect teamwork and morale. Budgets can only deal with future events that can be expressed in dollars.

EXHIBIT 9.1

Home Furnishings Store, Inc.: Forecast of Sales Revenues

Year	Sales Revenues		
		1st month	$ 20,000*
		2nd month	10,000
		3rd month	12,000
		4th month	14,000
		5th month	16,000
1	$240,000	6th month	18,000
2	320,000	7th month	20,000
3	400,000	8th month	22,000
		9th month	24,000
		10th month	26,000
		11th month	28,000
		12th month	30,000
			$240,000

* Assumes revenues will be relatively high the first month because of store's "grand opening."

Still, budgeting represents a remarkable achievement. It provides a way of summarizing the future in a single statement and in language that investors and creditors understand. Let us now show how operating plans may be translated into a cash budget:

Example: An entrepreneur plans to open a home furnishings store and she has estimated her sales revenues for the first three years (see Exhibit 9.1).

This revenue forecast is a result of the marketing plan that she worked out as part of her business plan. Although it is rough, the revenue forecast is the single most important estimate an entrepreneur can make. Most of the other estimates the entrepreneur must make are based on it. For example, a store with yearly revenues of $2,000,000 rather than $400,000 may call for:

- Five times as many salespersons
- Four times as much floor space
- Three times as much inventory of home furnishings

Having forecast her revenues, the entrepreneur next estimates the cost of the fixed and current assets she will need to support those revenues. Before we proceed with our example, we will describe and differentiate fixed and current assets.

Fixed Assets Fixed assets are resources whose use will benefit the entrepreneur for more than one year. An example is a building bought for $150,000. If the entrepreneur expects the building to last 25 years, then he or she would receive $150,000 worth of shelter benefits over the next 25 years—or $6,000 worth of benefits a year. Other examples of fixed assets include machines, land, trucks, desks, and even ashtrays.

These examples are resources the entrepreneur can touch and see, but fixed assets may also be intangible. For example, an inventor may sell an entrepreneur the patent rights for a new pollution-control device for $80,000. The entrepreneur might expect to benefit from the patent rights for the next 10 years. These rights cannot be touched or seen, but they are a long-lived asset that will provide benefits to the entrepreneur's business for more than one year. Other examples of intangible assets are licenses and goodwill.

Current Assets In contrast to fixed assets, current assets are resources whose benefits will last less than one year. Commonly, current assets are cash, accounts receivable, and inventories. Accounts receivable, the bills owed by customers who buy on credit, represent a current asset because the entrepreneur may expect to collect within a short time, such as a month. Similarly, inventory is a current asset because entrepreneurs usually expect to recover their investment in inventory by selling it within a short period after purchasing it from a supplier.

Example: Returning to our previous example, let us now assume that the entrepreneur's store will sell Scandinavian furniture. She has made the following estimates of start-up costs. She will:

- Construct a one-story, free-standing building with 5,000 square feet of floor space to display and store furniture. Cost: $150,000 at year zero.
- Keep a base inventory of furniture high enough to support twice the average monthly budgeted (or forecast) revenues; in addition, buy enough inventory monthly to cover the following month's budgeted revenues. She plans to pay for all inventory within a month of purchasing it. Cost: $36,000 at year zero.
- Put an asphalt surface on a parking lot next to the building. Cost: $16,000 at year zero.
- Finance those customers who buy on credit. She is assuming that all sales will be credit sales, with customers taking a month to pay, on the average.
- Buy fixtures, office equipment, and a half-ton delivery truck. Cost: $26,000 at year zero.
- Incorporate the venture with a lawyer's help. Cost: $2,000.
- Design a record-keeping system with the help of an accountant. Cost: $1,000.
- Buy a three-year prepaid insurance policy. Cost: $6,000.
- Buy city, county, and state licenses. Cost: $1,000.
- Promote the store's grand opening. Cost: $2,000.

EXHIBIT 9.2 *Home Furnishings Store, Inc.: Cash Budget to Estimate Money Needs*

	Before Start-Up	Month After Start-Up 1	2	3	4
Expected sales revenues		$ 20,000	$ 10,000	$ 12,000	$ 14,000
Cash inflow					
Collections from credit customers		0	20,000	10,000	12,000
Cash outflow					
Purchasing inventory	$ 36,000	$ 6,000*	$ 7,200	$ 8,400	$ 9,600
Paying operating expenses		6,400	6,400	6,400	6,400
Subtotal	$ 36,000	$ 12,400	$ 13,600	$ 14,800	$ 16,000
Buying fixed assets	$192,000				
Buying other assets	12,000				
Subtotal	$240,000				
Total cash outflow	240,000	12,400	13,600	14,800	16,000
Cash-flow summary					
Total cash inflow		$ 0	$ 20,000	$ 10,000	$ 12,000
Total cash outflow	$240,000	12,400	13,600	14,800	16,000
Surplus or shortage	(240,000)	($ 12,400)	$ 6,400	($ 4,800)	($ 4,000)
Cumulative shortage	(240,000)	(252,400)	(246,000)	(250,800)	(254,800)
Money needs					
Maximum shortage	$262,800 ←				
10% allowance for contingencies	$26,280				
Total money needs	**$290,000‡**				
Cash balance at start of month	$290,000	$ 50,000	$ 37,600	$ 44,000	$ 39,200
Surplus or shortage	(240,000)	(12,400)	(6,400)	(4,800)	(4,000)
Cash balance at end of month	$ 50,000	$ 37,600	$ 44,000	$ 39,200	$ 35,200

* Obtained by multiplying the next month's revenues by 60 percent (60% × $10,000 revenues in *second* month = $6,000 purchase cost in *first* month).
† Assumes expected revenues of $30,000 in *thirteenth* month after start-up.
‡ Rounded upward to nearest thousand.

She now groups these cost items into three categories—current assets, fixed assets, and other assets—to arrive at the total cost of assets at year zero:

Current assets:		
Accounts receivable	$ 0	
Inventory	36,000	$ 36,000
Fixed assets:		
Building	$150,000	
Equipment and fixtures	26,000	
Parking lot	16,000	$192,000
Other assets:		
Prepaid insurance	$ 6,000	
Professional fees	3,000	
Promotional costs	2,000	
Licenses	1,000	$ 12,000
Total assets		$240,000

5	6	7	8	9	10	11	12
$ 16,000	$ 18,000	$ 20,000	$ 22,000	$ 24,000	$ 26,000	$ 28,000	$ 30,000
14,000	16,000	18,000	20,000	22,000	24,000	26,000	28,000
$ 10,800	$ 12,000	$ 13,200	$ 14,400	$ 15,600	$ 16,800	$ 18,000	$ 18,000†
6,400	6,400	6,400	6,400	6,400	6,400	6,400	6,400
$ 17,200	$ 18,400	$ 19,600	$ 20,800	$ 22,000	$ 23,200	$ 24,400	$ 24,400
17,200	18,400	19,600	20,800	22,000	23,200	24,400	24,400
$ 14,000	$ 16,000	$ 18,000	$ 20,000	$ 22,000	$ 24,000	$ 26,000	$ 28,000
17,200	18,400	19,600	20,800	22,000	23,200	24,400	24,400
(3,200)	(2,400)	(1,600)	(800)	$ 0	$ 800	$ 1,600	$ 3,600
(258,000)	260,400)	(262,000)	(262,800)	(262,800)	(262,000)	(260,400)	(256,800)
$ 35,200	$ 32,000	$ 29,600	$ 28,000	$ 27,200	$ 27,200	$ 28,000	$ 29,600
(3,200)	(2,400)	(1,600)	(800)	0	800	1,600	3,600
$ 32,000	$ 29,600	$ 28,000	$ 27,200	$ 27,200	$ 28,000	$ 29,600	$ 33,200

Instead of constructing the building, the entrepreneur could lease a building and its parking lot, thus reducing the asset costs from $240,000 to $74,000. If she did lease, she would probably have to pay rent in advance, covering at least the first month or two.

So far, the entrepreneur has estimated what it would cost just to open for business. She now must go one step further and estimate what it would cost to stay open through the first year, by month:

Monthly Cash Expenses (excluding cost of goods sold):	
Entrepreneur's salary	$2,400
Part-time employee wages	1,200
Advertising	600
Electricity, heat, telephone	400
Delivery	400
Accounting, legal	400
Supplies	200
Other	800
Total	$6,400

EXHIBIT 9.3 *Home Furnishings Store, Inc.: Beginning and Ending Balance Sheets*

Assets	Beginning	Ending	Equities	Beginning	Ending
Current assets			Liabilities	$ 0	$ 0
Cash	$ 50,000	$ 33,200[a]			
Accounts receivable	0	30,000[b]	Owners' equity		
Inventory	36,000	42,000[c]	Common stock	$290,000	$290,000
Subtotal	$ 86,000	$105,200	Retained earnings		1,000[f]
			Subtotal	$290,000	$291,000
Fixed assets					
Building	$150,000	$144,000[d]			
Equipment	26,000	23,400[d]			
Parking lot	16,000	14,400[d]			
Subtotal	192,000	181,800			
Other assets	12,000	4,000[e]			
Total assets	$290,000	$291,000	Total assets	$290,000	$291,000

[a] Obtained directly from Exhibit 9.2 (cash balance at end of twelfth month).
[b] Obtained directly from Exhibit 9.2 (all revenues in twelfth month will be owed by customers at month's end).
[c] Assumes a base inventory ($24,000) plus enough inventory ($18,000) to support the thirteenth month's budgeted revenues of 30,000.
[d] Reflects depreciation of fixed assets during year (see Exhibit 9.4).
[e] Reflects write-off of prepaid expenses during year (see Exhibit 9.4).
[f] Obtained directly from Exhibit 9.4 (assumes profits will be plowed back into the venture).

EXHIBIT 9.4 *Home Furnishings Store, Inc.: Income Statement (for first year of operations)*

Sales revenues		$240,000[a]
Cost of goods sold		144,000[b]
Gross profit		96,000
Operating expenses		
Administrative and selling	$76,800[c]	
Depreciation	10,200[d]	
Write-off of prepaid expenses	8,000[e]	95,000
Operating profit		$ 1,000

[a] Obtained from Exhibit 9.2 by adding monthly budgeted revenues
[b] Obtained by multiplying total budgeted revenues of $240,000 by 60 percent (because the gross margin is 40 percent).
[c] Obtained from Exhibit 9.2 by adding monthly operating expenses.
[d] Obtained as follows:

Building depreciation	= $150,000 ÷ 25-year life	=	$ 6,000
Equipment depreciation	= 26,000 ÷ 10-year life	=	2,600
Parking lot depreciation	= 16,000 ÷ 10-year life	=	1,600
			$10,200

[e] Obtained as follows:

Professional fees	=	$3,000
Insurance	=	2,000 (one third of $6,000 prepaid insurance policy expires during year)
Promotional costs	=	2,000
Licenses	=	1,000
		$8,000

Note that these monthly expenses are unlikely to change with revenues. That is, first-year revenues could be double the $240,000 forecast—and yet monthly expenses would not be significantly greater than $6,400. The only expense item likely to increase significantly is part-time wages, since as revenues increase, the entrepreneur will probably need to add more part-time salespersons to wait on customers.

To these costs, the entrepreneur should add the purchase cost of furniture sold. These purchase costs, as mentioned earlier, would vary with revenues. Assuming a profit margin of 40 percent, the entrepreneur would realize a gross profit of $40 on every $100 sales of furniture:

$100	paid by entrepreneur's customers (Revenues)
60	paid to entrepreneur's suppliers (Cost of Goods Sold)
$ 40	contribution to all other expenses and to profit (Gross Profit)

Having collected the cost figures, the entrepreneur may now go ahead and draft a cash budget for the first year. One method appears in Exhibit 9.2. Note that this budget shows:

- Expected *inflows* and *outflows* of cash
- The amount of money needed to finance the venture
- The cash balance at the end of each month

As shown in Exhibit 9.2, the entrepreneur needs $262,800, assuming that things will go as planned. They rarely do—so the entrepreneur adds a cushion of 10 percent to the $262,800 to allow for unevenness in the flow of money in and out of the venture and to absorb any unexpected bills. Rounding the figure to the nearest $1,000, the entrepreneur arrives at $290,000, the total amount she must raise to launch the venture.

Besides a cash budget, the entrepreneur should prepare beginning and ending balance sheets plus an income statement. These financial statements are shown in Exhibits 9.3 and 9.4. Note that most of the figures come from the cash budget and that the balance sheets assume that all the entrepreneur's assets would be financed through the sale of common stock. This assumption is unrealistic. Shortly, we will discuss other, more realistic ways of financing new ventures. Note also that the income statement shows that the venture will be profitable during its first full year of operation.

EQUITY CAPITAL VERSUS DEBT CAPITAL

Once entrepreneurs have estimated how much money they need to finance their ventures, they must then decide what fraction of this money should come:

- From investors, as *equity* capital
- From creditors, as *debt* capital

The ratio of debt to equity capital is a controversial topic. At one extreme, commercial bankers generally recommend that entrepreneurs and their investors put in at least one dollar of their own money for every one dollar they borrow. At the other extreme, some entrepreneurs prefer to put in as little of their own money as possible and still keep 100 percent control of their ventures.

Differences arise because bankers in general are not risk takers. They are in the business of renting depositors' money, not risking it. So they tend to shun ventures backed by small amounts of investors' money, because it is the investors' money that protects them when adversity strikes. As losses occur, investors' money bears the first impact of loss; and so the greater the amount of investors' money, the greater the likelihood that the bank will recover its loan.

On the other hand, entrepreneurs are risk takers. Many are willing to risk their life savings in their ventures, if they have to. Some try to sell stock in their ventures to investors. By doing so, they may raise all the money they need, lessen the risk to their personal savings, and still keep control of their venture:

Example: The entrepreneur in our earlier example needs $290,000 to finance her venture and has only $40,000 in savings. Her first choice is to float 4,000 shares of common stock at a par value of $20 each.

She buys 2,000 shares herself at $20 each, and then persuades friends to buy the remaining 2,000 shares at $80 each, giving her a total of $200,000.

The rest—$90,000—she may borrow readily from a commercial bank. With $200,000 of investors' money behind her, most banks would be willing to lend her the $90,000. The $200,000 she has raised accounts for nearly 70 percent of the total needed to finance her venture, and banks are generally satisfied if the ratio of equity capital to total capital is only 50 percent.

This example demonstrates a method of beginning a venture on a shoestring. With just $40,000 of her own money, the entrepreneur was able to raise $290,000 and still keep 50 percent control. There are other ways as well, as the following example illustrates:

Example: A youthful entrepreneur, Terry Allen, learned that a 180-student schoolhouse on four acres of land was about to be sold at a sealed-bid auction. With visions of a skiers' lodge, he turned in a bid of $24,610. He based his bid on the news that a nearby schoolhouse one third the size had sold for $8,200. Multiplying $8,200 by 3, he came up with $24,600, and then added an extra $10 so that he would outbid anyone else using the same logic.

Mr. Allen won the bid with only seven days to raise the money. Since he had graduated from Harvard Business School recently, he had little money of his own. After going over the idea with friends, he raised the entire $24,610 in one day and kept 50 percent of the equity as his reward for putting the venture together.

EXHIBIT 9.5

Chateau L'Ecole: Beginning Balance Sheet

Assets		Equities		
Improvements	$70,000	Bank loan		$ 70,000
Schoolhouse	24,610	Owners' equity		
Organizational costs	24,610	Mr. Allen	$24,610	
		Others	$24,610	49,220
Total	$119,220	Total		$119,220

Mr. Allen spent his nights and weekends changing the old schoolhouse into Chateau L'Ecole, a 140-bed skiers' dormitory. To make the changes, he needed $70,000 more which he got by borrowing on the strength of his friends' signatures. His beginning balance sheet appears in Exhibit 9.5.

Without putting in a single penny of his own money but by investing his ideas and energies, Mr. Allen created a skiers' lodge and owned 50 percent of it. Incidentally, he broke even the first ski season.[2]

The fact that Mr. Allen had no money did not discourage him. As his Harvard professor had told him:

> Money is no obstacle . . . since money could always be found to back a venture because so many people have it who do not have the ideas or energy to invest it. Furthermore, having any money at all could limit the imagination. For example, if a person had $5,000, he would look for a business he could buy with that amount. But if he had no money, he would not be confined by financial limitations, and could look for a much larger business to buy.[3]

For the entrepreneur, it is generally safer to finance a new venture with more investors' money than creditors' money because:

- Creditors' money involves a definite promise to repay the lender. Almost all loans require the borrower to meet a repayment schedule that demands not only repayment of the loan but also payment of interest—usually monthly. Failure to meet this twin obligation could force the entrepreneur's venture into bankruptcy.
- Investors' money, on the other hand, does not involve a definite promise to repay. Investors buy shares of stock at their own risk. Later, if they want to sell their shares, they cannot force the entrepreneur to buy them back. Investors are on their own to find somebody willing to buy their shares. Investors are not always entitled to a return on their investment—unless the venture makes a profit and declares a dividend.

The lack of a sharply defined financial obligation makes investors' money attractive to entrepreneurs. However, some entrepreneurs prefer to run their ventures with *no* investors' money except their own. Such a man was entrepreneur H.L. Hunt:

> [When Mr. Hunt died in 1974] at the age of 85, he had amassed an estimated personal fortune of $2 billion, putting him on a par with J. Paul Getty and Howard Hughes as one of the world's richest men. The exact extent of his wealth is unknown because Mr. Hunt *never* invested in anything that he could not own outright, and he had *no* outside stockholders in the businesses he did control.[4]

Unlike Mr. Hunt, some entrepreneurs who want 100 percent ownership of their ventures try to put in as little as they can and borrow as much as they can. Such entrepreneurs generally want to answer to nobody but themselves. But they may be deluding themselves. The entrepreneur's freedom to act may be as limited with creditors as with investors. Creditors with large stakes in the entrepreneur's venture may threaten to take over if the entrepreneur fails to pay bills or to repay loans.

SOURCES OF MONEY—EQUITY CAPITAL

One of an entrepreneur's most puzzling questions is where best to raise money. As shown in Exhibit 9.6, a bewildering variety of sources awaits the entrepreneur. The sources range from private to governmental. We will begin by looking at sources of equity capital (or investors' money); later, we will examine sources of debt capital (or creditors' money).

Venture-Capital Firms

Venture-capital firms generally invest in entrepreneurs whose ventures promise to grow rapidly. They tend to favor manufacturing ventures, especially in idea-rich, high-technology industries like electronics. Typically, a venture-capital firm receives more than 1,000 requests for money each year, many of which stand little chance of success. Out of every 100 requests:

- 80 are dropped after less than a day's study
- 10 are dropped after a week's study
- 8 are dropped after a month's study
- 2 are accepted after one or more months of detailed study

Most of the requests that are dropped within a day lack business plans. Most venture-capital firms will not even look at a written request for money unless it is accompanied by a business plan.

There are many types of venture-capital firms, among them:

Traditional partnerships: These are often established by wealthy families to manage a portion of their money aggressively by investing in small businesses.

Professionally managed pools: These are formed from institutional money and operate like traditional partnerships.

EXHIBIT 9.6 *Selected Sources of Capital*

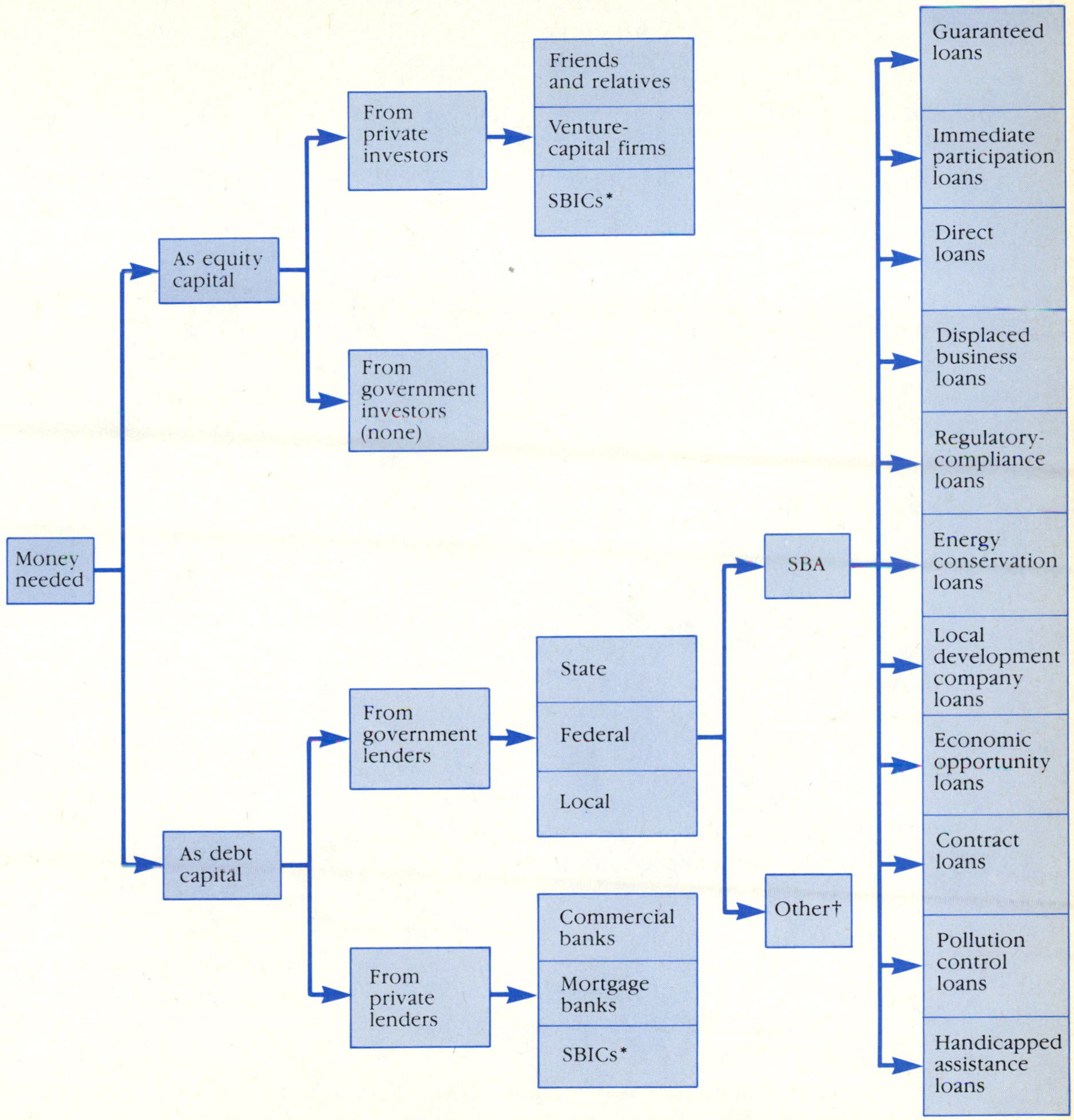

* Small Business Investment Companies.

† Including the U.S. Departments of Commerce, Housing and Urban Development (HUD), and Transportation (DOT).

Investment banking firms: Such firms occasionally form investor syndicates for venture proposals.

Insurance companies: These tend to be more conservative and often require a portion of equity capital as protection against inflation before they will lend to smaller businesses.[5]

Small Business Investment Companies

Small Business Investment Companies (SBICs) are another source of equity capital. SBICs began to form in 1958 after Congress passed the Small Business Investment Act. The purpose of this legislation was to encourage private investors to finance entrepreneurs. The act gave them an incentive to form SBICs, which they would run as private, profit-motivated businesses. In addition:

- Investors would invest only in small businesses, especially in high-risk ventures boasting new products with promising market potential, unusually favorable competitive positions, the possibilities of growth through favorable acquisition, and outstanding, aggressive management.

EXHIBIT 9.7 *Where Venture Capital Is Invested*

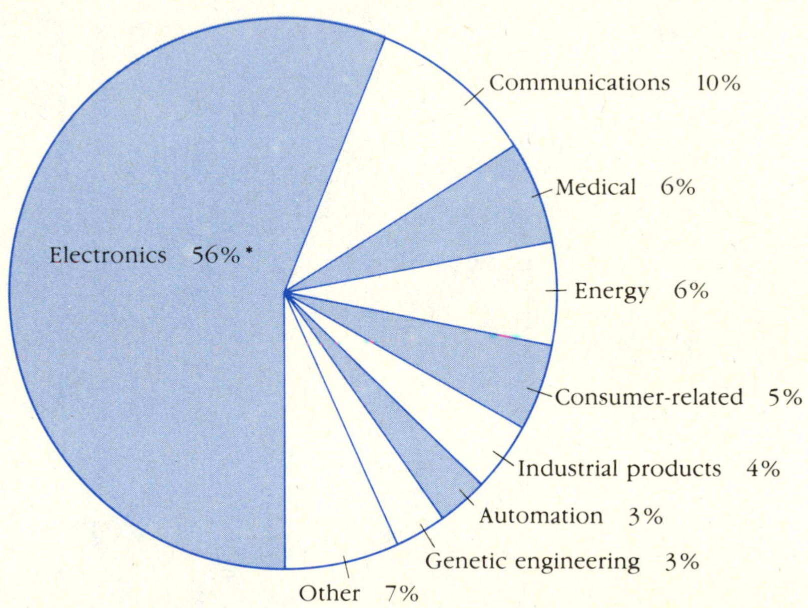

*Includes computers

Source: Capital Publishing Corporation, as reported by Peter A. Holmes, "The Boom in Risk Capital," *Nation's Business*, September 1983, p. 26.

- The SBA would oversee the SBICs, including their licensing and regulation.

In 1985, there were more than 375 SBICs scattered throughout the nation. Some are run by commercial banks; some by engineers, scientists, or experts in technical fields; others by lawyers, accountants, or other specialists. They all have one thing in common: the willingness to assume risks for a share of owners' equity, though in varying degrees. Some SBICs act like commercial banks and prefer to make loans rather than buy shares of stock, but they are the exception rather than the rule.

A popular misconception about venture-capital firms is that they also invest in so-called mom-and-pop shops—the corner drugstore or the neighborhood restaurant. They do not. Their interest lies mostly in ventures that promise to grow rapidly in revenues and profits. As dramatized in Exhibit 9.7, they find high-technology industries such as electronics and communications especially attractive. In contrast, SBICs often take a more balanced approach in their investment choices than do venture-capital firms:

Example: Traditionally, SBICs have been the workhorses of venture capital, investing more in traditional businesses than in flashy new fields such as electronics. "Venture capitalists are realizing that everything is not high technology, and some of the older industries that aren't as sexy still have a lot of growth," explains Barbara Stack, vice president of Rand Capital Corporation, a Buffalo SBIC.

Of the three deals Rand has participated in this year, only one is founded in electronics. Besides investing $150,000 in an electronics company that invented an energy-control device, Rand also invested $300,000 in a manufacturer of wood furniture founded 50 years ago. Ms. Stack believes that both companies are positively affected by the economy:

- The electronics company benefits from a concern about controlling the use of energy.
- The furniture company benefits from a growing trend among home-owners to buy high-quality furniture.[6]

SBICs are similar to the venture-capital firms we discussed earlier. They expect precisely the same kinds of information from entrepreneurs, so entrepreneurs must have their business plans in hand when they go to an SBIC for financial help. Otherwise, they stand little chance of success.

Big Business

Still another source of equity capital is big business. Many of the nation's major corporations have formed departments that seek out promising entrepreneurs to invest in. Their motives are mixed, ranging from a desire to have their money earn more money to a desire to identify candidates for acquisition later.

Regardless of the motivation, investment by big business into small business is a healthy idea; corporations can supply not only equity capital but also managerial skills. Often, it is not lack of money that plagues the entrepreneur but rather lack of managerial skills. Major corporations have such skills in abundance. A partial list of major corporations now aggressively seeking out promising entrepreneurs reads like a *Who's Who* of American business: Exxon Corporation, Ford Motor Company, Monsanto Corporation, and Standard Oil of Ohio.

Other Sources

In addition to the sources of equity capital we have already discussed—venture-capital firms, SBICs, and big business—there are many other sources. According to one study, equity capital is more likely to be raised not from venture-capital firms, but from entrepreneurs themselves or from friends and relatives:

> Even if we take into account the various government programs that aid small-businesspeople and minority entrepreneurs, it is clear that formal institutions provide very little capital for new companies.
>
> Most venture capital comes from the entrepreneur's own resources or from family and friends. This "earnest money" reassures bankers who

EXHIBIT 9.8 *Sources of Money for Entrepreneurs Who Begin from Scratch*

The most important resource is the entrepreneur's personal resources.

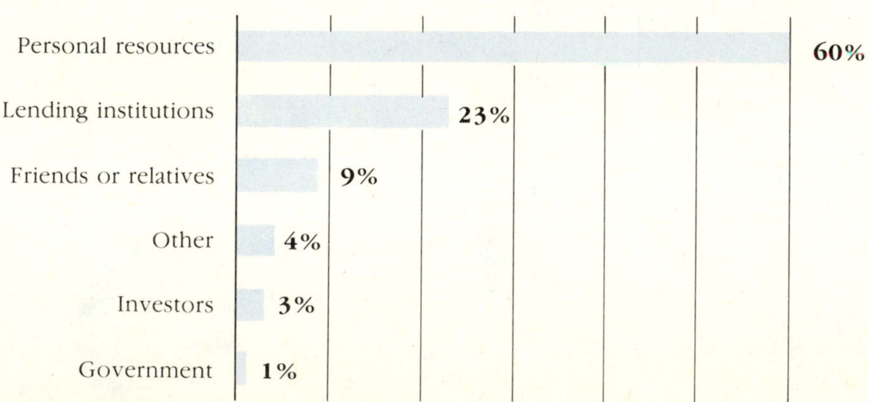

Source: Adapted from National Federation of Independent Business Research and Education Foundation, "Small Business in America," 1981.

EXHIBIT 9.9 *Sources of Money for Entrepreneurs Who Buy an Existing Business*

As with entrepreneurs who begin from scratch, personal resources are the most important source of money for those who buy existing businesses.

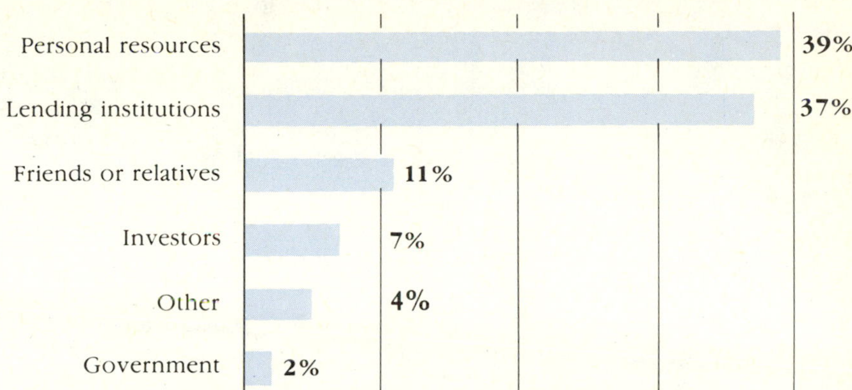

Source: Adapted from National Federation of Independent Business Research and Education Foundation, "Small Business in America," 1981.

often refuse to lend until entrepreneurs have locked themselves in by mortgaging their homes to the hilt and hustling everyone they know.

Such personal sources accounted for 90 percent of the initial financing for the new businesses we studied in this country and Italy. The rest comes from private investors who regularly invest in new companies, men often talked about in Texas as "good old boys."[7]

According to another study, by the National Federation of Independent Business, an entrepreneur's personal capital is the best source of equity capital. As Exhibits 9.8 and 9.9 illustrate, personal resources are the most important sources of capital for:

- Entrepreneurs who begin from scratch.
- Entrepreneurs who buy out existing businesses.

SOURCES OF MONEY—DEBT CAPITAL

So far, we have discussed ways of raising equity capital. Let us now turn to ways of raising debt capital. Many entrepreneurs believe that banks often lend money to ventures that have yet to earn their first dollar and that the SBA often lends money to unborn ventures. Both beliefs are erroneous. Most bankers reject the loan applications of would-be entrepreneurs unless:

- A wealthy friend or relative guarantees repayment of the loan by co-signing the bank note.

- The entrepreneur offers personal holdings such as a house or top-rated bonds as security for the loan.
- The entrepreneur needs the loan to construct a building, which can be repossessed without loss of dollar value if the venture fails.

However, there are various ways that entrepreneurs may borrow money—before and after they launch their ventures. We will look first at private lenders such as commercial banks, then at government lenders such as the SBA.

Private Lenders

There are many private lenders, ranging from commercial banks to storefront finance companies, from insurance companies to relatives. Of these, commercial banks offer entrepreneurs the most help. Besides lending money, banks offer a host of other services, such as:

- Professional financial advice
- Financial references
- Credit information
- Trust administration
- Transfer of funds

Commercial bankers are as indispensable to entrepreneurs as lawyers are. Entrepreneurs should strike working relationships with a banker months before they launch their ventures. According to the SBA:

> Too many entrepreneurs go to their banker only when they need to borrow money. If the entrepreneur deals with her banker in day-to-day financial matters, the banker can get to know her and her business. Not only will the banker often give aid and advice on current financial operations, but when she really needs to borrow money, the banker will be familiar with her business and will be better able to evaluate her loan application.[8]

Commercial banks make two major kinds of loans: short-term loans and long-term loans.

Short-term Loans As a rule, commercial banks like to see a fast turnover of loans, so they tend to make short-term loans—that is, loans that fall due within one year. Such loans generally finance inventories or finance customers who buy on credit. The entrepreneur then repays when inventories are sold or when customers pay their bills. Take this example:

Example: An entrepreneur opens a store to sell air conditioners. He must build up his inventory of air conditioners in the spring, just before the summer selling season. His need is only temporary, so he may take out a short-term loan to buy the air conditioners. He would then repay the loan when his inventory of air conditioners was sold and paid for by customers.

Because these loans last a short time, they often are made on an *unsecured* basis. Collateral is not required because the bank relies on the entrepreneur's credit standing unless the borrower's credit standing is poor or not yet established. Then the lender may require collateral as protection against possible default on the loan. Loans backed by collateral are called *secured* loans.

This example points up an important feature of short-term loans. They satisfy the entrepreneur's temporary need for money. Such loans are also called *self-liquidating* loans.

Long-term Loans In contrast to short-term loans, long-term loans help satisfy the entrepreneur's permanent need for money. Long-term loans run for more than one year and enable the entrepreneur to finance the purchase of assets with long useful lives, such as buildings and land, machinery and trucks. Such loans generally are repaid from profits.

Long-term loans may also enable the entrepreneur whose venture is growing rapidly to finance the permanent expansion of inventories as well as customers who buy on credit. A comparison of long-term and short-term financing needs appears in Exhibit 9.10. The following example shows

EXHIBIT 9.10 *Comparison of Long-term and Short-term Financing Needs*

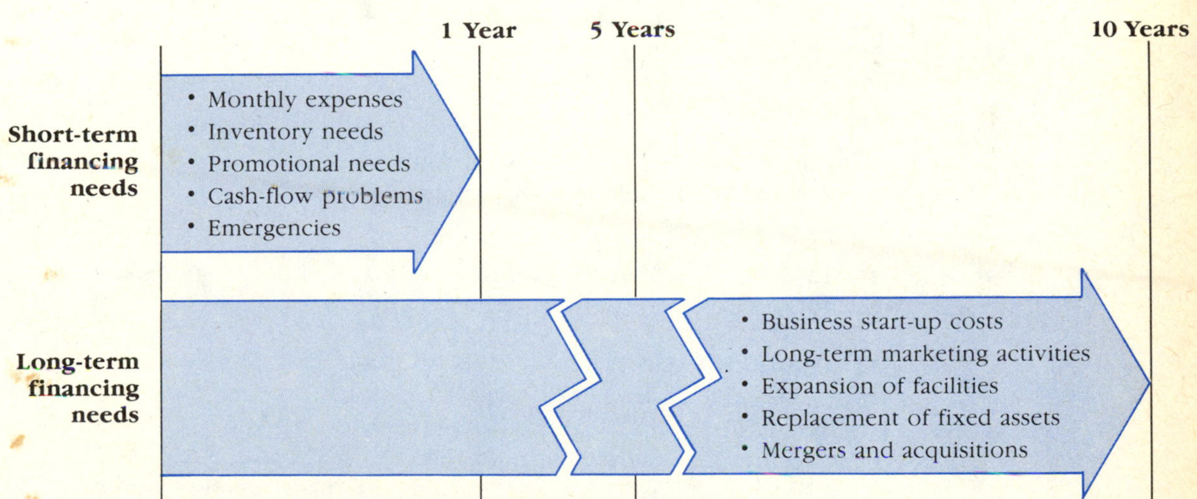

Source: Adapted from Robert J. Hughes and Jack R. Kapoor, *Business* (Boston, Mass.: Houghton Mifflin Company, 1985), p. 424. Copyright © 1985 by Houghton Mifflin Company. Used by permission of the publisher.

how long-term loans work:

> **Example:** An entrepreneur who owns a small machine shop needs a $15,000 turret lathe. Lacking the necessary cash, he takes out a $15,000 loan to buy the lathe. If he continues to be successful, the entrepreneur would then repay the loan out of profits plowed back into his venture.
>
> The entrepreneur and the bank agree to a repayment schedule that calls for the $15,000 loan to be repaid in five yearly payments of $3,000 each plus interest. Note that this kind of loan enables the entrepreneur to build up his equity over the five-year life of the loan—in the same way that a homeowner builds up equity each time he makes payment on a mortgage loan.

Supplier Credit

This source of debt capital works only for entrepreneurs who enjoy a good credit rating. Others have to pay their suppliers in cash. By allowing suppliers to finance them, entrepreneurs benefit from the cash released for other purposes. An example will show how this kind of financing works:

> **Example:** An entrepreneur who owns a tire supply store buys tires monthly. Her supplier offers credit terms of 30 days, meaning that payment is expected 30 days after the entrepreneur receives a supply of tires. If she sells out her inventory roughly once a month, then she really needs no money of her own to finance the purchase of tires.

Government Lenders

There are many government lenders, not only at the federal level, but at the state and local levels as well. At the federal level, such lenders include the SBA and the U.S. Department of Commerce. At the state and local levels, lenders generally include agencies that are designed to boost economic development. Of all such lenders, federal and otherwise, the SBA offers entrepreneurs the most help. To qualify for SBA help, businesses must:

- Be independently owned and operated and not dominant in their fields
- Be unable to get private financing on reasonable terms
- Qualify as small under the SBA's size standards, shown in Exhibit 1.2 on page 8.

In 1985, the SBA had more than 20 lending programs for entrepreneurs. A few are briefly described as follows.

Guaranteed Loans Under this program, entrepreneurs may borrow from a commercial bank with the SBA guaranteeing the bank to pay back part of any loss suffered by the bank. Here, the SBA may guarantee up to 90 percent of the loan amount, not to exceed $500,000. Such loans may be made for as long as 15 years. Through this program flows most of the SBA's lending activity.

Immediate Participation Loans If the entire loan amount is unavailable from a bank and if an SBA-guaranteed loan is also unavailable, then the

SBA may agree to finance the entrepreneur jointly with the bank. This decision is often made very quickly. The SBA and the bank each put up a share of the money, with the SBA's share not to exceed $150,000.

Direct Loans Under this program, loans may not exceed $350,000. These loans are made and serviced by the SBA itself rather than by banks.

Displaced Business Loans These loans enable entrepreneurs to stay in business or to relocate if the SBA determines that an entrepreneur's business has suffered financially because of a government project. Such loans may cover purchasing or construction on other property, whether or not the entrepreneur owned the original property occupied by the business.

Regulatory Compliance Loans Under this program, entrepreneurs may borrow money to help comply with government laws that otherwise would cause them undue financial harm. Examples of such laws are the Occupational Safety and Health Act and the Clean Air Act.

Solar and Other Energy Conservation Loans This program offers loans to help entrepreneurs save energy by covering such purposes as the production of energy from wood or grain, the use of windmills to generate electricity, and the burning of garbage to produce energy.

Local Development Companies (LDCs) Under this program, the SBA works through a profit or nonprofit corporation founded by local citizens who want to boost their community's economy. The SBA may lend up to $500,000 for each small business to be helped by an LDC.

SPECIAL PROGRAMS FOR MINORITY ENTREPRENEURS

Since the late 1960s, a number of special programs have surfaced to help minority persons become entrepreneurs. Local agencies, such as Chambers of Commerce and LDCs, as well as federal agencies like the SBA and the U.S. Department of Commerce, support these programs. Some of their programs include:

Economic Opportunity Loan Program Under this program, the SBA may make or guarantee loans to minority entrepreneurs only. The most that may be borrowed under this program is $100,000 for up to 15 years.

MESBIC Program A MESBIC is a Minority Enterprise Small Business Investment Company, owned and run by an established industrial or financial concern that combines money and management resources for assistance to minority entrepreneurs. Its major purpose is to marshal the skills of big business, banks, and the federal government to help develop minority entrepreneurs. Individuals or companies may form MESBICs by putting up at least $150,000 of their own money. After investing most of this sum in minority ventures, the MESBIC may then increase its original capital fifteenfold through a combination of federal and private financing. Like SBICs, MESBICs may either buy shares in minority ventures or lend them money. Take this example:

Example: A MESBIC decides that a minority manufacturer who needs $50,000 to start production should be financed in this way:

- $10,000 would be a 15-year loan from the MESBIC
- $40,000 would be a 15-year loan from a commercial bank, 90 percent of which would be guaranteed by the SBA

Note that the bank's exposure to loss would be only $4,000—or 8 percent of the total loan amount of $50,000.

So far, our discussion has centered on federal loan programs. There are many other federal programs that do not lend money, but can help entrepreneurs to upgrade their managerial skills or to get federal contracts. Similar programs often exist at both the state and local levels as well. In the next chapter, we will look at these programs in some detail, especially those sponsored by the SBA.

SUMMARY

Financing a new venture often frustrates the would-be entrepreneur. This frustration stems from the entrepreneur's failure to estimate money needs wisely and lack of knowledge of where best to seek money.

Perhaps the best way to go about estimating money needs is to prepare a business plan. Its centerpiece is the cash budget, which translates the entrepreneur's operating plans into dollars. This budget covers the entrepreneur's money needs before and just after start-up of the venture.

Preparation of a cash budget does not guarantee that entrepreneurs will get the money they need from money lenders and investors. It does, however, improve their chances. Today, investors and creditors rarely entertain requests for money unless entrepreneurs have worked out cash budgets as part of their business plans.

After estimating how much money is needed to finance the venture, the entrepreneur should:

- Estimate what fraction of the money should come from investors (equity capital) and what fraction from creditors (debt capital)

- Decide where to go to raise the money

It generally is safer to have more investors' money than creditors' money, since creditors' money involves a definite promise to pay a debt, while investors' money does not.

There are many sources of money. Investors' money may come from:

- Venture-capital firms and SBICs
- Big business and investment bankers
- Friends, relatives, and most important, the entrepreneur's own resources

On the other hand, creditors' money may come from:

- Federal agencies, especially the SBA
- Commercial banks and suppliers
- State and local agencies
- Friends and relatives

DISCUSSION AND REVIEW QUESTIONS

1. Explain why the business plan is so important in estimating money needs for a new venture.
2. Explain the difference between equity capital and debt capital. Which is preferable? Why?
3. Why do entrepreneurs tend to ignore budgeting as a financial tool?
4. Define these terms: *budgeting, fixed assets, current assets, secured loan, SBIC, MESBIC, long-term loan.*
5. Do commercial banks generally help finance an entrepreneur who is just starting out? Explain.
6. What are the hazards of financing a new venture with debt? Explain.
7. Why do venture-capital firms, commercial banks, and the SBA generally ask for a business plan?
8. How would you, as an entrepreneur, go about estimating how much money is needed to launch your venture?
9. In preparing a cash budget, which figure is the single most important estimate? Why?
10. How do these SBA loan programs differ: Guaranteed Loans, Direct Loans, and Immediate Participation Loans?
11. How may repayment of a long-term loan increase the entrepreneur's equity in a venture?
12. Why should an entrepreneur strike a working relationship with a commercial bank early on?
13. What services do commercial banks offer besides making loans?
14. Describe two programs designed to help minority entrepreneurs finance their ventures.
15. Do SBA loan programs compete with private lenders like commercial banks? Explain.

NOTES

1. Reprinted with permission from Bank of America, NT&SA, "Understanding Financial Statements," *Small Business Reporter*, Vol. 14, No. 6, Copyright 1980.
2. Adapted from Patrick R. Liles, *New Business Ventures and the Entrepreneur* (Homewood, Ill: Richard D. Irwin, 1974), p. 129.
3. Ibid.
4. "Entrepreneurs: Just a Country Boy," *Time*, December 9, 1974, p. 44 [Reprinted by permission from TIME, the Weekly Newsmagazine; Copyright Time Inc. 1974]
5. LaRue Tone Hosmer, U.S. Small Business Administration, *A Venture Capital Primer for Small Business* (Washington, D.C.: U.S. Government Printing Office, 1980), p. 6.
6. "How Venture Capitalists Share the Wealth," *Venture*, October 1980, p. 32.
7. Adapted from Albert Shapero, "The Displaced, Uncomfortable Entrepreneur," *Psychology Today*, November 1975, p. 86.
8. U.S. Small Business Administration, *Financing . . . Short and Long Term Needs* (Washington, D.C.: U.S. Government Printing Office, 1965), p. 33.

CASE 9A *Teddi's Restaurants*

When he came to this country from Greece, Steve Caloudis owned only the clothes on his back and spoke not a word of English. Today, he owns three restaurants that ring up sales revenues of $2.1 million a year.

His success has caught the eye of shopping center developers throughout the state. "They want me because of my record," says Mr. Caloudis. "It's a good feeling, but I'm not sure I should keep expanding. I'm happy with what I've got."

Background

To Mr. Caloudis, hard work is a way of life. "Work is a habit, and I've never grown out of it," says Mr. Caloudis. Indeed, he began working when he was 12, selling apricots and grapes to tourists in Greece. When he was 18, Mr. Caloudis left Greece for New York City, where he hired on as a dishwasher at seven dollars a week. His hours were from 6 A.M. to 6 P.M. six days a week.

Mr. Caloudis continued to work in restaurants and bars, mostly as a waiter. His objective was to learn the restaurant business "inside out." To meet that objective, he often "did a lot of extra work for nothing." For example, he worked with the chef, the bartender, the cleaning crew—on his own time, without pay.

His appetite for work paid off. He finally became manager of one of the city's biggest downtown restaurants.

That turned out to be his last promotion, for Mr. Caloudis decided to go into business for himself. He was sure he was ready and he had saved $11,000. After looking around for a month, he zeroed in on a 40-seat coffee shop that was for sale.

His First Venture

The owner wanted $25,000 for the shop. But before he would buy, Mr. Caloudis wanted to assure himself that he could make a go of the business. For a week, he stood 12 hours a day outside the coffee shop, asking customers just one question: "What attracts you to this location?"

Although his family thought $25,000 was too much to pay for a coffee shop, Mr. Caloudis felt strongly that he was buying "clientele and not salt shakers and coffee cups." He was sure that if he upgraded the menu and gave customers "more of a variety," he could double revenues in a year.

He bought out the owner for $25,000, making no attempt to negotiate a lower purchase price. His beginning balance sheet appears in Exhibit 9A.1.

To swing the $15,000 loan, Mr. Caloudis had the help of his wife, Mary, who did the banking for the advertising agency she worked for. When he applied for the loan, the Caloudis name was already familiar to the bank.

Mary Caloudis helped her husband in still another way. An attorney was teaching business law at a local college. One of his students was Mrs.

EXHIBIT 9A.1

Ted's Restaurant, Inc.: Balance Sheet (July 1, 1965)

Assets		Equities	
Cash	$ 500	Bank loan	$15,000
Equipment	2,000	Owners' equity	10,500
Goodwill	23,000		
Total assets	$25,500	Total equities	$25,500

Caloudis. When she told him about her husband's plans to go into business for himself, the attorney offered to incorporate the business at a small fee. The attorney still counsels Mr. Caloudis on all legal matters—though now, of course, at his usual fee.

The restaurant was a quick success. In fact, soon after Mr. Caloudis took over, patrons began lining up outside at 11:15 A.M. for lunch. Word had spread that he had enlarged the menu, improved the service, and that he called each customer by name. Revenues soared (see Exhibit 9A.2).

A Second Restaurant

Mr. Caloudis's success soon drew the attention of shopping center developers. Impressed by the restaurant's performance, the owner of Southgate shopping center told Mr. Caloudis: "I have a place for you in Southgate. You'd be a good tenant for us."

Again, his family was skeptical about the idea. After all, he was making a lot of money where he was. So why move? "My family told me I was overextending myself financially," says Mr. Caloudis.

True to form, he went against their opinion. He estimated it would cost $120,000 just to install equipment, fixtures, and furniture. "When you go into a shopping center, all you get is four walls and a ceiling," says Mr. Caloudis. "The rest is up to you." Unwilling at the time to sell his other restaurant, he had to look elsewhere for money to finance his new venture. So, he sold his house for $40,000 and borrowed $80,000 from a bank, using as collateral the market value of his other restaurant.

Unexpected Problems

When it opened in 1969, the new restaurant was not a runaway success—as his first restaurant had been. "I never stopped to think about whom to cater to," says Mr. Caloudis. "I was too busy running the other restaurant and also setting this one up. In fact, I was putting in an 18-hour day."

EXHIBIT 9A.2

Ted's Restaurant, Inc.

Year	Sales Revenues	Notes
1964	$ 35,000	Under former owner
1965	60,000	Under Mr. Caloudis
1966	110,000	
1967	190,000	Seating capacity expanded from 40 to 86 seats
1968	190,000	

EXHIBIT 9A.3

Teddi's Restaurant at Southgate

Year	Sales Revenues	Notes
1969	$300,000	Restaurant is opened
1970	300,000	Foreign meals added
1971	310,000	Open kitchen changed to closed kitchen
1972	375,000	
1973	375,000	
1974	465,000	Cocktail lounge and party room added

The problem of "whom to cater to" now took up most of Mr. Caloudis's time. To solve the problem, he talked to customers, other businesspersons, and his wife. From these talks, he found that the shopping center drew its shoppers mostly from middle-income families. So he decided to change his image:

- He changed the restaurant's name from Ted's to Teddi's. Why? Because Ted's suggests the image of a truck stop.
- He upgraded the quality of the menu. "People wanted home-cooked meals," says Mr. Caloudis. So he added meals with a foreign flavor.

Despite these changes, revenues failed to go up until 1971, when Mr. Caloudis borrowed $30,000 to carpet the restaurant and to change from an open to a closed kitchen. "That improved the atmosphere," says Mr. Caloudis. "You can't offer broiled Florida scampis and champagne to customers with an open kitchen staring them in the face." His revenues picked up immediately (see Exhibit 9A.3).

In 1973, opportunity knocked again. This time, the developer of the Parmatown shopping center asked Mr. Caloudis to become a tenant. Despite his family's opposition, Mr. Caloudis said yes, but only after the developer agreed to help finance the $200,000 cost of the new restaurant. "The only way to get ahead is to use other people's money," says Mr. Caloudis. His new restaurant was an instant success, as shown in Exhibit 9A.4.

Another Opportunity

Mr. Caloudis's success soon moved another shopping center developer to ask him to take over a bankrupt restaurant in Richmond Mall. Its owners had gone under after just six months of business.

EXHIBIT 9A.4

Teddi's Restaurants, Inc.: Sales Revenues: 1974–1978

Year	Southgate	Parmatown
1974	$465,000	—
1975	510,000	—
1976	525,000	$450,000
1977	550,000	465,000
1978	610,000	510,000

EXHIBIT 9A.5

Teddi's Restaurants, Inc.: Sales Revenues: 1979–1981

Year	Southgate	Parmatown	Richmond
1979	$635,000	$515,000	$415,000
1980	720,000	580,000	510,000
1981	760,000	705,000	660,000

The bankrupt owners offered Mr. Caloudis the equipment and furnishings for $25,000. After inspecting the restaurant, Mr. Caloudis estimated it would take another $175,000 to make it over to his own taste.

Again, his family thought it would be a mistake for him to buy another restaurant. "You'll lose everything," they told him, but Mr. Caloudis went ahead anyway. To make a long story short, he again succeeded. In fact, it took just three years for this restaurant to catch up with the other two (see Exhibit 9A.5).

A newspaper reporter recently asked Mr. Caloudis: "What's the secret to all this success?" The reply: "We've learned what the public wants. They like family-type, home-cooked meals—along with the right price, plus good service and a clean establishment."

Credits Wife for Success

Mr. Caloudis knows that he probably never would have made it without his wife, Mary. "She's been by my side for 17 years," says Mr. Caloudis. Working as a team, they still put in 12-hour days. And being fully involved has paid off for both.

Shopping center developers still beat a path to Mr. Caloudis's door, seeking him as a tenant. They always come away impressed with his grasp of details. For example, he keeps in his head such financial details as these:

- Payroll costs as a percentage of revenues, broken down by restaurant and by month for the past two years
- Sales revenues and before-tax profits, broken down by restaurant and by year for the past 17 years

His strong memory helps him spot trends and danger signals quickly. "That's why my restaurants have never had a losing month," says Mr.

EXHIBIT 9A.6

Teddi's Restaurants, Inc.

Item		1981 Breakdown per Sales Dollar
Sales revenues		$1.00
Costs		
Food	$0.42	
Overhead	0.26	
Labor	0.22	0.90
Profit		$0.10

Caloudis. "I always know where I stand and where I'm going. You can't get along without figures in a business like mine."

Indeed, he is one of the most efficient restaurateurs in the state. In 1981, out of every sales dollar, 10 cents was left over as profit (see Exhibit 9A.6). Compared to the industry average of 4 cents, it becomes obvious that Mr. Caloudis is a rare manager indeed.

Organization

Mr. Caloudis receives almost all the profits himself. No outsider owns a single share of stock. Of the 1,500 shares outstanding, he owns 1,400 shares and his daughter 100. Yet his business is organized as a Subchapter S corporation, which permits as many as 25 shareholders.*

In addition to this corporation, Mr. Caloudis owns four others. The Subchapter S corporation serves as the management company, while the others serve as operating companies (see Exhibit 9A.7).

To help him run all five corporations, Mr. Caloudis relies on just three persons: his wife, daughter, and son-in-law. They hold all the key positions. "It's all in the family," says Mr. Caloudis. His organizational chart appears in Exhibit 9A.8.

Altogether, Mr. Caloudis employs 190 persons. "I hire the best," says Mr. Caloudis. "My turnover is low compared to other restaurants. Only 12 percent a year. If I hire cheap employees, my costs are going to go up. That's why I go after the best."

* Later, in 1984, Subchapter S corporations became known as S-corporations and the number of shareholders permissible became 35—as discussed in Chapter Seven.

EXHIBIT 9A.7 *S&M Management Company, Inc.: Corporate Structure*

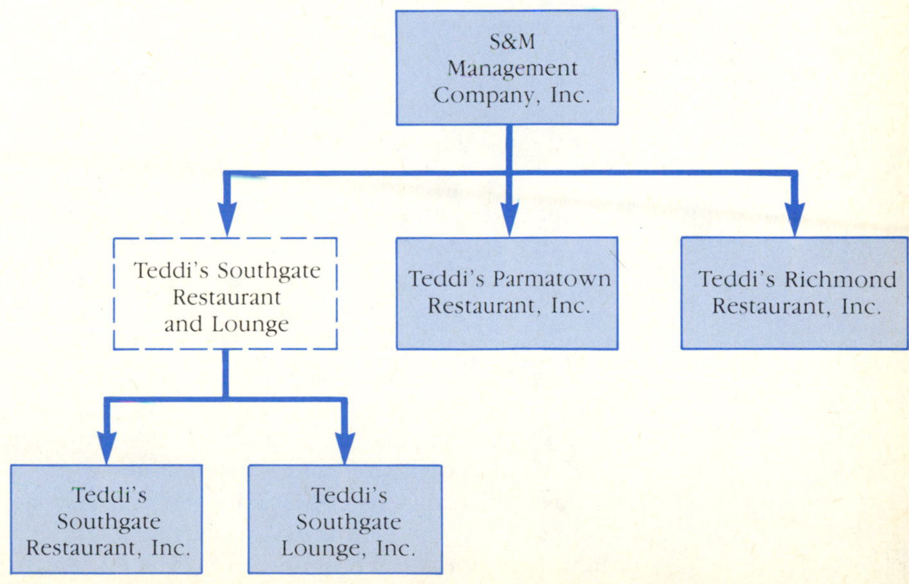

EXHIBIT 9A.8 *S&M Management Company, Inc.: Organizational Chart*

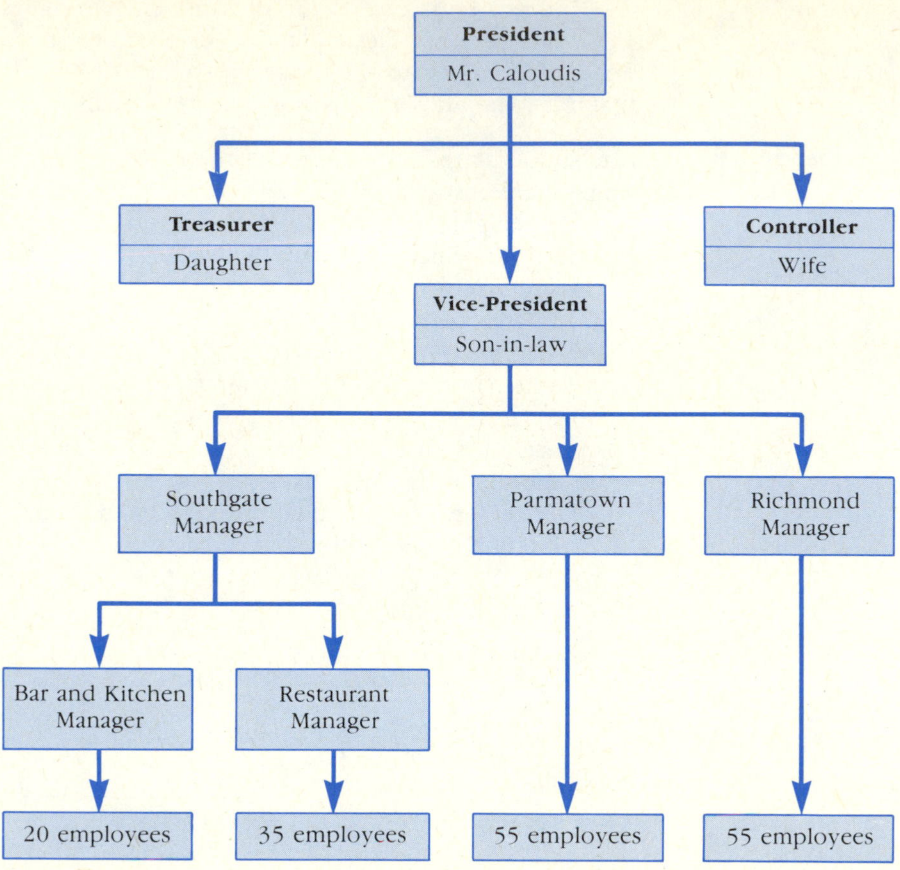

Controlling Performance

He controls his employees' performance by setting standards and rewarding them if they do well. "Your employees have to know what you expect of them," says Mr. Caloudis, "and they appreciate knowing. I pay them well." For example, he pays his dishwashers five dollars an hour. Mr. Caloudis himself was paid only 10 cents an hour to wash dishes when he first came to this country. "How dimes have changed," he says in jest.

Mr. Caloudis also believes in treating his employees humanely. "In a capitalistic system, we have to learn to share. I even lend employees up to $300 each, without interest. And I never get mad when they make mistakes. Self-respect is important. I know every one of my 190 employees by name. They know I mean it when I say, 'How are you?' I even have a policy that my managers cannot fire an employee without first consulting

EXHIBIT 9A.9

Teddi's Restaurants, Inc.: 1981 Income Statement

Sales revenues		$2,125,000
Cost of goods sold		861,000
Gross profit		$1,264,000
Operating expenses		
Payroll	$468,000	
Office*	164,000	
Rent	119,000	
Payroll taxes	49,000	
Depreciation	47,000	
Utilities	38,000	
Interest	36,000	
Supplies	36,000	
Advertising	33,000	990,000
Operating profit		$ 274,000

* Includes such expenses as accounting, entertainment, insurance, legal, office payroll, telephone, and travel.

me. I don't like the word 'fire.' It's bad for morale." Employees enjoy such fringe benefits as a pension plan, profit-sharing, medical insurance, paid vacations, and business-interruption insurance.

Mr. Caloudis is especially proud of his management team. Every manager came up through the ranks, working at jobs ranging from dishwasher to chef. "We develop our own managers," says Mr. Caloudis. One example is his daughter. She started when she was just 12 years old. Now 24, she is treasurer of the business.

Sets Goals

Looking back, Mr. Caloudis says: "I knew what I wanted to do, and I did it. My record speaks for itself. And my credit is triple-A. Nobody asks me when I'm going to pay. Instead, they ask how much do I want." He has never submitted his financial statements to Dun & Bradstreet, the national credit-rating firm. "I don't need them," says Mr. Caloudis. A recent income statement appears in Exhibit 9A.9.

Looking ahead, Mr. Caloudis has set a goal of $5.0 million in revenues by 1986, up from $2.1 million in 1981. To reach that goal, he may have to add two restaurants. Yet he has second thoughts about further expansion. For one thing, his family opposes the idea of "expansion for expansion's sake." For another, Mr. Caloudis, now 53 years old, has been training his son-in-law and daughter to take over.

But Mr. Caloudis continues to feel pressures to expand. In the past month alone, two shopping center developers have asked him to set up restaurants in the centers they are now building. One will be the largest shopping center in the state, with 260 shops.

EXHIBIT 9A.10 *Outside and Inside Views of a Teddi's Restaurant*

Source: The Cleveland Press, Cleveland, Ohio.

Photographs of one of Mr. Caloudis's restaurants appear in Exhibit 9A.10.

Questions

1. If you were Mr. Caloudis, would you expand again? Explain.
2. Comment on how Mr. Caloudis has organized his business.
3. What accounts for Mr. Caloudis's success?
4. Comment on Mr. Caloudis's attitude toward his employees.
5. Looking at Exhibit 9A.9, how would you adjust the income statement to arrive at a better estimate of profit?

CASE 9B *Swisshelm Department Store, Inc.*

John Carollo bought a small department store for $120,000. He paid the sellers $30,000 cash and gave them a 5-year note on the remaining $90,000 at an interest rate of 15 percent a year.

A graduate of Stanford University with honors, Mr. Carollo had worked for 11 years with the Sears, Roebuck Company. His experience there included:

- Selling men's suits and appliances on the floor
- Managing a men's clothing department
- Serving as assistant branch manager.

All along, his ambition was to have his own department store. Sears, he believed, would be a good place to learn every aspect of department-store operations. After all, Sears is the nation's biggest retailer.

Mr. Carollo worked for 10 years to learn the business. Then he started to search for a small department store in a small city. A year went by before he learned from a banker that a department store was for sale in New Philadelphia, a city of 16,000 persons. Three months later, he and the sellers agreed on the purchase price of $120,000.

One week after he took over, Mr. Carollo and his accountant sat down to prepare a cash budget. It was now early August. Mr. Carollo knew that he would need a short-term loan to build up his inventory in anticipation of high consumer demand in September, when schools start, and again in December, when Christmas buying is in full swing.

The cash budget helped him decide how much to borrow and when to borrow. After analyzing past records, he came up with these estimates:

Sales Revenue	Forecast
June (actual)	$24,000
July (actual)	20,000
August	28,000
September	52,000
October	44,000
November	76,000
December	96,000
January	22,000
February	32,000

Monthly Expenses	
Rent	$3,000
Depreciation	500
Other expenses	900
Wages and salaries:	
August	$2,800
September	3,200
October	3,200
November	3,600
December	3,600
January	2,800

- Sales would be:
  30 percent for cash
  70 percent for credit
- Of the credit sales:
  80 percent would be paid within *one* month of purchase
  20 percent would be paid within *two* months

EXHIBIT 9B.1 *Swisshelm Department Store, Inc.: Cash Budget Worksheet*

	August	September	October	November	December	January
Cash inflow						
Sales revenues						
Credit sales						
Collections from						
One month before						
Two months before						
Subtotal						
Cash sales						
Total cash inflow						
Cash outflow						
Inventory purchases						
Wages and salaries						
Rent						
Other expenses						
Interest						
Total cash outflow						
Cash gain or loss						
Borrowings						
Opening cash balance						
Balance before borrowing						
Borrowings						
Ending cash balance						
Cumulative borrowings						

- Credit sales outstanding on August 1 consisted of:
  $14,000 from July
  $ 3,360 from June
- Gross profit on sales would be 25 percent.
- Enough inventory would be purchased monthly to cover the *next* month's budgeted sales.
- All inventory purchases would be paid for in the *same* month they were made.
- A *minimum* cash balance of $8,000 would be maintained.
- The cash balance was $19,000 on August 1.
- All borrowings would be in multiples of $1,000 and would be made or repaid on the *first* of the month.
- Interest at 1 percent a month would be paid when borrowings were *repaid in full*.

Questions

1. How much should Mr. Carollo borrow to meet seasonal demand? When should he repay his borrowings? (Prepare a cash budget on a *separate* piece of paper, using the worksheet in Exhibit 9B.1 as a guide.)
2. How profitable does Mr. Carollo expect the store to be during the six months covered by his budget? (Prepare an income statement).
3. Why is the cash budget useful to both Mr. Carollo and his banker?

CASE 9C *New-Venture Financiers*

According to a newspaper editorial, "each day in this country 1,000 firms are formed, more than 900 change hands, and another 930, on the average, are discontinued."

So what chance have I to start a business? True, the SBA supplies all sorts of information in the way of conferences and pamphlets. And it offers many types of loans. Its loan-guaranty program, for example, offers loans up to $500,000. But I don't need that much money.

Sure they say that the federal government, the world's largest buyer of supplies and services, will buy anything from paper clips to battleships. There are bids and many sources of help, such as these:

- U.S. Senate Select Committee on Small Business
- U.S. House Select Committee on Small Business
- Small Business Division of the U.S. Department of Justice

Well, that's all well and good. But what about the little guy?

We don't want the early headaches that go with big and middle-size business. We want a challenge, an opportunity to use our little business, a chance to leave our own mark of achievement in this work-a-day world. Here are a few samples of what we think is the right ideology of small business in the democratic sense, a way of life, possibly a hearkening back to the good old days:

- A one-room pizza kitchen that blossomed into a block-long semiautomatic frozen pizza factory for former restaurateurs.
- Milady's Wigs, a small shop that cannot keep up with the demand. Women who have lost their hair because of sickness or after some operation, as well as bald men, are eager to pay $100 for wigs made by an entrepreneur.
- New England's ski resorts, which started with the Nansen Ski Club and prospered in every New England state. For the small businessperson, these, along with summer cabins and motels, spell out entrepreneurship and a certain prestige.

One could go on telling of ventures that began small and prospered:

- The coffee vending machine
- A wiping cloths firms that grew out of a rag business
- An unknown detergent venture that got the jump on the soap giants in this country
- The Irish bubble gum, a cure for a surplus beet crop
- A shamrock farm to catch St. Patrick's Day patriots

But they have to get started. And that's where *New-Venture Financiers* could help. Small businesspersons cannot always qualify for bank or

SBA loans. But they have an idea, and they should have the opportunity to start their own venture and leave their memorial to free enterprise.

Questions

1. Is there a need for New-Venture Financiers—an agency, public or private, to help those "little guys" who cannot qualify for financial help from banks or the SBA?
2. When young people seek their first job, they are asked, "What experience do you have?" Is the entrepreneur with an idea but no money or credit in this same situation? Explain.

Source: Adapted with permission from Henry M. Cruickshank and Keith Davis, *Cases in Management* (Homewood, Ill.: Richard D. Irwin, 1962), pp. 26–29. Copyright © 1962 by Richard D. Irwin, Inc. Reprinted by permission of the publisher.

10 ORGANIZATIONAL PLANNING

QUESTIONS FOR MASTERY

Why is organizational planning important?

How does one define skill needs?

How important is the help of professionals such as accountants, bankers, lawyers, and insurance agents before launching a venture?

How does one go about fulfilling skill needs and building a staff?

What kinds of counselling help are available from both private and government sources?

Good order is the foundation of all good things.

Edmund Burke

Major corporations employ hundreds of knowledge workers. In contrast, would-be entrepreneurs generally cannot afford the luxury of such expert help. They often have no recourse but to stand alone.

How can entrepreneurs fill their needs for skilled, knowledgeable support? Help does exist, often for no fee. To make the most of such help, entrepreneurs should first ask themselves two questions:

- What skills do I need to launch my venture successfully?
- How can I get the help of men and women armed with those skills?

NEED FOR ORGANIZATIONAL PLANNING

In this complex age, few entrepreneurs are equipped with all the business skills they need to survive on their own. Until World War II, entrepreneurs worked in a business world of few regulations, few taxes, few records, few

EXHIBIT 10.1 *Circular Nature of Organizational Planning*

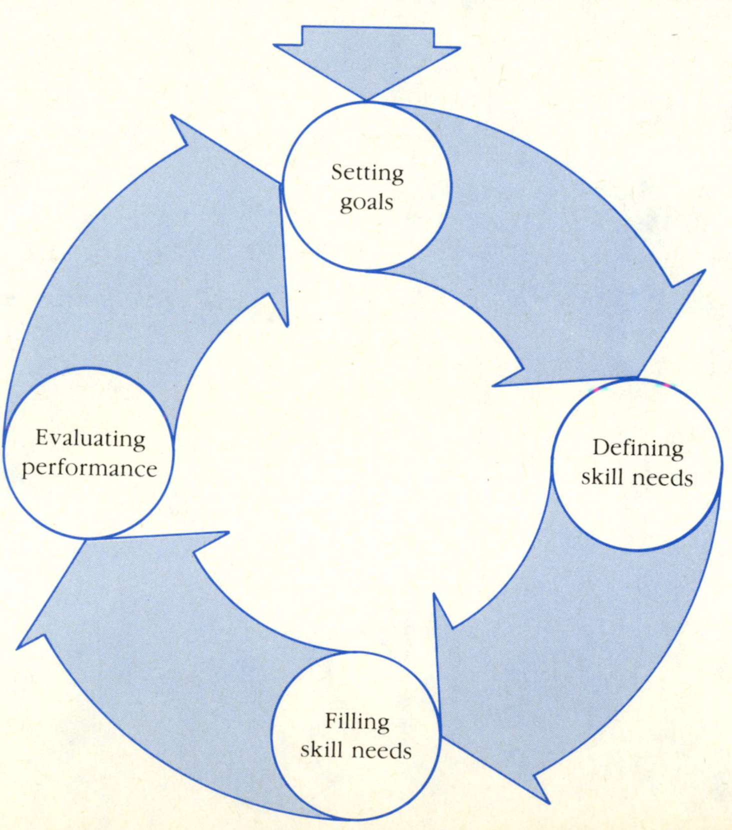

big competitors, and no computers. Since that time, simplicity has given way to complexity. Entrepreneurs can no longer be their own troubleshooters, lawyers, bookkeepers, financiers, tax experts, and systems analysts.

To survive and grow, entrepreneurs need help and should be able to identify precisely what kinds of help they need. To do so, they need to plan their organization before they launch their venture. As indicated in Exhibit 10.1, the organizational planning is circular in nature. It has a key role in the business plan because it is the organization that carries a venture, its goals and all its personal and operating relations.

Despite the need for it, organizational planning is ignored by many entrepreneurs who fail to see how important it really is. But its value was recognized even in Biblical times:

> The Bible tells of the advice Moses received from his father-in-law, Jethro. Feeling that Moses was making too many decisions himself in governing his people, Jethro said, "The thing that thou doest is not good. Thou wilt surely wear away, both thou, and this people that is with thee; thou art not able to perform it thyself alone."
>
> Moses followed this advice and did a better job of organizing. In the words of the Scripture: "Moses harkened to the voice of his father-in-law and did all that he said. And Moses chose able men out of all Israel, and made them heads over the people, rulers of thousands, rulers of hundreds, rulers of tens. And they judged the people at all seasons: the hard causes they brought unto Moses, but every small matter they judged themselves."[1]

DEFINING SKILL NEEDS

An organization is any team of people who work together to meet common goals. For example, a professional football franchise may hire 45 players, each with different skills, to fill its cavernous 80,000-seat stadium. Whether they fill it depends largely on how well they play as a team. Losses usually mean empty seats. That is why coaches spend so much time each year scouting college players.

> **Example:** A football franchise's all-pro defensive tackle is about to retire. The coach is looking hard for a replacement who earned at least all-conference honors as a defensive tackle, weighs at least 260 pounds, is at least 6 feet 4 inches tall, sprints 40 yards in less than 5.0 seconds, bench-presses at least 450 pounds, and plays with the "hurts."

This is a tall order to fill. But note that the coach knows precisely what he needs to win. Equally important, he knows precisely what kind of player he is looking for to meet that need.

EXHIBIT 10.2 *Identifying Skill Needs*

Step Number	Description of Step	Skill Needed	Expert Best Suited to Meet Need: Entrepreneur	Other
1	Decide to go into business	Knowledge of self	√	
2	Analyze yourself	↓	√	
3	Choose product or service	↓	√	
4	Research markets	Knowledge of marketing research		Marketing researcher
5	Forecast sales revenues	↓		Marketing researcher
6	Choose site	↓		Marketing researcher
7	Develop production plan	Knowledge of chemical engineering	√	
8	Develop marketing plan	Knowledge of marketing		Advertising account executive
9	Develop organizational plan	Knowledge of skill needs	√	
10	Develop legal plan	Knowledge of law		Lawyer
11	Develop accounting plan	Knowledge of accounting		Accountant
12	Develop insurance plan	Knowledge of insurance		Insurance agent
13	Develop financial plan	Knowledge of finance		Loan officer
14	Write cover letter	Knowledge of venture	√	

Entrepreneurs should define their skill needs in a similar way. There is a catch, though. Usually they cannot afford to hire, for example, a fulltime marketing researcher or a fulltime accountant. Even so, entrepreneurs should plan their organization as if they *could* afford them. Only by going through such a procedure can they assure themselves that needed skills have not been overlooked.

Entrepreneurs should thus define their organization in terms of skills rather than in terms of persons. For example, if a chemical engineer were about to go into plastics manufacture, he might begin defining his organization by asking himself: What skills do I need to earn a net profit of $30,000 on sales revenues of $500,000 by the end of my first year in business?

Note how precise this goal is. It gives the entrepreneur a target to aim for as well as a measure of performance. He might have said: "My goal is to make a profit." But such a fuzzy goal is meaningless. How much profit? By when? More will be said about goals in Chapter Twelve.

Let us assume that this particular chemical engineer has worked at nothing but engineering since graduating from college. A resourceful person, he has just invented a new process to make fiberglass-reinforced plastic for sports cars like the Corvette. This process is faster and cheaper than the present one. For the past two years, he has worked nights and weekends in his garage workshop perfecting the new process.

Our chemical engineer is now ready to exploit his invention by creating a new venture. He has set a first-year goal of $500,000 of revenues and now needs to define the specific skills he needs to make his venture a reality.

A good place to begin is with the business plan. Following the outline of the business plan presented in Chapter Six, he might set up a table like the one in Exhibit 10.2 to identify the skills he needs.

The engineer decides that he is best qualified to complete six of the steps shown in the exhibit. For the rest, however, he recognizes that he must rely on outside experts. To find those experts he turns to the Chamber of Commerce. Its members come from every walk of business life and are usually aware of which professionals are competent and reputable.

Commercial bankers are another good source of information about professionals—often a better source than the Chamber of Commerce. Bankers see the work of professionals first-hand; Chambers of Commerce often do not and thus judge professionals on reputation alone.

GETTING THE RIGHT PROFESSIONALS

In his quest for help, the engineer in our example should seek professionals who also work in his industry. For example, accountants can specialize in chemicals or lawyers can specialize in musical recordings. By using such specialists, the engineer may profit from the professional's experience with similar problems in other businesses in the same industry.

Before opening for business, the entrepreneur generally needs the following kinds of professional help:

- An accountant to set up books
- A lawyer to advise on legal matters
- A banker to advise on financial matters
- An insurance agent to make sure the venture is protected from dangers that cannot be foreseen or controlled

But the work of these professionals does not stop when entrepreneurs make the first pound of product or close the first sale. Rather, the need for these services continues throughout the life of the venture. Entrepreneurs have an ongoing need for:

- An accountant to prepare monthly income statements and quarterly balance sheets
- A banker to help finance expansion or renewal
- A lawyer to do legal checkups at least once a year and to bring the entrepreneur up to date on such things as tax, labor, and worker-safety laws
- An insurance agent to make sure the growing venture is safely covered against the unknown

BUILDING A STAFF

Accountants, bankers, lawyers, and insurance agents provide an entrepreneur with outside professional help, but the entrepreneur also needs inside help. In some ventures, getting such help poses few problems because the entrepreneur may choose to be the only employee. For example, entrepreneurs who start their own employment agency may need only themselves and a telephone answering service to start out. After business begins to pick up, they may then have to add a receptionist or another interviewer.

But many entrepreneurs do not choose to begin as one-person ventures. The chemical engineer mentioned earlier is one such entrepreneur. He expects revenues of $500,000 the first year in his fiberglass-reinforced plastic business. Based on his intuition and his experience in the field, he realizes that, to support that level of revenues, he will need two chemical operators, one foreperson, and one secretary-bookkeeper besides himself.

Job Descriptions

The engineer's experience with other chemical companies serves him well in defining what work needs to be done. He does not need an organizational planning expert to make a study for him. Still, he should prepare an organizational plan, complete with job descriptions that detail:

- Who does what
- Who has what authority
- Who reports to whom

Such job descriptions need not be fancy. They may be as simple and straightforward as the one for a gas station attendant shown in Exhibit 10.3.

Job descriptions spare entrepreneurs the disease that attacks many ventures, especially as they grow and add more men and women. The disease is called organizational muddle. It generally is caused by the entrepreneur's failure to plan the organization. Typically, entrepreneurs allow their organizations to evolve naturally, with everybody reporting to them or with some employees reporting to two or more bosses. The resulting mix-ups often lead to anger and frustration, waste and duplication of work. As Marvin Bower puts it: "Like a good golf swing, an organization should become so well grooved that people can go about their jobs without thinking twice about who does what."[2]

Job descriptions are one aspect of the organizational plan. The entrepreneur should also define the personal qualifications needed for above-average performance in each position. To expect less from one's employees could result in a merely average venture. Earlier, we defined an organization as a team of people working together to meet common goals. It follows, then, that the more qualified the team, the greater the likelihood of success.

EXHIBIT 10.3

Sample Job Description

Job Title:	Gas station attendant
Job Statement:	Finds out customer needs and performs minor services for motorized vehicles such as operating a gas pump, and checking and replacing engine fluids.
Major Duties:	1. Cheerfully greets customers and offers service. 2. Performs minor services to motorized vehicles: a. Operates gas pump. b. Checks oil, radiator, and battery fluid levels, adding oil or water where requested. c. Cleans windshield. 3. Notifies customer of total service cost and collects payment.
Minor Duties:	Helps mechanics when requested and keeps service office neat.
Relationships:	Reports to station manager or to mechanic, when manager is absent.

Source: U.S. Small Business Administration, *Business Basics: Job Analysis, Job Specifications, and Job Descriptions* (Washington, D.C.: U.S. Government Printing Office, 1985), p. 20.

Organizational Charts

No organizational plan is complete without an organizational chart. Such a chart traces the lines of responsibility and authority between jobs. In a new venture, an entrepreneur may have to wear several hats, as would be the case with the chemical engineer in our earlier example. His organizational chart might look like the one in Exhibit 10.4.

EXHIBIT 10.4 *Organizational Chart*

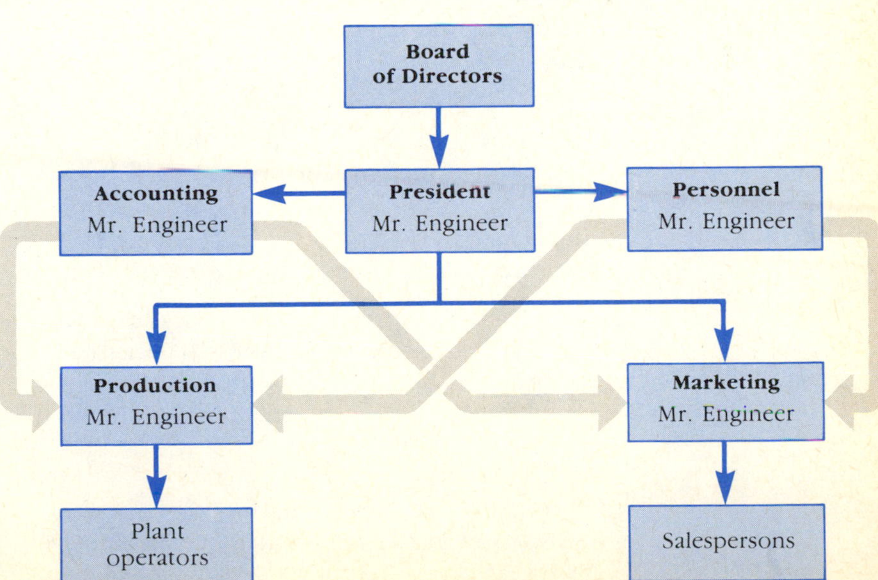

This kind of organization is called *line-staff*. Note in the exhibit that each jobholder reports to a single boss, represented by a solid line connecting their boxes. There is no overlap. But note also that those holding the staff jobs of accounting and personnel have some control over those holding the line jobs of production and marketing, represented by shaded lines connecting their boxes. Although this may seem like an overlapping of authority, it is not. To see why, let us define what we mean by line and staff:

> **Line authority:** Line positions give the people in authority the right to lead those under them. They are the ones who may say "do it and do it now." The strength of their authority usually stems from their power to hire and fire.
>
> **Staff authority:** Staff positions possess power that is subtler than line authority. People in staff positions have the right to exercise their expert knowledge in solving marketing and production problems. As line managers may say "do it and do it now," staff managers say "you *ought* to do it in this way because it's the best way."

In other words, line authority is the power of authority that one person has over another, and staff authority is the power of knowledge that one person has over another.

Another way to distinguish between line and staff is to say that line is charged with getting the product out and closing the sale. Staff, on the other hand, is charged with getting out ideas to keep the venture profitable and competitive. It is not enough for staff to simply generate ideas, however; they should also be adept at putting their ideas to work. Exhibit 10.5 compares line and staff work.

So far, we have focused on the line-staff form of organization. There are others, among them:

> **The line organization:** Every jobholder reports to a single boss; no one has a staff function. This form of organization is common to ventures with fewer than 10 employees.
>
> **The functional organization:** A jobholder may report to two or more bosses. With this kind of organization, a production foreperson may report directly to the accountant, the purchasing agent, and the researcher as well as to the production manager.

The functional organization usually leads to chaos. With two or more bosses, a jobholder may never know where to turn when a problem comes up, and there is no single boss who is responsible for the way jobholders perform. Obviously, entrepreneurs should drop this form of organization from their list of choices.

Attitudinal Problems The line organization is a practical choice for ventures that start small, but once they begin to grow beyond 10

EXHIBIT 10.5 *Comparison of Line and Staff Work*

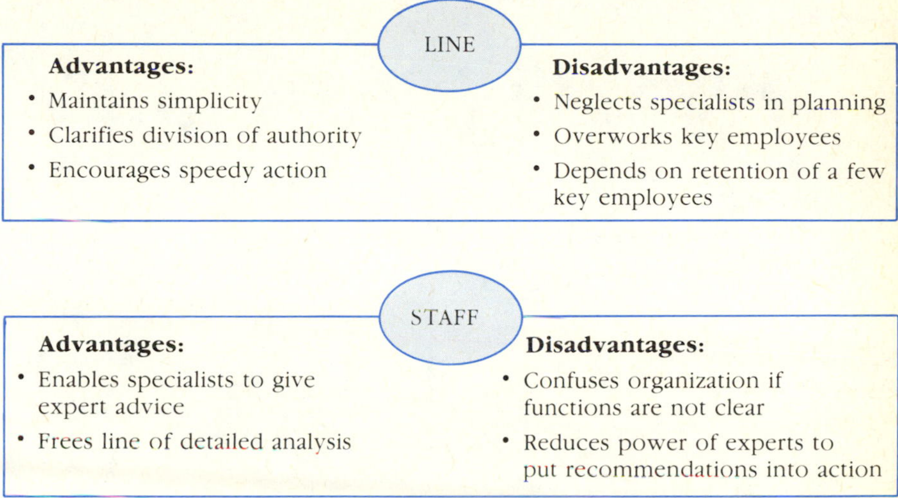

Source: Adapted with permission of Macmillan Publishing Company from *The New Management* by Robert M. Fullmer. Copyright © 1974 by Robert M. Fullmer.

employees, entrepreneurs should consider switching to a line-staff form of organization. This switchover often causes some knotty problems, especially in ventures that have grown quickly. When entrepreneurs give up one of their many hats to a newly hired accountant or to a marketing researcher, veteran jobholders are likely to resent the change by treating the staff persons as intruders. Their attitude often is reflected in such statements as:

> We got along without them before, so why do we need them now? Besides, what do they know about the way we do things around here? They never even get their hands dirty. They're just overhead. Why, they don't even know how our products are made. Who needs them?

The best way to solve this attitudinal problem is not to let it arise in the first place. Before they open for business, entrepreneurs should plan their organization as if they could afford to hire persons to fill each staff job. They should do the kind of organizational planning done by the engineer in our earlier example who:

- Drafted descriptions for each job, both line and staff
- Defined the qualifications of persons to fill those jobs
- Prepared an organizational chart showing who reports to whom, with the engineer himself filling most of the jobs slots at the start

With such an organizational plan, each jobholder would know from the start how the entrepreneur plans to run the venture. They would also

EXHIBIT 10.6 *Management Versus Professional Help*

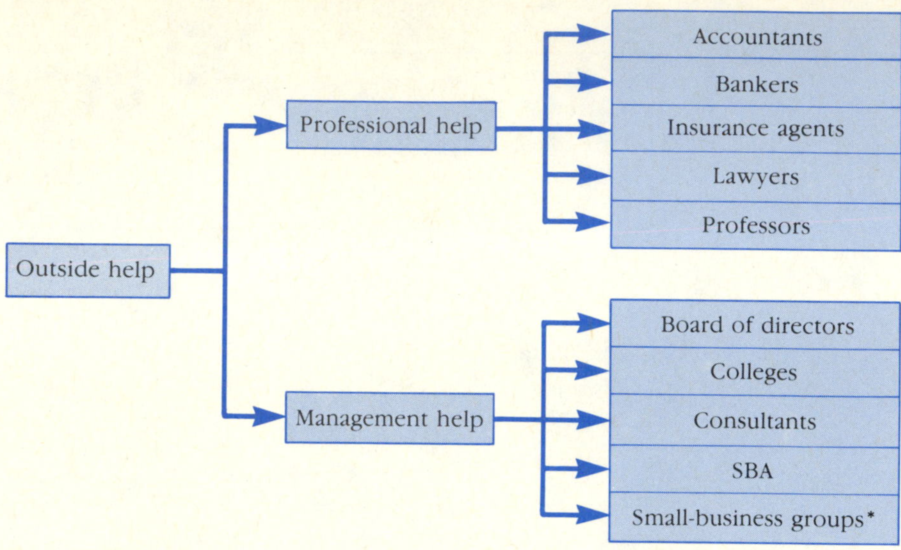

* Generally with Chambers of Commerce.

know that the entrepreneur is wearing many hats only temporarily. Later, as the venture grows, knowledge workers would be hired to wear those hats, thus enabling the entrepreneur to spend more time charting the venture's future.

Limitations Entrepreneurs should also be aware of the limitations of organizational charts. Although they do symbolize how an entrepreneur plans to get the work out, they often impress more than they express. Few ventures run precisely the way their organizational charts indicate. In a growing venture, organizational charts soon become dated; unpredictable events often change the course of an entrepreneur's plans. For this reason, wise entrepreneurs update their organizational charts at least once a year.

Creating an organizational chart forces entrepreneurs to crystallize their thinking before opening their businesses. In order to put a chart together, they must think about what work should be done to make their venture profitable and how the work should be done. Without such thought, organizational charts may have no more value than doodles on a scratch pad.

A chart is also limited since it cannot show how all the jobs within a venture tie into one another. To try to do so would result in a chart with solid and broken lines crisscrossing the page in undecipherable confusion. A good organizational chart is simple and highlights only key jobs and lines of authority. A good organizational chart must communicate if it is to be effective.

To bring an organizational chart to life, entrepreneurs generally need help, especially when they begin with few employees. In Chapter Nine we discussed the need for financial help. We will now discuss the need for management help, focusing on these sources:

- Boards of directors
- Management consulting firms
- The federal government, especially the SBA
- Trade associations, Chambers of Commerce, and small-business organizations

Exhibit 10.6 contrasts management with professional help.

FULFILLING SKILL NEEDS—BOARDS OF DIRECTORS

Potentially, boards of directors offer the entrepreneur a wealth of help, especially as problem solvers. Elected by shareholders, the directors are legally responsible for the venture and are given full authority. In theory, they do such things as these:

- Choose the president and other officers of the venture
- Delegate power to run the day-to-day affairs of the venture
- Set policy on paying dividends, financing major spending, and executive pay, including the entrepreneur's salary

If the venture is a sole proprietorship or a partnership, the entrepreneur does not have to form a board. However, every state requires that a corporation have a board to protect shareholders. This requirement holds even if the entrepreneur is the sole shareholder.

Board Myths

Studies show that, because entrepreneurs tend to ignore their boards, more than 90 percent of all boards fail to perform. In a study, Professor Myles L. Mace of Harvard University found that:

> The generally accepted roles of boards—that is, selecting top executives, determining policy, measuring results, and asking discerning questions—have taken on more and more of the characteristics of a well-established myth, and there is a considerable gap between the myth and reality.[3]

One myth exploded by Professor Mace's study is that the board selects the president. He found that in most corporations the directors do not, in fact, pick presidents—except when faced with unexpected deaths. Commenting on this function of the board, one executive said:

> The old concept that the stockholders elect the board, and the board selects the management, is fiction. It just doesn't apply to today's

corporations. The board does not select the management; the management selects the board.[4]

Another myth exploded by Professor Mace's study is that board members set goals and ask wise, probing questions. He found, instead, that board members generally are passive. Like puppets, they dance to strings pulled by entrepreneurs. Since they are chosen by entrepreneurs, board members tend to act as their representatives, not as their challengers. Rarely do they ask sharp questions about falling profits, for example. Nor do entrepreneurs encourage such questions. Their attitude is: "It's my money and my company, so I'll do as I please." Friendly board members share this attitude and ask, "Why bother interfering?" In contrast, this entrepreneur took an enlightened attitude toward his board:

Example: "No one around here ever asks the boss a tough question—so I decided to form a board of directors to give myself a few peers to talk to," says Ray Peterson, owner and president of Industrial Fabricating Company in Stratford, Connecticut. If he worked for a large corporation, Mr. Peterson says he would have six or seven "equals" to swap ideas with; his board of directors helps provide similar feedback.

Mr. Peterson formed the board in 1981. One year later, the maker of metal casings had sales of slightly over $2 million, only a small improvement over the previous year's $1.8 million. Yet Mr. Peterson is enthusiastic about the board's impact on the company, and he expects the board's suggestions to eventually help earnings. "The best thing about it is it makes me think," he says.

Mr. Peterson's board has already made an important contribution to savings, in response to board probing. Mr. Peterson was forced to admit one of his products was unprofitable. He dropped it immediately. By the way, he pays his board $200 a meeting. "They do it for the experience," says Mr. Peterson. "They gain as much knowledge and insight as I do."[5]

Getting the Right Board Members

Of course, some boards do perform well, especially as problem solvers. How should entrepreneurs select people who will contribute to the success of the venture to serve on their boards? Preferably, board members should be drawn from the community's ranks of:

Successful entrepreneurs: Ideally, any such candidates should be familiar with the entrepreneur's industry. For example, an entrepreneur about to create a computer services venture might appoint to the board a retailer who sells small-business computers.

Professionals: Generally, these would include accountants, bankers, lawyers, or professors. For example, the same entrepreneur might appoint to the board a professor of computer sciences.

Not everyone agrees that it is wise to put professionals on boards of directors. One dissenting voice belongs to entrepreneur William Wayne, who writes:

EXHIBIT 10.7 *Role of Board of Directors*

In theory, one of the board's main duties is to elect officers capable of running the venture successfully.

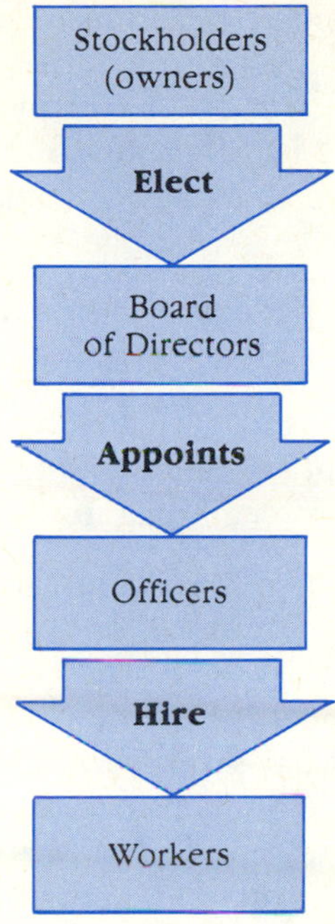

Source: Adapted from Robert J. Hughes and Jack R. Kapoor, *Business* (Boston, Mass.: Houghton Mifflin Company, 1985), p. 74. Copyright © 1985 by Houghton Mifflin Company. Used by permission of the publisher.

> Never put an attorney on the board of directors. Attorneys know the legal considerations, but they don't know the business considerations. You will find yourself with a lot of nit-picking questions which have legal implications but contribute in no real way to the business. You will have a lot of conversation, high bills, and slow progress.[6]

Entrepreneurs should also keep their board small. A board with more than five members may become unmanageable and unproductive. It is better to spend some time selecting five problem-solving members than to hastily assemble ten members incapable of anything but idle talk.

In Exhibit 10.7, note where the board of directors fits into the organizational structure of a corporate venture.

FULFILLING SKILL NEEDS—MANAGEMENT CONSULTANTS

The Value of Management Consultants

Outside consultants may also be sources of help to the entrepreneur. Giving advice to management about management has grown into a $4-billion-a-year industry. Management consulting has often been a much-maligned profession—opinions vary widely about its worth.

Entrepreneurs, in particular, seem unhappy with consultants. A typical criticism might be as follows:

> In most cases, outside consultants simply don't solve the problem. They may be fully qualified and can give endless technical advice, but they can't tell us how to put their knowledge to practical use. Quite often I have had to take off my own coat and work with such fellows, doing more explaining of our problem to them than they do explaining their special knowledge to me.[7]

If clients complain about their consultants, consultants also complain about their clients. For example, consultants claim that their clients:

- Wait too long before seeking help
- Want someone to hold their hand rather than an unbiased analysis of the problems plaguing them.

Despite the complaints from both sides, however, management consulting continues to thrive. Perhaps the best proof of its acceptance is its rapid growth. As C. Northcote Parkinson put it, "There must be a great demand for efficiency experts since they are in such large supply."[8]

What should entrepreneurs do to ensure that they get their money's worth from consultants? First, entrepreneurs should know what it is they want to know. The sharper the focus of their questions, the better the answers they will get. Instead of asking broad questions such as, "What advertising method should I use to reach my prospective customers," they should first ask well-focused questions such as these:

- Who are my customers? Where are they? In what census tracts?
- How do they buy? At what price? In what quantities?
- What motivates them to buy?

Getting the Right Consultants

How can entrepreneurs check a consultant's credentials? Testimonial letters are generally worthless. Only the big firms have well-established reputations, and their high fees are beyond the reach of most entrepreneurs. Unlike medicine and law, management consulting is not considered a profession. In fact, anyone with printed business cards can claim to be a magician of the entrepreneurial world. There is no law requiring that men or women have a masters degree in business administration, five years of industrial experience, and passing grades on a comprehensive test administered by the state before they can become practicing consultants.

The big firms have formed a group called the Association of Consulting Management Engineers (ACME). Its purpose is to raise the standards of consultants to a professional level. ACME suggests, for example, that entrepreneurs should watch for such unprofessional practices as these:

- High-pressure salesmanship that promises quick, sure results
- Preliminary surveys offered cold at a fixed fee

- Requests for fees in advance
- Offers to consult at a low fee until results are shown

Despite ACME's efforts, consulting still has a long way to go before it reaches the status of a profession. Entrepreneurs must therefore do some investigating of their own before they decide upon a consultant. Questions they should ask are:

- How long has the consulting firm been in business?
- What is the background of their consultants?
- What entrepreneurs has the firm served?
- What do these entrepreneurs say about the quality of the firm's work?
- Has the firm had experience applicable to the entrepreneur's problem?

FULFILLING SKILL NEEDS—FEDERAL GOVERNMENT

Let us now look at the sources of help offered by the federal government. Since the 1950s, the idea that entrepreneurs need management help to survive and grow has spread like a spider's web, stretching to virtually every corner of the country. Exhibit 10.8 shows the many sources of management help now offered at little or no fee to entrepreneurs, both before or after they go into business for themselves. Different services are available to entrepreneurs who go into a high-technology business than to those who go into a low-technology business because of the greater level of management sophistication required to launch a high-technology venture.

Note that Exhibit 10.8 covers not only federal help but also help from other sources such as community colleges and universities, Chambers of Commerce, and organizations made up of small businesses. Exhausting this long list could only help entrepreneurs in their efforts to get the right advice.

Heading the list is the SBA. Since it was founded in 1953, the SBA has helped hundreds of thousands of entrepreneurs. Still, most entrepreneurs have the mistaken view that the SBA only lends money or guarantees repayment of loans made by commercial banks. Even *more* important, however, the SBA strives to help entrepreneurs prepare themselves better for the job ahead. Any entrepreneur can spend money. The SBA's programs try to help entrepreneurs spend it wisely. As one small-business expert puts it:

> No small business ever failed because of a lack of funds. The supply of funds and the availability of cash to meet obligations is merely a thermometer that measures the wisdom and discipline with which the entrepreneur has committed his funds. When and if he runs clean out of working cash, his thermometer reading is zero. It indicates his inability to live within his means.[9]

EXHIBIT 10.8 *Sources of Help for Entrepreneurs*

Management Help Offered by—	Where Available	BEFORE they go into a business whose technology is—		AFTER they go into a business whose technology is—	
		High	Low	High	Low
U.S. Small Business Administration					
Counseling by:					
Staff	N				✓
Service Corps of Retired Executives	N				✓
Active Corps of Executives	N				✓
Small Business Institutes	N			✓	✓
Small Business Development Centers	S	✓	✓	✓	✓
Prebusiness workshops	N		✓		
Nonaccredited courses and seminars	N				✓
Publications	N		✓		✓
U.S. Department of Commerce					
Seminars and workshops	N			✓	✓
Publications	N	✓	✓	✓	✓
Other federal agencies (Example: IRS*)					
Seminars and workshops	N				✓
Publications	N				✓
State, county, and local governments					
Counseling	S				✓
Seminars and workshops	S				✓
Publications	S				✓
Local development corporations and similar companies					
Counseling	N				✓
Seminars and workshops	N				✓
Universities					
Accredited courses	S	✓	✓	✓	✓
Nonaccredited courses and seminars	S				✓
Publications	S	✓	✓	✓	✓
Counseling	S				
Community colleges					
Accredited courses	S				✓
Nonaccredited courses and seminars	N				✓
Counseling	S				✓
Small-business groups (Example: NFIB†)					
Seminars and workshops	S				✓
Counseling	S				✓
Publications	N				✓
Large corporations (Example: Bank of America)					
Publications	N		✓		✓
Counseling	S				✓
Trade associations					
Publications	N			✓	✓
Seminars and workshops	N			✓	✓

*U.S. Internal Revenue Service
†National Federation of Independent Business

N = Nationally
S = Some parts of nation

Though obviously an exaggeration, these comments underscore the central importance of management skills in any venture, big or small. What counts most is the entrepreneur's skill at managing resources, and money is only one of these. The SBA offers entrepreneurs four major management-counseling programs to upgrade their management skills and to help them get federal contracts. These are:

- SCORE (Service Corps of Retired Executives)
- ACE (Active Corps of Executives)
- SBI (Small Business Institute)
- SBDC (Small Business Development Center)

SCORE Program

If entrepreneurs need help in launching a venture, they can get it free through SCORE. All of its members are retired executives who enjoyed successful careers in either small or big business. All are volunteers.

Under this program, the SBA tries to match the expert to the need. For example, if an entrepreneur needs a marketing plan and does not know how to put one together, the SBA will pull from its list of SCORE counselors a person with marketing experience and knowledge.

ACE Program

As with SCORE, ACE is designed to help the entrepreneur who cannot afford expensive consultants. The SBA recruits ACE volunteers from virtually every industry. All ACE members currently enjoy successful careers, generally as entrepreneurs themselves.

Together, SCORE and ACE have about 12,000 counselors working out of 350 chapters throughout the country. In 1985 alone, they counseled more than 120,000 entrepreneurs about their problems and opportunities.

SBI Program

This program draws on the talents available at colleges and universities. It involves students working towards advanced degrees as well as professors of business administration. Under the professors' guidance, these students work with entrepreneurs to help solve their problems. Earning degree credit for their work, the students are graded on how well they solve the entrepreneur's problem. In 1985, 510 colleges and universities took part in the program, counseling more than 10,000 entrepreneurs.

SBDC Program

This is the newest of SBA's management-counseling programs. Established in 1976, SBDCs are designed to draw together the various disciplines—including technical and professional schools—of a university and make their knowledge available to new and existing small businesses. In 1985, universities in 31 states were taking part in this program.

In a way, the SBDC program parallels the widely acclaimed Research and Extension Service of the U.S. Department of Agriculture. This agricultural service mobilizes through state universities all of the nation's latest technical and management advances in farming and makes sure that this knowledge reaches all farmers.

Cooperation among Programs

These four counseling programs often merge, if it is in the best interests of the entrepreneur. It is not uncommon, for example, for both SCORE and ACE counselors to work closely with an SBI professor to solve an entrepreneur's pressing problem. These programs also work together to offer:

- Pre-business workshops
- Small-business management courses
- Seminars on special topics such as taxation

Often, these programs are called upon to give special workshops throughout the country to deal with unique problems. One such workshop encourages women to consider small business as a career option. Another deals with Vietnam veterans and their problems as entrepreneurs.

Minorities also benefit from the SBA's Minority Enterprise Program as well as from special workshops. The main goal of the Minority Enterprise Program is to help close the gap between minority entrepreneurs and other American entrepreneurs. The SBA has joined with local communities, commercial banks, and major corporations to increase the number of minority entrepreneurs. Under this program, the SBA tries to match minority persons who want to become entrepreneurs with sound business opportunities. The SBA then works closely with the minority person, often helping with financial statements and occasionally with preparing a business plan. SCORE, ACE, SBI, and SBDC counselors are deeply involved in this effort.

Of the many programs offered by the SBA, the foregoing are the most helpful to the entrepreneur about to launch a venture. These same programs are also helpful to those already in business for themselves.

FULFILLING SKILL NEEDS—TRADE ASSOCIATIONS

Trade associations aim to help their members survive and grow. Such associations are uniquely qualified to do so, because their expert help and guidance relate *directly* to the entrepreneur's industry. There are more than 2,500 trade associations in the country, one for virtually every industry.

Many trade associations offer skilled help in a wide range of subjects, such as research, finance, labor relations, tax aspects, government regulations, and marketing. They also offer expert guidance in helping entrepreneurs to:

- Pursue new opportunities in the marketplace
- Take advantage of the latest technology
- Adopt the latest operating methods
- Solve operating problems
- Increase sales revenues
- Read market trends

EXHIBIT 10.9 *Selected Services Offered by Trade Associations*

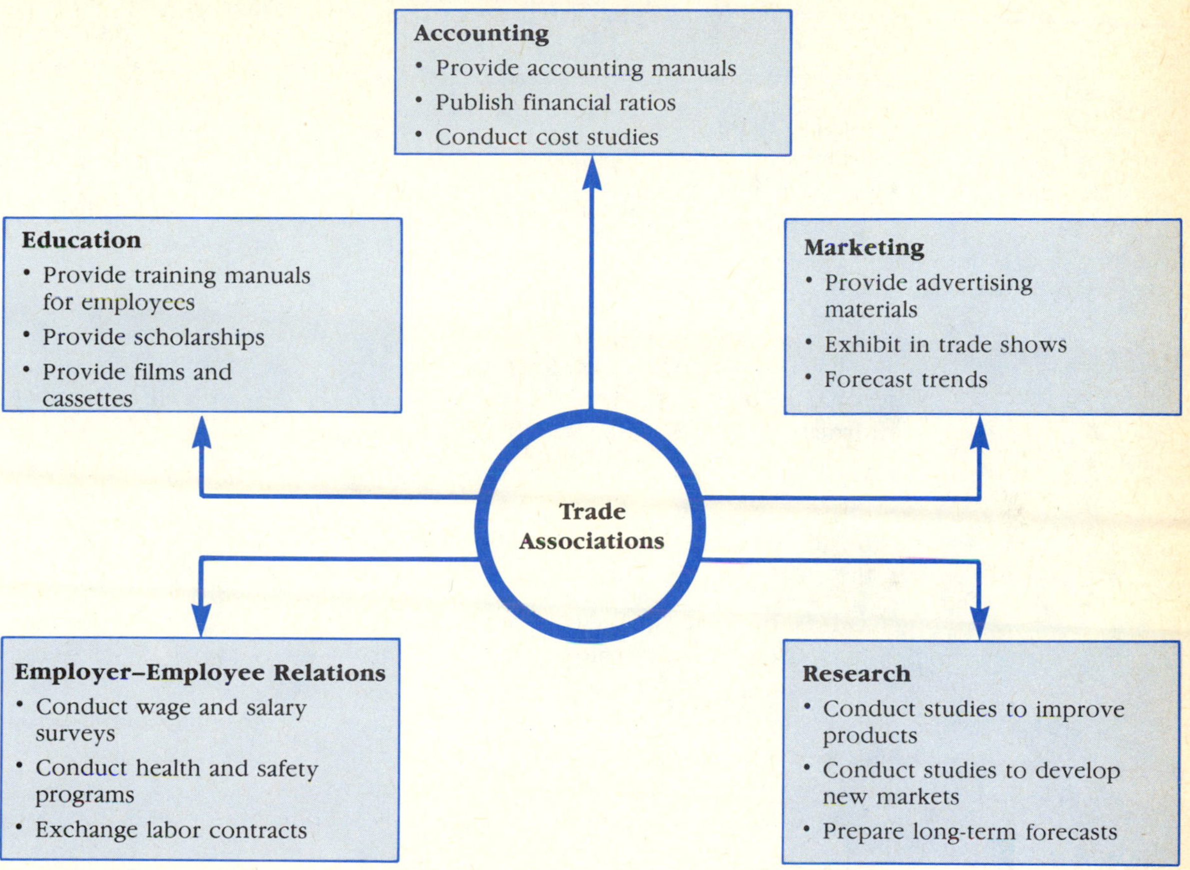

Source: U.S. Small Business Administration, Association Services for Small Business (Washington, D.C.: U.S. Government Printing Office, 1984).

Some idea of the many services offered by trade associations is outlined in Exhibit 10.9, which provides a composite picture of trade associations. Keep in mind, however, that not all associations offer all of these services to their members.

Even so, entrepreneurs should join the trade association in their industries, since the benefits usually far outweigh any individual's contribution. The costs to belong are reasonable—membership dues are usually a fraction of one percent of the venture's yearly sales revenues. "Considering the services available, the forward-looking entrepreneur will regard association dues not as an expense but as a form of investment toward improving the venture."[10]

OTHER SOURCES OF HELP

Many groups besides the SBA help entrepreneurs. One that stands out is the Bank of America. Ten times a year, it publishes the *Small Business Reporter* on topics as diverse as:

- Bicycle stores
- Retail nurseries
- Cocktail lounges
- Bookstores
- Sporting goods stores
- Shoe stores
- Apparel manufacture

Each issue focuses on just one industry. For example, the issue devoted to bicycle stores contains 20 pages packed with well-researched information on 25 topics, among them:

- Marketing research and store location
- Initial inventory and pricing
- Business records and store design
- Financing and personnel[11]

This journal costs the entrepreneur only two dollars. Similar information is also available from the SBA and from many trade associations.

Networking

Networking is still another excellent source of help that now enjoys widespread popularity. Entrepreneurs network by meeting regularly and discussing mutual problems and opportunities.

Small-business organizations have been founded all over the country for just this purpose. One such organization is the Council of Smaller Enterprises of Cleveland which, in 1985, had a total membership of 7,200 entrepreneurs, the largest number in the country. It offers educational programs and fringe benefits tailored to the needs and wants of its members as well as networking.

Women and minority entrepreneurs in particular have found networking to be an effective problem-solving tool. Take this example drawn from a column in *The Wall Street Journal*:

> **Example:** Ruth Lambert and her partner, Dianna Minnick, were hesitant to use a consultant to help them in their $2 million-a-year real-estate-forms business. Ms. Lambert says their reluctance was a matter of gender. "Men have no personal script against getting help. But women do; they get into I made the apple pie all by myself."
>
> However, the partners aren't trying to run their New Haven company, Forms & Worms Inc., alone anymore. They joined a group of 10 women business owners who meet monthly to help each other with business

problems. Known as the Chief Executive Roundtable, the group is sponsored by the New York-based American Woman's Economic Development Corporation and includes women who own and operate companies in the New York area with annual sales of $1 million to $10 million.

"You are alone at the top," says Doris Colgate, president of Offshore Sailing School Limited. "The roundtable gives me the opportunity to hear what someone else has to say. They are much more capable of analyzing a problem sometimes because I am too close to it."

The women have helped each other with an array of problems: important customers who chronically pay late, conflicts between partners, troublesome employees, financing expansion. "You get suggestions that are real and actionable," says JoAnn Friedman, president of Health Marketing Systems Inc. "There aren't many people who will tell you that you have a pimple on your nose."[12]

We have barely scratched the surface. There is help available everywhere and entrepreneurs need only to look for it. They may not be able to hire a $50,000-a-year marketing researcher or a $500-a-day consultant, but they can always use the many free services available from such sources as the SBA.

SUMMARY

In general, entrepreneurs stand alone. They cannot afford the expert help that large corporations have at their disposal, so they must be resourceful, and take what help they can get—especially free help from organizations like the SBA. To benefit from such help, entrepreneurs should first answer questions such as these:

- What skills do I need to launch my venture successfully?
- How can I go about finding men and women armed with these skills?

In defining their skill needs, entrepreneurs should think in terms of skills rather than persons. To do that, they should begin with the business plan, identifying all the skills needed to complete each step and then identifying who has those skills.

The organizational plan should have two parts, one dealing with inside help and the other with outside help. In determining inside help, entrepreneurs should take pains to define:

- Who does what
- Who has what authority
- Who reports to whom

In assessing their need for outside help, entrepreneurs should take equally great pains to define what kinds of professional and management services they need. One source of management help often ignored is the board of directors.

There are many organizations dedicated to giving entrepreneurs a helping hand, among them:

- The federal government, especially the SBA
- Chambers of Commerce and organizations made up of small businesses
- Universities and community colleges
- The Bank of America
- Trade associations

DISCUSSION AND REVIEW QUESTIONS

1. Explain the need for organizational planning.
2. Explain how skill needs should be defined, using an entrepreneur you know as an example.
3. How helpful are organizational charts? Explain.
4. Define these terms: *organization, job description, organizational chart, line authority, staff authority, board of directors, ACME.*
5. Why do boards of directors tend to be ineffectual? Can they be made to work well? How?
6. If you were about to start a venture, what skills would you prefer to have on your board of directors? Explain.
7. Why don't sole proprietorships and partnerships have boards of directors? Should they?
8. How would you, as an entrepreneur, go about estimating the skills needed to launch your venture successfully?
9. Describe how entrepreneurs can get help at little or no fee.
10. How do the SCORE, ACE, SBI, and SBDC programs differ? Do they overlap? How?
11. How would you go about getting the right consultant?
12. What is "organizational muddle" and how can it be prevented?
13. Describe line-staff organization. When should you use this organizational structure?
14. Why is preparation of a business plan so vital in planning your organization?
15. Which is more important, management skill or money? Explain.

NOTES

1. Marvin Bower, *The Will to Manage* (New York: McGraw-Hill, 1966), p. 123.
2. Ibid., p. 153.
3. Myles L. Mace, "The President and the Board of Directors," *Harvard Business Review*, March–April 1972, p. 38.
4. Ibid., p. 43.
5. Adapted from "Choosing a Board," *Venture*, April 1982, p. 25.
6. William Wayne, *How to Succeed in Business When the Chips Are Down* (New York: McGraw-Hill, 1972), p. 107.

7. Perrin Stryker, "What's Your Problem," *Fortune*, March 1953, p. 107.
8. C. Northcote Parkinson, "A Hard Look at Efficiency Experts," *New York Times*, Sunday Magazine Section, April 3, 1960, p. 31.
9. Louis L. Allen, *Starting and Succeeding in Your Own Small Business* (New York: Grosset & Dunlap, 1968), p. 28.
10. U.S. Small Business Administration, *Association Services for Small Business* (Washington, D.C.: U.S. Government Printing Office, 1984), p. 6.
11. "Bicycle Stores," *Small Business Reporter* (San Francisco: Bank of America, 1981), pp. 1–18.
12. Sanford L. Jacobs, "Women Chief Executives Help Each Other with Frank Advice," *The Wall Street Journal*, July 2, 1984, p. 17.

CASE 10A *Kerscher Elevator Company*

After suffering heavy operating losses in 1982, the Kerscher Elevator Company has rebounded to post modest profits. The main reason for its poor performance was an employee's embezzlement of $175,000. This problem still persists, so the president and sole owner, John Blatt, is still struggling to keep the company afloat. He has just prepared a plan that he believes will help ensure the company's future.

Background

Founded in 1912, Kerscher Elevator prospered until the 1960s. When Mr. Blatt bought the company in 1978, the company was in "beat-up, rundown condition," says Mr. Blatt. "The company's building was a mess. The roof leaked, the washroom had no running water, and the windows had been shattered by vandals. Worse, the company had lost all respect in the community. Believe me, the company was all but dead." Undaunted, Mr. Blatt "plunged into deep water and bought the company anyway."

Mr. Blatt had worked for eleven years in the elevator division of Reliance Electric, a billion-dollar company, before striking off on his own to buy Kerscher Elevator. "I just hated working for a company that big," says Mr. Blatt. "I felt boxed in and couldn't stand the endless meetings. They were so boring. Besides, my job was a dead-end job, although I enjoyed going to Las Vegas and other resort cities on trouble-shooting jobs." Mr. Blatt had joined Reliance Electric soon after he was discharged from the U.S. Navy, where he had worked for four years as a nuclear engineer under the renowned Admiral Hyman Rickover. Before his stint in the Navy, Mr. Blatt attended Ohio State University, where he studied industrial management.

Mr. Blatt inherited his entrepreneurial spirit from his father, whom he deeply admired. A successful entrepreneur, his father owned a small retail automobile dealership selling Studebakers and Willys. "He did well enough to put me through college," says Mr. Blatt. "It was my dad who always encouraged me to be my own boss."

Financial Sacrifice

When he left Reliance Electric in 1977, Mr. Blatt was earning $60,000 a year as manager of elevator construction and technical service. His first two years with Kerscher Elevator, however, he paid himself only $15,000 a year. "It was worth the sacrifice, just to be my own boss," says Mr. Blatt. "I was reduced to scrambling for a living, and instead of working 40 hours a week, I found myself working 80 to 100 hours a week. Funny thing is, I really enjoyed it."

Mr. Blatt's wide travels as a trouble-shooter with Reliance Electric enabled him to observe firsthand the operations of virtually every other elevator company in the country. Long entertaining the thought of owning his own elevator company, he made mental notes of which companies "seemed ripe for purchase at a low price." He chose the Kerscher Elevator

EXHIBIT 10A.1 *Kerscher Elevator Company: Balance Sheet At Time of Purchase (September 30, 1977)*

Assets			Equities		
Current assets			Current liabilities		
Cash	$15,000		Note payable	$15,000	
Accounts receivable	42,000		Accounts payable	26,000	$ 41,000
Inventories	11,000	$ 68,000			
			Long-term liability		
Fixed assets			Note payable		100,000
Land	$ 5,000				
			Owners' equity		
Building	47,100		Common stock		10,000
Equipment	2,000				
Vehicles	18,000	72,100			
Goodwill		10,900			
Total assets		$151,000			$151,000

Company, which "was going under before my very eyes. I was sure I had the drive and imagination to turn the company around," says Mr. Blatt.

He bought Kerscher Elevator for $120,000, financing the purchase with just $10,000 of his own money and borrowing the rest from the seller. Interest was 8 percent, and the term of the loan was 10 years. "Not a bad deal," says Mr. Blatt. "The banks never would have given me such generous terms." His beginning balance sheet appears in Exhibit 10A.1. Note that Mr. Blatt also loaned the company $15,000 to purchase inventories of elevator parts and to finance customers until they pay their bills, as well as to repair and renovate the building, which had become an "eyesore."

When he bought the company, Mr. Blatt had decided to take in a partner whose experience with the elevator industry complemented his—someone who was an expert in sales and purchasing. Mr. Blatt, on the other hand, was an expert in installing and repairing elevators.

Although he had incorporated his new company and made the total investments, Mr. Blatt had agreed, in writing, to share the company and all future dividends equally with his partner. In essence, then, Mr. Blatt had an equal partner who had invested not a single penny of his own money. "It was my way of letting him know that I needed and appreciated his skills," says Mr. Blatt. "In my eyes, he was my partner and I always spoke of him as such, even though the company was a regular corporation and not a general partnership."

Turning the Company Around

Kerscher Elevator had suffered a string of operating losses under the prior owner. "The challenge was awesome," says Mr. Blatt. "My partner and I agreed that our most pressing problem was to brighten the company's

EXHIBIT 10A.2 *Kerscher Elevator Company: Operating Performance Before and After Purchase*

	1977*	1978	1979	1980	1981	1982	1983
Sales revenues	$312,000	$417,500	$667,500	$896,900	$1,396,500	$ 907,500	$969,000
Cost of sales	242,000	301,100	510,000	639,400	999,500	654,000	615,000
Gross profit	$ 70,000	$116,400	$157,500	$257,500	$ 397,000	$253,500	$354,000
Operating expenses	92,000	104,300	125,500	258,300	374,900	339,400	315,600
Operating profit	$(22,000)	$ 12,100	$ 32,000	$ (800)	$ 22,100	$(85,900)	$ 38,400
Interest		8,000	11,300	16,000			
Profit before taxes	$(22,000)	$ 4,100	$ 20,700	$(16,800)	$ 22,100	$(85,900)	$ 38,400
Income taxes		200	1,100				
Net profit	$(22,000)	$ 3,900	$ 19,600	$(16,800)	$ 22,100	$(85,900)	$ 38,400

* Under prior owner

badly tarnished image. The question was, How?" After much thought, the two partners decided that Mr. Blatt would become the company's "Mr. Outside," making himself visible in the community as a volunteer to service groups and civic organizations. He would make himself available to serve the community at a moment's notice and, in this way, make every effort to boost the company's image.

At the same time, he would be "beating the bushes" to recapture clients lost by the prior owner. Here he would stress that Kerscher Elevator's new and aggressive management would focus on supplying better service than any competitor. For example, the company would be ready to respond "instantly—at any hour of the day and night—if a client's elevator broke down."

Mr. Blatt's partner, on the other hand, would be the company's "Mr. Inside," directing his energies at running the shop. He would be responsible for getting the work done right the first time and on time. He would also run the office and make sure that records were kept up to date and clients paid their bills on time.

The partners' strategy paid off immediately. As shown in Exhibit 10A.2, sales revenues moved steadily upward through 1981, although profits were erratic. "It surely was a heady feeling to know that it was our strategy that saved the company from certain bankruptcy," says Mr. Blatt.

National Recognition

To turn the company around, Mr. Blatt spent "part of almost every day" working to change its image. Soon after he and his partner took over the company, he was elected president of the small-business branch of the local Chamber of Commerce. In 1980, he was elected to be a delegate to the White House Conference on Small Business. Because of his volunteer work, Mr. Blatt soon won national recognition—President Jimmy Carter awarded him a special citation and *Inc.* magazine quoted him as follows:

> When I bought the Kerscher Elevator Company in 1978, its image was going down. Our building was an eyesore. It leaked like a sieve, vandals attacked the property on weekly sorties, and our 23,000 square-foot factory was so cluttered that we could barely fit a pick-up truck on the floor.
>
> We figured the business would be dead in less than a year if we didn't improve our image immediately. My partner and I then joined civic organizations like the Kiwanis and Rotary Clubs. We did work at the city zoo—a $1,000 job for which we charged $1. The public exposure was excellent, and we met more people in the process.
>
> Now we've budgeted about $5,000 a year for giveaways such as tickets for local sporting events, that we donate to local public television station auctions. We also help finance the college educations of deserving youth.
>
> The result? We now employ 14 repairmen, up from just 4 in 1978, when we started.*

Workforce When he and his partner took over the company, Mr. Blatt was aware that image and solid performance must go hand in hand. "It was vital," says Mr. Blatt, "to hire, train, motivate, and mold all employees in the image of excellence that we wanted to project."

Mr. Blatt had to hire his employees through the International Union of Elevator Constructors, which runs a closed shop, meaning that workers must first join the union before hiring on with elevator companies. The union supplies the labor for Mr. Blatt, although he retains the right to hire and fire specific employees. "If I need a worker," says Mr. Blatt, "I just pick up the phone and call the union. I don't have to advertise for help or call an employment agency."

The elevator industry rivals both the automotive and the steel industries in the generosity of its wage structure. In 1984, elevator mechanics earned an average base wage of $18.87 an hour plus fringe benefits of $5.14 an hour. "Not a bad wage," says Mr. Blatt. "In fact, my employees have often drawn more pay than me, and I'm the company president. My employees make more money than most college professors."

As well paid as his employees are, Mr. Blatt still goes to "extraordinary lengths" to make sure they meet his expectations of excellence. His promotional brochure claims:

> The Kerscher team is kept constantly on the cutting edge of the state of the art in vertical transportation by attendance at KERSCHER COLLEGE. Our commitment is that our employees will be the best trained elevator

* Adapted from "The Company Image: How Much is it Worth?" *Inc.*, November 1980, pp. 44–45.

persons in the area. Our supervisory personnel work directly with the field mechanics to reach this goal.

The Kerscher professional service team includes elevator mechanics and helpers with experience on hundreds of different makes and models of elevators. No other local company has as much breadth of talent as Kerscher's carefully selected team.

"I'm a poor motivator," says Mr. Blatt. "I'm not very good at it, and yet I need workers who are motivated to excel at providing service. It's not uncommon for elevators to break down in the dead of night or on a holiday. In such emergencies, our answering service gets on the phone immediately to persuade a mechanic to repair the elevator. But to get someone to come in at odd hours is often as easy as pulling teeth. Why, the other day I had to send a taxi to a mechanic's house to get a repair job done in a downtown office building."

At present, Mr. Blatt employs 17 men and women, of whom 14 work in the field and 3 in the office. "Our organization is a lot leaner than it was in our growth days," says Mr. Blatt. "We had too much overhead." Mr. Blatt's organizational chart appears in Exhibit 10A.3. Although he is its chairman, he has never called a meeting of the company's board of directors.

Note that the organizational chart omits mention of Mr. Blatt's partner. "We parted in 1982," says Mr. Blatt. "We got tired of each other. We just couldn't get along and it took me four years to do something about our relationship. Had I known in 1978 what I know now, I never would have formed a 50-50 working partnership. We ran the company as equals, even though I had put up all the money to buy it."

EXHIBIT 10A.3 *Kerscher Elevator Company: Organizational Chart*

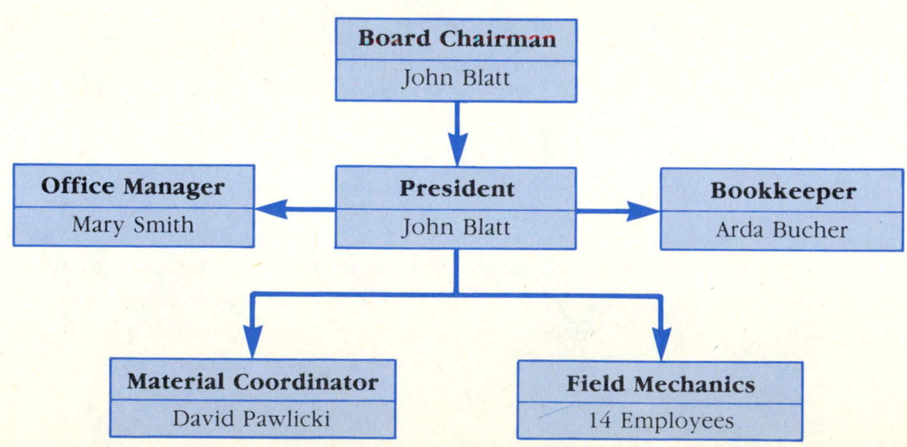

Market Segments

Kerscher Elevator markets its services within a 75-mile radius of its offices. "Any building with an elevator is a potential client," says Mr. Blatt. "In my marketing area alone, more than a thousand buildings have elevators of some kind."

Indeed, elevator service is in constant demand because buildings, tall or short, must now be accessible to the handicapped. Mr. Blatt says that two factors put building owners "at the mercy" of elevator service companies like his:

- The complexity of today's elevator systems. A single elevator system may have more than 10,000 separate parts, each one capable of causing a breakdown in elevator service.
- The technology of elevator systems. Manufacturers differ sharply in their designs as they try to outdo each other by using the latest advances in electronic technology.

These two factors complicate Kerscher Elevator's ability to service its clients properly. "That is why our training program, which I like to call the KERSCHER COLLEGE, is so necessary," says Mr. Blatt.

Kerscher Elevator recently diversified into the market for the handicapped with a complete line of porch lifts, residential elevators, stair climbers, dumbwaiters, and power-lift chairs. "We recognize this segment as a rapidly-growing market into which we have moved with deliberation," says Mr. Blatt. In the next two years or so, Mr. Blatt plans to continue his diversification efforts by "invading the escalator market. This market is also growing rapidly," he says, "and we ought to exploit it, although not now."

Competition

Kerscher Elevator is the second largest elevator service company in its marketing area. The largest is Shindler of North America, which also manufactures elevator systems. "Competition in the industry for service work is severe and getting worse by the week," says Mr. Blatt. "To survive in this industry, you have to know your competition—their strengths and weaknesses." See Exhibit 10A.4 for a list of Mr. Blatt's competitors, their market shares, and his remarks about their services.

Competition has become so severe that Otis Elevator, the nation's largest manufacturer of elevators, has just begun a "price-cutting war to obtain a wider base for their local servicing operation." Mr. Blatt adds that Shindler of North America has "fabricated stories to make Kerscher Elevator look bad." He responds to these competitive pressures by exploiting his company's agility. "Response time is our niche in the marketplace," he says. "We respond quicker and faster than our competitors when clients need us. In bidding on a service job, for example, we're never more than fifteen minutes from a decision on a client's elevator problem; our competitors take a week or two. In fact, it usually takes me no more than a couple minutes to price a service job."

EXHIBIT 10A.4 *Kerscher Elevator Company: Competition*

Name	Number Of Field Mechanics	Local Service Sales	Remarks
Shindler of North America	20	$1,300,000	Strong connections
Otis	3	300,000	Lowering prices to cheapen competition
Toledo	3	200,000	One-man show
Davis-Newcomber	3	200,000	Non-union
Montgomery	4	100,000	Only in neighboring state
American Home Lift	1	80,000	Residential market only
Westinghouse	1	35,000	Treats area as a visiting company
Plunger-Lift	1	5,000	Man visits once a month
Dover	1	2,000	Sold one big job and is now trying to enter local market

Even so, Mr. Blatt is especially worried about the price-cutting war now underway. "I've always priced to value," says Mr. Blatt. "My clients have always been willing to pay a premium for the excellent service I give. They want fast, reliable, dependable service, and they know I have staked my reputation on giving such service." Despite the price war, Mr. Blatt has drafted these objectives for 1984:

- To work with union workers to achieve a profit margin of 48 percent through improved job planning and scheduling
- To develop an effective quality control program, ensuring high-quality products and service at competitive prices and reducing callbacks* to three per day
- To design an inventory control system that reduces the investment in inventory by 10 percent
- To develop office procedures to ensure that all customers with contracts are routinely serviced and not overlooked
- To improve communications within the office to spark instant response to customer complaints
- To brighten the appearance of the company by keeping the shop and office both clean and orderly at all times and by improving lawn care and snow removal

Financial Crisis

As noted earlier, the company turned around dramatically under Mr. Blatt's leadership until 1982. That year, near-disaster struck—the company's bookkeeper, over a period of four months, embezzled $175,000 of

* A term that refers to "calling back" an employee to work overtime during odd hours to repair an elevator.

cash. "Funny thing is, I hired her because she had impeccable references and, to top it off, she tested just great," says Mr. Blatt.

The embezzlement began the very day that Mr. Blatt put his accounting system on computer. "From day one, my newly-hired bookkeeper stole my cash wholesale," says Mr. Blatt. Operating losses for the first month after the computer system was put in were $60,000 and the second month, $70,000.

When he discovered the embezzlement, Mr. Blatt fired both the bookkeeper and the computer service. "When I took over the bookkeeping myself, I began making profits again," says Mr. Blatt. Although he still keeps records manually, Mr. Blatt is "not soured on computers. When I installed the computer system, I got bad advice from a certified public accountant, who was also a friend of mine. Next time, I'll be better prepared for the computer."

Although the embezzlement happened more than two years ago, Mr. Blatt is still preoccupied with its aftermath. He has sued for $250,000 both the bookkeeper and the employment agency that recommended her. The U.S. Internal Revenue Service, in turn, has sued Mr. Blatt for failing to deposit social security taxes for his employees, since the bookkeeper had taken these payments along with other money in her embezzlement.

At the same time as the embezzlement, Mr. Blatt and his partner were "in the throes of negotiating a business divorce." Plagued with so many problems, Mr. Blatt was so distracted that he began to neglect the day-to-day operation of his business. As a result, in 1982, sales revenues dropped to $907,500 from $1,396,500 the year before and profits vanished as operating losses of $85,900 were incurred. "It was the worst period of my life," says Mr. Blatt, "but I never doubted my ability and courage to turn the company around, a second time."

The Second Turnaround

Taking stock of himself and his company, Mr. Blatt decided to stick to the philosophical course he had set originally. He would not panic and he would continue to focus on excellence to regain lost customers and gain new ones. He would not compromise his principles or engage in any price-cutting war. Although this strategy has not worked as well as he would have liked, Mr. Blatt has turned the company around once again. In 1983, sales revenues rose to $969,000 and profits came to $38,400. "Coming on the heels of that whopping big loss the year before, I couldn't be more pleased," says Mr. Blatt. His 1983 income statement and balance sheet appear in Exhibits 10A.5 and 10A.6. Exhibit 10A.7 traces his sales and profit performance since 1978.

Optimistic, Mr. Blatt prepared both a financial plan and a marketing strategy for 1984. The plan appears in Exhibit 10A.8 and the strategy in Exhibit 10A.9. He is so confident of his future that he is now seriously considering relocating to the nearby Control Data Business Technology Center. Founded by the giant Control Data Corporation, this center helps

EXHIBIT 10A.5

Kerscher Elevator Company: 1983 Income Statement

Sales revenues		$969,000
Cost of sales		615,000
Gross profit		$354,000
Operating expenses:		
Office salaries	$130,500	
Interest	30,100	
Travel, entertainment	26,800	
Office supplies, postage	16,100	
Insurance	15,500	
Building rent	14,400	
Depreciation	13,100	
Professional fees	13,100	
Covenant not to compete	12,500	
Automobile and truck	8,200	
Employee benefits	6,600	
Utilities, security	4,100	
Dues and subscriptions	2,800	
Advertising	2,700	
Tooling	2,500	
Temporary help	2,100	
Personal property taxes	1,900	
Licenses	1,500	
Repairs and maintenance	900	
Penalties	700	
Freight	700	
Education	700	
Equipment rental	500	
Contributions	400	
Bad debts	200	
Miscellaneous	7,000	315,600
Operating profit		$ 38,400

its tenants, small-businesses like Mr. Blatt's, by providing:

- Layout and space design help
- Basic utilities such as heat and air conditioning
- A security system for controlling after-hours operations
- Word processing
- Clerical services
- Equipment leasing
- Shipping and receiving
- State-of-the-art computer services

It also provides the services of information specialists and a complete business and technical library that offers automated literature searches. "Of course, I cannot move into the Center until I resolve my financial problems," says Mr. Blatt. A view of the Center appears in Exhibit 10A.10.

EXHIBIT 10A.6 *Kerscher Elevator Company: Balance Sheet (December 31, 1983)*

Assets			Equities		
Current assets			Current liabilities		
Accounts receivable	$144,900		Bank overdraft	$ 4,000	
Inventories	168,400		Accounts payable	75,100	
Other	8,700	$322,000	Long-term loan (current)	61,900	
			Payroll deductions	68,700	
Fixed assets			Miscellaneous	35,100	$244,800
Equipment	$ 5,900				
Furniture and fixtures	9,900		Long-term liabilities		
Vehicles	37,000		Installment notes	$ 17,600	
	$ 52,800		Long-term loan	162,500	
Less: Accumulated depreciation	37,200	15,600	Owed to former partner	44,300	
				$224,400	
Other assets			Less: Current portion	61,900	162,500
Covenant not to compete	$ 31,200				
Miscellaneous	2,100	33,300	Other liabilities		
			Covenant not to compete		31,200
			Owners' equity		
			Common stock	$ 10,000	
			Retained earnings	(77,600)	(67,600)
Total assets		$370,900			$370,900

EXHIBIT 10A.7 *Kerscher Elevator Company: Sales and Profit Performance*

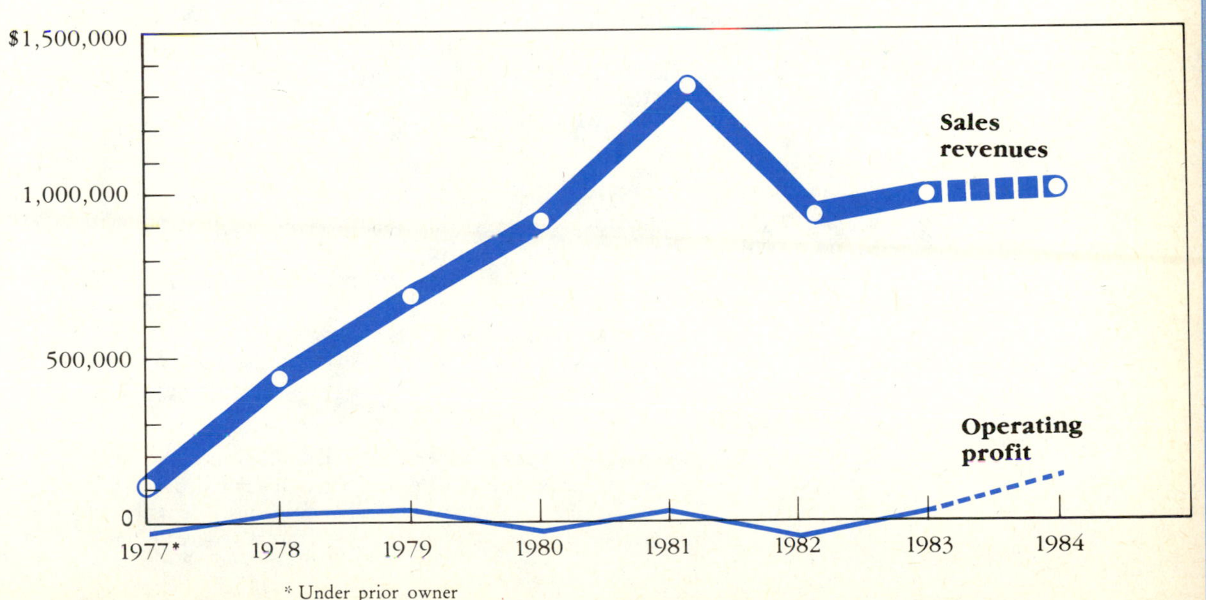

EXHIBIT 10A.8

Kerscher Elevator Company: 1984 Financial Plan

Sales revenues		
Maintenance	$600,000	
Repair	300,000	
Construction	75,000	
Handicap	5,000	$980,000
Cost of sales		
Maintenance	$300,000	
Repair	200,000	
Construction	66,000	
Handicap	14,000	580,000
Gross margin		$400,000
General and Administrative		250,000
Operating profit		$150,000
Less: Profit-sharing		15,000
Profit before taxes		$135,000

EXHIBIT 10A.9

Kerscher Elevator Company: Marketing Strategy

Product

We will maintain these product lines: Maintenance, repair, construction, and residential. We will expand our repair efforts through clearly stated specification sheets and simple price lists. We will sell Kerscher as "The Elevator Professional" and seek profitable opportunities to so demonstrate. We will seek to sell our product differentiation, including professionalism, personal attention, contractual freedom, insurance, company strength, 75-year experience, local ownership.

Price

We will work from a standard price book and will later upgrade it to reflect actual competitive expenses. We will carefully price major contracts to reflect superlative service and will clearly demonstrate what we are selling so as to differentiate it from the competitor. We will always consider "Why should the customer buy from Kerscher?" If we have no good answers, we will not pursue that market segment.

Promotion

We will utilize appropriate trade shows and related opportunities to position Kerscher in the forefront. We will selectively advertise to promote the theme: "Professionals in vertical transportation." Personal selling will remain the backbone of our efforts with a profit-sharing bonus program geared to reward superior success. We will utilize a company brochure to help build company recognition. We will remain active in civic affairs to maintain our present positive reputation.

Distribution

We will continue with direct company salespersons in the present market. We will continue to serve an area 75 miles around. We will remain alert to governmental opportunities, or favored customers, to operate satellite branches. We will remain alert to the opportunity to consult or educate in remote areas where the profits remain attractive.

EXHIBIT 10A.10 *Kerscher Elevator Company: View of Control Data Business Technology Center*

Questions

1. What accounts for the company's recent problems?
2. Comment on Mr. Blatt's entrepreneurial and managerial traits.
3. What are the key factors for success in a business like this one?
4. What are the company's prospects?
5. What should Mr. Blatt do now?

CASE 10B *Hobson Manufacturing Company, Inc.*

A year ago, Charles Hobson launched a one-man machine shop in an abandoned service station. Orders have just begun to pick up and Mr. Hobson now wants to devote most of his time to marketing and to hire a full-time machinist.

So far, Mr. Hobson has received help from his wife, who keeps the books, and from moonlighting machinists. Recently, he placed an advertisement for a machinist in the local newspaper. One of the applicants was George Benson. Selected information from his application appears below:

Age	27
Marital status	Married
Dependents	3

Own home	Yes
Kind of work desired	Machinist
Hobbies	Music, swimming
Previous experience	Machinist—Cole Manufacturing Machinist—Ward Manufacturing
Education	Graduate of West Tech
References	Mr. Ray Moon, Cole Manufacturing Mr. Ira Mack, Ward Manufacturing

When he interviewed the applicant, Mr. Hobson was impressed. The applicant appeared to be clean-cut and ambitious. Mr. Hobson then checked his references. Mr. Benson's former boss gave this information:

Reason for leaving	Fired
Would you rehire?	No
Additional information	Mr. Benson was unhappy with company policies

Question If you were Mr. Hobson, would you hire Mr. Benson? Why?

CASE 10C *James Thornton*

James Thornton began working with aluminum products shortly after he completed high school. He started out installing aluminum gutters, doors, and windows and later learned how to put up aluminum siding. When his employer expanded the plant, Mr. Thornton was named foreman of operations.

Three years later, with family backing and a $60,000 bank loan, Mr. Thornton started a small factory that produced aluminum doors and windows. He was sure his practical knowledge would help him succeed.

For the first eight months, however, the plant, which Mr. Thornton had designed himself, seemed to be operating inefficiently. Although work was getting done, he was sure that the process could be improved. He made several changes, but he was not pleased with the results. He was also having trouble marketing his products. The customers he knew through his previous employer were hesitant to give up their reliable source of supply, and Mr. Thornton was too busy in the plant to spend much time prospecting for new business.

Worried about failure, Mr. Thornton decided to retain a consultant who could help him with layout planning and marketing. Fred Riley, the consultant he chose, had presented him with a long list of businesses for whom he had consulted. Impressed by the size of the list and with the promises Mr. Riley had made, Mr. Thornton decided on the spot to hire him.

During the first week, Mr. Riley sat down with Mr. Thornton several times, looked over the invoices, and inspected the plant layout. Mr. Riley then suggested that Mr. Thornton broaden his geographic area. But Mr. Thornton balked at this idea because "increased shipping costs would sharply reduce my profits."

Mr. Riley also suggested that Mr. Thornton hire salespeople by placing advertisments in local newspapers. Although the advertisements did not bring in new customers as he had hoped, Mr. Thornton hired one person, Bruce Stephens, who generated $80,000 in local sales over the next six months.

Mr. Riley's last suggestion dealt with layout changes that would improve productivity. Only a few costly changes were actually put into effect. Although the plant looked a little better, Mr. Thornton decided to reassess his accomplishments since hiring the consultant:

- He had paid the consultant a healthy fee for his services.
- The advertising and sales promotional schemes had not been very helpful.
- The costly layout changes had not improved productivity significantly.
- The consultant's other suggestions would remain in the file, unused, since Mr. Thornton was not ready to risk more money to put them into effect.

Questions

1. Should Mr. Thornton have hired a consultant?
2. What other sources might Mr. Thornton have used to help him with his operating problems?
3. What steps should Mr. Thornton have taken in evaluating the consultant's qualifications?
4. What should Mr. Thornton do with the unused suggestions?

Source: U.S. Small Business Administration, *Sources of Assistance and Information for Small Business* (Washington, D.C.: U.S. Government Printing Office, 1979), pp. 18–19.

PART 3 MANAGING THE ONGOING VENTURE

11 ACCOUNTING

QUESTIONS FOR MASTERY

How important is accounting?
What are the uses of accounting?
How do income statements and balance sheets differ?
What are the limitations of accounting?
What is the importance of cash flow?

Frequent accounting makes for lasting friendship.

Lucas Pacioli

The entrepreneur is accountable for the performance and health of a venture. How profitable is my venture? How wisely have I invested the moneys entrusted in my care by shareholders or creditors? What is my venture worth, at least on paper? These are just a few of the questions that an accounting system should help answer. We have already touched on accounting in earlier chapters. In this chapter, we will focus on the ways entrepreneurs can use accounting to give them the information they need to act and decide.

THE USES OF ACCOUNTING

Perhaps because accounting raises images of green eyeshades, yellow paper pads, and red ink, entrepreneurs often think that accounting is something better left to accountants. Although it is the accountant who designs the entrepreneur's accounting system, the entrepreneur needs the information supplied by the system in order to plan and control the venture. As indicated in Exhibit 11.1, investors, lenders, and government agencies also

EXHIBIT 11.1 *Users and Selected Uses of Accounting Information*

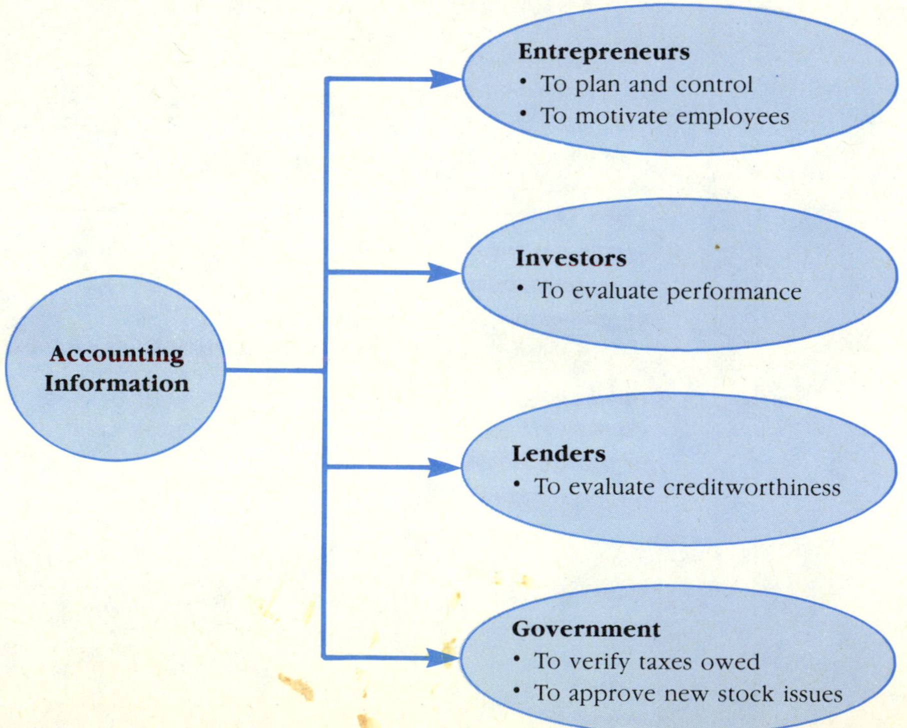

need the entrepreneur's accounting information. Failure to recognize these needs may explain why some ventures make little profit or fail completely.

Entrepreneurs often blame their failures on problems such as these:

- Low sales revenues
- Wrong mix of inventory
- High operating expenses
- Insufficient working capital
- Too much money tied up in fixed assets

Yet, with a well-designed accounting system, entrepreneurs can spot these problems early and then head them off. It is not enough for an accounting system to be well designed and carefully run. Unless the entrepreneur takes action based on the information generated by the system, the system is useless. Three different entrepreneurs, for example, may use precisely the same accounting system—the same set of records and reports, the same means of collecting data—but with wholly different results:

- In one venture, the system may be useless because the entrepreneur never acts on the information collected—and his employees know it.
- In the second venture, the system may be helpful because the entrepreneur uses the information as a general guide for planning and control and has educated her employees to use it in the same spirit.
- In the third venture, the system may be worse than useless because the entrepreneur overemphasizes the importance of the figures and therefore takes unwise actions.

Elements of a Good Accounting System

What should a good accounting system do? An accounting system is more than journals and ledgers and worksheets. The best system:

- Generates reports, tax returns, and financial statements quickly
- Ensures a high degree of accuracy and completeness
- Collects and processes information at low cost
- Minimizes the incidence of theft and fraud[1]

There is no such thing as one best accounting system applicable to all businesses, big or small. Any system will work as long as it meets these goals. For example, the owner of a fruit stand may use the back of an envelope to keep records. And if that is all he needs to stay on top of the job, it is enough. Or, take the entrepreneur who runs a women's dress shop with the help of one salesperson. Her accounting system may consist of just these parts:

- Daily cash register receipts
- A checkbook
- Monthly bank statements
- A file of unpaid bills
- A file of charge slips

Armed with the information yielded by this system, the entrepreneur's accountant may prepare her tax returns readily. She may know the dress shop so well that no other financial statements are needed. But if the shop joined a chain of 100 shops, some changes would have to be made. For one thing, the figures that the entrepreneur keeps in her head, such as daily receipts, would have to be recorded in order to communicate them to persons not on the spot.

- These figures would be used by the chain to make decisions about both her shop and the chain as a whole.
- Her performance as a manager would be measured by these figures, and then compared with that of other shop managers in the chain.

Her accounting system would become more formal, complex, and time-consuming than before. To enable the chain to make valid comparisons among shops, it would have to be the same system used by all other shops.

The bigger the venture, the more complex the accounting system. When the dress-shop entrepreneur was managing alone, with just one salesperson to look after, her need for records was slight. She could see things on the spot that executives of a 100-shop chain must find out about from written reports.

Example: The dress-shop entrepreneur scarcely needs detailed records on her inventory of dresses. She simply can look at her inventory position any time she needs to and reorder accordingly. But, if her shop belonged to a 100-shop chain, all reorders would be handled by purchasing agents at headquarters or perhaps by computer. These reorders would be based on inventory information that she would give the chain weekly.

Need for an Accountant

Regardless of the simplicity of their ventures, entrepreneurs should call in an accountant to help design their accounting system. Designing a good system takes professional skill, especially as a venture begins to grow. Long gone are the days when entrepreneurs could do it all themselves:

> A Greek restaurant owner in Montreal had his own bookkeeping system. He kept his accounts payable in a cigar box on the left side of his cash register, his daily cash returns in the cash register, and his receipts for paid bills in another cigar box on the right.
>
> When his youngest son graduated as a chartered accountant, he was appalled by his father's primitive methods. "I don't know how you can run a business that way," he said. "How do you know what your profits are?"
>
> "Well, son," the father replied, "when I got off the boat from Greece, I had nothing but the pants I was wearing. Today, your brother is a doctor. You are an accountant. Your sister is a speech therapist. Your mother and I have a nice car, a city house, a country home. We have a

good business, and everything is paid for. So, you add all that together, subtract the pants, and there's your profit."[2]

Today, no entrepreneur should launch a venture without an accountant's help. Their services are vital. As with their choice of bankers or lawyers, entrepreneurs should take pains to get the right accountants. Often, however, entrepreneurs view the accountant's role as a passive one. Accountants can do much more than merely prepare tax returns. In their more creative roles, they:

- Design accounting systems that best suit the management needs of entrepreneurs
- Suggest changes in accounting systems as ventures grow
- Help entrepreneurs analyze their financial statements to both spot problems and spy trends
- Help entrepreneurs raise money by preparing special financial statements for prospective investors or creditors
- Help chart the future by translating entrepreneurs' operating plans into cash budgets
- Help entrepreneurs save taxes at the federal, state, and local levels

An entrepreneur should look for and obtain the right accountant months before launching a venture. In their search for an accountant, entrepreneurs should use guidelines such as these:

- Get the names of experienced, reputable accountants from other entrepreneurs
- Narrow the list to those who work mostly with small businesses, preferably in the same industry as the venture
- Choose a certified public accountant (CPA)

A CPA designation means that the accountant is a college graduate who passed a qualifying state test. It helps assure the entrepreneur that the accountant is a professional. Let us also add that only a CPA can certify—or *legally* guarantee—the truth of the entrepreneur's financial statements

Accounting for a Purpose

Accounting is not an end in itself—it should never be done for its own sake, as some entrepreneurs seem to believe. Rather, accounting exists to serve some worthwhile purposes, such as these:

- To help solve problems
- To help pursue opportunities
- To help express future plans
- To keep track of what is happening

These purposes all add up to planning and control, which are discussed in the next chapter. Any accounting system should help entrepreneurs answer these key questions:

- Is my venture earning a profit? If the answer is "no," then entrepreneurs should find out why, so they can do something about it. And even if they are earning a profit, they should find out if it is as high as it should be—and what part of the venture is producing the profit.
- What is my venture worth? Entrepreneurs and their shareholders invest their money in the hope of earning some return, so the entrepreneur should know whether the equity in the venture has gone up or down, and why.

Answers to these two questions and others are available only after accountants have put together two important financial statements: the income statement and the balance sheet, discussed in the next section.

FINANCIAL STATEMENTS—THE INCOME STATEMENT

Definition

The income statement tells entrepreneurs how well they are doing, whether they have earned a profit or not. Entrepreneurs should prepare an income statement at least every three months, if not once a month. Lucas Pacioli, who wrote the first accounting textbook in 1494, commented on the frequency of income reporting, saying, "Books should be closed each year, especially in a partnership, because frequent accounting makes for lasting friendship."[3]

What does an income statement look like? In its simplest form, an income statement looks like the one in Exhibit 11.2. Note that profits are what remain after operating expenses have been deducted from sales revenues. Profits are the net effect of two opposing flows on money:

- Money flowing into the venture from sales made to customers, either for cash or for credit (generally called *sales revenues*)
- Money flowing out of the venture from costs earned in connection with making those sales (generally called *operating expenses*)

The breakdown in Exhibit 11.2 is typical only for ventures in the service industries, which do not sell a product. For those industry groups that do—retailing, wholesaling, or manufacturing—the income statement should also include an item called *cost of goods sold* (see Exhibit 11.3).

EXHIBIT 11.2

Computer Services, Inc.: Income Statement (for year ending December 31, 1985)

Sales revenues	$200,000
Operating expenses	180,000
Operating profit	$ 20,000

EXHIBIT 11.3 *Atlas, Inc.: Income Statement (for year ending December 31, 1985)*

Sales revenues	$200,000
Cost of goods sold	120,000
Gross profit	$ 80,000
Operating expenses	60,000
Operating profit	$ 20,000

For retailers, cost of goods sold generally represents what they paid wholesalers for the products they sold to customers. For wholesalers, it represents what they paid to manufacturers for the products they sold to retailers. For manufacturers, it represents, for just those products sold to customers, the cost of converting raw materials into finished products plus the cost of raw materials.

Exhibit 11.4 shows how financial flows differ depending on whether a venture deals with a product or a service.

Control

As in all businesses, control is simply a means by which entrepreneurs may check their progress against their goals. The following example shows how the income statement may help entrepreneurs exercise control:

Example: In December 1984, an entrepreneur set a profit goal of $18,000 on revenues of $190,000 for the year 1985. She budgeted her cost of goods

EXHIBIT 11.4 *Basic Financial Flows*

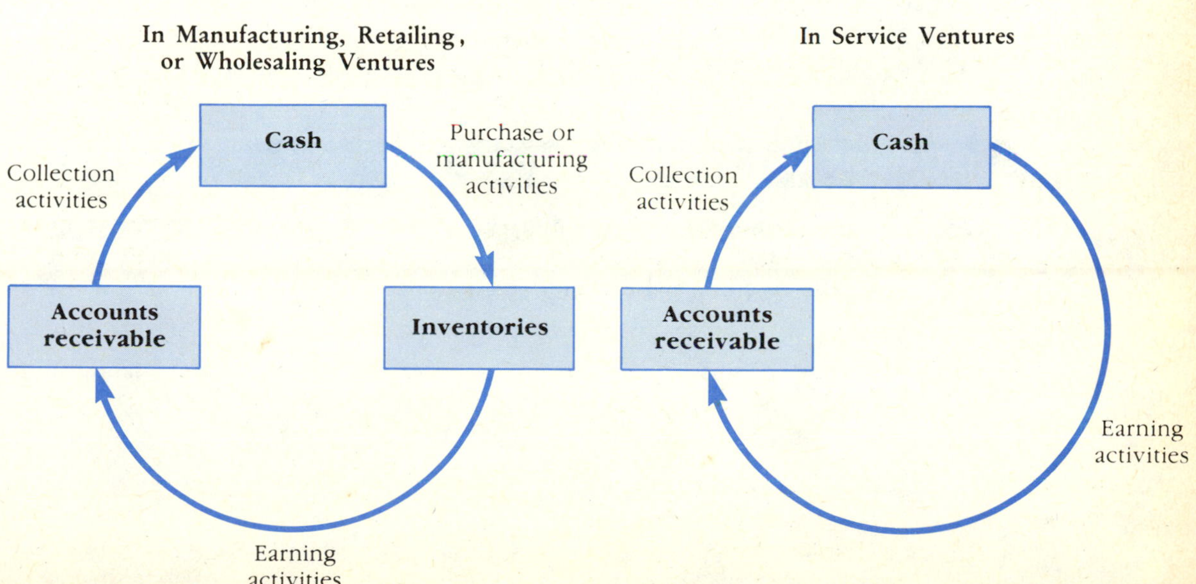

EXHIBIT 11.5

Atlas, Inc.: Performance Report

	Performance		
	Actual	Budgeted	Difference
Sales revenues	$200,000	$190,000	+$10,000
Cost of goods sold	120,000	114,000	+ 6,000
Gross profit	$ 80,000	$ 76,000	+$ 4,000
Operating expenses	60,000	58,000	+ 2,000
Operating profit	$ 20,000	$ 18,000	+ 2,000

sold and operating expenses at $114,000 and $58,000 respectively. How well did she do? To answer that question, turn to Exhibit 11.5, which compares actual with budgeted performance.

It appears that the entrepreneur performed well. Profits and revenues both topped expectations. She ran her venture not only more efficiently than expected but probably also more effectively.

- She was more *efficient* in the sense that she earned more profit for each dollar of revenues than expected.
- She was more *effective* in the sense that she probably earned a greater dollar return on investment (not shown in the exhibit) than expected.

Note that this example traces the entire cycle of planning and control. The entrepreneur began the year by translating her operating plans into dollars (budget). She ended the year by measuring her actual performance (income statement) and then comparing it with budgeted performance. Such comparisons give the entrepreneur reliable signals that often trigger further investigation. In our example, the entrepreneur did well. But if she had fallen short of her profit goal of $18,000, that fact alone would have signaled her to find out why and take remedial action.

FINANCIAL STATEMENTS—THE BALANCE SHEET

Purposes

As the income statement summarizes how well a venture has done over time, the balance sheet summarizes its financial health at one point in time. The balance sheet tells entrepreneurs:

- What their ventures are worth, at least on paper
- What they have invested in assets such as inventories, land, and equipment
- How these assets were financed, that is, where the money came from to buy them
- Who has what claims against these assets

These are just a few of the questions that balance sheets help the entrepreneur answer. To clarify our understanding of the balance sheet, let us use an example:

Example: An entrepreneur, George Corrales, is about to lease space in a shopping center to sell men's shoes. On February 1, he deposits $20,000 in a bank account opened in the name of his venture: Corrales Men's Shoes, Inc. His beginning balance sheet appears in Exhibit 11.6.

EXHIBIT 11.6

Corrales Men's Shoes, Inc.: Balance Sheet (February 1, 1985)

Assets		Equities	
Cash	$20,000	Owners' equity	$20,000

This balance sheet says the venture has assets of $20,000 cash, with Mr. Corrales, as the sole shareholder, having a 100 percent claim against that cash. On February 2, he borrows $10,000 from a commercial bank. His new balance sheet appears in Exhibit 11.7. This balance sheet says the venture has assets of $30,000 cash. Now the bank has a one-third claim against total assets and the entrepreneur a two-thirds claim. On February 3, the entrepreneur buys 400 pairs of shoes from a supplier for $10,000 cash. His new balance sheet appears in Exhibit 11.8.

EXHIBIT 11.7

Corrales Men's Shoes, Inc.: Balance Sheet (February 2, 1985)

Assets		Equities	
Cash	$30,000	Bank loan	$10,000
		Owners' equity	20,000
	$30,000		$30,000

EXHIBIT 11.8

Corrales Men's Shoes, Inc.: Balance Sheet (February 3, 1985)

Assets		Equities	
Cash	$20,000	Bank loan	$10,000
Inventory	10,000	Owners' equity	20,000
Total	$30,000	Total	$30,000

Note that the right-hand side of the balance sheet did not change between February 2 and 3. Only the left-hand side changed. The entrepreneur simply exchanged one asset—cash—for another—inventory—and received as much as he gave up. The key point here is that he really is no better off today than yesterday, because his equity of $20,000 remains unchanged. On February 4, the entrepreneur sells 10 pairs of shoes for $1,000 cash. His new balance sheet appears in Exhibit 11.9.

EXHIBIT 11.9

Corrales Men's Shoes, Inc.: Balance Sheet (February 4, 1985)

Assets		Equities		
Cash	$21,000	Bank loan		$10,000
Inventory	9,500	Owners' equity		
		Common stock	$20,000	
		Retained earnings	500	20,500
Total assets	$30,500	Total equities		$30,500

Note that the entrepreneur's equity has increased by $500, to $20,500 because he made some profitable sales. He sold shoes that had cost him $500 for $1,000—a 100 percent markup—giving him a profit of $500. His new income statement is shown in Exhibit 11.10.

Turning to Exhibit 11.11, note how the income statement in Exhibit 11.10 ties into the February 4 balance sheet in Exhibit 11.9. The income

EXHIBIT 11.10

Corrales Men's Shoes, Inc.: Income Statement (for four days ending February 4, 1985)

Sales revenues	$1,000
Cost of goods sold	500
Gross profit	$ 500

EXHIBIT 11.11 *How Income Statement Ties into Balance Sheet*

Balance sheet
(February 4, 1985)

Assets		
Cash		$21,000
Inventory		9,500
Total assets		$30,500
Equities		
Bank loan		$10,000
Owners' equity		
Common stock	$20,000	
Retained earnings	500	20,500
Total equities		$30,500

Income statement
(for four days ending February 4, 1985)

Sales revenues	$1,000
Cost of goods sold	500
Gross profit	$500

statement gives the details behind the changes that have taken place within the category of the balance sheet called retained earnings.

Without the income statement, the entrepreneur might never know what his sales revenues and operating expenses are. He also might never know what his profits are. For example, he paid himself a $500 cash dividend on February 5, and his new balance appears in Exhibit 11.12. At first glance, this balance sheet suggests that the entrepreneur made no profit. As we know, his profits were $500 on revenues of $1,000. The net change in retained earnings is recorded as zero because he paid himself a $500 cash dividend, as shown by his new income statement (see Exhibit 11.13).

EXHIBIT 11.12

Corrales Men's Shoes, Inc.: Balance Sheet (February 5, 1985)

Assets		**Equities**		
Cash	$20,500	Bank loan		$10,000
Inventory	9,500	Owners' equity		
		Common stock	$20,000	
		Retained earnings	0	20,000
Total assets	$30,000	Total equities		$30,000

EXHIBIT 11.13

Corrales Men's Shoes, Inc.: Income Statement (for five days ending February 5, 1985)

Sales revenues	$1,000
Cost of goods sold	500
Gross profit	$ 500
Dividends	500
Added to retained earnings	$ 0

Although the balance sheet tells the entrepreneur that his worth is $20,000, this is true only on paper. The true worth of his venture cannot be known until he tries to sell out. His venture could be worth more or less than $20,000, depending on what a prospective buyer is willing to pay. This is an important point, because entrepreneurs often believe that balance sheets report the real worth of their ventures. Accountants do not try to measure what a venture is worth, unless the entrepreneur wants to sell out.

A Confusing Term

Accountants generally define a balance sheet as a statement that lists assets on one side and liabilities and owners' equities on the other side. This definition is accurate but incomplete. It does not describe, for example, the other messages that balance sheets try to convey. Among these messages are the following:

- The right-hand (equities) side of the balance sheet tells how entrepreneurs have financed their venture
- The left-hand (assets) side tells how entrepreneurs invested the funds entrusted to their care

Assets and equities always balance, because all assets of a venture must be claimed by someone—either by investors or by creditors. And because the total dollar amount of these claims cannot exceed the total dollar amount of assets to be claimed, it must always follow that:

$$\text{Assets} = \text{Equities}$$

The term *balance sheet* is an unfortunate one. It suggests that there is something good about the balance between assets and equities. On the contrary, the balance tells nothing about the financial health of a venture, so accountants now recommend such terms as *position statement* or *statement of financial condition*. But the term *balance sheet* is so firmly rooted that few companies have adopted either of the two recommended terms.

FINANCIAL STATEMENTS—THE CASH BUDGET

So far, discussion has focused on the income statement and the balance sheet. Important as these two financial statements are, they fall short in one vital respect. They tell little about cash flow—the lifeblood of any venture. To be sure, the income statement measures operating results during a certain period, and the balance sheet measures the assets carried forward into the next period and the equities in those assets.

Yet neither statement measures cash flow. This fact escapes many entrepreneurs. They assume that, if their venture is earning a profit, it must be financially sound. This is not necessarily so. In fact, even in the midst of soaring profits, entrepreneurs often have to scurry for loans to pay bills. What they soon learn seems paradoxical: when it comes to paying the bills, profits are not the same thing as cash in the bank. An example may help explain this seeming paradox:

> **Example:** A wholesaler begins a venture on January 1 with a $15,000 inventory and $24,000 cash. She pays her bills promptly, and she bills customers 30 days net. She keeps an inventory equal to sales expected during the next 30 days.

EXHIBIT 11.14

Income Statements

	Actual January	Projected February
Sales revenues	$20,000	$32,000
Expenses	15,000	24,000
Profits	$ 5,000	$ 8,000

One month later, the wholesaler looks at her first income statement with pride. "A $5,000 profit isn't bad for a beginner," she says. Her January income statement appears in Exhibit 11.14, along with her projected income statement for February.

One day later, her banker calls to say she has run out of cash. "How come?" replies the wholesaler. "I made a profit of $5,000 in January. How can I possibly be out of cash?"

The missing cash is tied up in inventory and in bills owed by customers. The wholesaler had plowed her profits of $5,000 back into the business to build up inventories in anticipation of February sales of $32,000. She had used up the $24,000 cash on hand as of January 1 for the same reason.

How might the wholesaler have avoided this cash-flow problem? One way would have been to prepare a cash budget, as discussed in Chapters Six and Nine to forecast how much cash would flow in and out of the venture. The cash budget answers the vital question, Are we likely to pay our bills on time? The wholesaler's cash budget appears in Exhibit 11.15.

Had she prepared a cash budget, the wholesaler would have noted that she would run out of cash by the end of January, unless she raised more.

The lesson the wholesaler learned is that the sales dollar does not necessarily return when the inventory is sold, thus creating a drain on cash. In accounting terms, the lag is called *accounts receivable*. This lag may tie up cash for weeks or even months, depending on credit terms. What really

EXHIBIT 11.15

Cash Budget

	January	February	March
Sales revenues	$20,000	$32,000	$40,000
Cash inflows from sales	0	20,000	32,000
Cash outflows for inventory	24,000	30,000	30,000
Cash gain or loss	($24,000)	($10,000)	$ 2,000
Beginning cash	24,000	0	(10,000)
Ending cash	$ 0	($10,000)	($ 8,000)

EXHIBIT 11.16 *The Entrepreneur's Most Vital Financial Statements*

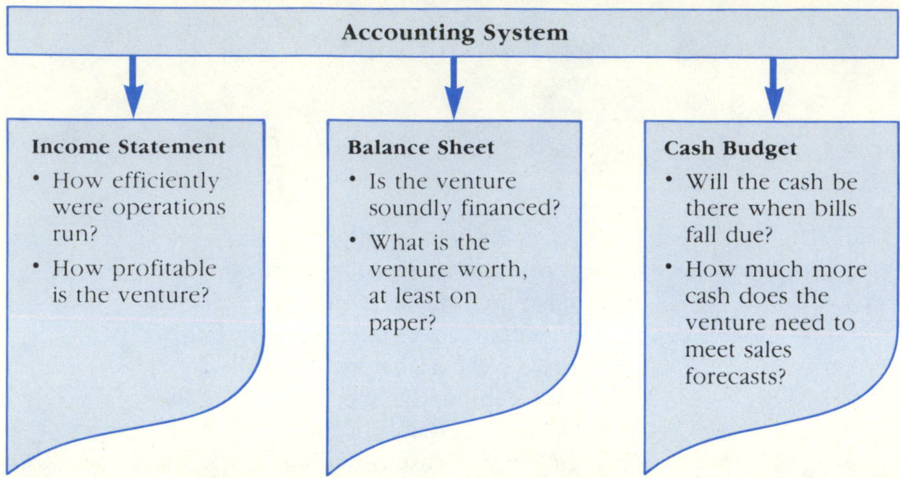

matters in a cash budget is not the volume of sales at any given time, but how soon the entrepreneur gets paid for products sold. Also keep in mind that, even when the dollars do come in, the entrepreneur may need to plow them right back into the venture to carry new inventory.

Accounts receivable and inventory are the heart of the cash-flow problem. Offsetting them are *accounts payable*, that is, what the entrepreneur owes suppliers but does not have to pay today. It is the balance and timing between these two sets of items that determines just how much cash the entrepreneur will have available at any particular time.

Depreciation is another item that complicates the cash-flow problem. Many entrepreneurs believe that depreciation is a source of cash. They are mistaken. Actually, depreciation is merely a faucet that allows the entrepreneur to tap the flow of cash as it goes from sales down to net income. It enables the entrepreneur to pay less taxes because it reduces net income. But, unless there *is* a cash flow to tap, depreciation is just another accounting item on paper.

Exhibit 11.16 compares selected purposes of the cash budget with those of the income statement and the balance sheet.

LIMITATIONS OF ACCOUNTING

As mentioned earlier, accounting does not measure what a venture is worth. It has other limitations that bear mention also. A common belief is that accounting figures are precise and exact. They are not. Neither the income statement nor the balance sheet can give a precise picture of a venture. The figures in them are rough. The main reason for their imprecision is that all ventures are highly complex bodies, made up of highly dissimilar parts such as cash and policies, materials and incentives, buildings and morale, equipment and human beings. It is impossible to add all these dissimilar parts together to form a precise picture of a venture.

Accounting is limited to recording only those facts that can be expressed in dollars, such as the $10,000 purchase of inventory or the receipt of a $1,000 bill from a lawyer. Note that these are hard, objective, verifiable facts. But accounting cannot put a dollar value on teamwork, for example. Nor can it report that a competitor has come out with a better product. It follows, then, that entrepreneurs should not expect to find in financial statements all the vital facts about their venture. Nonfinancial information is often as vital, if not more vital, than financial information.

Still another limitation is that assets are recorded at the price the entrepreneur paid for them, or cost. This cost stays on the books even though the value of the asset may increase.

Example: If an entrepreneur were to buy a plot of land for $20,000, this asset would be recorded at $20,000. If one year later a buyer comes along and offers the entrepreneur $40,000 for the land, the entrepreneur has strong evidence that it is really worth $40,000 and not $20,000. Yet recommended accounting practice disallows changing the records to reflect the $20,000 gain in value.

So the values at which assets are listed in the balance sheet do *not* always reflect what they could be sold for. As a rule, the older an asset, the lower the probability that its book value matches its value to a prospective buyer.

Yet another limitation is that the balance sheet reflects dollars of differing purchasing power. For example, the balance sheet may show:

- Cash that reflects purchasing power today
- Inventory stated in dollars that reflect purchasing power of a month ago
- Machinery stated in dollars that reflect purchasing power of 5 years ago
- A building stated in dollars that reflect purchasing power of 10 years ago

To reinforce our understanding of this limitation, let us use an example:

Example: Assume that an entrepreneur bought a $2\frac{1}{2}$ ton truck for $15,000 in 1978 and another $2\frac{1}{2}$ ton truck, just like the first one, for $25,000 in 1985. The entrepreneur's balance sheet would show both trucks at their *original* cost, unadjusted for price inflation:

First $2\frac{1}{2}$ ton truck =	$15,000	(in 1978 dollars)
Second $2\frac{1}{2}$ ton truck =	25,000	(in 1985 dollars)
	$40,000	

Accountants have suggested several ways of solving this problem. The most promising one is to apply a price index that reflects changes in the purchasing power of the dollar. That way, each asset on the balance sheet would be valued in dollars that reflect the same purchasing power.

Thus, if the first truck was purchased when the price index was 100 and the second truck when the index was 160, the dollar value of the first truck would go up 60 percent:

First $2\frac{1}{2}$ ton truck = \$25,000 (in 1985 dollars)
Second $2\frac{1}{2}$ ton truck = 25,000 (in 1985 dollars)

Despite its limitations, accounting does enable entrepreneurs to compress many complex events into just a handful of financial statements: the income statement, the balance sheet, and the cash budget, among others. That, indeed, is an important and remarkable achievement.

SUMMARY

Accounting enables entrepreneurs to make better decisions, supplying them with the information they need to keep on top of their ventures. Among other things, accounting enables entrepreneurs to see how profitable they are and whether they have wisely invested the money entrusted in their care by investors and creditors.

Accounting systems need not be elaborate. There is no such thing as one best system applicable to all businesses, big or small. In general, the best system is one that:

- Generates reports quickly and ensures a high degree of accuracy
- Collects and processes information at low cost

Generally, the end product of an accounting system is a set of financial statements. Among them are:

- The income statement, which reports how profitable a venture has been over a given period of time
- The balance sheet, which reports the financial health of a venture at one particular point in time
- The cash budget, which is a forecast of all cash inflows and cash outflows

To design an accounting system, the entrepreneur should call in an accountant. The entrepreneur should then retain the accountant to do such creative things as:

- Suggest changes in the accounting system as the venture grows
- Help the entrepreneur raise money by preparing special financial statements for prospective investors or creditors

Accounting has its limitations. It cannot, for example, measure what a venture is really worth; it can only report its paper value. Nor can it measure such intangible assets as teamwork, morale, incentives, and the entrepreneur's health. In short, accounting cannot give a precise and complete picture of the entrepreneur's venture. Still, accounting is an important and remarkable tool.

DISCUSSION AND REVIEW QUESTIONS

1. Why would you, as an entrepreneur, have need for an accountant?
2. What are the main objectives of a good accounting system?
3. Why is *balance sheet* a poor term?
4. Define these terms: *accounting system, income statement, profit, control, CPA, cash budget, depreciation.*
5. Explain some of the limitations of accounting. Can they be corrected? Explain.
6. Is it enough for an entrepreneur to have an accounting system that is well designed and carefully run? Explain.
7. How would you, as an entrepreneur, use the information generated by your accounting system?
8. Which financial statement is most important to the entrepreneur: the income statement, the balance sheet, or the cash budget? Explain.
9. When it comes to paying the bills, are profits the same thing as cash in the bank? Explain.
10. Explain why you, as an entrepreneur, should take at least two basic courses in accounting—one course dealing with principles of accounting and the other with management accounting.
11. How does the income statement tie into the balance sheet?
12. What procedure would you follow to get the right accountant?
13. How often should income statements and balance sheets be prepared? Why?
14. What is usually the heart of the cash-flow problem? Explain fully.
15. Why is accounting so important and remarkable an achievement?

NOTES

1. Robert N. Anthony and James S. Reece, *Accounting* (Homewood, Ill.: Richard D. Irwin, 1983), p. 108.
2. Attributed to Walter J. Cross in *The* [Montreal] *Gazette* by *Reader's Digest*, May 1973, p. 151. Reprinted by permission of *The* [Montreal] *Gazette* and *Reader's Digest.*
3. John J. Geijsbeek, *Ancient Double-Entry Bookkeeping* (Denver, Colo.: John J. Geijsbeek, 1914), p. 27.

CASE 11A *Majestic Molding Company, Inc.*

Margaret Ware Kahliff views with pride one of her latest achievements. She took over an ailing plastics company and improved its performance dramatically. Thanks to her, after-tax profits leaped from $7,000 to $115,000 annually in just three years. But sales revenues rose only slightly, from $1.4 million to $1.6 million a year.

Mrs. Kahliff is now wondering how best to increase her revenues at a time when raw materials are so hard to come by.

Background

Mrs. Kahliff caught the entrepreneurial fever from her father. He owned and managed a furniture store, a hardware store, and a funeral home in an Arkansas hamlet of 1,500 called Charleston.

Her father was a compulsive achiever. Besides managing three businesses at once, he served on the school board and ran the Methodist Sunday School. "He expected us to achieve, so we all did," says Mrs. Kahliff. And, indeed, they did: one brother, Carroll Bumpers, now heads two Greyhound subsidiaries in Phoenix, Arizona; another brother, Dale Bumpers, became a United States senator from Arkansas; and Mrs. Kahliff heads a plastics company employing 102 persons. Speaking of her father's influence, Mrs. Kahliff says, "If we kids made a 'B' in some subject and not an 'A,' father wanted to know how come? He never talked about money, but he talked about integrity and character."

Mrs. Kahliff recalls that her father once said, "There's nothing worse than an empty-headed woman who talks all the time. I know we're never going to get you to stop talking, so we had better train your mind." She proceeded to train her mind at the College of the Ozarks. Years later, the college bestowed upon her an honorary doctorate of humanities in recognition of her many achievements in business.

Creates Vending Machine Venture

Mrs. Kahliff launched her first entrepreneurial venture at age 14, when she produced her own radio program. Later she helped finance her college education by singing at a public dance hall—until her father found out and stopped her. "To think you'd use God's gift at a public dance hall," he told her.

Soon after college, she married a small businessman who received a Dr Pepper franchise in a town 1,000 miles from Arkansas. The franchise failed. Out of need, Mrs. Kahliff decided to go into business for herself with her husband's help. The business she chose was vending machines. And she began with just $300 of her own savings and a $1,000 bank loan. Her beginning balance sheet appears in Exhibit 11A.1.

On this shoestring, Mrs. Kahliff parlayed one vending machine into 500 vending machines ten years later. Her revenues soared from zero to $3.5 million a year. She credits this success to "knowledge, knowledge, and knowledge."

EXHIBIT 11A.1

Ware Vending Company: Beginning Balance Sheet

Assets		Equities	
Cash	$ 100	Bank loan	$1,000
Vending machine	1,000	Owner's equity	300
Other assets	200		
Total assets	$1,300	Total equities	$1,300

When Mrs. Kahliff went into the vending-machine business, she knew nothing about it. A friend of hers had told her in passing that the "coming thing in vending machines was cups not bottles." After sounding out vending machine suppliers and local bankers, she decided to plunge into the business.

To learn about the business, she talked to suppliers and attended sales seminars. She also took courses in accounting and marketing. "I was like a sponge, soaking up all the knowledge I could," says Mrs. Kahliff.

Sells Venture

She did so well she paid off all of her husband's debts. And later, she merged her business into a giant conglomerate—Servomation, Inc.—for 47,000 shares of common stock.

Meanwhile, she divorced her first husband and married William Kahliff, who had started his own plastics company during World War II.

Although she no longer headed her own business, Mrs. Kahliff did not lose her habit of winning. She soon became group president at Servomation. And by her third year there, her division ranked second in profitability among the company's 200 divisions.

About that time, her second husband died. She inherited his business lock, stock, and barrel—with all shares of company stock now in her name. She was now head of one company and group president of another. And she found herself working 80 hours a week and sometimes more.

This grueling work schedule all but overwhelmed her. She continued to do well at Servomation. But she soon found it physically impossible to oversee the affairs of Majestic Molding. As a result, the company began to flounder. In just one year, net profits plunged from $40,000 to $7,000. And it looked as though the company would soon find itself awash in red ink. Worse yet, the company was now so cash-poor it could not pay its bills on time.

Accepts New Challenge

Drastic problems call for drastic solutions. So, Mrs. Kahliff quit her job at Servomation to devote her full time to Majestic Molding. She soon found that her husband had picked the wrong man to succeed him as company president. His successor was a chemical engineer who had been with the company for three years. Although competent as an engineer, he knew little about running a plastics business. "One of his first acts," says Mrs. Kahliff, "was to abolish paid lunch hours. That, on top of his inability to get along with his workers, destroyed morale. Within three months, we had a union in the plant."

By mutual agreement, the engineer soon left. Mrs. Kahliff then took over the day-to-day operations of the business. Overnight she began to put into practice the knowledge she gained running her own vending-machine business and managing a division for a conglomerate.

"How well you do depends largely on how well the people under you do," says Mrs. Kahliff. Looking around her, she soon found that the engineer was not the only nonperformer. Such persons were everywhere, and they were gradually replaced. In fact, of the ten managerial employees she inherited, just one still works for her. She now has 102 employees, most of them hand-picked. "I test and interview almost every job applicant," she says. "I can't afford to be wrong."

Turns Company Around

In just three years, Mrs. Kahliff worked a minor miracle, reversing the downward trend of profits dramatically, as shown in Exhibit 11A.2.

Her success became the talk of the town. She soon found herself in demand as a luncheon speaker. And she accommodated them by talking on "How to Get to the Top in a Man's World." Today, speaking requests flood in at such a high rate that she accepts only one in ten requests.

Besides turning over the work force, what other changes did Mrs. Kahliff make to earn such high marks for competency? For one thing, she put in several big-business practices:

- A cost-accounting system, including a chart of accounts, to keep daily tabs on costs and leaks. "How can you price a product unless you know, to the penny, what it would cost to make?" says Mrs. Kahliff.
- Tuition-free education to all employees who take courses in high school or in college. "I've had as many as 16 employees in school at one time at my expense," says Mrs. Kahliff. "I won't promote anyone unless they prepare themselves for a better job."
- A sharp separation between line and staff work. In fact, she carries this separation to extremes by placing her plant not under one manager but under two—each with equal but separate responsibilities and authorities. "I don't want the production manager to buy raw materials and still take a physical count," says Mrs. Kahliff. "That's wrong." Says

EXHIBIT 11A.2

Majestic Molding Company, Inc.

Year	Sales Revenues	Net Profits
1981	$1,400,000	$ 7,000
1982	1,450,000	27,000
1983	1,510,000	91,000
1984	1,620,000	115,000

EXHIBIT 11A.3 *Majestic Molding Company, Inc.*

Mrs. Kahliff of her organizational chart, "I keep changing it at least once a year."

She took one look at her production process and decided to change that, too. Molding machines and raw materials were scattered helter-skelter throughout the plant. "It was messy and dirty," she says. Today, production is clean and orderly, flowing in a straight line from raw material storage through production and finally into finished-product inventory. (See Exhibit 11A.3)

Makes Sweeping Changes

Mrs. Kahliff also modernized her plant, replacing old molding machines with the latest models. And she added a recycling process that all but eliminates waste. "We don't throw away anything," says Jack Kulasa, who is in charge of purchasing and inventory control.

With her employees' welfare in mind, Mrs. Kahliff installed an exhaust system to cut air pollution and she initiated a safety program to keep employees safety-conscious. Soon after, a government representative enforcing the Occupational Safety and Health Act inspected the plant and gave it a clean bill of health. The inspector told Mrs. Kahliff upon completing his rounds, "This is one of the finest plastic injection molding plants I have had the privilege of visiting."

Of course, these sweeping changes took money, mostly hers. When she took over, the company's coffers were all but empty. She pumped $300,000 of her own money into the company. In addition, she borrowed $100,000 to enlarge the plant.

Motivated more by challenge than by money, Mrs. Kahliff draws a salary of just $35,000 a year. "I'm interested more in building up my equity in the business than drawing a big salary," says Mrs. Kahliff. One of her personal goals at this time is to build up a million-dollar equity. She is just $50,000 shy of that goal.

Marketing

Has she set any long-range goals? No. "I've been too busy surviving to think about where we should be five years from now," says Mrs. Kahliff. "But now that the company is on its feet, I'm going to think about the future, especially about ways to create more customers.

Today, her plant makes two kinds of products. One kind is called proprietary, meaning products made to the company's own design for sale directly to wholesalers or retailers. One such product is the Majestic Duck, a decorative piece for the home, office, or garden.

The other kind is called secondary, meaning products made to the design of other manufacturers. Into this category fall such diverse products as snowmobile wheels, shower knobs, tape cartridges, and football cleats—all made to order and all made to customer design.

Tape cartridges account for 38 percent of the company's revenues, up from 3 percent in 1981. This heavy dependence on one customer, which happens to be giant RCA, worries Mrs. Kahliff.

Today, products made for other manufacturers supply 75 percent of the company's revenues, while products made to Majestic's own design account for only 25 percent of revenues.

For both types of products, Mrs. Kahliff's marketing mix consists almost solely of word-of-mouth advertising. She employs no salespersons, nor does she advertise. But recently she hired an advertising agency to draw up flyers promoting the Majestic Duck. Nearly all her customers are repeat customers, landed by her late husband. "We've managed to keep them because we produce a quality product and deliver on time," says Mrs. Kahliff.

One of her biggest problems has been the short supply of raw materials. It seems that, under pressure from federal agencies, oil refineries no longer remove benzene from gasoline. And since resin is made from benzene, one of the company's most important raw materials is in short supply. RCA cartridges, for example, are made from resin.

Questions

1. What is Mrs. Kahliff's most pressing problem? Why? How would you suggest she solve it?
2. Comment on Mrs. Kahliff's attitude toward goal setting.
3. Comment on Mrs. Kahliff's marketing strategy.
4. Is Mrs. Kahliff more an entrepreneur than a manager? Explain.
5. What should Mrs. Kahliff do now?

CASE 11B *Henry Mercer*

After a slow start, Henry Mercer's venture grew to the point where the simple records on which he had depended for information became inadequate. So he sought help in designing a set of accounting records that would help him to manage his venture.

Mr. Mercer got the idea for his venture while serving as a pharmacist's mate in the U.S. Navy. In his off-duty hours, he carried on experiments in the pharmaceutical laboratory on his ship. And although he had only a high school education in chemistry, he developed several chemicals that seemed to have commercial possibilities. Of these, the most promising seemed to be a liquid which, when sprayed into the air, tended to neutralize foul odors.

After his discharge from the Navy, he worked in a drugstore and continued his experiments in his spare time. To test the market potential of his spray, he bottled a small quantity under the trade name of *AirNu*—and then went after customers.

Several competing products were already on the market. At first, he had a hard time convincing anyone that *AirNu* was in any way superior to them. Some of his prospects—principally hospitals, jails, and other institutions—agreed to try *AirNu*, however. And several of these trials resulted in sales.

Gradually, business increased to the point where, two years after he left the Navy, Mr. Mercer quit the drugstore to devote full time to his venture, which he named the Mercer Chemical Company.

At first he carried on alone, with help from his wife on the paperwork. Mrs. Mercer had studied bookkeeping at a business college. His records consisted of:

- A checkbook
- A file of unpaid bills
- A file of paid bills
- A memorandum record of sales to, and sums owed by, customers

Mr. Mercer kept company funds in a separate bank account. And each week he drew a check for $200 on this account and deposited it in the

Mercer family account. The original capital of the venture came from savings Mr. Mercer had accumulated during his Navy days. It totaled about $2,000. At the end of another year, Mr. Mercer decided to hire:

- A person part-time to help manufacture *AirNu*
- A full-time salesperson to visit drugstores and supermarkets in an effort to break into the consumer market

The manufacture of *AirNu* was simple. Operations were carried out in the basement of the Mercer home. But storage space there was getting so crowded that Mr. Mercer thought he would soon have to move his venture into more spacious quarters.

At about this time, Mr. Mercer became concerned about the adequacy of his records. He discussed the matter one evening with James Finnerty, controller of a large chemical company. Mr. Finnerty was a friend of Mr. Mercer's father.

Mr. Finnerty listened to the story of Mercer Chemical's birth and growth with interest and some surprise—and then offered these observations:

> The favorable response of tough-minded industrial buyers to *AirNu* should please you. It indicates your product has merit. A successful business requires more than a good product, however. It also requires good management.
>
> To manage the business, you need, among other things, records. The records for your business do not need to be as elaborate as those used in the large company I work for.
>
> The need for good records is especially important in view of your decision to hire people. Furthermore, as your business grows, you likely will need to borrow from a bank. And the bank will surely want to study the facts about your progress before lending you any money.
>
> If, as you say, you plan to introduce other products, records showing cost and profit by product will become increasingly important. In fact, good figures on your experience with *AirNu* might turn up some valuable information that would help you make your company more profitable.

Questions

1. Describe as completely as you can the kinds of information that you think Mr. Mercer needs to have in order to manage his business.
2. How would you go about preparing a balance sheet for the Mercer Chemical Company? What items would probably be shown on such a balance sheet—and how would you obtain the dollar amounts for each item?

CASE 11C *Melissa's Health Food Store, Inc.*

Tomorrow, Melissa Moran will open a new health food store. She plans to sell "foods the way nature made them." In preparing for the opening, she has already spent these sums of money:

$11,000	for equipment
10,300	for inventory
700	for advertising and publicity
400	for legal and accounting services
400	for lease deposit
200	for licenses and permits

The company's bank balance is $2,000.

Question Prepare a beginning balance sheet, assuming that Mrs. Moran and her co-investors bought $25,000 worth of common stock.

A month later, Mrs. Moran took pride in her performance. Her revenues reached $8,000 and her expenses totaled $7,600. An expense breakdown follows:

$5,400	for cost of health foods sold
1,200	for salaries (including Mrs. Moran's)
400	for rent
200	for advertising
200	for utilities
200	for other expenses

Question Prepare an income statement for Mrs. Moran's first month of business.

12 PLANNING AND CONTROL

QUESTIONS FOR MASTERY

What are the problems of growth?
How does one set goals?
How do planning and control interact?
What is the best way to plan and control performance?
What are such planning and control tools as management by objectives, budgets, and profitgraphs?

Planning and control go together like love and marriage.

Marvin Bower

In creating their ventures, entrepreneurs are both thinkers and doers. They are thinkers when they think through the steps of their business plans, and they are doers when they carry out these steps. These two processes are actually parts of one inseparable process. Thinking leads to doing; then doing leads to rethinking; and rethinking leads again to doing—until finally the venture is created.

Called planning and control, this circular process is as vital to the health of a venture after its birth as it is before. In this chapter we shall discuss planning and control for the ongoing venture, focusing on coping with the problems of growth, setting goals, budgeting, and using the profitgraph (or breakeven chart).

PROBLEMS OF GROWTH

Almost all entrepreneurs want their ventures to grow. Often, though, growth takes place haphazardly because entrepreneurs forget the lessons they learned before launching their ventures—namely, that planning and control help keep their ventures on track.

Before the birth of their ventures, entrepreneurs tend to plan their moves carefully before they act. Later, the results of their actions may force them to rethink their moves, leading in turn to better actions. But, once their ventures get underway, entrepreneurs often ignore planning and control. One reason may be that planning and control are easily put off until a tomorrow that never seems to come.

Some entrepreneurs are like the climber who, after scaling the mountain, slips off the peak. They contribute to their own failure by not continuing to plan and control their progress. To them, planning takes place only before, not after, the birth of their venture. This failure to continue planning is often the reason that so many ventures grow haphazardly, stand still, or go under.

Four Stages of Growth

New ventures rarely take off like an Olympic sprinter. Generally, they start slowly, sometimes inching along at a snail's pace.

Example: Without some contracts in hand, an entrepreneur who leases factory space to make vinegar expects the first few months to be lean. It most likely will take some time to:

- Debug the vinegar-making equipment, to make sure the vinegar it makes uniformly meets the quality standards of prospective customers
- Make vinegar with negligible waste, at low cost
- Convince prospective customers, especially food chains, to buy the vinegar, generally on a trial basis

Meanwhile, with sales limping along, the cash drain becomes severe as bills and wages must be paid. There is little relief until the marketplace begins to accept the entrepreneur's vinegar. Then, and only then, do cash inflows begin to match and finally overtake cash outflows—perhaps months after start-up.

Many ventures follow the pattern of growth shown in Exhibit 12.1. Generally, however, entrepreneurs fail to handle the later stages of growth as well as they do the earlier stages. They tend to do well in bringing their venture through the *prebirth* and *acceptance* stages, despite the fact that progress in these stages often meets with obstacles. In the acceptance stage, entrepreneurs may struggle to break even as they introduce unique products. Usually in this stage they are so close to their ventures that they can spot obstacles and act quickly to remove them.

The *breakthrough* stage follows. Until then, the rate of growth is slow—so slow that it often passes unnoticed, but in the breakthrough stage, the rate of growth is so fast that entrepreneurs often cannot keep up with it. Caught unprepared, they often blunder. Sales revenues continue to spiral upward as problems begin to surface and cry out for attention. These problems might have to do with:

Cash flow: Will we have the cash when it comes time to pay bills?
Production: Are we keeping costs down in a way consistent with making a high-quality product?

EXHIBIT 12.1 *Stages in the Growth of a Venture*

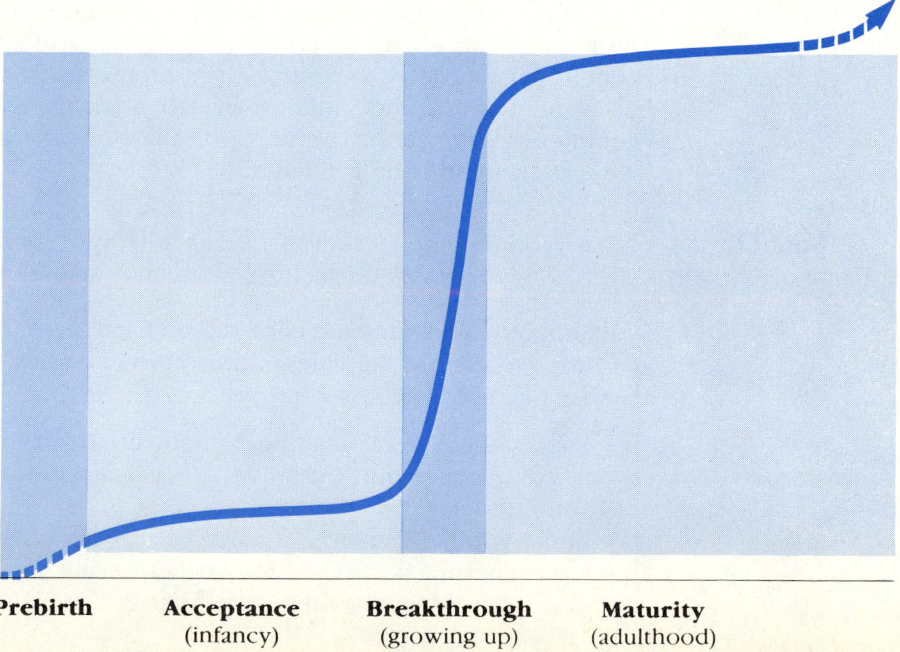

Quality: Are we handling customer complaints by guaranteeing uniformly high quality?
Delivery: Are we delivering promptly on all customers' orders?

At the same time, competition may become more severe. In the face of all these pressures, entrepreneurs often react rather than respond. They apply inadequate solutions to problems. When revenues suddenly begin to level off or slip, they may add such specialists as an accountant, a quality-control analyst, or a customer-services representative to relieve their problems. Costs go up momentarily, squeezing profits further. Meanwhile, entrepreneurs regain the flexibility they lost shortly after breakthrough and the cycle of growth begins to repeat itself as they pass through the *maturity* stage.

Consider this example of an entrepreneurial venture that avoided, through wise planning, the problems that often accompany fast growth:

Example: If every successful computer-accessory company started the way Tallgrass Technologies Corporation did, venture capitalists would have to find another line of work. David Allen didn't use any venture capital to start his company in Lenexa, Kansas, and he didn't have much use for bank loans either—until Tallgrass's sales surpassed $20 million a year. "We just bootstrapped ourselves," says the 36-year-old entrepreneur.

Tallgrass has had to cope with dazzling growth. Sales of its data storage products were only $1 million in 1982, when the company had 14 employees. This year, sales are expected to hit $60 million, and there are 280 employees. "Such quick success has ruined a lot of new businesses," comments Jeffry Timmons, professor of entrepreneurial studies at Babson College. "Uncontrolled growth often can be fatal."

Typically, inexperienced entrepreneurs expand production, shipping, and marketing operations as fast as they can, but they are unable to manage their greatly enlarged enterprises. "They don't have adequate manufacturing or inventory controls," Mr. Timmons says. They don't realize that costs have gotten out of hand and the company is losing money until it is too late.

That was never the case with Tallgrass. Mr. Allen deliberately set out to avoid the sort of cash-flow problems that overwhelm many growing businesses by buying components on 45- and 60-day terms and then selling COD. Retailers became accustomed to paying on delivery.[1]

Entrepreneurs as Managers

Some entrepreneurs tend to be good at creating and nursing a venture through infancy but not as good at carrying its growth through to maturity. Other ventures never even survive infancy. Why do some ventures take off while others do not? One answer may be that all the qualities that enable entrepreneurs to succeed during the venture's infancy may not be helpful at the breakthrough stage. At that point, they should change hats and work at being managers as well as entrepreneurs by:

- Surrounding themselves with men and women who know more than they do about many aspects of the venture
- Orchestrating the skills of such persons into efficient production
- Keeping abreast of the latest management methods

In becoming managers they should not give up their entrepreneurial bent. On the contrary, they should continue to seek out new opportunities, at the same time striking a balance between exploiting such opportunities and solving problems. Otherwise, their ventures may top out with little prospect for future growth.

A Management Consultant's Study

The management consulting firm, McKinsey & Company, made a study of fast-growing ventures. Its purpose was to describe these ventures and analyze the management processes adopted by successful ventures to solve the problems of growth. One finding dealt with complexity and size:

> One of the most important and, at the same time, most difficult organizational requirements imposed by complexity is to ensure that the role played by the entrepreneur evolves with growth. Although the nature of this role change depends on several factors—the individual style and ability of the entrepreneur, the rate at which complexity increases—we can trace some general patterns.
>
> When complexity is low, the chief executive typically knows all the details of the business and spends most of his time carrying out such major functions as:
>
> - Raising capital
> - Selling to key accounts
> - Thinking up new products
> - Hiring and training people
>
> As complexity increases, however, the number of decisions and activities outstrips the time available, and the entrepreneur must rely increasingly on other persons to perform major functions.
>
> At this point, a major shift in emphasis occurs. The entrepreneur must spend more time selecting, motivating, allocating, and evaluating key personnel. Furthermore, he must devote a larger share of his waking hours to strategic planning to ensure that new products are developed and that old products and markets are trimmed off if they are unprofitable or take a disproportionate share of management time.
>
> Finally, almost inevitably, the entrepreneur takes on a host of other activities, such as dealing extensively with the government, serving on corporate boards, and so forth. As a result, by the time his company is highly complex, the entrepreneur's life has changed dramatically—or should have.[2]

These general patterns of behavior are depicted in Exhibit 12.2.

EXHIBIT 12.2 *Complexity and the Changing Role of the Entrepreneur*

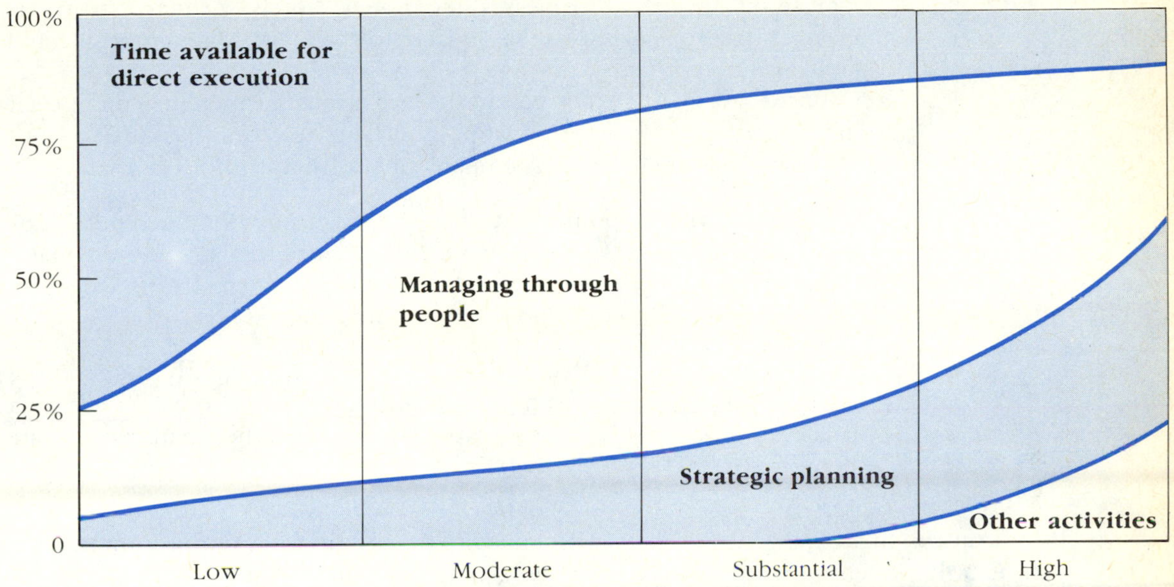

* Time allocation is representative but varies widely with the industry and the entrepreneur's style.

Source: Adapted from Donald K. Clifford, Jr., *Managing the Threshold Company* (New York, N.Y.: Mckinsey & Company, Inc., 1973), p. 21.

SETTING GOALS

To help keep their ventures alive and well, entrepreneurs should set goals, just as they did before launching their venture. The act of setting goals is especially vital once a venture begins to grow rapidly and add more workers. That is when the entrepreneur, as manager, must lead others toward meeting the venture's goals. As Robert Townsend, former board chairman of the Avis Rent-A-Car Corporation, puts it:

> One of the important functions of a *leader* is to make the organization concentrate on its goals. In the case of Avis, it took us six months to define goals, which turned out to be: We want to become the fastest-growing company with the highest profit margins in the business of renting and leasing vehicles without drivers.
>
> This goal was simple enough so that we didn't have to write it down. We could put it in every speech and talk about it wherever we went. And

it had some social significance, because up to that time Hertz had a crushingly large share of the market and was thinking and acting like General Motors.

It also included a definition: renting and leasing vehicles without drivers. This let us put the blinders on ourselves and stop considering the acquisition of related businesses like motels, hotels, airlines, and travel agencies. It also showed us that we had to get rid of some limousine and sight-seeing companies that we already owned.

Once these goals are agreed on, the leader must be merciless on himself and on his people. If an idea that pops into his head or out of their mouth is outside the goals of the company, he kills it without a trial.[3]

As Mr. Townsend points out, the key to such single-minded pursuit of goals is concentration. Once they set goals, entrepreneurs should make sure that every employee understands and pursues them. In the words of Peter F. Drucker, noted author-lecturer-consultant:

> No other principle of effectiveness is violated as constantly today as the basic principle of concentration. . . . Our motto seems to be: "Let's do a little bit of everything" . . . we scatter our efforts rather than concentrate them. . . .[4]

The Timing of Goals

In setting goals, entrepreneurs need to determine what requires immediate attention and what requires long-range planning. With tongue in cheek, *The New Yorker* draws this distinction between immediate and long-range goals:

- Long-Range Goals:
  Health—more leisure
  Money
  Write book (play)—fame///??
  Visit India
- Immediate Goals:
  Pick up pattern at Hilda's
  Change faucets—call plumber (who?)
  Try yoghurt??[5]

If only it were this easy to set goals for an ongoing venture. If asked what their goals are, entrepreneurs are most likely to say, "To make a profit, of course!" But they must learn to be as precise about their business goals as *The New Yorker* list is about personal goals.

It is true that a venture must make a profit if it is to survive and grow, but, as mentioned in Chapter Two, profits are simply a reward for a job well done—the sale of a product or service that customers need or want. In this view, profits are a yardstick that measures how well entrepreneurs are satisfying their customers. Generally, the higher the profits, the better their customer satisfaction; and conversely, the lower the profits, the poorer their customer satisfaction. Stating that profits are the only goal of the venture is vague and provides little benefit to its growth.

Building on Strengths

To set meaningful goals, entrepreneurs should look first at their own strengths and skills. What can their venture do best? Self-examination is perhaps the most creative step in goal setting, for it may lead the entrepreneur to exciting challenges: to invade wholly new markets, to drop a product, or to add a product. The approach of setting goals based on one's strengths is built on these assumptions:

- In a highly competitive economy, success generally favors the venture that does its job with superior skill. Being an average performer may be almost as risky as being a poor one, especially in fast-moving markets like electronics and chemicals.
- A venture may create new buyer demand by the job it does if it does the job well.
- A venture's product or service may be outdated quickly, but its profile of special skills will tend to continue for years to come.

One board chairman had this to say about the cardinal importance of building on strengths:

> Investors, financial people, and others from time to time ask about us. What's our productive capacity? How many tons will we ship? How do we figure depreciation? What profit will we make three years from next Michaelmas? And so on. All useful questions—no doubt.
>
> But rarely, if ever, do they ask the one, real, gutsy question—which is—what have you got for an organization? What sort of people are they? How do you recruit and train them? Who is going to run the business—and do the thinking for it—5 years from now, 10 years, 20 years? This is the business. The rest is spinach.[6]

Management by Objectives

One method of translating the insights gained from identifying a venture's strengths into concrete goals is *management by objectives*(MBO). Practiced widely among giant corporations, MBO is a powerful tool. Its power lies in the simplicity of its premises:

- The clearer the entrepreneurs' idea of what they want to do, the better the odds that they will succeed—if their intent is to make the most of their venture's skills and talents.
- True progress can only be measured in relation to entrepreneurs' goals.

MBO is simple to grasp, yet the literature teems with articles and books about it. Most of them deal with goal-setting methods or with the propriety of one kind of goal as opposed to another. Few deal with what one author calls the hierarchy of goals:

> In some orderly way, we must relate the grand-design type of goal with the much more limited goals lower down in the organization. And we have to examine how one type of goal can be derived from another.[7]

Let us now examine how MBO might work in an ongoing venture, focusing first on long-range goals and then on immediate goals:

Example: An entrepreneur owns a Buick dealership. His hierarchy of long-range goals looks like this:

- To rank each year among the top ten Buick dealerships in the nation as measured by the number of new models sold yearly and the ratio of after-tax profits to sales revenues.
- To be known in the community as a dealership that offers equal employment opportunities for minority persons and the physically handicapped.
- To always be mindful of our responsibilities to our employees and to the community in which we work, in order to create a climate of warmth in which people may give their best to the dealership and to the community.
- To sell quality Buicks at reasonable prices, backed by excellent customer-oriented services. To meet strong competition from other dealerships, we must always give our customers superior service. Above all, we must be marketing-minded.
- To base our decisions on information collected and analyzed in light of the latest management tools. To compete profitably, we must be able to reach decisions and take action promptly and accurately. Our margin for error is wafer-thin. For example, less than two cents of every dollar we took in last year was left for dividends and for financing our future growth.

The entrepreneur's immediate goals look like this:

- To increase new-car sales to 2,400, up from 2,100 last year
- To increase return on sales to 2.2 percent of sales, from 2.0 percent last year
- To increase return on investment, to 10.0 percent annually, from 9.0 percent last year
- To establish a pension plan for all employees
- To beautify the grounds by planting elm trees

Note how these two lists of goals descend in order of importance, giving the entrepreneur a clear idea of how much attention he should give to each item. By separating the goals into short and long-run lists, he also clarifies what needs to be done immediately.

Not only are the goals clear to the entrepreneur, but they are also explicit enough to be shared directly with employees. To make sure he has their support, the entrepreneur should set his goals with the help of key employees—his new-car sales manager, service manager, and controller.

Guides to Action

Note the balance among the goals listed in the example. Not only are these the goals of the dealership itself but also those of all its employees. When managers have a voice in setting goals, commitment is more likely to filter through each layer of the organization, from the entrepreneur to the floor sweeper. The deeper the commitment, the greater the likelihood that the goals of the organization will be met. As Dr. Douglas McGregor, the eminent behavioral scientist, puts it:

> The central principle . . . is that of integration: the creation of conditions such that the members of the organization can achieve their own goals *best* by directing their efforts toward the success of the enterprise.[8]

Finally, note that all of these goals are actually guides to action. They:

- Facilitate decision making by helping the entrepreneur and his employees choose the best course of action in the solution of a problem or the pursuit of an opportunity.
- Clearly suggest specific courses of action. "To make profits" is a vague guide to action, but "to rank each year among the top ten dealerships" is a precise guide.
- Suggest ways of measuring the dealership's performance. The entrepreneur can tell how close he comes to the top ten by comparing his new-car sales with those of other dealers throughout the nation. This measure is much more useful than such an empty statement as "to compete in the new-car field."
- Challenge and excite the entrepreneur and his employees. Without such goals, the venture may lose its spirit and risk stagnation. Goals should not be too demanding, of course. Goals that are challenging but achievable spur performance best.

Action Plans

Setting goals is just the beginning. Next, the entrepreneur must decide how best to meet those goals. This calls for the development of action plans that:

- Lay out in precise detail the steps necessary to achieve each goal
- Fix the responsibility for each step, be it the entrepreneur or a key employee
- Set deadlines for each step

Action plans should be designed to make things happen. Without such plans to breathe life into them, goals become meaningless. One example of an action plan is the business plan, described in Chapter Six.

Control

Setting goals and drafting action plans alone are not enough. Entrepreneurs should also measure their progress at frequent intervals. To do that, they need information that tells them whether their goals are being met.

Called *control*, this process of measurement helps assure entrepreneurs that their own actions, as well as those of employees, are on target. The key element of the control process is information that permits entrepreneurs to compare actual performance with planned performance. This information allows entrepreneurs to measure not only their performance but also the propriety of their goals and action plans—and if need be, to adjust them.

Example: The entrepreneur in our earlier example worked out the following action plan for his new-car sales manager:

To help meet our goal of increasing new-car sales from 2,100 to 2,400 Buicks a year, you should:

- Send all salespersons to a salesmanship course at a local college to improve their ability to close a sale
- Work with our advertising agency to create eye-catching television commercials with an appealing message
- Invite all old customers to visit our showroom by letter and then by a follow-up telephone call
- Meet with me and our controller each Monday at 10 A.M., to review our sales performance for the previous week

Action plans can be simple. They need not be fancy and elaborate, although it is a good idea to put them into writing, since a permanent record leaves little room for argument later.

BUDGETING

In Chapters Six, Nine, and Eleven, we discussed the cash budget. We said it was the centerpiece of the business plan because it translated the would-be entrepreneur's operating plans into dollar terms. This translation best enables entrepreneurs to talk about their plans with outsiders such as bankers and venture capitalists before launching their ventures.

Budgets play an equally vital role after entrepreneurs get their ventures underway, as tools for both planning and control. Again, the focus is usually on dollars. To see how budgeting might work in an ongoing venture, let us look at this example:

Example: The entrepreneur in our earlier example expressed his new-car sales in units, as shown in Exhibit 12.3. This unit budget would be used by the new-car sales manager to control the performance of her salespersons. Units, not dollars, have real meaning to salespersons and are an effective way of communicating goals to them.

But at the sales manager's level, dollars assume importance as a control. To meet her unit goal of 2,400 new-car sales, the sales manager might overreact and tell her salespersons to sell at discounts or accept trade-ins that erode profit margins. To avoid that problem, the entrepreneur would

EXHIBIT 12.3

New-Car Sales Budget—Units

	Quarter				
Model	First	Second	Third	Fourth	Total
Small	200	300	300	200	1,000
Medium	100	150	150	100	500
Large	200	250	250	200	900
	500	700	700	500	2,400

prepare another budget, this one translating units into dollars (see Exhibit 12.4).

This control system is still incomplete, because the sales manager may overspend in her efforts to meet her unit goal of 2,400 new-car sales, so the entrepreneur must prepare a third budget, dealing with selling expenses (see Exhibit 12.5).

Armed with these three budgets, the entrepreneur can control the performance of his new-car sales department. By providing them with the information they need to make sound decisions, these budgets encourage the sales manager and her salespersons to do their best. These budgets also enable:

- The entrepreneur to evaluate the performance of his sales manager
- The sales manager to evaluate the performance of her salespersons

EXHIBIT 12.4

New-Car Sales Budget (net of trade-in)

	Quarter				
Model	First	Second	Third	Fourth	Total
Small	$1,200,000	$1,800,000	$1,800,000	$1,200,000	$ 6,000,000
Medium	900,000	1,350,000	1,350,000	900,000	4,500,000
Large	1,500,000	2,250,000	2,250,000	1,500,000	7,500,000
	$3,600,000	$5,400,000	$5,400,000	$3,600,000	$18,000,000

EXHIBIT 12.5

New-Car Selling Expense Budget

	Quarter				
Item	First	Second	Third	Fourth	Total
Salaries	$300,000	$300,000	$300,000	$300,000	$1,200,000
Commissions	150,000	225,000	225,000	150,000	750,000
Advertising	30,000	60,000	90,000	60,000	240,000
Telephone	1,500	1,500	1,500	1,500	6,000
Total	$481,500	$586,500	$616,500	$511,500	$2,196,000

These evaluations of performance may result in promotions and merit increases in salary or remedial action and even dismissals. However, budget figures should never be the only judge of a person's performance. For example, suppose an unexpected recession hits the nation and causes unemployment to rise sharply. New-car sales slump nationwide. As a result, the sales manager fails to meet the goal of 2,400 new-car sales. Should she be penalized? No. Her failure was due to events beyond her control. In any case, it would be the responsibility of the entrepreneur, not the sales manager, to foretell such a slump and adjust the budget accordingly.

Return on Sales Versus Return on Investment

So far, we have touched on ways the entrepreneur can control the performance of his new-car salespersons and their manager. But what about the entrepreneur himself? Because he alone is accountable for the dealership's efficiency and effectiveness, he should be evaluated for performance in these two areas. Two of his budgeted goals are:

- Return on sales, which measures efficiency, of 2.2 percent
- Return on investment, which measures effectiveness, of 10.0 percent a year

At year's end, the entrepreneur would then compare his actual performance with budgeted performance. For example, a return on investment of 10.5 percent would tell the entrepreneur that he had managed his dealership well.

Never confuse these two yardsticks of performance. Often, entrepreneurs say, "My return is just 2 percent," creating the impression that their return on investment is 2 percent. They more likely are talking about return on sales. Learn to distinguish between them. Exhibit 12.6 shows how they differ.

EXHIBIT 12.6 *Return on Sales vs. Return on Investment*

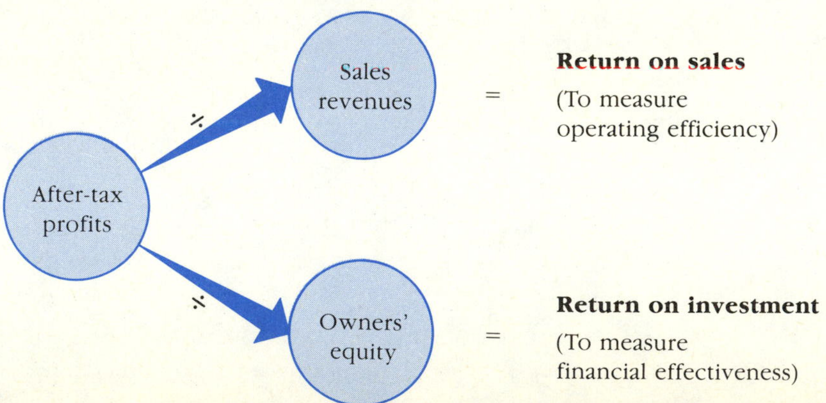

EXHIBIT 12.7

Example: Computing Return on Sales

Sales revenues = \$100.00 (\$1.00/unit × 100 units/year)
Expenses = 99.00 (\$0.99/unit × 100 units/year)
Operating profit = \$ 1.00

$$\therefore \text{Return on revenues} = \frac{\text{Operating profit}}{\text{Sales revenues}} \times 100$$

$$= \frac{\$1.00}{\$100.00} \times 100$$

$$= 1\%$$

EXHIBIT 12.8

Example: Computing Return on Investment

Operating profit = \$1.00
Owners' equity = 0.99

$$\therefore \text{Return on owners' equity} = \frac{\text{Yearly operating profit}}{\text{Owners' equity}} \times 100$$

$$= \frac{\$1.00}{\$0.99} \times 100$$

$$= 101\% \text{ a year}$$

Example: An entrepreneur buys a product in the morning for 99 cents and sells it in the afternoon for one dollar. She does business this way 100 days a year. What are her return on sales and her return on investment?

- Her return on sales is 1 percent, computed as shown in Exhibit 12.7.
- Her return on investment is 101 percent a year, computed as shown in Exhibit 12.8.

The important measure of performance is the return of 101 percent because it tells how effectively she used her investment of 99 cents—how well she managed her resources to produce results. Though less important, the return on 1 percent tells how efficiently she did business—how much she has left over as profit for each dollar of sales.

More will be said about return on sales and return on investment in Chapter Thirteen.

Reporting Performance

To make the best use of budgets, entrepreneurs should establish a system that compares actual performance with budgeted performance. Such comparisons may be made on the back of an envelope or even on scraps of

EXHIBIT 12.9 *Report on Actual and Budgeted Sales—Units*

	Small Model			Medium Model			Large Model		
Quarter	Budgeted	Actual	Difference	Budgeted	Actual	Difference	Budgeted	Actual	Difference
First	200	220	+20	100	110	+10	200	180	−20
Second	300	280	−20	150	150	—	250	220	−30
Third	300	310	+10	150	140	−10	250	230	−20
Fourth	200	180	−20	100	110	+10	200	190	−10
Total	1,000	990	−10	500	510	+10	900	820	−80

paper, but an organized chart of comparison like the one in Exhibit 12.9, provides a clear and concise picture.

Note how this quarter-to-quarter comparison gives off immediate signals. For example, in the first quarter, actual performance topped budgeted performance for both small and medium models. This signals the entrepreneur that the new-car sales department peformed well with those models. On the other hand, the sales department did poorly with large models, falling 20 cars short of the budgeted quarterly goal. Because this figure is 10 percent off budgeted performance, the entrepreneur must find out what happened and then take remedial action.

PROFITGRAPH

Uses of the Profitgraph

Another helpful planning and control tool is the profitgraph.[9] Few entrepreneurs make use of this tool, although it is remarkably versatile. Profitgraphs can give entrepreneurs visual answers to these questions:

- How many pounds of my product must I make and sell before I begin to make a profit?
- At what percentage of capacity must I run my plant before I begin to make a profit?
- How much must my sales revenues increase to justify hiring another salesperson? Or a receptionist?

The profitgraph may also give entrepreneurs visual answers to "what if" questions, such as, what would happen to my profits if:

- Fixed costs increases 10 percent but volume, prices, and variable costs stay the same?
- Sales volume drops off 10 percent but prices, fixed costs, and variable costs stay the same?
- Sales volume goes up 10 percent but prices, fixed costs, and variable costs rise 5 percent?

These sample questions underscore how handy and versatile a tool the profitgraph can be. Entrepreneurs may apply this tool to the venture as a whole or to parts of the venture as well.

Example: An entrepreneur has been profitably operating a restaurant in a shopping center for six years. Her success has encouraged her to think seriously about leasing space in another shopping center for a second restaurant. Before she can make this decision, she needs to know how many customers she must average daily before she begins to make a profit. To answer that question, the entrepreneur and her accountant have estimated that:

- Variable costs will be $0.40 on each $1.00 of sales.
- Fixed costs will be $36,000 a month.
- The average customer will spend $10.00 for a meal.

Using this information, the entrepreneur can construct a profitgraph like the one in Exhibit 12.10. As shown, the new restaurant would begin to make a profit when its monthly revenues top $60,000—or at least 6,000 customers a month. Note that in constructing the profitgraph, the entrepreneur:

- Drew a straight line parallel to the horizontal axis to show that fixed costs ($36,000 a month) would be the same regardless of the number of customers patronizing the new restaurant

EXHIBIT 12.10 *Profitgraph*

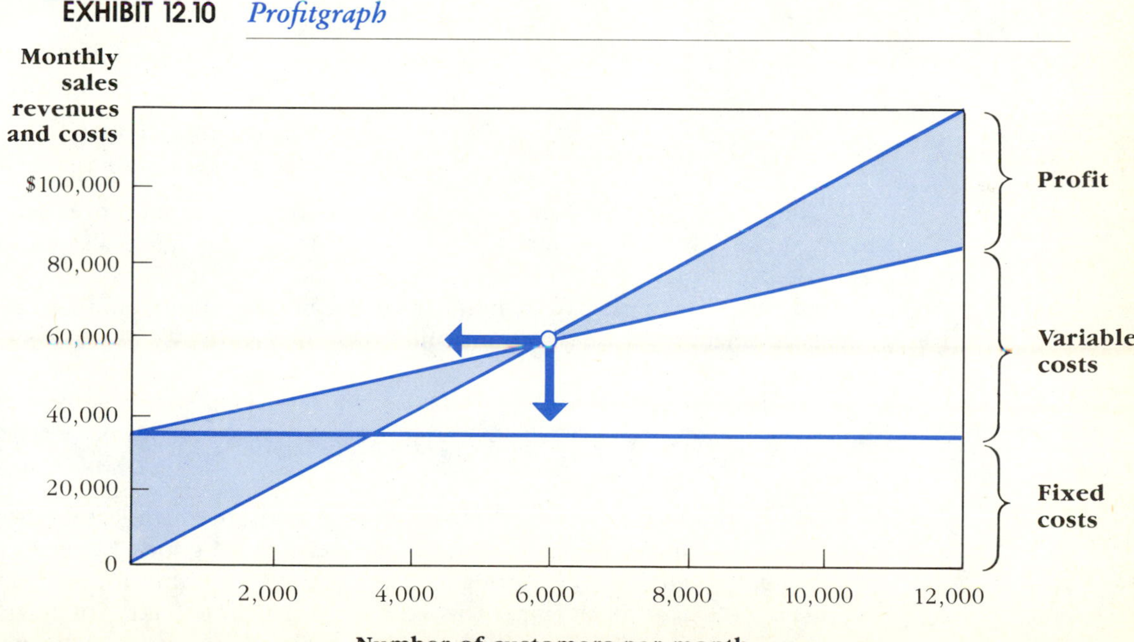

- Drew a second straight line beginning at \$36,000 on the vertical axis and increasing at the rate of \$0.40 per \$1.00 of sales or \$4.00 per average customer to show total costs
- Drew a third straight line beginning at zero and increasing at the rate of \$10.00 per average customer to show total revenues

The point at which the revenue and total-cost lines intersect is the point at which revenues match total costs. In other words, it is the point at which the entrepreneur would make neither a profit nor a loss, but would break even.

Limitations of the Profitgraph

One word of caution about profitgraphs like the one described in the example: the volume-price-cost relationships are valid only within relevant ranges of volume. For instance, if monthly volume in our example were to drop to 4,000 customers, then the entrepreneur would undoubtedly slice her fixed costs by taking such actions as these:

- Eliminating the job of hostess and permitting customers to seat themselves
- Closing the restaurant on Sundays because volume is lowest that day

Instead of constructing a profitgraph, the entrepreneur could have found the point at which she would begin to make a profit through the following calculation. First, she would estimate the contribution to fixed costs made by each customer (\$10.00 selling price − \$4.00 variable cost = \$6.00). This means that \$6.00 out of each \$10.00 sales is left over to cover fixed costs. Then she would divide this unit contribution into monthly fixed costs:

$$\frac{\$36{,}000/\text{month}}{\$6.00/\text{customer}} = 6{,}000 \left\{ \begin{array}{l} \text{customers a month} \\ \text{needed to cover fixed costs} \\ \text{and begin to make a profit} \end{array} \right.$$

Although this computation gives the entrepreneur her breakeven point, it does not have the versatility of the profitgraph, which is also useful as a tool for visualizing the answers to a host of "what if" questions. The entrepreneur can anticipate a number of possible scenarios and see the effects of changes in sales volume and costs on profits.

SUMMARY

A venture often passes through four stages of growth: prebirth, acceptance, breakthrough, and maturity. Entrepreneurs tend to be good at launching and bringing their ventures through the acceptance stage, but they are not always as good at managing their ventures through breakthrough and maturity. One reason is that they tend to ignore a lesson they learned before they launched their ventures—namely, that planning and control help keep a venture on target.

As elements in a circular process, planning and control are as vital to the health of a venture after its birth as before. This process begins with setting precise goals, both immediate and long-range. Goal setting is critical for these reasons:

- The clearer the entrepreneur's idea of what should be done, the greater the chances that it will be done.
- True progress can only be measured in relation to the entrepreneur's goals.

The second step requires entrepreneurs to draft action plans to meet their goals. These plans should be similar to the business plan, which is a form of action plan.

The third step requires entrepreneurs to measure their progress at frequent intervals. This process is called control. It helps assure entrepreneurs that their actions, as well as those of their employees, are progressing according to plan. The key to any system of control is the information that enables the entrepreneur to compare actual with planned performance. Such information lets entrepreneurs know where they stand, and more important, in what direction they may be moving.

Budgeting and profitgraphs are two tools that help entrepreneurs plan and control more effectively. Budgets generally serve as a standard against which actual performance may be compared. Profitgraphs, on the other hand, visually show the impact of volume, price, and costs on profit.

DISCUSSION AND REVIEW QUESTIONS

1. Explain the process of planning and control in a venture. Why is this process circular?
2. Why do entrepreneurs tend to avoid the process of planning and control in their own ventures?
3. Why is it vital to set precise goals? Give two examples of precise goal setting.
4. Define these terms: *immediate goals, long-range goals, action plans, return on sales, return on investment, efficiency, effectiveness.*
5. What is meant by MBO?
6. Which is the better measure of venture performance, return on sales or return on investment? Explain.
7. How would you, as an entrepreneur, go about setting goals for your venture?
8. In your opinion, why do so many entrepreneurs fail to plan and control their ventures in the ways suggested in the chapter?
9. Why is budgeting a vital tool for both planning and control?

10. Why is the profitgraph such a versatile tool in planning and control? Give two examples of how this tool may be used.
11. Why is it vital for small businesspersons to be managers as well as entrepreneurs?
12. Does an entrepreneur's venture necessarily stop growing when it reaches the maturity stage in its growth cycle? Explain.
13. What is the most important principle in the pursuit of goals? Why?
14. What is meant by the hierarchy of goals? Give an example.
15. What do profits measure? Explain fully.

NOTES

1. Adapted from Sanford L. Jacobs, "High-Tech Firm Avoids Perils that Accompany Fast Growth," *The Wall Street Journal*, December 10, 1984, p. 27.
2. Adapted from Donald K Clifford, Jr., *Managing the Threshold Company* (New York, N.Y.: McKinsey & Company, Inc., 1973), pp. 21–22.
3. Adapted from Robert Townsend, *Up the Organization* (New York: Alfred A. Knopf, 1970), pp. 129–130.
4. Peter F. Drucker, *Managing for Results* (New York: Haper & Row, 1964), pp. 12, 13.
5. Quoted by H. Igor Ansoff, *Corporate Strategy* (New York: McGraw-Hill, 1965), p. 43.
6. David W. Ewing, "Corporate Planning at a Crossroads," *Harvard Business Review*, July–August 1967, p. 86.
7. Charles H. Granger, "The Hierarchy of Objectives," *Harvard Business Review*, May–June 1964, p. 64.
8. Douglas McGregor, *The Human Side of Enterprise* (New York: McGraw-Hill, 1960), p. 49.
9. As mentioned in Chapter Six, the profitgraph is often called a breakeven chart, which mistakenly suggests that the entrepreneur's goal is to break even rather than to make a profit. *Profitgraph* is suggested as a better term.

CASE 12A *Newe Daisterre Glas*

In 1982, Alfred Brickel founded Newe Daisterre Glas (*new dawn glass* in Old English) to create stained-glass windows and other works of glass art. His fledgling company has already designed and built the world's biggest kaleidoscope, mostly out of glass. But sales revenues have failed to match Mr. Brickel's reputation for artistic excellence. In fact, he has laid off half his workforce, cutting it from eight to four employees. He is wondering what to do to build up demand for his unique service.

Background

The son of a physician, Mr. Brickel qualifies as a dyed-in-the-wool entrepreneur. Although only 25 years old, he has worked on and off as an entrepreneur for 11 years. At 14, he set up his own landscaping business in the summer. Then at 16, bored with school, he left home for Bloomington, Indiana. There, he did odd jobs while earning his high school diploma.

Mr. Brickel's next stop was college, where the dean promptly expelled him for poor attendance and even poorer grades. After a brief stint clerking in a grocery store, he enrolled at another university to study art. This time he stayed four years, graduating with a bachelor of arts degree. In his junior year, he earned most of his living by painting houses on his own.

In his senior year, Mr. Brickel decided to go into the glass art business—by accident. As he sat in his parents' living room one December day, his eye caught a replica of a stained-glass window, used as a Christmas decoration. Its beauty fired his imagination. And that was the unlikely beginning of a hobby that led him three months later to set up his own business turning out works of glass art.

Still a senior at college, Mr. Brickel worked at his new venture part time and also moonlighted in a bar four hours a night. All told, he was putting in 90 hours a week studying and working. After graduation, he gave up his job as a bartender to work full time at organizing his new venture and researching his market. His beginning balance sheet appears in Exhibit 12A.1.

EXHIBIT 12A.1

Newe Daisterre Glas: Balance Sheet (June 1, 1982)

Assets		Equities	
Cash	$1,000	Liabilities	$ 0
Supplies	800	Owner's equity	6,000
Equipment	2,400		
Organizational costs	1,100		
Prepaid expenses	700		
Total assets	$6,000	Total equities	$6,000

Takes Partner

Although he himself put up the entire $6,000 out of savings, Mr. Brickel took in Dale Mitchell as an equal partner. With the help of a lawyer, they drew up articles of co-partnership which specified that:

- The two partners would share equally in the firm's profits.
- Mr. Brickel would oversee all design, production, purchasing, financial, and employee relations activities.
- Mr. Mitchell would oversee all marketing and public relations activities.

On the advice of his lawyer, Mr. Brickel also hired a certified public accountant (CPA) to design a simple bookkeeping system. "Every day I set aside time to make entries in my books," says Mr. Brickel. "Every three months the CPA picks them up to prepare an income statement and a balance sheet. He also does my tax returns for the city, county, state, and federal governments."

But Mr. Brickel finds such financial statements unhelpful. "My business is so small, I can easily keep on top of things," says Mr. Brickel. "There's little that goes on that I don't know about. I'm here day and night. Besides, my people and I are like a close-knit family. Each of us is interested in doing what's best for the others in the family."

From the start, Mr. Brickel's education stood him in good stead, especially in design. And what he did not know, he quickly picked up through trial and error and from a 77-year-old glasscutter. "There are only eight left in the whole country," says Mr. Brickel. "In the 1930s, there were more than 1,500. It's really a dying art."

One of a Kind

Mr. Brickel's business is indeed unique. His creations range from a stained-glass jack of diamonds to a turn-of-the-century ticket booth, from individualized Christmas ornaments to custom-made fiberglass kayaks. He also does such unique things as slicing a beer bottle in half, gluing the bottom slice to the neck, and creating beer-bottle goblets for drinking. But his bread-and-butter trade comes from original stained-glass windows. Photographs of his creations appear in Exhibit 12A.2.

Perhaps his proudest creation is a kaleidoscope that may be the world's biggest. Ordered by a nightclub appropriately called The Kaleidoscope, it weighs 425 pounds and measures 12 feet in length and 3 feet in diameter. Mr. Brickel made it out of pulleys, rocks, glass, posters, and plywood. Today it sits unappreciated in his downtown studio waiting for a buyer with $3,000 to spare. He had to repossess it from the nightclub owner because "the guy couldn't pay."

Mr. Brickel's business is unique in other ways too. For example, he turns down repeat orders. "Everything I do is a one-of-a-kind, handmade thing," says Mr. Brickel. "I don't like to repeat myself. I'm not a mass producer." Although in business to make a profit, he regards himself more as an artist than a businessman. He aims to bring back the esthetics of hand craftsmanship, an "ancient craft that some people think is dead." Clearly, he has no illusions about becoming the Tiffany's of the Midwest.

EXHIBIT 12A.2 *Newe Daisterre Glas, Inc.: Examples of Glass Art*

All of his four coworkers echo his business philosophy. For example, his vice president, Delbert Morrow, says: "The important thing is that we love what we do. We have ambitions only to the point of comfort, but we do get good money for what we do." Indeed, no item sells for less than $40, with most items selling at prices in excess of $200.

Unit prices may be high, but revenues have failed to take off. In May 1983, revenues peaked at $12,800. But, by June 1984, monthly revenues had dropped off to half as much. This sharp drop forced Mr. Brickel to reduce his workforce from eight to four employees. "I hated to do it," says Mr. Brickel, "but I had no choice. There wasn't enough work for them."

All his coworkers exhibit an artistic bent. In fact, Mr. Brickel recruited them from classes he gives in glass art at his alma mater. None of them draws more than $150 a week in wages. And Mr. Brickel himself often draws less. "It's a labor of love," says Mr. Brickel. "We could all be making much more working for some big outfit."

Steps to Boost Sales

Mr. Brickel has looked for ways to boost revenues to levels that would enable him to rehire the artists he laid off. "I feel a responsibility toward them," says Mr. Brickel. "If I could drum up more sales, I could also increase their wages. Let's face it, $100 to $150 a week doesn't go very far these days." To boost revenues, Mr. Brickel has already taken these steps:

- He replaced Mr. Mitchell with Mr. Morrow, whose main charge is to find new customers and, equally important, to come up with new product ideas. One idea he came up with was the manufacture of custom-built kayaks.
- He incorporated his business. It had been a two-way partnership. The new company was capitalized at $500, the minimum allowable in the state. Mr. Brickel put up the entire $500 himself, getting in return 80 percent of the stock. He gave Mr. Morrow and another coworker each 10 percent of the new company. Mr. Brickel's reason for doing so was his belief that "one way to make the company grow is to have employees with a vested interest."
- He installed a cost-accounting system to keep closer tabs on the cost of each job as it passes through production.
- He applied for a three-year $10,000 loan from a local bank, telling them he needed the money to increase wages, promote the company and its products in a wider market, purchase more materials, and expand into new product lines.

Mr. Brickel was sure these steps would lead to "much higher revenues." His financial statements, dating from the time he incorporated his business to July 1984, appear in Exhibits 12A.3 and 12A.4. A photograph of his workshop appears in Exhibit 12A.5.

EXHIBIT 12A.3 *Newe Daisterre Glas, Inc.: Balance Sheet (July 31, 1984)*

Assets			**Equities**		
Current assets			Current liabilities		
Cash	$ 40		Accounts payable		$ 3,240
Accounts receivable	2,380		Other liabilities		
Inventory	3,960		Loan payable, officer		16,120
Work in process	4,240	$10,620			
Equipment and fixtures		17,000	Owners' equity		
			Common stock	$ 500	
			Retained earnings	7,760	8,260
Total assets		$27,620	Total equities		$27,620

EXHIBIT 12A.4 *Newe Daisterre Glas, Inc.: Income Statement (for four months ending July 31, 1984)*

Sales revenues		$19,140
Cost of sales		
Purchases	$5,960	
Less: Ending inventory	3,940	
Materials used	2,020	
Labor	6,460	
	8,480	
Less: Work in process	4,240	4,240
Gross profit		$14,900
Operating expenses		
Rent	$3,640	
Utilities	1,000	
Automobile	780	
Insurance	660	
Office supplies	460	
Maintenance	460	
Advertising	240	
Legal and audit	160	
Travel	120	
Telephone	100	
Rubbish	20	7,640
Operating profit		$ 7,260

EXHIBIT 12A.5 *Newe Daisterre Glas, Inc.: View of Workshop*

Questions

1. If you were Mr. Brickel, what would you do to boost sales revenues?
2. Comment on Mr. Brickel as an entrepreneur.
3. How well has Mr. Brickel done so far?
4. Comment on the way Mr. Brickel organized and financed his venture.
5. If you had the chance, would you invest in Mr. Brickel's venture? Why or why not?

CASE 12B *James Stanton*

James Stanton took his savings and some money his parents had left him and started in business for himself. It wasn't a large business, but it did give him the pleasure of being his own boss.

Mr. Stanton's product was a painted wooden toy train priced at $20.30 each. It was a well-built toy, designed like the hand-made toys of his grandfather's day.

An energetic person, Mr. Stanton soon had production rolling. His only start-up problem was paint. But he soon solved the problem by finding a supplier who promised him the quality of paint needed.

At the end of his first six months in business, Mr. Stanton took pride in his first income statement, show in Exhibit 12B.1. He hoped it would be

EXHIBIT 12B.1

James Stanton: Income Statement (for six months ending December 31)

Sales revenues			$11,620
Cost of goods sold			
Beginning inventory		$ 210	
Purchases of materials	$ 7,010		
Labor	11,340		
Rent of machines and space	2,930	21,280	
		$21,490	
Ending inventory		16,090	5,400
Gross profit			$ 6,220
Other expenses			
Advertising and selling		$ 2,120	
Interest		70	2,190
Operating profit			$ 4,030

EXHIBIT 12B.2

James Stanton: Balance Sheet (December 31)

Assets		Equities	
Cash	$ 430	Note payable	$ 4,200
Inventory	16,090	Accounts payable	3,840
		Owner's equity	8,480
Total assets	$16,520	Total equities	$16,520

the first in a long series of reports showing business "in the black." His balance sheet appears in Exhibit 12B.2.

Question Comment on Mr. Stanton's performance to date and his prospects for the future.

Source:

This case was prepared by Charles A. Bliss as a basis for class discussion rather than to illustrate effective or ineffective handling of an administrative situation. Reprinted by permission of the Harvard Business School.

CASE 12C *Sidney Jordan*

Sidney Jordan owned a small manufacturing plant that made hinges and small hardware used on kitchen cabinets. When he began three years ago, Mr. Jordan took a five-year, $110,000 loan from a commercial bank, using his private home as collateral.

During the first two years, Mr. Jordan was barely able to keep afloat. After meeting his bank obligations, he was able to take only a small salary for himself. In the third year, he decided to make several changes to boost sales and profits.

Mr. Jordan began to quote lower prices than he had before, in the hope that higher volume would lead to more profits. His reduced prices did improve volume, but this higher volume brought increased overtime as his employees worked to fill orders. When he realized how costly overtime had become, he decided to hire extra employees instead. This decision created crowded conditions that led to enormous inefficiency. Because of the crowded conditions, he could only purchase the materials that he needed and could not take advantage of quantity discounts from suppliers.

In addition, the larger volume of business meant higher accounts receivable and higher cash needs so, although he was needed to oversee production, he spent more and more of his time on the telephone trying to get customers to pay more quickly.

When the February installment of his loan came due, Mr. Jordan found that he was unable to meet it. He could not even pay his own salary. He asked the bank for more money, but he was told that he had exhausted his credit. The bank agreed to let him postpone several payments until his cash flow improved.

When he looked at his books at year's end, Mr. Jordan found that he had earned even less than the year before. He had little recourse but to ask his family to help him keep the business afloat.

Questions

1. How did Mr. Jordan's managerial decisions affect the success of his business?
2. How important was "the people factor" in Mr. Jordan's business?
3. What specific money factors influenced the changes in this business?
4. How would you have tried to make this business more profitable?

Source: U.S. Small Business Administration, *Success and Failure Factors in Small Business* (Washington, D.C.: U.S. Government Printing Office, 1979), pp. 26-27.

13 FINANCIAL ANALYSIS AND COMPUTERS

QUESTIONS FOR MASTERY

How does financial analysis fit into the pattern of planning and control?

What are the methods of analyzing financial statements and interpreting results?

What are the ways of evaluating investment opportunities?

How can computers be used to improve performance?

What should you consider in selecting a computer?

When you can measure what you are speaking about, and express it in numbers, you know something about it.

Lord Kelvin William Thomson

As their growing ventures strive toward maturity, entrepreneurs often fail to strike a balance between being entrepreneurial and being managerial. As mentioned in Chapter Twelve, entrepreneurs who excel at launching new ventures often do poorly at managing their growth. This is not because they lose the spark of entrepreneurship, but rather, because they fail to plan and control well.

Such entrepreneurs generally fail to use their financial statements to spot problems before they occur, or they make unwise investment decisions, or they refuse to consider computers to help them plan and control. In this chapter, an extension of Chapters Eleven and Twelve, we shall focus on analyzing financial statements, evaluating investment opportunities, and selecting and using computers.

ANALYSIS OF FINANCIAL STATEMENTS

To plan and control their ventures well, entrepreneurs should become skilled at analyzing the numbers in their financial statements. Many entrepreneurs believe that financial analysis should best be left to their accountant. Although it is the job of accountants to design accounting systems and prepare financial statements, it is not their job to analyze and interpret the numbers in the statements. That is the entrepreneur's responsibility.

Doing business is certainly not all numbers. In fact, few business problems can be solved solely by the collection and analysis of numbers, financial or nonfinancial. Often, there are important factors that merit equal consideration but cannot be reduced to numbers, such as teamwork and the entrepreneur's management skills.

Even so, analysis of financial statements can help the entrepreneur make sound decisions, especially in the areas of planning and control. As advice to entrepreneurs who put their trust in numbers alone as well as to entrepreneurs who put their trust in intuition alone, this quotation bears mention:

> The real trouble with this world of ours is not that it is an unreasonable world, nor even that it is a reasonable one. The commonest kind of trouble is that it is nearly reasonable, but not quite. Life is not illogical; yet it is a trap for logicians. It looks just a little more mathematical and regular than it is; its exactitude is obvious, but its inexactitude is hidden; its wildness lies in wait.[1]

The Essence of Financial Analysis

Comparison lies at the heart of all analyses of financial statements. For example, the statement "a venture earned a profit of $10,000" is, by itself, meaningless. The $10,000 becomes meaningful only if compared with some standard, such as last year's profit or this year's budgeted profit—as discussed briefly in Chapter Twelve.

Note that such comparisons are precise and concrete. Comparisons, however, may also be imprecise and intuitive. For example, if the venture had sales revenues of $10 million, we would know intuitively that a $10,000 profit is a poor return—a return of just one tenth of a penny for each dollar of sales.

The comparisons that are most meaningful to entrepreneurs are those that relate to the goals entrepreneurs set for themselves, as described in Chapter Twelve. The comparisons are intended to tell entrepreneurs how well they are meeting their goals. As we have discussed before, entrepreneurs usually have both financial goals—sales revenue and return-on-investment targets—and nonfinancial goals—psychic satisfaction, workers' satisfaction, and social awareness. Entrepreneurs should, of course, balance the two kinds of goals in measuring their ventures' performance. Of the goals that can be reduced to numbers, the most meaningful one is to earn a satisfactory return on the moneys invested in a venture consistent with maintaining its financial health. Note the two-sided nature of this goal:

- To earn a satisfactory return
- To maintain financial health

We shall now discuss how entrepreneurs should analyze financial statements to see how well they have done financially.

Earning a Satisfactory Return

The best yardstick to use in assessing return is called *return on investment* (ROI). It is computed by dividing net profit by investment. ROI tells entrepreneurs how many cents they earn in a year for each dollar of investment, in the same way that interest tells savers how much they earn for each dollar of savings at a bank. Investment may be defined in three different ways:

- Total assets
- Owners' equity
- Permanent capital

That means entrepreneurs may compute three different ROIs. Which yardstick is best? The answer depends on what entrepreneurs want to measure, described as follows:

Return on total assets: This yardstick should be used if entrepreneurs want to measure how well they have invested all the money entrusted in their care, regardless of where it came from. Therefore, they should include as sources of money not only shareholders but also short-term creditors, such as suppliers, and long-term creditors, such as mortgage banks.

Return on owners' equity: This yardstick should be used if entrepreneurs want to measure how well they have invested only the money entrusted in their care by shareholders. This yardstick appeals especially to existing and prospective shareholders, because it is the entrepreneur's duty to run the venture in the shareholders' best interests.

Return on permanent capital: This yardstick should be used if entrepreneurs want to measure how well they have invested all the long-term money entrusted in their care. It takes into account not only the investment made by shareholders but also any long-term loans made by commercial banks, mortgage banks, bondholders, and so on.

The sum of owners' equity and long-term debt is called *permanent capital* because it reflects the total amount needed to finance fixed assets and the fraction of current assets not otherwise financed by short-term creditors.

Maintaining Financial Health

Besides desiring a satisfactory return on investment, shareholders also expect their investments to be protected against excessive risk. For example, entrepreneurs could boost their return on owners' equity if they

EXHIBIT 13.1 *Selected Key Ratios in Financial Analysis*

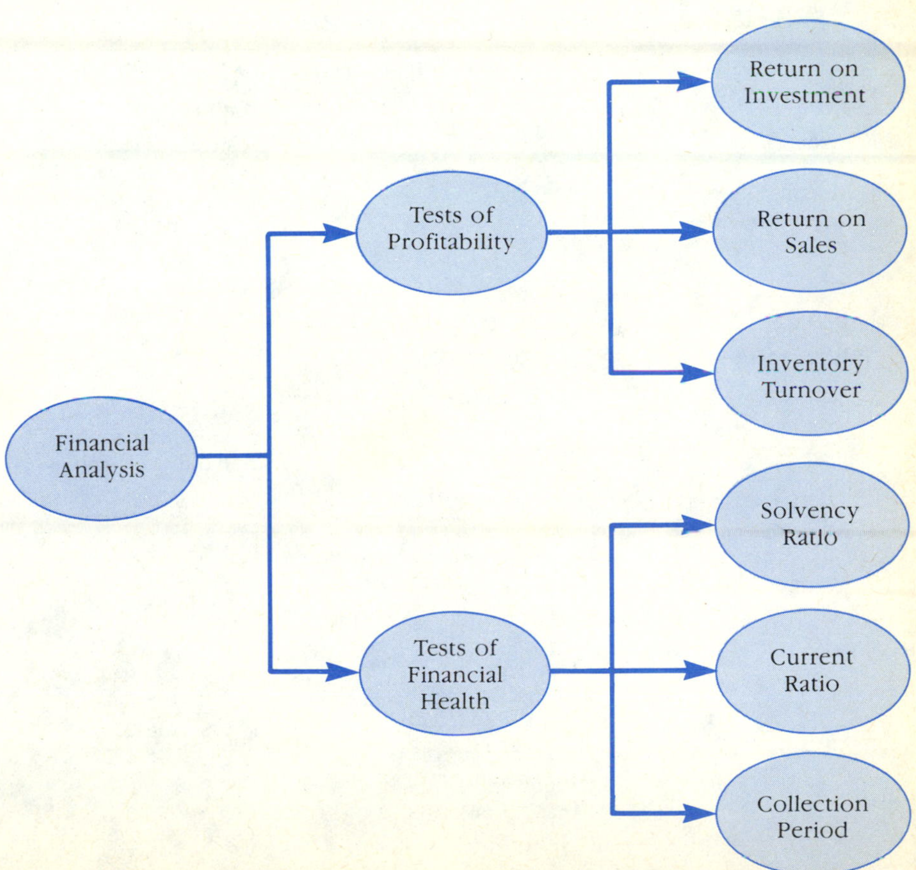

financed an expansion solely by borrowing from a commercial bank. This action might boost the shareholders' return, but only at the shareholders' increased risk of losing their investment. By financing the expansion with a loan, entrepreneurs must both repay the loan and pay interest. Failure to do both could throw a venture into bankruptcy.

To measure their degree of protection against risk, entrepreneurs may use any one of several yardsticks. One relates total debt to total assets; another omits current debt and relates just long-term debt to permanent capital. These yardsticks and others are described in an upcoming section of this chapter called "Tests of Financial Health."

Ratio Analysis

To evaluate their financial performance, entrepreneurs should use a technique called *ratio analysis.* Although dozens of ratios may be computed from just one set of financial statements, generally only a handful will be helpful to entrepreneurs. In the discussion that follows, and as shown in Exhibit 13.1, we have grouped the ratios into two categories:

- Tests of profitability
- Tests of financial health

EXHIBIT 13.2 *Financial Statements for Zeno Products, Inc.*

Balance Sheet (December 31, 1985)

Assets			**Equities**		
Current assets			Current liabilities		
Cash	$ 40,000		Accounts payable	$ 80,000	
Accounts receivable	100,000		Notes payable	40,000	
Inventories	160,000	$300,000	Accrued expenses	20,000	$140,000
Fixed assets					
Land	$ 40,000		Long-term liabilities		
Building	240,000		Loan payable		
Equipment	320,000	600,000	(12% interest)		300,000
			Owners' equity		
			Common stock	$200,000	
			Retained earnings	260,000	460,000
Total assets		$900,000	Total equities		$900,000

Income Statement (1985)

Sales revenues	$1,000,000
Cost of goods sold	700,000
Gross profit	$ 300,000
Operating expenses	164,000
Operating profit	$ 136,000
Less: Interest on loan	36,000
Profit before taxes	$ 100,000
Income taxes (30%)	30,000
Net profit	$ 70,000

We shall compute ratios for the various yardsticks of performance based on the financial statements of a fictitious venture called Zeno Products. These statements appear in Exhibit 13.2.

TESTS OF PROFITABILITY

Return on Investment As explained earlier, entrepreneurs may estimate their return on investment by using any one of three ratios, depending on whether they see investment as being total assets, owners' equity, or permanent capital. Computations are made as follows.

$$\text{Return on Assets} = \frac{\text{Net Profit} + [\text{Interest} \times (1 - \text{Tax Rate})]}{\text{Total Assets}} \times 100$$

$$= \frac{\$70{,}000 + [\$36{,}000 \times (1 - 0.30)]}{\$900{,}000} \times 100$$

$$= \underline{\underline{10.6\% \text{ a year}}}$$

$$\text{Return on Owners' Equity} = \frac{\text{Net Profit}}{\text{Owners' Equity}} \times 100$$

$$= \frac{\$70{,}000}{\$460{,}000} \times 100$$

$$= \underline{\underline{15.2\% \text{ a year}}}$$

$$\text{Return on Permanent Capital} = \frac{\text{Net Profit} + [\text{Interest} \times (1 - \text{Tax Rate})]}{\text{Owners' Equity} + \text{Long-Term Liabilities}} \times 100$$

$$= \frac{\$70{,}000 + [\$36{,}000 \times (1 - 0.30)]}{\$460{,}000 + \$300{,}000} \times 100$$

$$= \underline{\underline{12.5\% \text{ a year}}}$$

Note that in estimating the return on assets or on permanent capital for Zeno Products, we added the after-tax expense of interest to net profit. It is common practice to do so because assets are financed by both shareholders and creditors, and the ratio should reflect the return to both; otherwise the returns would have been understated. In arriving at net profit, interest on debt is subtracted as expense, but earnings on owners' equity are not. So, net profit should be adjusted upward to reflect its value as a return not only on the investment made by shareholders but also on the loans made by creditors.

Note also that the adjustment is made by multiplying the interest expense by the complement of the tax rate. Because interest expense is

EXHIBIT 13.3

Example: Effect of Taxes on Interest Expense

	Without Interest	With Interest
Sales revenues	$300,000	$300,000
Operating expenses	240,000	240,000
Operating profit	$ 60,000	$ 60,000
Interest expense	0	20,000(c)
Profit before taxes	$ 60,000	$ 40,000
Income taxes (30%)	18,000(a)	12,000(d)
Net Profit	$ 42,000(b)	$ 28,000(e)

Note that interest expense of $20,000 (c) reduces net profit not by $20,000 but by only $14,000 (b–e). This venture pays $6,000 less in taxes (a–d) with interest expense than it does without interest. Thus, the effective cost of interest is only $14,000 (b–e) or simply [c × (1–tax rate)] because of the effect of taxes.

tax-deductible, it must be partially offset by the effect of taxes. For example, if a venture's tax rate is 30 percent, every dollar of interest costs only 70 cents after taxes. See the example in Exhibit 13.3 for a detailed explanation of how the actual cost of interest is reduced by taxes.

Return on Sales Revenues

Also referred to as profit margin, return on sales revenues measures how efficiently entrepreneurs are managing their operations. It tells them how many cents are left over for each dollar of sales. To use this yardstick in analyzing Zeno Products, divide net profit by sales revenues, as follows:

$$\text{Return on Sales Revenues} = \frac{\text{Net Profit}}{\text{Sales Revenues}} \times 100$$

$$= \frac{\$70{,}000}{\$1{,}000{,}000} \times 100$$

$$= 7.0\%$$

This figure enables entrepreneurs to compare their operating efficiency with that of other ventures in the same industry. Public figures are available for most industries so that entrepreneurs can rate themselves. If their return on sales is low, it means they are inefficient, a sign that the venture is unhealthy and needs attention.

As mentioned in Chapter Twelve, a common mistake is to consider return on sales the best measure of financial performance. Rather, return on investment holds the greater significance because it takes investment into account—the resources that are the foundation of both sales revenues and profits.

Another Look at Return on Investment

Intuitively, we know that the more we make for each dollar of sales and the more sales we make for each dollar of investment, the greater our return on investment will be. These relationships may be expressed as follows:

$$\frac{\text{Net Profit}}{\text{Investment}} = \frac{\text{Net Profit}}{\text{Sales Revenues}} \times \frac{\text{Sales Revenues}}{\text{Investment}}$$

In short, this equation suggests that entrepreneurs may improve their return on investment in two ways:

- By improving the efficiency of their operations, resulting in more profit for each dollar of sales
- By making better use of their assets, resulting in more sales for each dollar of investment

Inventory Turnover

Inventory turnover measures how well entrepreneurs are managing their inventories. Whether inventories are large or small depends mostly on the kind of industry and the time of year. A fertilizer dealer, for example, with a large inventory in early spring is in a strong position to satisfy farmers. That same inventory in the late fall spells trouble. One way to tell whether inventories are high or low for Zeno Products is to relate inventory to cost of goods sold, as follows:

$$\text{Inventory Turnover} = \frac{\text{Cost of Goods Sold}}{\text{Inventory}} = \frac{\$700{,}000}{\$160{,}000} = 4.4 \text{ times a year}$$

On the average, therefore, Zeno Products is selling out its inventory 4.4 times a year.

If their industries are seasonal, entrepreneurs should make sure they relate average inventory to cost of goods sold. To do so they should use the average of the beginning and ending inventories or even the average of monthly inventories in their calculations, rather than simply the year-end inventory.

TESTS OF FINANCIAL HEALTH

So far, we have discussed only those yardsticks that measure how well entrepreneurs manage their operations and their assets. We shall now look at those yardsticks that measure how well they manage the finances of their ventures, focusing on:

- Solvency
- Liquidity
- Customer credit

Solvency The term *solvency* refers to a venture's ability to repay long-term debts when due, including interest. Naturally, the more solvent a venture, the better protected its shareholders are from possible bankruptcy. To measure such protection, entrepreneurs should use *debt ratio* and *times interest earned*, as follows, using Zeno Products as a model:

$$\text{Debt Ratio} = \frac{\text{Total Liabilities}}{\text{Total Assets}} \times 100$$

$$= \frac{\$140{,}000 + \$300{,}000}{\$900{,}000} \times 100$$

$$= \underline{\underline{48.9\%}}$$

Note that debt ratio simply measures the degree to which a venture's assets are financed by creditors. Generally, a debt ratio of less than 50 percent is considered favorable. A variation on this yardstick is to omit current assets and to relate only long-term debt to permanent capital, as follows:

$$\text{Debt Ratio} = \frac{\text{Long-Term Liabilities}}{\text{Owners' Equity} + \text{Long-Term Liabilities}} \times 100$$

$$= \frac{\$300{,}000}{\$460{,}000 + \$300{,}000} \times 100$$

$$= \underline{\underline{39.5\%}}$$

Though widely used, these yardsticks do not by themselves measure financial soundness. To complete their analysis, entrepreneurs should also measure times interest earned:

$$\text{Times interest earned} = \frac{\text{Operating Profit before Interest}}{\text{Interest Expense}}$$

$$= \frac{\$136{,}000}{\$36{,}000}$$

$$= \underline{\underline{3.8 \text{ times}}}$$

Times interest earned measures how low profits may drop without straining a venture's ability to pay interest when due. Here, with operating profit exceeding interest 3.8 times, Zeno Products seems financially sound, its shareholders amply protected against financial ruin.

Liquidity Another yardstick that measures exposure to debt is *current ratio*. Estimated by relating current assets to current liabilities, this yardstick measures a venture's ability to pay short-term bills when due, computed as follows for Zeno Products:

$$\text{Current Ratio} = \frac{\text{Current Assets}}{\text{Current Liabilities}}$$

$$= \frac{\$300{,}000}{\$140{,}000}$$

$$= \underline{\underline{2.1 \text{ to } 1}}$$

The rule of thumb is that a current ratio of 2 to 1 is good, because it means that current assets could shrink 50 percent in value and still cover short-term bills. An even tougher test of liquidity is the *quick ratio*, which omits inventories. It is computed as follows for Zeno Products:

$$\text{Quick Ratio} = \frac{\text{Cash} + \text{Accounts Receivable}}{\text{Current Liabilities}}$$

$$= \frac{\$40{,}000 + \$100{,}000}{\$140{,}000}$$

$$= \underline{\underline{1 \text{ to } 1}}$$

This yardstick measures a venture's ability to pay short-term bills if a real crisis strikes, by assuming that inventories would be worthless. Generally, a quick ratio of 1 to 1 or better is considered good.

Customer Credit *Collection period* measures the degree to which a venture finances customers who buy on credit. The entrepreneur should determine whether the actual amount of uncollected sales—or accounts receivable—closely matches the amount expected to stay uncollected, given the entrepreneur's credit terms. For example, if a venture gives its credit customers 30 days to pay up, it normally would expect to have only the last month's sales owed to it.

To apply this yardstick to Zeno Products, we make two computations, as follows:

$$\text{Receivables Turnover} = \frac{\text{Credit Sales}}{\text{Accounts Receivable}}$$

$$= \frac{\$1{,}000{,}000}{\$100{,}000}$$

$$= \underline{\underline{10 \text{ times}}}$$

$$\text{Collection period} = \frac{\text{Days in the Year}}{\text{Receivables Turnover}}$$

$$= \frac{360}{10}$$

$$= \underline{\underline{\text{36 days' sales owed}}}$$

In this example, the "36 days' sales owed" means that a venture carries its credit customers for 36 days, on the average. If its credit terms call for customers to pay up in 30 days, then a collection period of 36 days is considered good. The rule of thumb is that a collection period should not exceed $1\frac{1}{3}$ times the expected payment period.

EVALUATION OF INVESTMENT OPPORTUNITIES

So far, we have discussed how entrepreneurs should evaluate their financial performance, focusing on how to spot problems most effectively. In this section, we shall discuss how entrepreneurs should evaluate investment *opportunities* such as these:

- Whether to lease or buy
- Whether to expand a plant
- Whether to make or buy a product
- Whether to add another retail outlet
- Whether to acquire another venture in order to diversify
- Whether to replace a machine with one that reduces operating costs

Each of these questions involves a choice that may make or break a venture, because the decision may commit the entrepreneur to a way of doing business that allows little opportunity for change.

Perhaps no other area is as crucial to success as making the right investment decision. Let us now look at some yardsticks that help entrepreneurs to measure their investment opportunities, among them:

- Cash payback
- Return on original investment
- Return on average investment

Cash Payback

The most popular yardstick of investment worth is simple to understand and easy to apply. *Cash payback* may be defined as the time required for the cash produced by an investment to equal the cash required by the investment. An example will show how this yardstick works:

Example: An entrepreneur owns a machine shop that makes many kinds of nuts and bolts. He carries a large inventory of steel stock as well as finished product. In an effort to cut costs, he is now mulling over an opportunity to buy a forklift for $18,000 that may save him $6,000 cash a year in inventory-handling costs.

Should the entrepreneur buy the forklift? To help answer that question, he estimates that it would take 3 years to recover his investment ($18,000 investment ÷ $6,000 savings per year). Whether this payback period is short enough depends upon his own criteria. He may have decided:

- To accept all investment opportunities with cash-payback periods of less than four years
- To reject all those with payback periods of four years or more

In this example, the entrepreneur decides to buy the forklift.

As a yardstick of investment worth, cash-payback period has a serious flaw. It fails to take into account savings earned after the payback period. In other words, it ignores what happens after the forklift has paid back the $18,000 investment. If the forklift's useful life were just three years, then the return on the $18,000 investment would really be zero, and the investment would be worthless no matter how short the cash-payback period was. The entrepreneur would have made the wrong decision.

To offset this drawback, entrepreneurs should measure the size and duration of cash return beyond the payback period. Another example will show how an entrepreneur might do that.

Example: The entrepreneur must choose between two kinds of forklifts, each of which has the same payback (see Exhibit 13.4).

Which forklift should the entrepreneur buy? The two forklifts would be equally desirable as investments if he looks only at payback. But it is clear from Exhibit 13.4 that the entrepreneur should choose Model A, because it not only recovers his cash investment of $18,000 but also promises to earn a return beyond the second year.

Cash payback has another flaw. It fails to take into account the fact that a dollar received today is worth more to the entrepreneur than a dollar received a year or more from now, since other investment opportunities may be available for today's dollar. If he has cash tied up for many years in a forklift, the entrepreneur loses the opportunity to invest that same money in more profitable ways.

EXHIBIT 13.4

Example: Payback on Forklifts

		Cash Savings			
Forklift	Cash Outlay	First Year	Second Year	Third Year	Cash Payback Period
Model A	$18,000	$9,000	$9,000	$9,000	2 years
Model B	18,000	9,000	9,000	0	2

EXHIBIT 13.5

Example: Payback on Forklifts

Forklift	Cash Outlay	Cash Savings First Year	Second Year	Third Year	Cash Payback Period
Model A	$18,000	$9,000	$9,000	$9,000	2 years
Model B	18,000	13,000	5,000	9,000	2

Example: The entrepreneur must again choose between two kinds of forklifts, this time with the cash flows shown in Exhibit 13.5.

Which forklift should the entrepreneur buy? Each one pays back its initial investment in two years and earns the same total cash savings of $27,000. Yet Model B is better than Model A because it promises to earn more savings earlier. With Model B the entrepreneur would have $4,000 more to reinvest at the end of the first year—a fact that the entrepreneur might neglect if he looks only at payback. As the saying goes, a bird in the hand is worth two in the bush.

Return on Investment

Let us now look at another yardstick of investment worth. As discussed earlier in the chapter, *return on investment* (ROI) tells entrepreneurs how much they may earn yearly on each dollar invested. ROI is a helpful guide because it enables entrepreneurs to compare their estimates of return with their cost of money.

Example: An entrepreneur who owns a chain of frozen-custard stands is thinking about building another outlet. Her chain is now earning an ROI of 10 percent a year—each dollar of investment earns ten cents a year after taxes.

Here, the 10 percent reflects the entrepreneur's cost of money. Every dollar that she and her shareholders take from the venture and apply toward another investment opportunity costs them ten cents of lost return, so any opportunity they consider must at least recover that ten cents for it to be worthwhile.

The entrepreneur is looking at two possible sites for the new frozen-custard stand. Both sites would require the same investment of $100,000, but sales revenues, expenses, and profits would differ (see Exhibit 13.6).

Which site should the entrepreneur choose? If her cost of money is 10 percent, she should choose Site A, because its ROI would be 20 percent a year:

$$\text{ROI}_A = \frac{\$20{,}000 \text{ a year}}{\$100{,}000} \times 100 = 20\% \text{ a year}$$

The entrepreneur should not choose Site B, because its ROI would be

EXHIBIT 13.6

Example: Choosing a Site

	Site A (yearly)	Site B (yearly)
Sales revenues	$220,000	$200,000
Operating expenses	180,000	180,000
Operating profit	$ 40,000	$ 20,000
Taxes	20,000	10,000
Net profit	$ 20,000	$ 10,000

only 10 percent a year:

$$ROI_B = \frac{\$10{,}000 \text{ a year}}{\$100{,}000} \times 100 = 10\% \text{ a year}$$

Now let us assume that Sites A and B are in neighborhoods that do not overlap but are instead ten miles apart. In that case, the entrepreneur might consider building frozen-custard stands at both sites, since Site B also promises to earn at least 10 percent a year. The reasoning here is that the entrepreneur should make as many investments as possible that promise to return at least 10 percent a year, which is her cost of money.

Note that the entrepreneur estimated her ROI by relating net profit to original investment. Another widely-used approach is to relate net profit to average investment. With this approach, the entrepreneur assumes that the frozen-custard stand would wear out gradually over its estimated useful life.

Example: If expected to last 10 years, the $100,000 frozen-custard stand would depreciate at the rate of $10,000 a year. At the end of the tenth year, the investment would shrink to zero. Thus, the average investment outstanding would be $50,000 ($\frac{1}{2} \times \$100{,}000$). Note that the ROI at both sites would be much higher:

$$ROI_A = \frac{\$20{,}000 \text{ a year}}{\$50{,}000} \times 100$$
$$= 40\% \text{ a year (versus 20\% using original investment)}$$

$$ROI_B = \frac{\$10{,}000 \text{ a year}}{\$50{,}000} \times 100$$
$$= 20\% \text{ a year (versus 10\%)}$$

Conflicting Results

So far, we have touched on three yardsticks for measuring investment worth:

- Cash payback
- Return on original investment
- Return on average investment

These three yardsticks give highly different results. In fact, one yardstick may give figures twice those given by another. An investment that shows a return of 10 percent on original investment may show as much as 20 percent on average investment.

Since the mid-1950s, many large corporations have switched to a yardstick called *present value* to resolve such confusion. It is beyond the scope of this textbook to explain this yardstick in detail. It measures the true rate of return offered by an investment opportunity by taking into account the timing of cash returns and outlays over the entire useful life of an investment opportunity. The other yardsticks do not consider these factors.

Another Application

To reinforce our understanding of investment analysis, let us review still another example.

Example: An entrepreneur who owns a laundry needs a new dryer. Two competing suppliers have submitted bids:

- Dryer A requires a cash outlay of \$10,000 and promises to return \$12,000 the first year.
- Dryer B requires a cash outlay of \$15,000 and promises to return \$17,700 the first year.

Each dryer has a useful life of one year and the entrepreneur's cost of money is 10 percent. Which dryer should he buy? He would estimate the ROI as follows:

$$\text{ROI}_{\text{A}} = \frac{\$12{,}000 - \$10{,}000}{\$10{,}000} \times 100 = 20\% \text{ a year}$$

$$\text{ROI}_{\text{B}} = \frac{\$17{,}700 - \$15{,}000}{\$15{,}000} \times 100 = 18\% \text{ a year}$$

At first glance, it may seem to the entrepreneur that Dryer A is the better investment because its ROI is higher than Dryer B's. But if he takes a closer look, he will find that Dryer B is better. The \$5,000 of extra cash required by Dryer B promises to return \$700 more cash than Dryer A, and the ROI on that extra \$5,000 is 14 percent:

$$\begin{aligned}\text{ROI}_{\text{B}-\text{A}} &= \frac{[(\$17{,}700 - \$15{,}000)]_{\text{B}} - [(\$12{,}000 - \$10{,}000)]_{\text{A}}}{\$15{,}000_{\text{B}} - \$10{,}000_{\text{A}}} \times 100 \\ &= \frac{(\$2{,}700)_{\text{B}} - (\$2{,}000)_{\text{A}}}{\$5{,}000_{\text{B}-\text{A}}} \times 100 \\ &= \underline{\underline{14\% \text{ a year}}}\end{aligned}$$

Because the 14 percent exceeds the entrepreneur's 10 percent cost of money, he would buy Dryer B.

These explanations barely scratch the surface on how best to measure the worth of investment opportunities. It is a complex subject. We wish merely to stress the need for carefully weighing the desirability of an investment opportunity by use of the yardsticks described.

In Chapters Four and Nine, we approached investment analysis from the viewpoint of entrepreneurs about to launch their venture. In this chapter, however, we have approached investment analysis from the viewpoint of entrepreneurs whose venture is established and growing. These viewpoints differ sharply. In this chapter, we looked at bits and pieces of an expanding and changing investment puzzle while in Chapters Four and Nine, we looked at the whole investment puzzle with all the pieces, as designed by the entrepreneur, already in place.

COMPUTERS

Until the late 1970s, entrepreneurs largely ignored computers as a way to help them do better jobs of planning and control. One deterrent was the high cost of computers. That situation has changed. With the invention of the microchip, a computer the size of a fingernail, the cost of computers has dropped dramatically. As a result, both computer hardware and software are today well within the budgetary reach of many entrepreneurs. *Hardware* has to do with the computer equipment itself; *software*, with the written instructions that tell computers what to do.

As shown in Exhibit 13.7, the computer revolution has already begun to engulf small business. By 1995, experts predict there will be a computer on almost every entrepreneur's desk. They likely will be as common as typewriters. At present, computers already enable entrepreneurs to do bookkeeping tasks easily. They can:

- Prepare income tax returns as well as financial statements on the basis of continuous records of revenues, costs, assets, liabilities, and so on
- Process customer orders and keep track of cash balances, accounts receivable, accounts payable, and inventory levels

Just a Beginning

The foregoing is only a sampling of the uses to which entrepreneurs may put the computer, both now and in the years to come. Just how fast the computer revolution has moved, and still is moving, is described in this 1979 quotation:

> In 1950, a computer with the same capacity as a human brain would have had to be the size of New York City and would have used more power than the subway system. In 1980, that computer would be the size of a television set. By 1990, it will be smaller than a human brain and will run on a transistor radio battery.[2]

EXHIBIT 13.7 *Estimated Number of Small Businesses Buying Computers*

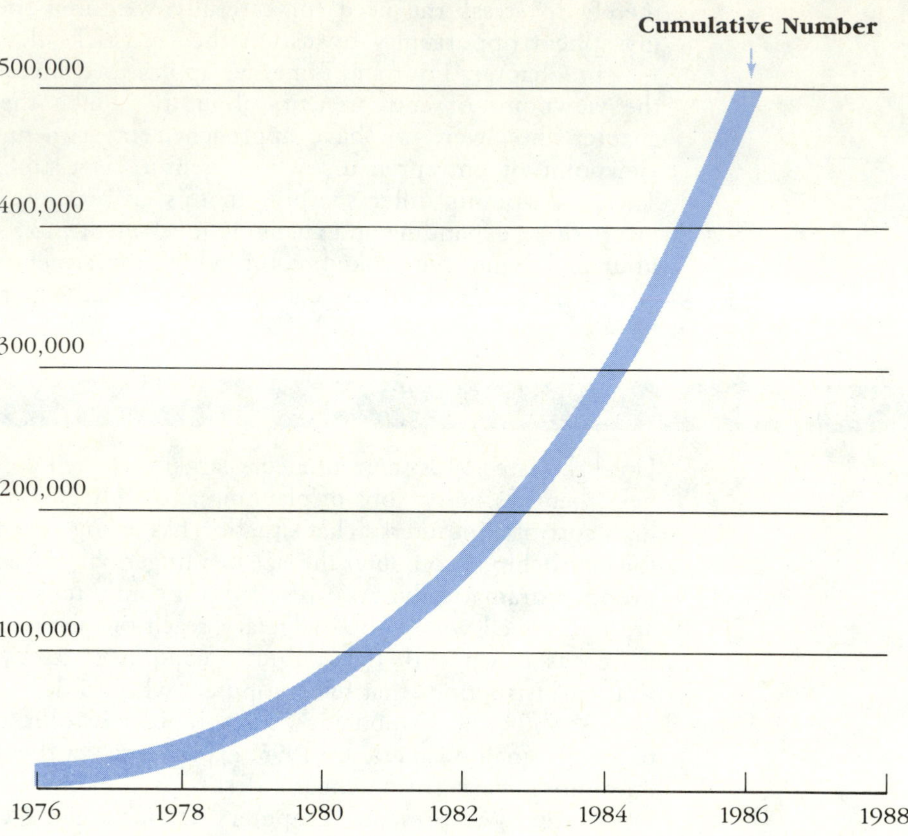

Sources: Various Articles from Data General Corporation and *The Wall Street Journal*

Few entrepreneurs can afford not to consider the use of a computer in their own ventures. The computer's ability to do the old bookkeeping tasks more efficiently is undoubted. Much more important, however, is its ability to help entrepreneurs plan and control their ventures more effectively. Computers can be used for:

- Managing projects such as plant expansion or introduction of new products
- Analyzing financial statements, as discussed earlier in this chapter
- Analyzing sales by product and by customer
- Scheduling production to minimize downtime
- Analyzing "what if" situations, such as those posed in our discussion of the profitgraph in Chapter Twelve

EXHIBIT 13.8 *Some Benefits of Using a Small Business Computer*

Applications	Reduce labor expense	Shorten billing cycle	Carry less inventory	Increase sales	Control costs	Manage cash	Plan and control growth
Accounts payable	●				●	●	●
Accounts receivable	●	●	●	●		●	●
Business modeling				●	●	●	●
General ledger	●			●	●		●
Inventory control	●	●	●	●	●	●	●
Order entry	●	●	●	●		●	●
Payroll	●				●		●
Word processing	●			●			

Source: Data General Corporation, *The Insider's Guide to Small Business Computers* (Westboro, Mass.: 1980), p. 8.

Exhibit 13.8 summarizes some of the benefits of using computers. This example shows how a computer helped an entrepreneur to plan and control his venture more effectively:

Example: Donald Hoover is a partner in a painting contracting firm in Strasburg, Pennsylvania. His firm employs 20 persons. Mr. Hoover uses a computer to run the company's payroll, accounting, and job estimating operations.

Mr. Hoover says that their initial investment in the computer was about $3,000. "I do the programming with some help from a software consultant," says Mr. Hoover. His sales revenues have grown from $50,000 to $500,000 a year. "The computer is probably what has helped us gain a competitive edge in this business, as well as maintain our growth without additional overhead costs," asserts Mr. Hoover.[3]

A Breakthrough

Few industries change as dramatically as the computer industry has. One new development of special significance to entrepreneurs is the optical memory system, which will enable them to develop extensive data bases that include all past and present information useful to them in managing their ventures. Just how dramatic a breakthrough this development may be is explained as follows:

> Although the computer industry has grown dramatically since its birth 40 years ago, memory systems have changed little. Optical memory systems are now ready for the big time, replacing the magnetic tapes, hard disks, and floppy disks that have stored information since the early 1950s.

Magnetic technology has served the industry well, but now the mature technology has reached the theoretical limits of its capacity. Top electronics researchers are having difficulty finding new ways to squeeze more information into a limited space. The optical memory advantage is that a single disk can hold two million pages of information.

That's *600* times more information than a floppy disk can hold—at a cost competitive with today's floppy disk. In fact, the entire *Encyclopedia Britannica* and the *American Heritage Dictionary* could probably fit on one optical disk. Clearly, optical memory systems will strongly benefit those entrepreneurs who are beginning to find their old magnetic memory systems inadequate for the steadily increasing use of extensive data bases.[4]

Seeking Computer Help

When entrepreneurs first consider using computers, they are often puzzled about how best to go about it. Generally, three options are open to entrepreneurs:

- Service bureaus
- Time sharing
- Use of in-house computers

Before deciding which option to adopt, an entrepreneur would be well advised to hire a computer consultant. A competent consultant can save money and hassles for the entrepreneur who knows little about computers. In selecting a consultant, the entrepreneur might follow a process like this one:

> The computer consultant's compensation, in most instances, should not be based solely on the amount of time he devotes to the client's business. The business can protect itself by contracting for a series of specific deliverables for which a fixed dollar amount is paid.
>
> A first step is ensuring that the computer consultant understands your business. The consulting engagement can begin with the consultant's preparing a problem statement that includes a narrative of the present business operation, identification of problem areas, and definition of information needs. The report must be prepared using the language and terminology of the client's business.
>
> After that, the client determines whether the computer consultant understands the business well enough to propose operating improvements. If the client isn't satisfied, he has not risked the present operation and has minimized expenditure. If the client is comfortable with the consultant's understanding of the business, the next step is commissioning a proposal for action.
>
> The contract must specify the results provided by the computer system, using language and terminology that the client can easily understand. Too often, entrepreneurs agree to purchase specific hardware and software, only to discover later that they do not solve their business problems.

Seek a computer consultant who can communicate on your terms. Avoid those who begin by discussing solutions. Avoid those who are enamored of a particular hardware or software technology. Avoid consultants who can't explain what they are doing because it is "too technical."[5]

Service Bureaus This option generally appeals to entrepreneurs who are about to use a computer for the first time. The computer itself is located at the service bureau, so the entrepreneur must carry raw data to the service bureau for processing. Several days later, the service bureau returns the analyzed data to the entrepreneur. As a rule, entrepreneurs should seek out service bureaus that will:

- Do a feasibility study of the entrepreneur's need for computer help—mostly to identify and define problems and opportunities that lend themselves to solution by computer
- Help the entrepreneur tailor the collection of raw data into a form suitable for acceptance by the computer
- Train entrepreneurs and their employees in the smooth operation of their computer system, focusing on the timely and accurate collection of data

In essence, when entrepreneurs hire a service bureau, they are hiring the services of computer experts. As such, service bureaus are always available to help entrepreneurs run their systems smoothly. A disadvantage is that service bureaus focus mostly on bookkeeping tasks like payroll, not on tasks having to do with planning and control.

Time-sharing This option generally appeals to more sophisticated entrepreneurs, mostly because time-sharing enables them to make fuller use of the computer. Where service bureaus are largely limited to bookkeeping tasks, time-sharing enables the entrepreneur to store mountains of data in the computer's memory, update the data continuously, and recall any of the data instantly. Among the sophisticated applications available are:

- Preparing a company history of financial information, focusing on income statements and balance sheets
- Preparing forecasts of sales revenues, operating expenses, and profits
- Computing financial ratios such as return on investment
- Tracking inventory, production, and quality control data

As with service bureaus, time-sharing enables entrepreneurs to use computers without having to buy or lease their own systems. Time-sharing does, however, require entrepreneurs to install computer terminals in their offices. A telephone line connects the terminal to an outside computer, thus enabling the entrepreneur to "talk" to the computer, or vice versa.

One disadvantage of time-sharing is that it costs more than a service bureau does. An entrepreneur must install either a teleprinter or a keyboard

EXHIBIT 13.9 *The Microcomputer*

The microcomputer has dramatically changed the way many entrepreneurs do business.

and television-like screen called a *CRT* (cathode ray tube) when installing a terminal.

Customer service is an advantage that time-sharing and service bureaus have in common. Time-sharing companies generally help entrepreneurs to identify and define where computers can best help them manage their ventures more efficiently. These companies also help train entrepreneurs and their employees in the smooth use of time-sharing systems.

In-house Computers This option generally appeals to the entrepreneur whose venture has grown to a size that may justify the purchase of an in-house computer. Often, such entrepreneurs have already been exposed to computers, either through service bureaus or time-sharing. Before buying a computer, however, entrepreneurs should first study:

- Precisely what their needs are and what they are projected to be
- At what costs these solutions would be justifiable.

The better the study, the better the chances that entrepreneurs will buy the in-house computer best able to serve their needs. They should expect their computers not only to do the routine bookkeeping tasks but also special tasks, especially in the areas of planning and control. As they master computer technology, entrepreneurs may also program their computers to do tasks tailor-made to their own needs, such as helping them to:

- Decide whether to add new products
- Decide whether to expand their ventures
- Decide which products to keep and which to drop
- Decide whether to lease or buy new pieces of equipment

Minicomputers vs. Microcomputers

Entrepreneurs have two options for in-house computer systems—minicomputers or microcomputers. They differ in these ways:

A *minicomputer* is a general purpose computer that can be programmed to do a variety of tasks and is generally designed so input can be entered directly into the system. For example, data such as a sales order is put into the computer at the same time the order is written. A minicomputer can be operated by users who don't have special computer knowledge. The costs for minicomputer equipment begin around $25,000 and range to more than $200,000.

The *microcomputer* is a household word if not quite yet a universal household system. It is inexpensive, small, lightweight, and can be set on a desk. Such computers run programs that do an astonishing variety of tasks and can be easily operated by personnel who do not have special computer knowledge. Prices for microcomputers begin at $1,000. They can satisfy the needs of many entrepreneurs, although they usually handle only one task at a time. There are available, however, supermicrocomputers capable of doing more than one task at a time. These cost $5,000 and up.[6]

The advantages and disadvantages of the three options open to entrepreneurs who are considering the computer are summarized in Exhibit 13.10.

Computers are now an unshakeable fact of life, first in big business and now in small business as well. As mentioned earlier, few entrepreneurs

EXHIBIT 13.10 *Advantages and Disadvantages of Three Computer Options*

	(1) Service Bureaus	(2) Time-Sharing	(3) In-House Computers	
			Mini	Micro
Hardware costs	None	Some	High	Low
Software development costs	None	Some	High	High
Computer training needed	None	Some	Some	Some
Availability of applications	Poor	Fair	Good	Good
Privacy of records	Poor	Fair	Good	Good

can afford to ignore this marvel of modern technology. It can help the entrepreneur in a variety of ways, from routine bookkeeping tasks to complex analyses. With correctly prepared input data and programs, computers do not make mistakes.

SUMMARY

Analysis of their financial statements can help entrepreneurs make sound decisions, especially in the areas of planning and control. In their analysis, entrepreneurs should keep in mind that their main financial goal is to earn a satisfactory return on the money invested in a venture, consistent with maintaining its financial health.

Ratio analysis is the technique used to analyze financial statements. Among the more important ratios are return on investment, return on sales, debt ratio, and current ratio. By themselves, ratios are meaningless, but when compared with some standard they can give entrepreneurs valuable insights into their performance.

Investment decisions involve choices that may make or break a venture. Such decisions often commit the entrepreneur's resources for years to come, so entrepreneurs must evaluate their investment opportunities wisely, using these yardsticks of investment worth:

- Cash payback
- Return on original investment
- Return on average investment

Each of these yardsticks has drawbacks that entrepreneurs must be aware of, and they should adjust their decisions accordingly.

The computer revolution has overtaken small business. A remarkably versatile tool, the computer can help entrepreneurs not only with routine bookkeeping tasks but also with creative tasks such as deciding whether to acquire another venture or to add a product.

Entrepreneurs generally have three options in selecting computers:

- Service bureaus
- Time-sharing
- In-house computers

DISCUSSION AND REVIEW QUESTIONS

1. How does analysis of financial statements help entrepreneurs plan and control more effectively?
2. What is the main financial goal of a venture? Why?
3. Can problems or opportunities be solved solely by the collection and analysis of numbers? Explain, using examples.
4. Define these terms: *ratio analysis, permanent capital, cash payback, cost of money, average investment, computer software, time-sharing*.

5. Explain the three ways of estimating return on investment. Which way is best? Why?
6. If a venture makes a profit of $15,000, is its performance good or bad? Explain.
7. What are the best ways to measure the financial health of a venture? Explain fully.
8. Why is the *after*-tax cost of interest used in estimating the return on permanent capital or the return on total assets?
9. How do solvency and liquidity differ? Which one is more important to a venture's financial health? Why?
10. Explain the pitfalls of cash payback as a way to measure the worth of an investment opportunity. How might you avoid these pitfalls?
11. What is meant by the saying, "A bird in the hand is worth two in the bush"?
12. Why would investment decisions be critical to you as an entrepreneur?
13. Besides routine bookkeeping tasks, what creative tasks can computers perform for the entrepreneur?
14. What advantages do service bureaus have over time-sharing and in-house computers? Disadvantages?
15. How should an entrepreneur go about selecting a computer?

NOTES

1. Quoted by Robert N. Anthony and James S. Reece, *Accounting* (Homewood, Ill.: Richard D. Irwin, 1983), p. 501.
2. Adapted from Christopher Evans, *The Micro Millennium* (New York: Viking Press, 1979), p. 55.
3. Adapted from Jonathan Dover, "A Systematic Approach to Get On-Line," *Inc.*, September 1980, p. 90.
4. Drawn from several sources, including *Breakthrough* and *Scientific American*.
5. Richard D. Helppie, Superior Consultant Company, West Bloomfield, Michigan, "Programming Your Computer Guru," letter appearing in *The Wall Street Journal* (Midwest ed., March 8, 1985), p. 25. Reprinted with the author's permission.
6. Michael M. Stewart and Alan C. Shulman, U.S. Small Business Administration, *How to Get Started with a Small Business Computer* (Washington, D.C.: U.S. Government Printing Office, 1984), p. 3.

CASE 13A *Computer Clubs of America, Inc.*

Founded by Elaine Stevens Angle in 1983, the Computer Clubs of America is the first venture of its kind in the country. It works on the same principle as racquet clubs, by charging membership dues and hourly fees for computer "court time." Computer Clubs even features in-house "pros" to guide learners along the path to computer literacy. Its logo appears in Exhibit 13A.1.

In business just four months at her first club in Hudson, Ms. Angle already wants to franchise her idea nationwide. "We just can't start shipping hamburgers across the country," says Ms. Angle. "In a service business like ours, the traditional franchising mechanism may not be appropriate. So we must take pains to come up with a franchise system that works best for us."

Ms. Angle now seeks $440,000 to build two more clubs, claiming that sum would enable her venture to grow to fifth-year after-tax profits of $1.9 million on sales revenues of $8.3 million. She has just prepared an 88-page business plan and mailed it to several venture-capital firms in the state.

"I'm not at all sure how the venture-capital firms will respond to my business plan," says Ms. Angle. "Although we're part of the computer industry, which is high-tech, we do not develop software. Nor do we manufacture computers. We're simply a club that teaches computers in a user-friendly way." Excerpts from her business plan follow.

Executive Summary

Our goal is to build a highly profitable corporation by enabling people to absorb computer technology optimally and then make it work for them either personally or professionally. Our major first steps are to franchise our concept into a nationwide network of computer clubs, modeled on the one in Hudson.

EXHIBIT 13A.1 *Computer Clubs of America, Inc.: Company Logo*

The purpose of this business plan is to convince venture capitalists to be our partners in achieving that goal.

The market for services like ours is, of course, excellent. The nearly universal need to be computer literate has exploded into a market expected to reach $3 billion by 1985. Our *unique* concept for capturing a significant market share is similar to that of a racquet club. Like the racquet club, our computer clubs will offer all the needed computers, software, and a "club pro" in an office setting for use by club members for a fee.

The club concept's appeal is evidenced by the major press coverage we have enjoyed in virtually every major publication in the area. One result is that we have already received twelve requests for franchises.

That our club concept works is confirmed by our membership surveys, which show that 80 percent would join again. By the way, our prototype unit in Hudson unexpectedly broke even in June, which is only the fourth month that we have been in business.

An excellent group of consultants and advisors helped us create both our venture and our business plan, particularly Dr. Joseph Seton Smith of The Center for Venture Development.

We need $440,000 to build two more clubs now. This sum, plus additional funding later, will enable us to achieve a growth rate resulting in fifth-year after-tax profits of $1.9 million on sales revenues of $8.3 million.

This is a high-risk offering, but we are extremely well-positioned to exploit one of the nation's fastest-growing markets. Even so, the prototype's success should significantly reduce the financial risk borne by such investors as venture-capital firms. Our balance sheet as of June 30, 1983 appears in Exhibit 13A.2.

EXHIBIT 13A.2 *Computer Clubs of America, Inc.: Balance Sheet (As of June 30, 1983)*

Assets			**Equities**		
Current Assets			Current Liabilities		
Cash	$19,400		Notes payable	$24,000	
Accounts receivable	9,100		Accounts payable	23,200	
Inventory	1,000	$ 29,500	Interest payable	1,900	
Fixed Assets			Taxes payable	1,800	$ 50,900
Furniture and fixtures	$38,200		Long-term Liabilities		
Hardware	28,800		Notes payable—Angle	$26,700	
Leasehold improvements	10,200				
Software	5,300		Notes payable—Freeland	10,000	
	$82,500				
Less: Accumulated depreciation	5,200	77,300	Other notes payable	32,000	68,700
Other Assets		2,400	Owners' Equity		
			Common stock	$40,500	
			Retained earnings	(50,900)	(10,400)
Total Assets		$109,200	Total Equities		$109,200

Our Concept and Its Uniqueness

The "brass ring" is the idea upon which we will build our club concept into a nationwide network of franchises located in communities clustered around large metropolitan markets. This network of community-based clubs will form the Computer Clubs of America.

As mentioned earlier, the club concept is uniquely analogous to the familiar racquet club. The analogy is carried further in the person of a "club pro," who provides guidance and education in the use of hardware and software. A unique and exclusive self-paced curriculum called the *Guided Learning Method** is used by members to gain computer literacy. A relaxed and informative atmosphere, conducive to learning is maintained. Computer supplies, reference books, software, and other materials are sold in our "pro shop."

In a time when *Business Week* publishes feature stories about "computer shock" and says "wild proliferation" dominates the confusing computer market, our uniqueness is a powerful advantage. In fact, the national computer weekly, *InfoWorld*, has told us they know of no other business using the club concept and has asked that we write an article for publication.

Pursuit of Excellence

To achieve fifth-year sales revenues of $8.3 million, we must first earn a reputation for excellence in our area market. That requires us to have both a high-quality corporate services group serving prestige clients and a highly successful cluster of computer clubs. It also requires us to put a high priority on:

- Developing proprietary products and services that help us to keep well ahead of competitors
- Designing accounting systems that help us to control operating costs
- Attracting and developing the best available talent—men and women who not only possess a sound knowledge of computers but who are able to communicate that knowledge to others

We took the first step toward our sales goal in March 1983, when we opened our prototype club in Hudson. Our objective was to use this site to test:

- The appeal of the club concept to prospective members
- The ability of the club concept to successfully deliver computer learning to members

We intend to open two more clubs by the spring of 1984, or sooner, depending on the speed of financing. Expansion strategies beyond our metropolitan area will be carefully researched during Year One.

An outside view of the computer club in Hudson appears in Exhibit 13A.3, along with Ms. Angle.

* Trademark

EXHIBIT 13A.3 *Computer Clubs of America, Inc.: A View of Elaine Stevens Angle and the Computer Club*

Capturing and Maintaining Market Leadership

It is important to point out that our potential spreads far beyond the initial market thrust of the computer club in Hudson and its current concept for computer training.

At this point, however, our strategies must focus on protecting our unique club concept for delivering computer training. Since ideas can best be protected by high-quality work and by growth in sales and profits, it is vital that we move quickly to expand nationwide—without, of course, sacrificing quality and excellence in our initial marketing activities.

The fast growth of competitive offerings in just the last six months suggests that competition will be fierce. Hastily assembled computer classes are being offered by high schools, by universities, and by retail computer stores on virtually every corner. Moreover, this market will continue to attract large corporations. We intend to beat our competitors by maneuvering around them with well-positioned offerings and with aggressive marketing methods. Specifically, we plan to:

- Acquire copyrights and trademarks to identify our programs and services that are distinctive and unique. One example is our *Guided Learning*

Method, which combines self-paced learning with tutorial instruction in a user-friendly atmosphere. This intensely personal format for delivering knowledge and services will form a fundamental part of our club concept.

- Use multi-media advertising and computer telemarketing to build and sustain traffic flow through our computer clubs. Preparations for expansion nationwide will begin by marketing our club concept selectively.

Moreover, the racquet club concept for our computer clubs gives us an edge in the marketplace. For example:

- *Marketing* of the computer club concept is enhanced by the consumer's instant familiarity with the racquet club concept.
- *Profitability* is enhanced by the consumer's acceptance of membership fees and "pro shop" sales of software and other products.
- *Cost efficiency* is enhanced by the bundling of services designed around the use of the same equipment and personnel. Too, "racquet club hours" offer members access to computers outside the fringes of the regular workweek, thus further increasing the efficiency of our operations.
- *Our image of success* is enhanced by our reputation for a distinctively high-quality service, one that is preferred over other training methods as the "right" place to acquire computer literacy.

Some Marketing Problems The foregoing discussion creates the impression that marketing our club concept will pose few, if any, problems. To balance the discussion, let us now touch on some of the problems:

- We are a small company attacking a giant, fast-moving market, one that will attract many larger and stronger companies as competitors. There will also be a scarcity of entrepreneurial and technological talent to fuel our growth.
- The club concept will be difficult to protect against competitors who would choose to imitate us. But, as mentioned earlier, we believe that protection is best served by high-quality performance and superior marketing strategies.
- The so-called "fearful-computer-illiterate" market will mature and begin to decline by the end of the decade. Vigilant sensitivity to advances in technology and their market exploitation will be vital to our long-term survival and growth.

Future Leadership in the "Tech-Knowledge Age"

Recognizing that the dawn of microcomputers in 1978 was less than six years ago, we are vividly aware that our society is advancing at more than just a normal evolutionary pace.

With the industrial revolution having provided the runway and technology the vaulting pole, our society now finds its entire weight poised at full compression upon the force of a new era as the information explosion catapults us toward a whole new way of doing things.

The magnitude of change created by this new era is just now becoming widely apparent. We foresee that, in a few short years, the most powerful personal technology will be the majestic marriage of the microcomputer with both video and telecommunications. Such a union will provide us with all but unlimited capability for the delivery of human ideas. And, with the union of these converging technologies will come the full arrival of what we call the "Tech-Knowledge Age."

These phenomena will provide our company with new markets as well as new ways to serve these markets, through our nationwide network of franchised computer clubs. Technological change and confusion will not end but instead will increase with lightning speed, requiring learning services for technical skills not even defined yet.

In short, our continued leadership in the marketplace will be made possible by our ability to continue providing people, in their own communities, with an ever-expanding set of state-of-the-art resources for absorbing the latest advances of the "Tech-Knowledge Age."

Management Team and Organization

We will reach an employment level in the first year of 22 full-time and at least 6 part-time employees. Two of the new employees will work in our corporate services group designing corporate course materials as well as refining our *Guided Learning Method.*

From June through December 1983, we plan to devote about 70 percent of our managerial energies to such high-priority pursuits as:

- Raising venture capital
- Designing technology-based programs
- Selecting sites for new computer clubs
- Interviewing and hiring employees
- Evaluating and selecting software
- Designing shop space

During the fall of 1983, our company will seek to hire a strong operations and financial management person. Her job will be to enhance our ability to:

- Maintain profitable operations
- Develop accounting systems that help to control costs
- Design financial systems that alert us to cash flow problems

Exhibit 13A.4 shows the projected growth in personnel from 1984 through 1988.

Profiles of Key Managers

In our pursuit of excellence, we have already enlisted the talents of several men and women capable of growing with our company. Their

EXHIBIT 13A.4

Computer Clubs of America, Inc.: Growth in Corporate Personnel (1984–1988)

	Number of Personnel				
Position	**1984**	**1985**	**1986**	**1987**	**1988**
Chief Executive Officer	1	1	1	1	1
Chairman of the Board	1	1	1	1	1
Vice President of Operations	1	1	1	1	1
Director of Instructional Technologies	1	1	1	1	1
Director of Membership	1	1	1	1	1
Secretaries and Assistants	1	2	3	4	4
Consultants	3	6	10	15	15
Instructional Designers and Writers		1	1	1	1
Machine Language Programmers		1	1	2	2
Finance Officer		1	1	1	1
Clerks		1	2	3	3
Office Manager			1	1	1
	9	17	24	32	32

profiles follow:

Elaine Stevens Angle, Chief Executive Officer Recently named to *Who's Who of American Women*, Ms. Angle brings more than 18 years of business experience to our company. Her strong managerial background adds depth to our ability to develop business applications.

A consultant for ANACOMP-Computer Management from 1978 to 1980, Ms. Angle was involved in strategic planning. Her prior background includes consumer marketing, advertising, product management, and product development.

Ms. Angle holds several patents for the development of a small electric appliance. With a marketing education from Northwestern University and graduate work in business administration at Harvard University, Ms. Angle developed the racquet club model for the computer club concept. She also developed the self-paced learning curriculum called the *Guided Learning Method*.

Eric Arnold, Board Chairman One of the foremost microcomputer consultants in the state, Mr. Arnold has developed and taught many of the microcomputer courses at the University of Akron. He studied engineering at Bucknell University and then changed majors to receive a degree in music composition and education.

Mr. Arnold has also studied at the graduate school of business administration of Kent State University. His professional background combining education with microcomputers also includes extensive development work in such related state-of-the-art technologies as video and telecommunications.

Mr. Arnold is in great demand by business for his abilities to custom-design and instruct microcomputer training programs. He is also expert at consulting with executives to meet their specific needs for microcomputer applications.

Susan Arnold, Director of Instructional Technologies A graduate of the University of Akron with a degree in elementary education, Ms. Arnold taught for seven years before becoming an instructional workshop designer and coordinator for a television station. She brings strong microcomputer teaching and design capabilities to our staff.

Diana Freeland, Director of Membership An honors graduate in English from the University of California at Berkeley, Ms. Freeland's background has been in educational administrative areas and in the development of communications skills. She is knowledgeable in the use of, and teaching of, word processing. Ms. Freeland is responsible for public relations as well as member recruitment and member services.

David Richard, "Club Pro" Mr. Richard joined us after having managed and instructed a computer day-camp program. He received his degree in education from the University of Akron and is currently completing his masters work in computer-based education there. He is the "Club Pro" at the Computer Club of Hudson.

Lynn Rojahn, Consultant With more than 20 years in the computer industry, Ms. Rojahn began with IBM as a systems engineer in applications development. She received her degree in mathematics from Chatham College in Pittsburgh. In 1979, she shifted to the field of microcomputers and joined us after an independent consulting career as a personal computer applications programmer.

Stock Summary and Private Placement Disclaimer*

The company was incorporated as the Computer Clubs of America, Inc., on January 5, 1983, with a total of 750 shares of common stock authorized for sale. As of September 1983, 308 shares have been issued to 14 investors, 7 of whom are employees or relatives.

The information contained in this business plan is confidential and is intended for the persons to whom it is transmitted by the company. Any reproduction of this plan, in whole or in part, or the divulgence of any of its contents without the prior written consent of the company is prohibited.

No person has been authorized to give any information or to make any representations other than those contained in this plan in connection with the offering thereby, and, if given or made, such other information or

* Prepared by the company's attorney.

representations must not be relied upon as having been authorized by the company.

This plan does not constitute an offer to sell or solicitation of an offer to buy any securities other than the securities offered hereby, nor does it constitute an offer to sell or solicitation of an offer to buy from any person in any state or other jurisdiction in which such offer would be unlawful.

Offers and sales of common stock will only be made to persons who have the knowledge and experience to evaluate the merits and risks of the investment and who have the economic means to afford the illiquidity of the securities offered hereby.

EXHIBIT 13A.5

Computer Clubs of America, Inc.: Five-year Growth Plan: Addition of Clubs in Beachwood, Columbus, Pittsburgh, and Cincinnati

Year 1 1984	Year 2 1985	Year 3 1986	Year 4 1987	Year 5 1988
Prototype Club: Hudson	Prototype Club: Hudson	Prototype Club: Hudson	Prototype Club: Hudson	Prototype Club: Hudson
CC of A, Inc.	*CC of A, Inc.*	*CC of A, Inc.*	*CC of A, Inc.*	*CC of A, Inc.*
Club # 1 Beachwood	Club # 1 Beachwood	Club # 1 Beachwood	Club # 1 Beachwood	Club # 1 Beachwood
Club # 2	Club # 2	Club # 2	Club # 2	Club # 2
Club # 3	Club # 3	Club # 3	Club # 3	Club # 3
	Club # 4	Club # 4	Club # 4	Club # 4
	Club # 5	Club # 5	Club # 5	Club # 5
		Club # 6	Club # 6	Club # 6
		Columbus *Franchise*	Columbus *Franchise*	Columbus *Franchise*
		Club # 1	Club # 1	Club # 1
		Club # 2	Club # 2	Club # 2
			Club # 3	Club # 3
			Club # 4	Club # 4
				Club # 5
				Club # 6
			Pittsburgh *Franchise*	Pittsburgh *Franchise*
			Club # 1	Club # 1
			Club # 2	Club # 2
			Club # 3	Club # 3
				Club # 4
				Club # 5
				Club # 6
				Cincinnati *Franchise*
				Club # 1
				Club # 2
				Club # 3

The information set forth herein is believed by the company to be reliable. It must be recognized, however, that predictions and projections as to the company's future performance are necessarily subject to a high degree of uncertainly and no warranty of such projections is expressed or implied.

Immediate Financial Needs

Our five-year growth plan calls for the launching of three franchises by 1988, with each franchise operating a cluster of six computer clubs. Our growth plan appears in Exhibit 13A.5.

As mentioned in the Executive Summary, we will need $440,000 to build just two units, both modeled on the computer club in Hudson. In Exhibit 13A.6, we show how the $440,000 would be spent. Exhibits 13A.7 and 13A.8 show our five-year income statement and cash flow projections.

EXHIBIT 13A.6

Computer Clubs of America, Inc.: Uses of $440,000 Investment

$ 67,900	IBM and Apple microcomputers
64,100	Corporate use equipment
63,000	Professional development program
60,000	Furniture and fixtures
25,000	Kick-off marketing expenses
25,000	Pre-opening expenses
23,000	Software library
20,000	"Pro shop" inventory
18,000	Leasehold improvements
16,500	Computerization of club's administrative controls
15,000	Management recruiting
10,000	Facility design and interior decorating
10,000	Patent and trademark work
9,300	Refinement of *Guided Learning Method*
3,200	Telemarketing development
10,000	Miscellaneous
$440,000	Total uses

EXHIBIT 13A.7

Computer Clubs of America, Inc.: Five-year Projected Income Statements (In Thousands of Dollars)

	1984	1985	1986	1987	1988
Sales revenues					
Corporate sales	$ 251	$1,139	$2,314	$3,200	$3,500
Club sales	537	1,778	3,131	3,295	3,375
Franchise sales	0	156	437	795	1,387
Total sales revenues	$ 788	$3,073	$5,882	$7,290	$8,262
Operating expenses	1,198	2,450	3,902	4,734	4,838
Profit before taxes	$ (410)	$ 623	$1,980	$2,556	$3,424
Federal income taxes	0	0	743	1,156	1,482
Profit after taxes	$ (410)	$ 623	$1,237	$1,400	$1,942

EXHIBIT 13A.8

Computer Clubs of America, Inc.: Five-year Cash Flow Projections (In Thousands of Dollars)

	1984	1985	1986	1987	1988
Cash inflows					
Cash customers	$ 537	$1,515	$2,905	$3,603	$4,046
Credit customers	223	1,371	2,766	3,533	4,002
Total cash inflows	$ 760	$2,886	$5,671	$7,136	$8,048
Cash outflows					
Operating expenses	$1,013	$2,038	$3,427	$4,284	$4,604
Asset acquisitions	346	400	200	0	0
Repayment of loans	16	26	0	0	58
Interest	2	0	0	0	30
Federal income taxes	0	0	743	1,156	1,482
Total cash outflows	$1,377	$2,464	$4,370	$5,440	$6,174
Cash surplus (Shortage)	$ (617)	$ 422	$1,301	$1,696	$1,874

Questions

1. What is the potential for companies like Ms. Angle's in the computer industry? What lies ahead?
2. What are the keys to successfully franchising a computer club like Ms. Angle's?
3. If you were a venture capitalist, would you invest in the company? Why?
4. Comment on Ms. Angle's entrepreneurial traits.
5. What suggestions, if any, would you make to improve Ms. Angle's business plan?

CASE 13B *Pete's Garage*

Unincorporated, Pete's garage operates as a gasoline station and repair shop. Its owner is Peter Bingham. In business for himself for 10 years, Mr. Bingham has always paid his bills promptly.

Most of his repair work comes from small truckers. He also overhauls school buses under contract with the local school district.

It is now September and Mr. Bingham would like to borrow $10,000 to buy antifreeze and tire chains. He believes his current customers will need these goods in the winter to come. He has always lacked the cash to stock such goods and he is still cash-poor.

Mr. Bingham has never borrowed from a bank before, but he knew that his banker would ask for his latest financial statements, so he had his accountant prepare the financial statements shown in Exhibit 13B.1.

When he sat down with his banker, Mr. Bingham told him he would earn a 35 percent gross profit on the sale of antifreeze and tire chains. He also promised to repay the $10,000 loan by February 1, since customers usually buy these goods during October, November, and December—and not later.

EXHIBIT 13B.1

Pete's Garage: Balance Sheet (August 31)

Assets		**Equities**	
Cash	$ 1,000	Accounts payable	$ 2,000
Accounts receivable	12,000	Owner's equity	72,000
Inventory	9,000		
Building and fixtures	52,000		
Total assets	$74,000	Total equities	$74,000

Pete's Garage: Income Statement (for year ending August 31)

Sales revenues		$200,000
Cost of sales		122,000
Gross profit		$ 78,000
Operating expenses		
Salary	$18,000	
Other	54,000	72,000
Operating profit		$ 6,000

Questions

1. If you were the banker, what other information would you like before making a decision? Why?
2. Where would you get the additional information?
3. On the information given, does this loan look like a sound investment? Why?

Source: This case was developed in 1966 by John B. McCarter for use by Central National Bank of Cleveland.

CASE 13C *Cedar & Associates, Inc.*

Robert Pizzuli, founder of Cedar & Associates, has just received from his accountant the financial statements appearing in condensed form in Exhibits 13C.1 and 13C.2. The company makes specialty chemicals. Mr. Pizzuli has asked you to help him analyze the financial statements.

EXHIBIT 13C.1

Cedar & Associates, Inc.: 1984 Income Statement

Sales revenues	$1,023,000
Cost of goods sold	801,100
Gross profit	$ 221,900
Selling and administrative expenses	173,000
Operating profit	$ 48,900
Interest expense	2,800
Profit before income taxes	$ 46,100
Income taxes	13,100
Profit after taxes	$ 33,000

EXHIBIT 13C.2 *Cedar & Associates, Inc.: Balance Sheet (December 31, 1984)*

Assets			**Equities**		
Current Assets			Current Liabilities		
Cash	$ 99,200		Notes payable	$ 92,200	
Accounts receivable	177,600		Accounts payable	38,900	
Inventories	308,400		Income taxes payable	7,200	$ 138,300
Prepaid insurance	13,000	$ 598,200	Owners' Equity		
Fixed Assets			Common stock	$964,700	
Plant and equipment	$892,800		Retained earnings	85,600	1,050,300
Less: Accumulated depreciation	302,400	590,400	Total Equities		$1,188,600
Total Assets		$1,188,600			

Questions

1. Calculate the following ratios: return on assets, return on owners' equity, return on sales revenues, receivables turnover, inventory turnover, current ratio, quick ratio, and times interest earned.
2. What questions would you ask Mr. Pizzuli, based on these ratios?

14 MARKETING

QUESTIONS FOR MASTERY

What is marketing?
How important is marketing research?
How should marketing research be carried out?
How do the various marketing activities fit together to form a marketing mix?
How can one take advantage of the opportunities available in exports markets?

You can tell the ideals of a nation by its advertisements.

Norman Douglas

The entrepreneur's main goal is to create satisfied customers at a profit. Marketing helps to do that by moving products or services out of the hands of the entrepreneur and into those of customers. There is a wide spectrum of marketing tools, each one reinforcing the other, including:

- Marketing research
- Advertising and sales promotion
- Personal selling
- Pricing
- Packaging and distribution
- Service

In this chapter, we shall focus on each of these marketing activities, paying special attention to marketing research and the preparation of marketing plans. The final section of the chapter will explore the special field of export marketing.

MARKETING RESEARCH

Many experts claim that marketing research is the most important marketing activity of all. Why? Because it helps satisfy the never-ending need for knowledge about markets, including:

- What products or services to sell
- Where to sell them, in what quantities, at what prices
- What competitors are selling, where they are, how strong they are

A venture's survival and growth depend largely on the quality of its marketing research. It is just as vital to do research after a venture begins as it is before. Yet marketing research tends to be ignored by entrepreneurs. The belief that it is an activity that only giant corporations can afford is erroneous. Marketing research falls within reach of every entrepreneur, no matter how small. Defining, finding, and analyzing the facts about markets are activities any entrepreneur can master. To show what marketing research is like, let us go through an example:

Example: One of the simplest full-time ventures is the corner newsstand in big cities like New York. If the entrepreneur is doing a successful job selling newspapers and magazines, he is doing marketing research. Before telling his supplier how many newspapers he wants each day, the entrepreneur has settled some important marketing matters.

He knows how many newspapers he usually sells on each day of the week—a fact he has on tap from his own experience. Then our entrepreneur checks the weather each day and considers what effect it may have on the number of people in town and in the mood to stop and buy a newspaper. He uses this second fact in deciding how many papers to buy each day.

The two facts are not enough, though. Our entrepreneur next checks to see if there are any special events, conventions, or meetings that might bring additional customers by his corner. He might even go so far as to check to see what stores are having special sales. This is a third fact that he uses in his decision-making process.

Because our entrepreneur is really on his toes, he checks the early edition to see if there are any special news events that may add extra customer interest. When his newspapers arrive, he may make a quick survey to see if there is any news item of special interest that he may be able to exploit for extra sales—a fourth fact he has in his possession.

Our entrepreneur goes through this process before he tells the supplier how many papers he wants. This process is called marketing research—in short, getting all the facts available on:

- Customer interest
- Market potential
- Market mood
- Environmental conditions[1]

A Mistaken Attitude

This example shows why marketing research falls within reach of every entrepreneur—and why it bears strongly on success. Chances are that most entrepreneurs do marketing research before beginning their venture. For example, decisions about where to locate their venture, what sales revenues to expect the first year, and how much money they need to finance their venture—all are usually based on facts, not opinions. After start-up, however, entrepreneurs often fail to get new facts, mistakenly assuming that their markets will not change.

This attitude is dangerous. Unless they remain in tune with their markets, entrepreneurs may soon find themselves without customers. Today, buying habits change so quickly that success belongs largely to those entrepreneurs who keep a close watch on their markets and, if necessary, quickly change their line of products or services to keep pace. For example, public taste has shifted away from the hot dog toward the gyro, the taco, and the pizza:

- The gyro, a Greek creation of lamb, tomato, and onion, has replaced the hot dog in many eastern cities.
- The taco, a Mexican concoction of ground meat and spices, has become a short-order favorite in the Southwest.
- The pizza is now one of the most popular snacks among 21- to 34-year-olds, according to the Gallup poll.

Exhibit 14.1 underscores the process of marketing research as an activity that any entrepreneur can master. The process itself is both logical and straightforward to follow.

EXHIBIT 14.1 *Marketing Research Process*

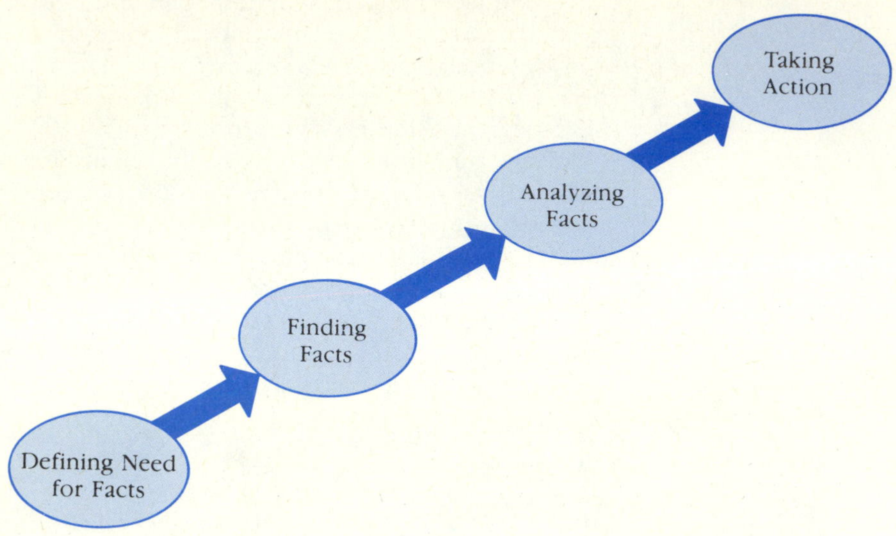

Kinds of Facts

So far, we have touched on the purposes of marketing research. Let us now examine the kinds of facts it can generate. Consider an entrepreneur who is about to make pocket calculators. With the help of marketing research, the entrepreneur can uncover many facts about the market by asking questions about these topics:

Nature of product: What is the product like, both physically and chemically? How is it used? How is it made?

Nature of market: How big is the industry? What is the industry like? Where are customers concentrated?

Market size and outlook: How many can be sold yearly? How many have been sold yearly in the past five years? What factors affect the outlook for the market?

Pricing: How have prices changed over the past five years? What influences price? What will future prices be like?

Production: What product specifications should the production process meet? How should the product be packaged? What patent rights should be purchased?

Competition: Who are competitors? Where are they? What is their production capacity? What are their strengths and weaknesses? What is the outlook for capacity?

Marketing: Through what channels are products sold? Out of each marketing dollar, roughly how much is spent for advertising, sales promotion, personal selling, and servicing?

Although this set of questions applies specifically to manufacturing, much of it also applies to retailing, services, and wholesaling.

More Research Questions

The preceding list of questions helps to expand our understanding of marketing research. To clinch our understanding, let us now explain it in another way. Again using pocket calculators as our example, we can see that marketing research helps entrepreneurs to answer such questions as these:

- Who is buying or will buy
  What pocket calculator in
  What quantities of
  What specifications at
  What price in
  What kind of package against
  What competitors?
- What competitors are supplying pocket calculators with
  What capabilities at
  What plant sites with
  What capacities?
- What opportunities are there for us with
  What calculators of
  What quality at
  What price under
  What marketing conditions in
  What quantities at
  What future periods?

Uses of Marketing Research

Marketing research replaces opinion with fact. Getting the facts helps offset the risks of doing business in today's fast-changing markets. All too often entrepreneurs ignore facts that bear heavily on their success and can be obtained readily. Instead, they make decisions on the basis of opinion or impulse. Working without facts, entrepreneurs may decide to take such actions as these:

- Add a new product because their nearest competitor just did
- Draft a new plan to build revenues because they think it will work
- Add a new service because they hear that customers like it

Small wonder, then, that so many entrepreneurs fall by the wayside. They lose sight of the fact that their success begins and ends with the *customer*; their one key to success is to know what attracts customers better than their competitors do.

It is the entrepreneur's unique job to anticipate, adjust to, and capitalize on the sweeping changes that mark our times. In this regard, Professor Theodore Levitt of Harvard University has this to say:

> An essential starting point is always to ask oneself: "What kind of society will we have in, say, five, ten, or twenty years? What does it mean for

my company and its orientation?" Had the railroads asked themselves these germinal questions fifty years ago, they might now be making less frequent trips to Washington with tin cup in hand.[2]

Setting Realistic Goals

The more facts they have, the better may entrepreneurs forge niches in the marketplace that are specially suited to their skills and desires.

Example: A videocassette rental business in Michigan offers door-to-door pickup and delivery of tapes, the only outlet in the area to do so. The store also delivers dinner for an extra $5 to $8 a person. The results? Although it charges more for rentals than other stores, its services are so popular that the business opened seven outlets in its first four months of operation.[3]

To find their niches, entrepreneurs should be futurists, always looking ahead. As such, they should get the facts that enable them to:

- Identify which markets are the most profitable to go after
- Identify soft spots in market coverage
- Choose new products or services that customers want
- Find out why existing products or services are selling well or poorly
- Set realistic market goals

Setting realistic market goals is the logical end of marketing research. If they fail to set such goals, entrepreneurs are unlikely to know where they stand and, equally important, in what direction they are moving, as in this example:

Example: A tire dealer sold 10 percent more tires than he did the year before. "It's the best year I've had so far," he said. But what he did not realize was that his growth was not keeping up with the growth of his market area. The area's population had grown by 30 percent.

Even though his sales went up 10 percent, the tire dealer was not getting his share of the market. Instead, he was falling behind. But that fact had escaped him entirely.[4]

Definition of Market

We have been using the word *market* without defining it. There is no one best definition since, depending on its context, the word *market* may have many different meanings.

People sometimes use it to refer to a specific location where products are bought and sold. A large geographic area also may be called a *market*. Sometimes it refers to the relationship between the demand and supply of a specific product or service. It has this meaning, for example, in the question, "How is the *market* for diamonds?" At times, it also is used to mean the act of selling something.[5]

As used in this book, however, the word *market* refers to groups of individuals or organizations seeking products or services in the entrepreneur's industry. It is assumed that these groups have the desire, the buying power, and the willingness to buy the entrepreneur's products.

Market Segmentation

Market segmentation is the process of dividing a total market into market groups of customers who have similar needs for either a product or a service. Thus, a market segment would be any group of customers who share one or more traits that make them have similar product needs.

Example: A clothier located in a large city may decide to direct his marketing efforts at young professional men between the ages of 21 and 34. Therefore, he would carry only those suits, shirts, and other apparel that his marketing research told him would probably appeal to upwardly-mobile young men.

As this example suggests, the market segmentation approach requires the entrepreneur to focus on just one part or just a few parts of the total

EXHIBIT 14.2 *Selected Ways of Segmenting Markets*

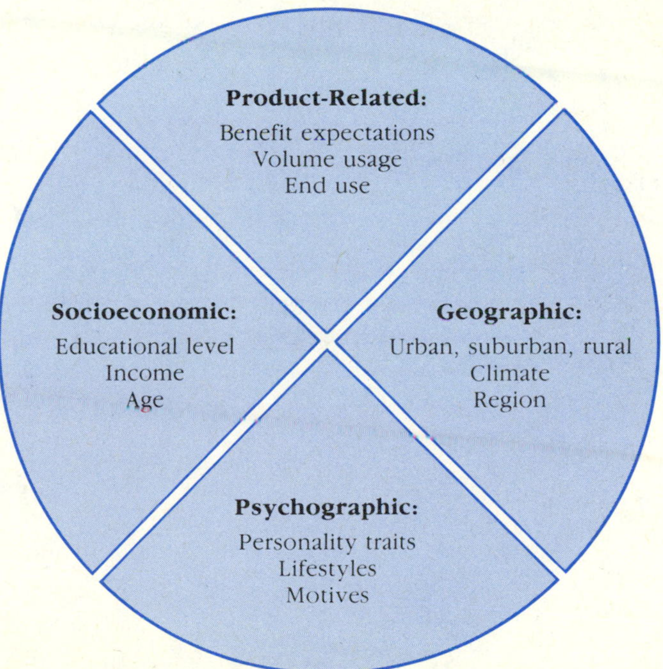

Source: Adapted from William M. Pride and O. C. Ferrell, *Marketing* (Boston, Mass.: Houghton Mifflin Company, 1985), p. 46. Copyright © 1985 by Houghton Mifflin Company. Used by permission of the publisher.

market rather than all of it. Exhibit 14.2 shows some of the ways that entrepreneurs may segment their markets. As shown in the exhibit, the ways to segment may be grouped into four categories:

- Product-related
- Geographic
- Psychographic
- Socioeconomic

Product-Related Factors

Here entrepreneurs may divide the market according to the benefits that customers expect from the product. By using marketing research to learn which benefits customers want, entrepreneurs may be able to divide customers into groups. For example:

- One group of camera customers may be looking for a product that takes reasonably good pictures, is easy to operate with a minimum amount of adjustment, and is inexpensive, while another group wants top-quality pictures and is willing to go to any expense.

Other product-related ways to segment markets include volume usage and end use. For instance, to satisfy customers who use a product in a certain way, some feature—say color, size, or texture—may have to be designed precisely to make the product easier to use, safer, or more convenient. In addition, special pricing or sales promotion activities may have to be created.

Geographic Factors

Geographic factors—such as climate, terrain, and natural resources—may also influence customers' product needs. Entrepreneurs may divide their markets into regions because some geographic factor causes customers to differ from one region to another. For example:

- Pizza Hut changes its pizzas from one region to another because customer preferences vary by region. Easterners want lots of cheese, Westerners prefer a greater variety of ingredients, and Midwesterners like both.[7]

Climate is also commonly used as a geographic segmentation factor because it has such a broad effect on people's behavior and product needs. Just think of the wide variety of product markets that are affected by climate. A few examples would include air conditioning and heating equipment, clothing, yard equipment, sports equipment, and building materials.

Psychographic Factors

Although many psychographic factors could be used to segment markets, the three most common are personality traits, motives, and lifestyles. Examples of personality traits that entrepreneurs may use to segment markets are gregariousness, compulsiveness, competitiveness, extroversion, introversion, ambitiousness, and aggressiveness. Marketing based on personality traits is useful when a product is similar to many competing products and customer needs are not affected significantly by other segmentation factors.

In marketing their products, entrepreneurs should select personality traits that are valued by many people in our culture. For example, an entrepreneur may promote a product as "not for everyone" but for those who are "independent," "strong-minded," or "outgoing." Entrepreneurs who take this approach need not worry about measuring the actual number of people who have the positively valued trait—they can simply assume that a sizable proportion of people in the target market either have it or want to have it.

Motives are the internal energizing forces that move an individual toward a goal. To some degree, motives influence what people buy and, therefore, may be used to divide markets. Product durability, economy, convenience, and status are all motives that may affect the types of products purchased and the choice of stores in which they are bought.

When segmenting a market according to a motive, an entrepreneur must examine the customers' reasons for making a purchase. For example, one motive for the purchase of lawn power mowers is convenience.

Socioeconomic Factors

Socioeconomic factors are commonly used to divide markets. Such factors are closely related to customers' product needs and purchasing. Socioeconomic factors can also be measured readily through observation or surveys. Consider the types of product markets that are segmented according to age:

- Some examples are clothing, diet foods, automobiles, and toys. Exhibit 14.3 shows a possible segmentation scheme for the toy market. Note that with the exception of the twelve-to-adult segment, the segments contain relatively small cross-sections. The divisions are narrow because children's needs for toys change rapidly; a toy that entertains children at age two rarely interests them at age five.

Income is often used to divide a market because it strongly influences people's product needs. It affects their ability to buy and their aspirations for a certain style of living. Examples of product markets segmented by income include housing, furniture, clothing, automobiles, food, and certain kinds of sporting goods.

How Marketing Research is Done

In a giant corporation, the president may draw on many in-house resources for marketing research. Such corporations have marketing research departments staffed with high-powered professionals, many with master's degrees in business administration. Du Pont, for example, has more than 500 professionals in its marketing research department.

EXHIBIT 14.3 *Segmentation of the Toy Market*

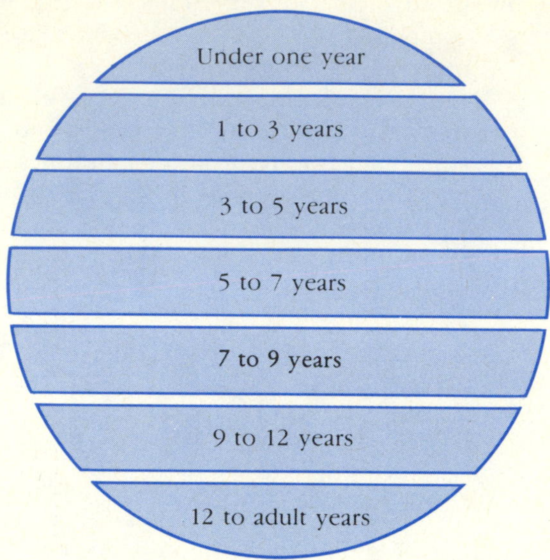

Source: Adapted from William M. Pride and O. C. Ferrell, *Marketing* (Boston, Mass.: Houghton Mifflin Company, 1985), p. 47. Copyright © 1985 by Houghton Mifflin Company. Used by permission of the publisher.

But few entrepreneurs can justify hiring a marketing researcher, let alone establishing a marketing research department. So how do entrepreneurs get the facts about their markets? They can get the facts by:

- Tapping information already compiled by public libraries, trade associations, Chambers of Commerce, the U.S. Department of Commerce, suppliers, and the marketing research departments of local daily newspapers
- Buying the services of a marketing research firm
- Organizing a part-time marketing research effort within their own venture

Perhaps the best way to begin is by using statistical data already worked up by Chambers of Commerce, trade associations, and the U.S. Department of Commerce. Often available at no fee, such information yields the greatest return on the time and effort spent by the entrepreneur. As already mentioned in Chapter Eight, entrepreneurs may use U.S. Census Bureau data to draw profiles of their markets by estimating:

- The percentage of persons in their marketing area who are under 10 years old, 10 to 19, 20 to 30, and so on
- The average yearly income per family
- The percentage of families who own their home
- The percentage of families who own automobiles

From such statistical data, entrepreneurs may draw all kinds of useful conclusions about their markets, as this example shows:

Example: An entrepreneur who owned a supermarket could readily measure her market potential as follows:

22,000	Population of Dover (from U.S. Census Bureau)
× $6,000	Per capita income yearly (from U.S. Census Bureau)
$132,000,000	Gross income per year
× 0.14	Percentage spent on groceries (from trade association)
$ 18,480,000	Total market potential

She might then go one step further and estimate her share of the market. Her yearly sales revenues are $3,696,000, so her share of the market would then be 20 percent:

$$(\$3{,}696{,}000 \div \$18{,}480{,}000) \times 100 = 20\%$$

The entrepreneur might now carry her analysis one step further and compare her store's performance with that of other supermarkets in the area. There are three competing supermarkets. She estimates that her competitors are averaging sales of $4,928,000 a year:

$$(\$18{,}480{,}000 - \$3{,}696{,}000) \div 3 = \$4{,}928{,}000$$

Clearly, our entrepreneur's work is cut out for her. Competitors are doing 33 percent better than she is:

$$[(\$4{,}928{,}000 - \$3{,}696{,}000) \div \$3{,}696{,}000] \times 100 = 33\%$$

Of course, such analysis does not explain why her performance falls short. But it does raise these pertinent questions:

- Why are competing supermarkets attracting more customers?
- What are they doing to attract customers that I am not doing?
- What changes should I make in advertising, sales promotion, and personal selling to boost sales?
- Am I offering the right mix of food products?

Answers to such questions may lead to further marketing research. Our entrepreneur may, for example, decide to do a consumer survey to find out:

- What homemakers in her marketing area want in a supermarket
- How they choose a supermarket
- Their general feelings about supermarkets

Need for Professional Help

If initial marketing research leads entrepreneurs to the decision to do a consumer survey, they might design and do the consumer survey themselves, with help from employees, but they would be wise to hire the services of a marketing researcher instead. Consumer research is not for beginners. It takes the skills of a professional to work up a questionnaire free of bias—the basic requirement for a survey.

Designing a questionnaire requires more than simply asking questions. Questions should be designed in ways that produce the most accurate replies. The very wording of a question may imply a bias and thus influence the reply.

Besides helping to draft bias-free questions, a marketing researcher may also be helpful in designing the survey itself. In consumer surveys, for example, it would be impractical and costly to interview all homemakers. A better approach would be to select a representative sample of homemakers. Selecting a representative sample requires skill and ingenuity.

Example: The Gallup poll uses a random sample of only 1,500 voters to learn the political preferences of a nation of more than 240,000,000 people. This sample is called *random* because every voter in the nation has the same chance of being chosen for the sample.

On a random basis, Gallup picks 300 sections of the nation and chooses 5 voters in each one. Then Gallup sends interviewers to poll them.

How accurate have Gallup's readings of the voters' likes and dislikes been? Remarkably accurate. Its national election polls have erred only 1.5 percent.

Sampling is not a job for amateurs. Entrepreneurs need professional help to make sure their sample is representative. Otherwise, the results will be misleading and worse than no research at all.

Although some aspects of marketing research, such as sampling, require some professional advice, entrepreneurs should do as much of the research themselves as they can. They might begin by keeping a file of marketing facts that includes data from trade publications and articles from magazines and newspapers. Taken singly, these facts may seem trivial. But when filed and studied over the years, they can be a fertile source for marketing research. For example:

- *The Wall Street Journal* may carry information on marketing trends, alerting entrepreneurs to changes in customer needs and tastes in their market.
- The local newspaper may publish data on population shifts, alerting entrepreneurs to opportunities emerging outside their immediate marketing area.
- Trade publications may publish articles on highly successful ventures, alerting entrepreneurs to production, financial, or marketing methods they might try.

Exhibit 14.4 diagrams the approach to finding facts we have just described.

EXHIBIT 14.4 *General Approach to Finding Facts*

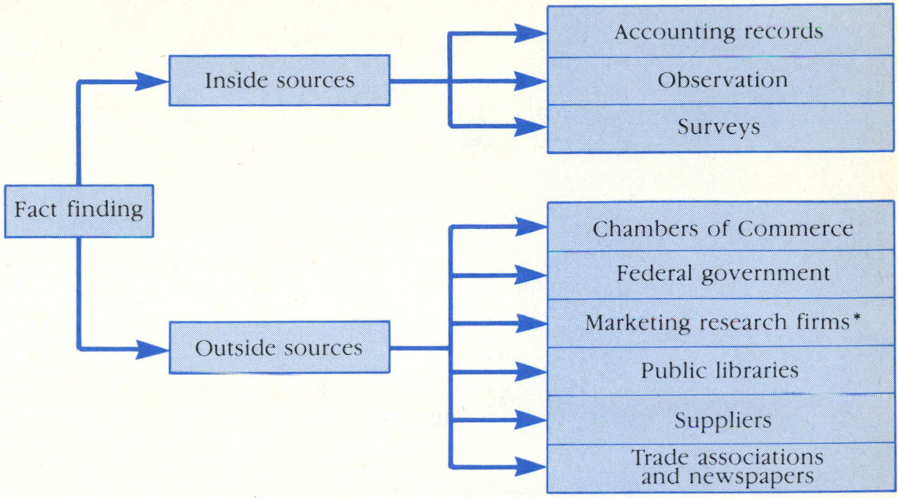

* Or advertising agencies that do marketing research.

MARKETING MIX

Elements of a Marketing Mix

After identifying and researching their market, entrepreneurs are ready to decide how best to create new customers and to keep those they already have. To the layperson, all that is needed is selling. But selling is merely the last step in a series of marketing steps, including:

- Distribution channels
- Pricing
- Advertising
- Personal selling
- Sales promotion
- Packaging
- Service

For example, when a customer goes to a drugstore to buy toothpaste, this is the last step in the marketing process. The drugstore entrepreneur and the toothpaste manufacturer have already spent huge sums on the other steps just to convince customers to buy that particular brand of toothpaste at that drugstore. Let us now look at each marketing step.

Distribution Channels

What is a distribution channel? Every manufacturer, wholesaler, retailer, and service firm is part of a distribution network. The network's purpose is to move products from producers to users.

Distribution channels are controlled mostly by manufacturers. It is the manufacturer, not the retailer or the wholesaler, who usually decides how best to move products from the plant to the final user. No matter how good the product may be, the entrepreneur who produces a product or service may fail if:

- The product reaches the user too late
- Distribution costs are too high
- The product is not distributed as widely as competing products

So, to market their products profitably, manufacturers should decide whether to sell directly to users or through middlemen such as manufacturers' agents, wholesalers, distributors, or retailers.

Exhibit 14.5 shows the various channels of distribution open to the entrepreneur. In the manufacturer-to-user channel, for example, the entrepreneur sells directly to the user and no middleman is involved. Manufacturers may use this channel when:

- They sell from their plant
- They sell through the mail
- They have salespersons who sell door to door

Entrepreneurs often begin by selling their products through manufacturers' agents, because they cannot afford to hire full-time salespersons. Only after they have grown can they justify hiring salespersons.

EXHIBIT 14.5 *Various Channels of Distribution*

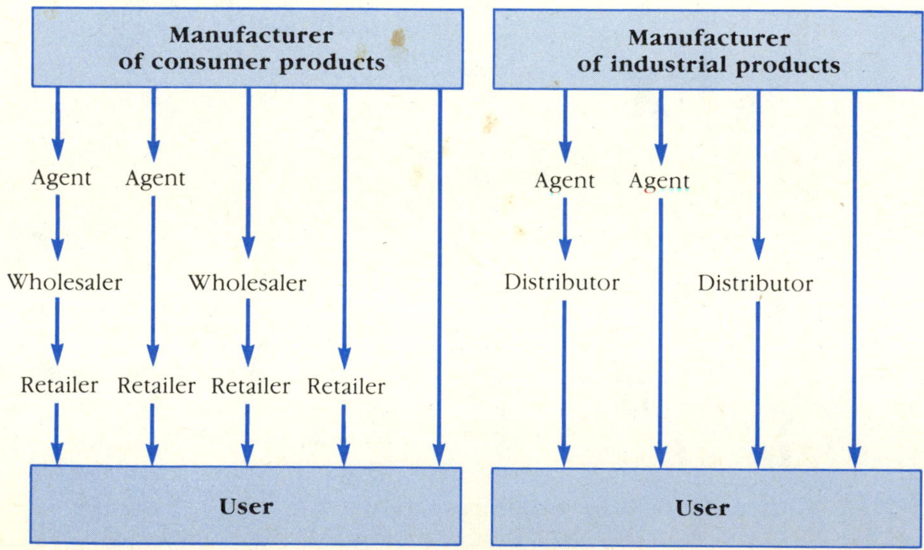

Pricing

Entrepreneurs and other businesspersons are more mysterious about pricing than about any other aspect of their businesses. Few reveal how they go about setting prices. In many cases, setting a price poses no problem—especially when the entrepreneur's product is identical to that of competitors. Rational customers will not pay a higher price than they know is being charged elsewhere for a product they regard as identical. In such cases, all that the entrepreneur can do is follow competitors—and hope to keep costs within prices.

But in other cases, setting a price does pose a problem, especially to entrepreneurs with new products. Such entrepreneurs often charge as much as the market will bear—and so they should—for often it is the promise of high profits on their innovations that encourages them to risk money on research. This pricing practice is called *skimming*. It generally works well if:

- It is most likely that a high price will not discourage customers from buying the new product.
- The cost of developing the new product is high, and it may become obsolete in a short time.
- The entrepreneur's patent position on the product is strong.

High prices and high profits also tend to fire up competitors, who may then invade the market with innovative products of their own.

Another pricing practice for new products is called *penetration pricing*. With this practice, the entrepreneur sets a low initial price in an effort to capture customers quickly. It generally works well if:

- Customers are more likely to be sensitive to the price of the new product. That means a lower price would boost total revenues to levels higher than they would be with a higher price.
- The low price is likely to discourage competitors from invading the market.

Both practices generally lead to the same profit picture in the long run. With either pricing practice, the entrepreneur's goal is to maximize profits:

- With skimming pricing, by charging a *high* price for low volume
- With penetration pricing, by charging a *low* price for high volume

Pricing Mechanics

How are prices computed? The entrepreneur generally needs more than the simple arithmetic of costs and profits to set prices. Yet many entrepreneurs seem to price on a cost-plus basis. This approach is a natural one, because entrepreneurs cannot survive unless they take in more than they pay out. The easiest formula for the entrepreneur to use is this one:

$$\text{Price} = \text{Costs} + \text{Fair Profit}$$

But this simple formula cannot guarantee the entrepreneur a profit. Why? Because cost and profit estimates hinge on volume estimates—and volume hinges on the right price, among other things. For example, an entrepreneur with idle plant capacity and a growing market may temporarily cut prices to boost revenues.

To improve our understanding of pricing, let us look at some noncost questions that each innovative entrepreneur should answer before setting a price:

- How unique is my product? Is it different enough to command a premium price?
- How will distribution channels influence my price? What is the normal industry practice on discounts at each level of distribution? What is the industry practice on prices, credit terms, and volume discounts?
- How will competitors react to my price? Will they cut prices, improve old products, increase service?
- What market conditions will influence my price? What role do inflation, employment level, and federal tax policies play? How do rate of technological change, excess capacity in the industry, and foreign suppliers affect my price?
- Are there any legal restrictions that may influence my price?

Even psychology may enter into the pricing decision. We need only look at the reluctance of some firms many years ago to raise the price of candy bars above five cents to see an example of psychological influences on pricing. For a long time, it was deemed wise to reduce the size of the bar instead of raising the price. At some point, however, the psychological benefits of a stable pricce were outweighed by the psychological benefits of a larger candy bar and prices began to rise.[8]

Deciding upon a price for a new product is a complex process; but for old products, the entrepreneur generally has no pricing decision to make. The entrepreneur need only decide whether to make and sell the product at its current market price.

Pricing for Wholesalers and Retailers Setting prices may pose problems not only for innovative entrepreneurs who manufacture new products but also for wholesalers and retailers who sell established products. To be sure, many of the retailer's prices are set by competitors. On many products, though, retailers are free to set their own prices. How do they do it? They generally use a *markup* approach. Markup is simply the difference between selling and purchase cost:

$$\text{Markup} = \text{Selling Price} - \text{Purchase Cost}$$

For retailers, the overall markup of all products should be high enough not only to cover expenses but also to earn a profit. In practice, markup is expressed not in dollars but as a percentage of either selling or purchase cost. The simple formulas are:

$$\text{Markup percentage on retail price} = \frac{\$\ \text{Markup}}{\$\ \text{Retail Price}} \times 100$$

$$\text{Markup percentage on purchase cost} = \frac{\$\ \text{Markup}}{\$\ \text{Purchase Cost}} \times 100$$

Let us now go through an example to show how a retailer may apply markup percentages in order to set prices:

Example: An entrepreneur runs a camera shop located in a suburban shopping center. In anticipation of the spring selling season, she has just purchased a line of cameras for $66 each. She would like to get a 40 percent markup on retail price. At what price should she sell these cameras? The entrepreneur sets her price by using this simple formula:

$$\text{Retail Price} = \frac{\text{Purchase Cost}}{100\% - \%\ \text{Markup on Retail}} \times 100$$

$$= \frac{\$66}{100\% - 40\%} \times 100$$

$$= \underline{\$110}$$

She would price her new line of cameras at $109.95 each (just below the $110 figure).

Advertising

Entrepreneurs use advertising to communicate about their products or services to customers, focusing mostly on benefits to customers if they buy. Entrepreneurs may also try to convince customers that their products are superior to those of competitors. Their message may take any one of several forms, such as:

- A two-column, 5-inch advertisement in a local newspaper, describing the product the entrepreneur is offering. The advertisement may also dramatize the ideas that surround the product—ideas designed to lead customers to think well of the entrepreneur's venture, by making it clear that it is an honest venture to buy from and publicizing the venture's role in bettering the quality of life in the community. In this way, a venture can build a good reputation for itself among customers, suppliers, investors, and the press.
- Multicolored posters splashed across storefronts heralding the specials of the day.
- Thirty-second spots on television or radio telling customers why they should buy a certain product.
- Large neon signs flashing above a building, inviting customers to stop in for a look at the latest products.

As a rule of thumb, advertising offers the cheapest way to get a message across. It can build revenues at a lower cost per sale than any other way. Few entrepreneurs can afford not to advertise. At the same time, few can afford to spend $600,000 for 60 seconds of prime time on national television. Entrepreneurs should make every advertising dollar count through careful planning. They should create advertising that:

- Communicates the desired message
- Reaches customers a sufficient number of times
- Sells the product
- Earns a return on the advertising dollars spent

These goals are easy to set down on paper. To measure progress against them, however, is extremely hard. Even giant corporations with million-dollar advertising budgets find it hard to measure how well their advertising messages get across. Still, entrepreneurs should keep these goals in mind when mapping their advertising campaigns, always striving to deliver the right message to the right audience at the right time.

Many entrepreneurs, however, do not plan. For example, during a recession, some may drop advertising in the mistaken belief that it is an unnecessary cost. Or some may advertise only when a media salesperson drops in with an attractive deal. But astute entrepreneurs plan their advertising by consciously deciding on budgets, messages, and media.

Budgeting the Advertising Expenditures Entrepreneurs should tie expenditures to goals. For example, an entrepreneur may be introducing a new line of products for the youth market. Her goal may be revenues of $200,000 for the first year. How much should she spend on advertising to reach that goal?

This decision should be made, however, only after two other questions have been answered: What should my advertising message be? What media should I use?

Preparing the Advertising Message Before writing a message, the entrepreneur should examine the market, estimating its size, income, age, and so on. Only by getting this information can entrepreneurs prepare messages that appeal directly to their audience.

Note that getting the answers is really doing marketing research. Without the facts, the advertising message is likely to misfire. While writing their advertising messages, entrepreneurs should place themselves in the customer's shoes and ask:

- What is so unique about my product?
- What can it do for customers that competing products cannot? Will it save them money? Will it last longer? Is it of better quality?
- How can I convince prospective customers that my product is better?

Examples of attention-getting messages appear in Exhibit 14.6.

EXHIBIT 14.6 *Examples of Advertisements*

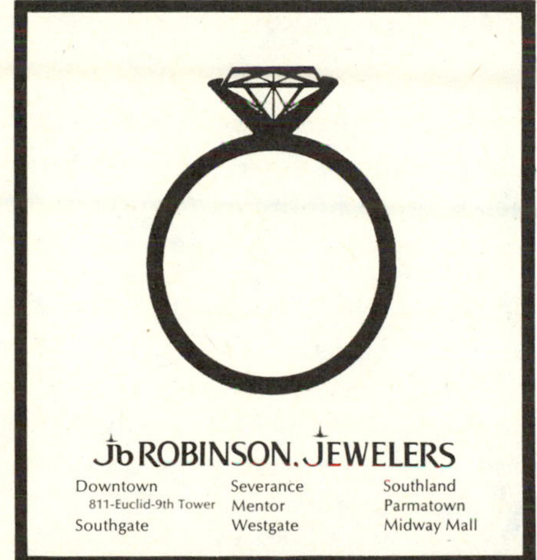

Sources: Top left, created by Carr Liggett Advertising, Inc., for Don's Lighthouse Inn. Top right, Marcia M. Polevoi. Left, Intercontinental Advertising.

Selecting Media Because few entrepreneurs are advertising experts, it behooves them to work with advertising agencies. Agencies can be especially helpful in mapping out advertising campaigns. They are also adept at preparing messages of professional quality, for newspaper or magazine advertisements, or for radio or television commercials.

Advertising agencies are also qualified to recommend what media entrepreneurs should use to get their messages across. Media account for about 90 percent of advertising costs, so entrepreneurs can ill afford to pick the wrong medium. Advertising agencies can help them to decide among such media as these:

- Radio or television
- Newspapers or magazines
- Handbills or direct mail
- Yellow Pages or outdoor signs

Example: Several years ago, Cleveland homemaker Marion Landis had a problem—dirty windows. There was no product on the market that would make the grimy film on her windows disappear. She solved the problem in her laboratory—her kitchen—by inventing Mr. Glass, a nontoxic window cleaner that really works.

It works so well that Ms. Landis has set up her own firm, Ultra-Fine Products, Inc., to market the product. It is now sold nationally and has a national trademark. She credits much of her success to television talk-show interviews. "Following one interview, people were lined up outside stores . . . waiting for them to open so they could buy Mr. Glass," she recalls.[9]

Turning to Exhibit 14.7, note the shares of the advertising dollar captured by selected media. Newspapers are the most popular medium, followed closely by television.

Personal Selling

This marketing step takes over where advertising leaves off. Advertising coaxes the customer to buy; it stimulates interest. But advertising rarely closes the sale. Entrepreneurs must also rely on personal selling—meeting customers face to face to help them make up their minds.

Interaction Between Advertising and Personal Selling Because their goal is to create loyal customers, entrepreneurs should strike the right balance between advertising and personal selling. To put it another way, entrepreneurs should decide how best to mesh their *push* strategy with their *pull* strategy. Take this example:

Example: A customer is looking for a new, low-priced, two-door automobile. An advertisement in the local newspaper catches her eye. A dealer is offering a $300 rebate on the purchase of any automobile of a certain low-priced model. Her interest whetted, the customer decides to visit the dealer's showroom. That is *pull strategy*, because it was the dealer's advertisement that stimulated the customer to take a look.

As the customer steps into the showroom, a salesperson offers to show her the new models and answer any questions. The salesperson reminds her that the $300 rebate is offered for a limited time only, so the customer had better act quickly. Two days later, she decides to buy—in part because the salesperson was knowledgeable, helpful, and courteous. That is *push strategy*.

Note how these two strategies reinforce each other. Without advertising, the customer might not have set foot in the dealer's showroom; and

EXHIBIT 14.7 *Comparison of Selected Media in Advertising Expenditures*

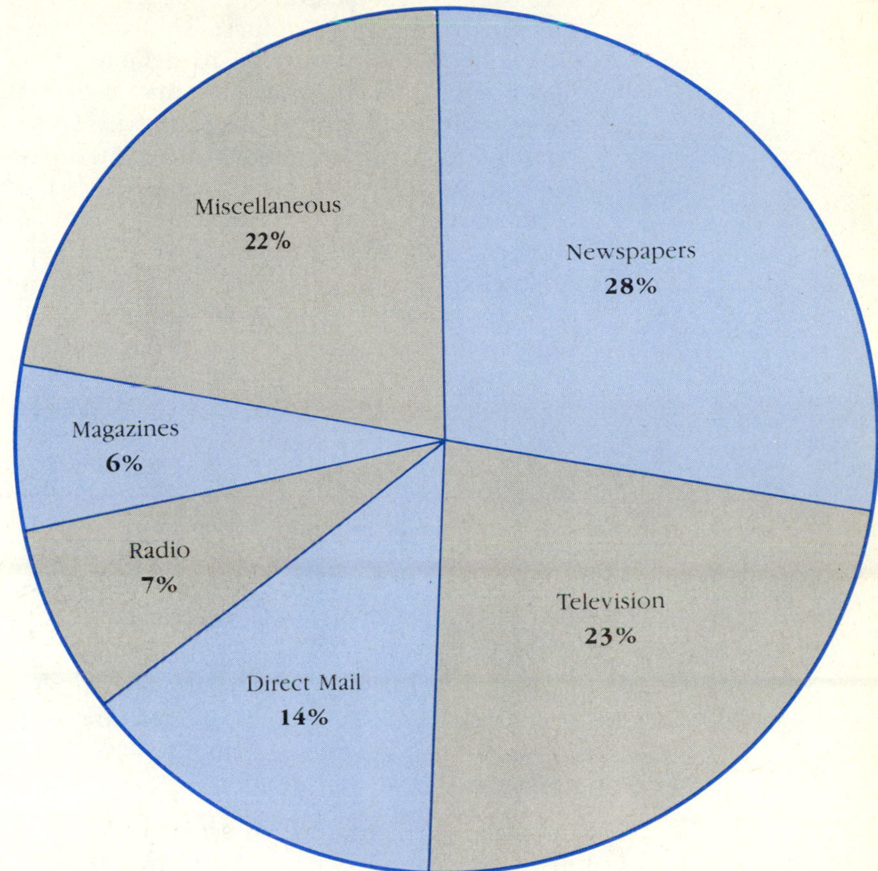

Source: U.S. Department of Commerce, *Statistical Abstract of the United States* (Washington, D.C.: U.S. Government Office, 1984), p. 567.

without personal selling, the dealer might not have sold the customer an automobile.

The Selling Process

Although no two selling situations are precisely alike, salespersons generally rely on a seven-step process. A brief explanation of each step follows:

Prospecting: In this first step, marketing research would suggest which potential customers are most likely to buy the product. This step enables salespersons to focus on only those prospects who are willing and financially able to buy the product.

Approaching Customers: Since first impressions are vital, the salesperson makes every effort to discover the customer's needs and how the product can meet those needs.

Presenting the Product: In this step the salesperson underlines the product's benefits to the customer as well as the ways in which it surpasses the competitor's product.
Demonstrating the Product: This step reinforces the presentation and calls for the salesperson to demonstrate the product's superior qualities. In this step the prospect may also test the product personally.
Overcoming Objections: Here, the salesperson gives the prospect an opportunity to raise objections or ask questions, giving the salesperson a chance to overcome the objections that might block a sale.
Closing the Sale: This is the most important step, calling for the salesperson to ask the prospect to buy the product.
Following Through: This last step requires the salesperson to follow through on the order to make sure that the product is delivered on time, in the right quantity, and of the right quality. Equally vital, the salesperson assures the customer that he or she will help if problems arise before or after delivery of the product.

Finding the Right Salespersons Personal selling varies in importance by industry. In retailing, for example, personal selling is indispensable. Salespersons give a store its personality; they help mold its image, and they help keep its customers from going elsewhere. Therefore, each salesperson should always try to satisfy the needs of customers. The true test of a good product is a satisfied customer.

To build a nucleus of loyal customers, entrepreneurs should find the right salespersons. One way to do so is to hire an employment agency that specializes in placing salespersons. Before going to such an agency, entrepreneurs should first decide:

- What the salespersons are expected to do
- What their salary and fringe benefits will be
- What their prospects for promotion are

In industries other than retailing, the requirements for salespersons vary widely. In manufacturing, for example, the salesperson is usally a highly educated expert in the field:

> **Example:** The sales engineers for a manufacturing company sell lathes to machine shops. As technical experts, they may also train their customers' machinists on how to run and care for the lathes. And they may even help design lathes that better satisfy their customers' special needs.

Similarly, salespersons in wholesaling must be deeply knowledgeable about their products. Take this example:

> **Example:** Salespersons for a hardware supplier may sell to hardware retailers as many as 10,000 different items made by dozens of manufacturers. They must know all the items and their strengths and weaknesses, so

they can help satisfy customer needs. On top of that, they must keep their customers posted on supply and price trends. Besides closing sales, these salespersons must also:

- Answer complaints
- Keep daily records
- Prepare sales reports
- Help draft new advertising and promotional programs

As these examples illustrate, salespersons often qualify as managers, since they manage the relations between a venture and its customers. Success or failure often depends on their performance.

Sales Promotion

Sales promotion makes both advertising and personal selling more effective. It may take many forms, such as:

- Contests to spur salespersons to sell more. An automobile dealer, for example, may offer its top salesperson a two-week, all-expenses-paid vacation in Hawaii.
- Special price discounts to introduce a new product. Discounts may also be used to sell slow-moving or obsolescent inventory.
- Free samples to introduce a new product. Cosmetics manufacturers, for example, may give away tubes of a new face lotion at shopping centers.
- Piggyback premiums to introduce a new product. In such a promotion, an unrelated item is attached to a product. A manufacturer, for example, may attach plastic flowers to boxes of detergent.
- Exhibitions to build up a product's image. A manufacturer, for example, may buy a booth at a trade show in order to demonstrate a product to many potential customers.

Let us now see how one entrepreneur used sales promotion to solve a summer problem:

Example: Each summer the clothier, Stuart and Burns, offers customers $25 off on a new, tailor-made suit for each old suit they bring in. This promotion has worked so well that sales during the normally slack summer months of July and August almost match sales during May and June, the traditional peak months for the sale of suits.

The promotional flyer the clothier mails to customers appears in Exhibit 14.8. Note how persuasively the clothier gets the message across.

Packaging and Servicing

So far, we have discussed the five main marketing steps: distribution channels, pricing, advertising, personal selling, and sales promotion. Two other steps bear discussion:

Packaging: For some products, the package can be almost as important as its contents. An aerosol can of hair spray, for example, does a better job than a squeeze bottle of spray. In packaging their product, entrepreneurs should also consider whether the package protects the

EXHIBIT 14.8 *Promotional Flyer*

Source: Stuart & Burns.

product against damage under normal shipping conditions and whether the package combines attractiveness with sales appeal. This question is especially important in such industries as cosmetics and perfumes, wines and jewelry.

Service: This marketing step deals with keeping customers satisfied. An appliance dealer, for example, may stock spare parts and repair appliances if they break down unexpectedly. Without this service, the customer may become frustrated and never buy another appliance from the dealer.

Service is directed not only at products but also at customers. For example, some department stores now provide for the care of babies while mothers shop.

Service is indispensable in manufacturing industries. Manufacturers often send their engineers to customers' plants to help cure machine breakdowns or solve production bottlenecks. By doing so, the manufacturer keeps the customer satisfied and, at the same time, helps assure future orders.

One sure-fire way of gaining customer confidence is to guarantee product performance. That means accepting all returns without question, within reason. For example, a clothier who guarantees quality would hardly be duty-bound to take back a suit, say, *six* months after a customer bought it.

Guarantees of product performance can be a vital tactic in the entrepreneur's marketing strategy. Both sales revenues and profits are likely to improve dramatically when an entrepreneur uses a guarantee.

PREPARING A MARKETING MIX

After learning what it takes to create customers, entrepreneurs are ready to prepare their marketing mix. Its ingredients, of course, are the marketing steps previously discussed:

- Distribution channels
- Pricing
- Advertising
- Personal Selling
- Sales promotion
- Packaging
- Service

Because these steps—either singly or in combination—create customers, it is helpful to think of them as ingredients forming a marketing mix. It is up to the entrepreneur to mix the ingredients in amounts that will give the most for each marketing dollar. As one management consultant puts it:

> The entrepreneur, as the marketing man, is a kind of cook who is continually experimenting with new blends and new kinds of ingredients. He hopes ultimately to come out with the ideal combination that will produce the highest amount of sales at the lowest practical cost. In a sense, he is balancing a number of variables in which the contribution of each element to the total result is often extremely difficult to measure.[10]

Marketing mix varies widely from industry to industry. Even within an industry, marketing mix may vary among competitors, and it will also vary during the life of a venture:

Example: Just before launching a men's shoe store, an entrepreneur places a three-column advertisement in the local newspaper heralding the store's opening. He also hires a model to pass out circulars in front of the store for three days before the opening. So his preopening marketing mix consists of advertising and sales promotion.

Once the entrepreneur opens the store, however, advertising diminishes and personal selling becomes the main ingredient in his marketing mix. Generally, customers are unsure about the style and size of the shoes they want. A salesperson is needed to help customers make up their minds.

After peak selling seasons like Christmas and Easter, the entrepreneur offers discounts to sell old inventory. At these times, his marketing mix consists of personal selling as well as some advertising and sales promotion.

Marketing is an Attitude

The goal of marketing is to find a mix that creates satisfied customers at a profit; but often, entrepreneurs avoid deciding which ingredients are likely to work best. Why? Because they believe that the marketing mix is the exclusive province of sophisticated, billion-dollar corporations. Yet the principle of a marketing mix is simple—and it may even be easier to apply in small ventures than in large corporations.

After preparing their marketing mix, entrepreneurs should take pains to keep accurate records of marketing costs. Among other things, their records should enable them to compare each salesperson's salary with the revenues he or she generates, in order to single out those who are doing well and those who are not.

Because marketing is also largely an *attitude* toward goals and their achievement, entrepreneurs must keep their ventures market-oriented at all times. Some entrepreneurs tend to take their existing markets for granted. That is a mistake. Although products may seem to remain unchanged from year to year, markets are in fact changing and it is a delusion to believe otherwise.

Entrepreneurs should also keep in mind that new products are the lifeblood of vigorous ventures. New products exploit changing markets, open new vistas, spark new investment, and charge a venture with excitement and vigor.

EXPORT MARKETING

Our discussion of marketing would be incomplete without touching on the vitality of export markets, although the U.S. share of world export sales has dropped sharply since 1955. Such markets are generally overlooked or ignored by entrepreneurs. Yet foreign markets often offer a fertile source of sales opportunities—billions of dollars worth of products and services are exported yearly to virtually all 135 countries in the world. Of the total volume, less than 5 percent is accounted for by small business. The reasons that entrepreneurs tend to shun export markets are threefold:

Their fear of the unknown: Many entrepreneurs believe that their lack of knowledge about export markets is an insurmountable barrier. They reason that it is hard enough doing business locally where information about markets is at their fingertips, let alone trying to do business abroad where information may be much less accessible.

Their fear of long-distance relationships: Many entrepreneurs believe that any relationship with a foreign country would be too hard to control smoothly. These entrepreneurs may be used to exercising on-the-spot control over local markets. In their view, foreign markets that may be thousands of miles away would be all but impossible to control. They often perceive any such relationship as unstable, untidy, and more than likely to unravel—with unhappiness all around.

Their fear of the complex: Many entrepreneurs believe that the very act of initiating a relationship abroad is too complex even to think about. Such entrepreneurs believe that it is beyond them to grasp the complexities of language, legal systems, and money matters that often differ sharply from those at home.

Abundant Help Available

These fears are real, yet healthy, for no entrepreneur should ignore the risks involved in exporting. Yet such fears may quickly dissolve once entrepreneurs avail themselves of the professional help, much of it free, available within the federal government and Chambers of Commerce. For example, the first question asked by an entrepreneur who is considering foreign markets may be: How can I find out if there really is a market for my product or service abroad?

Answers to this question may take just minutes to get by tapping the information stored in a computerized file kept by the U.S. Bureau of International Commerce (BIC).[11] BIC, by the way, has information on more than 150,000 foreign importing organizations in 135 countries. Largely through its computerized file, BIC enables entrepreneurs to:

- Find agents or distributors in virtually every country of the world.
- Get up-to-the-minute direct sales leads and representation opportunities from overseas. Some business in Paris, for example, could be spotted instantly by an entrepreneur, say, in Denver.
- Get a detailed profile on an individual foreign company. A typical report, for example, would cover background information on the company, kind of organization, years in business, number of employees, size of company, sales area, method of operation, products handled, names of officers, general reputation in financial circles, and names of the company's trading connections.

Other Federal Services

Besides these computerized services, BIC also offers the entrepreneur a host of personal services, among them:

Free counseling: In Washington and other places, BIC offers guidance, in-depth counseling, and scheduling of appointments with knowledgeable officials in other federal agencies. This is a one-step service designed to give the entrepreneur the most amount of information in the least time.

Publications: Thousands of government reports and booklets describing the sales opportunities available abroad are available to entrepreneurs. One example is a survey of the sales opportunities for suppliers of machine tools in Australia, Germany, Mexico, and Sweden. For each country, this report lists the major users of machine tools, along with other vital marketing information such as which machine tools are the most salable.

Promotional events: In 1984 alone, the U.S. Department of Commerce scheduled 220 promotional events, including trade fair exhibitions, international marketing shows, and trade missions to fertile markets such as the Republic of China. Each year, this federal department publishes a calendar listing each promotional event by product and by service.

Workshops: The U.S. Department of Commerce also conducts workshops throughout the country on export marketing. They also hold seminars and organize mini-courses on export marketing, generally in cooperation with local universities or community colleges.

The foregoing describes help available from the federal government. Equally helpful are local Chambers of Commerce. Many have special departments devoted to spurring and helping local businesses sell their products abroad. Like the federal government, they organize trade missions, hold trade shows, and publish brochures on how best to expand into foreign markets.

Yet, despite the governmental and private help, many entrepreneurs fail to consider the sales opportunities available to them abroad; and if they do, they often ignore seeking professional help. A recent true story follows:

> **Example:** A U.S. company launched a frozen food venture in a major country in the Far East before it realized that most homes in the market area did not have freezers. Had the company first checked with the U.S. Department of Commerce, they probably never would have made so costly a mistake.[12]

Preparing a Marketing Plan

To best serve a foreign market, an entrepreneur should prepare a separate marketing plan. Such a plan would rely heavily on marketing research already done by others, mostly by:

- The U.S. Department of Commerce

- Local Chambers of Commerce
- The foreign countries themselves

Only after collecting and analyzing all available information should entrepreneurs prepare their marketing plans, following a procedure much like this one:

- Identify the most desirable market for their products or services
- Identify potential buyers within that market
- Prepare a proposal describing their products
- Develop terms of sale that would satisfy the foreign buyer while protecting the entrepreneur's best interests[13]

To prepare such a plan, entrepreneurs should seek the help of lawyers versed in drafting international sales contracts. An experienced lawyer can help entrepreneurs describe what they have to offer in plain and concise language. It is vital that the foreign buyer have a clear and precise idea of the entrepreneur's proposal. The lawyer can also help protect the entrepreneur's best interests when it comes time to negotiate a sales contract with the foreign buyer by determining what kind of legally enforceable contract will help the entrepreneur in his or her quest to maximize profit while minimizing risks in the foreign market.

SUMMARY

Selling often is equated with marketing, but selling is just one end of the marketing spectrum. At the other end is marketing research. In between fall such activities as pricing, distribution, advertising and sales promotion, packaging and servicing. Thus, marketing is a many-sided activity, involving all the steps entrepreneurs must take to get their products or services into the hands of customers.

Marketing research is perhaps the most important of these activities. Before preparing their marketing plans, entrepreneurs should first search out the facts about their markets, facts that help answer such questions as these:

- What products to sell, where, in what quantities, at what prices
- What competitors are selling, where they are, how strong they are

The answers to these questions provide entrepreneurs with solid information on which to build their marketing plans. It is these answers that suggest, for example, advertising in trade magazines as the best way to stimulate demand for a particular product. Without such direction, entrepreneurs are likely to miss their market.

To prepare their marketing plan, entrepreneurs should seek the help of experts such as advertising agencies and marketing research firms. Advertising agencies can help entrepreneurs prepare professional copy and help them choose the proper media for getting their advertising messages across to customers. Marketing research firms can provide the expert help needed to design consumer surveys and to select representative samples.

Entrepreneurs should take pains to prepare their marketing plans in the form of a marketing mix. This means blending advertising, personal selling, and the other marketing activities into combinations that are likely to produce the highest amount of revenue at the lowest cost.

Export markets offer entrepreneurs a fertile source of sales opportunities. To capitalize on such opportunities, entrepreneurs should first seek help from the U.S. Department of Commerce or local Chambers of Commerce. Next, they should prepare separate marketing plans for their foreign markets. It is also important that they seek help from lawyers to make sure their best interests are protected when a sales contract is negotiated with a foreign buyer.

DISCUSSION AND REVIEW QUESTIONS

1. Why is marketing research one of the most important marketing activities? What questions does it help answer?
2. Describe the various ways that marketing research may be done.
3. Describe the steps needed to develop an advertising message that stimulates customer interest.
4. Define these terms: *marketing*, *random sampling*, *advertising*, *market*, *markup*, *market segmentation*, *BIC*.
5. Why is the marketing mix so vital to the success of a venture? How is it prepared?
6. How would you, as an entrepreneur, seek the facts before introducing a new product?
7. How do advertising and sales promotion differ? Give examples.
8. How do pull strategy and push strategy differ? How do they reinforce each other? Give two examples.
9. What kinds of professional help do entrepreneurs generally need to prepare their marketing plans? Explain fully.
10. Why is personal selling so critical to entrepreneurial success in most industries?
11. How do penetrating pricing and skimming pricing differ? Under what conditions would it better to use one rather than the other?
12. How would you, as an entrepreneur, go about exploring sales opportunities in foreign countries?
13. Do the words *selling* and *marketing* mean the same thing? Explain fully, giving an example.
14. A small manufacturer of outdoor, portable swimming pools has the problem of choosing his channel of distribution. What are his alternatives? Which alternative would you recommend he pursue? Why?
15. Compare a manufacturer's marketing mix for a product sold to other manufacturers with the mix for a product sold through retailers to consumers.

NOTES

1. Adapted from U.S. Small Business Administration, *Marketing Research* (Washington, D.C.: U.S. Government Printing Office, 1968), p. 2.
2. Theodore Levitt, *Innovation Marketing* (New York: McGraw-Hill, 1962), p. 120.
3. "Brainstorming on Marketing," *Boardroom Reports*, May 1, 1985, p. 16.
4. Adapted from Arthur W. Cornwell, U.S. Small Business Administration, "Sales Potential and Market Shares," *Small Marketers Aids* No. 112 (Washington, D.C.: U.S. Government Printing Office, 1972), p. 1.
5. William M. Pride and O. C. Ferrell, *Marketing* (Boston, Mass.: Houghton Mifflin Company, 1985), p. 40.
6. The author is wholly indebted to both Dr. William M. Pride and Dr. O.C. Ferrell of Texas A & M University for this discussion.
7. Christy Marshall, "Pizza Hut is Cooking Up Recipe for Future Growth," *Advertising Age*, February 6, 1978, p. 45.
8. John C. Lere, *Pricing Techniques for the Financial Executive* (New York: Wiley, 1974), p. 1.
9. "The Entrepreneurial Woman," *Cleveland Woman*, May 1981, pp. 38–39.
10. Harvey C. Krentzman, U.S. Small Business Administration, *Managing for Profits* (Washington, D.C.: U.S. Government Printing Office, 1968), p. 6.
11. BIC is a division of the U.S. Department of Commerce.
12. Adapted from "Doing Business Abroad," *Boardroom Reports*, December 1, 1980, p. 6.
13. D. Mark Baker and Glade F. Flake, U.S. Small Business Administration, "Negotiating International Sales Contracts," *Management Aid No. 247* (Washington, D.C.: U.S. Government Printing Office, 1979), p. 2.

CASE 14A *Peabody's Cycling Systems, Inc.*

In 1976, Richard Peabody launched his own venture—to sell motorcycle accessories. At the time, his long-range goal was to retire in ten years with an equity of $1 million. It is now 1980, and he is far short of that goal. To help achieve this goal, Mr. Peabody is wondering whether to buy out a competitor or to open a second store in a sprawling shopping mall—or do both now.

Background

In the last 15 years, Mr. Peabody has owned 15 motorcycles. "Motorcycles are a mania with me," says Mr. Peabody. "Gas-guzzling automobiles aren't for me. Motorcycles are superior. They give me that heady feeling of freedom and gusto that I crave." Indeed, he once rode a motorcycle from coast to coast and back in 49 days in the dead of winter.

A veteran of the Vietnam War, Mr. Peabody first gave serious thought to going into business for himself when he left the U.S. Army in 1970. His war experiences had convinced him that he would be "miserable unless I were my own boss. I wanted greater control over what I wanted to do in life. And, having my very own business seemed the best way to do that."

Although taking orders annoyed him, he credits his tour of army duty with maturing him. "I went in wet behind the ears and came out a man." Trained as both an artilleryman and a wheel-and-truck vehicle mechanic, he rose from private to motor sergeant of his battery in just 14 months. "I learned some valuable lessons," says Mr. Peabody. "The army taught me patience and how to get along with people. They also taught me how to fix almost anything that's broken."

To prepare himself for a venture of his own, Mr. Peabody enrolled in a community college that featured a complete accredited curriculum in small-business management. Once enrolled, however, he decided to go after a dual degree, in accounting as well as small-business management.

Often on the dean's list, he once earned straight A's one quarter carrying a full load of courses and working 50 hours a week as a gas station attendant. With time out for cycling trips to Florida and California, he earned his dual degree in five years. A year later, in 1976, he launched his own venture. His beginning balance sheet appears in Exhibit 14A.1.

GI Bill Helpful

"Thank heaven for the GI Bill of Rights," says Mr. Peabody. "I never would have realized my dream without it, because no bank would help me. I knew I needed $65,000 to open my doors for business. And all I had in my name was a piddling $222 in cash and a motorcycle worth $2,800. I don't blame the banks for refusing to risk their depositors' money to help me get started."

Even so, Mr. Peabody soon found that all the GI Bill did was "open doors." Its purpose is to reward veterans by helping them adjust to civilian

EXHIBIT 14A.1

Peabody's Cycling Systems, Inc.: Beginning Balance Sheet (February 15, 1976)

Assets			Equities	
Current assets				
Cash	$10,350		Long-term loan	$40,000
Inventory	26,000	$36,350	Owners' equity	500
Fixed assets				
Shelving and fixtures	$ 2,400			
Other	1,000	3,400		
Other assets				
Organizational cost	$ 250			
Prepaid rent	500	750		
Total assets		$40,500		$40,500

life. "Grateful as I am for the GI Bill, I sure wish the U.S. Veterans Administration had held my hand when I applied for a $65,000 loan. Instead, they sent me to the SBA because they were in charge of all veterans' loans.

"I was so naive that I thought it would be a breeze getting an SBA loan. It wasn't. The red tape, you just wouldn't believe. They fooled around for eight months before I finally got my loan.

"What really got to me was that I probably was better prepared and better qualified than anybody else for a loan. Would you believe my business plan was 44 pages long—and they still wrapped so much red tape around me that I could barely move? And, when I finally got my loan, it was for $40,000 and *not* the $65,000 called for by my business plan. You talk about frustration!"

A Novel Solution

At one point, he was so frustrated that he went to a former professor of his for relief. After listening to Mr. Peabody's litany of complaints about government red tape, the professor suggested to Mr. Peabody that he write a letter to the head of the SBA in Washington, Mitchell Kobelinski, and send it special delivery.

His professor's suggestion worked. Just days later, a letter came from Mr. Kobelinski himself stating that his office would look into Mr. Peabody's complaint "immediately." On that very same day, Mr. Peabody received a telephone call from the SBA loan officer he had been working with. "Mr. Peabody, your loan application looks in order," said the loan officer. "I'm sure our loan-review committee will approve it in a day or so, and you'll have your check for $40,000 the day after that."

"Wow, I couldn't believe it," says Mr. Peabody. "I was so happy that I didn't even remind the loan officer that I really needed $65,000, not the $40,000 they had agreed to lend me. I wanted to leave well enough alone."

Marketing Research

Until now, all Mr. Peabody had was a business on paper. His business plan was his blueprint, containing forecasts like those in Exhibits 14A.2 and 14A.3. He was sure that he had thoroughly researched the market for motorcycle accessories. He found, for example, that, on the average, motorcycle buyers belong to the middle and upper-middle income brackets. They own either so-called street or off-the-road motorcycles, not customized ones (or "choppers"). Mr. Peabody also found that this street and off-the-road market was largely ignored by merchants in his area, which boasted a population of 1.7 million. In fact, of the 84 merchants listed in the Yellow Pages, only two served this market aggressively. Perhaps his most astonishing findings about motorcyclists were that, in 1974:

- 59.8 percent were married
- 46.2 percent were college graduates
- $14,200 was their median income
- $16,800 was their average income
- 25 was their median age

These statistics belie the Hell's Angels image often depicted in the movies. "I had no idea the average motorcyclist was so well off," says Mr. Peabody. "My friends still don't believe me when I tell them who my

EXHIBIT 14A.2

Peabody's Cycling Systems, Inc.: Projected First-Year Income Statement

Sales revenues		$102,000
Cost of goods sold		
Beginning inventory	$10,000	
Delivered cost of purchases	85,000	
Merchandise available for sale	$95,000	
Less: Ending inventory	28,000	67,000
Gross profit		$ 35,000
Operating expenses		
Salaries and wages	$23,000	
Rent	10,800	
Depreciation	2,600	
Utilities	1,800	
Advertising	1,650	
Payroll taxes	1,500	
Miscellaneous	1,400	
Telephone	1,200	
Delivery and travel	1,050	
Insurance	600	
Stationery	600	
Maintenance	600	46,800
Operating loss		($ 11,800)

EXHIBIT 14A.3 *Peabody's Cycling Systems, Inc.: Profitgraph from Business Plan*

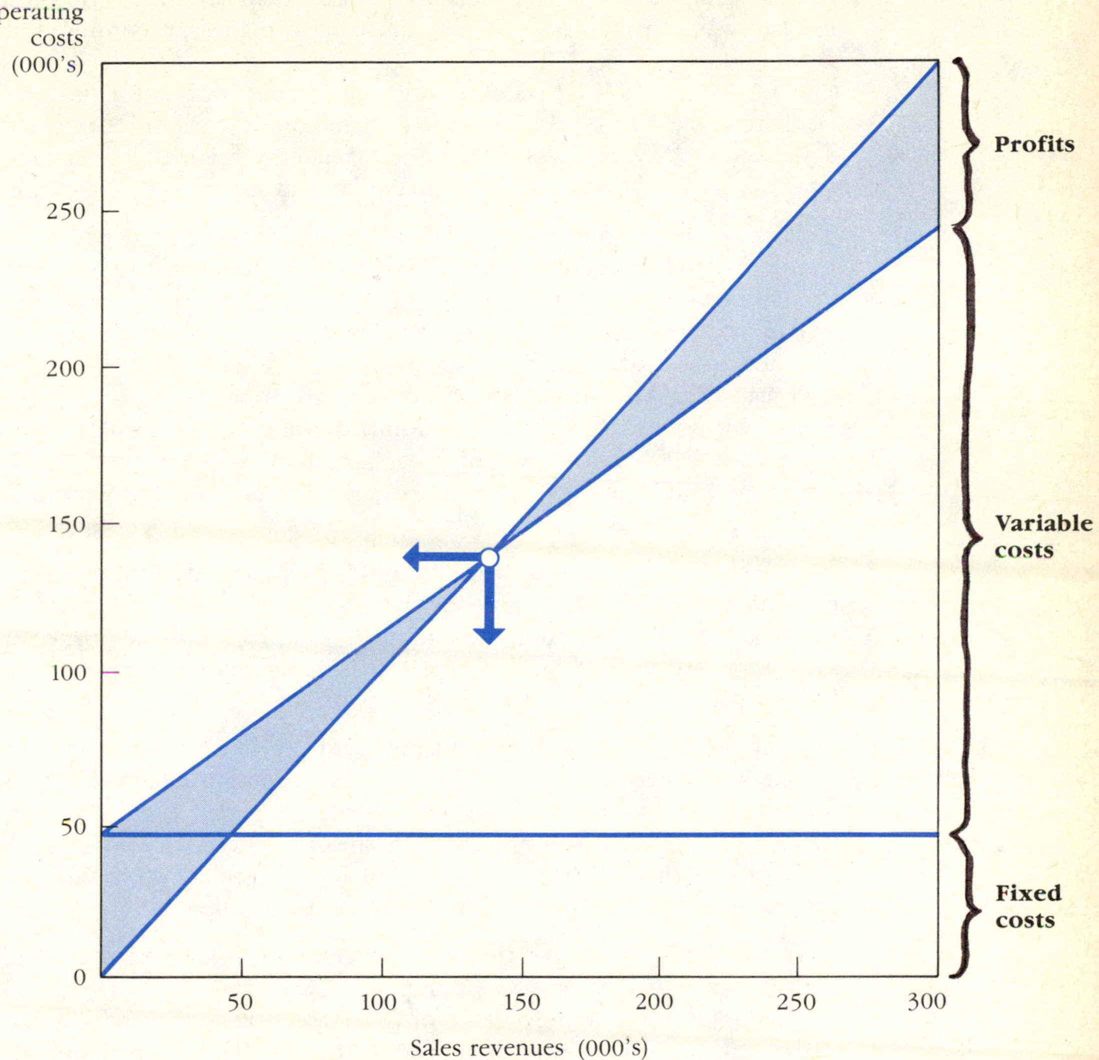

customers are, that motorcyclists are better educated and make more money than the average American." Other information that he unearthed included the following:

- The industry is growing at a rate of 15 percent a year, with accessory sales growing at the even greater rate of 25 percent a year.
- Parts and accessories make up 40 percent of the money spent on motorcycling each year.

"Clearly, I was in the right market at the right time, and I was the right person to exploit the market. The match was near-perfect. I knew motorcycling inside out; I enjoyed it more than anything else; and my market was soaring. Believe me, those facts made me confident that I would succeed."

In March 1976, Mr. Peabody opened his doors for business in Bedford. (See Exhibit 14A.4.) He had looked at just one other site, in Twinsburg. "My business plan made it real easy for me to pick the right site," says Mr. Peabody. His business plan had specified that the right site offer:

- A free-standing building, 50 to 100 feet off the street, with a basement for storage of inventory
- Ample parking for both motorcycles and automobiles, both in front and in back of the building
- Cheap rent—no more than $7 per square foot of space
- Closeness to a freeway intersection, no more than two miles away
- At least 2,000 square feet of floor space
- A full-windowed facade, to afford ample display of motorcycle accessories

With these guidelines firmly in mind, Mr. Peabody settled on the site in Bedford. It had been empty for three years. "It was an ideal site," says Mr. Peabody. "Funny thing is, it used to be a place to make pornographic movies. There were so many complaints from nearby residents that the city fathers had to shut it down."

Legal Form of Organization

A year before he opened for business, Mr. Peabody hired a lawyer to "make sure I was covered legally." He had known the lawyer personally for nine years; and he was impressed with his experience in corporate law, lease contracts, and zoning law. On the lawyer's advice, Mr. Peabody decided that the Subchapter S* form of legal organization would be best for his venture. Excerpts from his business plan follow:

> The attractive aspect of the Subchapter S corporation is that it allows losses incurred by a small company like mine to be distributed to shareholders on a percentage-of-investment basis. Shareholders may then treat these losses as tax deductions from their other income, up to the extent of their investment.
>
> Thus, a $1,000 loss to a shareholder in the 30 percent tax bracket would mean a $300 return on his investment because of tax savings. . . . Profits, if distributed to shareholders as dividends, are taxed, not at the corporate level, but at the shareholders' level only—thus avoiding the double taxation that shareholders of regular corporations must pay on dividends.

* Later, in 1984, Subchapter S corporations became known as S-corporations.

EXHIBIT 14A.4 *Peabody's Cycling Systems, Inc.: View of Bedford Store*

It cost Mr. Peabody $250 to incorporate. He pays his lawyer a $400 retainer each year. "All that means," says Mr. Peabody, "is that I can pick up the phone and get a one-sentence answer to a legal problem. It's a real comfort to know my lawyer is there for help when I need him."

Marketing Strategy

Mr. Peabody's marketing research had revealed that motorcyclists complain most about service. "That's why I decided to sell accessories only and not motorcycles also," says Mr. Peabody. His research had also revealed that the accessory market, although looked upon by most dealers as a sideline, was actually more profitable than the motorcycle market. (See Exhibit 14A.5.) "By specializing in this aspect of the business, I could offer my buying public more of what they wanted. That way, I could encourage them to spend more money at my store." Excerpts from his business plan follow:

> I plan to offer my customers goods and services that they want, at fair prices, in an atmosphere that makes them feel comfortable. My marketing strategy will attempt to attain a steady clientele, by being a place where shopping is pleasant and where employees are knowledgeable and courteous. My customers will *always* be satisfied that they are getting the most for their dollar, and that they have been treated *fairly*. Services will include:
>
> **Wheel truing and spoking:** Few dealers now offer this service, which requires special tools that the average motorcyclist does not have.
>
> **Installation of parts:** Most motorcyclists possess neither the tools nor the mechanical knowledge to install parts and accessories themselves.
>
> **Tire changing**
>
> I intend to sell motorcycle parts and accessories, karts and accessories, and snowmobile accessories at the retail level. My business will be unique because it will be aimed at a specific market. And my advertising, sales promotion, pricing, and store atmosphere will be aimed at attracting that market.

EXHIBIT 14A.5

Peabody's Cycling Systems, Inc.: Top 20 Motorcycle Accessories

1 Helmets
2 Luggage racks
3 Sissy bars
4 Eye protection
5 Apparel
6 Tires
7 Safety bars
8 Handle bars
9 Fairings
10 Saddlebags
11 Seats
12 Fenders
13 Exhaust systems
14 Windshields
15 Gloves
16 Footpegs
17 Boots
18 Tubes
19 Lighting equipment
20 Grips

The buying habits of my potential customers are varied. For example, motorcyclists who compete regularly are more likely to buy large quantities of the basic essentials, such as oil and spark plugs, and then come back to replace parts that have broken.

The average street rider, however, buys only when the need arises. On the other hand, the competition rider will buy during the week to make his or her motorcycle track-ready for weekend racing. In contrast, the road rider tends to buy only on rainy days or on weekends. Because of these buying habits, I will attempt to aim my sales at these markets:

- The replacement market created by competition motorcyclists who are incredibly hard on their equipment and who are always searching for something to make them go faster.
- The original market created by street motorcyclists who want to improve the appearance of their motorcycle or to equip it for touring or foul-weather touring.

Competition

As part of his marketing research, Mr. Peabody also looked at how strong his competitors were. He began by choosing 21 names at random from the Yellow Pages, which covers a county with a population of 1.7 million. Next, he visited each competitor, posing as a potential customer.

"I then recorded my impressions on 3-by-5 cards, as soon as I left their store," says Mr. Peabody. In most cases, I found that my competitors were courteous and friendly. I did find, however, two areas in which they were lacking. One was their poor display of merchandise; the other was their failure to greet me as I walked into their store."

To lure customers away from his competitors, Mr. Peabody planned to rely mostly on advertising and on his reputation as a "motorcycle pro." His business plan called for:

- Placing advertisements in community newspapers and the Yellow Pages
- Broadcasting 10-second spots on radio

Pride in Performance

In January 1981, Mr. Peabody reflected on the five years that had gone by since he first began doing business in Bedford. "I'm proud of what I've accomplished so far," says Mr. Peabody. "My careful planning has really paid off." His sales revenues topped $660,000 in 1980. To help reach that sales level, Mr. Peabody acquired another accessory store in nearby Tallmadge for its book value of $20,000. This store had rarely turned a profit. 'It was ripe for acquisition," says Mr. Peabody. "The owner tried to run the store on an absentee basis, and it just didn't work out."

Mr. Peabody financed the acquisition with $5,000 of his own money as a loan and by borrowing $15,000 from a commercial bank. He also incorporated the newly acquired store because of the "SBA's first-lien position with my Bedford store."

At both stores, sales have grown steadily, almost dramatically. Note in the table of sales revenues that Tallmadge sales doubled the first full year after he had taken over:

Year	Sales Revenues at— Bedford	Tallmadge
1976	$ 87,000	$ 90,000*
1977	169,000	90,000*
1978	227,000	110,000*
1979	324,000	220,000
1980	392,000	270,000

* Under prior owner

Reasons Behind Sales Performance

Mr. Peabody believes that this performance stems not only from "careful planning but also from a unique marketing strategy and unequaled customer service. Service is the key in this business," says Mr. Peabody. "That's what creates repeat customers."

He also credits his 12 employees for much of his success. Turnover, by the way, is zero. His employees are young, ranging in age from 14 to 33. "I try to make my employees feel as if they're more than just spokes on a wheel," says Mr. Peabody. "I do that by constantly asking them their ideas on how to run the two stores better." He surveys his employees at least once a year, often getting responses like the one appearing in Exhibit 14A.6.

According to Mr. Peabody, what is unique about his marketing strategy is his monthly newsletter. "The newsletter is my most effective advertising tool. It goes only to genuine customers who have signed onto an exclusive mailing list of more than 7,000 names, all of them cyclists." Each of these 7,000 cyclists has met and visited with Mr. Peabody at one of his two stores. "Small wonder that my combined operation is now the largest in the state," says Mr. Peabody.

An Unexpected Turn for the Worse

In 1980, the economy momentarily took a turn for the worse. As a recession set in, Mr. Peabody's two stores unexpectedly found themselves cash-poor, despite rising sales. That year, "a strong spring turned into a soft summer. By fall, conditions had stabilized. Yet my instincts told me to build up inventories anyway, even at the expense of my cash position," says Mr. Peabody.

He wanted to prepare for 1981 by purchasing large quantities of up-to-date, high-quality accessories. "My strategy was to seek sales opportunities while my more cautious competitors were placing their orders with suppliers. It would give me an edge. Believe me, availability of lots of high-quality merchandise is one of the keys to success in the motorcycle accessory business."

EXHIBIT 14A.6

*Typical Response to Employee Survey**

Memo to: Employees
Subject: Survey to Help Improve Our Operations

Please do not discuss your answers with anyone else. I would like individual responses, and will collect the information and discuss it with you as a group. Be honest.

1 What five products should we expand into or carry in more depth?
Answer: Dirt bikes more in depth
Mini bikes
Leather vests
Selling ski jackets in winter

2 What five products should we drop or carry substantially less of?
Answer: Plastic fenders
Knapsacks
Belt buckles
Locks
Most of the stuff on the shelves above the spark plugs

3 What area should we place more emphasis on in 1982?
Answer: Don't know

4 What area should we place less emphasis on in 1982?
Answer: Touring stuff

5 What can we do to attract more customers in 1982?
Answer: Put a sign out by the street so people can see the store better. Have Peabody's T-shirts on sale. Not real expensive but always have on sale. Everyone likes them!!

6 What can we do to sell our existing customers more products in 1982?
Answer: Be nice to them. Show them products and explain them. Tell them your opinion about the product and just be real nice and smile a lot. Don't be grouchy!

7 How can we better serve our customers in 1982?
Answer: Have something on sale every week. Better information on bikes. Descriptions of questionable items.

8 How can I better serve you? What means of communication can I use to better serve us all?
Answer: We should have meetings over a pizza or something at Mama Mia's. Get to know each other better.
You serve me good and I really can't think of how you can serve me better. Maybe a little raise. I don't really think I'm being underpaid; it's just that everyone likes raises.

* Answers given by a 15-year-old employee

A shortage of cash ordinarily would not disturb Mr. Peabody. "I've survived in the past with little or no salary, and I could do it again," he says. "But I need cash now to keep expanding, to keep improving the quality of my service to customers. Sure, my sales have been great, but I've succeeded without the benefit of a full-fledged service center.

"Not having such a facility has caused me to lose business. Why? Because, although many cyclists are do-it-yourselfers, many of them are not inclined to make repairs or to install accessories. They just don't have the time, knowledge, or tools needed to do so.

"The result is that they often purchase accessories elsewhere, or not at all. That hurts my sales. People have come to trust Peabody's. So they would welcome a single, high-quality service center to solve their repair and installation problems."

A Possible Solution

Bent on adding a service center in the spring of 1981, Mr. Peabody decided to seek a $40,000 loan from a commercial bank. His letter to the bank, justifying his request for the loan, follows:

> In Bedford, 7,600 square feet of the former Bob Kay American Motors–Jeep dealership have become available with favorable lease terms. This vacated property is less than one block from the existing store, and in a much more visible location. The large, glass-enclosed showroom that once housed new cars will now house the retail store, while a remote building that had been the body shop will become a service center.
>
> A third corporation will be formed in an effort to isolate the service center, with its inherent higher liability exposure, from the other two corporations.
>
> The service center will cost money. A comfortable estimate is $40,000. Of that sum, $20,000 will be for machinery and equipment, $10,000 for leasehold improvements and advertising, and the rest for working capital.
>
> Because of the poor cash-flow position created in 1980, neither the Bedford nor the Tallmadge store will have the moneys needed for this expansion. Of course, cash will also be needed to move the retail store into the vacated showroom mentioned above.
>
> Peabody's Cycling Systems of Tallmadge, Inc. has a very favorable position as a borrower. This corporation has a vast, unencumbered inventory and little current debt. Its debts to both Peabody's Cycling Systems of Bedford, Inc. and to Richard Peabody are long term.
>
> A lien position could be offered by the service center, too, on its machinery and equipment. The personal signature of Richard Peabody is also offered.
>
> So, we propose that a loan of $40,000 be granted immediately to Peabody's Cycling Systems of Tallmadge, Inc. The loan will be used to form Peabody's Cycling Systems Service of Bedford, Inc.
>
> For your review, we have attached the latest balance sheet for Peabody's Cycling Systems of Tallmadge, Inc. (Exhibit 14A.7). We will call you in a day or so to set up a meeting, either at our Tallmadge store or at your bank, whichever your prefer. Thank you for giving our proposal the attention it deserves.

EXHIBIT 14A.7

Peabody's Cycling Systems of Tallmadge, Inc.: Latest Balance Sheet (January 1, 1981)

Assets		Equities	
Inventories	$68,000	Loan, Euclid Bank	$ 9,000
Fixtures and equipment	6,000	Loan, Richard Peabody	16,500
Goodwill	6,000	Loan, PCS* of Bedford	24,000
Cash	3,000	Common stock	500
Prepaid rent	2,000	Retained earnings	36,500
Truck	1,500		
Total assets	$86,500	Total equities	$86,500

*Peabody's Cycling Systems

Questions

1. What accounts for Mr. Peabody's good sales performance? What role did his business plan play, if any?
2. If you were the bank, would you grant Mr. Peabody the $40,000 loan he now seeks for the installation of a service center? Why?
3. Comment on Mr. Peabody's approach to managing his employees.
4. Could Mr. Peabody have avoided his cash crisis in 1980? How?
5. What suggestions would you make to Mr. Peabody to help him reach his goal of retiring with an equity of $1 million just ten years after he went into business for himself?

CASE 14B *Mid-Texas Helicopter*

After retiring as an Air Force helicopter pilot, Eric Berke returned to his home town in mid-Texas to open a helicopter charter service in partnership with his wife. They spent two years researching the local market. As part of their fact-finding, they talked to:

- Chambers of Commerce
- Major pipeline companies
- Oil-well suppliers
- Oil-well drillers

These organizations responded so favorably that the Berkes were convinced their new service would fill a need. Fortified by this knowledge, they then opened an account with a local bank, applied for credit with an oil company, and established a line of credit with a major helicopter supplier. They also rented a house, moved their family, and rented hangar and office space. In addition, Mr. Berke negotiated a rental contract for a four-seat helicopter.

Staffing posed no difficulty, for Mrs. Berke joined her husband as an equal partner in the venture. She would run the office, keep books, and help land new clients while Mr. Berke did the flying. But there was one nagging problem: they weren't sure what price to charge.

They knew that similar helicopter services in Dallas were charging $60 to $70 an hour, but they weren't sure whether they could charge that much in their own area. They did have some information on fixed costs that could help them set a price:

- $1200 monthly rental on helicopter, including insurance
- $600 monthly rental for office and hangar
- $200 monthly advertising expenses
- $200 monthly office expenses

In addition, the Berkes found it would cost them:

- $8.40 per engine hour for aviation fuel
- $8.00 per engine hour for helicopter use
- $1.00 per engine hour for oil
- $0.60 per engine hour for repairs

The Berkes also estimated that each would need to take out $600 a month to supplement their retirement income and maintain their standard of living.

During their fact-finding, the Berkes learned that other operators kept their helicopters busy for about 60 percent of normal business hours, or about 120 hours a month. They already had promises of work that they believed would enable them to meet this average.

Questions

1. If we assume that the Berkes intend to add 10 percent of expenses for profit, what is the lowest price they should charge for each hour of helicopter service? What price should they *actually* charge? Why?
2. Prepare a profitgraph on the basis of at least two other prices than the one determined in Question 1 (use graph paper). For each assumed price, when would the Berkes begin to make a profit?

Source: Adapted from a case prepared by the SBA.

CASE 14C *Michael Jackson, Incorporated*

At age 25, Michael Jackson is one of the hottest stars in the pop music world. CBS Records considers him to be its biggest asset. He has won a record-breaking total of eight Grammy Awards, and his recent *Thriller* LP sold more than 27 million copies in the year it was launched. At one point, fans were buying the *Thriller* album at the incredible rate of one million copies every four days.

Why is Michael Jackson so popular? Admittedly, he has a charismatic personality and many talents. However, some credit for his success is due to the promotional efforts that have been aimed at making him a popular entertainer.

Michael Jackson was determined to make *Thriller* a big success. He spent $1.2 million of his own funds to produce the fourteen-minute *Thriller* video that was viewed on MTV, the music-video cable television station, by audiences across the United States. The video showed him dancing and singing, but there was an added twist—a monster-movie motif.

In addition, two separate video presentations were created and performed by Michael Jackson—*Billie Jean* and *Beat It*. Both of these are considered video classics. While MTV is an excellent promotional medium for all music performers, these video excerpts have quadrupled Michael Jackson's worth as a movie musical star.

The *Thriller* LP involved some strategic teamwork. To expand Michael Jackson's listener audience, Eddie Van Halen, a heavy-metal rock musician, performed on the album. In an attempt to create a worldwide appeal, Michael Jackson teamed up with British star Paul McCartney in the duet "The Girl Is Mine."

An extensive array of paraphernalia—including T-shirts, posters, buttons, and trading cards—can be purchased displaying Michael Jackson's sculptured features. For $15, a person can purchase a Michael Jackson eleven-inch doll, garbed in the red-and-black outfit he wore for the *Thriller* video. Plans have been made for a new line of leather jackets sporting the Michael Jackson trademark. Soon we may even be seeing Michael Jackson's face on a postage stamp issued by a country in the Caribbean.

Anyone attempting to wear a single glove will be considered a Michael Jackson imitator because his symbol is a single, silver-sequined glove. The glove is not new; he has been wearing it for about six years. However, it has only recently become a well-recognized symbol. Invitations sent out for his party in New York's American Museum of Natural History were printed on white gloves.

The *Thriller* success has led to numerous new opportunities for the star. Plans have been drawn up for a movies part, a biography, a concert tour with his brothers, and Pepsi commercials. PepsiCo is one of the many companies that have been attracted by Michael Jackson's popularity. As part of its "choice of a new generation" advertising campaign, Pepsi has contracted Michael Jackson and his brothers to appear in a series of advertisements.

Questions

1. What marketing tools are being used in the marketing of Michael Jackson?
2. Which ingredient in the marketing mix is especially important in marketing an entertainer's overall image?
3. Evaluate PepsiCo's decision to spotlight the Jacksons as part of its advertising campaign.

Source: William M. Pride and O. C. Ferrell, *Marketing* (Boston: Houghton Mifflin, 1985), pp. 342–344.

15 CREDIT AND COLLECTION

QUESTIONS FOR MASTERY

What is credit?

What types of credit are there?

What are the advantages and disadvantages of credit?

How important is it to age accounts receivable?

What are collection procedures?

Words pay no debts.

William Shakespeare

This is the age of mass credit. Although mass marketing began about 75 years ago with department stores, mail-order houses, and chain stores, mass credit did not begin until 45 years ago, and it has grown dramatically since World War II. Consumer credit—personal loans, service credit, installment-purchase loans—soared from $8 billion in 1946 to $181 billion in 1982. Exhibit 15.1 depicts the rapid rise.

In most industries, entrepreneurs must give credit or lose customers. Although credit helps to create customers, it also creates the risk that customers may not pay. It is vital that entrepreneurs understand how to give credit without risking failure. In this chapter, we shall give entrepreneurs the tools to understand and use credit to their advantage.

USES OF CREDIT

Today, consumers are bombarded with invitations to enjoy all manner of products and services right now and pay for them later. Most consumers accept freely, without feelings of guilt. No longer is it shameful to go into debt. In fact, the nation's prosperity depends on widespread use of charge accounts, mortgage loans, bank loans, credit cards, and other means by which customers get products before they can afford them fully. So deep is this dependence that any outbreak of resistance to credit would most likely afflict the nation with joblessness or even economic paralysis.

Credit is a way of life. To survive and grow, entrepreneurs should learn how best to give credit and, at the same time, how best to avoid nonpaying customers. If we look at each industry group, we find that credit supports:

- About 95 percent of all sales by manufacturers
- About 90 percent of all sales by wholesalers
- About 50 percent of all sales by retailers and by service firms

These high percentages mean that entrepreneurs will probably find themselves in the financing business as well. Whenever customers buy on credit, entrepreneurs are, in essence, advancing them the money to buy. To do so means that entrepreneurs must have large sums of money tied up in accounts receivable. Clearly, they should manage their use of credit carefully, or they may find themselves in financial trouble, as did this entrepreneur:

Example: Jack Woolson, owner of Woolson Filling Stations, developed a serious credit problem. Expanding from two to six stations in a three-month period, he personally hired all employees and trained them in the handling of credit.

Within another three months, he found that a very large number of old accounts receivable were uncollectible. It took his accountant an additional two months to determine that two of the new station attendants,

EXHIBIT 15.1 *Build-up in Consumer Credit*

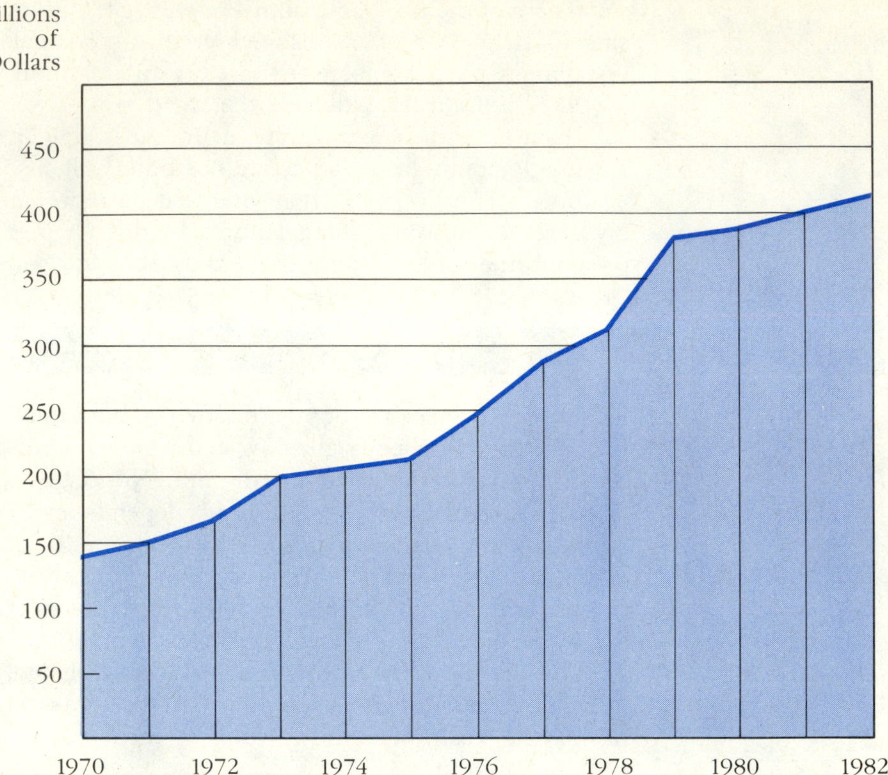

Source: U.S. Department of Commerce, *Statistical Abstract of the United States* (Washington, D.C.: U.S. Government Printing Office, 1984), p. 503

who worked evenings only, were granting credit to customers unauthorized to receive it. They had, in fact, given credit to customers on the firm's list of poor credit risks.

The firm's credit procedures called for having all credit sales checked at the home office every day. Because of the overload of work in the office, this important procedure had been bypassed and the resulting losses had occurred.

Mr. Woolson could have avoided his losses had he maintained the original procedures that worked so well. His lack of planning and poor credit discipline proved to be costly.[1]

Entrepreneurs do have the right to charge their customers interest for financing their purchases, and many entrepreneurs do just that. In some industries the sale of credit brings in more profit than the sale of products. One example is the automobile industry: "According to *The Wall Street*

EXHIBIT 15.2

The Cost of Uncollected Accounts

If the ratio of before-tax profits to sales is . . .	. . . then, for every $1,000 of uncollected accounts, additional sales in these amounts would be needed to recover the lost profit
20%	$ 5,000
15	6,700
10	10,000
5	20,000
2	50,000

Journal, more than half the dealers' average profit per new car comes from the financing charges."[2]

Credit is a source of profit that few entrepreneurs can afford to ignore. However, products should not be used as tools for credit. Remember, the main purpose of credit is to help sell products, and not the other way around.

Credit and Cost

Credit can also be costly, unless entrepreneurs take pains to control their costs of credit and collection closely. Just how costly credit can be, is underscored by Exhibit 15.2 and by this example:

Example: An entrepreneur sells $1,000 worth of lumber on credit to the Nemo Corporation, which manufactures office furniture. She has done business with Nemo before. Although at times she had to send two or three invoices, Nemo eventually paid the bill. The entrepreneur's ratio of before-tax profits to sales revenues is 5 percent.

Three months go by, and the amount is still outstanding. When the entrepreneur pursues the collection, she finds that Nemo has gone out of business. Note in Exhibit 15.2 that, at a profit-to-sales ratio of 5 percent, the entrepreneur must sell $20,000 of additional lumber to offset the $1,000 that she cannot collect.

KINDS OF CREDIT

There are two kinds of credit. One is called *commercial credit*, which is credit that one entrepreneur may give to another. Equally important is *consumer credit*, which is credit that entrepreneurs may give to individual customers.

Commercial Credit

In retailing or services, entrepreneurs often can choose whether to sell for cash or credit. They usually do not have that choice in wholesaling or

EXHIBIT 15.3 *Sample Dun and Bradstreet Report*

Summary: For quick appraisal and an overview of the company—the D&B Rating, company history and operation performance.

Special Events: Contains late-breaking news—that may affect your decisions about a firm—like criminal proceedings, bankruptcies, burglaries, fires or other disasters.

Payments: A brief review of the company's payments including dates, high credit terms, amounts owed and past due, and time period since last sale so you can evaluate how *you* will be paid.

Changes: Alerts you to shifts in management, business expansion or changes to legal structure, such as the incorporation of a proprietorship. Or changes in location or business name, so you can keep your records current.

Update: Assurance that your report contains the latest information because it has been verified by a scheduled D&B review.

Dun & Bradstreet, Inc.

BE SURE NAME, BUSINESS AND ADDRESS MATCH YOUR FILE

ANSWERING INQUIRY

This report has been prepared for:

THIS REPORT MAY NOT BE REPRODUCED IN WHOLE OR IN PART IN ANY MANNER WHATEVER.

DUNS: 00-007-7743
GORMAN MANUFACTURING CO INC
GORMAN PRINTING
(Subsidiary of Gorman Holding Companies Inc)
492 KOLLER ST
(formerly 400 KOLLER ST)
(and Branches and Divisions)
SAN FRANCISCO CA 94110-0012
TEL: 415 872-9664

CHIEF EXECUTIVE: LESLIE SMITH, PRES

DATE PRINTED
AUG 23, 198–

COMMERCIAL PRINTING
SIC NO.
27 51

SUMMARY	
RATING	3A3
STARTED	1965
PAYMENTS	SEE BELOW
SALES F	$18,931,956
WORTH F	$3,482,600
EMPLOYS	500 (150 here)
HISTORY	CLEAR
FINANCING	SECURED
CONDITION	FAIR
TREND	DOWN

SPECIAL EVENTS 8/20/8– On August 19, 198–, subject experienced a fire due to an electrical short in one of their printing machines. Damages amounted to $35,000, which was fully covered by their insurance company.

PAYMENTS (Amounts may be rounded to nearest figure in prescribed ranges)

REPORTED	PAYING RECORD	HIGH CREDIT	NOW OWES	PAST DUE	SELLING TERMS	LAST SALE WITHIN
07/8–	Ppt	1500	-0-	-0-	N30	1 Mo
07/8–	Ppt	500	-0-	-0-	N30	2-3 Mos
07/8–	Ppt	750	-0-	-0-	N30	2-3 Mos
07/8–	Slow-15	17000	6000	-0-	2 10 N30	1 Mo
07/8–	Slow-15	10000	500	-0-	2 10 N30	1 Mo
07/8–	Slow-30	3000	500	-0-	2 10 N30	1 Mo
07/8–	Slow-60	3000	3000	3000	N30	2-3 Mos
07/8–	Slow-60	2000	2000	2000	N30	2-3 Mos
06/8–	Ppt	7000	300	-0-	N30	2-3 Mos
06/8–	Ppt	5000	2500	-0-	N30	1 Mo
05/8–	Ppt	1000	-0-	-0-	EOM	2-3 Mos
05/8–	Slow-30	12000	2500	2500	N30	2-3 Mos
05/8–	Slow-30	2500	1000	1000	N30	2-3 Mos

Payment experiences reflect how bills are met in relation to the terms granted. In some instances payment beyond terms can be the result of disputes over merchandise, skipped invoices, etc.

CHANGES 03/17/8– Subject moved from 400 KOLLER ST to 492 KOLLER ST on March 11, 198–.

UPDATE 08/17/8– On August 17, 198– KEVIN J. HUNT Sec-treas stated for the six months ended June 30, 198– profits were up compared to same period last year.

FINANCE 03/17/8–

	Fiscal Dec 31, 198–	Fiscal Dec 31, 198–	Fiscal Dec 31, 198–
Curr Assets	7,151,675	7,055,442	6,770,968
Curr Liabs	3,379,403	4,015,903	4,192,046
Other Assets	1,354,469	1,336,009	1,309,375
Worth	4,056,901	3,893,231	3,482,600
Sales	26,577,608	20,432,522	18,931,956
Net Income	767,364	64,451	32,892

Fiscal statement dated Dec 31, 198–

Cash	$ 212,597	Accts Pay	$ 1,921,028
Acct Rec	1,733,380	Bank Loans	1,795,000
Inventory	4,439,597	Other Curr Liabs	476,018
Prepaid Exp	385,394		
Curr Assets	6,770,968	Curr Liabs	4,192,046
Fixt & Equip	1,271,811	L.T. Liab-Other	405,697
Other Assets	37,564	CAPITAL STOCK	50,000
		RETAINED EARNINGS	3,432,600
Total Assets	8,080,343	Total	8,080,343

(Continued)

THIS REPORT, FURNISHED PURSUANT TO CONTRACT FOR THE EXCLUSIVE USE OF THE SUBSCRIBER AS ONE FACTOR TO CONSIDER IN CONNECTION WITH CREDIT, INSURANCE, MARKETING OR OTHER BUSINESS DECISIONS, CONTAINS INFORMATION COMPILED FROM SOURCES WHICH DUN & BRADSTREET, INC. DOES NOT CONTROL AND WHOSE INFORMATION, UNLESS OTHERWISE INDICATED IN THE REPORT, HAS NOT BEEN VERIFIED. IN FURNISHING THIS REPORT, DUN & BRADSTREET, INC. IN NO WAY ASSUMES ANY PART OF THE USER'S BUSINESS RISK, DOES NOT GUARANTEE THE ACCURACY, COMPLETENESS, OR TIMELINESS OF THE INFORMATION PROVIDED, AND SHALL NOT BE LIABLE FOR ANY LOSS OR INJURY WHATEVER RESULTING FROM CONTINGENCIES BEYOND ITS CONTROL OR FROM NEGLIGENCE. 9 R2-25(750320)

Present Key to Ratings

Estimated Financial Strength			Composite Credit Appraisal: High	Good	Fair	Limited
5A	Over	$50,000,000	1	2	3	4
4A	$10,000,000 to	50,000,000	1	2	3	4
3A	1,000,000 to	10,000,000	1	2	3	4
2A	750,000 to	1,000,000	1	2	3	4
1A	500,000 to	750,000	1	2	3	4
BA	300,000 to	500,000	1	2	3	4
BB	200,000 to	300,000	1	2	3	4
CB	125,000 to	200,000	1	2	3	4

Dun & Bradstreet, Inc.

GORMAN MANUFACTURING CO INC
SAN FRANCISCO CA

AUG 23 198

This report has been prepared for:

PAGE 2
CONSOLIDATED REPORT

THIS REPORT MAY NOT BE REPRODUCED IN WHOLE OR IN PART IN ANY MANNER WHATEVER.

FINANCE (Cont'd) Annual sales $18,931,956; cost of goods sold $16,777,064. Gross profit $2,154,892; net income $32,892; dividends $29,640; monthly rent $2,500. Lease expires 1999. Fire insurance on mdse & fixt $6,000,000.

Submitted by Kevin J. Hunt, Sec-Treas. Prepared from statement(s) by Accountant: Fred Mitchel, San Francisco, CA. Prepared from books without audit.

Other assets are tangible, composed of miscellaneous deposits and deferred items. Other current liabilities and long term liabilities are notes due on equipment.

On Mar 15, 198- Kevin J. Hunt, Sec-Treas, referred to the above figures as still representative.

He stated that sales for the 12 months ended Dec 31, 198- were up compared to the same period last year. Profit for the period was down but is expected to increase. Kevin J. Hunt stated that the net worth decreased at 12/31/8-, attributed to the purchase and retirement to treasury of a portion of the capital stock.

Current debt is in excess of net worth. Inventory is large in relation to sales and working capital is light compared to volume transacted.

PUBLIC FILINGS 03/17/8- On Mar 25, 198-, a suit in the amount of $500 was filed against Gorman Manufacturing Co Inc. by Z Henric Assoc.(Docket #27511) in San Francisco, CA. Cause of action was Goods sold and delivered.

Financing statement dated Jan 28, 198- against Gorman Manufacturing Co Inc. in favor of Swinger Corp., Malibu, CA. Amount $2,000. File #741170. State CA. Assignee: San Francisco, CA. Collateral: equipment.

On March 17, 198- Kevin J. Hunt reported action filed by Z Henric Associates was due to damages caused by faulty printer and has been settled. Count records reveal suit was withdrawn.

BANKING 03/8- Balances average moderate six figures. Account open over three years. Loans extended to low seven figures, now owes low seven figures, secured by accounts receivable and inventory, and relation satisfactory.

HISTORY 03/17/8- LESLIE SMITH, PRES KEVIN J. HUNT, SEC-TREAS
DIRECTOR(s): THE OFFICER(s)

Incorporated California May 21, 1965. Authorized capital consists of 200 shares common stock, no par value.

Business started 1965 by principals. 100% of capital stock is owned by parent.

LESLIE SMITH born 1926 married. Graduated from the University of California, Los Angeles, June 1947. 1947-1965 was the general manager for Raymor Printing Co.San Francisco, CA. 1965 formed subject with Kevin J. Hunt.

KEVIN J. HUNT born 1925 married. Graduated from Northwestern University, Evanston, IL, in June 1946. 1946-1965 was the production manager for Raymor Printing Co., San Francisco, CA. 1965 formed subject with Leslie Smith.

Related Companies: Through the financial interest of Gorman Holding Companies Inc., the Gorman Manufacturing Co Inc. is related to two other sister companies (Smith Lettershop Inc, San Diego, CA and Gorman Suppliers Inc., Los Angeles, CA). These sister companies are also engaged in commercial printing. There are no intercompany relations.

OPERATION 03/17/8- Subsidiary of Gorman Holding Companies Inc.,Los Angeles, CA, which operates as a holding company for its underlying subsidiaries. Parent company has two other subsidiaries. There are no intercompany relations between parent and subject. A consolidated financial statement on the parent company, dated Dec 31, 198- showed a net worth of $7,842,226, with a fair financial condition indicated.

Commercial printing, engaged in letterpress and screen printing. Sells for cash 30% balance net 30 days. Has 1,000 accounts. Sells to commercial concerns. Territory: Nationwide. Nonseasonal.

EMPLOYEES: 500 including officers. 150 employed here.

FACILITIES: Rents 40,000 sq. ft. in 1 story concrete block building in good condition. Premises neat.

LOCATION: Industrial section on side street.

BRANCHES: Subject maintains a branch at 1073 Boyden Road, Los Angeles, CA.

07-23)9D9 /5)0039/02 00000 052

THIS REPORT, FURNISHED PURSUANT TO CONTRACT FOR THE EXCLUSIVE USE OF THE SUBSCRIBER AS ONE FACTOR TO CONSIDER IN CONNECTION WITH CREDIT, INSURANCE, MARKETING OR OTHER BUSINESS DECISIONS, CONTAINS INFORMATION COMPILED FROM SOURCES WHICH DUN & BRADSTREET, INC. DOES NOT CONTROL AND WHOSE INFORMATION, UNLESS OTHERWISE INDICATED IN THE REPORT, HAS NOT BEEN VERIFIED. IN FURNISHING THIS REPORT, DUN & BRADSTREET, INC. IN NO WAY ASSUMES ANY PART OF THE USER'S BUSINESS RISK, DOES NOT GUARANTEE THE ACCURACY, COMPLETENESS, OR TIMELINESS OF THE INFORMATION PROVIDED, AND SHALL NOT BE LIABLE FOR ANY LOSS OR INJURY WHATEVER RESULTING FROM CONTINGENCIES BEYOND ITS CONTROL OR FROM NEGLIGENCE. 9 R2-25(750320)

Finance: The essential components of the company—assets, sales, liabilities and profits—are revealed to you including comments that sum up the figures and trends.

Public Filings: Identifies specific dates of suits, judgments, tax liens and filings (if any).

Banking: Loan experience and banking relationships are presented, giving you further insights into a company's purchasing power and liquidity.

History: The company's principals or owners are identified. You can easily determine whether their past business experiences and expertise complement the company's operations.

Operation: Completes your overall picture of a company—what it does, where it is located and the size of its floor space.

Present Key to Ratings

	Estimated Financial Strength		Composite Credit Appraisal			
			High	Good	Fair	Limited
CC	75,000 to	125,000	1	2	3	4
DC	50,000 to	75,000	1	2	3	4
DD	35,000 to	50,000	1	2	3	4
EE	20,000 to	35,000	1	2	3	4
FF	10,000 to	20,000	1	2	3	4
GG	5,000 to	10,000	1	2	3	4
HH	Up to	5,000	1	2	3	4

manufacturing, mostly because:

- Buyers desire to scan the delivered products before paying the seller
- Buyers need to have the purchase financed by the seller
- Buyers depend on the seller to deliver the product to locations far from the seller's site

Entrepreneurs cannot be too careful in their credit decisions. Selling to the more stable industries, such as chemical companies, rarely poses a credit problem. Corporations like Du Pont, for example, are almost as solid as the U.S. Treasury. But in many industries the reverse is true, especially in so-called fragmented industries, which are marked by ease of entry. Example are housing construction and dress manufacture.

The Key Question How can entrepreneurs protect themselves from bad credit risks? How can they tell whether buyers will make good on their promises to pay? Naive entrepreneurs rely on blind trust. Astute entrepreneurs put their trust in the buyer's known credit reputation. The key question is: Will the buyer pay promptly?

To answer this question, it is wise for entrepreneurs to turn to credit-rating firms like Dun & Bradstreet for help. This well-known firm reports on how promptly businesses pay their bills. Their files have up-to-date credit ratings on over 5.3 million businesses. Here is what they have to say about credit:

> Credit is based on confidence. Confidence in what? It is confidence in two things: Integrity, or willingness to pay, and ability. When we say a man is a good businessman, we generally mean he has been a good businessman in the past. Our only guide, imperfect though it may be, to what a man is today, or what he may be in the future, is a study of his past. Hence, the painstaking, often time-consuming effort . . . to gather the facts concerning past business performance.[3]

Through a system of letters, numbers, and symbols, Dun & Bradstreet gives entrepreneurs who sell to other companies this vital information:

- What kind of business the buyer is in and how it is managed
- The buyer's latest income statement and balance sheet
- An estimate of the buyer's financial strength
- A record of the buyer's promptness in paying bills

Sample Credit Report On the basis of this information, entrepreneurs may better judge whether the customer will pay promptly. A sample Dun & Bradstreet credit report appears in Exhibit 15.3. Note that:

- The business has a credit rating of 3A3, which means it has a financial strength of $1,000,000 to $10,000,000 and a good credit rating.

EXHIBIT 15.4

Business Credit Terms

Terms	Meaning
2–10–30	2 percent discount for first 10 days; bill due net on day 30. Sales date coincides with date of shipment, not when sale is closed.
2–10–30 E.O.M.	2 percent discount for first 10 days, bill due net on day 30— but both days are counted from the *end* of the month in which the sales are made.
2–10–30 M.O.M.	2 percent discount for first 10 days, bill due net on day 30—but both days start from the fifteenth of the month *following* the sales date.
2–10–30 R.O.G.	2 percent discount for first 10 days, bill due net on day 30—but both periods start from the date of receipt of the product, not from the date of sale.
C.O.D. (Cash On Delivery)	Bill due upon delivery of product.
C.B.D. (Cash Before Delivery)	Product is prepared and packaged by seller, but shipment is not made until buyer pays in full.

In the *Payments* section, note such terms as *2-10-30*. This shorthand means that customers get a two percent discount by paying within 10 days. Customers who fail to take advantage of the discount must pay their bills within 30 days. Commonly used credit terms are explained in Exhibit 15.4.

The purpose of cash discounts is to persuade credit customers to pay their bills faster, thus reducing the entrepreneur's investment in accounts receivable. As borne out by Exhibit 15.5, credit customers also benefit substantially.

EXHIBIT 15.5

How Credit Customers May Benefit from Cash Discounts

If entrepreneur offers credit terms of...	...then credit customers, by taking advantage of cash discounts, can earn an annual interest rate* of
1–10–30	18%
2–10–30	36
3–10–30	54
1–10–60	7
2–10–60	14
3–10–60	22

* FORMULA: $I = \frac{D}{(G - D)(T \div 360)} \times 100$

where I = annual rate of interest earned by credit customer
D = amount of cash discount offered to credit customer
G = amount of bill owed the entrepreneur
T = the days' difference between the discount and net payment dates
360 = the number of days in a year (rounded)

Consumer Credit

Especially vulnerable to financial loss are entrepreneurs who sell directly to individual customers on credit. To screen such customers, entrepreneurs should first settle two vital questions:

- How much credit can the customer safely absorb?
- Does the customer have a history of paying bills promptly?

To get the answers, entrepreneurs should begin with the credit applicants themselves by having them fill out credit applications. Then, entrepreneurs should get a credit report on each applicant from the local credit bureau. This report enables them to:

- Verify the information volunteered by the applicant
- Determine whether the applicant pays promptly

After comparing the application and the credit report, they can decide whether to give credit. The promptness with which applicants pay their bills is the most important factor in this decision.

Credit bureaus have such information on virtually every person who has bought on credit at one time or another. Some idea of the size of the credit-checking industry may be gleaned from these statistics: The Associated Credit Bureaus of America, the largest trade association of its kind, has a membership that includes 2,200 credit bureaus, serving 500,000 businesses in 36,000 communities. The association also has 1,300 collection bureaus.

Let us end our discussion of credit by listing some of the advantages and disadvantages of giving credit to customers:

Credit Advantages

- Credit customers are likely to become repeat customers.
- Credit enables customers to buy products or services they might otherwise have to do without.
- Credit customers tend to overspend.
- Credit customers pay less attention to prices.
- Credit sales require less selling effort.
- Credit customers tend to buy products of higher quality.
- Credit is a convenience to customers who dislike carrying cash.

Credit Disadvantages

- Credit forces entrepreneurs to finance their customers, thus tying up money in accounts receivable.
- Credit refusal may cause ill will.
- Credit customers are more likely to abuse the privilege of returning products.
- Credit may cause entrepreneurs to borrow and repay with interest.
- Credit adds to the cost of doing business, because of investigations and bookkeeping needed to keep records, bill customers, and collect payments.

COLLECTION POLICIES AND PROCEDURES

At one time or another, most entrepreneurs have some trouble collecting from credit customers. Slow or nonpaying customers can severely strain the entrepreneur's financial resources.

Example: The owner of a women's dress shop makes a $100 sale on credit. Unless the customer pays, the entrepreneur may lose at least $70 and possibly more. Why? Because it cost her $70 to buy the dress from a wholesaler, and the $30 markup is designed to cover other expenses, such as rent, utilities, and the salaries of salespersons, as well as profit.

As the saying goes, a sale is not a sale until the customer pays in full. Otherwise it is a bad debt. Often, all it takes is a little prodding to get a customer to pay; but sometimes entrepreneurs are saddled with bad debts that could have been avoided had they looked into their customers' credit history. Besides investigation, a good way to avoid bad debts is to design a collection system that:

- Traces accurately the history of each customer, until the account is closed
- Alerts the entrepreneur the moment a customer is past due
- Separates credit customers into three categories: current; past due; and suspended, meaning the customer's account has been turned over to a collection agency or to a lawyer
- Updates customer accounts daily, meaning that cash from customers is posted daily
- Protects account files from theft, fire, or destruction

These principles underlie all sound collection systems. Details will vary from venture to venture, especially regarding the use of forms and files, office machines and computers. It behooves entrepreneurs to follow these principles to the letter. They can ill afford to be lax since, after all, uncollectible accounts erode profits, and may even cause failure.

Aging of Accounts Receivable

Perhaps the backbone of any collection system is the analysis of accounts receivable—the amounts owed by customers. Entrepreneurs should prepare aging schedules that keep track of how old each debt is and thus measures the quality of the receivables. Such a schedule helps entrepreneurs to spot overdue accounts that demand extra attention. An example of an aging schedule appears in Exhibit 15.6.

Note that the aging schedule works as a control device. It not only tells entrepreneurs the make-up of their receivables but also directs their attention to accounts that are severely overdue. Aging schedules may be prepared for individual customers as well as commercial customers.

EXHIBIT 15.6

Aging Schedule

Age	Amounts Owed by Customers (Receivables)
Not past-due	$13,600
01 to 30 days past-due	5,400
31 to 60 days past-due	1,200
61 to 90 days past-due	800
More than 90 days past-due	400
Total owed	$21,400

Collection Procedures

No matter how well designed a collection system may be, it is worthless unless it spurs action. Entrepreneurs should pursue each past-due customer promptly and doggedly. To be effective, follow-up procedures should move through a series of collection steps, each step more pressing than the one before, until customers have either paid their bills or been written off the books as bad debts. Generally, collection action should follow the sequence described as follows:

Reminding the credit customer: As mentioned earlier, the entrepreneur's aging schedule should flag past-due customers who need a reminder. Reminders normally go out after a grace period of 5 to 10 days from the day that payment fell due. The best reminder is warm and gentle. Why? Because, so far, the failure to pay reflects neither unwillingness nor inability to pay. There could be any number of reasons why an account is past due. The customer may have overlooked the bill, for example. Or the customer may have been troubled by an emergency that delayed payment.

Seeking a response: This step should be taken only after the gentle reminder produces no response. Stronger in tone, the second reminder asks customers why they have not paid. There may still be some good reasons why delinquent customers have not yet paid. For one, the entrepreneur may have made a billing error. Or customers may be dissatisfied with the products they purchased. Or they may be temporarily short of cash.

Pressing for payment: If gentle persuasion fails, entrepreneurs have no recourse but to press for payment. They have reminded delinquent customers twice of their promises to pay. These customers have twice failed to respond. Entrepreneurs must now assume that these customers do not intend to pay.

In pressing for payment, entrepreneurs have several avenues open to them. They may continue to write letters, each one more severe in tone. Or they may turn the accounts over to collection agencies or to lawyers. Both are expert at coaxing past-due customers to pay their bills. Often, the mere threat to sue or to repossess a product gets results.

Collection agencies offer the entrepreneur their expert knowledge of persuasive collection methods. Moreover, once past-due credit customers find out that their account has been turned over to a collection agency, they tend to pay rather than risk further damage to their credit ratings.

Such agencies usually charge 25 to 50 percent of each account collected. Although some past-due customers prefer to pay the business directly, the business must still pay the fee when the customer settles the account.

The courts are the entrepreneur's final recourse if the collection agency fails. If the amount owed is small, the problem may be resolved in a small claims court. For larger claims, however, the entrepreneur may have to sue to collect. In either case, the entrepreneur must face a costly and time-consuming procedure.

Such recourse invariably leads to unhappiness on both sides. It also reflects poorly on both the entrepreneur and the customer—on the entrepreneur for misjudging the customer's willingness to pay and on the customer for breaking the promise to pay promptly.

Taking final action: When this step is reached, all else has failed. Since they now know it is unlikely that they will ever collect, entrepreneurs have no choice but to write off the amounts owed them. The delinquent customer may have skipped town or disappeared to another address in the same city, leaving no forwarding address—or the customer may simply be a deadbeat.

Collection Period

So far, discussion has focused on collection of individual past-due accounts. Another question that merits discussion is: How may entrepreneurs measure their total credit-and-collection performance? One yardstick is the collection period. Discussed in Chapter Thirteen, collection period tells entrepreneurs how many days' revenues are tied up in accounts receivable. In other words, How long does it take, on the average, to collect from credit customers?

Example: A women's fashion shop rang up revenues of \$900,000 in 1985. Of this amount, \$730,000 reflects charge-account sales. The shop's year-end balance sheet shows accounts receivable of \$100,000. What is its average collection period? It is computed as follows:

$$\text{Daily credit revenues} = \frac{\$730{,}000}{365 \text{ days}} = \$2{,}000 \text{ per day}$$

$$\text{Collection period} = \frac{\$100{,}000}{\$2{,}000 \text{ per day}} = 50 \text{ days}$$

EXHIBIT 15.7 *Diminishing Returns on Slow-Paying Customers*

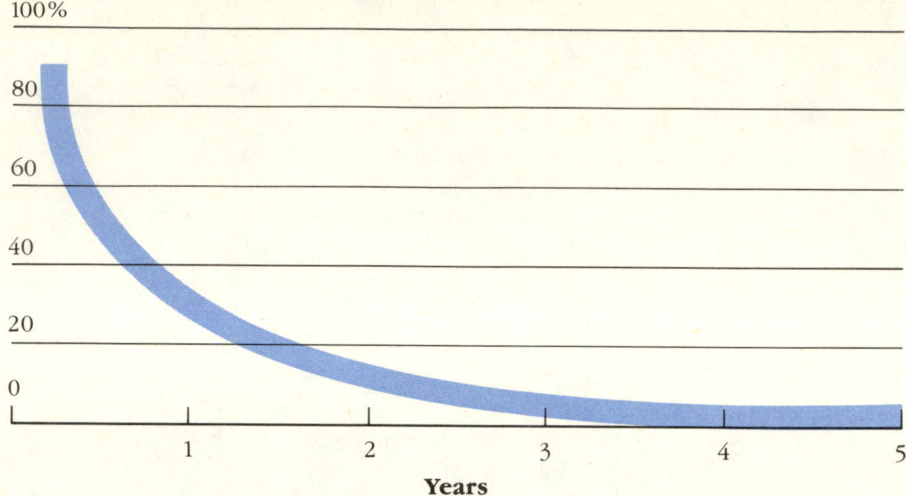

How good a job of credit and collection is the shop doing? We cannot tell without also knowing its terms of sale. On net selling terms of 30 days, a collection period of 50 days might mean the shop is performing just below par, but, on net selling terms of 60 days, it would mean the shop is performing well.

Another way to measure credit-and-collection performance is for entrepreneurs to compare their collection periods with those of others in the same industry. Although Dun & Bradstreet does compute the collection period for nearly a hundred industries, such information is unavailable for many industries.

Entrepreneurs should keep a sharp eye on credit customers. The older a bill becomes, the tougher it gets to collect, as shown graphically in Exhibit 15.7. In extreme cases, loose granting of credit may even lead to bankruptcy, as it did for this entrepreneur:

Example: Robert Richards once owned a service station. Unlike many owners, Mr. Richards had planned his venture carefully. He and his wife had saved almost $24,000, and he had waited until he found what he considered an almost ideal site for a filling station. With eight years' experience as a mechanic behind him, Mr. Richards bought all new equipment for which he paid $16,000 in cash. With $8,000 left over for working capital, he was confident that he would succeed.

By all accounts, the business should have succeeded. Sales increased during every one of the 13 months that Mr. Richards was in business. Moreover, all his bills were paid, and he was getting the business into a position where he could have made "some good money real soon."

Mr. Richards's actual financial situation was far worse than the sales record indicated, however, because much of his capital was tied up in accounts receivable that he could not collect. Despite good intentions and a big "No Credit" sign at the door, Mr. Richards was softhearted. As he put it: "See that sign? I mean what it says. You can't afford to get started in a credit business because you can never pinpoint the deadbeats. I don't want to extend credit to anyone, but the problem is to say so in a nice way. You know what I mean—so I won't lose their business."

Apparently, Mr. Richards never acquired that knack, for he lost over $8,000 in bad debts in less than a year. In desperation, he stopped giving credit altogether. As a result, his revenues dropped almost to half. Mr. Richards was so discouraged by this drop that he sold the station for just $10,000.[4]

Credit Cards

One way that entrepreneurs may avoid the problems connected with consumer credit is through the use of either bank or national credit cards. Such plans may benefit them in several ways. For example, use of credit cards sharply reduces investment in accounts receivable, and may even eliminate it altogether. Moreover, it is not the entrepreneur but the bank or the credit card company that bears the burden of credit management and collection. The SBA describes the credit card process as follows:

> Credit card service is available from the entrepreneur's regular commercial bank. Receipts from bank credit card purchases can be deposited daily so that they may be *immediately* credited to the entrepreneur's checking account.
>
> The bank assumes all credit risks so long as the entrepreneur follows instructions for approval of credit card purchases. Typically, these instructions require the entrepreneurs to check the validity of the card against a master list of canceled cards and contact the credit service before accepting the customer's card for purchase above a certain limit.
>
> In return for this service, the bank charges a percentage of total credit card sales.
>
> The national credit services run on a similar basis, but they do not offer the advantage of daily credits to the business's checking account. As with bank credit cards, the business must follow established procedures and, by so doing, eliminates any risk connected with uncollectible accounts. Normally, national credit card companies remit to the business twice monthly and charge a fee based upon a percentage of total credit card sales.
>
> Credit card services are especially vital for businesses with a large number of relatively small accounts. They eliminate the need for credit approval, invoice preparation, record maintenance, and collections. They also minimize the entrepreneur's commitment of capital and virtually eliminate the risk of uncollectible accounts. From a marketing

viewpoint, the availability of instant credit could often encourage a customer to buy immediately, rather than postpone the decision to a later date or bypass it completely.[5]

THE FUTURE ROLE OF CREDIT

Credit will continue to play a prominent role in the economy. Thanks to electronic wizardry, a checkless, cashless society may evolve by the year 2000. In such a society, money would transfer electronically, making the use of cash and checks largely unnecessary.

Credit cards are already playing a vital role in this new era of instant money, forming the nucleus around which consumers organize their financial dealings. Consumers now may use their credit cards to:

- Get cash from commercial banks or from other businesses
- Charge purchases of products internationally as well as nationally
- Pay bills automatically

From a technological viewpoint, a checkless, cashless system is more feasible than many entrepreneurs may realize. If there are delays in putting it into effect, they are due to social, not technological, problems. Still to be resolved are such questions as these:

- How should credit customers be identified? Some alternatives are by fingerprint or by voiceprint. Identification is perhaps the thorniest problem. There must be a way to make credit cards fail-safe so that their loss or theft does not result in electronic robbery.
- Who should have access to a customer's credit file? Under what circumstances? The question of privacy is a major issue in the relatively simple process of determining who is eligible for credit and how much.

If it becomes a reality, the cashless society will probably handle finances more cheaply, more quickly, and more efficiently. Already, many industries other than banking are studying the possibility of a cashless society and what it will mean to them. There are three reasons for believing that such a society may be just around the corner:

- Most of the electronic technology needed to make it possible is already available.
- In the years to come, the nation's financial system will need the cashless society to avoid being overcome by the sheer volume of paper.
- The federal government supports the idea of a cashless society because it knows that some people—from gamblers and racketeers to white-collar professionals and blue-collar moonlighters—receive payments in cash so there is no record.

SUMMARY

Today, credit is a way of life. To survive and grow, entrepreneurs should learn how best to grant credit and, at the same time, avoid the problem of nonpaying customers. When they grant credit, entrepreneurs advance money to customers to buy products or services.

There are two kinds of credit. One is commercial credit, which entrepreneurs grant to other ventures. The other is consumer credit, which they grant to individuals.

Because they are likely to have large sums of money tied up in accounts receivable, entrepreneurs cannot be too careful in screening credit applicants. They should find out whether each applicant has a history of paying bills promptly. Credit histories on individuals are available from local credit bureaus and on businesses from Dun & Bradstreet.

At one time or another, most entrepreneurs have some trouble collecting from credit customers. Slow or nonpaying customers can severely strain the entrepreneur's financial resources. Besides investigation before granting credit, a good way to avoid bad debts is to design a collection system that alerts the entrepreneur the moment an account is past due. Entrepreneurs should pursue each past-due account promptly and doggedly; the older a bill becomes, the tougher it gets to collect.

Credit will continue to play a prominent role in our economy. Chances are that a cashless society will evolve by the year 2000. This dramatic change will help solve the paperwork problems now plaguing the nation's financial system while making it easier for customers and entrepreneurs to do business.

DISCUSSION AND REVIEW QUESTIONS

1. Explain why credit is so vital an activity in our economy.
2. Explain the difference between commercial credit and consumer credit.
3. How would you, as an entrepreneur, go about avoiding bad debts?
4. Define these terms: *credit, credit report, 2-10-30, past-due account, aging schedule, collection period, cashless society.*
5. Do you believe we soon will have a checkless, cashless society? Why?
6. How would you, as an entrepreneur, benefit from granting credit to customers?
7. What is the best measure of an entrepreneur's performance in credit-and-collection activities? Explain.
8. Explain why entrepreneurs who grant credit are also in the financing business.
9. Why do manufacturers make almost all their sales on credit?
10. Describe the steps an entrepreneur should take in collecting an overdue bill.
11. How does the aging schedule help to minimize bad debts?

12. If you owned a theater or a bowling alley, why might you be reluctant to grant credit?
13. Do you agree with the statement, "Credit is a source of profit"? Explain your answer fully.
14. If an entrepreneur has an average collection period of 28 days, is that good or bad? Explain fully.
15. At what point should an entrepreneur write off a past-due account as a bad debt?

NOTES

1. Harvey C. Krentzman, U.S. Small Business Administration, *Managing for Profits* (Washington, D.C.: U.S. Government Printing Office, 1968), p. 106.
2. Quoted by Hillel Black, *Buy Now, Pay Later* (New York: William Morrow, 1961), p. 112.
3. *Ten Keys to Basic Credits and Collections* (New York: Dun & Bradstreet, 1972), p. 11.
4. Adapted from Kurt B. Mayer and Sidney Goldstein, U.S. Small Business Administration, *The First Two Years: Problems of Small Firm Growth and Survival* (Washington, D.C.: U.S. Government Printing Office, 1961), pp. 128–129.
5. U.S. Small Business Administration, *Business Basics: Credit and Collections* (Washington, D.C.: U.S. Government Printing Office, 1985), p. 29.

CASE 15A *American Steel Fabricating and Machinery Company, Inc.*

Nolan Williams began his fabricating business in 1975. Six years and four expansions later, his business had expanded from a one-man operation to 40 employees. In 1981, sales revenues topped $1.3 million. Now he is wondering whether to reorganize his company for future growth—and if so, how?

Background

A native of Texas, Mr. Williams came to Cleveland at age 18. At the time, becoming an entrepreneur was the furthest thing from his mind. He wanted only to get a job, any job. But he soon found that Cleveland employers wanted men with skills. And he possessed none.

Upon hearing from a friend that welding paid high wages, Mr. Williams enrolled in a 9-week welding course. He did well in the course. Soon afterward he got his first job, working in a metal-fabricating company as a welder. While there, he acquired a second skill: tool and die design.

After changing jobs several times—but always observing and learning—Mr. Williams decided to strike off on his own. He had been thinking about it for several years. He saw how others ran their metal-fabricating companies, and he became convinced that he could do as well, if not better. "I wanted to do something on my own," he says. "I knew I had the ability to get things done and the self-confidence that I could make it."

Gets Help

Only three months passed from the moment Mr. Williams made his decision until he opened for business. It was 1975, and he was 28 years old.

But before he got underway, Mr. Williams talked to successful entrepreneurs like Julian Madison, one of Cleveland's best-known architects. Mr. Williams made mental notes of the advice he received. For example, he was told to form relationships with a banker, a lawyer, and an accountant, in that order. So he did.

Mr. Williams wasted little time assembling a management team. Together they picked a plant site, ordered welding equipment, set up a bookkeeping system, raised cash, and moved in. His beginning balance sheet appears in Exhibit 15A.1.

Mr. Williams's corporate charter authorized him to issue 500 shares of stock at a par value of $10 each. He issued 100 shares to himself and 150 shares to others, leaving 250 shares unissued. Mr. Williams paid only $200 for his shares; the others paid nothing. It was Mr. Williams's way of paying them for their help in getting his business started.

Although he spent $3,000 for welding equipment and hand tools, he really needed "at least $25,000 to equip the plant properly to compete for customer orders." After struggling for three months, he received a $20,000 loan from the Central National Bank to finance purchase of additional equipment. Meanwhile, to survive, he had "borrowed two welding machines from another company, which had idle capacity."

EXHIBIT 15A.1

American Steel Fabricating and Machinery Company, Inc.: Balance Sheet (July 1, 1975)

Assets		Equities		
Cash	$ 100	Loan payable		$3,000
Equipment	3,000	Owners' equity		
Organizational costs	2,000	Williams	$1,000	
Prepaid expenses	400	Others	1,500	2,500
Total assets	$5,500	Total equities		$5,500

Long Hours

During the first year, he found himself working 14 hours a day, 7 days a week. "It was quite a change from my old job," says Mr. Williams. "My family rarely saw me. My business became my life."

He found that his lack of managerial experience was a real drawback. Until then, he had never tried to get things done through others. "I had never supervised anyone before," says Mr. Williams. "But I was in it, so I soon learned. In fact, I haven't stopped learning." What had pulled him through in the early years was his knowledge of shopwork and his "desire and determination to succeed."

One major mistake still bothers him. Early in the business, he formed an alliance with a friend. Their talents appeared to mesh. Mr. Williams's strong suit was production; the friend's was marketing. But soon after learning the business and moving up to a vice presidency, the friend resigned to form his own venture. Not wishing to have a competitor as a shareholder, Mr. Williams bought back his friend's shares of stock for $20,000, although the friend had received his shares without paying a single penny for them. "That was my biggest mistake," says Mr. Williams.

Financial Performance

Mr. Williams ended his first year—1976—with a loss of $5,000. He also lost money in succeeding years, until, in 1981, he turned the corner with before-tax profits of $170,000 on revenues of $1.3 million. His 1981 income statement appears in Exhibit 15A.2. Mr. Williams is proud of the statement, mainly because he still shoulders a heavy burden of debt. He borrowed heavily when he began, and he has continued to borrow, mostly to finance four expansions. So, he watches his "profit position closely—and more importantly, cash flow." A balance sheet from 1981 appears in Exhibit 15A.3.

Mr. Williams continues to expand his business. This year he acquired 51 percent control of another steel-fabricating company in Solon, Ohio, and he is searching for still another company to buy into, to make machinery rather than weld it.

Mr. Williams's lawyer was especially helpful in the Solon acquisition, as were his accountant and banker. The lawyer handled negotiations and the legal aspects of acquisition, the accountant audited the books of the seller, and the banker helped him finance the purchase.

EXHIBIT 15A.2

American Steel Fabricating and Machinery Company, Inc.: Income Statement (for year ending July 31, 1981)

Gross sales revenues	$1,300,700	
Less: Returns and discounts	71,600	$1,229,100
Cost of goods sold		856,800
Gross profit		$ 372,300
Operating expenses		
Office salaries	$ 84,300	
Taxes*	39,400	
Interest	17,900	
Insurance	14,300	
Freight	12,100	
Hospitalization	10,200	
Accounting	5,800	
Truck and auto	5,500	
Telephone and telegraph	4,900	
Selling	4,900	
Maintenance	4,100	
Office supplies	3,600	
Auto leasing	2,400	
Legal	1,200	
Depreciation	1,200	
Advertising	1,000	212,800
Operating profit		$ 159,500
Other income		11,400
Before tax profit		$ 170,900
Federal income taxes		0
Net profit		$ 170,900

* Includes city income tax, franchise tax, personal property tax, real estate tax, and other taxes.

EXHIBIT 15A.3

American Steel Fabricating and Machinery Company, Inc.: Balance Sheet (July 31, 1981)

Assets		
Current assets		
Cash	$ 55,600	
Accounts receivable	144,700	
Notes receivable	2,600	
Raw material inventory	55,700	
Work in process	67,400	
Prepaid expenses	21,500	$347,500
Fixed assets		
Plant and equipment	$267,300	
Accumulated depreciation	79,600	187,700
Other assets		4,900
Total assets		$540,100

Equities		
Current liabilities		
Accounts payable	$140,300	
Notes payable	54,800	
Accrued taxes	22,900	
Other	6,300	$224,300
Long-term loans		135,900
Deferred federal taxes		6,500
Owners' equity		
Common stock	$ 17,900	
Paid-in capital	7,200	
Retained earnings	148,300	173,400
Total equities		$540,100

Marketing Strategy

To achieve growth, Mr. Williams has weathered some rugged competition. There are roughly 200 other metal-fabricating companies in Cleveland, 20 of which employ more than 100 persons. So, the industry is highly fragmented—a fact that he believes works to his advantage.

To wean customers away from competitors, Mr. Williams focuses on big business. In fact, his clients read like a *Who's Who* in manufacturing: Xerox, Westinghouse, General Motors, Cummins Engine, Warner and Swasey, Otis Elevator, Harris-Intertype, and Thompson-Ramo-Wooldridge.

To snare new customers, he uses a marketing mix made up almost solely of personal selling. Neither advertising nor sales promotion plays a role. Instead, he calls on purchasing agents himself—but only after determining whether they need his services. "I always do my homework before I pay them a visit," says Mr. Williams, "and it has paid off."

EXHIBIT 15A.4 *American Steel Fabricating and Machinery Company, Inc.: Organizational Chart, July 1, 1981*

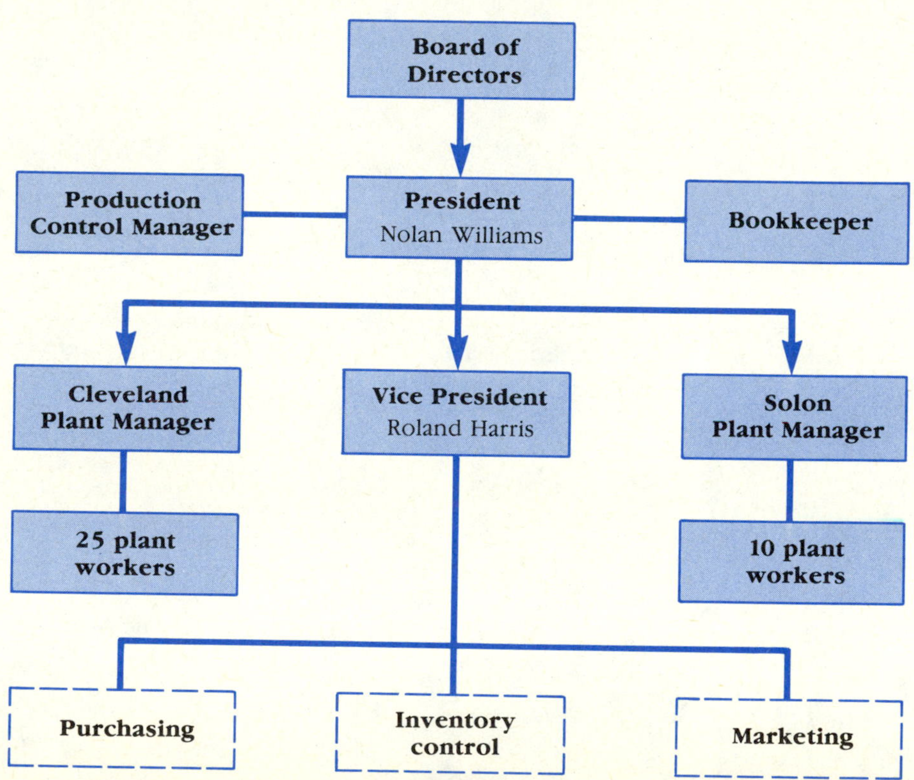

Only one salesman helps Mr. Williams. The salesman's job is to retain existing customers, while Mr. Williams's is to land new customers. Mr. Williams alone handles customer complaints. He is sensitive to complaints of any kind. He personally answers each one the day it is received. "We sell quality and service," says Mr. Williams, "so we can't afford to fall short."

To help ensure quality, he employs only skilled welders who qualify as craftsmen. This philosophy affects his entire organization. For example, his foremen have a combined work experience of 45 years, his accountant is a Certified Public Accountant, and his layout person is a graduate mechanical engineer. His organizational chart appears in Exhibit 15A.4.

Mr. Williams enjoys a rapport with employees that is rare in metal-fabricating circles. So good are his relations with employees that none of them belong to a union. Recently, the Teamsters Union tried to organize all plant workers, but they turned the union away.

Production Capability

Mr. Williams's Cleveland plant is equipped to deliver the full range of welding services demanded by his clients. "We sell our capabilities to do a job," says Mr. Williams. "That's what customers look for." The plant covers 50,000 square feet, roughly the size of a football field. When he first went into business, his plant covered only 1,000 square feet. A photograph of the plant appears in Exhibit 15A.5.

EXHIBIT 15A.5 *American Steel Fabricating and Machinery Company, Inc.: View of Cleveland Plant*

The plant houses such equipment as welding machines, brake presses that bend steel, a shear to cut steel, a burning machine to cut steel patterns, and a punch press. There is no inventory problem because Mr. Williams runs a job shop, meaning work starts only after a customer orders it—he never produces in anticipation of orders. His backlog of orders averages three months. "I begin to worry when it gets down to one month," says Mr. Williams.

"My door is always open to employees," says Mr. Williams. "If they have a problem, they're free to come in and discuss it with me." As a result, his turnover among welders and fitters is so low it excites envy among competitors. Among laborers, however, turnover is high.

Besides being fair and open with employees, Mr. Williams also looks after them. For example, he offers such fringe benefits as Blue Cross and Blue Shield. Soon he will introduce life insurance at low group rates.

As for himself, Mr. Williams avoids estate planning of any kind. He does not even have a will. "My lawyer is after me about that," he says, "but I'm too young to think about it seriously." Nor has he groomed anyone to take over if he should suddenly become physically incapable of running the business.

Currently, Mr. Williams is spending much of his time merging his Solon acquisition into the company. "We've had lots of problems out there," says Mr. Williams, "problems we never found out about until after we bought 51 percent control." He is also considering how best to reach his sales goal of $10 million a year by 1987. "That's an ambitious goal," he says. In 1981, his revenues stood at $1.3 million.

Questions

1. What accounts for Mr. Williams's success?
2. Comment on Mr. Williams's entrepreneurial traits.
3. Do you believe it was wise for Mr. Williams to acquire a second plant? Explain.
4. Comment on Mr. Williams's relations with his workers.
5. If you were Mr. Williams, would you, have gone deeply into debt to achieve your sales goals? Explain.

CASE 15B *Charlane's Fashions, Inc.*

An entrepreneur owned a pair of small but highly profitable stores specializing in women's wear. For years she had placed orders only for her normal needs, usually in the $500 to $1,000 range. She bought most goods from the top ready-to-wear manufacturers in New York, always without difficulty. Her credit reputation was excellent—she paid her bills on time, never made unauthorized returns, and always behaved, from the suppliers' point of view, in a most exemplary way.

EXHIBIT 15B.1

Charlane's Fashions, Inc.: Balance Sheet (July 31, 1980)

Assets		Equities	
Current assets	$41,000	Current liabilities	$ 5,100
Fixed assets	4,300	Owners' equity	40,200
Total assets	$45,300	Total equities	$45,300

Charlane's Fashions, Inc.: Income Statement (for six months ending July 31, 1980)

Sales revenues	$100,500
Operating expenses	89,300
Operating profit	$ 11,200
Federal income tax	2,400
Net profit	$ 8,800

She had started from scratch, so it was with some pride that she went over her latest financial statements (see Exhibit 15B.1). She had indeed come a long way in the five years she had been in business for herself.

Heady with success, she decided to open nine new stores the next year, without investing additional money. She planned instead to rely solely upon the good will of her current suppliers to finance her expansion and to act as references for her new suppliers.

She kept her suppliers, new and old, in the dark about her ambitious plan to expand. She was sure suppliers would never suspect that she planned to add as many as nine stores in *one* year.

Her credit rating was excellent so she aroused little suspicion when, the following spring season, she flew to New York and began placing orders larger than previously. By June 20, she had placed more than 200 orders with suppliers, totaling more than $230,000. Most of these orders were placed with new suppliers.

The day of reckoning soon arrived. On August 8, she called a meeting of her creditors, to report that her company was in troubled financial straits (see Exhibit 15B.2).

EXHIBIT 15B.2 *Charlane's Fashions, Inc.: Balance Sheet (July 31, 1981)*

Assets			Equities		
Current assets			Current liabilities		
Cash	$ 900		Accounts payable	$503,100	
Inventory	314,400	$315,300	Payroll tax	23,300	
Fixed assets		5,500	Bank loan	3,800	$530,200
			Owners' equity		(209,400)
Total assets		$320,800	Total equities		$320,800

Less than a month later, the referee's office in the Central District of California judged her to be bankrupt. The new stores she had managed to open went down the drain along with her original two.

Questions

1. What really caused the entrepreneur's bankruptcy? If you had been the entrepreneur, what would you have done differently? Why?
2. Could the entrepreneur's creditors have prevented their losses? If so, how?
3. What was the company's operating loss in its last year?
4. What should the entrepreneur do now? Why?

Source: Case adapted from Sol Barzman, *Everyday Credit Checking*. © 1973 by Sol Barzman courtesy of John Shaffner Associates.

CASE 15C *Bingham Electrical Parts, Inc.*

Norton Bingham owned an electrical parts and supplies store in Los Angeles. Modestly successful over the years, Mr. Bingham sold his electrical products on credit terms of 2-10-30.

In 1980, Mr. Bingham's sales revenues were $480,000. On December 31, 1980, his accounts receivable were $60,000.

According to Dun & Bradstreet, collection periods for the electrical parts and supplies industry vary as follows:

Range	Collection Period
Top Fourth	38 days
Median	47
Bottom Fourth	60

Questions

1. On the average, how long does it take Mr. Bingham to collect from his customers?
2. How good is Mr. Bingham at managing his credit-and-collection activities?

16 HUMAN RELATIONS

QUESTIONS FOR MASTERY

What is human relations?

How important is participatory management?

What are the needs of workers and how can one satisfy those needs?

Why are wage and salary policies important?

How important are safety and health on the job?

After all, there is but one race—humanity.

George Moore

Far from being a mysterious science, human relations is often nothing more than good will and applied common sense. Much of an entrepreneur's success in human relations depends on simple things, such as making a store a friendlier place to work or making a plant more comfortable.

Entrepreneurs often ignore these simple things, especially when their ventures begin to grow. When they start their ventures, entrepreneurs often have only themselves and perhaps a few employees to manage. A strong sense of purpose binds owner and employees together. But the addition of new workers tends to loosen that bond unless entrepreneurs pay attention to so-called people problems. In this chapter, we shall discuss these problems by focusing on the responsibilities of entrepreneurs to recognize the needs of their workers and manage their workers in ways that help bring out their best.

THE IMPORTANCE OF HUMAN RELATIONS

So massive are many businesses today that workers lose all sense of human contact with their employers. In many manufacturing industries, for example, the high degree of mechanization robs workers of their sense of personal pride and often their identification with the product they help make. Many workers do not even know how customers use the product. The robotlike nature of much of their work thwarts their sense of self-respect. In the words of Fyodor Dostoyevsky, the famed Russian author:

> If it were desired to reduce a man to nothingness, it would be necessary only to give his work a character of uselessness.[1]

A character of uselessness is imposed on much of the work done in plants, stores, and offices. Many workers feel they have been swallowed by a big, impersonal machine that robs them of their self-respect and identity. Out of this betrayal of the human spirit, the science of human relations was born to find ways to give workers a sense of usefulness and thus improve their performance on the job. One of the tenets of human relations is that life can be made more enjoyable by making work more meaningful.

Often, however, entrepreneurs lose sight of the importance of meaningful work in their rush to boost revenues. They soon find themselves saddled with workers who do poorly. Why? Because they are unhappy. The entrepreneur can buy:

- A worker's time
- A worker's physical presence at a given place
- A measured number of skilled muscular motions per hour

But the entrepreneur can*not* buy:

- The worker's enthusiasm
- The worker's initiative or idea-getting ability
- The worker's loyalty

Entrepreneurs must earn these valuable contributions from their employees. They can do so by recognizing that workers need to feel that the work they do really matters, that the entrepreneur is interested in them and appreciates what they do. Workers generally do better, for example, when they are singled out for individual attention. The recognition makes them feel they no longer are nameless cogs. In return for their loyalty and enthusiasm, they expect entrepreneurs to:

- Protect their right to work continuously, as long as they perform honestly and productively
- Give them a chance to advance as the venture grows
- Treat them as human beings, with dignity and respect

Entrepreneurs should keep in mind that every worker, regardless of abilities, has the right to be treated with respect and dignity. In fact, entrepreneurs have a moral obligation to grant their workers that right.

PARTICIPATORY MANAGEMENT

One way for entrepreneurs to instill a strong sense of purpose in workers is to share decision making with them. The practice of shared decision making is called *participatory management*. Its message is this:

- The entrepreneur should recognize the social needs of workers as well as their need for money.
- Workers will respond with better performance and will help shape the venture's changing goals.

In essence, participatory management encourages entrepreneurs to seek out their workers' ideas and, in addition, to organize work around jobs broad enough to have meaning. Participatory management also encourages entrepreneurs to:

- Share decision making with workers
- Share authority and responsibility with workers
- Communicate openly and candidly—up, down, and sideways within the venture

This approach, however, may not work well with all employees. In fact, studies show that happy workers are sometimes merely happy—and

EXHIBIT 16.1

Record your answers in the appropriate area of the spectrum. For example, on the first question, if you answer "almost complete," put a check mark between "substantial" and "complete" but more toward the "complete" end of the continuous gray line. When you have answered each question, draw a line through the check marks from the top to the bottom of the chart. The result will be a profile of your managerial style.

Analysis of Managerial Style

		System 1 Exploitive Authoritative	*System 2* Benevolent Authoritative	*System 3* Consultative	*System 4* Participatory Group
Leadership	How much confidence is shown in subordinates?	None	Little	Substantial	Complete
	How free do they feel to talk to superiors about their job?	Not at all	Not very	Rather free	Fully free
	Are subordinates' ideas sought and used, if worthy?	Seldom	Sometimes	Usually	Always
Communication	How much communication is aimed at achieving organization's objectives?	Very little	Little	Quite a bit	A great deal
	What is the direction of information flow?	Downward	Mostly downward	Down and up	Down, up, and sideways
	How is downward communication accepted?	With suspicion	Possibly with suspicion	With caution	With an open mind
	How accurate is upward communication?	Often wrong	Censored for the boss	Limited accuracy	Accurate
	How well do superiors know problems faced by subordinates?	Know little	Some knowledge	Quite well	Very well

Motivation	Is predominant use made of 1 fear, 2 threats, 3 punishment, 4 rewards, 5 involvement?	1, 2, 3, occasionally 4	4, some 3	4, some 3 and 5	5, 4, based on group set goals
	Where is responsibility felt for achieving organization's goals?	Mostly at top	Top and middle	Fairly general	At all levels
Decisions	At what level are decisions formally made?	Mostly at top	Policy at top, some delegation	Broad policy at top, more delegation	Throughout but well integrated
	What is the origin of technical and professional knowledge used in decision making?	Top management	Upper and middle	To a certain extent, throughout	To a great extent, throughout
	Are subordinates involved in decisions related to their work?	Not at all	Occasionally consulted	Generally consulted	Fully involved
	What does decision-making process contribute to motivation?	Nothing, often weakens it	Relatively little	Some contribution	Substantial contribution

Source: Adapted from *The Human Organization: Its Management and Value*, by Rensis Likert.

not productive. Some workers can take only limited responsibility. They prefer to let others shoulder the main burden of responsibility.

Entrepreneurs should exercise care in unlocking the talents and energies of their workers. Participatory management is not for every venture. But there is an impressive body of evidence to suggest that it works well, especially among ventures that are struggling to keep pace with shifting markets or are growing at a fast pace.

Participatory management may not be for every entrepreneur, either. An entrepreneur with an authoritative style may find it hard to adapt to the expectations of a participative approach. How may entrepreneurs determine whether their managerial style is authoritarian or participative? One way is to use the chart in Exhibit 16.1 (pages 482 and 483), developed by Dr. Rensis Likert at the Institute of Social Relations of the University of Michigan.

DIFFERENT STYLES OF LEADERSHIP

Although the idea of participatory management was developed decades ago, it has become known only recently in the United States, where entrepreneurs still tend to be more autocratic than participatory. Turning

EXHIBIT 16.2 *Continuum of Leadership Styles*

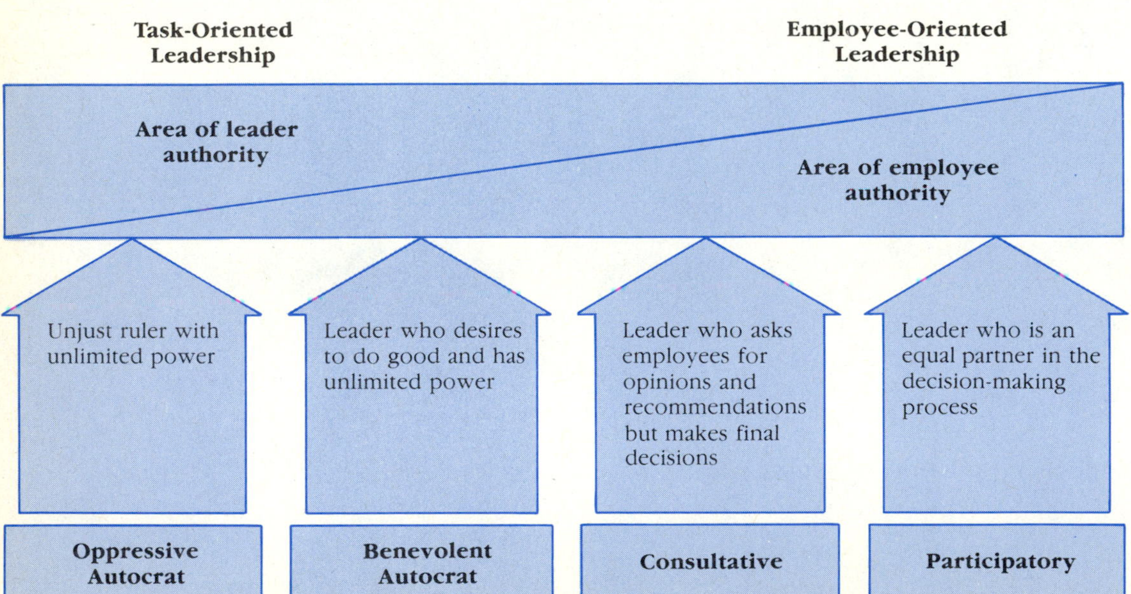

Source: Reprinted by permission of the *Harvard Business Review*. An exhibit from "How to Choose a Leadership Pattern" by Robert Tannenbaum and Warren H. Schmidt (May/June 1973).

to Exhibit 16.2, note the different styles of leadership that entrepreneurs may adopt:

Oppressive Autocrat: Entrepreneurs who adopt this leadership style are absolute dictators. They believe that they are always in the best position to judge what is best for employees. Moreover, they believe that the proper superior-subordinate relationship exists only when subordinates do precisely what they were told without questioning their superior.

Such leadership does not necessarily imply the use of force, but force may sometimes be used. Some employees respond well to this kind of leadership, but most do not.

Oppressive autocratic leadership appeals to two kinds of entrepreneurs—those who are uneducated and know of no better ways, and those who are self-centered and need this style in order to feel important.

Benevolent Autocrat: This style of leadership is both task-oriented and employee-oriented at the same time. Although these entrepreneurs are absorbed with the accomplishment of tasks, they do consider the wishes, feelings, and needs of employees. Benevolent autocrats try to do what is best for their employees, and keep them informed on the reasons for decisions.

Such entrepreneurs may ask employees for facts and information before making decisions, but they do not ask for their recommendations. Nor do they permit employees to make decisions or take part in the decision-making process.

Their attitude toward employees is warm, friendly, courteous, and respectful. They regard employees not as second-class citizens, but as equals in the human family. They do not make shows of rank to make themselves feel important. Nor do they make employees feel inferior. There is never any question, however, about who is in charge.

Consultative: In this style of leadership, entrepreneurs suggest courses of action to their employees. They are open to new alternatives and want the honest reactions of their subordinates. Their employees may be able to persuade them to accept different solutions. This style by no means leads to a one-person, one-vote situation, however. In the final analysis, entrepreneurs make the decisions themselves. They must accept full responsibility for these decisions, even if they have based them on bad advice.

Participatory: As already discussed earlier, this style of leadership requires complete involvement of subordinates in the decision-making process.[2]

Example: Perhaps the best-known practitioners of participatory management are the Japanese. They use it almost exclusively. Consider this example:

. . . Troubled by increasing costs and the three to six months' time that

> it took to ship zippers from Japan to the United Kingdom, Y.K.K. in 1969 invested $3.5 million in a British plant. The gamble... has been a mighty success. The plant has never been hit by a strike or a slowdown. . . . There is basically no difference in performance between British workers and those in Japan.
>
> Inside the plant, pop music throbs from loudspeakers while a multinational collection of American, West German, British, and Japanese machines turn out 6,000,000 zippers a month. . . . All men employees wear Y.K.K.'s jackets, which have the company initials proudly displayed on the breast pocket and no fewer than six zippers on the front, the pockets, and the cuffs.
>
> Japanese-style corporate paternalism is strong. Y.K.K. provides cut-rate bus service for employees and . . . is forever throwing morale-boosting, all-hands-welcome parties at [a local motel]. After work on Fridays, the Japanese make a point of dropping [into a pub] near the plant to socialize. . . .
>
> . . . John Davies, who represents the employees on the plant's Japanese-style "works committee," renders the final verdict: "We asked to finish at 4:30 P.M. instead of 5 on Friday; they gave us that. We asked for a Christmas holiday; they gave us that. We asked for a sickness scheme and they gave us that, too. These Japanese seem to understand us. I wouldn't want to work for an English firm again."[3]

The Japanese style is designed to create group unity through which entrepreneurs may achieve efficiency and a sense of teamwork. Recently, the Japanese style has made some inroads in the United States, especially among major corporations.

THE ENTREPRENEUR AS COACH

Today, the job of managing often is looked upon as the job of getting work done through others. Managing means much more, however. It also includes making it possible for others to work easily and productively, and at the same time bringing out the best in them. How can entrepreneurs help workers achieve their best?

First, entrepreneurs must want to help their workers become achievers. Some do not, holding fast to the idea that workers do not crave satisfaction from their jobs. This attitude may cause such problems as absenteeism and high turnover, shoddy workmanship and a weakening of the will to work.

What many entrepreneurs lack is an understanding of just how deeply managerial style can affect the survival and growth of their venture. They need to analyze their managerial style, using as a guide the questions shown earlier, in Exhibit 16.1. By answering such questions, entrepreneurs may learn a good deal about themselves as well as about the way they treat their workers.

As humorist Josh Billings once said, "It's not only one of the most difficult things to know yourself, but one of the most inconvenient ones, too." Although it may be an uncomfortable task, the more realistic the entrepreneurs' view of themselves, the better will be their performance as managers; for insights are the building blocks of personal growth. Growing entrepreneurs change because they want to and because they must, in response to insights gained on the job.

Self-image

Entrepreneurs cannot begin to know their workers without first knowing themselves. All entrepreneurs, whether they are aware of it or not, have self-images. They may, for example, see themselves as quick or slow, neat or sloppy, busy or lazy. Everything they feel, hear, or do is filtered through their self-images, so they are what their self-images allow them to be. In order for entrepreneurs to grow as managers, they must know—and change—their self-images. To twist an old saying, it is not what the entrepreneur knows that counts, but rather who he or she is.

Mainly through these processes of self-discovery and change of self-image, entrepreneurs learn how people work better. These processes go on continuously, yet many entrepreneurs ignore them in themselves and in their workers. When entrepreneurs do not understand how their employees see themselves and what motivates them, they cannot give their employees the tools they need to change. The result often is a poor product or slipshod service that jeopardizes survival and halts growth. Entrepreneurs cannot isolate themselves from their workers. At a conference of business leaders, Robert Townsend, former head of the Avis Corporation, offered these prescriptions:

> The boss should be constantly with the workers. So important is this that the paraphernalia of the boss should be entirely removed. He shouldn't have a mahogany office. He shouldn't have a limousine. He shouldn't have a space reserved outside for his car. He shouldn't be addressed by anything but his first name. And he shouldn't receive a salary more than five times that of the least of his employees. For all intents and purposes, that means his salary should not be in excess of [$60,000].
>
> What happens then? Well sir, morale is very high, workers have a sense of participation in the business, absenteeism all but disappears, and the problem is pretty well solved.[4]

A Creative Work Atmosphere

Entrepreneurs can learn the art of bringing out the best in their workers by observing the model presented by successful athletic coaches. Just as athletic coaches must be close to their players, so must entrepreneurs be close to their workers. Topflight coaches generally have teams that win consistently, mostly because the coaches know their job and have a knack for communicating that knowledge to their players:

- Players see their assignments with clarity because their coach helps them see.
- Players understand how to carry out their assignments because their coach has meticulously laid out the game plan and the plays necessary for use against competition.
- Players execute their assignments with West Point precision because their coach has created an atmosphere of fairness, confidence, and camaraderie, which generates the will to win.

Creating such a work atmosphere is difficult. No two players, or workers, are precisely alike. What appeals to one worker may repel another. Each worker is uniquely complex, so to help workers achieve their best, entrepreneurs must understand each worker's needs. According to psychologists, needs are what motivate us and the process of motivation is circular—a person feels a need, makes an effort to satisfy the need, and receives feedback that leads to a new need. Workers are motivated to behave in certain ways because of their need for certain things, among them money, security, and status.

Work helps satisfy all these needs. Weekly paychecks, for example, enable workers to buy food, clothes, and a house. Besides security, workers may also seek status through:

- Promotions
- Merit salary increases
- Learning new skills
- Invention of new products

The Hawthorne Experiment

Work helps satisfy a worker's physical and emotional needs. Workers want entrepreneurs to treat them as individuals, craving recognition for a job well done. A classic example of what happens when workers are treated as individuals was demonstrated by the now-famous Hawthorne Experiment.

Example: In the 1920s, Professor Elton Mayo of Havard University asked 2,000 workers at the Hawthorne plant of the Western Electric Company how they felt about their jobs, their bosses, and the company. The professor and his interviewers used checklists that carefully itemized every feature of the work situation. The lists included the lights, the materials used, the handling of equipment, rest periods, product knowledge, and so on. The workers, however, wanted to talk about other things. Surprisingly, the interviews themselves seemed to improve production.

The results of the interviews were so inconclusive that the research teams decided to try some experiments. They increased and decreased lighting, temperature, and rest periods. They changed room colors. They isolated groups from each other. No matter what the change, production improved. The Harvard scholars were stumped. Finally, they asked the workers, "What's happening?" "Oh, don't you know?" the workers replied. "We're something special."

Although the groups of workers did not know why, they knew they had been distinguished from all other employees. They were now something more than cogs in a machine. The special treatment had made these workers feel different about themselves and about their work. They recognized that their jobs were important, and so did their coworkers. They had achieved that something special—status, or the importance or prestige placed upon a work position by the workers themselves as well as by entrepreneurs.[5]

Giving Recognition to Workers

How can entrepreneurs help workers earn status, to gain better opinions of themselves and their jobs? Entrepreneurs may do it in a variety of ways, among them:

- Sharing decision making with workers, as mentioned in our discussion of group management.
- Applying the Golden Rule: "Behave to other people as we wish people to behave to us."
- Giving workers greater responsibility as soon as they are ready for it.
- Taking workers' ideas and suggestions to heart.
- Judging workers rigorously on merit and rewarding them accordingly.

Entrepreneurs who follow these suggestions are likely to succeed. By building up their workers' self-images and improving their status, entrepreneurs are likely to keep growing in stature themselves. The process feeds on itself. As the venture grows, talented men and women will be attracted to it. They generally prefer to work in a growing venture because growth creates opportunities for promotion. The possibility of promotion is, of course, one of the strongest incentives known for improved performance and for personal growth.

Additional Guidelines for Sharing

Entrepreneurs who want to keep their ventures growing must share the ventures with their workers. To foster that sharing, entrepreneurs should offer:

- A precise set of goals, shared by all workers, (as discussed in Chapter Twelve)
- An atmosphere of orderly growth that stimulates and rewards achievement of goals
- Challenging, exciting work to do
- Opportunities for personal growth
- An image that generates a sense of pride in a job well done

In managing their ventures, how do entrepreneurs earn their workers' respect and loyalty? Of course, there is no one best way to manage a venture. Each entrepreneur has a unique style of managing. But chances are that successful entrepreneurs are those who:

- Ask the right questions—questions that generate thinking, initiate action, and spawn improvement
- Weave old ideas into new patterns
- Have a knack for reducing a problem quickly and accurately to its barest elements, thus laying the groundwork for solutions that are simple and clean
- Communicate clearly
- Have a drive for quality and a vision for results
- Act vigorously
- Seek excellence day in and day out[6]

Pursuit of Excellence

Of these traits, perhaps the last is the most crucial one: the pursuit of excellence day in and day out. For, it is the entrepreneur who must set the tone in his or her own venture. As the famed football coach, Vince Lombardi, put it: "You don't try to win some of the time. You don't try to do things right some of the time. You do them right all of the time."[7]

Generally, excellence occurs as a result of expectations. If entrepreneurs expect excellence from their workers, it often will occur. If they do not, it will occur rarely. Only highly motivated workers are likely to make and sell superior products that cause customers to return again and again.

Entrepreneurs crave worker loyalty. Some entrepreneurs, however, believe that their workers should be blindly loyal to them. They expect workers to stick by them through good times and bad. And they expect workers to stick by them regardless of how the workers are treated.

Such false loyalty weakens rather than strengthens a venture. True loyalty means working up to one's capabilities, doing the best one knows how. True loyalty is to the job, not to the entrepreneur.

The McKinsey Study on Excellence

In the early 1980s, few business subjects sparked more interest than excellence, or more accurately, the pursuit of excellence. Thomas Peters and Robert Waterman wrote one of the many books on this subject. Called *In Search of Excellence*, the book made the *New York Times* best-seller list for 59 straight weeks. It examined the traits of such well-known giant corporations as IBM and 3M.

Although most authors focus on successful big businesses and what made them tick, others also have looked at successful smaller businesses. One such study that merits attention was done by the large management-consulting firm of McKinsey & Company. They found that successful smaller and midsized businesses:

Innovate as a way of life: Winners continue to generate a stream of new products, services, and ways of doing business that help them maintain their already-established competitive leadership.

Create and develop small market niches: It is important to expand into related niches only, where strengths such as distinctive technologies, good sites, and entrenched distribution channels already exist.
Compete on value, not price: Winners deliver products and services that provide consistently superior value to all their customers. Often, these products and services cost the customers more rather than less.
Develop a strong sense of mission: Winners have an unusually clear sense of their distinctive role—where they will compete and will not compete, what kinds of products they will and will not offer, what level of quality they expect to produce.
Attend to fundamentals: Winners worry about return on investment. They employ strong financial disciplines to generate cash flow—designated for the innovation of new products and for increases in organizational strength.
Attack bureaucratization: The winning companies consciously restrict overhead. They make use of temporary work groups and task forces to accomplish short-term goals.
Encourage experimentation: Unlike giant companies that fire or demote risk takers who fail, these companies bend over backwards to avoid punishing failure, so risk takers can learn from their failures and generate more solid new ideas.
Think like customers: Salespersons for some of these companies spend most of their time working in the customer's plant, looking for applications to save money or increase performance for that customer. They have learned that the best way to make money for themselves is to make money for their customers.
Motivate with money: Incentive pay tied to company performance tends to be much higher in these companies than at competitive companies in the same industries.
Set examples at the top: The entrepreneurs or heads of the winning companies show extraordinary perseverance, even obsession, about doing quality work. Despite their success, they continue to work hard and for long hours—64 hours a week on the average. They are deeply involved in the details of the business and can talk intelligently and intelligibly about their products or services, specific customer relationships, competitive positions, and the like.[8]

Maslow's Hierarchy of Needs

Our discussion of human relations would be incomplete without some mention of Dr. Abraham Maslow and his widely quoted study of human needs. Dr. Maslow classified all human needs in order of importance to the individual and presented them as a pyramid of five levels:

- Physiological
- Safety
- Belongingness and love

- Esteem
- Self-actualization[9]

According to Dr. Maslow, workers strive to satisfy these needs in ascending order. Once a lower level is satisfied, a worker will strive to satisfy the next level of need, as shown in Exhibit 16.3. Note that the first level is the satisfaction of *physiological* needs—air, water, and food. Once these needs have been satisfied, the worker needs protection from hostile environments such as criminals and cold weather. These needs form the second level, called *safety*.

The third level, called *belongingness and love*, refers to the worker's need for affection and the acceptance of others. The fourth level, *esteem*, refers to the worker's need for self-respect, self-esteem, and the esteem of others.

The fifth, and loftiest, level has to do with *self-actualization* needs. Activated only when all other needs have been satisfied, this level reflects the worker's desire to fulfill his or her highest potential as an individual.

EXHIBIT 16.3 *Maslow's Hierarchy of Needs*

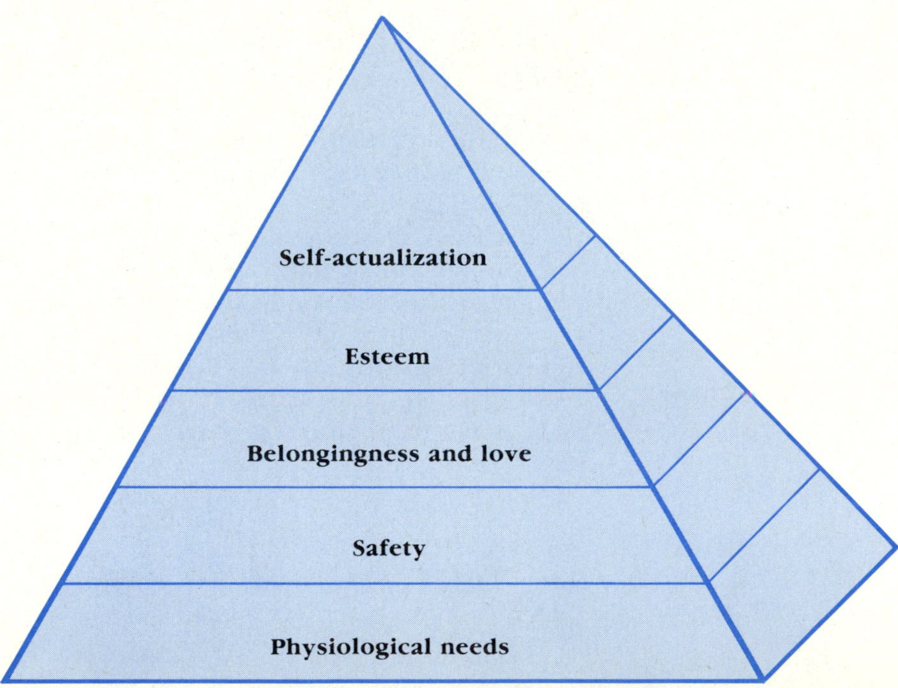

Source: Data for diagram based on Hierarchy of Needs in "A Theory of Human Motivation," from *Motivation and Personality*, 2nd edition, by Abraham H. Maslow. Copyright © 1970 by Abraham H. Maslow. Reprinted by permission of Harper and Row, Publishers, Inc.

Self-actualization refers to the worker's need to do what he or she is best suited to do, as athletes must compete and entrepreneurs must create.

Theory X and Theory Y

Two of the most widely quoted theories about human behavior are *Theory X* and *Theory Y*. Set forth by Douglas McGregor,[10] these two theories focus on the assumptions that entrepreneurs and other business leaders may have about employee motivation, as explained below:

Theory X: According to this theory, entrepreneurs assume that employees hate work and so will perform only if threatened with punishment. Such entrepreneurs have a low regard for employees, tending to bully them and to undermine their security with threats to fire them. When related to Maslow's hierarchy of needs, note that Theory X focuses on the first two levels: physiological needs and safety.

Theory Y: According to this theory, entrepreneurs assume that work is as natural as rest. These entrepreneurs believe that employees work hard to meet goals if they are committed to them. They also assume that employees want and seek responsibility and can use their creativity to solve problems. Theory Y relates to the higher levels of Maslow's hierarchy of needs: belongingness and love, esteem, and self-actualization.

The overriding reason for employing Theory Y rather than Theory X is that entrepreneurs are much more likely to succeed by satisfying the human needs of their employees than by ignoring them. Only by satisfying these needs will employees be strongly motivated to pursue excellence in their work. A comparison between Theory X and Theory Y appears in Exhibit 16.4.

EXHIBIT 16.4 *Comparison of Theory X and Theory Y*

Theory X	Theory Y
• Employees have little ambition.	• Employees crave responsibility.
• Threats are necessary to motivate employees.	• Employees dislike threats.
• Employees avoid work because they hate it.	• Work is as natural as rest.
• Employees avoid all responsibility.	• Employees want to satisfy their needs for esteem and self-actualization.

WAGE AND SALARY POLICIES

Good human relations help motivate employees to cooperate fully and do their best. But a human relations policy must be supported by attractive wage and salary incentives, since motivation and pay go hand in hand. Generally, highly motivated workers produce at a higher rate and hence merit more pay. In turn, they expect their pay to reflect the skills and energy they put into their jobs.

To attract and keep good workers, entrepreneurs should make sure their pay scale compares favorably with those offered by competitors. They must draft wage and salary policies that promote good human relations. One sound policy is to pay workers on merit, gearing their pay to performance.

Legal Obligations

Not matter how wages and salaries are set, the entrepreneur must meet certain legal obligations to workers. For example, entrepreneurs who pay more than $50 in quarterly wages must pay Social Security taxes. These payments require entrepreneurs to:

- Withhold a certain percentage of wages from each worker's paycheck
- Contribute a matching amount themselves
- Deposit withheld amounts and their own contributions in a bank, either monthly or quarterly, depending on the amount

Entrepreneurs need legal and accounting help to make sure they honor all legal obligations. New obligations are added from time to time, and old ones keep changing. Besides Social Security taxes, entrepreneurs must meet these legal obligations:

Federal income taxes: If they pay salaries and wages or have workers who report tips, entrepreneurs must withhold a certain amount from each worker's paycheck.

Workers' compensation insurance: If they have full-time workers, entrepreneurs must protect workers from loss of income from injury on the job.

State unemployment insurance: If they pay wages, entrepreneurs must contribute to a fund that will be drawn upon when any of their workers are laid off but are willing and able to work.

Federal unemployment taxes: If they have four or more workers who put in 20 or more weeks a year, entrepreneurs must pay federal unemployment taxes that serve the same purpose as state unemployment insurance.

Federal wage and hour laws: If they sell across state lines, hold federal government contracts, or have revenues in excess of $500,000, entrepreneurs must abide by these laws that help avoid poverty by setting a minimum hourly wage. These laws also regulate child labor and worker health and safety.

Civil Rights Act, Title VII: If they have workers who are covered under the federal wage and hour laws, entrepreneurs must also abide by the Civil Rights Act that ensures that all job applicants and employees are treated fairly and equally, regardless of race, color, religion, sex, age, or ethnic origin.

Fringe Benefits

A form of pay, fringe benefits strongly influence the lives of workers. These benefits have given the average worker a standard of living higher than ever before. The average worker now receives the following benefits:

- Paid vacations, holidays, and "personal" days
- Life, unemployment, and medical insurance
- Pension plan and Social Security
- Paid leave for illness or jury duty

A moment's reflection will show that these are not really fringe benefits at all but are, in fact, a significant part of the entrepreneur's payroll. As shown in Exhibit 16.5, these benefits today cost the average employer about 37 percent of the yearly payroll—and the percentage keeps rising almost every year. In contrast, fringe benefits in 1930 cost the average employer just 3 percent of the total amount paid for wages and salaries. Generally, entrepreneurs must offer fringe benefits in order to:

- Attract and hold good workers
- Help upgrade the workers' quality of life
- Keep pace with benefits offered by competitors
- Meet legal obligations imposed by local, state, and federal governments

EXHIBIT 16.5 *Fringe Benefits as a Share of Total Payroll: 1985 vs. 1930*

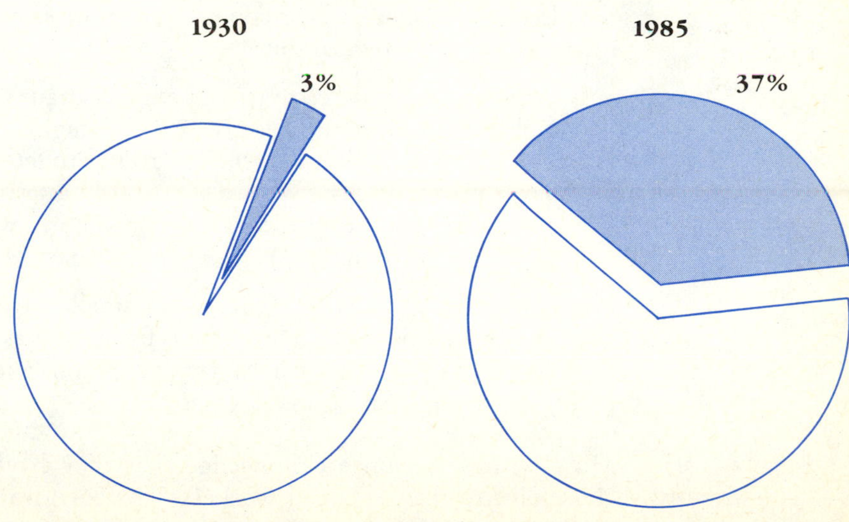

Source: "Labor Letter," *The Wall Street Journal*, (February 26, 1985), p. 1.

The most important of these reasons is to attract and hold good workers. Other things being equal, workers seek employers who offer a complete package of fringe benefits. This attitude often puts the entrepreneur at a disadvantage. Many entrepreneurs cannot afford to offer the same package of benefits as a giant corporation can, so they are often forced to compete for talent on other terms, such as the appeal of contributing to the growth of a promising venture.

Sooner or later, most workers come to expect the same fringe benefits no matter whom they work for. Fringe benefits are so common today that workers look upon them as a right rather than a privilege—they often equate fringe benefits with cash pay. If entrepreneurs fail to recognize worker expectations, they may be faced with governmental action that forces them to comply with workers' rights.

SAFETY AND HEALTH ON THE JOB

Convinced that business was not doing enough to make workplaces safe and healthful, in 1970 the federal government passed the Occupational Safety and Health Act (OSHA). This law requires all businesses to free their operations of hazards to workers. Although initially praised, this law has come under heavy fire from workers and businesspersons alike:

> Some workers have complained that the new work rules cramp their work styles. Others fear the federal government's power to shut down their workplace if it is considered unsafe.
>
> Businesspersons have complained that the law has added severely to their equipment costs and has vastly complicated their paperwork. They have also complained that many of the rules are petty.[11]

Lending weight to their complaints are these examples of the enforcement of OSHA's regulations:

- Businesses were ordered to take down guardrails 41 or 43 inches high and replace them with rails exactly 42 inches high.
- Businesses were ordered to replace round toilet seats with ones shaped like horseshoes.
- Mom-and-pop grocery stores and variety stores were ordered to provide separate restrooms for men and women.[12]

Especially plagued by OSHA are small entrepreneurs. In fact, the National Federation of Independent Business has charged OSHA with using small-business as "guinea pigs to establish legal precedents and to build up a record of successful cases."[13]

Safety Trend Upward

Most businesspersons acknowledge that they have become more safety conscious, to the benefit of workers. The cost, however, is high. In 1984 alone, business spent more than $6 billion to comply with OSHA. Most of this sum was spent on equipment with safety or pollution-control features.

The lesson here is that entrepreneurs should make sure their operations comply with OSHA. In designing a new plant, for example, the entrepreneur must make sure the plant will be free of high noise levels, toxic substances such as carbon monoxide, clutter, and a host of other health or safety perils. Entrepreneurs would be wise to consult with their lawyer to make sure they observe the letter and spirit of the law. A recent study by OSHA found that:

> Because the number of workplace accidents has fallen dramatically in the last decade, OSHA now conducts fewer routine safety inspections. According to statistics by the U.S. Bureau of Labor Standards, the total number of workplace injuries has fallen from 10.6 injuries per 100 full-time employees in 1973 to 7.5 injuries per 100 in 1983.
>
> OSHA's new policy is to conduct routine inspections in high-hazard industries only. Although businesses are still subject to inspections triggered by complaints and accidents, the agency is targeting companies with worse-than-average accident rates based on its industry-wide statistics.[14]

SUMMARY

The best human relations are founded on good will and applied common sense. Entrepreneurs who practice good human relations treat their workers with dignity and respect. Above all, they recognize that every worker is uniquely complex.

To keep their ventures running smoothly, entrepreneurs should instill a strong sense of purpose in their workers. One way to do that is by sharing decision making. This attitude generally yields high dividends, mostly because it helps satisfy the worker's desire for recognition.

There is no one best way to manage workers, for each entrepreneur has a unique managerial style. But entrepreneurs will probably succeed if they seek excellence at all times and treat their workers with respect. These two attitudes best set the tone for a venture.

Entrepreneurs should support good human relations with attractive salary and wage policies. Motivation and pay go hand in hand. Highly motivated workers expect their pay to reflect the skills and energies they put into their jobs. A policy that gears wages to individual merit should satisfy workers and promote good human relations.

Entrepreneurs must also be mindful of their legal obligation to workers. They need legal and accounting help to make sure they meet such obligations as federal income taxes on salaries and wages, workers' compensation insurance, and state unemployment insurance.

To attract and hold talent, entrepreneurs must offer fringe benefits. Today, fringe benefits are so common that workers look upon them as a right rather than a privilege. Many entrepreneurs, however, cannot afford to offer the same attractive package of benefits that giant corporations do, so they are at a disadvantage in the competition for talent.

The federal government also plays a role in improving human relations. In 1970, it passed the Occupational Safety and Health Act (OSHA), requiring businesses to make workplaces safer and more healthful for workers.

DISCUSSION AND REVIEW QUESTIONS

1. What does the term *human relations* mean to you? Cite some personal examples of good human relations.
2. Describe one way in which an entrepreneur may create a work atmosphere that brings out the best in workers.
3. What kind of entrepreneur is likely to earn the respect and loyalty of workers?
4. Define these terms: *participatory management, Theory X, managing, needs, self-actualization, fringe benefits, OSHA.*
5. Why are attractive salary and wage policies so vital to the success of a venture?
6. Are fringe benefits a right or a privilege? Explain.
7. What is the best way to measure the quality of human relations in a venture? Explain.
8. Describe the entrepreneur's legal obligations in the area of human relations.
9. Do you believe that OSHA discriminates against entrepreneurs, as some claim? Explain.
10. Does it always follow that happy workers are also productive workers? Explain.
11. How would you, as an entrepreneur, compete for topnotch talent if you could not afford to pay the same salaries that large corporations can pay?
12. Why has group management made less headway in the United States than in Japan?
13. Dr. Maslow classified human needs in a hierarchy of five distinct levels. Describe the characteristics of each level.
14. Comment on the following statement made by an entrepreneur: "We really need to take a hard look at behavior in our venture. Our workers are totally unmotivated. So nothing gets done when it should or in the way that it should be done."
15. Is there one best way to manage a venture that works for all entrepreneurs? Explain.

NOTES

1. Fyodor Dostoyevsky, *The House of the Dead* (London: William Heineman, 1915), p. 20.
2. Adapted from Kenneth H. Killen, *Management: A Middle-Management Approach* (Boston, Mass.: Houghton Mifflin Company, 1977), pp. 79–81. Used by permission of the author.
3. "Making Zippers: All the Way with Y.K.K.," *Time*, August 13, 1973, p. 76. Copyright 1973 Time Inc. All rights reserved. Reprinted by permission from *Time*.
4. Updated from William F. Buckley, Jr., "How to Stimulate Will to Work," Cleveland *Plain Dealer*, November 18, 1972, p. 11-A.
5. Adapted from U.S. Small Business Administration, *Human Factors in Small Business* (Washington, D.C.: U.S. Government Printing Office, 1965), p. 12.
6. Adapted from Rohrer, Hibler and Replogle, *Managers for Tomorrow* (New York: New American Library, 1965), p. 175.
7. From a film produced by the U.S. Small Business Administration, *The Habit of Winning* (1972).
8. Donald K. Clifford, Jr. and Richard E. Cavanagh, *The Winning Performance of the Midsized Growth Companies* (New York, N.Y.: McKinsey & Company, Inc., 1983).
9. Abraham H. Maslow, *Motivation and Personality* (New York: Harper & Row, 1970), pp. 35–47.
10. Douglas McGregor, *The Human Side of Enterprise* (New York: N.Y.: McGraw-Hill, 1960).
11. "Protecting People on the Job: ABC's of a Controversial Law," *U.S. News & World Report*, November 24, 1975, p. 70.
12. Ibid., p. 71.
13. Ibid., p. 71.
14. National Federation of Independent Business, "OSHA Reacts to Safety Trend," *NFIB Mandate*, March–April 1985, p. 8.

CASE 16A *National Rolled Thread Die Company*

Founded in 1946, National Rolled Thread Die Company has had just two losing years. Yet William Mau, who inherited the company from his father, is concerned about its future. Why? Because for the past 17 years, Mr. Mau has been working under a "rain cloud." In each of these years, the city fathers have suggested he move out to make way for urban renewal, and each year they have come back to tell him to wait another year." That's city hall for you," says Mr. Mau.

Background

Mr. Mau's father created the company because he found it hard to work for somebody else. "He was a bull-headed man," says Mr. Mau. "My dad was the classic entrepreneur—a driver. Never taking no for an answer. Always running a one-man show. He was quite a guy. I had a hard time getting along with him but I respected him."

Mr. Mau is hardly a chip off the old block. He is a mechanical engineer. "I never had what it takes to start up a business," says Mr. Mau. "By training, I'm more a professional manager than an entrepreneur. When I left the Army in 1946, my dad couldn't find room for me in the Mau empire. So I went to work for somebody else."

Then, in 1953, Mr. Mau's father became disabled. For years he had suffered from Parkinson's disease. By 1953 the disease had so consumed him that he could no longer market his products aggressively. He turned to his son for help, asking him to quit his job and join the company. Young William Mau did just that, because he "felt a family responsibility to help out."

Earns Several Promotions

Despite his illness, Mr. Mau's father remained in control of the company almost until his death in 1966. Meanwhile, Mr. Mau worked hard to hold the company together and introduce new managerial techniques. His work eventually earned him two promotions:

- In 1953, Mr. Mau started as company secretary, working mostly in marketing.
- In 1962, he moved up to a vice presidency.
- In 1966, he became president when his father died.

When Mr. Mau joined the company in 1953, the company's after-tax profits were $9,000 on sales revenues of $264,000. For the company's 1952 balance sheet, see Exhibit 16A.1.

Introduces New Managerial Style

As soon as he became president, Mr. Mau proceeded to remold the company in his own image. Where his father had been a driver, Mr. Mau would be permissive. Where his father had been a doer, Mr. Mau would be both thinker and doer. Where his father had fired incompetent employees, Mr. Mau would carry them, "matching their skills with available tasks." In short, he would humanize the company's work practices.

EXHIBIT 16A.1 *National Rolled Thread Die Company: Balance Sheet (December 31, 1952)*

Assets			Equities		
Current assets			Current liabilities		
Cash	$33,000		Accounts payable	$ 1,500	
Accounts receivable	10,000		Other	4,500	$ 6,000
Inventory	17,000	$60,000			
Fixed assets			Owners' equity		
Machinery and tools		27,000	Common stock	$68,000	
Other assets		2,000	Retained earnings	15,000	83,000
Total assets		$89,000	Total equities		$89,000

This managerial style was really a reaction to the way big business operated. Before joining his father, Mr. Mau had worked as an industrial engineer for a big steel company. "You tried to improve a worker's productivity in a way that was dehumanizing," says Mr. Mau. "You didn't consider the man. Only the productivity."

To this day, Mr. Mau talks eloquently about the "dehumanizing practices of big business." He deplores the big businesses that make drudgery out of work and reduce workers to little more than robots cranking out bolts all day. Mr. Mau has described the cycle toward boredom in this way:

- Increasing work productivity requires work simplification.
- Simplification means specialization.
- Specialization means each worker does one thing, all the time.
- The end is a stifling work atmosphere and an unhappy workforce.

Humanizing Performance

Mr. Mau's philosophy of treating workers as human beings has paid off. In the past 28 years, he has had no layoffs, no strikes, and no work stoppages. He says, "You've got to know each man; know his flexibilities; let him see where he's going; know what he's doing; and give him a feel for the product he's making.

"For some workers," he continues, "this means letting them shift from one machine to another and from one operation to another. For others, it may mean keeping them assigned to one job. I have two men running milling machines—a job that is considered monotonous work by some. Yet, one man is completely satisfied, doesn't want to do anything else, and is doing an exceptional job. The other man needs the mantle of confidence the highly repetitive job allows him to wrap around himself. He is, however, unhappy at whatever job he is assigned."

Why doesn't Mr. Mau fire the latter employee? "I inherited him from my father's regime," says Mr. Mau. "I feel he's a kind of legacy, and I won't let him go."

He has other problem employees, one of whom he considers an irritant. "He wants things run his way," says Mr. Mau. "He wants more efficiency, more foreman control, but only as it relates to the other workers, not to himself." Spurning ultimatums that can turn small disagreements into stormy battles, Mr. Mau deals with this employee simply. "I don't talk to him because we don't operate on the same wavelength. He will do what he feels he has to do. And in his own way he is highly conscientious and trustworthy."

Stressing the importance of giving workers a free hand, Mr. Mau says of one of his machinists: "He lays out his own work schedule under the guidance of a lead man, decides what steel to start with, what machine he'll be running. The important thing is that no one pays any attention to him. That's the way he wants it. He wants to be left to himself.

"Rarely does he find himself with nothing to do. I've seen him keep as many as five or six machines running—a planer, shaper, circular grinder, end miller, butt miller, and sidewheel grinder. Each machine does a different operation. And their operations must be coordinated to get our die blanks out to meet schedules."

No Pollyanna

In trying to avoid the pitfalls of many big manufacturers, Mr. Mau does not profess to be any management Pollyanna. "This isn't entirely unselfish," says Mr. Mau. "We recognize that we won't get the best out of the men unless we keep them in a good state of mind. Being small, we can't pay top wages. The average hourly rate is about $7.50. Surveys show that the worker's desire to be treated as a human being ranks with wages as a top priority. Those are the facts behind our approach."

All 18 workers on his payroll agree with this approach. One machinist, for example, says he prefers working for Mr. Mau because of the job security. During eight years with much bigger companies he was laid off for periods equal to three years. "Maybe the pay here is a little less than in a union shop, but I've been here 13 years and I've never been laid off," says the machinist. His remarks are echoed by his fellow workers. Another machinist says he prefers his present job to work he did for a Detroit automobile plant where "you had to get a relief man if you wanted to go to the washroom."

Mr. Mau punches a time clock along with his factory workers. Why? Because it helps him maintain his perspective "at a time when the badge of success in some big companies is the key to the executive washroom."

These views may not win him high marks in Chamber of Commerce circles, but they have helped him run a stable business. Revenues have gone up steadily since he took control of the company (see Exhibit 16A.2). Clearly, stability is the company's strongest characteristic. When Mr. Mau came in 1953, there were 15 employees; in 1981, there were 18. In that 27-year span, revenues have tripled. "I'm proud of that record," says Mr. Mau.

EXHIBIT 16A.2 *National Rolled Thread Die Company: Sales Revenues and Profits*

Year	Sales Revenues	Operating Profit
1976	$568,000	$33,000
1977	642,000	39,000
1978	735,000	59,000
1979	848,000	63,000
1980	840,000	71,000

Marketing Strategy

It would be a mistake to credit that record solely to his humane treatment of employees. Much of the credit really belongs to the product he makes. National Rolled Thread Die now ranks as the nation's biggest independent manufacturer of flat thread-rolling dies. Most of its customers belong to the fastener industry, which uses the dies to make screws and bolts.

Except for his nephew, Mr. Mau has no salesforce to speak of. "Word-of-mouth advertising is how we get most of our new business," says Mr. Mau. "The word has gotten around that we do what few other die shops do. We make dies to a customer's specifications. Custom-made dies are our bread and butter. We tailor them to fit hand-in-glove with a customer's operations." See Exhibit 16A.3 for photographs of thread-rolling dies, and see Exhibit 16A.4 for a photograph of Mr. Mau's plant, where the dies are made.

To be sure, there are other die shops in the country that are much bigger, but they mass-produce dies. "They sell their dies off the shelf," says Mr. Mau. "We don't. We're too small to compete with them in their markets. And they're too big to compete with us in our markets." Thirty-five percent of his revenues stem from foreign markets. He has even sold 50 pairs of custom-made dies to a Russian company.

EXHIBIT 16A.3 *National Rolled Thread Die Company: Thread-Rolling Dies*

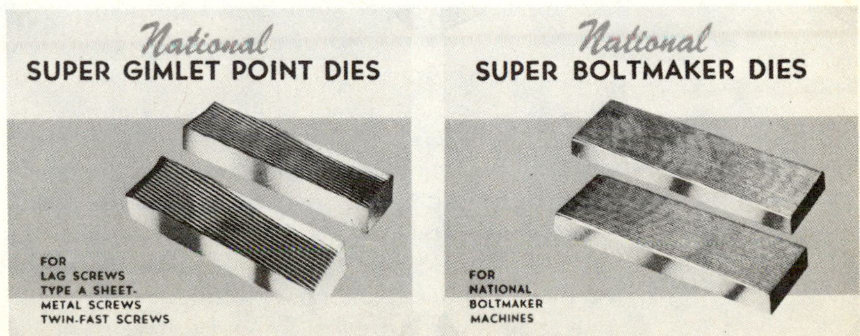

EXHIBIT 16A.4 *National Rolled Thread Die Company: Inside View of Plant*

The Future

Although his past performance pleases him, Mr. Mau worries about the future. For one thing, he worries about himself, especially about his managerial skills. "I don't set goals and budget my company's future," says Mr. Mau.

"I read all those high-sounding articles about goals, and I begin to wonder what's wrong with me. But I've read enough articles to know that even experts are at odds about them. Many techniques are tried today and discarded tomorrow, such as management by objectives. It leaves me confused. What do I do?

"You know, I don't even know what my costs are, by item. But as long as I satisfy my board of directors and shareholders, I guess I'm doing OK." Mr. Mau's board consists of just three persons: himself, his brother's widow, and the vice president of a local steel company.

Another thing that worries him is urban renewal. "I've been under the gun on urban renewal for 17 years," says Mr. Mau. "Every year the city fathers tell me I'll have to move. Then they come back telling me to hold up on plans to move. I don't have a concrete plan, though maybe I should have one at all times, because I know I'll have to move some day. In any case,

I've found it to be a study in futility to draw up a new plan each year to meet the ever-changing business scene. When the time comes, I'll establish a plan."

Still another problem is that his machinery is getting old. "I should replace most of my machinery with newer models and methods," says Mr. Mau, "but I don't have the money to do it. I could borrow the money, but I've never worked with debt. In fact, I've never believed in debt. What I like is a clean balance sheet. My board feels the same way. We've always expanded with retained earnings. But new techniques require capital outside our means."

Employee absenteeism also bothers him. "We used to have little absenteeism," he says, "but among the recent hires it's really gotten out of hand. I guess it's a way of the life these days, and you have to put up with it."

Mr. Mau has just called a special meeting of his board to go over these problems. Recent financial statements appear in Exhibits 16A.5 and 16A.6.

EXHIBIT 16A.5 *National Rolled Thread Die Company: 1980 Income Statement*

Sales revenues		$840,000
Cost of goods sold*		612,000
Gross profit		228,000
Other expenses		
Salaries†	$91,000	
Other	66,000	157,000
Operating profit		$ 71,000

* Includes raw materials, direct labor, utilities, and depreciation.
† Covers salaries of four men, including Mr. Mau.

EXHIBIT 16A.6 *National Rolled Thread Die Company: Balance Sheet (December 31, 1980)*

Assets			**Equities**		
Current assets			Current liabilities		
Cash	$ 20,000		Accounts payable	$ 14,000	
Accounts receivable	98,000		Other	36,000	$ 50,000
Inventory	96,000				
Marketable securities	175,000	$389,000	Owners' equity		
Fixed assets			Common stock	$ 68,000	
Plant and equipment		$104,000	Retained earnings	417,000	$485,000
Other assets		42,000			
Total assets		$535,000	Total equities		$535,000

Questions

1. What should Mr. Mau do now? In the long run?
2. Comment on Mr. Mau's philosophy on human relations with employees.
3. Is Mr. Mau more a manager than an entrepreneur? Explain.
4. Comment on Mr. Mau's reluctance to go into debt.
5. How well has Mr. Mau performed as head of the company? Explain.

CASE 16B *Welcome to the Big Time*

In just seven years, Dwight Hawkins, originally a carpenter, has built his construction firm into the second largest home-building firm in Jacksonville, Florida. Last year alone, Hawkins Home, Inc., constructed more than 500 homes. Hawkins Home stands out among local land developers because it does an effective job of responding quickly to customer needs and problems, while keeping construction costs well below average.

Mr. Hawkins credits the firm's effectiveness to what he calls "flexible organization." Each of his six field construction managers has broad decision-making authority. In his words, "I encourage each field manager to run his construction project as if it were his own business. I'm a jack of all trades, and I expect my managers to be, too.

"They don't come running to me to wipe their noses for every little problem. They know what needs to be done, and so I stay out of their way and let them get on with it." Mr. Hawkins has often told visitors and customers that they won't find any red tape at Hawkins Home.

During the past year, as commercial building has begun to catch up with the residential boom, Mr. Hawkins has been thinking seriously about diversifying into commercial construction. Unfortunately, Hawkins Home lacks the funds to buy or lease the heavy equipment needed to build schools, stores, and small office buildings.

At this point, the most promising alternative seems to be a merger with Interstate Builders, Inc., a large Chicago-based commercial builder. Interstate's legal staff has worked out a very tempting stock-trade arrangement.

From a financial viewpoint, the merger proposal looks good, but Mr. Hawkins is now having second thoughts about how well he and his firm would fit into Interstate's huge operations. In the first place, he deplores the long time it takes to get something through the bureaucratic machinery at Interstate. For example, by the time a bid has passed through the engineering, planning, and legal departments at Interstate, ten months have gone by. At Hawkins Home, the bid cycle rarely take more than three months. Mr. Hawkins also doubts Interstate's ability to adapt to the wide variation in small-scale commercial jobs. Finally, Mr. Hawkins is not enthusiastic about the prospect of reporting to the president of Interstate indirectly, through three layers of management. During the recent merger talks, it took Mr. Hawkins three trips to Chicago and a half-dozen meetings before he even met Interstate's president.

Questions

1. Contrast the organizational styles of the two firms.
2. How do you suppose Mr. Hawkins's field managers would respond to working in an organization like Interstate?
3. If you were Mr. Hawkins, what organizational concessions would you demand from Interstate before agreeing to a merger?

Source: Robert Kreitner, *Management* (Boston: Houghton Mifflin, 1983), pp. 262–263.

CASE 16C *The Disgruntled Employee*

For the past eight years, Brian Taft has worked as a machinist for Roy Regan, the founder and sole owner of a small machine shop. Mr. Taft is an uncommonly moody person, but one of his sullen moods has never lasted for more than one week before.

When his latest moody period began—about six weeks ago—Mr. Taft simply quit speaking to Mr. Regan. He also quit speaking to the other six employees of the machine shop.

Another strange thing about the matter is that Mr. Taft's work has not suffered at all, in either quality or quantity.

Mr. Regan does not know how to handle the problem. He has tried talking with Mr. Taft to find out what is troubling him, but Mr. Taft refuses to say anything. His long silence is beginning to have a bad effect on the morale of the whole machine shop.

Mr. Regan is afraid to take any kind of corrective action for fear Mr. Taft's performance may drop. Mr. Regan keeps reminding himself that Mr. Taft is much more efficient and knowledgeable than anyone else who has ever worked for him. In fact, when Mr. Taft goes on vacation, two people are needed to replace him.

Question What should Roy Regan do?

Source: Case written by Kenneth H. Killen of Cuyahoga Community College.

17 PURCHASING AND INVENTORIES

QUESTIONS FOR MASTERY

What is purchasing?

Why is efficient purchasing important?

How can one control inventories?

What is the relationship between purchasing and inventories?

Why are records necessary to plan and control inventories?

The buyer needs a hundred eyes, the seller not one.

Anonymous

Shopping for the best buys should rank high on the entrepreneur's list of priorities. Just as homemakers compare brands and prices at the supermarket to get the most for the least, so should entrepreneurs look sharply at markets and prices to get the best value for each dollar.

How well entrepreneurs do their buying may spell the difference between profit and loss. So they cannot afford to overlook the management of purchases or of inventories.

THE IMPORTANCE OF PURCHASING

The Effect of Purchasing on Profits

The goal of purchasing should be to improve a venture's profits, so entrepreneurs should make every effort to choose those materials, services, and sources of supply that best meet their needs at the lowest possible cost without sacrificing quality for price. To some entrepreneurs, the idea that purchasing can make or break a venture may seem farfetched. It is not. A look at the following ratios underscores its importance:

- Wholesalers spend 80 to 85 cents out of every sales dollar to purchase materials from suppliers for resale later.
- Retailers spend 60 to 70 cents out of every sales dollar to purchase materials from suppliers for resale to customers later.
- Manufacturers spend 20 to 50 cents out of every sales dollar to purchase raw materials from suppliers for conversion into finished product.
- Service firms spend 0 to 10 cents out of every sales dollar to purchase materials from suppliers for sale as part of the services they render.

Note how widely purchasing varies in its impact. It is vital in wholesaling and retailing, less so in manufacturing, and negligible in services. Despite its impact, entrepreneurs often overlook purchasing as a major function in their business.

Further evidence of why purchasing should rank as a major function is stressed in this statistic: in manufacturing alone, $1.2 trillion was spent for materials and services in 1981.[1] Its importance can also be seen by comparing spending for purchased materials and services with spending for other items (see Exhibit 17.1). Savings in purchase costs are likely to raise profits dramatically, as shown in Exhibit 17.2. Note that if the entrepreneur's profit-to-sales ratio is only 2 percent, purchase savings of only $1,000 would be equivalent to the profit earned on a sales increase of $50,000.

Purchasing, if done wisely, offers entrepreneurs a good way to cut costs and boost profits. In short, it pays to buy efficiently.

EXHIBIT 17.1 *How the Sales Dollar is Distributed: Based on the Experience of 100 Representative Businesses*

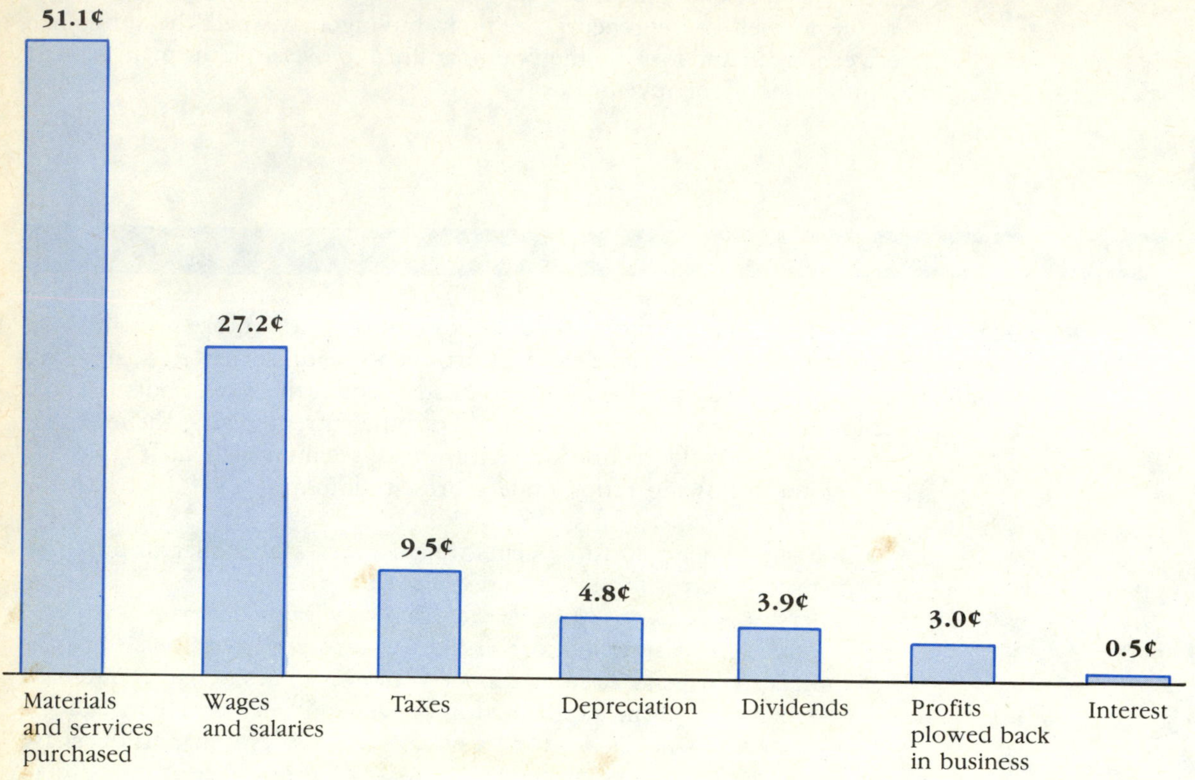

Source: Adapted from *Purchasing Handbook*, by George W. Aljian. Copyright © 1973 by McGraw-Hill, Inc. Used with permission of McGraw-Hill Book Company.

Complexity of Purchasing

Purchasing covers much more ground than the act of buying. In its broader sense, purchasing also requires the entrepreneur to:

- Pinpoint the need for materials and services
- Search out and select suppliers
- Settle with suppliers matters such as price and payment terms
- Negotiate the contract or order
- Make sure suppliers live up to their end of the agreement

It is the entrepreneur's responsibility to buy materials and services:

EXHIBIT 17.2

What Purchase Savings May Mean to the Entrepreneur

If the ratio of before-tax profits to sales is...	...then purchase savings of $1,000 would raise profits as much as a sales increase of
20%	$ 5,000
15	6,700
10	10,000
5	20,000
2	50,000

- Of the *right* quality
- Of the *right* quantity
- At the *right* time
- From the *right* supplier
- At the *right* price

More will be said about this vital responsibility in the paragraphs that follow.

PURCHASING MANAGEMENT

Entrepreneurs should plan their purchasing with the same care they devote to other activities of their ventures. Equally important, they should also measure their purchasing performance at least once a year, asking these questions:

- How do my purchasing costs measure up to those of my competitors?
- What are my losses from shrinkage, spoilage, and theft?
- Do I have too much money tied up in inventory?

The last question is especially vital. It relates to inventory turnover, the average number of times that inventory is sold out during the year. As mentioned in Chapter Thirteen, turnover generally is the best measure of how well entrepreneurs manage their purchases.

Example: Stein Brothers Company, an eastern food wholesaler, buys most of its produce directly from farmers in various parts of the country. Buyers represent the firm in scattered, local communities. Some of these communities are on the West Coast, and delivery to the East takes about eight days—a considerable time for perishable products. Because of this long lag between purchase and delivery, the company is forced to speculate a great deal on prices.

Practice varies with the season of the year and with the current habits of customers, but purchases must usually be made long before sales. Stein Brothers sells to supermarkets, institutions, and other wholesalers. Demand for any particular produce commodity varies continuously—

depending on the quality of the product when it arrives in the East and on the amount of the same commodity available from other suppliers.

Daily closing inventories must be taken because each salesperson must know the amounts of specific lots and items available for sale the next morning. The inventory is used to check out the sales for every case or bushel received in each railroad car or truck. Stein Brothers knows exactly how much profit is made on any given purchase. With an inventory turnover every two or three days—or more than 100 turnovers a year—the Stein Brothers office staff must always be on its toes to keep pace with changing market conditions.[2]

A yearly turnover of 100 is the average for wholesale grocers. A lower turnover, say 90, would be a signal that the entrepreneur is carrying slow-moving or spoiled produce. On the other hand, a higher turnover, say 110, would be a signal that the grocer is carrying fast-moving produce. If the level of revenues remains the same, the entrepreneur's investment in inventory is less with a turnover of 110 than with a turnover of 90. In general, the less money tied up in inventory, the better, as long as stockouts are held to an acceptable level.

The inventory turnover for wholesale grocers differs from that of most other wholesalers or retailers. Men's clothing stores, for example, have an average yearly turnover of 3; appliance stores, 4; and restaurants, 22. Manufacturers also have a broad range of turnovers. Some chemical manufacturers, turn over their inventory 100 times a year. In contrast, some steel fabricators have turnovers as low as 3. An entrepreneur's goal in purchasing would be to equal or better the industry average.

Purchasing Guidelines

Let us now look more closely at the general purchasing guidelines we mentioned earlier.

Buying the right quality: Entrepreneurs should make sure that purchased materials and services suit their needs. In manufacturing especially, entrepreneurs should make sure that raw materials meet their specifications exactly. Otherwise, the product they make may turn out faulty. In retailing, entrepreneurs should see to it that the products they buy from suppliers meet their customers' standards of quality. Otherwise, customers may desert them for a competitor.

Buying the right quantity: Because they may have large amounts of money tied up in inventory, entrepreneurs should make sure they buy the right amount of inventory. In retailing, for example, too small a purchase may result in a loss of customers because of empty shelves. Too large a purchase, on the other hand, may mean excess inventory that hikes costs and threatens to become obsolete.

Buying at the right time: The timing of purchases is equally crucial. For manufacturers, for example, buying at the right time means buying raw materials to meet production schedules without overloading warehouses with inventory. In times of inflation, it may mean buying raw materials just before a price rise. Entrepreneurs should study the forces of supply and demand in their markets. They should also try to foresee what the economy will be like in the years to come. Will there be a recession or prosperity? Will there be shortages in raw materials? If so, entrepreneurs may have to look for substitute materials or stock up on materials early.

Buying from the right suppliers: Picking the right supplier is one of the entrepreneur's most challenging decisions. A bad choice may cancel out the entrepreneur's meticulous plans regarding quality, quantity, price, and time of delivery. Some suppliers, for example, may be incapable of meeting the entrepreneur's precise specifications. Others may not be able to deliver on time. Still others may not sell at the right price. It is the entrepreneur's job to find the supplier who can offer the best mix on all these points.

Buying at the right price: Contrary to popular opinion, the right price is not always the lowest price. For one thing, a lower price may not supply the entrepreneur with the product quality that customers expect. A lower price may also mean poorer service from suppliers. In deciding on price, entrepreneurs should balance price with both quality and service. Quality must come first. Next comes service—suppliers must deliver materials of proper quality in the correct quantity on time. Price comes last. Why last? Because the entrepreneur gains little by negotiating a lower price only to lose out on quality and service.

The Purchasing Cycle

If manufacturers, retailers, and wholesalers follow the preceding process thoroughly, they are likely to purchase the right materials. Similarly, the SBA suggests that entrepreneurs follow the purchasing cycle for retailers described as follows:

Estimating needs: Before you buy, you must estimate what you will need until the next time you review the particular line of merchandise. For some items, determining what you need involves merely looking at inventory and past sales. For other lines, it concerns risky decisions—which styles to select and how much of each to buy. You do not want to be left with merchandise in stock when a style is outmoded or the season is past.

Select supplier: After estimating your merchandise needs, you must find a supplier who can provide it. Some merchandise can be bought from only one vendor; in this case, the only decision you have to make is whether to carry the line. For most merchandise, however, there are several suppliers among which you can choose. In these instances, you must evaluate price as well as service. Consider matters such as reasonable and reliable delivery, adjustment of problems, and help—with credit terms, with spacing deliveries, with inventory management, and in emergencies.

Negotiate purchase: This crucial third step involves the purchase price as well as quantities, delivery dates, single or multiple shipment deliveries, freight and packing expenses, guarantees on the quality of the merchandise, promotion and advertising allowances, special offers on slightly damaged materials or sell-outs, and so on.
Follow-through: Finally, to improve service, you must review your relationship with each supplier from time to time, to determine if changes should be made. As necessary, search for alternate or new suppliers.[3]

Although this example applies to retailers, it applies equally well, with variations, to manufacturers and wholesalers.

The following two examples deal with entrepreneurs who are manufacturers and highlight the need to follow sound purchasing procedures:

Example: Samuel Holtz, the owner of a small foundry, one day complained bitterly about the amount of defective material he was receiving. "The raw material is guaranteed to meet quality specifications so as to contain less than 0.005 percent impurities. For the past three weeks, though, our castings have been turning out rougher than they should. I'm sure that last shipment of raw material wasn't as pure as it should have been. What do I do now?"

Example: In another plant, Joseph White was wondering what to do about a new supplier from which he had just purchased electronic components. "I got a good price on the first shipment, and so signed an order for two more shipments. The bill I got for this last shipment is almost $600 over that of the first. I told the supplier to take it back or reduce the bill, and he said that his quotation gave him the right to increase prices as inflation and labor expenses rose for him. I know I could get the shipment for less elsewhere."[4]

INVENTORY MANAGEMENT

Let us begin by defining *inventory*. In manufacturing, inventory means the raw materials that are stored in warehouses to make a product. In retailing, on the other hand, it means the products for sale to customers that are stored in stock rooms and on display shelves.

Note here that inventory relates only to material goods. Services are excluded. Shoes may be stored in anticipation of sales, or raw materials may be stockpiled to make product, but how could the skills of a management consultant or a lawyer be stockpiled?

Why have inventory at all? Though rarely asked, this is one question that entrepreneurs should never overlook. Its answer strongly influences how best to plan and control inventories. Here are some reasons for having inventory:

- To avoid the loss of customers because product is not in stock
- To enable customers to look over a product before buying
- To capitalize on discounts in the price of raw materials
- To keep a plant from cutting back or shutting down
- To make product in quantities that minimize cost
- To speculate against increases in price and cost
- To assure customers of prompt delivery
- To protect against strikes

This list is by no means complete, nor does each reason stand by itself—many of them overlap. Whatever their reasons, entrepreneurs should decide why they need inventory before they plan and control their inventory levels.

Planning and Control

To plan their inventory, entrepreneurs should always begin by forecasting their revenues. At best, forecasts are intelligent guesswork. Only entrepreneurs with monopolies in unsaturated markets can tell precisely what the future demand for their products will be and thus exercise pinpoint control over their inventory. For most entrepreneurs, however, these questions defy precise answers:

- When should I order? Should inventory be replenished now?
- How much should I order? What quantity should be ordered?

Who knows, for example, what the demand for Valentine cards will be? Although the entrepreneur may forecast the demand for Valentine cards and order accordingly, the demand is sure to be zero after February 14, so the entrepreneur can ill afford to be far off in making the forecast. To decide on the right number of cards to order, the entrepreneur should rely on *inventory control.* This tool consists of a set of rules that strike a balance among conflicting pressures. Many of these pressures are shown in Exhibit 17.3. For example, the entrepreneur may wish to:

- Have an ample supply in stock at all times, so that orders can be filled promptly. That way, customers will be happy with the service and come back again and again.
- Keep inventories low in order to reduce the amount of money tied up in inventory. That way, more cash will be available for, say, expansion. Return on investment will also be higher, because investment will be less.
- Keep inventories high in order to maintain steady production despite up-and-down demand. That way, costly shutdowns and temporary layoffs will be avoided.

To strike a balance among these conflicting goals, entrepreneurs should apply the concept of turnover, mentioned earlier. Together with the

EXHIBIT 17.3 *Conflicting Pressures on Inventory Levels*

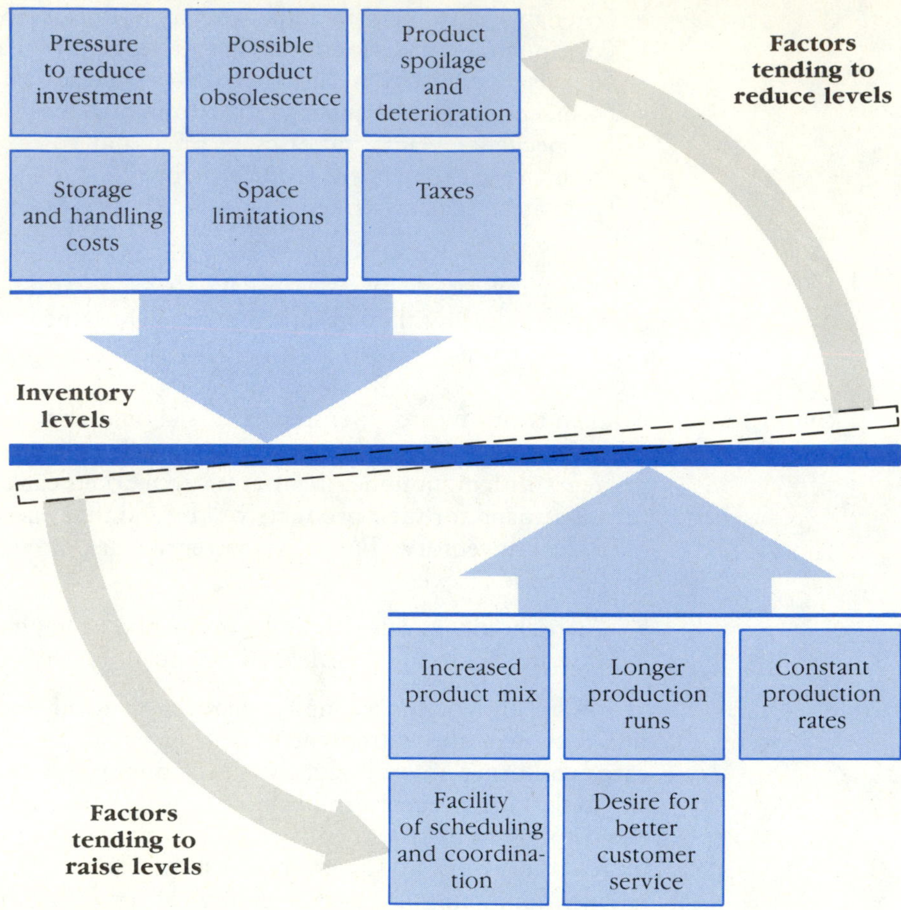

Source: Reprinted by permission of the *Harvard Business Review*. An exhibit from "Questions for Solving the Inventory Problem" by James I. Morgan (July/August 1963). Copyright © 1963 by the President and Fellows of Harvard College; all rights reserved.

forecast, turnover analysis enables entrepreneurs to estimate roughly how many months' supply should be on hand.

Example: A retailer of men's clothing forecasts revenues of $900,000 next year. In this industry, inventory turns over three times a year, on the average. How many months' supply should be on hand? How much investment should be in inventory? To answer these questions, the retailer would make the following computations:

$$\text{Months' supply} = \frac{12 \text{ months/year}}{3 \text{ turns/year}}$$

$$= 4 \text{ months' supply}$$

$$\text{Inventory investment} = \frac{\$900{,}000 \text{ revenues/year} \times 75\%^{5}}{3 \text{ turns/year}}$$

$$= \$225{,}000$$

These computations are only part of this entrepreneur's inventory control system. Control also involves evaluating the turnover of each item of inventory, such as shirts, ties, and topcoats.

As a way to judge inventories, turnover is by no means flawless. One flaw is that the very idea of turnover suggests that inventory should vary directly with revenues. That is, if revenues double, then inventory should also double, or if revenues should drop 50 percent, then inventory should be cut 50 percent. Not so. In fact, it is more likely that turnover will increase as revenues rise and drop off as revenues fall off.

Avoiding Formulas that Control Inventories

As with many other aspects of managing a venture, there is no one best way to control inventories. Many books and articles recommend various techniques to answer these questions:

- What is the best inventory level for a product?
- Where should inventories be kept?
- Should there be an inventory?

Such techniques generally do little for the entrepreneur. They result in simple formulas that may be applicable to mass production or to retail chain store operations, but not to smaller, growing ventures. The technique itself is not as important as the method of reasoning that entrepreneurs use to analyze their control of inventories:

> If [entrepreneurs] would apply a systematic approach to analyzing their inventory problems, they would be better able to resolve their different cases, and they would have better assurance that they are using the correct formulas.[6]

Record Keeping

As mentioned earlier, entrepreneurs should strive to have the right product in the right quantities at the right time in the right place. That is the goal of both purchasing and inventory management, as indicated in Exhibit 17.4. To meet that lofty goal, entrepreneurs must keep good records.

When they are just starting out, entrepreneurs generally can plan and control their inventories visually. They can readily see how much inventory they have on hand. They also know when and how much to reorder, the amount of time needed for delivery, and so on.

As their ventures grow, entrepreneurs need records to keep abreast of changing requirements. The need for records becomes even more pressing if the entrepreneur should delegate the responsibility for both purchasing and inventory management to someone else. At the very least, a good

EXHIBIT 17.4 *Goals of Purchasing Management and Inventory Management*

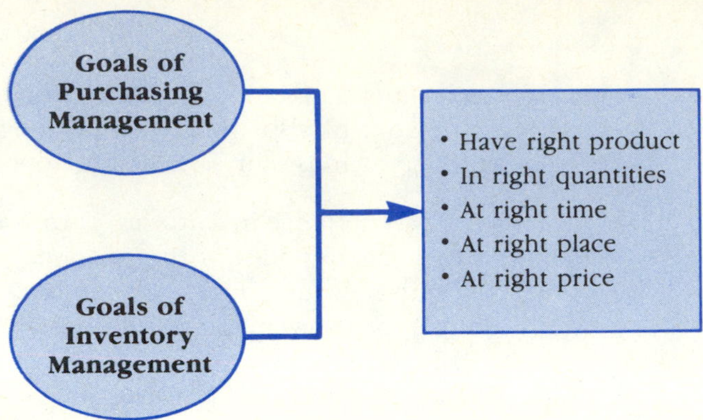

record-keeping system should enable entrepreneurs to keep track of:

- All orders received and all shipments made to customers
- The rates at which purchased materials are used
- Suppliers' quantities and delivery cycles
- Names of suppliers and their price lists
- Order cycles and quantities ordered
- Products returned from customers

These records enable entrepreneurs to handle their purchases and inventories efficiently.

Example: An entrepreneur decides to replace old tools that are worn out with new machine tools. To buy them, the entrepreneur sets a train of events in motion. First, the foreperson fills out a requisition stating the type and number of tools needed and gives it to the entrepreneur for approval. The entrepreneur then checks the requisition to make sure that:

- The cost of the tools is correct
- The description of the tools is adequate
- The quantity is sufficient
- The delivery date is reasonable
- Routing is clear

Next, the entrepreneur issues a purchase order, authorizing purchase of the tools requisitioned by the forepersons. The entrepreneur sends two copies of this purchase order to the supplier. One of these copies will be later returned with the promised delivery date noted by the supplier. Other copies of the purchase order go to the entrepreneur's accountant and to the foreperson.

When the shipment comes in, the foreperson verifies the tools and sends his receiving copy of the purchase order to the accountant, thus completing the purchasing cycle.

Often when a delivery date is crucial or a shipment is overdue, the entrepreneur must assume an even more active role. By every means available, the entrepreneur should negotiate with suppliers to speed up shipments. Doing so may prevent, for example, the shutdown of a plant due to shortages of vital raw materials.

Physical Inventory

To make sure that the actual amounts of materials on hand equal those shown in the inventory records, entrepreneurs should take physical inventory. If entrepreneurs then find that book inventory and physical inventory differ, they should adjust the records immediately. At the same time, if the difference is significant, entrepreneurs should find out why, in order to remedy the problem.

There are many reasons for any inventory shortage. For example, materials may have been pilfered, lost, thrown away, or overlooked when the physical inventory was taken. Or the entrepreneur may have poor receiving and billing procedures. Of these reasons, pilferage is the most easily understood. The other reasons are more subtle but equally damaging. For example:

- If an entrepreneur's receiving procedures are faulty, a receiving clerk may not be counting actual amounts received and comparing them with those on the supplier's packing list or invoice. If the amount received is less than that invoiced to the entrepreneur, the entrepreneur is paying for the difference.
- Merchandise may be sold to customers without being billed to them, through oversight or carelessness. In these cases, the entrepreneur will take a loss equal to the cost of the product and also lose the profit that should have been earned on the sale.
- Clerks may be accepting customer returns of merchandise that are no longer salable because of damage, stains, or packing defects. Entrepreneurs may be ignoring opportunities to return merchandise to suppliers when it arrives unfit for resale.[7]

According to the SBA, most entrepreneurs take careful steps to guard against theft, but few adopt serious procedures for protection from inventory shortages caused by factors such as poor receiving procedures, poor billing procedures, and merchandise damage.

Inventory Costs

To buy and hold inventories is costly. Yet many entrepreneurs count only the purchase price of materials and ignore the costs incurred after their purchase. These costs include:

- Storage and handling
- Interest, insurance, and property taxes
- Obsolescence and spoilage
- Paperwork

EXHIBIT 17.5 *The True Cost of Inventory*

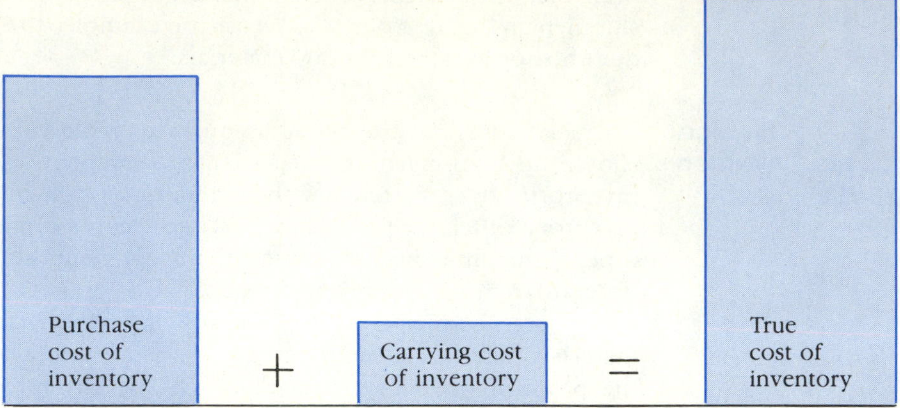

How significant are carrying costs? One estimate puts the average carrying cost at 25 percent of the purchase cost of inventory (see Exhibit 17.5). However, carrying costs differ sharply from industry to industry.

The main reason entrepreneurs ignore carrying costs may be that they rarely appear as such in accounting records. Interest charges and property taxes, for example, are easy to isolate and identify. But the other carrying costs are extremely hard to measure, particularly the cost of money and the cost of shortages.

Cost of money: Often overlooked, the cost of money is perhaps the most crucial of all carrying costs. Why? Because money not invested in inventory might be invested elsewhere, perhaps in plant expansion; the loss of the return from any such forgone opportunity is the cost of money tied up in inventory. It is especially hard to estimate this cost because it depends on an estimate of the return from other opportunities.

Cost of shortages: This cost is as hard to estimate as the cost of money. The costs connected with carrying too little inventory may be as severe as the costs of carrying too much inventory. Entrepreneurs often overlook this fact, because shortages are less visible than excesses. The cost of shortages may include:

- Revenues lost because the entrepreneur could not fill a customer's order out of inventory
- Excess costs incurred to speed up production or to break into the schedule of another product in order to avoid losing a customer's order
- Loss of goodwill and future orders

The costs of shortage defy computation. For example, if a $1,000 order is lost because of an inventory shortage, the cost of shortage for that order alone is precisely $1,000. But how many future orders from the same customer has the entrepreneur lost? That question is impossible to estimate with any accuracy, but is nevertheless a real cost to the entrepreneur.

SUMMARY

How well entrepreneurs do their buying and manage their inventories may spell the difference between profit and loss. Purchasing is a major entrepreneurial function along with finance, marketing, and production. On the average, more than 50 percent of every sales dollar is spent to purchase materials and services.

Entrepreneurs should plan and control their purchases with the same care they devote to the other activities of their ventures. Their goal should be to buy materials and services of the right quality, in the right quantity, at the right time, from the right supplier, and at the right price.

Generally, inventory turnover is the best measure of an entrepreneur's performance in managing purchases and inventories. A turnover equal to the industry average indicates acceptable purchasing and inventory management.

In most industries, inventory and purchasing are equally important. Without sufficient inventory, customers may be lost and services compromised. To plan and control their inventories, entrepreneurs should strike a balance among such conflicting pressures as product obsolescence, longer production runs, reduced investment, and better service.

To plan and control well, entrepreneurs should keep good records on all purchases and inventories. Records of all orders received and all shipments made to customers are especially important.

DISCUSSION AND REVIEW QUESTIONS

1. Are purchasing and inventory management equally important? Why?
2. If you were an entrepreneur, what tool might you use to judge your performance in managing your purchases and inventories? Why?
3. Explain why inventories may be necessary.
4. Define these terms: *turnover, inventory, inventory control, purchase requisition, carrying costs, cost of money, cost of shortage.*
5. Explain why purchase costs are not the only cost of inventory. Give one example.
6. How may sound purchasing and inventory-control practices help you, as an entrepreneur, to boost profits?
7. Is purchasing as important a function as finance and marketing? Explain.

8. In the purchase of a product or service, which comes first: quality or price? Explain.
9. Why should entrepreneurs keep good records on purchases and inventories?
10. Would you, as an entrepreneur, try to maximize inventory turnover in order to maximize sales revenues? Explain.
11. Why is it so hard to estimate the cost of shortages? The cost of money?
12. Why should entrepreneurs take a physical count of inventory at least once a year?
13. Why is the timing of purchases so crucial?
14. How do inventories differ among the manufacturing, retailing, and wholesaling industries?
15. Name some service industries that do carry inventories.

NOTES

1. U.S. Department of Commerce, *Statistical Abstract of the United States* (Washington, D.C.: U.S. Government Printing Office, 1984), p. 764.
2. Harvey C. Krentzman, U.S. Small Business Administration, *Managing for Profits* (Washington, D.C.: U.S. Government Printing Office, 1968), pp. 112–113.
3. Adapted from U.S. Small Business Administration, *Business Basics: Retail Buying Function* (Washington, D.C.: U.S. Government Printing Office, 1985), pp. 6–7.
4. Adapted from U.S. Small Business Administration, *Business Basics: Purchasing for Manufacturing Firms* (Washington, D.C.: U.S. Government Printing Office, 1985), p. 1.
5. Ratio of purchase cost to selling price.
6. James I. Morgan, "Questions for Solving the Inventory Problem," *Harvard Business Review*, July–August 1963, p. 95.
7. Adapted from U.S. Small Business Administration, *Business Basics: Inventory Management* (Washington, D.C.: U.S. Government Printing Office, 1985), p. 25.

CASE 17A *All-Trex Security Group*

In business for slightly more than a year, All-Trex Security Group is already generating sales revenues at the rate of $200,000 a year—precisely the fifth-year goal set by president Alan Lewis in his business plan. "What a great feeling to know that you're four years ahead of your fifth-year projection," says Mr. Lewis. The company offers security services such as armed guards and alarm systems.

Mr. Lewis's feelings of joy are tempered, however, by the painful knowledge that rapid growth often spawns a host of problems. "Right now our most serious problem is cash flow," says Mr. Lewis. "We're often cash-poor because our customers pay too slowly.

"One of our biggest and slowest-paying customers is City Hall. But what can you say to the city, to the mayor? Can you say, 'We'll stop providing you with security?'"

Mr. Lewis's new projections call for sales revenues of $1 million in three years. "I'm sure we can reach that sales level, but I want to make sure we do so profitably and without cash flow crises like the one we're having now."

Background

The cofounders of All-Trex are Mr. Lewis and Keith Lucas. "Keith and I decided to go into business for ourselves because our career paths failed to meet our expectations," says Mr. Lewis. "Opportunities for advancement were slim." Excerpts from their resumes appear in Exhibits 17A.1 and 17A.2.

Mr. Lewis prides himself on the fact that he once worked for two Fortune 500 companies and performed well. "Our strengths, Keith's and

EXHIBIT 17A.1

All-Trex Security Group: Excerpts From Alan Lewis's Resume

Education

In 1978, graduated from the College of Wooster with a degree in business economics and urban studies.

Work Experience

March 1984 to present—as president of All-Trex Security Group.
June 1983 to present—as a consultant for Webb Manufacturing.
June 1983 to September 1980—as manager of the NTSS* program at Cuyahoga Community College.
September 1980 to February 1983—as a jobholder with a number of companies, among them Milico Life Insurance and Clopay.
March 1978 to September 1980—as assistant employee relations manager at B.F. Goodrich.
September 1976 to March 1978—as security guard at the College of Wooster.

* Non-Traditional Summer School

EXHIBIT 17A.2

All-Trex Security Group: Excerpts From Keith Lucas's Resume

Education

December 1983 to present—as student majoring in small business management at Cuyahoga Community College.

June 1975 to September 1980—as student taking private police courses at Case Western Reserve University.

Work Experience

March 1984 to present—as cofounder and general manager of All-Trex Security Group.

June 1983 to March 1984—as security guard for Aetna Total Security.

April 1982 to June 1983—as security guard for Beach Security.

June 1980 to October 1981—as bank floor guard and FBI payroll messenger for Society National Bank.

March 1980 to June 1980—as security guard for Burns Security Services.

March 1979 to March 1980—as sergeant of security guards.

January 1979 to June 1979—as assistant sales manager for Ekco Home Products, selling cookware and other kitchen products.

April 1974 to November 1978—as mail handler for the U.S. Postal Service, loading and unloading mail trucks.

mine, include professionalism and excellent communications skills," says Mr. Lewis. "And, our thirst for knowledge is bottomless. We're always taking courses and attending seminars, especially in security and in small business management.

The idea for launching a venture and becoming entrepreneurs came in 1982, when the two men exchanged ideas on what to do with the rest of their lives. One idea that intrigued them was entering the security industry. There was ample evidence that security was one of the country's fastest-growing industries. As shown in Exhibit 17A.3, consumer spending for security is projected to rise sharply through 1988.

Thus evolved their decision to enter the security industry as entrepreneurs. First they prepared a business plan. "All the experts told us to prepare one, even though we were going to finance the business ourselves, Keith and I," says Mr. Lewis. "The business plan was really helpful to us. It forced us to think through the many steps required to start a business sucessfully."

In Business for Themselves

Two years passed before the two men opened for business, in March 1984, as the All-Trex Security Group. At first, the business was organized as a sole proprietorship, with Mr. Lewis as its only full-time employee. The business's beginning balance sheet appears in Exhibit 17A.4. Meanwhile, Mr. Lucas held two jobs, one part-time with All-Trex and the other full-time as a security guard with Aetna Total Security—until the volume of business would justify his joining All-Trex full-time.

Mr. Lewis is quick to acknowledge the help he received from the Minority Business Development Center at City Hall, which showed him how

EXHIBIT 17A.3 *All-Trex Security Group: Consumer Spending for Security*

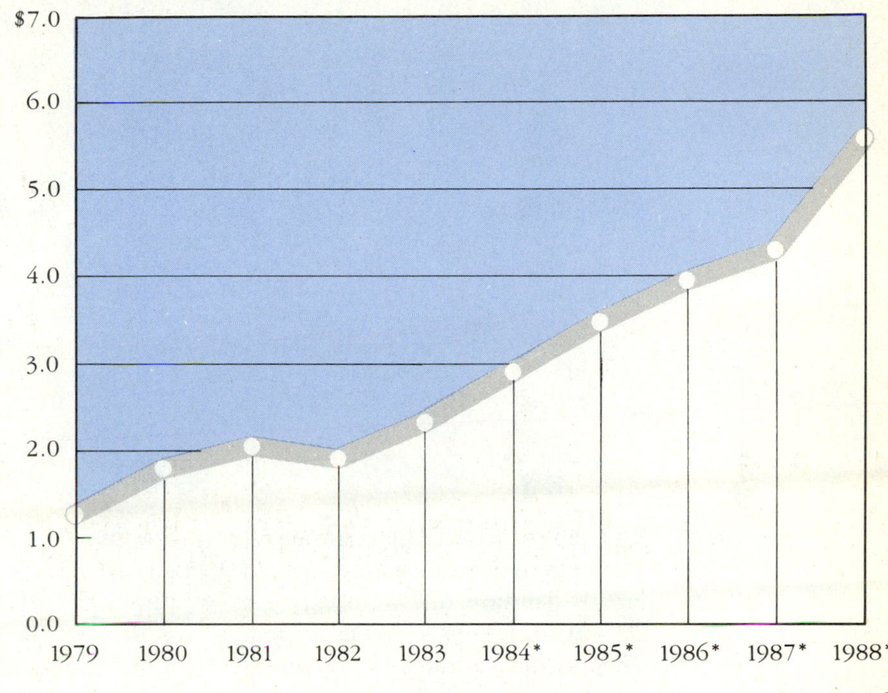

Source: Marcy Eckroth Mullins, "Security Spending," *USA TODAY*, Auguest 14, 1984, p. 36.

EXHIBIT 17A.4 *All-Trex Security Group: Beginning Balance Sheet (As of February 29, 1984)*

Assets			**Equities**		
Current Assets			Liabilities		
Cash	$27,000		Accounts payable	$ 0	
Accounts receivable	0		Loan payable to Mr. Lewis	44,100	$44,100
Inventories	0		Owner's Equity		0
Materials and supplies	300	$27,300			
Fixed Assets					
Equipment and fixtures		16,300			
Other Assets		500			
Total Assets		$44,100	Total Equities		$44,100

EXHIBIT 17A.5

*All-Trex Security Group: Evaluation of All-Trex's Progress**

In January 1984, Alan Lewis had his first meeting with us. At that time, he was in the early stages of developing ideas and a business plan for a new business. The two industries he was considering were human-resource consulting and the security business.

After evaluating Mr. Lewis's experience, qualifications, and interests, we advised him it would be unwise to open a consulting business. He lacked the reputation to build a successful practice. We then suggested that he start a business with a product that prospective customers could touch and see. He accepted our advice and decided to form a business that would offer armed security guards and sell security alarm systems.

Later, we provided Mr. Lewis with information and materials on the business plan, on start-up procedures, and on marketing. He also used the services provided by the Minority Business Development Center and began taking courses there in accounting, management, and marketing.

In summary, as a result of the help we provided, All-Trex is a growing business with 23 employees and with aggressive plans for expansion. In fact, All-Trex expects to hire at least six more employees within the next three months. Had Mr. Lewis gone instead into consulting, he would have employed at most three persons by this time.

* This evaluation of All-Trex was prepared by Patti DeRosa, head of the Small Business Resources and Technology Center.

to prepare a business plan, among other things. 'I can't say too much for the help they've given me," says Mr. Lewis. "They were also instrumental in my landing one of our largest accounts, City Hall."

Another group that helped Mr. Lewis was a local college's Small Business Resources and Technology Center. It aims to stimulate small and minority business growth throughout its area. Heading the Center is Patti DeRosa, whom Mr. Lewis also credits with much of All-Trex's success. Excerpts from her evaluation of All-Trex's progress appear in Exhibit 17A.5.

The Markets for Security

All-Trex strives to be an all-purpose security company. Numbered among its clients are major corporations as well as major governmental units. "Both types of clients are excellent," says Mr. Lewis, "although the government does the lion's share of the spending for security" as shown in Exhibit 17A.6.

Mr. Lewis and Mr. Lucas do not believe in focusing their efforts on just one market, so they have divided their company into two operating divisions, as shown in Exhibit 17A.7 and described as follows.

Protective Systems Division Headed by Carlton Garner, this division's marketing efforts cover residential, industrial, and government customers. The residential market is largely untapped, with less than 9 percent of all homeowners currently owning an effective security system. A recent newspaper article said:

EXHIBIT 17A.6 *All-Trex Security Group: Private vs. Government Security Spending*

1980 Total Security Spending = $36.2 Billion
Private Sector Markets
38%
Government Markets
62%

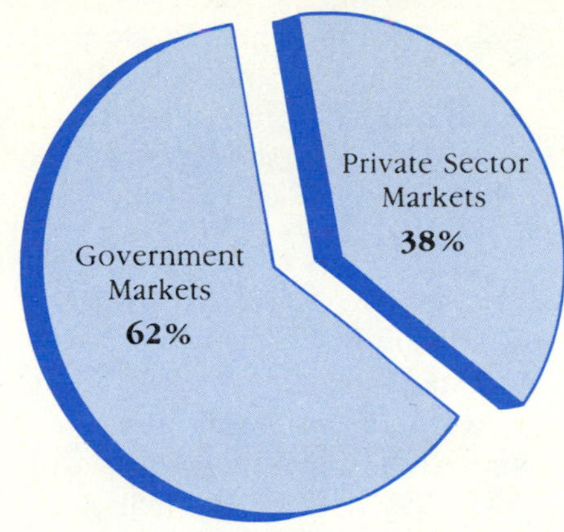

Source: "The Security Market Outlook," *Security Management*, (January 1985), p. 69.

EXHIBIT 17A.7 *All-Trex Security Group: Organizational Chart*

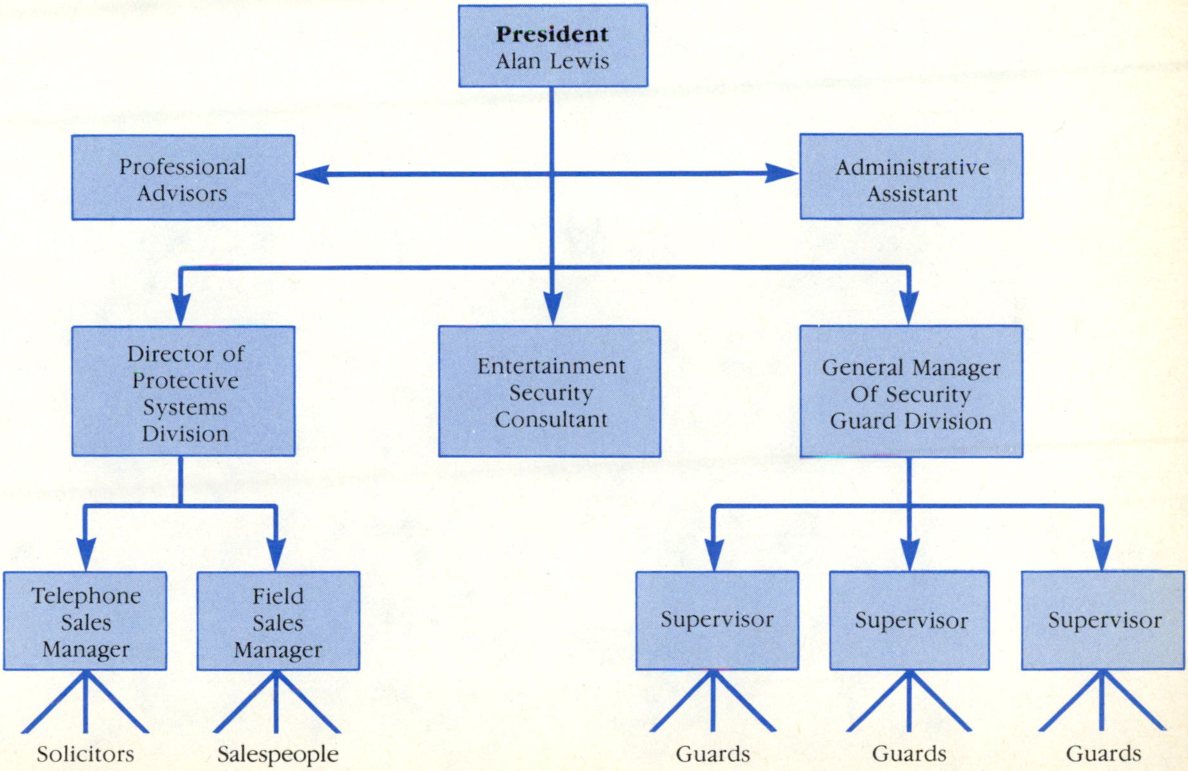

President
Alan Lewis
Professional Advisors
Administrative Assistant
Director of Protective Systems Division
Entertainment Security Consultant
General Manager Of Security Guard Division
Telephone Sales Manager
Field Sales Manager
Supervisor
Supervisor
Supervisor
Solicitors
Salespeople
Guards
Guards
Guards

recent newspaper article said:

> Given the fact that a residential burglary occurs every 15 seconds nationwide, and that these burglaries escalate into violent crimes 30 percent of the time when the home is occupied, security should obviously be the No. 1 priority upon moving into a new home or remodeling an old one.
>
> Burglars do not enjoy challenge, so the immediate goal for effective home security should be four to five minutes of deterrence. A thief who has not gained entry within that time will probably abandon the attempt.

To fill this need, All-Trex offers a variety of innovative products. All are user-friendly systems. Shown in Exhibit 17A.8 examining such a system are Mr. Lewis, Mr. Garner, and two co-workers. All-Trex offers new state-of-the-art electronic security systems that use buzzers and lights to warn of intrusion, fire, or smoke hazards. Because the system is wireless, installation cost has been reduced sharply. This system costs about $500. They also sell a new remote control system that turns the homeowner's telephone into a security monitoring device that dials authorities in case of an emergency. This system costs about $1,000.

All-Trex expects several major corporations including Honeywell,

EXHIBIT 17A.8 *All-Trex Security Group: View of Alan Lewis and Co-workers Examining an Electronic Security Alarm*

Inc., and Fargo and Company, to enter the residential market by the end of 1985. Soon, General Electric Company may also open a chain of service centers nationwide that would sell, install, and monitor home systems.

Currently All-Trex's strongest competitors are not the major corporations but the small street-corner shops; 15,000 such shops dot the country. Many of them are disreputable, often preying on the elderly. "That's deplorable," says Mr. Lewis.

Security Guard Division Headed by Mr. Lucas, this division provides armed and unarmed guards for a wide variety of individuals, such as:

- Highly visible corporate executives
- Well-know politicians like Congressman Louis Stokes
- Diplomats who carry large amounts of money
- Special events such as Labor Day picnics

This division also markets its services to local colleges and universities as well as to federal and municipal clients. "It's these large accounts that make money for us," says Mr. Lucas, "although it often takes some of them a long time, more than ten weeks, to pay us."

All-Trex tells potential clients that its employees are on call 24 hours a day to provide armed or unarmed, uniformed or plainclothes guards as well as professional bodyguards.

This division's stiffest competition stems from high technology. As shown in Exhibit 17A.9, retailers are now substituting electronics for guards to stop shoplifting. In 1984, 700,000 people were arrested nationwide for shoplifting, and only one shoplifter in ten is prosecuted. Retailers are paying more attention to this crime, and are installing sophisticated

EXHIBIT 17A.9 *All-Trex Security Group: Most Effective Anti-shoplifting Devices According to Retailers*

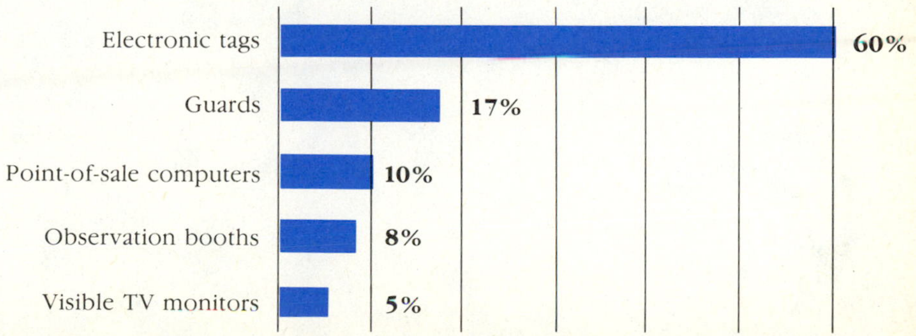

Source: Fighting Shoplifters," *The Wall Street Journal*, January 4, 1985, p. 11.

anti-theft devices. The most popular is a plastic tag about the size of a pocket comb that retailers can put on everything from dresses to fur coats. The tags, conveniently removed only by a special tool, set off an alarm when they pass through sensing devices located at exits.

Criminals often try to remove the tags or cover them with aluminium foil to fool the detection machines. Originally, retailers hid a tag inside each piece of merchandise, and many criminals were caught, leading to expensive and time-consuming prosecution. Now retailers generally pin the tags on the outside of garments to deter would-be thieves.

The Future Mr. Lewis is pleased with All-Trex's performance. "We've done well for a fledgling business," he says. "Sure we have our problems, but so does

EXHIBIT 17A.10 *All-Trex Security Group: Latest Income Statement (Five months ending May 31, 1985)*

Sales Revenues		$82,890
Operating Expenses		
Payroll	$61,720	
General and administrative	3,610	
Insurance and taxes	3,370	
Printing	1,650	
Depreciation	1,440	
Rent and electricity	1,260	
Uniforms	1,220	
Legal and accounting	1,050	
Telephone	770	
Training seminars and conferences	820	
Dues and subscriptions	760	
Office supplies	420	78,090
Operating Profit		$ 4,800

EXHIBIT 17A.11 *All-Trex Security Group: Latest Balance Sheet (As of June 1, 1985)*

Assets			Equities		
Current Assets			Current Liabilities		
Cash	$ 1,120		Accounts payable	$ 0	
Accounts receivable	12,460		Loan payable	750	$ 750
Inventories	0	$13,580	Long-term Liabilities		
Fixed Assets			Loan payable to Mr. Lewis		18,420
Office equipment	$ 6,730		Owners' Equity		
Security equipment	4,550		Common stock	$ 500	
	$11,280		Retained earnings	4,000	4,500
Less: Accumulated depreciation	1,440	9,840			
Other Assets		250			
Total Assets		$23,670	Total Equities		$23,670

everybody else." All-Trex's latest income statement and balance sheet appear in Exhibits 17A.10 and 17A.11.

"At our present rate of growth, it's likely that we'll become a million-dollar company in just two or three years," says Mr. Lewis. "And in just five to ten years we'll be a five-million-dollar company." He recently prepared the company's statement of goals, both short- and long-range for his staff, shown in Exhibit 17A.12.

One of Mr. Lewis's consuming ambitions is for All-Trex to be the largest minority security company in the state. To realize that ambition, he plans to rely heavily on his team of professional advisors, noted in Exhibit 17A.7. "We must grow in an orderly way," says Mr. Lewis. "That's why I need sound, expert advice." Among his present advisors are:

- Ms. DeRosa, who, as already mentioned, heads a college's Small Business Resources and Technology Center.
- A management consultant, who helps in strategic planning, cash flow, and market projections.
- A certified public accountant, who prepares income statements and balance sheets every six months.

All-Trex's board of directors rarely meets, mostly because Mr. Lewis prefers to consult with his team of professional advisors. "They've helped get me this far, and I know they will continue to help me grow," he says.

Questions

1. Comment on Mr. Lewis's latest sales projections.
2. What risks do you see in this industry?
3. What are the key elements for continuing to make the company successful?
4. Comment on Mr. Lewis's entrepreneurial and managerial traits.
5. Would you invest in the company? Why?

EXHIBIT 17A.12

All-Trex Security Group: Short- and Long-range Goals

Short-range Goals (1 to 3 years)

- Add two trucks.
- Form joint ventures
- Expand lines of service
- Open offices in two other cities
- Achieve sales revenues of $1 million a year

Long-range Goals (5 to 10 years)

- Expand markets
- Set up satellite office
- Establish training school
- Be the largest minority security company
- Achieve sales revenues of $5 million a year

CASE 17B *Zeus Fabricated-Metal Company, Inc.*

George Linsenmann has watched his venture leap from 2 to 33 employees in just three years. From the start, company offices have been located in one corner of a large, musty basement in an old, multistory factory building. Now that sales revenues are approaching $1 million a year, Mr. Linsenmann plans to move his venture to more spacious quarters, in an industrial park that looks like a college campus.

In keeping with his image as a successful entrepreneur, Mr. Linsenmann plans to outfit his company's cluster of new offices with modern furniture and equipment. Four suppliers have submitted bids:

Ferrell Company	$8,000
Hildebrand Company	7,500
Hudlin Company	7,200
Pearson Company	7,000

Clearly, if all four bidders are equally capable, Pearson should be the winner. But the choice is not that simple. Two of the bidders, Ferrell and Hildebrand, are also two of Mr. Linsenmann's most important customers. His sales manager has strongly urged him to award the contract to one or both of them:

> George, as I see it, you've got to choose between Ferrell and Hildebrand. I know their bids are higher than the others. But if you don't, we may lose their business. Besides, they've been loyal customers from almost the beginning. Everybody does it, George. Reciprocity is good business.

Reciprocity means that Mr. Linsenmann should place his orders with those companies that buy from him. Just how much fabricated metal have these two companies bought? Sales records show that, last year, Mr. Linsenmann sold them fabricated metal worth these amounts:

Ferrell Company	$43,000
Hildebrand Company	32,000

Questions

1. If you were Mr. Linsenmann, how would you award the order for office furniture and equipment? Why?
2. Is reciprocity ethical? Why?
3. If you were Mr. Linsenmann, how would you explain your decision satisfactorily to the losing bidders?

CASE 17C *Samantha Teen Shoppe, Inc.*

Samantha Martynak owned a store that specialized in clothes for teenagers. Located in a suburban shopping mall, the store was doing moderately well.

Last year, the store had:

- Sales revenues of $234,000
- A gross margin of 40 percent on sales
- An inventory turnover of three

One day, Mrs. Martynak learned from a supplier that her yearly turnover of three was below the average in her field, which was four.

This news prompted Mrs. Martynak to take a long, hard look at the clothes she carried. She soon found that she had been carrying some slow-moving styles. So she replaced them with items that turned over more quickly—four times a year.

Questions

1. Assuming all other costs remained unchanged, by how many dollars did Mrs. Martynak improve her cash position?
2. What related costs were affected by this increase in inventory turnover? Up or down?

18 TAXATION

QUESTIONS FOR MASTERY

Why are taxes necessary?

What is the difference between tax avoidance and tax evasion?

Why is tax planning important?

What are ways of saving or postponing taxes?

Why is it vital to keep good tax records?

In this world, nothing is certain but death and taxes.

Benjamin Franklin

Few subjects spark more controversy than taxes. Most taxpayers grumble about them; entrepreneurs are no exception. Few entrepreneurs enjoy poring over their federal income tax return, for example. As suggested in Exhibit 18.1, federal income taxes are just one of many taxes that entrepreneurs must pay. Entrepreneurs must know precisely what taxes they must pay and, equally important, how taxes may affect the survival and growth of their ventures.

THE NEED FOR TAXES

The English poet, Robert Herrick, in referring to taxes once wrote, "Kings ought to shear their sheep, not skin them." His remark strikes a responsive chord in the minds of most entrepreneurs. Even so, few entrepreneurs would quarrel with the need for some taxes. As Oliver Wendell Holmes, former chief justice of the U.S. Supreme Court, put it, "Taxes are what we

EXHIBIT 18.1 *Selected Tax Obligations*

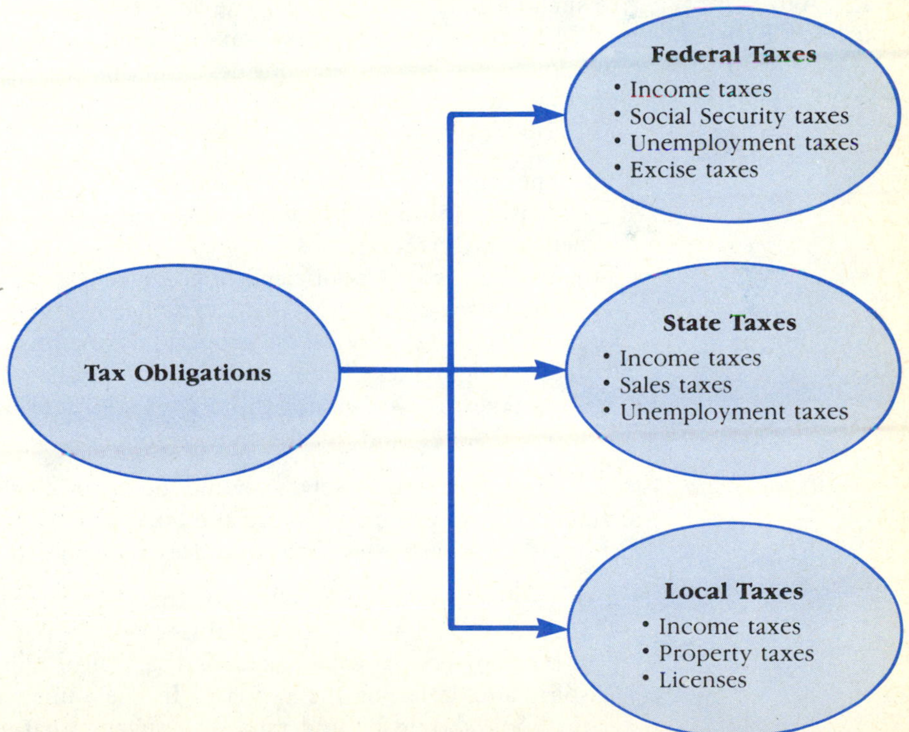

pay for a civilized society."[1] Because of taxes, for example:

- All persons are entitled to a high-school education, regardless of race, creed, or color, income level, or social standing.
- The poor, the handicapped, and the elderly are maintained at a decent standard of living.
- The nation is capable of defending itself against invaders.

There are many more benefits that taxes make possible. Despite the benefits, there is often vast disagreement about who should bear the burden of taxation. Raking business over the coals about the taxes they pay or do not pay has often been politically expedient. Admittedly, some profitable billion-dollar corporations pay no federal income taxes. Mindful of that fact, a congressman once sponsored a bill requiring giant corporations to make their income tax returns public:

> The annual reports published by giant corporations announce to stockholders that business is better and profits are improving. The tax statements of these same companies to Internal Revenue paint a picture that reduces their profit figure, which in effect reduces their total tax figure. Like the medieval European peasant, for their stockholders they wear wedding clothes; for the tax man they wear rags.[2]

Tax Avoidance Not Tax Evasion

Are such corporations breaking the law? No. In fact, no business, big or small, has any duty to pay more taxes than the law demands. But what the public often perceives is that businesses permit their tax accountants to cut corners in order to evade rather than avoid taxes. This erroneous perception needs correction:

- For one thing, tax savings boost the economy by helping to finance expansion into new products or new markets, thus serving customers better and creating jobs.
- For another, when politicians brand business for not paying enough taxes, they generally mean federal income taxes only. Business also pays Social Security taxes, property taxes, local taxes, and possibly even foreign taxes. These taxes merit the same attention as federal income taxes. As shown in Exhibit 18.2, all three levels of government—federal, state, and local—play significant roles as tax collectors.

Entrepreneurs themselves should be clear in their mind about the distinction between tax *avoidance* and tax *evasion*. Perhaps the best way to distinguish between these two practices is to say that:

- Tax avoidance has the blessings of the U.S. Supreme Court, the U.S. Congress, and the state legislatures.
- Tax evasion, on the other hand, is the willful failure to live up to the spirit and letter of the tax law. In the same vein, nothing in this textbook should be understood to suggest that entrepreneurs should apply evasive tax methods to their own ventures.

EXHIBIT 18.2 ***Share of Total Taxes* Collected by Federal, State, and Local Governments***

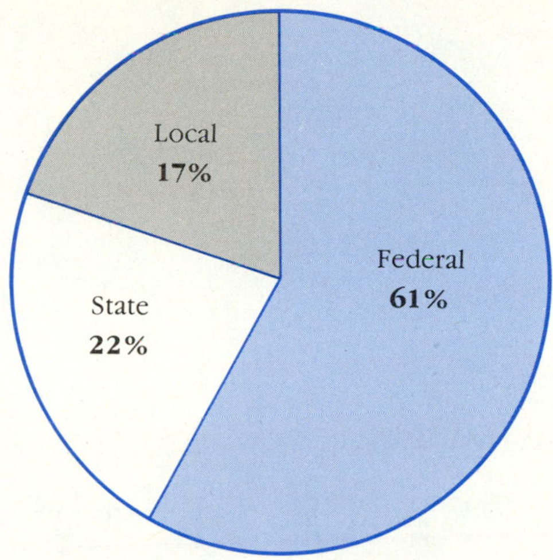

* Includes individual as well as business taxes.

Source: U.S. Department of Commerce, *Statistical Abstract of the United States* (Washington, D.C.: U.S. Government Printing Office, 1984), p. 273.

For the Greatest Good

Taxes flow in a circular direction. Money paid out in taxes has a way of coming back to entrepreneurs and other taxpayers in the form of benefits. *Time* magazine put it this way:

> The complacent observer of high taxes points out that all the money somehow comes back to the people. A fresh-water clam in the well-balanced home aquarium pumps through his voracious lungs nine gallons of water a day, yet the fish around it do not starve. Rather, the tank is purified in the redistribution. So the Government pumps it in, and pumps it out for the greatest good of the greatest number. That's the idea.[3]

TAX PLANNING

Tax laws change yearly, often in ways that strongly affect profits. Some changes may open the door to new tax savings, by hiking deductions or reducing tax rates. Some may boost taxes by wiping out tax shelters or shaving deductions. To keep abreast of such changes, entrepreneurs should rely on their lawyers or accountants for the latest tax information. Moreover, these professionals can help entrepreneurs to save taxes. Exhibit 18.3 shows how significant these savings may be.

EXHIBIT 18.3

What Tax Savings May Mean to the Entrepreneur

If the ratio of before-tax profits to sales is . . .	. . . then a $1,000 tax saving would boost profits* as much as a sales increase of
20%	$ 9,260
15%	12,350
10%	18,520
5%	37,040
1%	185,200

* Assumes a flat 46 percent corporate tax rate, which is the maximum.

Source: Adapted from *Key Moves to Cut Company Taxes* (Englewood Cliffs, N.J.: Prentice-Hall, Inc., 1980), p. 5.

Entrepreneurs also need tax help in areas other than federal income taxes. Equally complex are the laws covering:

- State, county, and municipal taxes
- Social Security taxes
- Estate taxes

We will now discuss various ways in which entrepreneurs may save or postpone taxes, focusing mainly on the U.S. Internal Revenue Code.

Legal Forms of Organization

How much a venture pays in federal income taxes depends strongly on which legal form of organization the entrepreneur chooses—the consequences of this choice may spell the difference between profit and loss. As discussed in Chapter Seven, entrepreneurs may choose one of several legal forms, among them:

- The regular corporation
- The S-corporation
- The general partnership
- The limited partnership
- The sole proprietorship

Regular Corporations Perhaps the first step in understanding corporate federal income taxes is to define what taxable income means. On the average, over a period of years, taxable income equals roughly the amounts that corporations report as book profit before federal income taxes in their reports to shareholders. In any given year, taxable income may differ sharply from book profit. This seeming contradiction comes about because the goals of *tax* accounting differ from those of *financial* accounting.

- The goal of tax accounting is to minimize taxes—by recognizing expenses as soon as is legally possible and by putting off recognition of revenues for as long as is legally possible. That way, tax payments are

EXHIBIT 18.4 *Sources of Federal Tax Revenues*

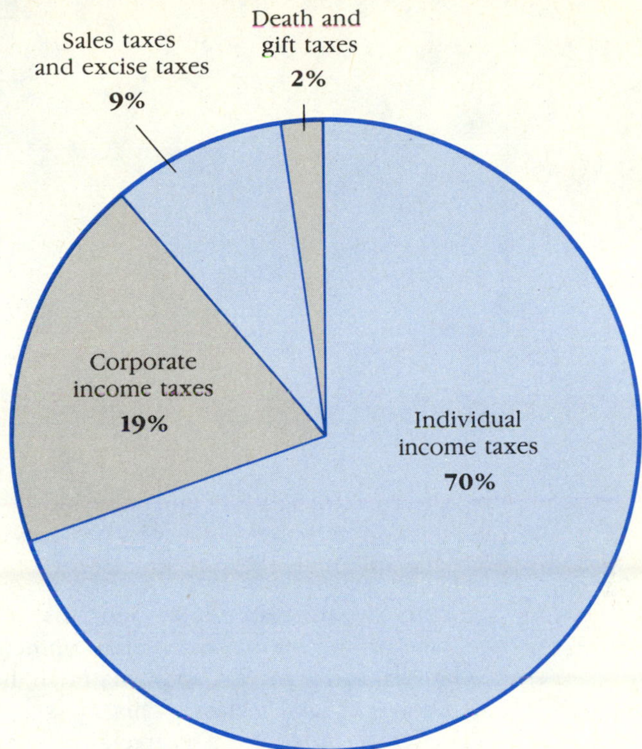

Source: U.S. Department of Commerce, *Statistical Abstract of the United States* (Washington, D.C.: U.S. Government Printing Office, 1984), p. 274.

postponed to later years. Note in Exhibit 18.4 that regular corporations contribute 19 percent of all federal tax revenues.

- The goal of financial accounting, on the other hand, is to report fairly the revenues, expenses, and profits earned.

The U.S. Internal Revenue Code, for example, permits entrepreneurs to use one depreciation method for tax purposes and another method for financial reporting purposes. Let us look first at the depreciation methods that may be used for tax purposes.

In 1981, a dramatic change took place in the tax law with passage of the Economic Recovery Tax Act of 1981. This act replaced a complex and slow depreciation system with one that is simple and allows depreciation over shorter time-periods. Called the Accelerated Cost Recovery System (ACRS), this new system permits entrepreneurs to depreciate most equipment over just a 3- or 5-year period *for tax purposes*. In contrast, under the old system, the average depreciable life was about 10 years. Moreover, buildings now qualify for either 10-year or 18-year depreciable lives, as

EXHIBIT 18.5

Depreciation Rates Under ACRS System

Year	Depreciation Rates for Assets With Depreciable Lives of 3 Years	5 Years	10 Years
1	33%	20%	10%
2	45	32	18
3	22	24	16
4		16	14
5		8	12
6			10
7			8
8			6
9			4
10			2
	100%	100%	100%

Source: U.S. Congress, *H.R. 4242* (Washington, D.C.: U.S. Government Printing Office, July 30, 1981), Section 201, pp. 61–62.

opposed to 40 to 50 years under the old system. Under the new system, the depreciation rules are alike for both new and used fixed assets. The four new classes of depreciable life are described as follows:

Three-year asset class: This class covers automobiles, light-duty trucks, and research-and-development equipment. Also covered are special tools, molds, some materials-handling devices, and racehorses.

Five-year asset class: This class covers almost all equipment not covered under the 3-year class, so 5-year assets include heavy-duty trucks, motors, lathes, office furniture, machines, and equipment, aircraft, drill presses, and a host of other equipment.

Ten-year asset class: This class covers mostly railroad tank cars and public utility equipment. Some buildings may also qualify.

Eighteen-year asset class: This class mostly covers buildings and other real property. It also includes some public utility equipment.

Shown in Exhibit 18.5 are the yearly rates at which entrepreneurs may now depreciate their costs of fixed assets for each of the first three classes just described. Note that the percentage of the asset's cost that can be depreciated each year will depend on the year the asset is put in service.

Note also that Exhibit 18.5 omits the 18-year asset class. The reason is that buildings and other real property are the exception to the principle that a single depreciation method and period apply to all assets within an asset class. Here, both the depreciation method and the period are determined on a property-to-property basis, using special tables prepared by the U.S. Internal Revenue Service.

Example: To estimate his depreciation expense, an entrepreneur plans to use two methods. To save taxes, he must use the ACRS method, but to

EXHIBIT 18.6

How Book Profit Differs from Taxable Income

	First Year	
	Book Profit	**Taxable Income**
Sales revenues	$300,000	$300,000
Operating expenses before depreciation	225,000	225,000
Operating profit before depreciation	$ 75,000	$ 75,000
Depreciation	15,000*	30,000†
Operating profit	$ 60,000	$ 45,000

* Using the straight-line method: $150,000 asset cost × 10 percent depreciation rate = $15,000
† Using the ACRS method: $150,000 asset cost × 20 percent depreciation rate = $30,000

report his financial performance to shareholders, he uses the straight-line method. This method assumes that his depreciable assets will provide equal benefits throughout their years of service.

To show why these different methods might be used for different purposes, let us assume that, in his first year, the entrepreneur has sales revenues of $300,000 and operating expenses of $225,000 before depreciation. Depreciable assets cost $150,000; their average useful life is 10 years. How would the entrepreneur's book profit differ from taxable income? They would differ as shown in Exhibit 18.6. Note that taxable income is $15,000 less than book profit. That means, of course, that taxes would also be less. However, the entrepreneur would end up paying the *same* total taxes over the life of his depreciable assets, regardless of depreciation method.

There is no deceit here. The entrepreneur is merely postponing some taxes until later years. This gives him more cash flow in the early years, as shown in Exhibit 18.7. And, of course, cash received this year is worth more than cash received in later years, because entrepreneurs may reinvest it sooner.

Remember that corporations are the only legal form of organization that the U.S. Internal Revenue Code recognizes as being a so-called legal person, separate and distinct from the owners. As a result, income tax rates for corporations differ from those applicable to either sole proprietorships or to partnerships. The only exception is the S-corporation, which is taxed as if it were a partnership. As shown here, corporations get tax breaks of up to $100,000 of their taxable income:

Taxable Income	Tax Rates
$ 0 to 25,000	15%
25,001 to 50,000	18
50,001 to 75,000	30
75,001 to 100,000	40
More than 100,000	46

This tax break recognizes the need to help small ventures survive and grow. To show its impact, let us now look at an example:

Example: Assume that a small corporation has a taxable income of $66,000. How much would it save in taxes with the tax break? Computations follow:

With tax break		
Taxable income		$66,000
Less: Federal income taxes		
On first $25,000 (× 15%) =	$3,750	
On next $25,000 (× 18%) =	4,500	
On next $16,000 (× 30%) =	4,800	13,050 ←
Net profit		$52,950
Without tax break		
Taxable income		$66,000
Less: Taxes ($66,000 × 46%)		30,360 ←
Net profit		$35,640

Thus, with the tax break, this corporation would save $17,310 in taxes ($30,360 − $13,050). Note, too, that net profit would be much higher: $52,950 versus $35,640.

S-Corporations As mentioned in Chapter Seven, an S-corporation is a hybrid form of organization, a cross between a regular corporation and a general partnership:

- Like a regular corporation, it enjoys limited liability.
- Like a partnership, it is not subject to corporate federal income taxes. Instead, its profits are taxed to the entrepreneur in the same way as the entrepreneur's salary and wages. Thus, it is free of the double taxation that plagues regular corporations and their shareholders.

S-corporations are especially attractive to wealthy people who prefer to invest in high-risk ventures. In the early years, losses incurred by ventures may shelter their other income from the full impact of taxes. An example will show how such tax shelters work:

Example: An entrepreneur is forming an S-corporation to open a small machine shop. He needs $250,000, 60 percent of which will come from a 5-year bank loan. The rest will be raised from wealthy individuals. He expects to lose $50,000 during the first two years of operation.

To help finance his venture, the entrepreneur has been talking to wealthy investors in the 50 percent income-tax bracket. How might he convince them to invest, even though he expects losses the first two years? One way is to demonstrate the high return they will receive in the first two years:

		First Two Years
• Return from investment tax credit	(10% × \$250,000)[4] =	\$25,000
• Return from loss flow-through	(50% × \$ 50,000) =	25,000
• Total return to investors		\$50,000

Investors benefit by \$50,000 because they are able to reduce their other taxable income by that amount, thus paying less in taxes than they would otherwise.

As the example shows, an investor may benefit personally even though a venture loses money, if the venture is organized as an S-corporation. Personal losses, however, may be claimed only up to the amount that each individual has invested.

EXHIBIT 18.7 *How Choice of Depreciation Method Affects Cash Flow*

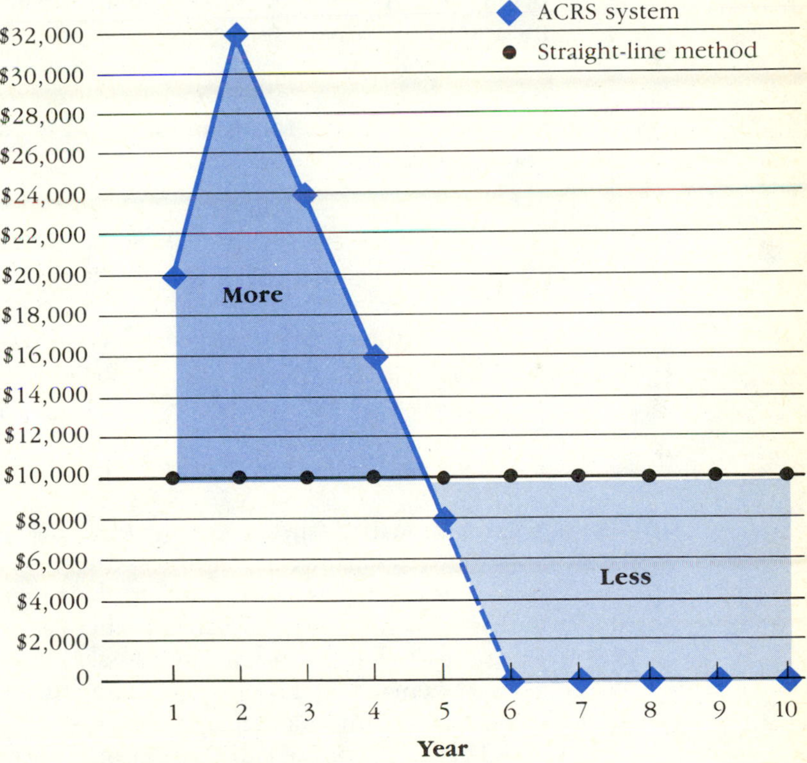

***Assumptions:**

(1) Asset cost = \$100,000

(2) Depreciation life = 5 years under ACRS system
= 10 years under straight-line method (which assumes asset will be in service for 10 years)

The ACRS system yields much more cash flow in the early years than does the straight-line method.

Partnerships and Sole Proprietorships These two legal forms of organization fall under almost precisely the same tax laws as the S-corporation. In a partnership, the partners themselves are taxed, not the partnership. The partnership merely serves as a pipeline through which profits or losses flow to the partners. To compute federal income taxes, each partner must report his or her share of the partnership's profit, even though some or all of it was plowed back into the business. In contrast, corporate shareholders must report only the cash dividends they receive.

Similarly, tax laws do not recognize the sole proprietorship as a separate and distinct legal entity, so sole proprietors are taxed as individuals. In contrast to corporations, sole proprietorships offer few opportunities for tax savings. Sole proprietors cannot take advantage of such corporate tax-sheltered benefits as life and health insurance, nor can they pay themselves tax-deductible salaries. Just two tax advantages are open to sole proprietorships—if their taxable income is low, individual tax rates may be lower than corporate tax rates; and if losses occur, sole proprietors may use those losses to offset their taxable income from other sources.

General partnerships, on the other hand, offer more tax-saving opportunities than sole proprietorships, though not as many as corporations. Tax law, for example, permits partners to engineer their tax consequences:

- Revenue and expense items can be contractually allocated to the partners so as to achieve the most favorable overall tax effect. A partner may, for example, earn 35 percent of the partnership's ordinary income and 40 percent of its capital gains, but only 10 percent of its losses.
- A partnership is privileged to lease or buy property or borrow money from its partners, all with predictable tax consequences. A partner may, for example, make a loan to the partnership, thus personally earning interest income while at the same time creating a corresponding interest-expense deduction for the partnership.[5]

Limited Partnerships

The traditional tax-shelter vehicle, of course, is the limited partnership. As mentioned in Chapter Seven, the partners are called limited because the tax law limits their personal liability to their investment, while denying them the right to take part in management. As with sole proprietorships and general partnerships, partnership losses flow straight to the limited partners. They may then save taxes by deducting those losses from their taxable income from other sources.

This completes our discussion of the legal forms of organization and their effect on federal income taxes. Let us now look briefly at some other areas that merit the entrepreneur's attention:

- Inventory valuation
- Investment tax credit

- Targeted jobs credit
- Energy tax credit
- Estate and gift taxes

Inventory Values and Taxes

Entrepreneurs should be aware that inventory values may strongly affect their tax bills, especially in times of fast-rising prices. The basic problem is how best to value the ending inventory. There are several ways to handle this problem, among them:

> **FIFO (First-In, First-Out):** In this method, entrepreneurs assume that the oldest materials are sold first. Ending inventory is thus made up of those materials purchased most recently. FIFO generally corresponds to the natural flow of materials through inventory. One exception is a coal pile, where coal on the outside rather than the inside is sold first.
>
> **LIFO (Last-In, First-Out):** In this method, entrepreneurs assume that the youngest materials are sold first. Ending inventory is thus made up of the oldest materials. LIFO generally corresponds to the economic flow of values through inventory.

Of the two methods, LIFO saves more taxes. With LIFO, if prices go up, taxes are lower because LIFO keeps book profits down. It matches present selling prices with present costs, which are also high. The spread is not so great. Let us now study an example that shows how LIFO yields less taxable income than FIFO:

Example: An entrepreneur runs a retail store. To save taxes, she is thinking of switching from FIFO to LIFO, because prices are rising rapidly. What tax savings will she realize, if she estimates that next year she will have:

- $200,000 of sales revenues
- $40,000 of operating expenses
- 2,000 units in beginning inventory
- 2,000 units in ending inventory
- 6,000 units of purchases
- A rise in the purchase cost of inventory from $10 a unit to $20 a unit

With the help of her accountant, the entrepreneur prepares Exhibit 18.8. As shown in the upper half of the exhibit, she first estimates the cost of goods sold under FIFO, then under LIFO. Next, she prepares two income statements to see the impact on both taxes and net profit.

Note that federal income taxes would be $4,000 less with LIFO than with FIFO ($12,000 under FIFO versus $8,000 under LIFO). Let us qualify our calculations here. We purposely assumed that prices would double in one year, from $10 to $20 a unit, to simplify the arithmetic. In real life, price increases would rarely be so steep.

EXHIBIT 18.8

How LIFO Saves Taxes: LIFO versus FIFO Computations

Items	Units	Unit Cost	Under FIFO	Under LIFO
Beginning inventory	2,000	$10	$ 20,000	$ 20,000
Purchases	6,000	$20	120,000	120,000
Available for sale	8,000		$140,000	$140,000
Ending inventory	2,000		40,000*	20,000†
Cost of goods sold	6,000		$100,000	$120,000

Income Statements

	Under FIFO	Under LIFO
Sales revenues	$200,000	$200,000
Cost of goods sold	100,000	120,000
Gross profit	$100,000	$ 80,000
Operating expenses	40,000	40,000
Taxable income	$ 60,000	$ 40,000
Federal income tax‡	12,000	8,000
Net profit	$ 48,000	$ 32,000

* Obtained by multiplying the unit cost of $20 by the 2,000 units in ending inventory.
† Obtained by multiplying the unit cost of $10 by the 2,000 units in ending inventory.
‡ We assumed a flat 20 percent corporate tax rate.

The U.S. Internal Revenue Code permits entrepreneurs to use LIFO for income-tax purposes, but only if they also use LIFO in their published financial statements to shareholders, commercial banks, or other interested parties. This is the only situation in which the Code requires entrepreneurs to use the same accounting method for both income tax and financial reporting purposes.

Investment Tax Credit

The U.S. Internal Revenue Code permits entrepreneurs to claim tax credits of 10 percent of the cost of certain fixed assets. This tax credit is a direct reduction of the federal income taxes owed, as opposed to a deduction that reduces taxable income. It applies only to such tangible assets as machinery and equipment. Buildings and intangible assets such as patents and covenants-not-to-compete are excluded.

Moreover, only assets with useful lives of three years or more qualify for the tax credit. If an asset's life is less than seven years, entrepreneurs may apply only a fraction of the maximum allowable credit, as shown below:

For fixed assets with a depreciable life of—	The investment tax-credit is—
3 years	6%
5	10
10	10
15	10

At present, the maximum amount of credit that entrepreneurs may claim each year is \$25,000 plus 90 percent of the tax bill in excess of \$25,000. To see how this tax credit works, let us go through an example:

Example: An entrepreneur plans to build a steel-fabricating plant. He estimates that the installed cost of all equipment will be \$500,000. He also estimates that, without the investment tax credit, his tax bill will be \$50,000. By how much will his tax bill be reduced by the tax credit? Computations follow:

\$50,000	Total investment tax credit (\$500,000 × 10%)
47,500	Total credit allowed \$25,000 + [90% × (\$50,000 − \$25,000)]
\$ 2,500	Unused investment tax credit

Any unused tax credits, as in our example, must first be carried back eight years, thus resulting in a tax refund. Then the entrepreneur may carry unused credits forward 15 years.

Some critics call the investment tax credit and other tax breaks "corporate welfare. These tax credits are outright subsidies to industry, in no way indistinguishable from such subsidies as food stamps for the poor."[6] Turning to Exhibit 18.9, note that in 1984–85, the investment tax credit alone accounted for tax-revenue losses of \$26.5 billion.

Targeted Jobs Credit

Entrepreneurs may avail themselves of the targeted jobs credit by employing certain disadvantaged people. This tax credit is equal to 50 percent of the first \$6,000 of wages per eligible employee for the first year of employment and 25 percent of such wages for the second year. Eligible employees include:

- Young men and women, ages 18 to 25, who come from low-income families
- Vietnam veterans
- Handicapped men and women
- Ex-convicts

For each of these categories, the employee must come from an economically disadvantaged family, defined as having incomes of less than 70 percent of the minimum living standard established annually by the U.S. Bureau of Labor Statistics. Let us now use an example to see how this jobs credit works:

Example: An entrepreneur hires three disadvantaged youths, each one certified to be an eligible employee for the jobs credit. Each of these employees receives wages of \$9,000 during the year. If the entrepreneur takes the tax credit, her tax bill will be reduced by \$9,000, computed as follows:

$$\text{Targeted jobs credit} = (\$6{,}000 \times 50\%) \times 3 \text{ employees} = \$9{,}000$$

EXHIBIT 18.9 *Federal Tax Revenues Lost from Business Deductions: 1984–1985 (in billions of dollars)*

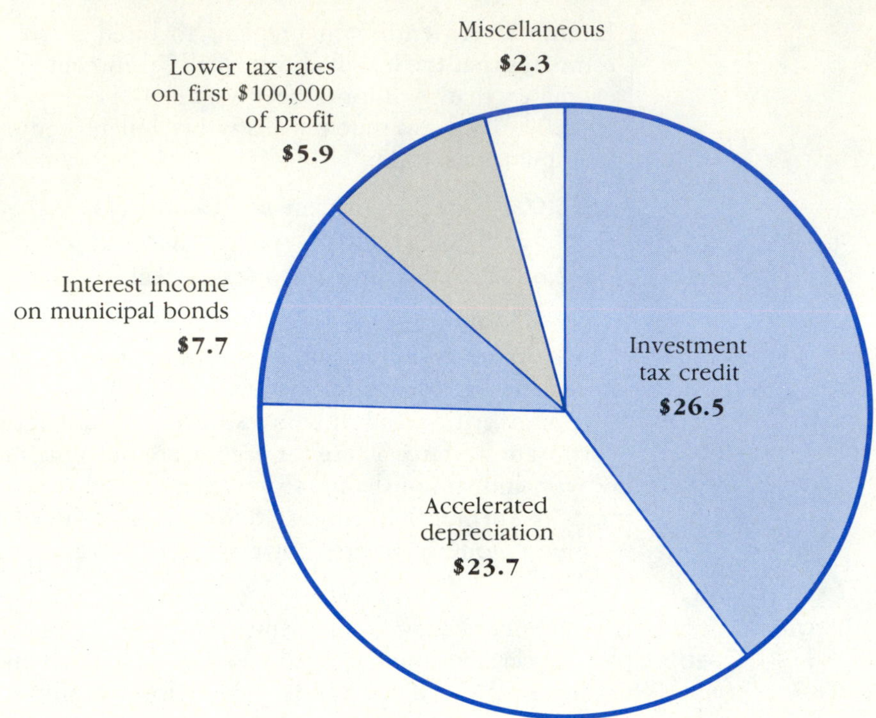

Source: U.S. Office of Management and Budget, quoted by "Endangered Loopholes," Cleveland *Plain Dealer*, December 18, 1984, p. 6-C.

Energy Tax Credit

Energy tax credits create incentives to save oil or natural gas. For example, the Tax Energy Act of 1978 enables entrepreneurs to take an investment tax credit of 20 percent of the cost of energy saving equipment, which is twice the normal rate. An entrepreneur who spends, say, $50,000 for recycling equipment may deduct 20 percent, or $10,000, from his tax bill.

This credit applies only to energy-saving equipment with a useful life of at least three years and uses a fuel other than oil or natural gas. Recycling equipment also qualifies.

Estate and Gift Taxes

Although we have focused on federal income taxes so far, we should also look at federal estate and gift taxes. Both taxes should be of major concern to every entrepreneur. Until passage of the Economic Recovery Tax Act of 1981, tax laws often led entrepreneurs and their spouses to follow certain tax-saving patterns to protect their estates. These exclusions included:

- Putting insurance policies in each other's names to avoid paying estate taxes on the money after death
- Legally sharing the ownership of a home or other assets

Under the 1981 tax law, there is no longer any motivation for such sharing. Entrepreneurs may now leave everything to their spouses *tax-free*.

The estate tax changes in the law have other effects. For example, the law now makes all taxable estates of $600,000 or less entirely exempt from federal taxes, no matter whom they are bequeathed to. It also lowers the maximum tax rate on estates from 70 percent to 50 percent.

Although it may appear best to leave all of an estate to a spouse, some tax experts suggest that entrepreneurs take advantage of another tax-free exclusion that applies to all estates—namely, to pass part of their estate to children or other persons rather than their spouse. Then, when the second spouse dies, that amount has already been passed along tax-free.

This exclusion is called the unified tax credit, because it may be used to cover tax-free gifts made before death. The following table shows how the unified tax credit and the amounts exempt from taxes are increased, beginning with 1985:[7]

Year of Death or Gift	Amount of Estate and Gift Tax Credit	Estate Transfers or Gift Amount Exempted from Tax
1985	121,800	400,000
1986	155,800	500,000
After 1986	192,800	600,000

One idea for entrepreneurs to consider is that *each* spouse is entitled to a unified credit allowance. Thus, in 1986, a husband and wife may give $1,000,000 tax-free to their beneficiaries. This amount increases to $1,200,000 in 1987. Moreover, these tax-free transfers may be further increased by taking advantage of the annual gift exclusion of $10,000 per recipient. Thus, a husband and wife may give $20,000 a year tax-free to any individual if they agree to split their gifts.

Today, with sound planning, an entrepreneur's family may have a net worth of more than $1 million and still avoid paying any estate taxes as property passes from one generation to the next. To achieve that result, the entrepreneur must do a sound job of planning with the help of an accountant, lawyer, or insurance agent. Planning for minimizing estate taxes should cover:

- Taking maximum advantage of the tax rules governing estates and gifts
- Making imaginative use of charities
- Using trust devices to prevent estate taxes from depleting capital in each generation

Other Federal Taxes

A variety of other taxes completes the federal tax structure. The most important are employment taxes and excise taxes on the sale of certain products and services.

Employment taxes: These cover Social Security and unemployment. Social Security tax laws require entrepreneurs to match their employees' contribution. In addition to Social Security, if entrepreneurs employ one or more persons for 20 weeks each during the year, they must pay federal unemployment taxes.

We shall discuss Social Security in more detail in the next chapter, which deals with insurance.

Excise taxes: Unlike the federal income tax, excise taxes affect revenues, not profits. Excise taxes apply mostly to the sale of selected products and services, such as the use of highways by trucks or the manufacture of alcohol and tobacco products.

KEEPING TAX RECORDS

Compliance with federal, state, and local tax laws requires a staggering amount of paperwork. Yet entrepreneurs must make sure that recording and withholding taxes, as well as reporting and paying taxes, are done accurately and promptly. For some entrepreneurs, these chores cause anxiety and confusion.

The best way to relieve this anxiety is to design an accounting system that also generates tax information. For example, an accounting system that turns out income statements should also provide data for preparing federal income tax returns. In any case, tax laws require entrepreneurs to keep permanent records on items such as these:

- Sales revenues and sales of products subject to excise taxes
- Tax-deductible expenses
- Inventories
- Names, addresses, and Social Security numbers of employees

The Entrepreneur as Debtor and Agent

In dealing with taxes, entrepreneurs must play a double role. As debtors, they pay federal income taxes on profits. As agents, they withhold federal income taxes and Social Security taxes from their own salaries as well as from the wages of employees in order to pass them on to the proper government agency.

Filing Tax Returns

To make sure they meet their tax obligations, entrepreneurs should keep tax calendars reminding them of tax due dates. Failure to file returns or pay taxes on time may bring stiff penalties, such as high interest charges, fines or even jail sentences.

The U.S. Internal Revenue Service (IRS) can hold the entrepreneur personally responsible for taxes owed by a venture even if it is incorporated. The IRS bears down especially hard on entrepreneurs who withhold income taxes and Social Security taxes from the wages of employees and then use these sums within their own ventures instead of passing them on to the government. Often, such illegal use of money occurs with the best of intentions. The entrepreneur fully intends to pay up, eventually. If payment is delayed for long, however, the IRS may penalize the entrepreneur severely.

Auditing

Because of computers, entrepreneurs may count on having their tax returns audited from time to time by the IRS. The government computers handle more than 135 million tax returns a year. They help the IRS to:

- Speed refunds
- Spot violators
- Make sure entrepreneurs file the right returns
- Check arithmetic accuracy
- Determine whether other taxes are owed before a refund is paid

There are two main reasons why an entrepreneur's tax return may be selected for audit. First, it may be selected at random. Second, and more serious, a return may be audited because it was prepared inaccurately or incompletely. When the IRS selects a return for audit, it usually examines:

- The entrepreneur's salary
- Revenues and expenses
- Inventories
- Large cash transactions
- Travel and entertainment expenses

Honest Differences of Opinion

Occasionally, the IRS does uncover fraud, but often, there is honest disagreement between the IRS and the entrepreneur on how certain items should be handled. They may disagree on:

- How revenues and costs should be allocated between years
- How fixed assets such as buildings should be depreciated
- How intangible assets such as licenses and covenants-not-to-compete should be amortized over their useful lives

Although such questions generally reflect true differences of judgment, the IRS often requires the entrepreneur to present proof of a questionable deduction.

Clearly, it is vital to be painstakingly thorough in all tax matters. To back their tax returns, entrepreneurs should keep good records, and must never violate the tax law. Ignoring these precautions may trigger enormous problems.

SUMMARY

Taxes are not intended to turn entrepreneurs into paupers. Rather, taxes are intended to enhance the quality of life by paying for the nation's defense, schools, welfare programs, and other vital services.

Entrepreneurs should understand the difference between tax evasion and tax avoidance. Tax laws change yearly, often in ways that affect profits. Some changes may lead to new tax savings, but others may lead to higher taxes. To avoid the complications such changes may create, entrepreneurs need the best tax advice available.

Legal forms of organization strongly influence the amount of federal income taxes an entrepreneur must pay. A venture may be organized as a sole proprietorship, a partnership, a corporation, or as some other form. The legal form selected depends mostly on the personal tax status of the entrepreneur and those who invest in the venture.

Entrepreneurs should be aware of the many ways to postpone or to save taxes. Accelerated depreciation is one way to postpone taxes. Tax-saving opportunities include the investment tax credit, the jobs credit, and the energy credit.

Federal income taxes are just one of many taxes that entrepreneurs must pay. Others include estate and gift taxes, employment taxes, excise taxes, and property taxes.

As tax managers, entrepreneurs must act as both debtors and agents. They must pay the taxes they owe and they must also collect certain taxes and pass them on to the proper government agency.

Computers enable the U.S. Internal Revenue Service to monitor closely the accuracy and completeness of income tax returns. Since there is a good chance that their returns will be audited some time, entrepreneurs must be ready to support every entry. To do that, they must keep accurate, complete, and up-to-date records.

DISCUSSION AND REVIEW QUESTIONS

1. Why should entrepreneurs keep up to date on changes in the tax law?
2. Do you believe it is ethical for entrepreneurs to figure their income one way for federal income-tax purposes and another way for financial accounting purposes? Why or why not?
3. Describe some of the ways that entrepreneurs may minimize their federal income taxes.
4. Define these terms: *taxable income, ACRS, straight-line depreciation, investment tax credit, targeted jobs credit, employment taxes, unified tax credit*.
5. Why is estate planning so vital? How would you, as an entrepreneur, go about it?
6. Explain how entrepreneurs act as both debtors and agents in managing the tax aspects of their ventures.
7. How do you, as an entrepreneur, benefit from the payment of federal income taxes?
8. How does the legal postponement of tax payments benefit the entrepreneur?
9. Why are S-corporations especially attractive to wealthy investors?

10. Why should entrepreneurs keep accurate and complete tax records?
11. How do LIFO and FIFO differ? Why does LIFO save taxes?
12. Why does the U.S. Internal Revenue Code give small corporations a tax break?
13. How significant can tax savings be to the entrepreneur? Give examples.
14. Do you believe that the tax incentives for energy-saving equipment are adequate? Explain.
15. Explain how tax evasion and tax avoidance differ.

NOTES

1. Oliver Wendell Holmes, *Compania de Tabacos v. Collector*, 275 U.S. 87, 100 (1904).
2. Robert J. Havel, "Vanik Sponsors Measure to Bare Firms' Tax Data," Cleveland *Plain Dealer* February 7, 1973, p. 1-B.
3. "Cover Story: Taxes: The Big Bite," *Time*, March 10, 1952, p. 27. [Reprinted by permission from *Time*, the Weekly Newsmagazine. Copyright Time Inc. 1952]
4. To stimulate investment in machinery and equipment, tax laws permit a credit against income taxes—here 10 percent of the shop's cost. This investment tax credit is discussed later in the chapter.
5. Adapted from Marc J. Lane, *Taxation for Small Business* (New York: Wiley, 1980), p. 54.
6. James J. Kilpatrick, "Tax Laws Build a Corporate Welfare State," Cleveland *Plain Dealer*, March 3, 1985, p. 4-D.
7. U.S. Congress, *H.R. 4242* (Washington, D.C.: U.S. Government Printing Office; July 30, 1981), Section 401, pp. 245–246.

CASE 18A *CWC Industries, Inc.*

Located in an inner city area, CWC Industries was "suffering from severe growing pains" in 1980. It had reached its manufacturing capacity and little room existed for expansion. Although it was earning $75,000 on sales revenues of $1.6 million, CWC found it hard to raise money to expand. "Every bank in town has turned us down," said Mary Jane Fabish, executive vice president. "It just doesn't make any sense."

Background

The two entrepreneurs most responsible for CWC's success are Ms. Fabish and Jerry Lancaster, founder and president. They have worked as a team since 1965, when Mr. Lancaster founded CWC. Before 1965, both had worked for Brooks Chemical, Mr. Lancaster as executive vice president, Ms. Fabish as office manager. Mr. Lancaster had hired Ms. Fabish at Brooks.

EXHIBIT 18A.1

CWC Industries, Inc.: Resume of Gerald Lancaster

Work Experience	
1965 to present	CWC Industries, Inc. Founder and president of an analytical testing laboratory that does work in the environmental sciences. This company is also the parent company of two wholly-owned subsidiaries, Continental Chemical Company and Excelsior Varnish & Chemicals, Inc. These two companies make and sell chemical specialties. Continental Chemical sells directly to the end user, mostly industrial and institutional. Excelsior Varnish sells mostly to jobbers who use private labels; its product line includes cleaners, floor finishes, paints, and varnish.
1949 to 1965	Brooks Chemicals, Inc. Began as technical director developing products. Was promoted to vice president of technical operations. In 1954, was promoted to executive vice president of the entire company, including its marketing operations.
Professionalism	
1949 to present	Professional Engineer, licensed to practice in Ohio, Pennsylvania, and Wisconsin
Present Activities	Air Pollution Control Association American Chemical Society National Association of Corrosion Engineers Water Pollution Control Federation
Education	
1960 to 1965	Case Institute of Technology Received master of arts degree in environmental engineering
1945 to 1949	Hiram College Received bachelor of arts degree in chemistry

EXHIBIT 18A.2

CWC Industries, Inc.: Resume of Mary Jane Fabish

Work Experience	
1965 to present	CWC Industries, Inc. Executive vice president. Oversees accounting, financial, marketing, and organizational aspects of the company. This company is also the parent company of two wholly-owned subsidiaries, Continental Chemical Company and Excelsior Varnish & Chemicals, Inc.
1956 to 1965	Brooks Chemicals, Inc. Office manager. Handled purchasing of raw materials, did costing of products, wrote technical bulletins.
1952 to 1956	Murray Ohio Manufacturing Company Secretary. Worked in production, personnel, and purchasing departments.
Activities since 1970	Council of Smaller Enterprises—Executive vice chairperson Chamber of Commerce—Member of board and of executive committee Ohio Motorist Association—Trustee Regional Advisory Council of U.S. Small Business Administration—Board member National Advisory Council of U.S. Department of the Treasury
Awards	
1971 and 1977	Chosen Woman of the Year by American Business Women's Association
Education	
1977	Dyke College Studied accounting
1970	Case Western Reserve University Studied marketing and creative writing

"Our talents mesh beautifully," said Ms. Fabish. "I take care of finances, marketing, and organizational planning. Jerry takes care of production, product development, and overall direction of the company. We share all of the decision making, Jerry and I. If we disagree, we hammer out the pros and cons. And every time, we end up acknowledging the strong points in each other's argument to come up with what we both agree to be a good decision." Their resumes appear in Exhibits 18A.1 and 18A.2.

Rapid Growth

Since its beginnings in 1965, CWC grew from sales of $40,000 to $1.6 million in 1980. "That's a dramatic growth rate," said Ms. Fabish, "even after adjusting for inflation." She credited CWC's success to Mr. Lancaster's "sheer guts, creativity, and willingness to take risks." With Ms. Fabish's help, Mr. Lancaster built CWC in two ways:

- Through acquisition of small chemical companies
- Through expansion into new markets

The acquisitions fulfilled Mr. Lancaster's dream of someday running a "full-blown chemical manufacturing company." When he first went into business for himself in 1965, Mr. Lancaster bought a service company called Zero Air Filter Company. It cost him just $10,000. No manufacturing was involved, just the servicing of air filters. "It wasn't very exciting, picking up and cleaning grease filters from restaurants," says Mr. Lancaster.

Even so, it was a beginning, one which Mr. Lancaster shortly parlayed into a manufacturing company. After two years of doing nothing but cleaning filters, he found out that a "sick" company called Continental Chemical was up for sale. Losing money at the rate of $1,200 a month, this company was in the same building as Mr. Lancaster's company. The owner was asking $75,000. Seeing the acquisition as an opportunity to become a chemical manufacturer at last, Mr. Lancaster decided to buy it.

The owner agreed not only to accept a $5,000 down payment but to finance Mr. Lancaster for five years at an interest rate of 7 percent a year. With the purchase of Continental Chemical in 1967, Mr. Lancaster became a manufacturer of specialty chemicals and coatings for maintenance work and water treatment.

Another Acquisition

Two years later, opportunity knocked again in the form of another acquisition, when Excelsior Varnish & Chemicals, Inc., came up for sale. This company manufactured paints, varnishes, and cleaning chemicals. Like Continental Chemical, this company was also losing money.

"The asking price of $120,000 was very reasonable," said Mr. Lancaster, "but we had to buy it on the spot, or so said the lawyer representing the seller. In fact, the lawyer was so demanding that we had to have the bank call him to tell him that under the then-prevailing 'truth-in-lending' regulations it was impossible to complete the transaction as quickly as he wanted it."

"Apparently he could understand that," said Mr. Lancaster, "and it was our bank that made the purchase possible. They loaned us the entire $120,000 we needed." For that purchase price, Mr. Lancaster received "inventory, receivables, cash, manufacturing equipment, and a customer list."

Period of Adjustment

For the next ten years, through 1979, both Mr. Lancaster and Ms. Fabish dedicated themselves to "turning these acquisitions around and making them profitable." Neither hard work nor sacrifice was a stranger to either of them. When Ms. Fabish joined Mr. Lancaster in 1965, she agreed to a salary of just $200 a month. She took the rest of her salary in options to buy stock, and when she later exercised her options, she ended up owning 25 percent of CWC.

"We all reminisce about the early days of eating wieners and beans," she said. "There were many times that we never took home a paycheck, but

EXHIBIT 18A.3

CWC Industries, Inc.: Comparative Income Statements (in thousands)

	1976	1977	1978	1979	1980
Sales revenues	$1,008	$1,105	$1,162	$1,396	$1,605
Cost of goods sold	469	511	540	681	712
Gross profit	$ 539	$ 594	$ 622	$ 715	$ 893
Operating expenses					
Factory and warehouse			$ 179	$ 162	$ 190
Selling	$ 499	$ 534	187	268	282
Administrative			186	217	302
Depreciation	12	20	25	19	14
Total operating expenses	$ 511	$ 554	$ 577	$ 666	$ 788
Operating profit	$ 28	$ 40	$ 45	$ 49	$ 105
Federal income taxes	3	6	9	10	30
Net profit	$ 25	$ 34	$ 36	$ 39	$ 75
Cash flow	$ 37	$ 54	$ 61	$ 58	$ 89

our employees always did. There were days when you could only go in the corner and cry like a child. But the next day, you knew you'd come back fighting because the competition was right around the corner."

Did their sacrifices and hard work pay off? The answer appears in their financial statements, shown in Exhibits 18A.3 and 18A.4. Note that both sales and profits have gone up each year.

Of course, it took more than sacrifice and hard work to achieve such sales and profit levels. "Jerry and I never would have made it without our employees. They helped us a lot, although I sometimes had to whip and scream and holler. Our philosophy was, and is, to get all our employees to feel as if they're part of the team." CWC shares its profits with employees. Every employee, including Mr. Lancaster and Ms. Fabish, receives proportionately the same bonus at year-end.

Rewards of Success

CWC's success brought with it community recognition. Word soon got around among businesswomen that Ms. Fabish was a successful entrepreneur. She was twice honored as "Woman of the Year" by the American Business Women's Association. This honor later led to her appointment to the board of the city's Chamber of Commerce. Only one of two women to be so recognized, Ms. Fabish now serves on the Chamber's executive committee along with members from "Fortune 500" corporations.

Moreover, in 1980, Ms. Fabish was elected by her peers as a delegate to the White House Conference on Small Business. At present, she is executive vice chairperson of the Council of Smaller Enterprises, which boasted a membership of 3,500 small businesses in 1980. This council is the largest one of its kind in the country, as a result of her efforts recruiting

EXHIBIT 18A.4 *CWC Industries, Inc.: Latest Balance Sheet (December 31, 1980)*

Assets			Equities		
Current assets			Current liabilities		
Cash	$ 89,000		Long-term debt (current)	$ 28,600	
Accounts receivable	248,900		Accounts payable	115,000	
Inventories	168,200		Accrued taxes	26,800	
Prepaid expenses	21,600	$527,700	Accrued expenses	53,000	
Fixed assets			Income taxes payable	22,200	
Land and buildings	$ 52,800		Dividends payable	3,300	$248,900
Equipment	132,200		Long-term debt		
	$185,000		Notes payable	$ 32,400	
Less: Accumulated			Lease payable	10,100	
depreciation	130,100	54,900		$ 42,500	
Other assets			Less: Current portion	28,600	13,900
Goodwill	$ 8,000				
Deposits	2,000	10,000			
			Owners' equity		
			Common stock	$ 26,300	
			Preferred stock	33,000	
			Paid-in capital	1,600	
				$ 60,900	
			Less: Treasury stock	9,000	
				$ 51,900	
			Retained earnings	277,900	329,800
Total assets		$592,600	Total equities		$592,600

small businesses. She led the recruiting effort that nearly tripled the council's membership, from 1,200 to 3,500.

Although she bemoans the fact that she never pursued a college degree, Ms. Fabish believes she has already earned an "MBA in the school of hard knocks. I've learned through doing." She often talks glowingly about her "crashing the good old boys' network in the city and becoming one of the guys."

Ms. Fabish believes it is a myth that women in business cannot get help when they need it. "Whenever I have a problem, I call on fellow businesspersons for help. They have never let me down. Often, just by discussing a problem with another person who's been there, I can work it out. Believe me, we can all learn from our competitors' experiences and mistakes—and I have."

Need for Expansion

In 1980, CWC was faced with an acute shortage of space. Located along with other manufacturers in a rambling, 99-year-old building complex, CWC needed room to meet the increased needs of its customers. (See Exhibit 18A.5.) "The only place to expand was into the street," said Ms. Fabish.

EXHIBIT 18A.5 *CWC Industries, Inc.: Views of Plant and of Chemical Laboratory*

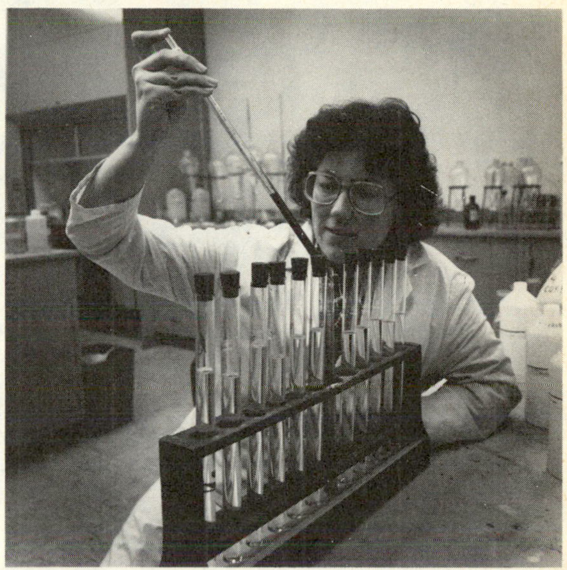

Ms. Fabish's frustration was short-lived. At about the same time, a company called Penreco, located in 12 adjoining buildings, decided to move out. It seems that Penreco had just dropped its line of chemical products because of labor problems. "What luck," said Ms. Fabish. "Jerry and I both saw Penreco's imminent departure as the answer to all our problems and prayers as a buy-out."

They wasted little time initiating talks with Penreco's management. "Penreco's plant was just what we needed," said Ms. Fabish. Their sprawling plant was four times the size of CWC's, and their equipment was more modern. Penreco's price was $900,000, but as shown in Exhibit 18A.6, CWC really needed an estimated total of $1,410,000 to complete its expansion.

"That was a lot of money for a little company like ours to raise," said Ms. Fabish. "But with our splendid record and reputation in the community, I was sure we could raise all of it through the banks."

With the help of their lawyers, CWC and Penreco soon negotiated a buy-and-sell agreement in principle. Penreco also gave CWC one year to buy them out. "Our work was now cut out for us," said Ms. Fabish. "It's one thing to have a list of customers, and another to deliver. We had to move in a hurry, Jerry and I, to raise the entire $1,410,000."

Inner City Location a Problem

Armed with resumes and financial statements, Ms. Fabish confidently approached the five largest banks in the city for a $1,410,000 loan. Each one turned her down. "They were so nice about it, too," said Ms. Fabish.

EXHIBIT 18A.6

CWC Industries, Inc.: Estimate of Investment Needs

To complete the proposed plant relocation and expansion, CWC will need an estimated total of $1,410,000 itemized as follows:

Amount	Item
$ 900,000	Purchase of Penreco plant (12 buildings with 3.10 acres of floor space; 3.04 acres of land; and equipment)
225,000	Working capital needed to expand
100,000	Boiler room equipment and installation
85,000	Dismantling and moving of existing equipment
50,000	EPA and OSHA controls and equipment
50,000	Office computer
$1,410,000	Total investment

On June 22, 1980, Penreco received from Cragin, Lang, Free & Smythe, Inc. an appraisal of $600,000 on the Penreco property. On December 1, 1978, the Industrial Appraisal Company appraised the total value of Penreco's equipment at $1,221,400. Upon their checking with the appraisers in December 1980, CWC's principals were informed that these values were still reasonably true.

Thus the total fair market value of the Penreco plant is about $1,821,400. The principals of CWC have negotiated a firm offer of $900,000 for the plant with Penreco's management.

"Many of the bank executives I knew on a first-name basis. Even so, because we were located in a 99-year-old building in the inner city, they strongly felt it would be too risky to lend us all that money."

These turndowns by local banks only served to strengthen Ms. Fabish's resolve. "I knew we were a solid company, and our income statements showed lots of profits (shown in Exhibit 18A.3) and our latest balance sheets showed lots of financial strength (shown in Exhibit 18A.4).

"No doubt about it, we were solid as the Rock of Gibraltar. So I wasn't about to take no for an answer. Somehow I was going to get the money Jerry and I needed to keep growing."

At this point, both Mr. Lancaster and Ms. Fabish knew they had to be creative in their financing. "You can't go to the banks with hat in hand," said Ms. Fabish. "You sometimes have to pound on the table and not give up. Not giving up—that's the hallmark of every successful small businessperson I know."

A Creative Solution

After numerous talks with other entrepreneurs, Ms. Fabish found that they had similar problems in the inner city. What did they do to solve their financial problems? Based on the advice she received, Ms. Fabish "packaged a creative financial proposal" involving help from:

- The Union Commerce Bank, which was the city's fourth largest bank
- The U.S Department of Housing and Urban Development
- The U.S. Small Business Administration (SBA)
- The planning commission of the city
- The Chamber of Commerce of the city
- The U.S. Department of Commerce

It took Ms. Fabish ten grueling months to prepare the proposal. "Being located as we were in the inner city, there was just no other way than to involve the government, both federal and local," said Ms. Fabish. "The red tape was unbelievable. The running I had to do from one group to another almost got me down. If I had it all to do over again, I'd be too tired." To justify CWC's request for money, Ms. Fabish's financial proposal had to show that:

- CWC would create a significant increase in jobs in the community
- A major share of the new jobs would go to residents of the surrounding community

Especially worrisome to Ms. Fabish was the tenuous nature of her relationship to each of the organizations involved in the proposal. Each one had to satisfy itself that the others were equally committed. If just one pulled out, Ms. Fabish's financial proposal would collapse "like a house of cards." Excerpts of her proposal appear in:

- Exhibit 18A.7, which shows how and from whom CWC planned to raise the entire $1,410,000 it needed in order to buy out Penreco and complete its expansion
- Exhibit 18A.8, which shows the loan conditions set by the bank, from whom CWC sought a $750,000 loan

EXHIBIT 18A.7

CWC Industries, Inc.: Tentative Sources of Money

To finance the proposed plant relocation and expansion, CWC's principals have obtained tentative commitments to a commercial bank loan, a HUD Action Grant and loan, and a loan from Penreco itself:

$750,000	Seven-year term loan from the Union Commerce Bank. Approval of this loan was granted subject to an SBA guarantee of two-thirds of the loan amount. In addition, CWC must obtain at least $300,000 from either investors, shareholders, or a 2 percent HUD loan, all of which must be subordinated to the Bank and to the SBA. Interest will be fixed at 12 percent.
$360,000	HUD Action Grant and loan. Of this sum, $230,000 would be a grant and $130,000 a loan payable in 10 years at 2 percent interest. Approval of both the grant and the loan are subject to firm financial commitments by private parties for the rest of the money needed.
$300,000	Penreco loan. Penreco is willing to finance this portion of the purchase price of their plant. Their loan will be payable in one year at 12 percent interest.

The principals of CWC have approached other banks and private investors, and have been turned down outright or have been offered terms that would place either an excessive drain on the company's cash flow or would force the principals to yield control of CWC to others.

EXHIBIT 18A.8

CWC Industries, Inc.: Loan Conditions Set by Bank

The $750,000 seven-year term loan from the bank will be secured by a first lien on all buildings, property, machinery, and equipment as well as on accounts receivable and inventories. It is also understood that all borrowings will be endorsed by Gerald Lancaster and Mary Jane Fabish. Reductions on the loan principal will be as follows:

Month	Monthly Reductions
1 to 12	$ 6,250*
13 to 48	8,333*
49 to 84	10,417*

The loan was approved subject to maintenance of a sound financial condition. It is further understood that all borrowings will be subject to these conditions:

- Minimum shareholders' equity of $686,000.
- Minimum working capital of $386,000.
- Ratio of long-term debt to shareholders' equity not to exceed 1.75 to 1.00.
- Quarterly financial statements and yearly audited financial statements.
- No additional borrowings other than trade and subordinate loans.

Finally, it is understood that CWC will maintain its major deposit relationship in the years ahead.

* Plus accrued interest

EXHIBIT 18A.9

CWC Industries, Inc.: Projected Income Statements (in thousands)

	1981	1982	1983	1984	1985
Sales revenues					
CWC Industries	$1,900	$2,270	$2,600	$3,070	$3,620
Penreco	1,020	1,500	2,000	2,500	3,000
Total sales	$2,920	$3,770	$4,600	$5,570	$6,620
Cost of sales					
CWC Industries	$ 840	$1,000	$1,200	$1,410	$1,670
Penreco	710	1,050	1,400	1,750	2,100
Total cost of sales	$1,550	$2,050	$2,600	$3,160	$3,770
Gross profit	$1,370	$1,720	$2,000	$2,410	$2,850
Operating expenses					
Administrative	$ 530	$ 570	$ 620	$ 760	$ 980
Selling	380	450	550	650	770
Factory and laboratory	290	370	430	510	610
Total operating expenses	$1,200	$1,390	$1,600	$1,920	$2,360
Operating profit	$ 170	$ 330	$ 400	$ 490	$ 490
Interest	120	110	100	90	80
Before-tax profit	$ 50	$ 220	$ 300	$ 400	$ 410
Income tax	—	80	120	160	170
Net profit	$ 50	$ 140	$ 180	$ 240	$ 240
Cash flow					
Net profit	$ 50	$ 140	$ 180	$ 240	$ 240
Depreciation	90	90	90	90	90
Total cash flow	$ 140	$ 230	270	$ 330	$ 330
Debt service	$ 75	$ 100	$ 100	$ 100	$ 125

- Exhibit 18A.9, which shows how profitable CWC expected to be after it acquired Penreco's complex of 12 buildings
- Exhibit 18A.10, which shows how financially sound CWC expected to be
- Exhibit 18A.11, which shows how many new jobs CWC expected to add

EXHIBIT 18A.10

CWC Industries, Inc.: Projected Balance Sheets (condensed) (in thousands)

	1981*	1982*	1983*	1984*	1985*
Assets					
Current assets	$ 980	$1,350	$1,730	$2,090	$2,510
Fixed assets	920	830	730	640	550
Other assets	40	40	40	70	70
Total assets	$1,940	$2,220	$2,500	$2,800	$3,130
Equities					
Current liabilities	$ 510	$ 760	$ 950	$1,120	$1,350
Long-term debt	980	870	780	680	530
Owners' equity					
Capital stock	130	130	130	130	130
Retained earnings	320	460	640	870	1,120
Owners' equity	450	590	770	1,000	1,250
Total equities	$1,940	$2,220	$2,500	$2,800	$3,130

* Year end.

EXHIBIT 18A.11

CWC Industries, Inc.: Employment Potential

To carry out its projected rise in sales, CWC must add to its workforce. CWC's most conservative estimates of the new jobs to be created follow:

	New Jobs to Be Added in:				
Year	Plant	Laboratories	Office	Total New Jobs	Cumulative Increase in Jobs
1981	4	1	2	7	7
1982	5	1	1	7	14
1983	5	1	1	7	21
1984	5	1	2	8	29
1985	5	0	1	6	35
Total	24	4	7	35	

As this table implies, within a matter of weeks after CWC acquires the Penreco plant, the principals will have to hire at least six new people to enable CWC to meet its expanding backlog of orders and its forward commitments to customers.

Questions

1. Why is CWC having trouble raising money to expand?
2. Comment on CWC's written proposal to raise $1,410,000 (see Exhibits 18A.6 through 18A.11).
3. Suggest financing alternatives other than the ones proposed by CWC. Would they be better? If so, how?
4. How have the managerial styles of Ms. Fabish and Mr. Lancaster contributed to CWC's growth?
5. If CWC's request for a $1,410,000 loan is turned down, what should Ms. Fabish and Mr. Lancaster do next? Why?

CASE 18B *Aristotle Pappas*

For the first few years after Aristotle Pappas opened his bookstore, he paid himself $8,000 a year even though his skills were worth $15,000, which had been his salary as branch manager of a bookstore chain. He worked long hours in his new venture, often seven days a week. Even so, he underpaid himself so that he could plow as much as possible back into the venture.

As the venture grew and prospered over the years, Mr. Pappas shortened his workweek. At the same time, he increased his salary to $40,000 a year. That salary, he felt, was more in keeping with his status as owner of the largest bookstore in town. Sales revenues were over $1 million annually.

The bookstore deducted his $40,000 salary as a reasonable business expense, but the IRS objected, and disallowed half the deduction. The IRS claimed that Mr. Pappas was paying himself a high salary to avoid reporting fat profits and paying dividends.

Mr. Pappas disagreed. So did his son, who was also his attorney. A week before they were to plead their case before the Tax Court, Mr. Pappas read an article that appeared in *The Wall Street Journal*:

> Small businesses that cheat on taxes will get a closer IRS look.
>
> Informed sources say possibly less than two-thirds of the nation's eight million small firms (generally those with assets of $1 million or less) are conscientiously paying the taxes they owe under the law. That compares with a 97 percent compliance rate for all corporate and individual taxpayers. IRS officials say small business compliance has slipped substantially over the past four years.
>
> To combat the problem, the IRS plans to begin next January screening all small-business returns by computer. That move alone is expected to hike tax revenues by as much as $42 million next year, says John Hanlon, an assistant IRS commissioner.*

* "Tax Report," *The Wall Street Journal*, June 14, 1972, p. 1.

Questions

1. Is Mr. Pappas's $40,000 salary a "reasonable business expense"? Why?
2. If you were Mr. Pappas, how would you argue your case before the Court?

CASE 18C *Ernest Allyson*

Ernest Allyson began in construction as a carpenter, working for a builder who specialized in additions and new homes. He worked with the same firm for eight years. When he decided to launch his own business, he was in charge of six other carpenters.

Mr. Allyson established his own firm because large parcels of land were being developed nearby and he was certain that, with his experience, he could receive a greater income. He rented a garage as his office, hired a work crew, and did subcontracting for about a year, gradually building up his own reputation.

In three years, Mr. Allyson's business grew so much that he needed additional space. He bought a building to house the tools and equipment that were accumulating. With more space, he was also able to buy materials at wholesale and stock them in his building, both for use by his three full-work crews and for sale to other builders.

After operating for four years on his own, Mr. Allyson looked at his business:

- He had three work crews who were kept busy full-time. Some employees had been with him for the full four years and he wanted to keep them.
- He wanted to expand his building so that he could display more of his supply inventory and increase sales.
- He purchased $22,000 in equipment in the past year alone and wondered if there was some way to recover those expenditures.
- He was beginning to think about saving some money for retirement.
- His taxes were rising sharply as the business grew. His accountant told him that his tax bill as a sole proprietor had been over $50,000 for the previous year.

Questions

1. Should Mr. Allyson consider changing his legal form of organization? How might a different form benefit him?
2. If Mr. Allyson is checking his tax return for deductions or savings, what should he look for besides normal operating expenses?

Source: U.S. Small Business Administration, *Taxes: Planning, Compliance, and Payment for Small Business* (Washington, D.C.: U.S. Government Printing Office, 1979), pp. 32–33.

19 RISK MANAGEMENT AND INSURANCE

QUESTIONS FOR MASTERY

How do the types of risk differ?

Why is it important to develop a program of risk management?

What are the different ways of dealing with risk?

What different types of insurance coverage are available?

How important is a pension program?

Oh, dry the starting tear, for they were heavily insured.

William Schwenck Gilbert

Our lives are fraught with risk from the very moment we draw our first breath. The fact that we can never know what tomorrow may bring is especially true in business.

Entrepreneurs soon find that risk is their constant companion, and their ability to manage it depends largely on their attitude. If entrepreneurs reject risk, they are most likely to blunder; but if they accept it, they can enhance their chances of survival and growth. In this chapter, we shall discuss how entrepreneurs may protect themselves and their ventures from risk, focusing on the use of risk management programs, insurance, and pension programs.

THE IDEA OF RISK

Risk defies easy definition. To the layperson, risk generally means the possibility of losing stamina, reputation, or self-image. To the entrepreneur, risk means the chance of financial loss. When we mention risk in this chapter, we mean financial risk, the kind that may result in dollar losses. Such losses may show up in the balance sheet or in the income statement as:

Reduced sales revenues: For example, if a fire reduces a plant to rubble, production stops until the plant is rebuilt. Meanwhile, revenues are lost.

Increased operating expenses: For example, a fire may cause the entrepreneur to move the venture into temporary but expensive quarters.

Reduced assets: For example, inventory or equipment may be stolen, or a major customer who owes the entrepreneur money may declare bankruptcy.

Increased liabilities: For example, the entrepreneur may fail to deliver on a contract or may lose a lawsuit.

Note that all of these potential losses have one thing in common: their occurrence cannot be foreseen. When such losses do occur, the entrepreneur is caught by surprise.

Three Types of Risk

As shown in Exhibit 19.1, risk may be classified into three main types: pure, speculative, and fundamental.

Risks qualify as *pure* if they may result in either a loss or no loss at all but with no possibility of gain. Examples are fire, theft, traffic accidents, and the death of a key person. There is little the entrepreneur can do to avoid pure risk. For example, any venture that owns a delivery truck faces the risk of accident, or any venture that owns a building faces the risk of fire that may create a financial loss.

EXHIBIT 19.1 *Types of Financial Risk*

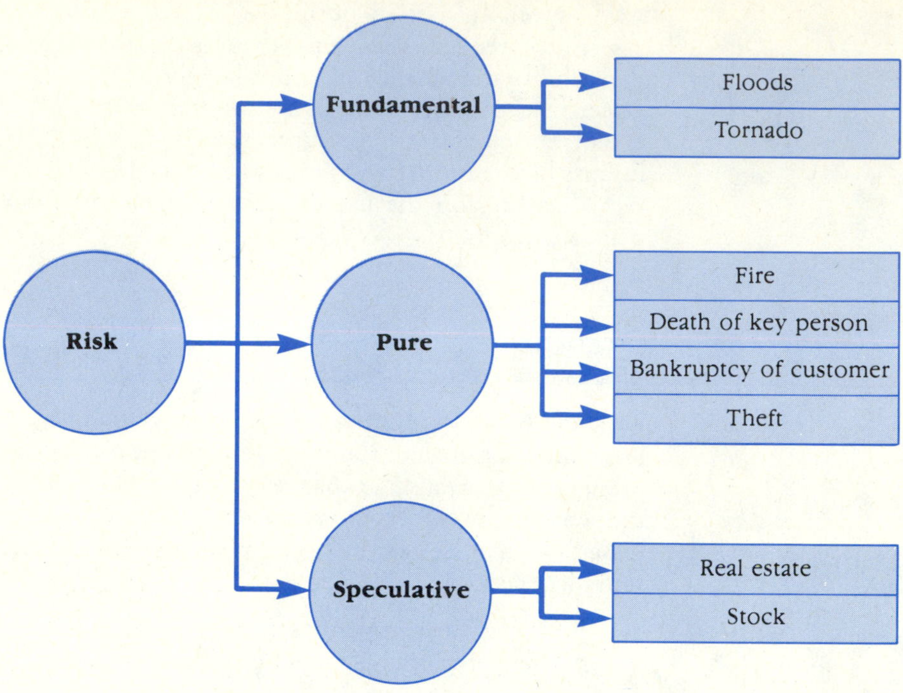

With pure risk, the entrepreneur can only lose or break even. With *speculative* risk, however, the entrepreneur may either gain or lose. For example, an entrepreneur may decide to invest in land on the chance that it will go up in value. Unforeseen events, however, may lower its value. Any such investment qualifies as speculative because it is the entrepreneur, not fate, who exposes the venture to loss.

Fundamental risk is the third type of risk. It differs from both pure and speculative risk in its impersonality. By *impersonality* we mean that fundamental risk plays no favorites. Fate does not single out just one venture and bypass all others. On the contrary, fundamental risk touches all ventures. It usually arises from the economic, political, social, or natural forces experienced by society. Some specific sources of fundamental risk are floods and earthquakes, inflation and war.

RISK MANAGEMENT PROGRAMS

It may seem self-evident that entrepreneurs are aware of all risks, especially those that may affect the survival and growth of the venture. Yet, entrepreneurs often ignore risk, especially risk that is not always apparent:

> [Risk] may exist in words inadvertently omitted from a label. Or it may be born of the enthusiastic promise of a salesperson. Risk may arise from the recommendation of an architect by the building supplies manufacturer if, as part of his sales promotion, he agrees to make the architect available—even though the architect is an independent contractor in every sense of the word.[1]

In short, entrepreneurs should fully analyze their exposure to loss. Only through such analysis may they protect their ventures against loss from pure risk. Although easy to state, this goal—to protect against possible loss—is difficult to carry off. The main reason is that risk management is more art than science, often defying precise analysis. Expert judgment plays the key role here. So entrepreneurs should seek the expert help of an insurance agent, who can design a program of risk management that:

- Pinpoints risks that may cause dollar losses
- Estimates how severe these losses may be
- Selects the best way to treat each risk

Pinpointing Risks

Because losses affect a venture monetarily, financial statements are a good starting point for pinpointing where losses may occur. The balance sheet, for example, may show a building valued at $200,000. The entrepreneur may then ask, "What could happen to destroy its value of $200,000?" Among many other possibilities, the entrepreneur might identify the risks of fire or boiler explosion.

By continuing in this vein, entrepreneurs may identify all of their points of exposure to loss. To make sure they have overlooked nothing, entrepreneurs should go through a checklist like the one in Exhibit 19.2.

For the entrepreneur, the job of pinpointing risks never ends. As a venture changes and grows, new risks arise. The manufacture of a new product, for example, may expose a venture to new risks. It is the entrepreneur's job to pinpoint these risks and gauge their possible effect on the venture.

Estimating How Losses May Affect a Venture

This step is perhaps the hardest one to carry out, for there are no checklists to help entrepreneurs estimate the effects of losses. It is generally a good idea to seek professional help. For example, lawyers can help entrepreneurs estimate their liabilities under the contracts they sign or estimate their liabilities for the hazards of a new product.

After estimating the dollar cost of each possible loss, entrepreneurs should estimate:

- How often the loss may occur
- How serious the loss may be

Such estimates are crucial. They tell the entrepreneur which risks offer the greatest loss and which offer the least loss. For example, chances may be

EXHIBIT 19.2 *Checklist for Pinpointing Exposure to Loss*

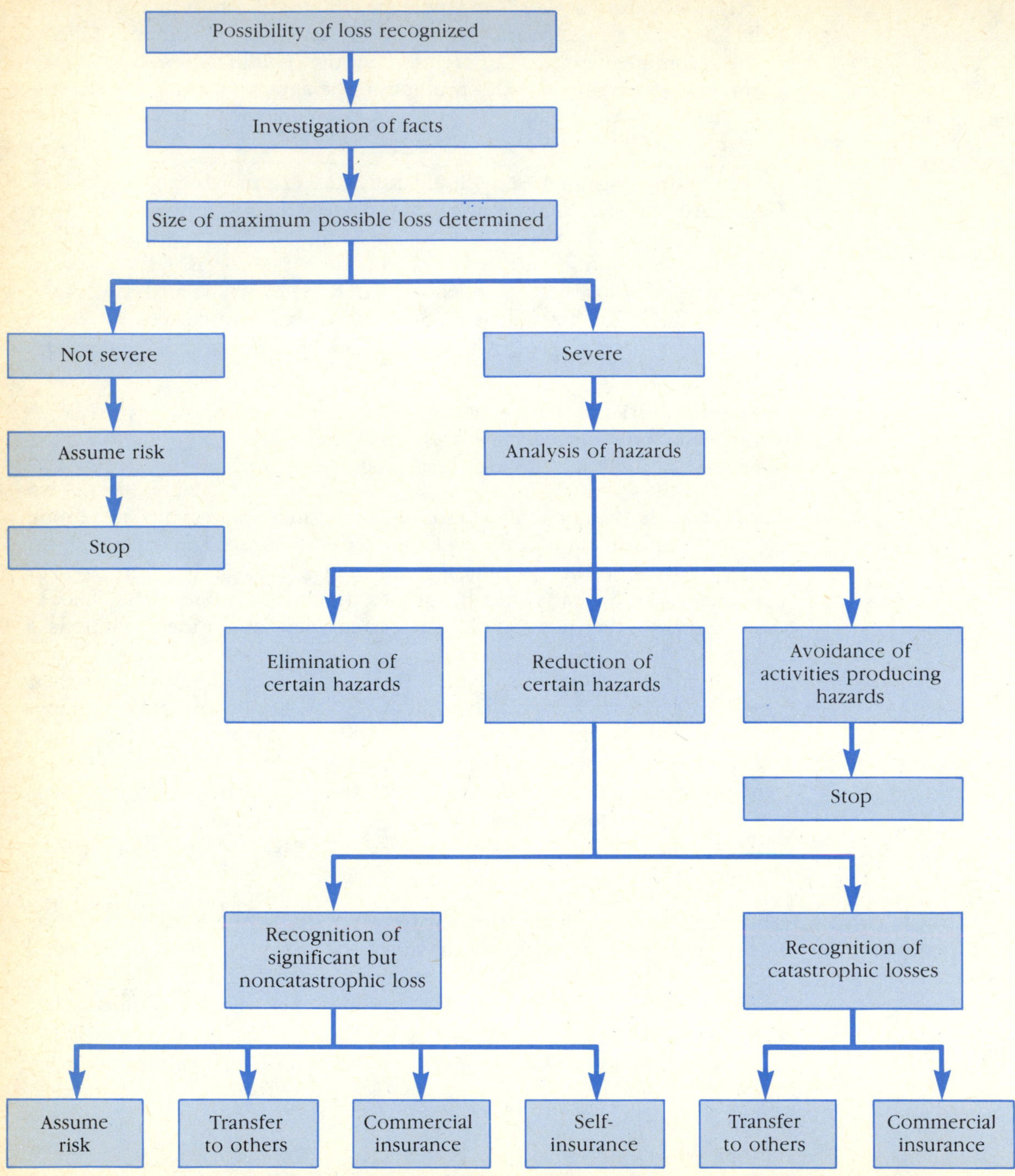

Source: Mark R. Greene, *Risk and Insurance*, South-Western Publishing Company, Inc., Cincinnati, 1968, p. 93. Reprinted by permission.

slim that a fire will break out; but if it does, it might ruin the venture. The entrepreneur cannot permit that to happen. One way to absorb that risk would be to shift it to somebody else, by buying protection, discussed as follows.

Selecting Ways to Deal with Risk

With the help of an insurance agent, entrepreneurs should select the best combination of ways to deal with risk. There are four choices open to entrepreneurs. They may choose to:

- Avoid risk entirely
- Absorb risk through self-insurance
- Prevent the occurrence of loss, cut the chances of its occurrence, or reduce its severity
- Shift risk to others, through insurance

Avoidance of risk is often practiced among entrepreneurs. For example, entrepreneurs may choose to lease rather than buy such assets as machines and trucks, thus bypassing the risks connected with owning them. Or entrepreneurs may choose to incorporate their ventures, thus avoiding many of the risks connected with the unlimited liability of general partnerships and sole proprietorships. Or they may choose to deposit at day's end all the cash taken each day, thus avoiding the risk of losing their cash to burglars after hours.

Self-insurance is rarely used by entrepreneurs, because it is too costly. Most entrepreneurs cannot possibly absorb risk by setting aside excess cash for that purpose. Generally, self-insurance makes sense only if an entrepreneur's asset values are small compared to sales revenues. One example is the entrepreneur who runs a management consulting firm out of a rented office.

Prevention is also practiced by entrepreneurs, although not to the same extent as avoidance of risk. To minimize their exposure to risk, entrepreneurs may:

- Design their plants, shops, or offices to minimize the chance of fire and accidents to workers
- Hold safety education programs for workers
- Inspect and repair safety devices regularly
- Protect assets by hiring guards, improving burglar alarms, and screening job applicants carefully

These practices help solve the problem of risk by preventing it or by lessening its impact. Even if problems do arise, losses are likely to be less severe. For example, an entrepreneur might install an automatic sprinkler system which may not prevent fires, but it will keep fire from spreading and causing even greater loss.

As shown in Exhibit 19.3, *transfer of risk* is the method most widely used by entrepreneurs. Because of its unique importance, it merits more attention than the three other methods.

EXHIBIT 19.3 *How Entrepreneurs Deal with Risk*

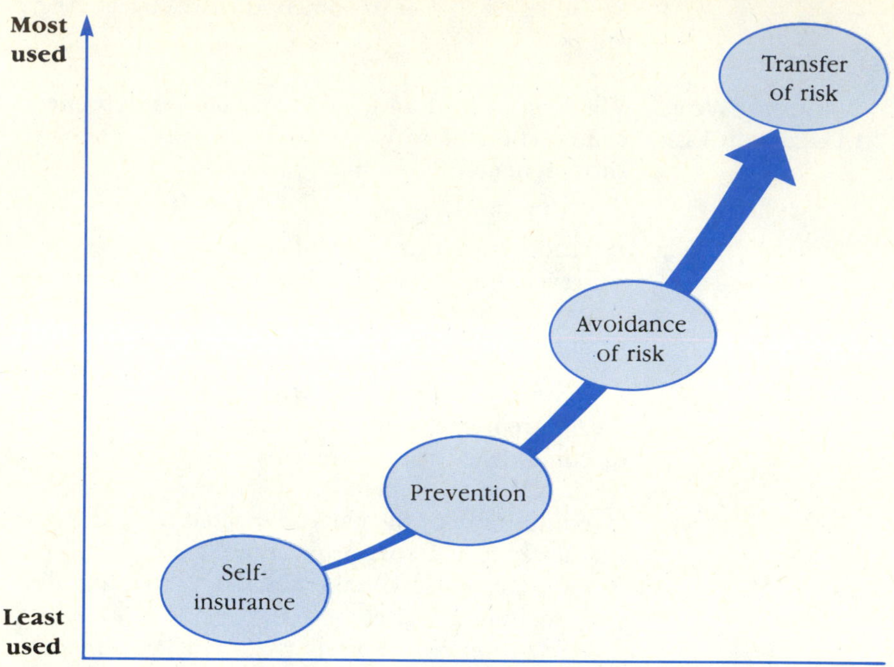

INSURANCE AND TRANSFER OF RISK

One way of dealing with risk is through insurance. What is insurance? In the words of a group of experts:

> Insurance . . . is the business of transferring pure risk by means of a two-party contract. In order for a particular risk technique to qualify as insurance, all of the requirements of the above definition must be met.[2]

Thus, insurance is simply a means of letting an outside party absorb risk. For a fee, called a premium, the outside party agrees to pay the entrepreneur a specified sum of money to cover losses suffered under conditions spelled out in a written contract, called an insurance policy. By buying such protection, the entrepreneur is, in essence, trading the uncertainty of a major loss—say, the loss of a $200,000 building through fire—for the certainty of a minor loss—the premium.

Example: An entrepreneur decides to protect her venture against loss of revenue that could occur if her star salesperson should die unexpectedly. To do so, she buys a $200,000 policy for $1,800 a year. This policy will provide her with $200,000 upon the untimely death of the salesperson.

This sum of money will help the entrepreneur survive the probable loss of revenue from such a tragedy.

How do insurers decide whether an entrepreneur's exposure to risk—as in our example above—is insurable or not? Basically, insurers say that a risk is insurable if it meets these four tests:

- The risk must exist in large numbers.
- Insured losses must be chance happenings that are beyond the entrepreneur's control.
- Losses must be readily measurable.
- Possible losses must be so severe that the entrepreneur is incapable of absorbing them.

Risk Must Exist in Large Numbers

This requirement is necessary to allow the law of averages to work for the insurer. Without this law, the insurance industry could not possibly survive. George Bernard Shaw described the workings of the law of averages as follows:

> An insurance company, sanely directed, and making scores of thousands of bets, is not gambling at all; it knows with sufficient accuracy at what age its clients will die, how many of their houses will be burnt every year, how often their houses will be broken into by burglars, to what extent their money will be embezzled by their cashiers, how much compensation they will have to pay to persons injured in their employment, how many accidents will occur to their motor cars and themselves, how much they will suffer from illness or unemployment, and what births and deaths will cost them: in short, what will happen to every thousand or ten thousand or a million people even when the company cannot tell what will happen to any individual among them.[3]

For example, because tens of thousands of ventures own trucks, insurers are willing to insure against accidents. In essence, each entrepreneur bets with the insurer whether his own truck will have an accident—with the odds being fixed mathematically by the insurer on the basis of historical facts showing frequency of accidents by truck size, age of driver, and so on.

The odds are fixed so that the insurer runs only the slightest risk of losing financially. When thousands of cases are considered, the probability that an accident will take place somewhere is certain, although the probability in any single case is uncertain.

Losses Must be Chance Happenings Beyond Control

One example of a chance happening incapable of control is a fire caused by lightning that guts a building. This great financial loss could not have been predicted by the entrepreneur. Its timing and severity were beyond the entrepreneur's control, so such a risk qualifies as insurable.

Another example is key-person life insurance. Here the risk is not whether the key person will die but rather when that person will die. The key person cannot control the time of death except by committing suicide. Insurers do pay death claims from suicide, but only if the policy has been in force for a certain period, usually two years. This practice, of course, belies the statement that losses must be controlled by chance alone.

Let us now look at some losses that often are uninsurable, namely those from theft or shoplifting. Since the mid-1960s, shoplifting losses have become so severe that insurers charge high premiums for theft insurance. In many of the nation's large cities, insurers often avoid selling theft insurance in areas earmarked by police as high-crime areas. The chances of loss in such areas are so great that insurers can ill afford to insure the entrepreneur's exposure to risk. Burglary and fire insurance are also often denied to high-crime areas.

Losses Must be Readily Measurable

Losses must be measurable in dollars and must be hard to falsify. Without this requirement, insurers would have trouble verifying losses.

Example: An entrepreneur insures a newly constructed building against fire. The building is appraised at $200,000. A year later, an explosive fire destroys the building, leaving in its wake only rubble and ashes. Note that such a loss is readily verifiable. The insurer has no recourse but to pay the entrepreneur $200,000 to rebuild.

Most losses, however, are not as cut-and-dried as the one in the example. The timing and severity of losses from a burglary, for example, are often hard to verify. The insurer often may have only the entrepreneur's word on the amount lost to burglars, especially for products that are portable and valuable, such as furs and jewels. Because such losses provide an opportunity for extensive fakery, insurers handle all such claims with extreme care.

Accidents on the job are another gray area, especially those injuries or ailments that defy precise diagnosis. One such ailment is the bad back. Insurance files bulge with records of persons who have collected huge sums of money because of bad backs, since medical science cannot yet spot and measure such ailments with precision. Physicians cannot measure precisely how injuries upset a patient's psychological well-being, either. The physician has only the patient's word to go on. As a result, insurers are extremely wary of such claims.

Possible Losses Must be Severe

Possible losses for exposure to risk must be so great that the entrepreneur cannot absorb them. An example is the loss of a factory from fire. The factory is insurable because its loss might ruin the entrepreneur. On the other hand, the possible loss of a 15-cent pencil from fire is not insurable, because the loss is trivial.

The preceding tests of insurability are by no means hard and fast. They vary from insurer to insurer, from situation to situation. They are only guides. Let us now look at some specific types of losses against which entrepreneurs may insure their venture. Some common examples of insurable risks are shown in Exhibit 19.4.

EXHIBIT 19.4 *Selected Insurable Risks*

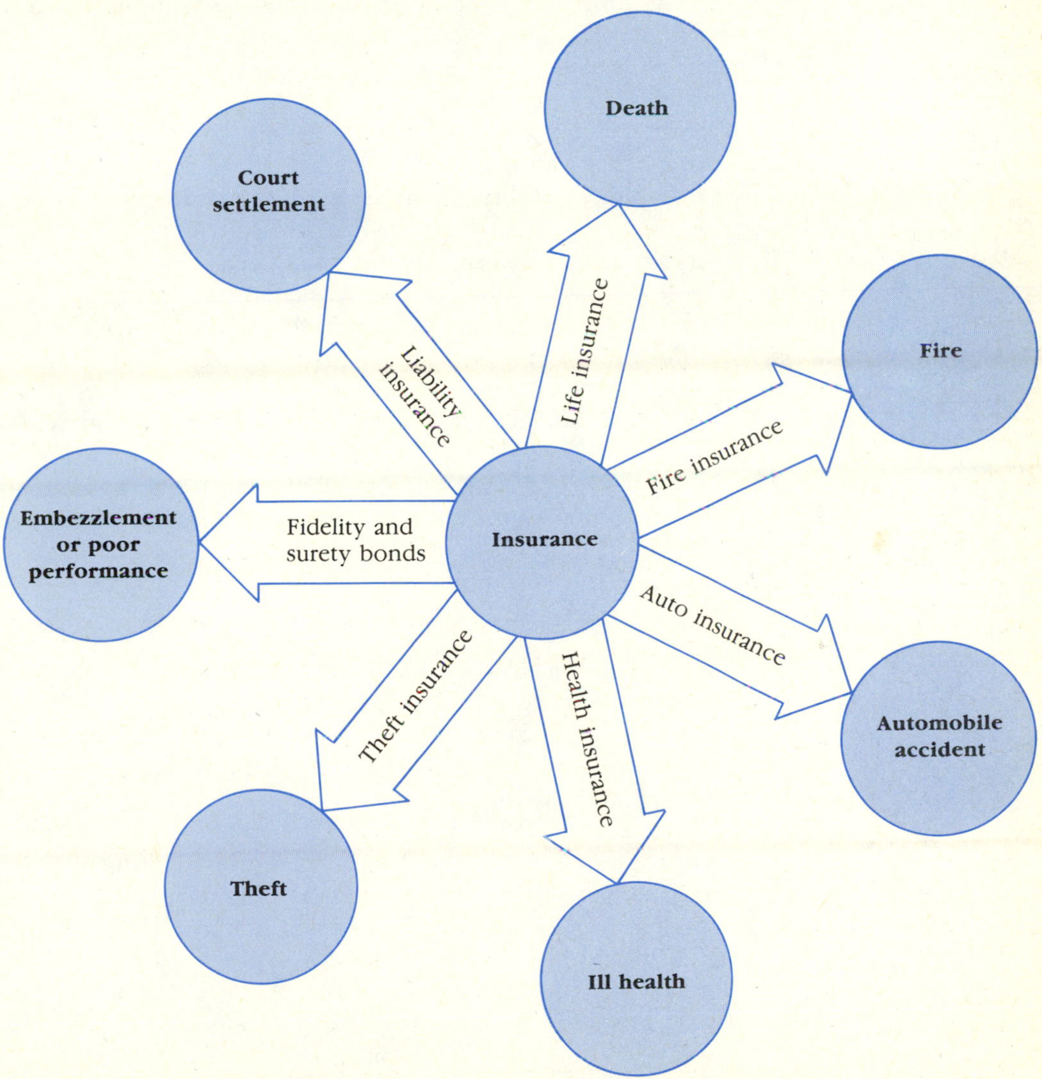

Source: Adapted from Samuel C. Certo, Max E. Douglas, and Stewart W. Husted, *Business* (Dubuque, Iowa: William C. Brown Publishers, 1984), p. 489. © 1984 Wm. C. Brown Publishers, Dubuque, Iowa. All rights reserved. Reprinted by permission.

TYPES OF INSURANCE COVERAGE

To protect their ventures against fire, windstorms, and other natural disasters, entrepreneurs may buy *property insurance*. This type of insurance generally covers such assets as buildings, equipment, and inventories. To discourage deliberate destruction of these assets, insurers often keep the face value of the policy below the book value of the assets.

Another important type of coverage is *liability insurance*. It protects against losses caused by negligence. For example, a customer may sue a manufacturer because he hurt himself by using his product, or a customer may sue a retailer because she tripped over an empty tin can and broke her leg. The liability judgments from such accidents often run into tens of thousands of dollars. With liability coverage, the insurer agrees to pay entrepreneurs for any liability claims assessed against them by the courts, but only up to the limit set forth in the policy.

Key persons are vital to the success of any venture. This is especially true in the sole proprietorship. To protect heirs from being forced to sell their ventures in order to pay estate taxes, entrepreneurs may buy *key-person life insurance*. This type of insurance may also be useful in partnerships, to buy out the heirs of a deceased partner. Entrepreneurs may also insure the lives of such key persons as creative chemists or star salespersons.

To protect their ventures against theft and fraud committed by employees, entrepreneurs may buy *surety bonds* from bonding companies. The face value of the policy is limited to the amount of cash, or to the value of products, accessible to employees.

Example: A father has a son who has fallen in with bad companions. The son is caught stealing and is sent to a reformatory. Upon his release, the son cannot get a job because of his record. A satisfactory employment record is necessary, however, if the son is to be rehabilitated, become self-supporting, and develop personal pride.

The father goes to a friend and asks that the boy be given a job that will demonstrate the boy's honesty. The friend refuses, fearing that he too may suffer a loss. The father then agrees in writing to repay the friend for any loss suffered because of the dishonesty of the boy, if he is hired. On this basis, the friend hires the boy.

This agreement is a personal surety contract of the type known as a *fidelity bond*. The obligation guaranteed is the son's honesty. The parties to the contract are the father, the son, and the friend who employs the boy. The risk is the uncertainty of loss arising from the son's possible dishonesty.[4]

FRINGE BENEFITS

The preceding types of insurance protect a venture from extraordinary financial loss. There are other types of insurance that protect not the venture but its employees. Often called fringe benefits, these types of employee insurance include:

- Life insurance
- Social Security
- Health and accident insurance

Life Insurance

Life insurance protects a family from loss of income upon the untimely death of its breadwinner. The basic form of life insurance is *term insurance*. It gives pure protection, meaning there is no savings plan connected with the insurance policy. The premium is just enough to cover the insured's death claim plus the insurer's expenses and profit. Term insurance gives protection only for an agreed-upon number of years, after which the insurer can charge higher premiums or even refuse to insure. Many ventures buy term insurance for their employees.

Another basic type of life insurance is *whole life insurance*, sometimes called straight life or ordinary life. It differs from term insurance in that premiums are paid throughout an employee's lifetime, with the whole amount of the policy payable upon the insured's death. The insurer cannot refuse to insure at any time during an employee's lifetime as long as premiums are paid promptly.

Each of the hundreds of different life insurance plans is but a variation of the two basic types of life insurance just discussed. In one variation, entrepreneurs may buy *group life insurance* if they employ four or more persons. This plan offers advantages that are denied to individuals. For one, medical examinations are usually waived, so employees may qualify under a group policy even if their health disqualifies them for a personal policy. Another advantage is that group premiums are low compared to individual premiums, with savings running 50 percent or more. Most group life insurance plans are contributory—an employee pays part of the premium, while the entrepreneur pays the rest.

Social Security

This is another vital form of protection. Run by the federal government, Social Security is a minimum kind of insurance. It provides families with income to live on when the breadwinner dies, retires, or is unable to work. Today, Social Security covers almost all of the nation's employees.

Because it is compulsory by law, economists often refer to Social Security payments as taxes rather than premiums. In 1985, the law required entrepreneurs to withhold 7.05 percent of the first $38,100 earned by each employee in a calendar year. Note in Exhibit 19.5 the yearly rise in Social

EXHIBIT 19.5

Rise in Social Security Taxes (1981 to 1989)

Year	Tax Rate Percent	Wage Base*	Social Security Taxes
1981	6.65	$29,700	$1,975
1982	6.70	31,800	2,131
1983	6.70	33,900	2,271
1984	6.70	36,000	2,412
1985	7.05	38,100	2,686
1986	7.15	40,200	2,874
1987	7.15	42,600	3,046
1988	7.51	†	—
1989	7.51	†	—

* Wage base was estimated by the U.S. Social Security Administration using a cost-of-living formula.
† Not established as of April 30, 1985.
Source: Author's communication with U.S. Social Security Administration (Washington, D.C.: April 30, 1985).

Security taxes scheduled through 1989. The law also requires that entrepreneurs pay sums equal to that withheld from the earnings of each employee.

It was the public desire for more financial security that led the federal government to initiate *social insurance*, with passage of the Social Security Act in 1935. Since then, the federal government has steadily expanded its social insurance programs. In fact, the government now spends tens of billions of dollars each year for such programs.

Health and Accident Insurance

This is still another vital form of protection. It protects employees against the high cost of hospitalization and physicians' services. The two most widely used insurance plans are Blue Cross and Blue Shield. Blue Cross pays hospital bills, whereas Blue Shield pays physicians' bills. Besides paying such bills, health and accident insurance often offers such benefits as these:

- Up to 26 weeks of wages if an employee cannot work because of accident or sickness
- A percentage of wages if an employee suffers permanent physical disability and can no longer work
- Lump sum payments if an employee is dismembered

PENSION PLANS

So far, our discussion has focused mostly on how entrepreneurs may protect their ventures against risk, against the unknown. We shall now discuss how entrepreneurs may protect themselves against the risk of financial hardship when they retire. Such hardship is a real probability unless entrepreneurs take pains to design financially sound pension plans.

Pension plans first appeared in the 1940s and have since grown to become a vital part of the nation's system of retirement. Today, economists often refer to this retirement system as a three-legged stool, supported by three sources of retirement income:

Social Security: As discussed earlier, almost all Americans can count on Social Security benefits when they retire. These benefits offer no more than a bare subsistence for people who have nothing else to live on.

Personal savings: This source of retirement income is beyond the reach of many entrepreneurs and their employees. As one congressional task force concluded: "If past performance is a guide, private savings cannot be expected to contribute significantly to raising the level of income in old age."[5]

Pension plans: This third source of retirement income offers perhaps the last hope for more than the bare subsistence that many entrepreneurs and their employees can expect from either Social Security or private savings.

Unlike the major corporations, however, many entrepreneurs cannot justify the cost of a private pension plan, either for themselves or for their employees, since private pension plans operate best with large numbers of both dollars and employees. But for small-businesses:

- The cost of administering a pension plan would be disproportionately high.
- Pension moneys, set aside and put to work earning a return, would be insignificant, because small groups mean a small pension fund.
- Failure is so common among new small-businesses that pension plans, if they exist at all, are more vulnerable to termination than those in major corporations.

Keogh Plan

For sole proprietors and partners who own at least 10 percent of a venture, this bleak picture has been relieved. In 1974, the U.S. Congress passed into law the Employment Retirement Income Security Act (ERISA) that enables many entrepreneurs as well as their employees to shelter their money from taxes while accumulating a nest egg on which to retire. Popularly called the *Keogh Plan*, this act allows entrepreneurs and their employees to set aside, *tax-free*, as much as 20 percent of their taxable income—with a limit of $30,000 a year—in a retirement plan.

The Keogh Plan works in this way: An entrepreneur's taxable income is $29,000. If she puts $2,000 a year into a Keogh Plan earning 10 percent a year, her nest egg at retirement very likely will be large enough to cover her financial needs. Turning to Exhibit 19.6, note that if she begins investing at age 35, by the time she reaches 65, she will have earned $285,000 in interest, giving her a grand sum of $345,000. Exhibit 19.7 traces the growth of

EXHIBIT 19.6

How Keogh Plan or IRA Builds Savings

Start Plan at Age	Total Amount You Deposit	Interest Earned	Total Savings at Age 65
25	$80,000	$848,600	$928,600
30	70,000	498,600	568,600
35	60,000	285,000	345,000
40	50,000	156,200	206,200
50	30,000	36,660	66,660
60	10,000	2,810	12,810

Note: Figures assume deposits of $2,000 a year at an interest rate of 10 percent.
Source: Data from *Thorndike Encyclopedia of Banking and Financial Tables* (Boston: Warren, Gorham & Lamont, 1980). Copyright © 1980, Warren, Gorham & Lamont, Inc. Reprinted by permission.

Keogh Plan savings at selected interest rates. The Keogh Plan has several features, among them:

- All of the entrepreneur's employees with three years or more of service must be included in the plan.
- All sums contributed to the plan are fully tax-deductible.
- All sums contributed are fully protected by law. In the event of a lawsuit, divorce, bankruptcy, or other financial problem, these sums cannot be taken away.
- All capital gains, interest, and dividends earned by the plan are not taxed until entrepreneurs begin to withdraw their retirement benefits. By then, entrepreneurs are more likely to be in a lower tax bracket.

To set up Keogh Plans, entrepreneurs should approach commercial banks, savings and loan associations, or insurance companies. Many of them have IRS-approved, tax-qualified master plans for investment of Keogh Plan moneys.

Another Tax Shelter

An Individual Retirement Account (IRA) is another tax shelter available to entrepreneurs and their employees. The IRA gives *every* working man and woman in the country the opportunity to set up a retirement plan and at the same time shelter a part of their paychecks from federal income taxes. According to the Economic Recovery Tax Act of 1981, every worker may set aside up to $2,000 a year toward retirement. What is more, the worker may deduct that money from his or her taxable income.

If they like, entrepreneurs may save for their retirement using both the Keogh Plan and the IRA. Thus, a sole proprietor or a partner may invest up to $30,000 a year or 20 percent of her income, whichever is less, in a Keogh Plan. She may also invest up to $2,000 a year in an IRA—for a total potential deduction from taxable income of $32,000 a year.

Rather than invest in an IRA, a worker may make a voluntary contribution to his corporate pension plan of up to $2,000 a year if the plan permits it. That, too, is deductible from the worker's taxable income. Mandatory contributions to corporate pension plans are not tax-deductible, however.

Looking again at Exhibits 19.6 and 19.7, note that the growth of savings at selected interest rates applies to IRAs as well as Keogh Plans.

EXHIBIT 19.7 *Growth of Keogh Plan or IRA Savings at Selected Interest Rates*

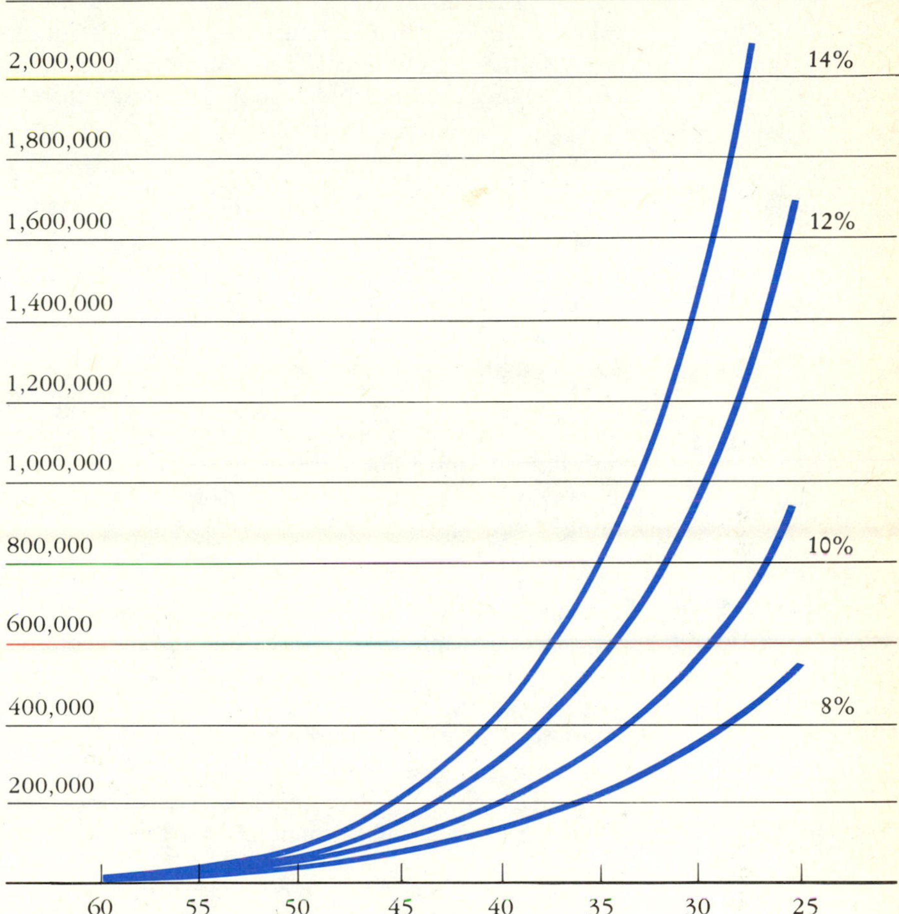

Source: Data from the *Thorndike Encyclopedia of Banking and Financial Tables.* Copyright © 1980, Warren, Gorham and Lamont Inc., Reprinted by permission.

SELECTING AN INSURANCE AGENT

Perhaps no industry is more carefully tailored to the needs of individual customers than the insurance industry. Insurers have something for virtually every entrepreneur, so entrepreneurs can readily buy the insurance program that best suits their own needs as well as those of their ventures. To do that, however, they need the expert help of an insurance agent. Licensed by the state, agents are qualified by training and experience to design an insurance program geared to the entrepreneur's needs.

In earlier chapters, we stressed the contributions that accountants, bankers, and lawyers can make to a venture's success. No less important are those that can be made by insurance agents.

Insurance is so complex a subject that few entrepreneurs understand it. These two examples underscore the need for entrepreneurs to seek expert advice:

Example: Ronald Gompertz, the owner of a small clothing store, was pondering over the last bill that he received from the insurance company. "These premiums are killing me. I must have insurance on everything under the sun, including my gold teeth. I have so many different policies that I wouldn't be surprised if some things were covered by two policies. There ought to be an easier way to get good insurance than this."

Linda Johnson, the owner of a small India import shop, seemed to have just the opposite problem. "Six months ago this shop was broken into and burglarized, and I am still trying to collect from my insurance company. They say my policy only covers robbery. Well, aren't they the same thing?"[6]

Selection Process

How do entrepreneurs go about selecting competent insurance agents? One way is to ask bankers or lawyers for the names of reputable agents. They are also likely to know which agents offer insurance programs in one package. Agents who offer a one-stop service sell all lines of insurance, including fire, health, liability, and life insurance.

The alternative to a one-stop service is a piecemeal service, in which the agent specializes in just one line, say fire insurance or health insurance. This alternative is less attractive than that of a one-stop service:

> Agents offering a one-stop service are more likely to do a painstaking job of analyzing all of the entrepreneur's insurance needs, because they earn a commission on not just one but many lines of insurance. Thus, such agents are more likely to favor the entrepreneur's interests rather than the insurer's on any settlement claims made by the entrepreneur.

Moreover, it is generally best to select an independent agent, one who represents a number of insurers. Independence permits the agent to shop for the policies that best fit the entrepreneur's needs. For example, if one insurance company fails to offer what the agent believes to be proper coverage at a reasonable premium, the agent may well decide to go to another insurer who will. Exhibit 19.8 highlights the desirable traits that entrepreneurs should look for in insurance agents.

To make sure their agents deal only with financially solid insurers, entrepreneurs should do some checking themselves. One good source of

EXHIBIT 19.8 *Traits of a Competent Insurance Agent*

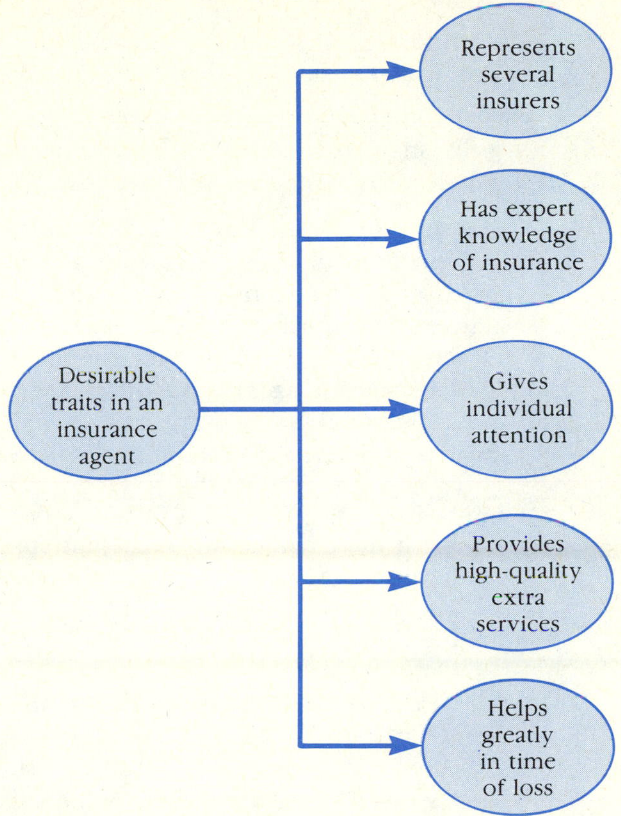

such information is *Best's Insurance Reports*, which rates each insurer's ability to pay claims promptly. Clearly, an insurer in financial straits may not honor an entrepreneur's claims—or, if it does, it may delay in paying them.

SUMMARY

Entrepreneurs should protect themselves and their ventures from any unforeseen events that may cripple survival or stunt growth. To reduce their chances of loss, entrepreneurs should know how best to deal with risk. There are four ways to do that:

- By avoiding risk
- By absorbing risk themselves

- By preventing a damaging event from taking place
- By shifting risk to others

To help them decide which approach to use, entrepreneurs should analyze their exposure to risk with the help of an insurance agent. The program of risk management produced by such an analysis should:

- Pinpoint risks that may cause dollar losses
- Estimate how severe such losses may be
- Select the best way to treat those risks

A pension plan should be a part of every entrepreneur's master retirement plan. In particular, the Keogh Plan offers sole proprietors and partners an opportunity to tax-shelter their moneys while accumulating a nest egg on which to retire.

In selecting the right insurance agent, an entrepreneur should look for an independent agent who offers a one-stop insurance service. Entrepreneurs should also make sure that the agent represents insurers that qualify as financially solid in *Best's Insurance Reports*.

DISCUSSION AND REVIEW QUESTIONS

1. What does risk mean to the entrepreneur? Give one example.
2. Explain the difference between pure and speculative risk. Give one example of each type of risk.
3. Explain the four ways of handling risk. Give one example of each.
4. Define these terms: *avoidance of risk, self-insurance, transfer of risk, premium, liability insurance, term insurance, ERISA*.
5. What is risk management? How might you, as an entrepreneur, go about setting up a program of risk management for your venture?
6. Explain why entrepreneurs should select insurance agents with the same care they select accountants, bankers, or lawyers. How would you, as an entrepreneur, go about selecting an agent?
7. Why do you, as an entrepreneur, need to protect your venture against such risks as fire and theft?
8. Describe some of the ways that an entrepreneur may help employees to protect themselves against financial loss. Why are they often called fringe benefits?
9. What is fundamental risk? Give one example.
10. Describe the four tests that insurable risks must meet.
11. Describe some of the ways that entrepreneurs may minimize their exposure to risk.
12. What is insurance? How does it work?
13. What is the Keogh Plan? How does it work? Who is eligible?
14. Why is it generally best for entrepreneurs to select *independent* insurance agents?
15. Why is key-person life insurance so vital to the survival and growth of certain ventures?

NOTES

1. H. Wayne Snider, *Risk Management* (Homewood, Ill.: Irwin, 1969), pp. 2–3.
2. Herbert S. Denenberg et al., *Risk and Insurance* (Englewood Cliffs, N.J.: Prentice-Hall, 1974). p. 149.
3. George Bernard Shaw, "The Vice of Gambling and the Virtue of Insurance," *Everybody's Political What's What* (Edinburgh: R. & R. Clark, 1944), p. 112.
4. Herbert S. Denenberg et al., *Risk and Insurance* (Englewood Cliffs, N.J.: Prentice-Hall, 1974), pp. 137–138.
5. Quoted by Ralph Nader and Kate Blackwell, *You and Your Pension* (New York: Grossman Publishers, 1973), p. 93.
6. Adapted from U.S. Small Business Administration, *Business Basics: Risk Management and Insurance* (Washington, D.C.: U.S. Government Printing Office, 1985), p. 1.

CASE 19A *Ramesh Shah*

After being on his own for eight years, mostly in the management of real estate properties, Ramesh Shah now wonders whether he is ready to "take a quantum leap" and launch a commercial bank in the United States and a manufacturing venture in India. "I've been building both my financial base and my credibility over the years to do something big," says Mr. Shah. "It's important to me, personally, to leave my footprints in the sands of history."

At present, Mr. Shah's personal net worth is $764,000, and his management company oversees seven real estate partnerships. Exhibit 19A.1 shows a view of one his real estate projects: Euclid Hills Chalet.

Background

Born in India, Mr. Shah earned a degree in electrical engineering from the University of Bombay in 1959. Soon after, he came to the United States on a student visa to pursue graduate study at the University of Illinois, where he earned a masters degree in electrical engineering. His thirst for knowledge later took him to Marquette University, where he earned a second masters degree, in business administration.

Although deeply attached to his homeland, he decided to stay and become a citizen of the United States. "The opportunities in this country are boundless," he says. Indeed, his academic credentials, especially in electrical engineering, were such that he had little trouble landing a job.

From 1962 to 1976, Mr. Shah worked at a succession of jobs. The first was with Allis-Chalmers, where he designed electronic instrumentation

EXHIBIT 19A.1 *Ramesh Shah: View of Euclid Hills Chalet*

for the steel and aluminum industries. Believing that his prospects for promotion there were poor, Mr. Shah became a computer systems manager with the Bailey Controls Company. "The experience was good for me," says Mr. Shah. "I began learning about the American way of doing business, which differs strongly from the Indian way."

Even so, Mr. Shah still was dissatisfied with his lot. Thoughts of someday breaking away and starting his own business began to intrigue him, as he came to realize that working for large companies like Allis-Chalmers and Bailey Controls was "stifling and gave me but a limited view of business. I was a tiny speck in a tiny corner of each company's universe and never saw how all the parts fit together to form a business," says Mr. Shah. "I was learning nothing about such vital parts of a business as finance, marketing, and production."

His frustrations were short-lived. He saw a blind advertisement in the local newspaper seeking applicants for an executive vice-presidency with a chemical manufacturer. From the advertisement, he could not tell whether the company was big or small. "It seemed a long shot to me," says Mr. Shah. "After all, I knew nothing about chemical manufacturing. But, because I had nothing to lose, I answered the ad anyway."

Entrepreneurial Beginnings

The company that needed managerial help was a small minority-owned business called Consul Chemical. The local Chamber of Commerce had helped finance the company. Theodore Bonda, the board member who represented the Chamber's interests, volunteered to interview Mr. Shah.* When Mr. Bonda interviewed Mr. Shah for the job, the tiny chemical company had sales revenues of less than $100,000 a year and showed no profit. "Mr. Bonda wondered why I would want the job," says Mr. Shah. "If the job were offered to me and I accepted, I would be taking a 50 percent cut in pay. But I told him my wife was a physician. So, my family's financial security would scarcely be jeopardized by my accepting the job. Besides, I welcomed the challenge of turning Consul Chemical around. The learning experience would prove useful to me when I later would go into business for myself."

So impressed was Mr. Bonda with Mr. Shah's credentials and answers to questions that he hired Mr. Shah on the spot. He soon found himself working twelve hours a day, six days a week. "It was a far cry from the job I left," says Mr. Shah. "It was strictly a nine-to-five job."

A quick study, Mr. Shah soon mastered the technology of the products manufactured by Consul Chemical. His duties included cost accounting, purchasing, taxes, production, and finance. He even learned to

* Mr. Bonda was also board chairman of Avis Corporation, one of the country's largest automobile rental firms. Mr. Bonda himself came up with Avis's slogan, known the world over: We try harder because we're No. 2.

drive a 5,000-gallon tank truck to make deliveries. "The experience was just what I wanted," says Mr. Shah. "I even swept floors."

Despite Mr. Shah's efforts, Consul Chemical failed six months after he had joined them. During that time, he did not draw a single penny in salary. "Our cash flow was so poor we had to let everyone else go. When we closed our doors for the last time, the company had a president, an executive vice president, and a bare cupboard. It was so sad."

Another Learning Experience

Out of a job, Mr. Shah believed he still was not ready to go on his own. He turned to Mr. Bonda for help and Mr. Bonda came through. He knew of a job opening at the local Chamber of Commerce, and hoped that Mr. Shah would be interested. The job would require him to help both current and future entrepreneurs to succeed. "The job was tailor-made for me," says Mr. Shah. "After a brief interview, I got the job, thanks to Mr. Bonda." The year was 1972.

Mr. Shah stayed with the Chamber of Commerce for four years. As its manager of new business development, he helped more than 200 entrepreneurs. "What a learning experience that was," says Mr. Shah. "It was the equivalent of earning a Ph.D. in entrepreneurship."

Indeed, this experience shaped Mr. Shah's thoughts on the kind of venture that would best suit his talents and personal goals. It would be in the management of such real estate properties as apartment complexes, motels, and shopping centers. He also observed that real estate was the "best way to build up equity."

Mr. Shah is quick to credit his wife, whom he met in India, for his decision to go into business for himself. "It was a family decision," says Mr. Shah. "I needed her strong support, moral as well as financial. She was behind me one hundred percent. She knew it would give me peace of mind to succeed as an entrepreneur in America. I needed the opportunity for self-expression that only entrepreneurship can give."

In Business For Himself

In 1976, Mr. Shah left the Chamber of Commerce and founded the Alpha Development Corporation. This corporation served as his springboard for acquiring and managing real estate properties. Each acquisition candidate was evaluated for its potential to appreciate in value quickly, an important criterion for Mr. Shah, since his personal goal was to be worth a million dollars by 1986, his tenth year in business. As shown in Exhibit 19A.2, he was worth $63,000 in 1976.

Six months went by before he made his first acquisition. After looking at 41 candidates, he zeroed in on an apartment complex called Forest Hills Manor, whose 28 units were occupied exclusively by retired women. Several features recommended the complex to Mr. Shah, among them:

EXHIBIT 19A.2

Ramesh Shah: Beginning Personal Balance Sheet (October 1, 1976)

Assets			**Equities**	
Current assets			Long-term liabilities	
Cash	$30,000		Mortgage loan	$27,000
Notes receivable	10,000	$40,000	Mr. Shah's equity	63,000
Fixed assets				
House	$38,000			
Furniture	5,000			
Vehicle	5,000	48,000		
Other assets		2,000		
Total assets		$90,000		$90,000

- It was fully occupied and had a waiting list of women seeking to rent apartments.
- Its rents were low and had not been raised for four years.
- Its owner wanted to sell because the resulting cash proceeds would enable him to move on to other, larger projects.
- Its location was good, just minutes away from the city's largest and most prestigious hospital.

Evaluating Real Estate

Besides these features, Mr. Shah looked closely at the profitability of the apartment complex. Here, his experience at the Chamber of Commerce stood him in good stead—he had evaluated such properties for many other entrepreneurs, so he had already mastered the techniques of investment analysis. He received audited income statements, audited balance sheets, and income tax returns for the past two years from the seller.

With these statements in hand, Mr. Shah estimated what the Forest Hills Manor was worth, from both his viewpoint and the seller's. To do so, he examined the investment's worth using both its present value and its book value. To determine its present value, Mr. Shah forecast cash flows over the next ten years. On a spread sheet, he estimated what the cash flows would be under existing management and then repeated this procedure to find the cash flows if he were to take over. In his calculations, Mr. Shah assumed that both he and the seller desired a return on investment of 10 percent a year. Next, he looked at the manor's book value, which measures the spread between total assets and total liabilities and thus reflects the seller's equity in the manor.

Armed with this information, Mr. Shah and the seller then negotiated a purchase price. Six months elapsed before they agreed to a price of $620,000. Meanwhile, Mr. Shah formed a general partnership of five investors, including himself. The partnership invested $64,000 and borrowed the rest from a commercial bank on a 25-year, $9\frac{1}{2}$-percent interest mortgage.

Thus, with just $64,000 of their own money at stake, Mr. Shah and his partners acquired Forest Hills Manor for $620,000. "That's typical of real estate," says Mr. Shah. "You can often buy property with just 10 percent or less of your own money and borrow the rest from a bank. That's how millionaires are made."

The Partnership and Management

To land his five partners, Mr. Shah made several presentations to prospective investors. He sought only wealthy individuals, primarily those in the 50 percent income tax bracket, who sought to invest in tax shelters that would appreciate in value.

So thorough was Mr. Shah's presentation that he readily convinced the investors to help finance the acquisition of Forest Hills Manor. The acquisition, by the way, very nearly failed to take place, when a partner who had already invested $16,000 decided to back out. Mr. Shah's bank agreed to make up the difference, and the acquisition took place at last.

As the general partner, Mr. Shah was responsible to the other four partners for the financial performance of Forest Hills Manor. The partnership itself was not involved in the day-to-day operations of the manor—it was solely an investment group and had no employees. The job of managing the manor was given instead to Mr. Shah's company, Alpha Development Corporation. With this arrangement, the company would charge the partnership a fee for managing the manor and carrying out these necessary tasks:

- Collecting monthly rentals from tenants
- Maintaining the buildings and grounds
- Marketing the apartment units
- Doing bookkeeping
- Preparing quarterly financial statements, such as income statements and balance sheets

In all of this, Mr. Shah stood to gain in several ways. As head of the management company, he would draw management fees; and, as an investor in the partnership, he would benefit financially from any appreciation of the property's value and from cash flow generated by operations.

To carry off the acquisition, Mr. Shah acknowledges the help received from his lawyer whom he had met when he worked for the Chamber of Commerce. "Without his expert knowledge of real estate law," says Mr. Shah, "I never would have been able to negotiate effectively with the seller. My lawyer knew all the intricacies of contract law and advised me on how best to protect my financial interests."

A Succession of New Acquisitions

Over the next five years, Mr. Shah acquired seven additional properties. In each one, he repeated the pattern that had worked so well for him in his first acquisition. Each was a partnership that he headed and invested in, and each was managed by his own Alpha Development Corporation. The seven

EXHIBIT 19A.3 *Ramesh Shah: Build-up in Asset Value of Alpha Development Projects (1977 to 1983)*

Project	Units	Year Acquired	Acquisition Value	Investment	Current Market Value
Forest Hills Manor	28	1977	$ 620,000	$ 64,000	$ 820,000
Euclid Hills Chalet	197	1979	2,000,000	400,000	3,200,000
Country Square Shopping Center	10	1979	385,000	21,000	650,000
Wetzel Spring Shopping Center	3	1980	790,000	113,000	980,000
Carriage Square Apartments	29	1982	751,000	60,000	800,000
Mentor Professional Building	20	1983	430,000	100,000	550,000
Marine Tower Condominium	26	1983	710,000	110,000	1,020,000
			$5,686,000	$868,000	$8,020,000

State Manor, acquired in 1982 for $520,000 and sold a year later for $620,000, has been omitted from this table. The investment was $110,000.

new acquisitions, coupled with the first one, cost a total of $6,206,000. "It's a wonderful feeling to know that I'm responsible for managing efficiently so much real estate," says Mr. Shah. "When I came to the United States twenty years ago, I never for a moment thought that I would succeed as an entrepreneur in the American tradition." Turn to Exhibits 19A.3 and 19A.4, and note the build-up in asset values with each acquisition since 1977.

To finance the acquisitions, Mr. Shah relied most on a loyal group of investors. "They have confidence in me and in my ability to make wise acquisitions," he says, "and I haven't disappointed them." Turning to Exhibit 19A.5, note how his investors have benefited.

Close Control

To control the financial performance of his projects, Mr. Shah relies not only on himself but on a cadre of managers. Each project's manager reports to him by 9 A.M. each Monday. "In an organization as far-flung as mine," says Mr. Shah, "I have to maintain fingertip control of each project."

Mr. Shah soon learned the importance of such close control when he took over the 197-unit Euclid Hills Chalet, shown in Exhibit 19A.1. Nestled high in a wooded setting, far removed from the hubbub of big-city life, this project seemed serene and peaceful. The very day he took over, however, he found anything but serenity. The seller had "shrewdly masked" the problems that plagued the project, among them:

- Numerous building code violations. The city had even threatened to shut the buildings down.

EXHIBIT 19A.4 *Ramesh Shah: Growth in Asset Value of Alpha Development Projects (1977 to 1983)*

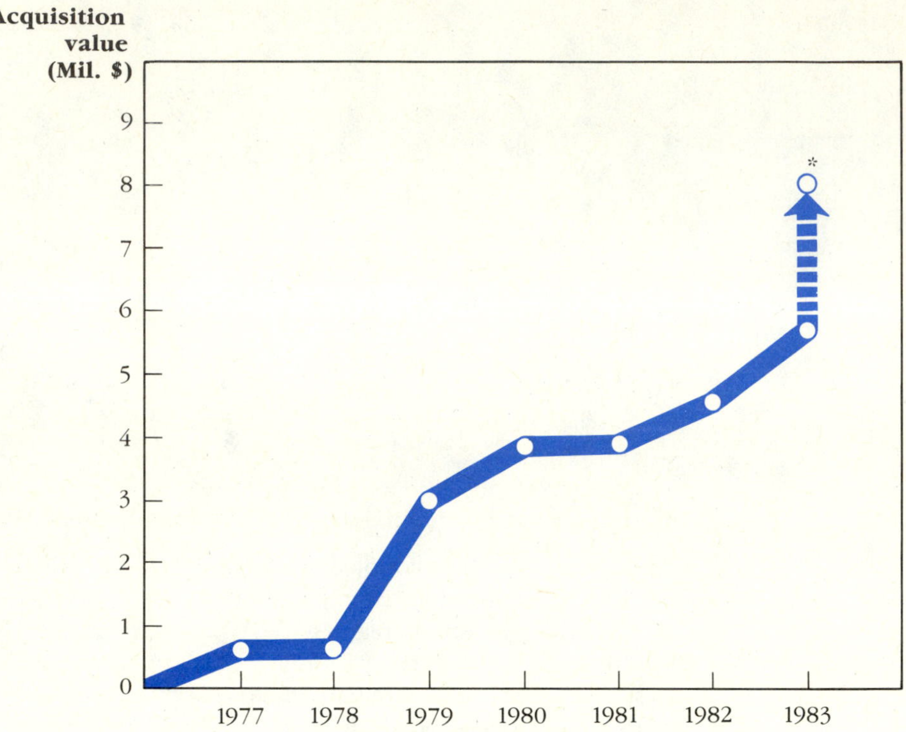

* Current market value

- A tenants' strike. The tenants had not paid rent for a full year. Instead, they deposited their rental payments in escrow.
- Lack of maintenance. The entire project was in disrepair. For example, the wood of 110 balconies had "rotted away so badly that they soon would be incapable of supporting the weight of a 150-pound person."

A Lesson Learned

"The prior owner had done a lousy job," says Mr. Shah, "and I never knew it until I took over. I now had to deal with a militant tenants' committee. They were right in every one of their grievances against the prior owner. My biggest problem was how best to convince them I would do right by them. I was scared, because I had taken a big leap when I acquired the project for $2-million.

Within six months, Mr. Shah restored peace in the project. He resolved the grievances of each of the tenants, and nearly all tenants began

EXHIBIT 19A.5 *Ramesh Shah: Financial Performance for Investors*

Project	Investment	Tax Benefit* to Investors	Cash Flow to Investors	Total Cash Flow to Investors
Forest Hills Manor	$ 64,000	$ 71,300	$43,400	$114,700
Euclid Hills Chalet	400,000	201,300	24,000	225,300
Country Square Shopping Center	21,000	31,200	16,000	47,200
Wetzel Spring Shopping Center	113,000	74,200	21,600	95,800
State Manor	110,000	36,500	1,000	37,500
Carriage Square Apartments	60,000	22,800	—	22,800
Mentor Professional Building	100,000	—	—	—
Marine Tower Condominium	110,000	—	—	—

* Assumes investors fall in the 50 percent income tax bracket.

to pay their rent on time. He also satisfied the city by correcting all code violations.

This experience taught Mr. Shah a lesson. Now he is never insensitive to the needs and wants of his tenants—he actively seeks out their grievances not waiting for them to come to him. This approach has worked. "I don't have any problems now," says Mr. Shah, "even when I raise the rent. My tenants trust me." Indeed, his managerial style requires his personal involvement with all tenants. He:

- Visits each of his seven projects at least twice a week, and talks not only with the project manager but also with any tenants he might meet by chance. "I'm a visible and not an absentee owner," says Mr. Shah.
- Writes a monthly newsletter that offers articles of interest to tenants, such as the names of new tenants, the birth of babies, the repaving of roadways, the renovation of a building, profiles of tenants who excel in community work, and even tenant suggestions on how to boost the quality of life in a project.
- Stages a picnic, at his expense, for all tenants once a year. At the picnic, he and his wife make sure they talk with each tenant at least once.

Organization

Mr. Shah complements his style of personal management with a formal one. As mentioned earlier, Alpha Development Corporation manages all seven of the real estate projects. Wholly owned by Mr. Shah, this corporation serves as the general partner of all projects. This means that Alpha Development is financially responsible to each investing partner of a project. Each project is run by a manager who reports to Mr. Shah in his capacity as president of Alpha Development. An organizational chart appears in Exhibit 19A.6.

To control the financial performance of each project, Mr. Shah sets monthly goals for his managers to meet. These goals are set with each manager's approval. For example, the manager of the Euclid Hills Chalet

EXHIBIT 19A.6 *Ramesh Shah: Organizational Chart*

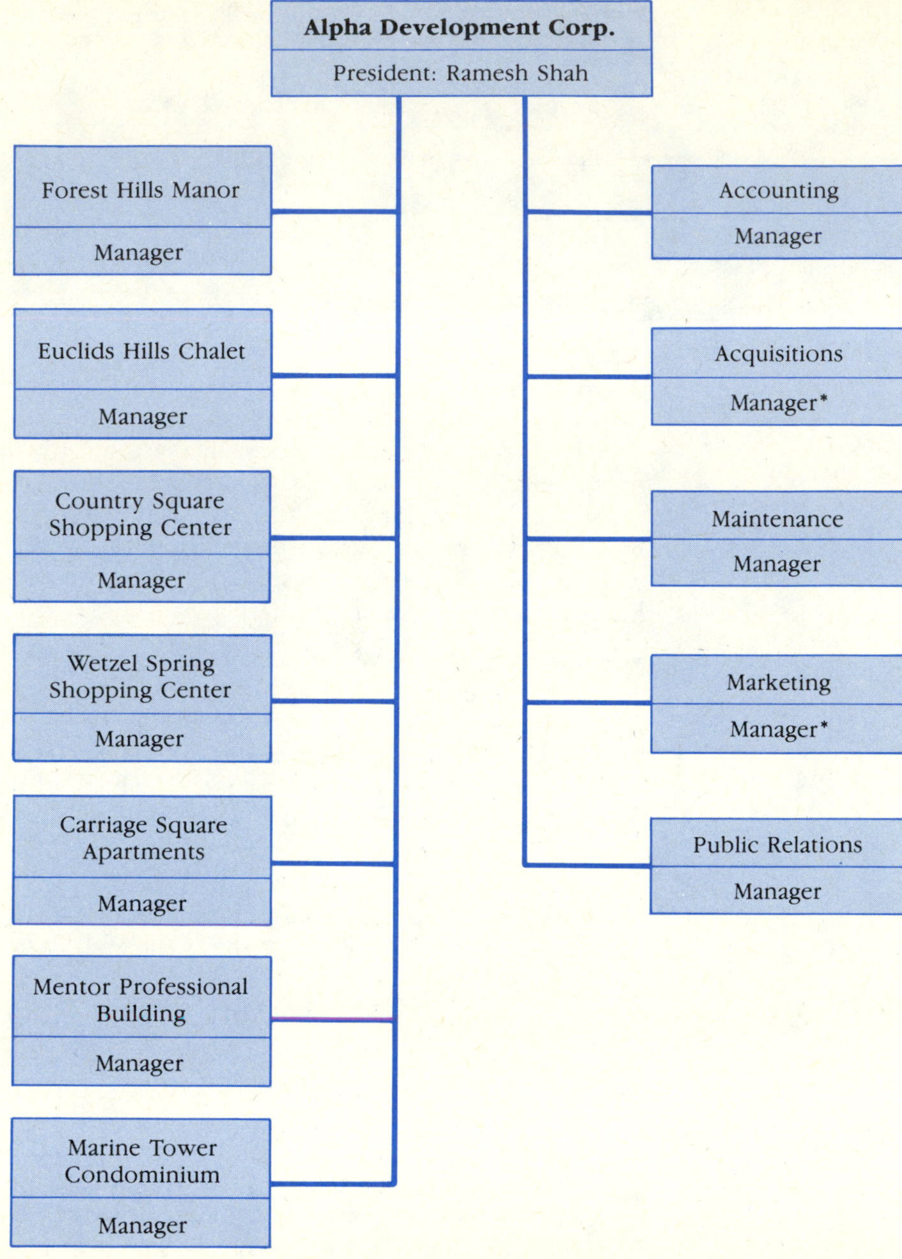

* Mr. Shah

has agreed to meet these goals in 1985:

- To sell at least 10 apartment units a month
- To maintain a bad debt ratio of less than 2 percent on total rental revenues
- To maintain an occupancy ratio averaging at least 90 percent a month
- To maintain a maintenance-expense ratio of no more than 10 percent on total rental revenues
- To resolve every tenant's complaint about maintenance within 72 hours after it is received

To help measure his managers' performance, Mr. Shah relies heavily on his microcomputer. Each month, the computer generates key expense data for each project. The computer also enables him to keep close watch over cash flow, giving him weekly cash positions for each project. "I'm very satisfied with the operation of my computer," says Mr. Shah. "The key was knowing what information I needed to control operations. Once I established that, the next step was getting the right kind of software. I didn't buy software already on the market. Instead, I had my nephew develop the software and I couldn't be more pleased with the results."

Thanks to the tailor-made software, Mr. Shah now does all of his accounting in-house, including tax returns and financial statements. See Exhibits 19A.7 and 19A.8 for the latest income statements and balance sheet for Euclid Hills Chalet.

The Future

Mr. Shah views his present position as just a beginning, a learning experience that will enable him to "take a quantum leap into the future." He is now seriously looking at other entrepreneurial ventures, such as a commercial bank in the United States and a manufacturing plant in his native India. He plans to undertake both ventures when he achieves a personal net worth of a million dollars. Now worth $764,000, he expects to reach that goal by 1986.

"There are 300 professionals of Indian descent in the city," says Mr. Shah. "We Indians must do what the Greeks and Jews have done in this country and build our own economic base. If I earn credibility among the many Indian physicians and scientists here, I know I can raise the money needed to take a quantum leap."

Questions

1. Comment on Mr. Shah's plans for the future.
2. What does it take to succeed in the real estate industry?
3. Comment on the financial performance of Mr. Shah's projects.
4. What are Mr. Shah's major problems?
5. Comment on Mr. Shah's entrepreneurial and managerial traits.

EXHIBIT 19A.7 *Ramesh Shah: Euclid Hills Chalet Three-year Income Statements*

	1982	1983	1984
Sales Revenues			
Rental income	$505,600	$512,000	$569,900
Other income	17,900	29,400	10,800
Total Sales Revenues	$523,500	$541,400	$580,700
Operating Expenses			
Utilities	$109,700	$116,100	$120,400
Management fees	33,700	15,900	20,600
Office	9,100	21,300	20,900
Maintenance, supplies	41,700	44,800	33,100
Wages	42,900	24,000	64,700
Insurance	3,300	6,400	5,700
Professional fees	9,300	8,400	9,400
Vehicle	1,100	2,900	2,400
Advertising	3,200	5,100	5,400
Painting, decoration	11,700	6,800	9,200
Repairs	31,600	32,200	25,200
Real estate taxes	42,600	42,400	40,300
Total Operating Expenses	$339,900	$326,300	$357,300
Operating Profit before Interest and Depreciation	$183,600	$215,100	$223,400
Interest	144,000	169,900	168,200
Operating Profit Before Depreciation	$ 39,600	$ 45,200	$ 55,200
Depreciation	121,500	120,700	124,700
Operating Profit	($ 81,900)	($ 75,500)	($ 69,500)

EXHIBIT 19A.8 *Ramesh Shah: Euclid Hills Chalet Latest Balance Sheet (As of December 31, 1985)*

Assets			Equities		
Current Assets			Current Liabilities		
Cash	$ 2,700		Payroll taxes payable	$ 5,100	
Cash advances	3,500	$ 6,200	Security deposits	55,600	$ 60,700
Fixed Assets			Long-term Liabilities		
Land	$ 306,100		First mortgage loan	$1,216,900	
Buildings, improvements	1,827,700		Second mortgage loan	180,000	
Less: Accumulated depreciation	(767,800)	1,366,000	Third mortgage loan	109,900	
			Note payable to Ramesh Shah	57,000	1,563,800
Other Assets			Variance Found in Audit		(8,700)
Real estate tax reserve	$ 19,800		Owners' Equity		
Syndication costs	48,100		Beginning equity	($ 103,800)	
Organizational costs	0		Operating loss	(69,500)	
Prepaid interest	6,800	74,700	Distributions	4,400	(168,900)
Total Assets		$1,446,900	Total Equities		$1,446,900

CASE 19B *Bailey Shoes*

Byron Bailey, working as sole proprietor, spent three years building up his retail shoe store. Mr. Bailey and his wife invested their life savings of $15,000 in the store. They were the co-owners, along with the bank that held the mortgage.

The shoe store was just beginning to break even when Mr. Bailey suffered a severe heart attack. His wife was overcome with shock, since Mr. Bailey was only 30 years old, vigorous, and bursting with energy. She blamed his heart attack on overwork. In her words:

> There's no doubt in my mind that Byron got sick because he tried to do everything himself. He's been carrying the entire workload himself. He'd work six and seven days a week, from dawn to dusk without any let-up. He hasn't taken a single vacation in the three years we've been in business for ourselves.
>
> How many times have I begged him to let me help out—even for a few hours. But he wouldn't listen. He thinks a wife's place is in the home. Now look at what's happened. If he pulls out of it, he's going to need a long rest at home. But meanwhile, who's going to run the store?
>
> He used to tell me, "I want you to take care of our home and the baby, and look pretty for me when I get home." Then I'd say, "What's the good of looking nice when you're not home to see me?" His whole life was wrapped up in that store.

Two days after he was stricken, Mr. Bailey died. The store faced a serious problem. George Dean, who was 63 years old and worked in the

EXHIBIT 19B-1

Bailey Shoes: Balance Sheet (August 31, 1980)

Assets		**Equities**	
Current assets	$27,200	Current liabilities	$18,000
Fixed assets	23,000	Mortgage loan	20,000
		Owners' equity	12,200
Total assets	$50,200	Total equities	$50,200

Bailey Shoes: Income Statement (for year ending August 31, 1980)

Sales revenues		$92,000
Cost of goods sold		64,400
Gross profit		$27,600
Operating expenses		
Mr. Bailey's salary	$15,000	
Other	12,400	27,400
Before-tax profit		$ 200

store as a salesman, kept things running, but Mrs. Bailey knew it was too much to expect him to keep doing that. Soon after the funeral, the store's accountant worked up the financial statements shown in Exhibit 19B.1.

Mr. Bailey had no will. Nor did he have much insurance—just a $10,000 G.I. life insurance policy. He had once told his wife that "wills and insurance policies are for older folk. I'm too young to think about stuff like that."

Questions

1. What should Mrs. Bailey do now? Why?
2. Had you been Mr. Bailey, what might you have done differently? Why?

CASE 19C *David Storm*

David Storm is president and sole shareholder of 13 corporations, each organized to run a taxi service. When he started out with just one cab, there was just one corporation. Each time he added a cab to his fleet, he created another corporation. "You've got to be smart to make it in this business," says Mr. Storm.

As required by local law, each of Mr. Storm's 13 corporations carries liability insurance of $25,000. This insurance enables each corporation to pay damages suffered by passengers or pedestrians injured in the negligent operation of its taxicab.

One smog-shrouded morning, one of Mr. Storm's cab drivers negligently struck a pedestrian, causing serious injury. The pedestrian sued the corporation.

The court awarded the pedestrian a judgment of $60,000, but the corporation lacked the cash to pay it. After collecting $25,000 on its insurance policy and $500 from its bank account, Mr. Storm had virtually exhausted the corporation's assets. Even the cab was beyond repair—worth only scrap value.

Questions

1. Can the pedestrian take action against Mr. Storm to recover the unpaid balance of $34,500 on the judgment?
2. Would Mr. Storm be personally liable for the pedestrian's injuries if he himself had been the driver on the day of the accident?

20 SOCIAL RESPONSIBILITIES

QUESTIONS FOR MASTERY

Why is social responsibility important?
How may property rights conflict with social rights?
What is the public's perception of business?
What are the problems of minorities, women, and the handicapped?
Why is consumerism important?

There is a point beyond which even justice becomes unjust.

Sophocles

If this is the age of computers and jets, it is also the age of nervousness. A vague feeling of helplessness, born largely of despair, plagues many entrepreneurs. Newspapers cry endlessly about the urban crisis, the energy crisis, the crime crisis, and a host of other crises.

Who is blamed for much of society's dis-ease? Business. Giant corporations, in particular, have become a favorite target of politicians and journalists alike. "Business is cold and heartless," we hear them say. "Business isn't doing enough to solve the nation's ills. Businesspeople are socially irresponsible. They think only of profits."

Unless reversed, this popular view bodes ill for the future of business. For one thing, it tends to discourage the best and the brightest from embarking on entrepreneurial careers. It also invites governmental interference and control.

In this chapter, we shall discuss the entrepreneur's social responsibilities, focusing on the meaning of social responsibility, the issues of civil rights and employment discrimination, and the impact of consumerism. Some of the popular arguments for and against social responsibility in business appear in Exhibit 20.1.

EXHIBIT 20.1 *Social Responsibility: Arguments For And against*

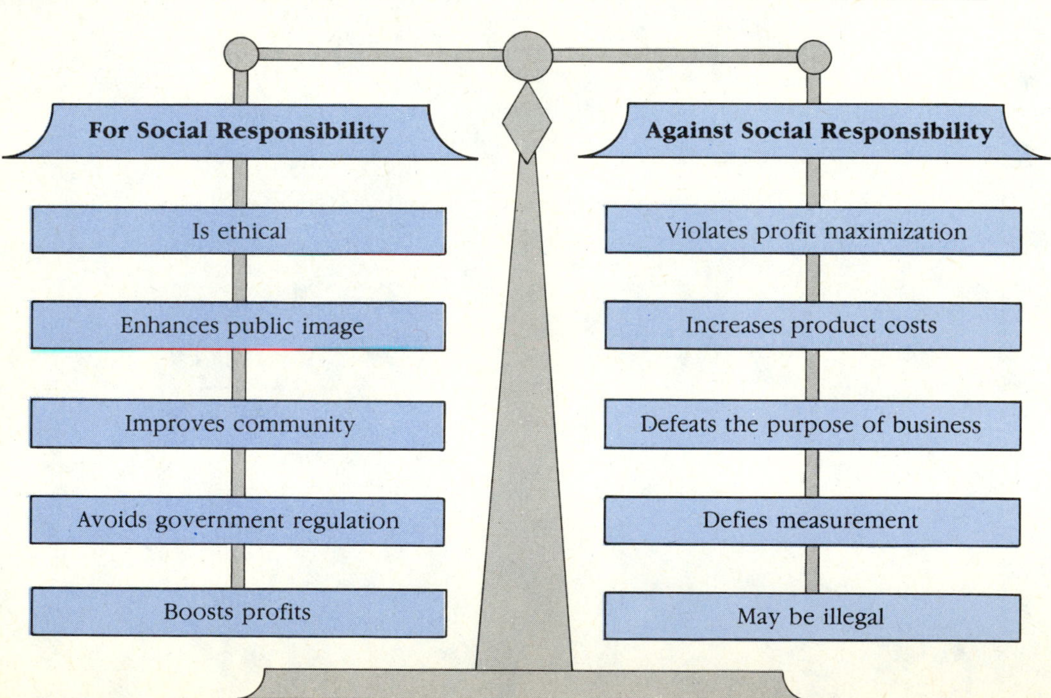

THE MEANING OF SOCIAL RESPONSIBILITY

"What's good for General Motors is good for the country," said a former president of General Motors. That remark sums up the sentiments of many entrepreneurs. They sincerely believe that what is good for their ventures is likely to be good for the community in which they invest their energies and moneys. They see their investment as sparking new products, new services, new jobs. Thus, especially as their ventures prosper, entrepreneurs see themselves as benefactors to the community.

Years ago, this narrow view generated little resistance. Today this view is no longer accepted by the public. As a result, there has been a steady erosion of the ideas basic to free enterprise, such as:

- Individualism
- Personal property rights
- Unhindered competition
- Limited role of government

Today, however, property rights are fast giving way to these social rights:

- Equal opportunity
- Justice
- Good health
- Clean air
- Survival
- Decent Income

Social rights are not eliminating property rights, but they are reducing their significance. In the words of Professor George Cabot Lodge of the Harvard Business School:

> Your right to enjoy your property is no longer subject merely to paying your taxes and obeying the laws. It is subject as well to the needs of the people who work for you and of the entire community. . . . It's not that property rights are wiped out, it's just that they become less important.[1]

Hostile Attitude Toward Business

What Professor Lodge is saying is that the good of the community should come before property rights, a concession that few entrepreneurs have been willing to make. Giant corporations have also been reluctant to do so, and many seem even oblivious of the social ills plaguing the nation.

As a result, the public has taken an increasingly hostile attitude toward business. The results of a poll taken by the Opinion Research Corporation of Princeton, New Jersey show the degree of hostility:

- Sixty percent of those questioned have a low opinion of American business.
- Fifty percent believe that profits run to 28 percent or more of sales revenues.[2]

EXHIBIT 20.2 *Public Confidence in Leaders of Major Institutions*

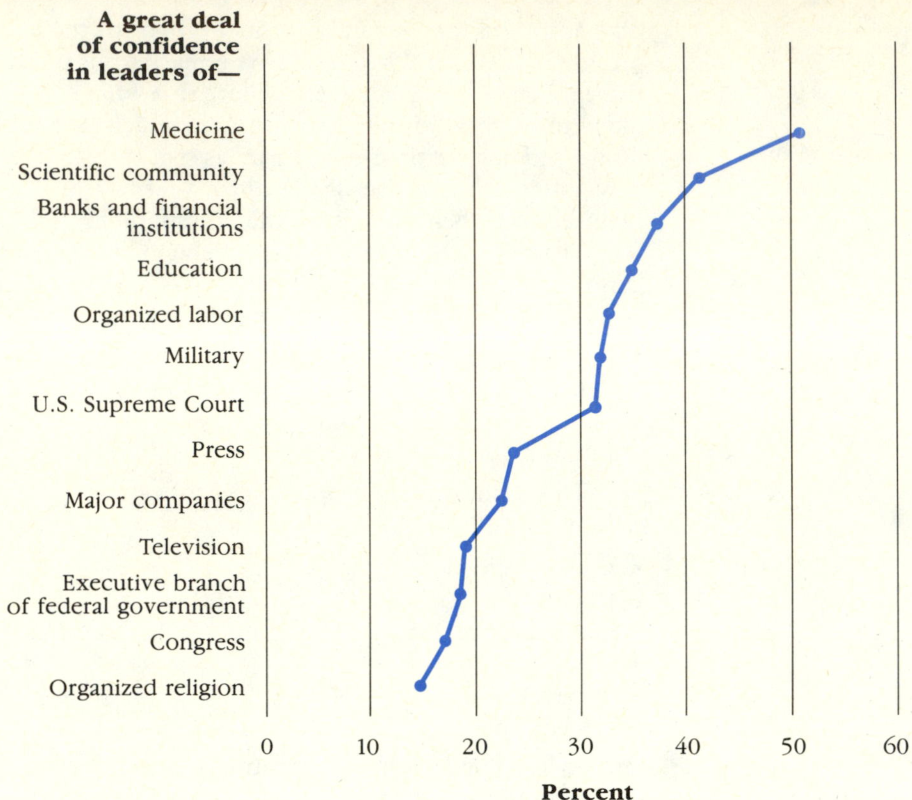

Source: U.S. Bureau of the Census, *Social Indicators III* (Washington, D.C.: U.S. Government Printing Office, 1980), p. xlii.

The second finding underscores the public's lack of knowledge about the true role of profits, which actually average only 4 cents out of every sales dollar. In any case, profit plays a vital role in keeping the economy healthy by attracting investors to finance new products and new markets that create new jobs.

Yet a misinformed public continues to believe that business is greedy and should somehow be punished—or at least regulated by the federal government to keep profits down. Note in Exhibit 20.2 that major companies rank low in public confidence.

Restoring Public Confidence

As members of the business world, entrepreneurs must share the blame for the public's distorted image of business. In their rush to sell products, entrepreneurs often create the impression that their goals are purely materialistic, and that they care little about social problems such as these:

- Air, noise, and water pollution
- Faulty products and slipshod service
- Discrimination against minorities, women, and the handicapped

In fact, many businesspersons, including entrepreneurs, *are* trying to do something about these problems, but they have failed to convince the public of their sincerity. Why?

American businesspersons are respected the world over for their superior knowledge and salesmanship. They are masters at selling air conditioners, automobiles, computers, and even ballpoint pens. But when it comes down to selling themselves to society by explaining their role in society, they do a poor job. Their message rarely gets across, especially to the young, who are not likely to be impressed, for example, by pages of statistics on steel tonnage or kilowatt-hours generated. Rather, they are looking for meaning in this complex world of computers and electronic wizardry. Materialism alone does not attract the young—a fact that business still largely ignores.

In a Gallup survey, a majority of teenagers rated businesspersons very low for their honesty and ethical standards (see Exhibit 20.3). "Many teens feel that businesspersons are only interested in profits and care little for the quality of life or the well-being of the public."[3]

EXHIBIT 20.3 *Gallup Youth Survey on Honesty and Ethical Standards of Major Occupations*

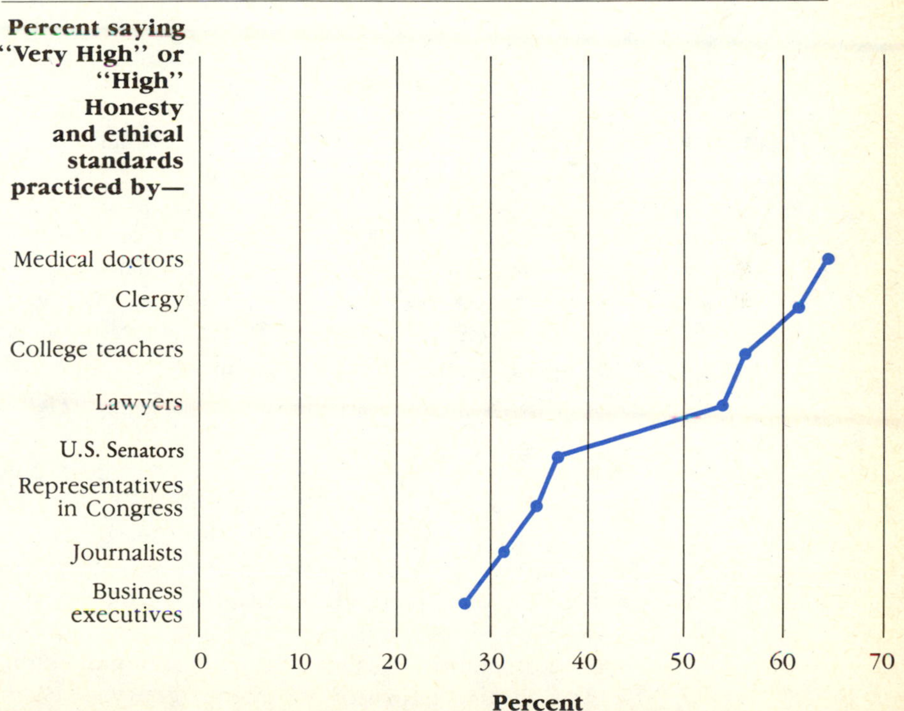

Source: George Gallup, "Doctors, Clergy Rate Highest," the Cleveland *Plain Dealer*, November 30, 1980. Reprinted by permission of George Gallup, Jr.

A Feeling of Helplessness

A melancholy tension grips entrepreneurs as well as the young. Few know how to overcome the sense of futility about problems such as inflation and the fouling of our environment. They know that the giant pieces of a new order are falling into place and they feel helpless. Why? Because the very size of each problem creates its remoteness from individual entrepreneurs. Entrepreneurs feels somehow connected to the problem but not to the means of solving it.

This feeling of helplessness can be overcome. Individual entrepreneurs may not be able to write legislation for the entire nation, but they can surely make their ideas known to those around them and take active roles to:

- Help clean the air
- Help make the streets safer
- Make their plants safer places to work
- Employ the handicapped, the poor, and minorities
- Participate in politics to help ensure the election of honest and intelligent public officials

Clearly, entrepreneurs must act in ways that enhance the community's well-being. However great their abilities to innovate and sell, if they cannot also use their skills to work for a safer and better community, they are incomplete businesspersons. In the words of economist Irving Kristol:

> Business tends to operate too narrowly within the constraints of "economic" concern. The businessman must act within the broader contexts of the "human" community.[4]

An Ominous Question

Indifference is a luxury few entrepreneurs can afford. The times cry out for action to preserve the nation's vitality. One observer went so far as to pose this ominous question: "Are we as a people and as a nation on the brink of the decline and fall of the United States of America?"[5]

It seems hard to believe that the nation's plight is so great that it triggers such a gloomy question. Yet, in his highly acclaimed television program, *America*, journalist Alistair Cooke saw these signs of decline:

- A disregard of law by those elected to uphold it
- A belief by many—in and out of government—that the end justifies the means
- The practice of deceit and hypocrisy in government, business, unions, religion, and elsewhere in society
- A perilous loss of credibility for nearly every category of national leadership, including politicians, the press, and the church
- An increasingly popular desire to live off the state on welfare subsidies and business subsidies.
- An acceptance of vulgarity, violence, and public indecency
- An inordinate love of show and luxury
- A moral indifference toward money corruption in politics and political corruption in government[6]

EXHIBIT 20.4 *Quality of Life in the United States: Indicators of Alienation*

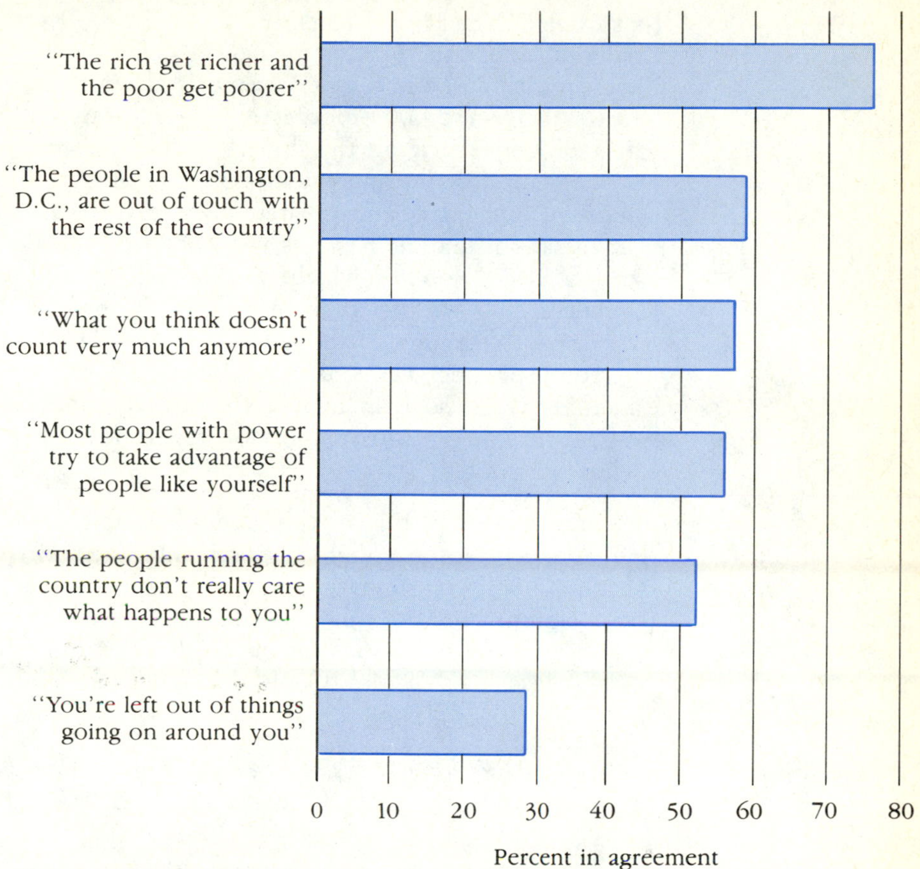

Source: U.S. Department of Commerce, *Social Indicators III* (Washington, D.C.: U.S. Government Printing Office, 1981), p. xlii.

How does the public perceive its quality of life? To answer that question, the U.S. Department of Commerce made a nationwide survey. Shown in Exhibit 20.4, the results of the survey suggest the "prevalence of substantial feelings of mistrust and hostility, inasmuch as over three-fourths of the respondents agreed that the 'rich get richer and the poor get poorer.'"[7]

Positive Action

These are not necessarily the worst of times. The past, too, was pock-marked with human imperfection. The hunger of the unemployed, the despair of the aged and the crippled, the pervasiveness of violence have been forgotten. Nor was the past spared the problems faced today, such as pollution and urban blight. Still, recognizing the imperfections of the past does little to soften the miseries of the present.

Let us now look at one example of a small business that is responsive to the social challenges of the times.

Example: When my partner and I bought the Kerscher Elevator Company of Toledo in 1978, its image was going down. Our building was an eyesore. It looked like a sieve, vandals attacked the property on weekly sorties, and our 23,000-foot factory was so cluttered that we could barely fit a pick-up truck on the floor.

We figured the business would be dead in less than a year if we didn't improve our image immediately. My partner and I then joined civic organizations like the Kiwanis and Rotary clubs. We did work at the city zoo, a $1,000 job for which we charged $1. The public exposure was excellent, and we met more people in the process.

Now we've budgeted about $5,000 a year for giveaways such as tickets for local sporting events, that we donate to local public television station auctions. We also help finance the college education of ghetto youth.

The result? We now employ 16 repairmen, up from just 2 in 1978, when we started.[8]

Similar examples have appeared all over the country. There is little doubt that, out of enlightened self-interest, entrepreneurs and other businesspersons are undertaking projects that enhance the well-being of their communities. But this is just a start. Businesspersons have a long way to go before they convince the public that they have, indeed, developed a social conscience. Ernest Conine, a writer for the *Los Angeles Times*

EXHIBIT 20.5

Selected Federal Legislation Requiring the Performance of Social Responsibilities

Agencies Created By Federal Legislation	Main Activities
Consumer Product Safety Commission	Attempts to minimize consumer complaints about product design and labeling
Environmental Protection Agency	Sets and enforces environmental standards regarding air, noise, and water pollution
Equal Employment Opportunity Commission	Investigates and resolves complaints of discrimination in employment based on race or sex
Food and Drug Administration	Sets standards for certain foods and drugs and issues licenses for the manufacture and marketing of drugs
Occupational Safety and Health Administration	Sets and enforces safety and health standards
Office of Federal Contract Compliance Programs	Assures that businesses holding federal contracts practice equal employment opportunity

commented:

> For public consumption, at least, most companies now endorse the creed enunciated in the Caterpillar Tractor Company code of business conduct: "The law is a floor. Ethical business conduct should exist at a level well above the minimum required by law."
>
> Unfortunately, professions of noble intent frequently have no discernible effect on the actual conduct of business.
>
> It still happens that a chemical firm neglects to tell its employees that they may become sterile through repeated exposure to a given production process. Some manufacturing companies still dump deadly pollutants into a lake or river with one hand while fending off environmental orders with the other. The examples go on and on.[9]

Often, entrepreneurs cannot choose to ignore social responsibility. Turning to Exhibit 20.5, note some of the federal legislation that created agencies that force entrepreneurs and other businesspersons to act in socially responsible ways.

CIVIL RIGHTS AND EMPLOYMENT DISCRIMINATION

Today, most businesspersons claim to be "an equal opportunity employer." Many are indeed working to erase bigotry and provide full equality of opportunity for all men and women by observing the spirit as well as the letter of the hiring practices law laid down by the federal government in 1964:

> It shall be an unlawful employment practice for an employer . . . to discriminate against any individual . . . because of such individual's race, color, religion, sex, or national origin.[10]

Good intentions do not, however, ensure good results. It is true that some progress has been made, but to many entrepreneurs, being an "equal opportunity employer" means simply being willing to consider minorities for employment. Few minority members move into managerial jobs. Those who do often find their progress ends with staff jobs entitled Equal Employment Opportunities Officer, Manager of Community Relations, or Director of Urban Affairs. The high visibility of such jobs smacks of tokenism. Few minorities find themselves in line jobs that count. Commenting on this problem, Professor Robert W. Nason of the Wharton School at the University of Pennsylvania, said:

> For most firms to date, institutional and overt racism make the commonly used claim of being "an equal opportunity employer" a mockery . . . a new and subtle deterrent to black mobility is institutional racism. In this case, individuals may justifiably feel they and fellow managers

hold no personal prejudice against blacks, yet there are real barriers to black mobility in management.

Most employment tests and screening criteria are standard for white subjects. A corporation often requires the black applicant to have higher qualifications than comparable whites. To the extent that seniority influences promotion, blacks newer in management are discriminated against.[11]

Minorities and Women

Entrepreneurs who pay only lip service to the principles of equal opportunity surely are not living up to their social responsibilities. Nor are only blacks denied equal opportunities. Women, Native Americans, Hispanics, and other minorities face similar problems. All the talk about equal opportunity cannot hide the fact that business still discriminates against minorities and women either openly or unconsciously.

Example: An executive search firm submitted the name of an exceptionally well-qualified woman for a corporate position. But she was not considered for the position. To find out why, the executive search firm questioned the corporation. Their dialogue follows:

"Why?"

"Her salary is too high."

"But women have always been underpaid; she must be outstanding to have reached that level."

"We have other candidates with pretty much the same qualifications for less pay."

"Pretty much?"

"Yes."

"Men?"

"Yes."

"Isn't it reasonable to assume that she could be better qualified than they are?"

"Maybe."

"Then you wouldn't be willing to see her?"

"No, she is too expensive."[12]

This dialogue bares the mask some employers wear. On the surface, they seem to welcome minorities and women. They radiate equal opportunity, but too often, they throw up hidden fences that keep minorities and women out. As they go over an applicant's credentials, they often let their own stereotyped attitudes influence them:

> One company sought to employ more minority males. And it would, too, except for one "problem." Its executives say, "The minority male is fine here at corporate headquarters, but we can't control him out in the divisions. He goes to pieces."[13]

Testing Job Applicants

Entrepreneurs are as guilty of such discriminatory behavior as their big-business counterparts are. Although they may mean well, when it comes down to hiring more minorities and more women, they often fall short.

One area where entrepreneurs and other businesspersons often discriminate unconsciously is in their tests for screening job candidates. What entrepreneurs must ask themselves is: Are the tests equally valid for all ethnic groups? Do those who perform well on tests also perform well on the job?

The best test is one that shows no bias toward any ethnic group. A study made by New York University concludes that unbiased testing is rare, but also saw the problems in using weighted tests:

> The circumstance that justifiably is of most concern to blacks is that members of their race may not score well on tests, even though their performance on the job is as good as that of whites. The solution, if the tests are otherwise valid, is to set a lower passing score for blacks; but this procedure, sensible and just though it may be, is forbidden in many federal and state jurisdictions.
>
> If there are two tests—one which works well for whites and one which works well for blacks, although both groups perform equally well on the job—the employer is faced with another dilemma under the present law. Which test shall he use? If he uses both tests for both groups, the effectiveness of the test that is valid for one group is diluted by adding the results of the invalid test. The logical answer is to employ one test for whites and another for blacks; but this is generally illegal.[14]

Perhaps the best solution to this dilemma is to use tests only as preliminary screens to reject applicants who score so low that their abilities to perform can be seriously doubted. In this model, less emphasis is placed on test scores, and the other information on the applicant assumes more importance.

The Handicapped

So far, our discussion has focused mostly on minorities and women. Another group that merits attention is the handicapped. In the rush for equal opportunity, the handicapped have been largely overlooked, yet discrimination against them is often more severe than that against minorities and women.

In recent years entrepreneurs and other businesspersons have begun to realize that the handicapped are as dedicated and talented as any other group. Studies show that to compensate for their disabilities, the handicapped often work harder than the able-bodied. Moreover, absenteeism among the handicapped often approaches zero.

So when they begin expanding their ventures, entrepreneurs should not pass up the opportunity to hire the handicapped. The experience is likely to be mutually rewarding.

THE IMPACT OF CONSUMERISM

The coming of consumerism can be traced to 1966, when Ralph Nader began making headlines with his exposes of unsafe automobiles. Since then, he has broadened his interests and helped launch a consumer movement that now spans the continent. Thanks largely to his efforts, consumers are no longer alone in the fight against dishonest businesspersons.

The main goal of the consumer movement is to help erase private abuses of the public interest. In essence, the consumer movement tries to:

- Teach consumers to care
- Make institutions more open, accessible, and accountable to consumers
- Educate consumers on their opportunities and their responsibilities to make changes
- Teach consumers how to learn what is going on, how to make complaints, and how to seek change

Today, almost every community has a consumer group. Such groups have already made their mark on entrepreneurs, other businesspersons, and even the federal government. In response to consumerism, the Federal Trade Commission (FTC) has hired hundreds of consumer specialists to spot-check businesses for violations of FTC rules, investigate complaints about faulty products or slipshod service, and educate consumers on how to avoid being taken in by dishonest businesspersons.

Even so, the nation's Better Business Bureaus processed more than 1.6 million consumer complaints in 1982. As shown in Exhibit 20.6, the worst offender—general mail order companies—accounted for 22.4 percent of all complaints and franchised auto dealers ran a distant second with 5.9 percent.

Two Opposing Views of Consumerism

Traditionally, the FTC has investigated mergers and other practices that could hamper free trade. Now that the FTC has joined the consumer movement, one FTC official described the behavior of business in this way:

> Every business is involved in some sort of misrepresentation. They're not all doing it maliciously, though. Some of them are doing it because they have to keep up with the competition that is doing it.[15]

This somewhat exaggerated statement echoes the attitude of Mr. Nader and other consumer advocates. In response, some entrepreneurs now go to extreme lengths to please the consumer while others believe that government—at all levels—has overreacted to consumerism. One such entrepreneur had this to say:

> The government has been pushed and badgered and harried by consumer groups, and it has acted before making a proper study of the matter under question. Some of our politicians . . . are going around the country

EXHIBIT 20.6 *Percentage of Complaints by Better Business Bureaus in 1982, by Industry*

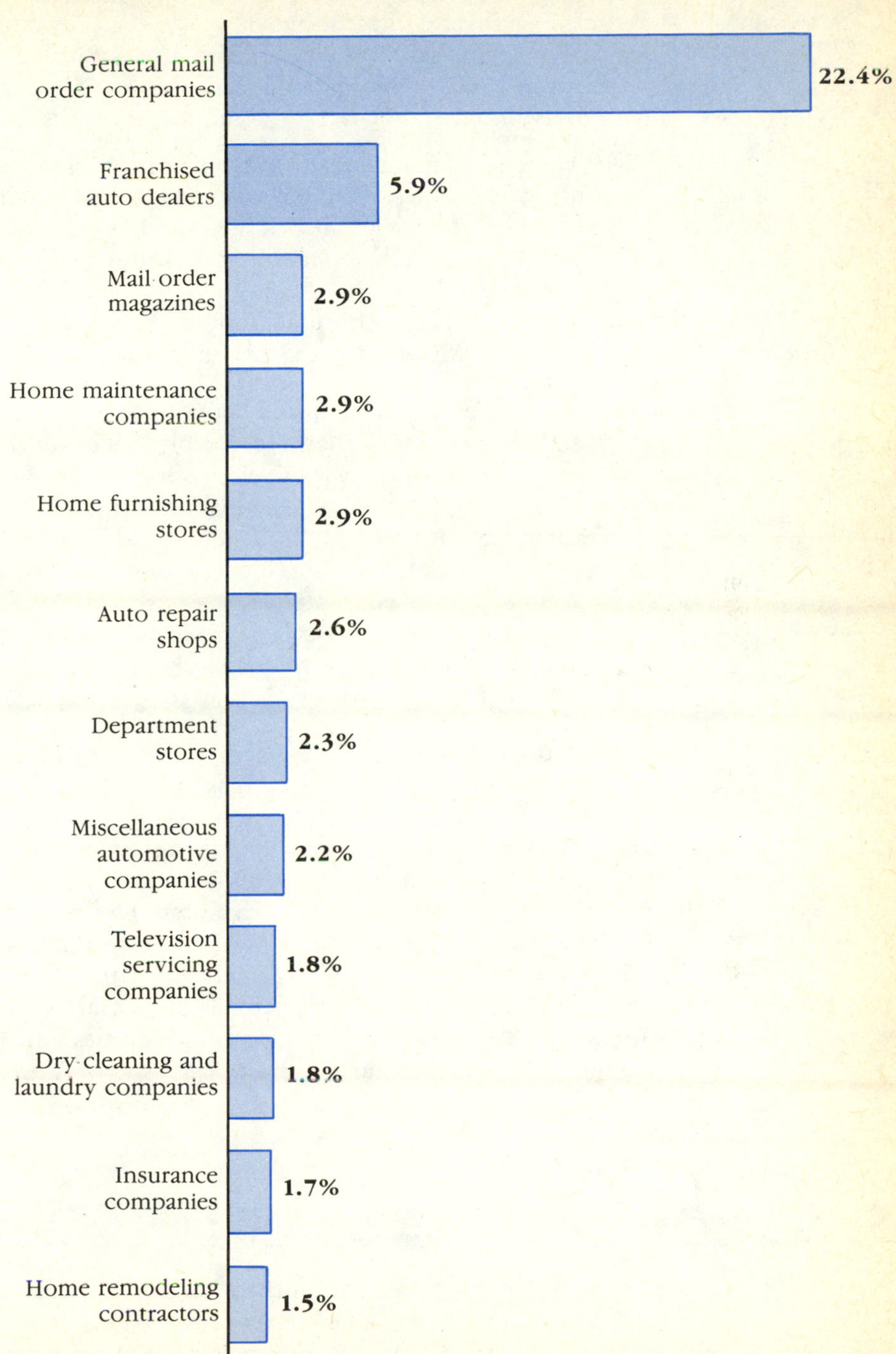

Source: The Council of Better Business Bureaus, "Businesses Under Fire," Cleveland *Plain Dealer*, July 6, 1983, p. 3-G.

> saying all clothing should be fire-proof without regard to how much this is going to cost the consumer.
>
> When you say, "Make all clothing flame-retardant," it gets out of control. People won't be able to afford their clothes. There would be no variety, no fashion. But to argue for it makes great politics.[16]

There is more than just a grain of truth in these remarks. The price of consumer protection is often a higher cost. Automobiles are a good example—prices rose dramatically in the 1970s because manfacturers were required to equip each automobile with safety belts and pollution controls.

Benefits of Consumerism

Despite its critics, the consumer movement has left its mark in many areas. For example, Mr. Nader and his colleagues have:

- Exposed the cozy relationship between some federal regulatory agencies and the industries they presumably watch over.
- Forced the Atomic Energy Commission to give verified assurances that back-up systems will work reliably if an atomic reactor breaks down.
- Drafted legislation to require federal chartering of corporations, a move that consumer advocates believe would make corporations legally accountable to consumers.
- Established Congress Watch, a group that promotes legislation on such matters as consumer protection and tax reform. It also follows and grades the performance of each congressman.

Although consumerism has struck fear in the hearts of many entrepreneurs, it has also encouraged tens of thousands of consumers. Remember, the only true test of a satisfactory product or service is a satisfied customer. If that test be their guide, entrepreneurs need never worry about doing the right thing.

Dr. Erika Wilson of California State University researched the question: What is the small-businessperson's stand on business responsibility in society? She found that only 12 percent of the 180 small-businesspersons she interviewed in Los Angeles felt no social responsibility at all. The remaining 88 percent mentioned responsibilities either to their customers, employees, or community. Responsibility to the consumer was most important—almost half referred to it specifically.[17]

SUMMARY

Social forces operate to influence business success no less than market forces do. Just as the wise person must give thought to what makes for a more fulfilling life, so must the entrepreneur give thought to what makes a better community in which to invest energy and money.

The idea that businesspersons must be socially responsible is relatively new. Although some have aggressively tackled the social problems facing society, many have not. Entrepreneurs must understand that the business of business is not simply profit but must also include the good of the community.

Because entrepreneurs and other businesspersons have been slow to change, the public's attitude toward them has become increasingly hostile. Polls show that most Americans have low opinions of businesspersons. They believe that businesspersons should exercise strong leadership to help solve problems such as these:

- Poor product quality
- Air, noise, and water pollution
- Discrimination against minorities, women, and the handicapped

One area where many entrepreneurs fall short is in the hiring and promotion of minorities, women, and the handicapped. Although often well-intentioned, many entrepreneurs are hamstrung by stereotyped attitudes toward these groups.

Consumerism has left its mark on business and the federal government. Thanks largely to consumer groups across the country, consumers are no longer alone in their fight against dishonest businesspersons in the marketplace. Consumerism is a force whose time has come. No entrepreneur can afford to deny its power.

DISCUSSION AND REVIEW QUESTIONS

1. Define what is meant by the social responsibilities of businesspersons. Give at least one example.
2. On the basis of your own observations, do you believe that entrepreneurs in your community are living up to their social responsibilities? Why?
3. How would you, as an entrepreneur, go about pursuing the principle of equal opportunity? What guidelines for hiring and promotion would you use?
4. Define these terms: *property rights, social rights, equal opportunity employer, institutional racism, consumerism, FTC, Congress Watch.*
5. Do you believe that consumerism helps or hinders the entrepreneur? Why?
6. Explain the true role of profits.
7. Explain how you, as an entrepreneur, would go about meeting your social responsibilities.
8. What must entrepreneurs and other businesspersons do to attract the young? Explain.
9. Comment on the results of the Gallup Youth Survey. Do you agree with the majority of teenagers who rate businesspersons very low for their honesty and ethical standards?

10. On the basis of your own observations, do you believe that job barriers against minorities, women, and the handicapped have been reduced? Explain.
11. Why is the testing of prospective employees often hazardous?
12. Do you believe that the quality of life in the country is declining or improving? Explain.
13. If an entrepreneur observes the law to the letter, does it also necessarily follow that his or her behavior is ethical? Explain, giving an example.
14. How may property rights conflict with social rights? Give one example.
15. What is the ultimate test of a satisfactory product or service?

NOTES

1. Quoted in "Radical in the Boardroom," *Forbes Magazine*, May 15, 1972, pp. 61–62.
2. John A. Davenport, "Free Enterprise's Forgotten Virtues," *The Wall Street Journal*, July 27, 1973, p. 10.
3. George Gallup, "Doctors, Clergy Rate Highest," Cleveland *Plain Dealer*, November 30, 1980, p. 6-C.
4. Quoted by Desmond M. Reilly, "Students View the Business Ethics Dilemma," *The Collegiate Forum*, Winter 1980, p. 10.
5. Roscoe Drummond, "Time to Deal with the National Decay Issue," Cleveland *Plain Dealer*, July 1, 1974, p. 5-B.
6. Ibid.
7. U.S. Department of Commerce, *Social Indicators III*, (Washington, D.C.: U.S. Government Printing Office, 1981), p. XXVII.
8. Adapted from "The Company Image: How Much Is It Worth?" *Inc.*, November 1980, pp. 44–45.
9. Ernest Conine, "Can You Rate Corporate Consciences?" Cleveland *Plain Dealer*, October 31, 1977, p. 19-A. (Reprinted by permission of the *Los Angeles Times*. Copyright 1977. All rights reserved.)
10. Civil Rights Act, Title VII (1964).
11. Quoted in "Calls Equal Opportunity a Mockery," *The Cleveland Press*, August 31, 1972, p. B-6.
12. Frances Lear, "EEO Compliance: Behind the Corporate Mask," *Harvard Business Review*, July–August 1975, pp. 139–140.
13. Ibid., p. 139.
14. Richard S. Barrett, "Grey Areas in Black and White Testing," *Harvard Business Review*, January–February 1968, p. 93.
15. Thomas S. Andrzejewski, "Idealist Untouchables Battle for Consumers," Cleveland *Plain Dealer*, April 9, 1972, p. 1-AA.
16. Larry Barth, "Says Consumer Law Can Go Too Far," *The Cleveland Press*, September 26, 1974, p. 2-B.
17. Erika Wilson, "Social Responsibility of Business: What Are the Small Business Perspectives?" *Journal of Small Business Management*, July 1980, p. 23.

CASE 20A *Sulcus Computer Corporation*

A high-technology venture, Sulcus Computer Corporation, has grown rapidly since its founding in 1979. In 1984, it earned after-tax profits of $213,000 on sales revenues of $2.1 million. Sulcus develops, makes, and markets microcomputer systems for the real estate industry, focusing on the land title market.

In 1984, Sulcus purchased Lawtomation, a company based in Washington, D.C., that specializes in management systems for law firms. Sulcus intends to win over the nation's law firms with the same methods it used to cement the land title market.

One of Sulcus's founders, Jeffrey Ratner, wonders whether his small firm can compete against giant corporations, such as IBM, in a market estimated to be as large as $10 billion a year. Mr. Ratner says, "We're playing hardball with the big boys and we think we'll be among the major league hitters. In three years, we'll either be a $100 million company or go bust."

Background

Sulcus's microcomputer systems are designed to perform the functions needed by these markets within the real estate industry:

- Title insurance firms and escrow companies
- Abstract companies* and mortgage bankers
- Financial institutions and law firms

Sulcus's most important product is a turnkey system, which consists of hardware, software, supplies, training, and support. In the turnkey system, Sulcus furnishes all the components and installs the microcomputer system *before* turning it over to the client, who then only has to "turn the key." This product is marketed nationwide through a network of distributors and dealers, regional representatives and branch offices. Mr. Ratner and a Sulcus microcomputer are shown in Exhibit 20A.1.

Company Financing

Founded by Mr. Ratner and Richard Gross, the company began its corporate life in November 1979 under the name of Ragtronics, Inc. Two years later, the company bought all of Mr. Gross's stock, leaving Mr. Ratner as the majority shareholder.

In March 1983, the company borrowed a total of $275,000 from three Small Business Investment Companies (SBICs). Licensed by the U.S. Small

* Abstract companies write concise histories, taken from public records, of the ownership of pieces of land. Each history includes a statement of all liens or liabilities to which the land may be subject that could affect a prospective purchaser.

EXHIBIT 20A.1 *Sulcus Computer Corporation: View of Jeffrey Ratner and a Sulcus Microcomputer*

Photograph by the Pittsburgh Press.

Business Administration, SBICs are venture capital companies that:

- Invest in, or lend to, small businesses only—especially high-risk ventures boasting new products with promising market potential, unusually favorable competitive positions, and sound, aggressive management.

The three SBICs received stock options for 152,700 shares of common stock that can be exercised only after Sulcus repays the loan of $275,000. This loan bears 12 percent interest, matures in 1990, and is subordinated to the company's debt to trade creditors and financial institutions.

Subordination means that a creditor agrees that the claims of a specified creditor or creditors must be paid in full before any payment can be made to him or her. Here, the three SBICs are subordinate creditors.

In September 1983, Sulcus sold 17,450 shares of its 7 percent convertible preferred stock for $45 a share in a private placement. The preferred stock is convertible into 401,350 shares of common stock. Preferred stock has preference, or priority, over common stock in receiving dividends, in obtaining assets in the event of liquidation, or in other matters specified before the sale.

Financial Performance

Since its founding in 1979, Sulcus has grown rapidly—so much so that it now qualifies as one of the most promising high-technology ventures in the country. In 1985, Sulcus placed 50th among *Inc.* magazine's 100 fastest-

EXHIBIT 20A.2 *Sulcus Computer Corporation: Sales and Profit Growth*

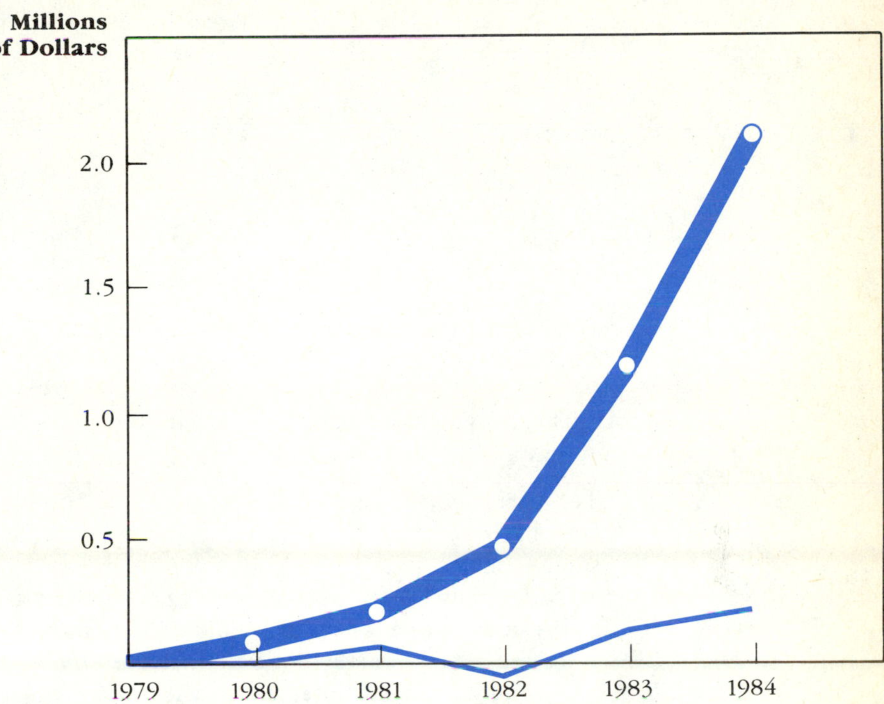

growing, public-owned small-businesses. To qualify for *Inc.*'s top 100 rankings, a small company must meet the following criteria:*

- The company is an independent corporation in a manufacturing, mining, wholesaling, retailing, or service industry. Banks, other financial institutions, and utilities are excluded.
- The company was publicly held as of December 31 of the previous year. The company's shares of common stock were necessarily traded either over the counter or on a listed stock exchange on that date.
- The company shows an operating and sales history of at least five years, with growth during its last fiscal year. Companies showing growth in the five-year base period but decline in sales in the last year are excluded.
- The company's sales five years ago were at least $100,000 but no more than $25 million.

As mentioned earlier, Sulcus posted after-tax profits of $213,000 on sales revenues of $2.1 million in 1984, compared to profits of $128,000 on sales of $1.3 million in 1983. This performance far exceeds that of 1982, when Sulcus lost $49,700 on sales of $448,000. Exhibit 20A.2 traces

* Curtis Hartman, "The 1985 *Inc.* 100," *Inc.*, May 1985, p. 62.

EXHIBIT 20A.3

Sulcus Computer Corporation: Three-year Income Statements

	1982	1983	1984
Sales Revenues	$447,800	$1,335,400	$2,148,400
Operating Expenses			
Cost of sales	$208,500	$ 381,800	$ 531,300
Selling and administrative	193,300	550,700	977,600
Research and development	93,700	216,500	334,800
Interest	100	26,700	34,700
Depreciation	9,800	18,200	29,600
Total Operating Expenses	$505,400	$1,193,900	$1,908,000
Profit Before Taxes	($ 57,600)	$ 141,500	$ 240,400
Federal Income Taxes	(7,900)	13,500	27,000
Profit After Taxes	($ 49,700)	$ 128,000	$ 213,400

Sulcus's growth. *Inc.* magazine describes growth companies like Sulcus in this way:

> Ten years ago, more than 80 percent of the companies on this year's *Inc.* list did not exist. Five years ago, most were still in the start-up stage—small, struggling, and privately held.
>
> Today they are in the front ranks of America's resurgent economy. If, as President Ronald Reagan predicted last January, we are on the verge of a second American revolution, then the chief executive officers of the *Inc.* 100 are the Minutemen of the 1980s, the growth leaders of the entrepreneurial age.*

In August 1984, Sulcus became a publicly owned company, selling 19 percent of its common stock for more than $1.8 million. In Exhibit 20A.3 Sulcus's three-year income statements appear; in Exhibit 20A.4, its two-year balance sheets.

Controlled Growth

Mr. Ratner has served as chief executive officer and board chairman since the company's founding in 1979. As such, he has been responsible for directing Sulcus's managerial and financial policies. During his leadership, Mr. Ratner has deliberately steered a course of controlled growth for Sulcus. A recent newspaper article praised Mr. Ratner for his restraint:

> In an industry rife with firms willing to rush a product to market and hope for the best, Sulcus has taken a slow, calculating course. For the better part of six years, Sulcus restricted its product to the land title industry, designing its computer software and hardware to automate real estate law, escrow, and title insurance firms.
>
> "We never intended to be a broad-brush computer company," says Mr. Ratner. "We want to know every nook and cranny in our customer's

* Ibid., p. 57.

EXHIBIT 20A.4 *Sulcus Computer Corporation: Two-year Balance Sheets*

	December 31 1983	December 31 1984
Assets		
Current Assets		
Cash and cash equivalents	$1,017,800	$3,006,200
Accounts receivable	37,800	48,100
Inventories	143,300	153,000
Other current assets	10,000	59,800
Total Current Assets	$1,208,900	$3,267,100
Fixed assets		
Equipment and fixtures	$ 104,200	$ 305,700
Less: Accumulated depreciation	30,600	59,600
Total Fixed Assets	$ 73,600	$ 246,100
Other Assets	$ 0	$ 10,600
Total Assets	$1,282,500	$3,523,800

	December 31 1983	December 31 1984
Equities		
Current Liabilities		
Notes payable	$ 0	$ 169,600
Accounts payable	50,400	72,600
Bonus payable	40,000	
Other liabilities	34,700	41,300
Deferred revenue	29,900	64,400
Taxes payable	13,500	27,200
Total Current Liabilities	$ 168,500	$ 375,100
Long-term Debt	$ 275,000	$ 275,000
Owners' Equity		
Preferred stock	$ 683,700	$ 0
Common stock	47,000	2,591,800
Retained earnings	108,300	281,900
Total Owners' Equity	$ 839,000	$2,873,700
Total Equities	$1,282,500	$3,523,800

business so we can add new products for them, make them more cost effective."*

Sulcus's strategy of giving birth to a section of the computer market and slowly nurturing its customers has worked well. By the time Sulcus began to mass-market its systems in 1983, they had been tested for nearly three years at several sites across the country, and a string of distribution centers was well established. In fact, Sulcus tailored its software to the real estate law and procedures in each state. Support services were in gear to respond to trouble, promising next-day replacement of any malfunctioning system.

In two years, Sulcus captured 75 percent of the 800 land title companies estimated to have automated their offices. "We literally dominate that market," says Mr. Ratner, "and the customers keep coming back. Once we automate their business, our customers tend to look to us to do everything."

Marketing Network

The far-flung nature of Sulcus's marketing network is illustrated in Exhibit 20A.5. To market its turnkey microcomputer systems efficiently, Sulcus designed a network made up of these parts:

Distributor-dealer network: Sulcus chooses its local distributors from among the entrepreneurial users of its products, so they can best

* Jeffrey Fraser, "Greensburg Firm Nurtures Software Niche," *The Pittsburgh Press*, May 10, 1985, p. B6.

EXHIBIT 20A.5 *Sulcus Computer Corporation: Location and Identity of Distributors, Branch Offices, and Representatives*

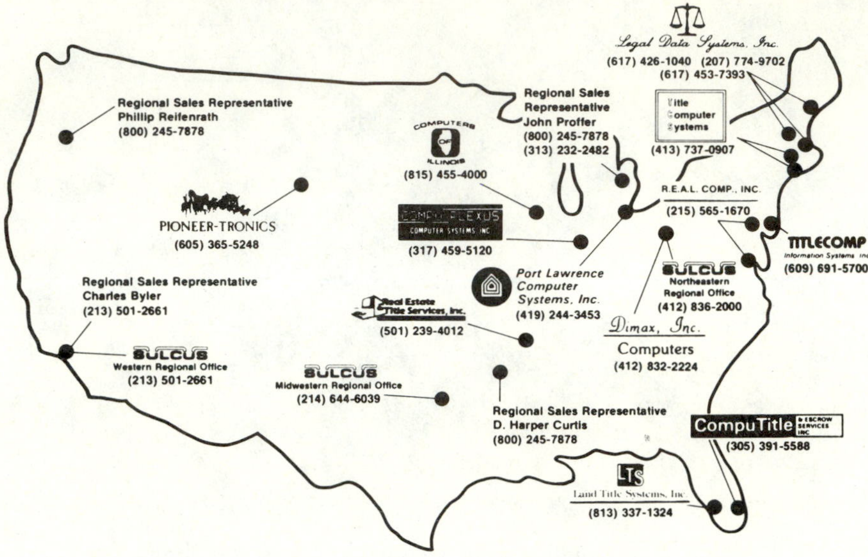

combine product knowledge and familiarity with customers' needs. Distributors are required to:

- Develop their own territories and markets
- Inventory all Sulcus products
- Have full-time sales, training, and support personnel available
- Organize and use the company's advertising and promotional programs

Branch Offices: The branch office provides regional support to the distributor-dealer network as well as the end users. Sulcus currently has branch offices in Dallas and in Los Angeles and others are planned in the Northeast and Midwest. Prompt response to user needs is enhanced and facilitated by these branch offices.

Regional representatives: The new regional representative program aims to expand Sulcus products into areas not currently serviced by distributors, dealers, or branches. Experienced salespeople also enable Sulcus to spread into new areas. At present, there are regional representatives in Oregon, California, Michigan, and Arkansas. Sulcus expects to add 20 to 25 regional representatives to carry out its marketing program.

EXHIBIT 20A.6 *Sulcus Computer Corporation: Family of Programs for Law Offices*

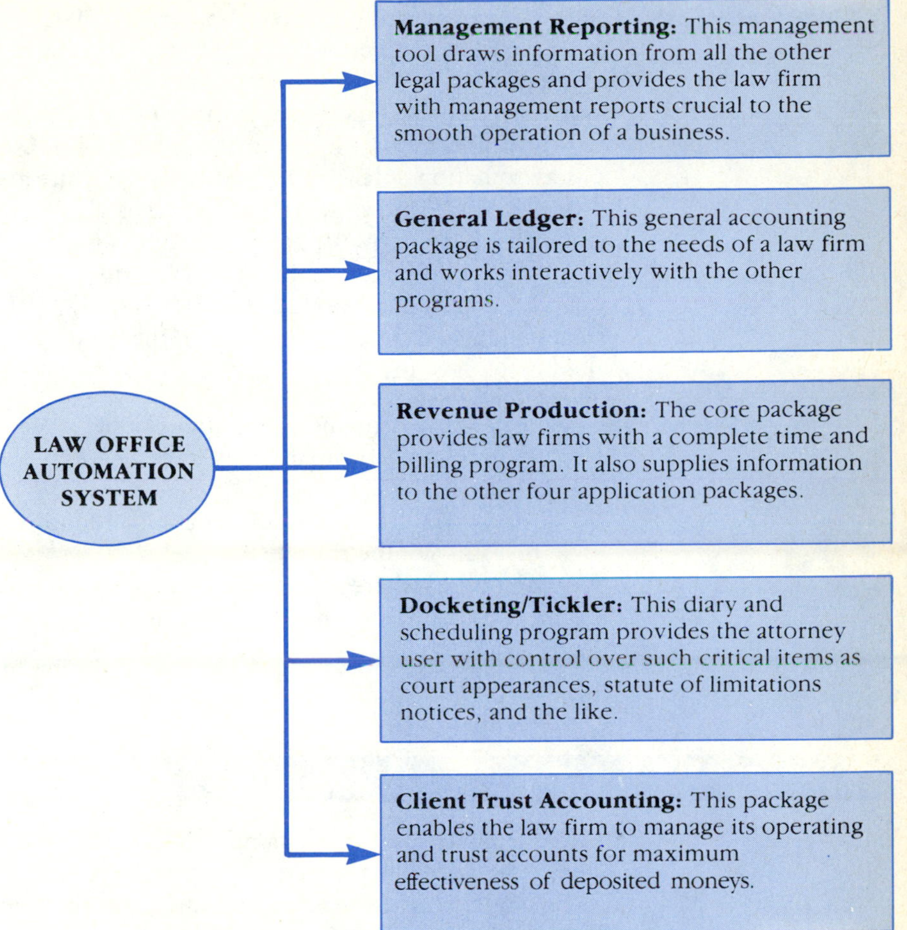

Advertising and Sales Promotion

In 1984, Sulcus's marketing efforts took a quantum leap. With a six-figure advertising budget, Sulcus expanded its reach in the marketplace, using a number of prestigious and industry-related publications. Advertisements and articles about Sulcus appeared in such publications as *The Wall Street Journal, ABA Journal, The National Law Journal, Legal Times, The American Lawyer, Title News, Financial Computing, National Thrift News, Legal Economics, Case & Comment, MicroBanker, Mortgage Banking*, and *Computers in Banking*.

In addition to advertising, Sulcus is active in trade shows, providing hands-on demonstrations to hundreds of its best prospects. The purchase of a 400-square foot, 12-foot high exhibit booth enables Sulcus to maintain its leadership in the ever-increasing competition of the national convention arena.

New Market

Sulcus is now poised to enter the market of law office automation. In November 1984, Sulcus acquired Lawtomation, a company specializing in management systems for law firms. "We believe we have a golden opportunity to be a major competitor in that market," says Mr. Ratner. "We know the needs of the small and medium-sized law office."

Lawtomation software and manuals have already been rewritten to fit Sulcus systems. A new line of computers is also being readied. Sales in the legal market have been estimated to reach as high as $10 billion. The stakes are so high that when Sulcus swoops down on the nation's 576,000 lawyers, it expects to compete successfully with IBM and other computer industry giants. Exhibit 20A.6 shows the family of programs that Sulcus will offer to law firms.

Questions

1. Comment on the financing of this publicly-held company.
2. Explain why this company has succeeded in the crowded computer industry.
3. If you were Mr. Ratner, would you expand into the legal market in light of the stiff competition?
4. Would you buy shares of common stock in the company? Explain fully.
5. Comment on Mr. Ratner's marketing strategy.

Source: This case was prepared by Professor Richard W. Shapiro of Cuyahoga Community College.

CASE 20B *John Bell*

John Bell comes from a poor family. Freshly discharged from the army, he landed a job with a manufacturing company that employs 11 persons. On his first day at work, the entrepreneur gave him 15 minutes of instruction and then told him to get busy. When asked if he understood what to do, Mr. Bell said yes.

Thirty minutes later, the entrepreneur returned. He noticed that Mr. Bell had not done the job properly. Angered, the entrepreneur yelled in front of the other workers, "I'll show you only once more how to do it. And you'd better pay attention or you're fired!"

Now Mr. Bell got the job done properly. Or so he *guessed*, because the entrepreneur came back to check several times but did not say a single word to Mr. Bell.

The next day, Mr. Bell failed to show up for work.

Questions

1. What would you have done had you been the entrepreneur?
2. To what extent must the entrepreneur use an autocratic approach when supervising relatively unskilled employees?

CASE 20C *Enterprise on Elton Street*

Joe Simak's neighbors on quiet, tree-shaded Elton Street were not surprised when he appeared early one spring morning equipped with ladders, brushes, and other painting equipment. Even the most casual observer could not fail to recognize that the well-maintained houses and manicured lawns reflected a pride of ownership among community residents. What did startle them, however, was the color that Joe was busily applying to the front of his home. It was fire-engine red.

Two days later, another eye-catcher appeared on the Simak residence—an illuminated sign that read: JOE's TELEVISION REPAIR. Both sides of the Simak family car were emblazoned with the identical message.

One evening about three weeks before he painted the house, Joe had read a magazine article entitled "The Joys of Being Your Own Boss." His reaction was one of enthusiastic acceptance. "This will be the most important day in our lives!" he jubilantly informed his startled wife, Florence.

Never one to dawdle, he set his new career plans in motion the very next day by giving his supervisor two weeks' notice of his intention to resign from his position as appliance repairman. Florence best describes the developments in Joe's enterprise after six months of operation, saying:

> Our life is in complete chaos, and I am at my wits' end. The phone rings at odd hours of the day and night. Strangers wander around the house. Our car is constantly being used to pick up or return television sets. We have no semblance of a meal schedule, and I am expected to serve coffee at any time to Joe and his customers.
>
> We are getting into financial troubles because our income is so irregular and because Joe charges low rates in order to attract business and undersell the competition.
>
> We have absolutely no social life and little privacy. Our daughter moved out last week because she couldn't stand conditions at home.
>
> Joe's former boss has called three times wanting him to come back to work, but Joe says he's competely happy where he is. When I urge him to locate his business elsewhere, he objects to paying rent and says it's more convenient to be at home.
>
> Meanwhile, the neighbors are beginning to object to the cars that are parked along the street and constantly move in and out of our driveway. Our own car—what's left of it—is always parked outside because the garage is filled with non-working TV sets that Joe plans to repair sometime.

Recently, Florence wrote to a nationally-syndicated newspaper columnist who offers advice on readers' problems. Her reply was: "Give your nutty husband an ultimatum—either he shapes up his operation in two weeks or you ship out!" When Joe received this word, he sighed and said:

> She just doesn't understand us entrepreneurs.

Questions

1. Should Joe relocate his business and raise his rates, in order to pay rent and other additional obligations?
2. Do Florence and Joe have a communications problem? If so, in what way and how may they correct the problem?
3. Should Joe promote Florence to vice-presidency of the firm? Why?

Source: This case was prepared by Frederick D. Wood of Cuyahoga Community College.

INDEX